This book is essential reading for any maritime ministry practitioner—a "must have" publication. Not for the bookshelf, but as a constant companion—to educate and stimulate about basic foundations and exciting opportunities for ministry in the seafaring world.

Rev. Canon Bill Christianson,
Secretary General of The Mission to Seafarers

We in the Apostleship of the Sea are indebted to Dr. Kverndal for taking on such a valuable work—from its foundational guidance to its "Wave of the Future." We are already using it to help shape our ministry in support of seafarers' all-important Seagoing Christian Community.

Commodore Chris York RN,
National Director of the AOS in England and Wales

Across denominational lines and across every ocean, this book offers all readers—from isolated chaplains to students of missiology—Roald Kverndal's important holistic approach to the worldwide ministry of this strong network of care and proclamation.

Rev. Dr. Jean R. Smith,
Executive Director, Seamen's Church Institute of New York
and New Jersey

How will we respond to the realities of change—both in the maritime industry and in the needs of seafarers, while keeping our commitment to the Great Commission? Once again, I have been challenged by Dr. Kverndal!

Rev. Philip H. Vandercook,
Co-Founder, Southern Baptist Global Ministries Intl.
of New Orleans

In this masterly synthesis, Kverndal combines his groundbreaking 1986 history, *Seamen's Missions: Their Origin and Early Growth,* with the current scene. Drawn largely on personal practice over half a century, his new book is written "from the heart" and thereby bears special authenticity.

Dr. Alston Kennerley,
Master Mariner, Professor/Research Fellow,
University of Plymouth

I believe this particular book will meet the long-felt need for a teaching tool to promote indigenous maritime ministry everywhere. It will surely help our churches both in Asia and the world to lay a thorough educational groundwork for such ministry. May God greatly bless it!

Rev. Josephine Shui-Wan Tso,
Past President, Evangelical Lutheran Church in Hong Kong

I am delighted that such a book should be published. For four decades I have had the privilege of researching the nations and peoples of the world for the successive editions of *Operation World.* Many of these nations are coastal and have a significant number of seafarers. Among these are Christian believers who need both fellowship and tools for outreach. Many more need to experience the Gospel for the first time, yet come from lands inaccessible to other means of witness—such as the Maldives, North Korea, Iran, Somalia, or Libya. My passionate interest in this ministry also comes from my year in Asia and the Pacific, serving on board the Operation Mobilization ship MV *Logos* during 1979. Reaching out to seafarers and promoting the planting of ship-based churches is a vital component of fulfilling the Great Commission—to make disciples of all nations and peoples. May this book be widely read and enlarge the vision of the Church of the Lord Jesus—by encompassing the mobile, multi-cultural community of the world's seafarers!

Patrick Johnstone

After many years of missionary service in Africa, Patrick Johnstone joined the leadership team of British-based WEC International as Research Director. Here he has authored both the widely used global mission resource *Operation World* and its companion volume *The Church is Bigger Than You Think.* His newest book is entitled *The Future of World Evangelization in the 21st Century.*

Also by the author

SEAMEN'S MISSIONS
Their Origin and Early Growth
A Contribution to the History of the Church Maritime

William Carey Library Publishers, 1986

See page 423 for more information

THE WAY OF THE SEA

The Changing Shape of Mission in the Seafaring World

Roald Kverndal

WILLIAM CAREY
LIBRARY

Published by
William Carey Library
1605 E. Elizabeth St.
Pasadena, California 91104
www.missionbooks.org

Cover Art by Lars Ekelund, Master Mariner, depicting Svenner Lighthouse at
the entrance to Oslo Fjord, Norway
Production Editor: David Shaver Sr.
Cover Design: Amanda Valloza

Produced under the auspices of the International Association for the Study of
Maritime Mission (IASMM), Secretariat: School of Theology, York St. John
College, York, England

Publication partially funded with major grants from the Lutheran World
Federation and the Seafarers' Trust of the International Transport Workers'
Federation; also with contributions by Korea International Maritime Mission,
Lutheran Advocates for Maritime Mission, Carol and Bill Matson, and Kirsten
and John Kverndal.

Printed in the United States of America

Library of Congress Cataloging-in-Publication Data
Kverndal, Roald.
  The way of the sea : the changing shape of mission in the seafaring world
/ Roald Kverndal.
      p. cm.
  Includes bibliographical references and index.
  ISBN 978-0-87808-366-4
1. Merchant mariners--Missions and charities. 2. Sailors--Religious life.
3. Navigation--History. I. Title.
  BV2670.K95 2007
  266'.023--dc22
                                    2007030393

With my love and devotion to

Our three daughters Evelyn, Jeanette, Marianne

Our eight grandchildren

Our three great-grandchildren

And all our yet unborn who will follow them

CONTENTS

PART I – History of Maritime Mission

SECTION 1 – Early/Premodern Era (Until 1920)

SECTION 2 – Ecumenical/Modern Era (1920-1974)

PART III – Perspectives on Maritime Mission

ABBREVIATIONS

AA	Alcoholics Anonymous
AOP	Apostleship of Prayer
AOS	Apostleship of the Sea (in Latin "Apostolatus Maris")
AOSUSA	Apostleship of the Sea of the USA
ASFS	American Seamen's Friend Society
BFBS	British & Foreign Bible Society
BFSS	British & Foreign Sailors' Society (later BSS)
BISS	British & International Sailors' Society
BIMCO	Baltic and International Maritime Council
CHIRP	Confidential Hazardous Incident Reporting Programme
CIS	Commonwealth of Independent States (former Soviet Union)
COSCO	China Ocean Shipping Company
CRC	Christian Reformed Church
CSR	Center for Seafarers' Rights (SCI NY/NJ)
FOC	Flag of Convenience
GSM	German Seamen's Mission
HIM	Harbour International Ministries
IASMM	International Association for the Study of Maritime Mission
IBMR	International Bulletin of Missionary Research
ICC	International Chamber of Commerce
ICCMFM	International Coordinating Committee for Maritime Follow-up Ministry
ICMA	International Christian Maritime Association
ICONS	International Commission on Shipping (Report)
ICOSA	International Council of Seamen's Agencies (later NAMMA)
ICS	International Chamber of Shipping
ICSW	International Committee on Seafarers' Welfare
ILO	International Labour Organisation
IMB	International Maritime Bureau
IMMTI	International Maritime Mission Training Institute (KIMM)
IMO	International Maritime Organisation
ISAN	International Seafarers' Assistance Network
ISCT	International Sailing Chaplains' Training
ISF	International Shipping Federation
ISM	International Safety Management (Code)
ISPS	International Ship & Port Facility Security (Code)
ISS	International Sailors' Society (Canada/S. Africa/Australia/NZ)
ISS	International Sports Sub-Committee (ICSW)
IT	Information Technology
ITF	International Transport Workers' Federation
ITF/ST	ITF/Seafarers' Trust
KHE	Korea Harbor Evangelism
KIMM	Korea International Maritime Mission (former Korea Seamen's Mission)

LAMM   Lutheran Advocates (f. Association) for Maritime Mission (f. Ministry)
LNG   Liquefied Natural Gas (carrier/terminal)
LPS   London Port Society
LWF   Lutheran World Federation
MARPOL   Prevention of Marine Pollution from Ships (Convention)
MCC   Maritime Christian Community
MOU   Memorandum of Understanding
MSNAC   Missions to Seamen in North America & the Caribbean
MSP   Ministering Seafarers' Program
MtS   The Missions to Seamen (later The Mission to Seafarers)
NAMMA   North American Maritime Ministry Association
NAMMAC   NAMMA Conference
NCCS   National Catholic Conference for Seafarers (later AOSUSA)
NIS   Norwegian International Shipping Register
NMBS   Naval & Military Bible Society (later NM&AFBS)
NMZ   Nederlandse Zeemanscentrale
NSM   New Sailor's Magazine
NUMAST   National Union of Marine, Aviation & Shipping Transport Officers
OPA90   Oil Pollution Act of 1990 (USA)
OPEC   Organization of Petroleum Exporting Countries
PMI   Port Ministries International (formerly SBSMF)
PRC   People's Republic of China
PRC   Piracy Reporting Centre (of the IMB)
PSC   Port State Control
RNMDSF   Royal National Mission to Deep Sea Fishermen
RO-RO   Roll-on/Roll-off (carrier)
SCFS   Seamen's Christian Friend Society
SCI   Seamen's Church Institute
SDT   Sreafarers' Discipleship Training
SHIP   Seafarers' Health Information Program
SIRC   Seafarers International Research Centre
SML   Sailor's Magazine (London version)
SMNY   Sailor's Magazine (New York version)
SMT   Seafarers' Ministry Training
SOLAS   Safety of Life at Sea (Convention)
STCW   Standards of Training, Certification & Watch-keeping (Convention)
SVP   Society of St. Vincent de Paul
TCM   Thames Church Mission
TEU   Twenty-foot Equivalent Unit (20'x8'x8' container)
TRC   Truth and Reconciliation Commission (South Africa)
UN   United Nations
USS   United Seamen's Service
USSR   Union of Soviet Socialist Republics (later CIS)
VLCC   Very Large Crude Carrier
WCC   World Council of Churches

CHRONOLOGY

1779   Naval and Military Bible Society (later NM&AFBS), world's first seafarers' mission organization, initiated in London by Methodist laymen.

1809   Naval Correspondence Mission begun by Baptist Rev. G. C. Smith in Penzance, Cornwall, in support of the British "Naval Awakening."

1812   Boston Society for the Religious and Moral Improvement of Seamen, commenced by Congregational Rev. Joseph Tuckerman.

1813   Thames Union Bible Society founded in London, as the first of several "Marine Bible Societies" to emerge in Great Britain, Northern Europe and North America

1814   "Thames Revival" ignited by the shipboard prayer-meetings initiated by Methodist layman Zebedee Rogers, a shoemaker in the docklands district of Rotherhithe, London.

1816   First "Seamen's Meetings" begun in New York by members of the Presbyterian "Brick Church," coordinated by Rev. Ward Stafford (also a Presbyterian).

1817   First "Bethel Flag" designed by Zebedee Rogers and hoisted on collier brig *Zephyr* as a call to shipboard worship in Lower Pool of London.

1818   Port of London Society founded March 18th, followed by dedication (May 4th) of former HMS *Speedy* as the world's first sanctuary for seafarers, known as the *Ark.*

1818   New York Port Society founded June 5th, followed by building of the world's first shore-based "Mariner's Church," opened in 1820 with Rev. Ward Stafford as pastor.

1819   British and Foreign Seamen's Friend Society and Bethel Union launched in London by Rev. G. C. Smith, in order to promote a global "Bethel Movement."

1819   First of three Sailing Chapel Missions to seafaring coastal communities of Norway (1819-1828), launched by London-based Congregational Rev. Carl von Bülow.

1822   William Henry Angas (a Baptist master mariner) ordained by BFSFSBU as the world's first "Missionary to Seafaring Men."

1822   Port of Dublin Society initiated by local naval officers, thereby becoming the first Anglican-affiliated seafarers' mission.

1822   Calcutta Bethel Society founded and floating chapel opened, with help
        of Baptist missionary pioneer, Dr. William Carey.

1822   Shipboard preaching under the Bethel Flag introduced in Whampoa,
        China, by Presbyterian missionary pioneer, Dr. Robert Morrison.

1822   Sydney Bethel Union Society founded by Australian Wesleyans and
        Anglicans.

1825   Episcopal Floating Church Society founded in London with help of
        naval officers, dedicating former HMS *Brazen* as an Anglican *Ark* in
        1829.

1825   Danish-Norwegian Church in Wellclose Square acquired by Rev. G. C.
        Smith as London Mariners' Church and metropolitan hub of his many
        diaconal initiatives.

1826   American Seamen's Friend Society founded in 1826 in New York as a
        national nondenominational agency, but with international reach
        (Reactivated in 1828).

1830   Dr. David Abeel (Dutch Reformed Church) arrives as first ASFS "Sea
        Missionary" in a future series of world ports.

1831   Havre de Grace British and American Seamen's Friend Society formed
        in France as first general seafarers' mission on mainland of Europe.

1833   British and Foreign Sailors' Society organized in London, continuing
        the combined ministries of both the PLS and the BFSFSBU, now
        renamed BISS and based in Southampton.

1834   Young Men's Auxiliary Education and Missionary Society founded by
        Episcopalians/Anglicans in New York (later becoming SCI NY/NJ).

1835   World's first "Sailors' Home" opened in Well Street, Wellclose Square,
        London, initiated by Rev. G. C. Smith and soon emulated elsewhere.

1835   Dr. John Ashley, pioneer of Anglican seafarers' missions, launched his
        personal 15-year anchorage ("roadstead") ministry in Bristol Channel.

1842   Amsterdam British & American Seamen's Friend Society founded by
        BFSS and ASFS acting in cooperation.

1843   Wesleyan Seamen's Missionary Society (later the Seamen's Mission of
        the Methodist Church) founded in London, eventually based at the
        Queen Victoria Seamen's Rest in East India Dock Road, Poplar.

1844   Thames Church Mission (Anglican) initiated naval officers and Trinity
        Brethren for sailing chapel ministry along London's River Thames.

1845   Methodist Bethelship Mission started among Scandinavian seafarers
        and immigrants in New York harbor by Swedish Rev. Olof Hedstrom.

1846   Seamen's Christian Friend Society founded in London, with Rev.
        George Teil Hill as principal promoter.

1856   The Missions to Seamen (Anglican) founded in London, facilitated by
        the nautical author and church-leader William H. G. Kingston, from
        now on becoming the global maritime arm of the Church of England.

1864   Norwegian Seamen's Mission (Lutheran) founded in Bergen, Norway,
        later emulated in Denmark (1867), Sweden (1869) and Finland (1875).

1881   Royal National Mission to Deep Sea Fishermen initiated by Ebenezer Mather, at that time Secretary of the Thames Church Mission.

1886   Committee for Church Ministry to German Seafarers Abroad formed in Hannover, eventually evolving into the German Seamen's Mission.

1893   An indigenous Dutch Seafarers' Home opened in Rotterdam by a Christian-based Seamen's Union ("De Zeemansbond") that would later evolve into the Netherlands Seamen's Center ("Zeemanszentrale").

1894   Société des Oeuvres de Mer (Society for Maritime Ministry) founded in France by the Assumptionists to promote outreach to fishers.

1896   International Transport Workers' Federation founded in London to coordinate maritime and other transportation-related unions worldwide.

1895   "Seamen's Branch" of the Apostleship of Prayer formed by British Jesuit priests (thereby becoming a precursor of the AOS in 1920).

1919   International Labour Organisation (ILO) established in Geneva to improve and monitor global labor conditions on land and sea.

1920   Apostleship of the Sea (AOS) initiated by three Catholic laymen in Glasgow, Scotland (organized in 1921, papal recognition in 1922).

1930   International Council of AOS established in UK (moving to Rome in 1952, eventually becoming part of the Vatican's "Pontifical Council for the Pastoral Care of Migrants and Itinerant People").

1932   International Council of Seamen's Agencies (ICUSA) formed in Philadelphia to promote cooperative maritime ministry in North America and the Caribbean (renamed NAMMA in 1991).

1958   International Maritime Organisation (IMO) established in London as a UN agency to facilitate "safer shipping and cleaner seas."

1969   International Christian Maritime Association (ICMA) founded in Rotterdam to promote global ecumenical cooperation, with Dr. Daisuke Kitagawa (WCC) as its first Secretary.

1973   Houston International Seafarers' Center opened as the first such ecumenical joint endeavor, followed by the first-ever ecumenical Port Chaplaincy Training School (1974).

1974   Korea Harbor Evangelism founded as the first-ever indigenous Asian maritime mission agency, headquartered in Seoul.

1976   International Committee on Seafarers' Welfare (ICSW) launched in London, in order to coordinate the implementation of ILO instruments relating to maritime welfare.

1977   "Ministering Seafarers' Program" launched by Rev. Ray Eckhoff, Lutheran Chaplain-Director of Tacoma Seafarers' Center in Pacific Northwest USA.

1981   Seafarers' Trust established by London-based International Transport Workers' Federation, to provide grants for the support of maritime welfare agency projects worldwide.

1982   Center for Seafarers' Rights, New York, co-founded by Dr. James Whittemore and Dr. Paul Chapman of SCI NY/NJ, prompting parallel ministries in London (MTS) and Barcelona (AOS).

1984   First documented History of the Seafarers' Mission Movement defended as ThD dissertation at University of Oslo, Norway, by Rev. Roald Kverndal, then Executive Secretary of NAMMA. Published 1986, as *Seamen's Missions: Their Origin and Early Growth.*

1986   First of several contact-building visits by ICMA delegations to Mainland China, subsequently (from 1990) also to Russia and former Soviet satellite states.

1989   "Seafarers' Covenant" adopted at International Congress on World Evangelization (Lausanne II) in Manila, the Philippines.

1990   International Association for the Study of Maritime Mission (IASMM) in Leeds, Yorkshire, as a research resource for the worldwide maritime ministry community.

1990   "NAMMA's Statement of Mission" (NASOM) unanimously adopted at NAMMAC, New Orleans.

1995   Seafarers International Research Centre (SIRC) established at Cardiff University, Wales, to provide reliable data on seafarers' safety and occupational health issues for the maritime industry and others.

1996   First non-Western doctorate in Maritime Missiology awarded by New York Theological Seminary to Rev. Jonah Won Jong Choi, founding President of Pusan-based Korea International Maritime Mission.

1997   Apostolic Letter Motu Proprio "Stella Maris" by Pope John Paul II reorganizes the AOS, while recognizing "God's People of the Sea" as primary agents of mission and ministry.

1997   ICMA's first "Seafarers' Ministry Training" held in Rotterdam to promote professional skill and spirituality among newly-appointed seafarers' chaplains worldwide.

2002   SIRC-researched "International Sailing Chaplain Training" endorsed by ICMA in order to build a worldwide network of professional seagoing chaplains.

2002   First-ever comprehensive Theology of Maritime Mission defended as ThD dissertation at University of Brussels, Belgium, by Church of Ireland-affiliated Rev. Paul G. Mooney, affirming the urgency of a paradigm shift to "seafarer-centered" lay peer ministry at sea. Published 2005, as *Maritime Mission: History, Development, A New Perspective.*

2004   A denominationally accredited "Seafarer Discipleship Training" plan proposed at ICMA Plenary Conference in New Orleans, to train and certify Ministering Seafarers for peer ministry on ships worldwide.

2006   "Consolidated Maritime Labour Standards Convention" adopted by ILO, combining over 60 existing instruments on seafarers' welfare issues, in order to become, when ratified, a long overdue "Seafarers' Bill of Rights."

FOREWORD

Ishmael Noko

I am happy to have this opportunity to write a foreword for this first comprehensive resource on Maritime Missiology. In the mid-1980s, when I assumed leadership of the Department for Mission and Development of the Lutheran World Federation, it happened to coincide with Roald Kverndal's arrival in Geneva to serve the Department as LWF Maritime Ministry Consultant. Coming, as I did, from a landlocked nation in Africa, I might perhaps be forgiven for never before having given much thought to the missiological significance of specifically seafaring people.

It was not long before I realized that here was a dimension of mission with wide, global implications. After previously working with refugees and displaced people around the world, I had already become aware of the close linkage between the gospels and people on the periphery, as potential carriers of the Good News. Yet only now did I discover how this is preeminently true of that mobile, marginalized sector of humanity known as People of the Sea.

Roald Kverndal's dissertation on *Seamen's Missions: Their Origin and Early Growth* (1986) provided, as far as I know, the world's first documented history of seafarers and the spread of the gospel. I welcome this second volume—carrying the story up to the present and tracing its theological contour. This is largely a logical outcome of the Author's subsequent travels as our consultant, constantly advocating the good cause around the world, particularly in the developing countries of the South and East, from where most of today's merchant mariners come.

In a world fragmented by the ferocity of hatreds fanned by religious fundamentalism and fear-based slogans, our hope as Christians is grounded in a God of peace and reconciliation, revealed through the Cross. In this kind of world, there is an urgent need for the type of dialogue in action, or "diapraxis," that characterizes maritime mission at its best. Such mission sees the face of Christ in others. In fact, the grassroots Christian communities emerging among today's multi-cultural ship's crews provide—through their daily walk of faith and human solidarity with those of other faiths—a sorely needed model for the church at large, in bearing authentic witness amidst the challenges of globalization.

While this book reflects the experience and insights of one who has devoted nearly his whole life to this field, a major strength is the vocational and denominational diversity represented by the Perspectives of so many others. As a result, *The Way of the Sea* will, I believe, fill a long existing void, not only in the maritime world, but far beyond. I therefore commend this volume to those engaged in ecumenical, interreligious and missiological studies and those providing ministerial formation, as well as all those interested in maritime life.

Ishmael Noko
General Secretary
The Lutheran World Federation

August 2006

PREFACE

Difficult tasks can be done immediately
Impossible tasks will take a little more time

This paraphrased version of the motto of the US Corps of Engineers aptly applies to its two famous early members, Meriwether Lewis and William Clark. In 1806, they finally fulfilled their seemingly impossible task—to cross and claim the country west of the Mississippi for America, all the way to the Pacific Ocean. In one sense, that statement could also apply to the completion of this book, exactly 200 years later—again in the Pacific Northwest.

This book's companion volume, *Seamen's Missions: Their Origin and Early Growth* (1986), was the outcome of a fifteen-year research odyssey (1968-1983). The relevant resource materials were incredibly "fugitive" in nature, literally scattered across the globe. The present book, *The Way of the Sea,* is the result of another fifteen-year preparation period (1991-2006), amidst the incessant challenge of change in the current climate of globalization.

The 1986 volume, as a doctoral dissertation and reference work, required particularly exhaustive treatment, together with an essential academic apparatus. If the result has been to pry open the doors of academia for Maritime Mission as a respected theological discipline, it will have made every day of those fifteen years well worth it. The *present* book, with its more comprehensive yet compact format, seeks to reach a wider readership. If this work can somehow contribute toward greater awareness and support in regard to historical reasons within both the Christian church and the public at large, the unique global role of the People of the Sea, every day of these further fifteen years will have been no less worthwhile.

There are also compelling historical reasons why so much time has elapsed. It took eighteen centuries before the beginning of any organized missionary movement among seafaring people. Moreover, a documented *history* of the movement would inevitably constitute a precondition for any theological *analysis* of the subject, such as in the current book.

My professor in the principles of theology, during seminary years in Norway, impressed a profound truth upon his students: As human beings, each one of us has a subjective set of personal presuppositions. These will inevitably affect every thought we have. No one can possibly be totally objective. It helps to know that—while we still struggle toward fairness. I do not claim, therefore, to be impartial in the pages that follow, neither in the selection of materials, nor in their interpretation. In both cases, the course of my life has colored my choices. That course has been diverse—ethnically, vocationally and denominationally. As a result, the challenge for me has been to make the subjective nature of such "biological baggage" serve an objective purpose in the body of the book.

Ethnically, a Norwegian-American background has led to experience in both nationally and internationally oriented seafarers' mission over the years. Vocationally, having first served as a seafarer, then later as a port chaplain, this has given me a sense of rapport with both. Denominationally, Lutheran affiliation has nurtured my ecumenical and holistic understanding of the Lord's Great Commission within the seafaring world. This seeks convergence around the uniqueness of both the person and rule of Jesus Christ as Savior and Lord. At the same time, it rejects the polarizing extremes of either universalistic betrayal or fundamentalistic perversion of the gospel (cf. Carter 1996, 195-199).

Rather than dwelling on issues of potentially divisive church tradition, the book seeks common ground on the basis of two widely recognized criteria—the one among Christians everywhere, the other among human beings regardless of religion: (1) *The Christian Bible,* however differently one may interpret it, holds unique normative status as source of authority for faith and life among all Christians. Scripture remains God's final word and, for us, our ultimate arbiter. (2) *The Universal Declaration of Human Rights,* adopted by the United Nations in 1948, does not yet have the force of law in every nation state. Yet, for governments and people everywhere, it remains a ringing challenge to the scourge of discrimination and any violation of human dignity and freedom.

While wishing to be "conservative" in principle, by adhering to both of these fundamental criteria, I offer no apology for seeking to be "radical" in applying them in practice. However, in another sense, I feel a sincere apology is due. I am among those who believe passionately in the power of forgiveness to transform both individuals and societies—and thereby the course of human history. As a Western-world white male claiming allegiance to the Christian faith, I wish to apologize for all the times I, like so many others, have failed to show solidarity with non-Western, non-white, female and male followers of other faiths or no faith. I would like this book to serve, in some measure, as a means of making amends.

A concerted quest for truth and reconciliation has never been more urgent. In a world where international terrorism is tearing away at the fabric of global human community, the issue is not to seek excuses, but to discover explanations—and address the disparities and disrespect that fuel fanaticism in the first place. Those familiar with seafarers know that nowhere can one find the concept of a one-world human community modeled more faithfully than among the nomadic, multi-ethnic, multi-faith ship's crews of today's seafaring world.

However pressing a priority it may be to promote a new world order—of economic justice, ecological sustainability and human solidarity—this is not the whole purpose of the book. Its ultimate rationale relates to the inviolable nature of humanity's God-given dignity. This includes the most basic human right of all—the freedom to form and follow one's own convictions in all matters of conscience. Such freedom necessitates universal access to all available options.

Consequently, the book tries to balance building human community with the human right of Christians and non-Christians alike to engage in *mission.* "Mission" means bearing witness, wherever this is inherent to one's faith. However, true mission—contrary to coercive proselytizing—can only claim to be authentic when following ways that do not infringe on the human rights of others. For current-day Christian mission, a crucial concern must be to raise awareness within the church at large of the *maritime* dimension of *global* mission. To that end, the book highlights the proven capacity of seafarers to carry with them, wherever they go, the gospel message— once entrusted by the Master to his first seafaring followers by the shores of the Sea of Galilee, now creating a key seagoing segment of today's "emerging church."

I am deeply grateful to each of the thirty-two contributors who have written the "Perspectives" that make up Part III of this book. Their views may not reflect those of the Author in every respect. Yet I would venture to say that both the diversity and expertise they provide constitute a unique enhancement of the whole enterprise. I am equally thankful for the contributions of others, most of them fellow-workers in the field, who have willingly shared their insights and experience throughout the years of writing this book. Many of them appear by name in the text. In the case of many more, they are too numerous to mention individually. Still, every single one has been no less meaningful to me and my work. The enhanced value of the book will be their reward. This applies in a special sense to all who have made this enterprise an object of prayer.

I do need to mention by name, though, the Norwegian pioneer and Professor of Missiology at my alma mater, Dr. Olav G. Myklebust. He became my unfailing mentor from the very beginning. To my brother John and sister-in-law Kirsten, my warm thanks for the writing refuge they repeatedly afforded me at their fjord-side cabin in Norway. I fail to see how I could have navigated the bewildering waters of 21st century electronic book production unless David Shaver—the former mariner who headed the publication of my 1986 History—had not come out of retirement to lend an indispensable hand. Also, I offer my sincere thanks once again to the talented team at William Carey Library.

Finally, this book would never have seen the light of day without the unflagging faith, skills, and sheer grit of the one person who, for me, will forever remain God's gift of grace in human form—my beloved Ruth.

Covenant Shores, Mercer Island/Seattle, Washington State, USA
New Year 2007, Roald Kverndal

INTRODUCTION

"I must go down to the seas again, to the lonely sea and the sky,
and all I ask is a tall ship and a star to steer her by . . . ."
John Masefield

THE PEOPLE

Seafarers—Who Are They?

The sea is an intrinsic feature of this book—as its title indicates. For anyone who has learnt to love that amazing element, it would hardly be possible to conceive of heaven without it. This author well remembers his dismay when, as a former seafarer and then freshman student of theology, he first pondered the prediction in Revelation 21:1. In the new order of celestial eternity, there would be simply "no more sea." How could that possibly be?

Apart from any personal prejudice, the sea is *primeval*. It was there from the beginning. The Spirit of God was "hovering over the waters," before any trace of dry land had begun to appear (Genesis 1:1-10). Since then, the sea has also seemed so *sovereign*. As has often been said, the sea recognizes no voice but the divine. Again, the sea, like God, is *global*. With all its majesty and might, it knows no divisions; it transcends all human boundaries.

There was, therefore, good reason for relief when a theological professor pointed to the particular context of that passage in Revelation. When, in the fullness of time, God reclaims his creation from the cosmic consequences of humanity's original fall, it is the *dark* side of the sea, the sea as a symbol of chaos, death and destruction, which will disappear. In dramatic affirmation of that final triumph, the sea will then give up its dead (20:13). By contrast, the ultimate future of both land and sea in all their infinite, natural beauty and grandeur may be left safely with the Lord who first created them, and who has promised to make "all things new" in the end (v. 5). For a practical affirmation of that conclusion by a master mariner, see Perspective by Captain Douglas (below).

The sea has not only served as an object of admiration. Through the ages, it has been both a source of bounty and a bridge of communication. As such, it has provided a livelihood for millions of people who have made their living on the waters. Elsewhere, in his vision of end-time events, the apostle John describes his momentous vision of a multi-ethnic throng "that no one could count," gathered before the throne of God (7:9). In that multitude there will also be people of the sea. They are the ones, the "seafarers" of the world, who constitute the subject of this book.

In the past, seafarers have also been called "seamen," "sailors," and "mariners." There is a small but growing number of women in this historically male-dominated occupation (according to the ILO, they made up between 1% and 2% in 2003). Given this trend, the gender-inclusive term "seafarer" is increasingly preferred, since it simply implies one who "fares," or travels, by sea, corresponding to a "way-farer" by land.

What are the population groups that share a specific relationship to the sea? Since the publication of the Apostolic Letter *Stella Maris* in 1997, most maritime mission agencies now share a common understanding of the term "people of the sea." This comprises three basic categories: (1) *Seafarers*— those who make their living on board merchant, fishing and other water-borne vessels. (Sometimes this group includes those who simply travel on such vessels for business or leisure). (2) *Maritime personnel*—port or off-shore workers, maritime students, maritime ministry personnel, and retired seafarers. (3) *Dependents*— related to any of the above.

One significant section of seafarers, *naval personnel*—those connected with the sea-related branch of a nation's armed forces—was included in earlier Christian-based outreach. With time, however, national military chaplaincy services have assumed that responsibility. As to the millions of people belonging to the global *fishing community,* these make up the largest category of seafarers worldwide. Again, because many fish-workers are women, the gender-inclusive word "fishers" is now often preferred to the term "fishermen."

How many seafarers are there in the world? Numbers vary according to the category in question. At the turn of the 21st century, there were 1,227,000 merchant seafarers worldwide (according to BIMCO/ISF 2000). Corresponding statistics for fishers quoted by the Apostleship of the Sea estimated 1,500,000 "industrial" or deep-sea fishers, and over 40 million "artisanal" or small-scale coastal fishers. In addition, there are many million inland waterway workers on lakes, rivers and canals. Together with maritime personnel plus their dependents, the Apostolic Letter *Stella Maris* estimated that, for people of the sea worldwide, "the figure climbs to 300 million."

Apart from this statistical overview of the different categories of people of the sea, what attributes do those who make up this particular people group have in common? There seems to be wide consensus that the following three characteristics continue to typify seafaring life: Danger—Discrimination—Depersonalization.

First, seafaring is one of the world's most *danger-prone* occupations. In the days of sail, at the mercy of wind and wave, it was quite common for a seafarer to be washed overboard by breakers, or torn from a storm-rent rigging. In addition, sailors were frequently the victims of starvation, disease and even torture in the name of "discipline." It is not surprising that, as late as in 1874, the Supervising Surgeon of the American Marine Hospital Service estimated the average life expectancy of a sailor, once he had left for sea, to be no more than twelve years. By the 1870s, cases of "coffin-ships" were commonplace, making un-seaworthy ships a pressing public issue.

Despite vast improvements in both safety and living conditions at sea, the life of the modern-day merchant seafarer is still subject to danger and deprivation. Though some of both remain inherent, much is the result of dehumanization due to the post-World War II phenomenon of "Flags of Convenience" (FOCs). The combined purpose of this bogus system of registering ships is solely to evade taxation and recognized standards of safety, justice and welfare.

Second, *pervasive discrimination* has pursued seafarers as a social class for centuries. The resulting public stereotype has shaped their self-image as "the least, the last and the lost." A popular legend maintained that deep-sea sailors would regularly deposit their conscience on a convenient deserted island when outward bound to remote destinations. Here they could then recover it just prior to returning home. There was good reason for such thinking. If life could be "hell afloat," it was normally no less than "purgatory ashore," not least because of the sailor's age-old social alienation there. The very name "Sailor-town" reflected the systematic segregation of that particular sector of a port city from "respectable" society. Here, covered by a cloak of convenient anonymity, sailors could find free play for pent-up emotions caused by abuse and privations at sea.

Details of past exploitation of seafarers ashore, as the prey of human predators aptly called "land-sharks," will follow later. The same applies to the different forms of current-day victimization of seafarers. Many such forms may be a fall-out of FOCs and the 9/11 aftermath. Recent examples of related discrimination can also be a consequence of the multicultural ethnicity of modern-day mariners.

The ongoing impact of globalization on the maritime industry has led to far-reaching ethnic and religious change in the international maritime workforce. During the 1970s, in order to reduce costs amid mounting cut-throat competition, ship operators went over to mass hiring of non- or weakly-unionized, low-cost labor from developing nations. Initially, these workers were mainly from Asia, though also from Africa and Latin America. From 1989, and the collapse of Communism in Eastern Europe and Russia, unemployed seafarers from former Soviet-bloc states eagerly joined this motley maritime work force. For the traditional seafaring nations in the West, this has meant mass unemployment and has placed their age-old vocation in jeopardy.

Recent studies in maritime anthropology on "Mixed Nationality Crews," by the Cardiff-based Seafarers' International Research Centre (SIRC), indicate that these seafarers often resolve potential tensions among themselves better than corresponding multi-cultural communities on shore do. A major problem, however, is the continuing intimidation—of seafarers who stand up for their rights—by blacklisting and other forms of anti-union intimidation. Vigilance against vestiges of racism and xenophobia is still called for in relation to multi-cultural ship's crews, as elsewhere in this globalized world. This is ironic when we know that ships transport over 90% of the world's trade, making today's international seafarers utterly indispensable to the rest of the human race.

Finally, from a sociological standpoint, a third characteristic seafarers have in common is the level of *depersonalization* of life on board a floating "total institution." Like residents of hospitals, military bases and prisons, ship's crews may live for long periods within the narrow confines of a self-contained society. In addition to the marginalization that inmates of all such places share, the very mobility of an ocean-going ship increases their social isolation even further. On the one hand, there is the interpersonal "weaning" process—physical separation from land-life with home, family and friends. On the other hand, there is the simultaneous pressure of the process of "sailorization"—conforming to the new demands of discipline and solidarity required by shipboard life, often safeguarded by severe sanctions. In recent years, reduced crew-size and turn-around time in port have raised the level of loneliness and stress even more.

Despite the physical danger, the incessant exploitation, and the inevitable isolation with which seafarers have always had to contend, society has been forced to recognize their justifiable reputation for courage and compassion, honesty and loyalty. Moreover, the seafaring vocation also has its rewards. Many still sense the lure of the sea's natural beauty, the freedom from conventions of shore life, and the challenge and promise of personal fulfillment. Meanwhile, as surveys continue to show, for most modern-day merchant mariners, the honorable urge to provide a better life for their families has now become a main motivation. In the developing world, the alternative would be far lower wages ashore or simply unemployment.

THE PURPOSE

"You Might as well Preach to the Mainmast!"

So said a skeptic, back in the 1800s, on hearing of plans to reach seafarers with the good news of the gospel. He was not alone. At the time, one minister frankly admitted that the mere sight of a sailor entering his church would have caused universal alarm and made everyone anxious to get him out again. There was, in the words of the Psalmist, seemingly no one who cared for the sailor's soul (Ps. 142:4). Why should they? It was widely held that the seafarer simply had no soul anyway!

One who knew sailors from first hand observation recorded a very different view. If a typical, infidel philosopher of the day were to tell honest Jack "that there was no First Cause, but that the world had made itself and still governs itself, the philosopher would stand in great danger of being thrown overboard" (*NMBS Annual Report*, 1820). One British mariner had long since written for the benefit of his compatriots, "Be pleased to understand . . .

although we have no churches, the same God you have on shore is ours at sea" (*The Seamen's Protestation,* London, 1642). All of which is already affirmed in another passage by the Psalmist, this time about merchant seafarers in particular. As they pursue their profession, these daily see "the works of the Lord, his wonderful deeds in the deep" (Ps. 107:23-24).

True, all of this went no further than to a faith in God's providence as Creator and Sustainer. Nevertheless, it was a faith in basic accord with the First Article of the Apostles' Creed. As such, it was a fruit of God's *general* revelation, in order to prepare human hearts for God's *special* revelation—of salvation, as conveyed through the Holy Scriptures.

Here, seafarers actually had a distinct advantage. Well might they try to cope with stress through a host of maritime superstitions, or suppress the burdens of conscience with reckless fatalism. Still, their characteristic honesty and their natural aversion to any suggestion of sham or hypocrisy would stand them in good stead. They needed no reminders of the depth of humanity's fallen condition. They knew they were sinners, if only by bitter experience of the consequences. What they lacked was access to the biblical message of forgiveness through faith in the sufficiency of Christ's sacrifice on the Cross. Once offered such a gospel of free grace, seafarers would prove as receptive to that message as any other vocational group— if anything, more so.

During the first two decades of the 19th century, a spiritual awakening spread among English-speaking seafarers and eventually beyond. This not only flew in the face of any remaining skepticism about seafarers' innate spirituality. Seafarers themselves took the initiative, as they gained access to the Word of God. All of this provided persuasive proof of seafarers' particular receptivity to the gospel, once it became available to them. In a remarkable way, they are reaffirming this characteristic in today's seafaring world.

The "Ethnic Revolution," emerging from globalization, has resulted in a high level of religious pluralism at sea. ICMA's 1987 Seafarers' Survey, while well received in other respects, admittedly under-reported statistics regarding seafarers with non-Christian religious affiliation. That fact invalidates its findings on that score. Although Catholic Filipinos still constitute a conspicuous exception, and while many former Soviet-bloc seafarers are Orthodox-affiliated, non-Christian faiths continue to predominate among current-day crews. Most of them are of Asian and therefore largely Muslim, Buddhist and Hindu background. Not surprisingly, chaplains often find that seafarers with a non-Christian religious affiliation manifest a deeper spiritual consciousness than common in the more secularized West.

This book is not limited to the subject of seafarers and their attributes alone. There are already many books in that category, although most of them omit any form of spirituality beyond superstitions. The ultimate aim of the present book is to explore the unique role of seafarers in promoting the revealed plan of the Creator and Redeemer of both land and sea. The "Great Commission" in Matthew 28:18-20 succinctly summarizes that plan and suggests that seafarers will have a key role in its implementation. The reason may well be because seafarers are not only themselves so *receptive* to the gospel. Seafarers are also especially qualified for partnership in the global *spread* of the gospel. Chapter 1 will discuss factors in the specific choice of seafarers for this task, namely not just their traits of character, but in particular their marginality and mobility. The intention of the book's title is to reflect this primary purpose.

The title *The Way of the Sea* comes from the King James Version of Matthew 4:15. Those words not only relate directly to Jesus' choice of a port city for most of his ministry. They also bring to mind how, according to the Book of Acts, the early Christians were known as "Those of the Way." In the title of this book, the words highlight those who, as people of the sea, still follow the one who is himself "the Way." (John 14:6). The sub-title, *The Shape of Mission in the Seafaring World,* underscores the *missionary* purpose of the book. In this case, the word "mission" covers a historic as well as a systematic approach; this applies to both mariners themselves and others involved in maritime life. Also, as will become apparent in the body of the book, the word "mission" implies an activity aimed at partnership "with" seafarers, rather than one targeted paternalistically "to" seafarers.

A further purpose is to promote public awareness of maritime mission and address this question: What is the appropriate location of maritime mission? The itinerant nature of the seafaring vocation identifies seafarers' mission as a form of *mobility ministry.* Because maritime mission and the mariner's workplace are so closely connected, it also qualifies as *industrial ministry.* The very nature of port-cities as centers of urban population makes maritime mission (also known as "port ministry") a strategic field of *urban ministry.* Given the high proportion of non-Christian faiths in today's maritime workforce, maritime mission has, in effect, become a vital frontier of global mission, and therefore a *cross-cultural ministry.* Both hospitality and advocacy for the marginalized have become so indispensable to authentic maritime mission that this may also be seen as *diaconal ministry.* Lastly, like other specialized, pastoral care chaplaincies that are on the fringes of the institutional church, maritime mission is a typical form of *sector ministry.*

Like mariners themselves, maritime mission has its own unique identity. As such, it transcends the many ministries (such as those mentioned above) with which it may have an inter-disciplinary relationship. In order to gain respect and acceptance in its own right, maritime mission needs to find expression in a dedicated discipline of "maritime missiology." Mission in general has, at long last, become accepted as a theological discipline known as "missiology." To contribute toward the emergence and integration of a corresponding *theological discipline of maritime missiology* in institutions of learning is therefore a major purpose of this book. In years to come, that discipline will, hopefully, reflect even more self-theologizing by Asians and others from the Two-Thirds World, since only they can adequately theologize from their own perspective.

The readership this book seeks to reach is mainly, but of course not limited to, three groups: (1) Future pastors, missionaries, and other church-related personnel, studying at theological, mission and Bible schools around the world. (2) Those considering, training for, or already engaged in, maritime mission, including teaching of same. (3) All involved in the maritime community. Consideration for these groups has guided the writing and organization of this book. However, it is the Author's hope that it will also benefit many others in the wider population among whom this area of social advocacy and ministry has remained largely unknown.

THE PLAN

Charting a New Course

The four hundred students and faculty gathered for morning devotions could hardly believe their ears. Were they really all guilty of violating God's commandment not to steal—and this even on a daily basis? After this Author's lecture series on "Maritime Missiology" at a theological seminary in mainly Muslim Indonesia some years ago, the president invited him to bring a farewell message. The question that caused such a stir was simply the following: Did they realize the implications of hundreds of gospel-deprived human beings arriving in their port-cities every day? *Not* providing them with an offer of the gospel was tantamount to robbing them of that God-given opportunity! This was just one of several similar incidents that all resulted in a repeated counter-question: So where are the *educational resources* to help us fill that void?

The answer was both embarrassing and challenging. There had never existed any updated history of this field of mission, nor any theology of its theory and practice, much less a book combining both in the same volume. Least of all was there anything even remotely appropriate for an inclusive readership, ranging from seminary students to seasoned practitioners, as well as the broader population. This book is an attempt to respond to those needs.

Gustav Warneck (1834-1910), the acknowledged founder of Protestant missiology, found he had to explore the historical development of the global mission enterprise before he could formulate an understanding of mission as a theological discipline. This reasoning relates just as much to maritime as to global mission. Understanding the *history* of maritime mission is a prerequisite for developing a *theology* of maritime mission, one that is rooted in reality— and therefore both inductive and truly contextual.

Winston Churchill has stated, "The farther backward you can look, the farther forward you are likely to see." Since this book is about Christian mission in the seafaring world, its historical part takes as its departure point the very beginning of the Christian Movement. It then follows the story right up to Christianity's Third Millennium. An earlier cut-off date would have allowed for greater historical perspective. However, this would have been difficult to justify, given the tumultuous global changes during the last quarter of the 20th century and into the current post-September 11th world. The implications for modern-day maritime mission have proved enormous.

This Author's 1986 study, *Seamen's Missions: Their Origin and Early Growth,* includes a tentative identification of different "eras" of maritime mission history. Some researchers have followed that particular "periodization," while others have adopted alternative criteria. Since the context of maritime mission is subject to continual change, not only its definition but also its division into eras is open to changing perceptions. Based on his own research, this Author has now arrived at the following threefold dialectic model: *Early or Pre-modern Era* (Thesis); *Ecumenical or Modern Era* (Antithesis); *Global or Post-modern Era* (Synthesis). A colleague, Fr. John Maguire, has pointed to a fascinating parallel with the triple-stage organizational dynamic so often seen in church history: a Formative or Charismatic Stage (emphasizing *evangelism);* a Transitional or Institutional Stage (highlighting *social concern);* a Trans-formational or Ecumenical Stage (underscoring *holistic balance).*

The systematic part of the book has two components, both of which combine to make up a "Theology of Maritime Mission." The Author has written the first of these as a "Systematic Overview." For the other component, he has invited colleagues and other individuals with special expertise in current issues to contribute a series of "Perspectives" on mission in the modern-day seafaring world.

Tracing the contours of a *Systematic Overview of Maritime Mission,* the Author has sought to be both biblically based and biblically balanced. Where there is essential goodwill, the common criterion of the Christian Bible holds the unique potential to transcend the daunting divisions between Christian denominations. The systematic overview is limited to a survey, thereby avoiding unnecessary duplication of material in the historical part. This overview follows the same model as in Part VIII of the author's 1986 volume. However, rather than seeking to formulate firm "Objectives," the overview follows the terminology of the widely recognized modern-day missiologist, David Bosch. It focuses instead on "Dimensions," depicting direction toward an *interim* definition—one that can relate to the constantly changing context of current maritime mission (Bosch 1991, 8-11, 511-12).

By inviting others to contribute to *Perspectives on Maritime Mission* the Author is following the precedent set by the successful *Perspectives on the World Christian Movement* of Dr. Ralph Winter and his colleagues at the US Center for World Mission (Winter 1979). Instead of following any rigid systematization, the emphasis in the choice of Perspectives has been above all on diversity. This applies to each of the following four areas: ethnicity, gender, theology and vocation.

It is the prayer of the Author that the resulting volume will not only provide a needful historical and theological mandate for maritime mission. Above all, may it serve the mandate of the Author of the Great Commission—in solidarity with today's and tomorrow's People of the Sea!

PART I

HISTORY
OF MARITIME MISSION

Section
1

Early/Premodern Era
(Until 1920)

1

PRE-ORGANIZATIONAL PHASE
(c. 30-1779)

BIBLICAL FOUNDATIONS (c. 30-70)

A philosopher of the pre-Christian era once faced the following question: "How many living are there in proportion to the dead?" The sage countered: "First you will have to tell me where I am to place seafarers—among the living or the dead?" (SML 1823, 124). That perception has persisted through the centuries. People have all too often regarded seafarers as a race apart. Landlubbers have seen them as a lower, and therefore separate, species compared with the rest of humanity. The history of Christian mission in the seafaring world bears witness to a reality that is radically different. The pre-history of that mission dates back as far as the dawn of the Christian era itself (Kverndal 1986, 3-67).

Christ's Choice of Seafarers as His First Followers

Seafaring as seen in the Bible

No one could have affirmed the humanity and dignity of those who earn their living on the waters more powerfully than the Son of God. It was mainly from this vocational group that he enlisted his very first followers on the shores of the Sea of Galilee. Just how radical such a reappraisal must have appeared to Christ's contemporaries is clear from the Covenant People's own history.

Hebrews held the sea in fear, at best in awe. With Passover as an annual reminder, they knew their nation owed its existence to a divine manifestation of mercy by means of the sea (Exod. 14:1-31). They could even exult that the Lord of Hosts could make his pathway through the great waters (Ps. 77:19). However, they revealed little wish to make their own pathway on an element they saw as the embodiment of arbitrary evil (Pss. 74:13-14; 107:25-27). Among their kinsfolk, only one Old Testament figure of note is recorded as having put to sea on his own volition, and he did so only because he saw no other avenue of escape from his God (Jonah 1: 1-3). For her sea-borne commerce, ancient Israel was content to rely on her Phoenician neighbors to the north (1 Kings 9:11, 26-28, 10:22).

It was from the Master that the Christian church was to inherit the incentive for a more positive attitude toward the world of the seafarer. It was, for example, the port city of Capernaum that he made "his own town" during much of his three-year ministry (Matt. 9:1, 17:24-25). Moreover, many leading events in the gospel narratives link the Lord with the sea, and the life of those who worked there (Matt. 8: 23-27, 14:22-36; Luke 5: 1-11; John 21: 1-14). For him, a boat became a favorite preaching place (Mark 4: 1-2; Luke 5:3).

The most dramatic affirmation of seafarers as a people group was the role Christ reserved for them in his master plan of human redemption. It was to these he not only entrusted his gospel message (Matt. 4: 18-22; Luke 5: 1-11). He commissioned seafarers to take that message to the whole world (Matt. 28:18-20; Acts 1:8). See also Anson 1954, 33-73; Yzermans 1995, 2-16.

Two Untenable Objections

Is it historically or logically justifiable to attribute the origin of seafarers' mission to Christ's calling of his first followers? Some have objected that Jesus called freshwater fishers, not ocean seafarers. True, the Sea of Galilee was landlocked, and those who plied its waters were mainly fishers. However, factors like square mileage, the level of salinity, and the precise work of those who had their living there, were not at issue when seafarers' mission organizations began burgeoning in the early 1800s. Early advocates of the movement saw fishers as seafarers, facing fears and sharing bonds with fellow seafarers everywhere. Among early advocates of the "Seamen's Cause," few arguments were more popular than the Master's choice of that category of seafarers as his first followers.

Another objection has been that Christ's primary purpose was to call his closest co-workers, not to start a special mission to seafarers. This line of argument denies Jesus' divinity, more particularly his foreknowledge. Whether he called them as *seafarers* may well be a subject of debate. The fact is, however, that the Bible repeatedly portrays Jesus as fully aware of the historic implications of all his actions.

Marginality and mobility

Many centuries were to elapse before any comprehensive mission among seafarers was organized. Still, the question remains: *Why did Christ select seafarers for his first followers?* It might seem presumptuous to claim to comprehend the motives behind any decision of the Lord (Rom. 11:33-36). However, in this instance, it is not difficult to discern at least two sociological factors, both of missiological significance: seafarers as social outsiders, as well as people constantly on the move, i.e. their historic *marginality* and their inherent *mobility.*

Marginality: Selecting such an underprivileged people group to communicate his gospel to the world would have been in complete accord with Christ's preferential option for the poor and disadvantaged, as laid out in his programmatic statement in Luke 4:16-21. Scripture reveals God as one who chooses the lowly and despised to shame the power-hungry and arrogant, "so that no one may boast" or challenge the sovereignty of his power and grace (Luke 1:46-55: 1 Cor. 1:26-31).

The God who reveals this special concern for those on the margins makes it clear that the same is required of the *people* of God. Both the Old and New Testaments represent *hospitality to the stranger* as a characteristic of all who claim the name of the Lord (Lev. 19:34; Matt. 25:35). John Koenig characterizes hospitality to the stranger as the "creative hub of God's redemptive work" in world mission (Koenig, 106). This is also the theme of Kaarlo Kalliala's 1997 book, *Strangership,* as well as this book's Perspective by Kjell Nordstokke.

Christ could hardly have chosen a vocational group more marginalized and removed from the rest of society than seafarers, given all the danger and deprivation endemic to their profession. Those first followers of Christ were not only seafarers; they were also *Galileans.* In recent years, missiologists have built a convincing case for the First Gospel's preoccupation with the "Matthew theme" as a key missiological concept. "Galilee of the Gentiles" was, in the eyes of the religious and ethnic elite in Jerusalem, a land living in the "darkness" of diversity (Matt. 4:15-16; Isa. 9:1-2).

Matthew was himself a *Galilean* Jew, and therefore a *marginalized* Jew. In his gospel narrative, he consistently emphasizes how God in Christ became incarnate as a *Galilean,* how he called *Galilean* seafarers as his primary disciples, and how he made the *Galilean* port city of Capernaum his home base. In so doing, he "accepts the rejected ones of the world and commissions them as his change agents..." (Hertig, 155-163). Entrusting both his gospel message and his global mission mandate to *seafaring Galileans,* Christ reveals mission, at its core, to be the crossing of every boundary and every barrier in order to reach those on the fringes of human society (1 Cor. 1:28; Gal. 3:28).

Mobility: Before the technology of modern-day media, when human mobility was still a precondition for providing communication for world evangelization, the itinerant role of seafarers was indispensable. Who other than these "nautical nomads" could possibly have provided such a natural network for carrying the Good News to where it was meant to go—to the ends of the earth (Acts 1:8, Rom. 10:15)?

Jesus must have been well aware that fishers on the Sea of Galilee belonged to a *worldwide* community of maritime migrants, even though their own craft might keep comparatively close to shore. Their vocation would make them among the most uprooted of all people groups, compelled to be constantly on the move. If that first generation of Christians, commonly called followers of "the Way," were to be true to their global mandate, they and succeeding generations would need to become not only a *wayfaring* community (Acts 9:2, 24:14). They would—by intentionally following "the Way of the Sea"—need to become a *seafaring* community (Matt. 4:15). In order to fulfill its destiny, the present Church Universal must also become—albeit in part—a *Church Maritime!*

Both the *marginality* and the *mobility* of the seafarer were crucial to a salvation plan that would be socially and geographically inclusive enough to become truly *global*. A renowned history researcher of the Early Church, John Foster, shows how that truth was already playing out in the second century:

> In the year AD 178 Celsus, a learned Greek, wrote a book to disprove the Christian religion. The Church was very young and really had no right to exist. Yet as a secret society, a vigorous underground movement, it was spreading through all the seaports of the Mediterranean. It had long ago reached Rome, and spread westwards to Gaul and Spain. From Alexandria it had gone up the Nile and down the Red Sea to the tip of Arabia. From Iraq it was reaching towards Persia. What had this anti-Christian writer to say? "Jesus collected round him ten or eleven bad characters, the crookedest of tax gatherers and sailors, and with them went hither and thither getting a living by disgraceful and importunate means." It seemed to Celsus enough to damn this cause to say that its first promoters were sailors. . . (Foster 1959, 110-113).

In contrast to Celsus' cynical appraisal, the very *morality* of seafarers would be just another factor affirming them as key carriers of the gospel. Attributes such as *courage* in the face of overwhelming peril, and *compassion* bred by professional solidarity, both of them reinforced by seafarers' proverbial *consciousness of the divine*, these were ethical characteristics that would, if anything, only complement their sociological marginality and mobility as global ambassadors for Christ.

Establishing the precise nature of Jesus' role in the origin of seafarers' mission depends on how such mission is defined. Structurally specific *organizations for maritime mission* (referred to collectively as "seamen's missions") did not begin before the early 1800s. However, Christ's choice of seafarers is not, as some would suggest, romantic speculation. It is a well-documented fact, one that—from the very beginning—has inspired seafarers' mission initiatives across both ethnic and denominational borders.

Other Biblical Foundations for Maritime Mission

The biblical foundations for maritime mission go beyond just Jesus' calling of seafarers as his first disciples. Bible passages linked to the sea, ships and seafarers may not deal with maritime mission as such. Nevertheless, maritime devotional literature, ever since the Post-Reformation era, is replete with examples of the application of such texts, often in a metaphorical manner. During recent years, whole books have been written about the relevance of maritime Bible passages to aspects of maritime mission (for example, by authors like Peter Anson, Jan Wristers and Robin Mattison).

Paul, "the Great Missionary"

Among the Apostles, the case of *Paul* is particularly remarkable. Although not a seafarer himself, he was born in the busy Mediterranean port city of Tarsus and therefore familiar with the maritime world from early on. Later, he recalls how, "in journeyings often," he was repeatedly in peril at sea, adrift a whole day and night, and shipwrecked no less than three times (2 Cor. 11:25-26). It is inconceivable that he who admonished others to seize every opportunity to preach and witness "in season and out of season" would himself have neglected the many opportunities his sea travels afforded him to share the gospel with seafarers.

The 27th chapter of the Acts of the Apostles includes Paul's words of witness for his Lord and encouragement for passengers and crew, as they face the foundering of their ship. It depicts him as clearly the only courageous and competent person on deck. In one sense, Christ himself *initiated* Christian mission to seafarers. However, among his followers, the portrayal of Paul shows him as *pioneering* such mission, serving as the first on biblical record to fill the role of ship's chaplain, while sailing on that storm-tossed grain-ship from Alexandria bound for Rome, some time around the year 60 AD.

Peter, "The Big Fisherman"

Many dramatic turning points in Simon Peter's turbulent life relate to the sea: First, his enthusiastic response when called to leave his nets (Matt. 4:18-20); then, his faltering faith when he tried to walk the waves (Matt. 14:25-33); subsequently, his reinstatement after that early morning beachside barbecue (John 21:1-19). Even more significant was Peter's "vision correction" on the roof-top of Simon the Tanner's "house by the sea" in the Mediterranean port city of Joppa (Acts 10:1-48). Without that epoch-making event, and its sequel in the Roman port of Caesarea to the north, Peter might have settled for a local Judaic sect, instead of devoting himself to the gospel's global destiny. As the Apostolic Council in Jerusalem (Acts 15) would soon confirm, it was from Joppa and Caesarea that the most defining development in the Early Church would emerge, its doors now "flung wide open to the whole world" (Yzermans 1995: 21-22).

Apart from such maritime-related references, the many Bible passages that mandate *global* mission apply no less to the *maritime* dimension of that mission. It is impossible to take *Christ's Great Commission* seriously without including, by inference, the people of the sea (Matt. 28:18-20, Acts 1:8). Part II of this book deals with the more *general* biblical foundations for maritime mission. It is these that constitute the broader basis for a biblically grounded theology of maritime mission.

EARLIER ENDEAVORS (70-1779)

Having established that seafarers were the first to whom Christ entrusted the gospel, why did almost 18 centuries roll by before his church collectively reached out to seafarers with that self-same gospel? Should not the church long before have instituted a targeted ministry for such an exposed yet vital vocation?

This is not to say that no form of Christian ministry among seafarers existed in earlier years. Recent research by maritime historians has highlighted how the Medieval Church, even prior to the extended voyages of the larger vessels in the Age of Discovery, did seek to serve seafarers through *traditional parish structures* (Cabantous 1983, 1990, 1991; Miller 1989, 1995, 2002). There is also evidence that a variety of *additional special efforts*, however inadequate, were made over the centuries to minister in Christ's name to the specific needs of those whose livelihood was on the waters. These endeavors fall into two broad categories: First, early forms of ministry at sea; second, early forms of shore-based ministry among seafarers.

Early Forms of Ministry at Sea

Prior to the Reformation

Understandably, it was at sea that the first manifestations of a "Church Maritime" seem to have surfaced. Unfortunately, sources are scant. However, it is clear that pioneer missionaries of the Early Church would seek to spread the faith whenever they put to sea, just like their great predecessor, Paul. Likewise, on board those massive triremes of ancient Rome, there were untold numbers of Christian galley slaves sailing as involuntary seafarers, chained to their oars for a faith they refused to renounce. Doubtless, they would have witnessed to that faith as best they could before both fellow slaves and their oppressors.

By the Middle Ages, the Roman Catholic Church, with its traditional piety and practical paternalism, was also seeking to safeguard the spiritual and moral life of those who spent much of their time at sea. Such measures could include special fast days for seafarers. Priests would sometimes attach sacred objects to the poop or mast, in order to comfort "shipmen in peril of death." In some cases, a ship might carry an altar, even a small chapel, whenever there was the prospect of a sea-going priest serving as part of the ship's complement. An example of medieval ship's chaplaincy is the priest accompanying the Norseman, Leif Erikson, on his epic voyage of discovery to North America around the year 1000 AD. During the 1960s, archeologists discovered authentic remains of a Viking village, dating from the year 1000, in L'Anse aux Meadows in Northern Newfoundland. This would make that unnamed Catholic cleric *the first seafarers' chaplain known to have reached the New World* (Yzermans 1995, 49-50; Kverndal 2000, 8-9).

With the Crusades, Franciscan friars would frequently leave with the transport ships and share the privations of the crew and others who sailed with them. At the advent of the Age of Discovery, Catholic monks and priests regularly accompanied the galleons of Portugal and Spain across every ocean. There is little doubt that they found a warm welcome. Less popular would be the provisions of ancient maritime codes like the Laws of Oléron. The church endorsed draconian penalties for such vices as drunkenness, gambling, blasphemy, and brawling. The later Black Book of the Admiralty admonished the medieval mariner, when ashore, to flee the company of "women unhoneste," and proclaimed "that no man be so bold as to ravish any woman upon pain of death." Finally, for such nefarious pursuits as piracy, wrecking, or carrying contraband, the Pope (who at this time claimed a kind of universal control over the high seas) could do no less than order excommunication.

The Post-Reformation Era

During the 16th century, the Reformation resulted in many reappraisals. At sea, "heretic" crews of Protestant nations automatically qualified as pirates. For their part, like their Catholic counterparts, they saw themselves as engaged in a campaign for the purity of the faith. In fact, for the mariners of England, this was no time for spiritual lethargy. With pragmatic piety, naval commanders and "Merchant Adventurers" like Francis Drake, Walter Raleigh, Sebastian Cabot and others knew that no venture could possibly succeed if they provoked the wrath of the Almighty. Whether they contemplated war or trade, they would not only combat cursing and "other scandalous actions." Where no ordained cleric was available, they would seek divine favor through instructions to their captains for "the Bible or other Paraphrases to be raid devoutly and Christianly to God's Honour, and for His Grace to be obtained and had by humble and heartie Praier of the navigants accordingly" (Hakluyt 1903, 199).

In 1492, Christopher Columbus made landfall at San Salvador in the Bahamas and laid claim to the Americas for Catholic Spain. Eighty-five years later, Francis Drake landed on the coast of California, evidently in the area of San Francisco Bay, and took possession of the new land in the name of Queen Elizabeth of Protestant England. Drake commanded his ship's chaplain, Francis Fletcher, to lead what many consider the *first Protestant service held in North America*. This happened to take place precisely 200 years before the founding of the first seafarers' mission organization in the world, in London in 1779.

The high endeavors of the Elizabethan era did not last into the 17th and 18th centuries. Although there were chaplains appointed from time to time, both on larger ships of war and East Indiamen, they were rare. Among those who did serve, several would prove to be less than competent at sea. Fortunately for the crews, there were exceptions. Among these was the chaplain on the ill-fated Danish-Norwegian Jens Munk Expedition. To his last breath, *Rasmus Jensen* continued ministering to his Scandinavian shipmates dying around him in the Arctic wastes of Western Hudson Bay, in the winter of 1619-20. No less significant were the unsung but loyal labors of the estimated 3,000 "Sick-Comforters," or lay chaplains, who served on Dutch East India vessels over the years (Moree 1995).

It would depend on the caliber of the commander of any given ship whether his crew would benefit by organized spiritual nurture at sea. Some would recognize a special responsibility for the spiritual welfare of crews under their charge. Among merchant ship captains of this category, those who often commanded the greatest respect were the Quakers. An example is Captain *Paul Cuffee* (1759-1817). The son of an African slave and his American-Indian wife, Cuffee was a native of Cuttyhunk Island near New Bedford, Massachusetts. He worked his way to the position of shipmaster, eventually shipowner, despite both poverty and prejudice. He provided inspiration for numerous fellow-ethnic ships' crews and shipbuilders of his day, also motivating black entrepreneurship and re-migration ventures to Africa (Kverndal 1986, 10).

Another form of ministry at sea was the steady flow of *maritime devotional literature* that emerged among Protestant seafaring nations following the Reformation. With the recent discovery of printing, coupled with the rediscovery of the biblical principle of the priesthood of all believers, devotional aids and manuals of moral guidance proliferated both ashore and, from the late 1500s, also at sea. Although the concept was, in some respects, indebted to Roman Catholic precedent, specialized literature offering spiritual guidance specifically for *seafarers* was entirely new.

This novel form of devotional literature, often called "Mariners' Manuals," contained meditations on maritime-related and other biblical passages, as well as prayers for all occasions, including deliverance from storms, enemies and dangerous diseases. Among early British versions of these manuals by both Church and Non-conformist authors, several remained popular for years to come, also in the American Colonies. Authors included Samuel Page, John Wood, Josiah Woodward, James Janeway, John Flavel and John Ryther. Their works were supplemented in the early 1700s by the maritime authorship of New England's controversial "Keeper of the Puritan Conscience," Cotton Mather. Meanwhile, Nordic, Dutch and German clergy like John Heitman, Hugo Grotius and Mauritius Rochels, respectively, developed devotional aids of similar content. These, too, were in ongoing demand.

Early Forms of Shore-based Ministry among Seafarers

Prior to the Reformation

Centuries before the printed word could accompany the seafarer on his travels to distant lands, the Roman Catholic Church was ministering from shore through both intercessory prayer and, where possible, sacramental ministry. It would also dedicate churches, chapels and chantries along the coasts to one of several seafaring saints, like St. Clement, St. Christopher, St. Nicholas, St. Elmo, St. Columba and St. Brendan. Very often, one would dedicate a sanctuary to the Virgin Mary, known also as *Stella Maris* or "Star of the Sea" (Num. 24:17). Seafarers and their dependents would widely seek the intercession of both Mary and maritime saints.

Here and there, pious hermits would spend their lives in solitude on rocky headlands, praying for the souls and safety of medieval mariners, while at the same time tending a beacon or bell to warn them of imminent danger. They became the pioneers of modern-day lighthouse and coastguard services. In major ports, a monastery might provide a "maison-dieu" (hostel) where weary travelers could find refreshment. Here, sick or injured seafarers could also find care. In the sailortown district of medieval Rome, there was not only hostel accommodation but also an oratory, or prayer chapel, available for people of the sea. Elsewhere, for example in Amsterdam, there was a 15th century Sint Olof's Kerk, dedicated to the patron saint of Norsemen, where mariners could find special worship facilities.

The Post-Reformation Era

In the post-Reformation era, seafaring Protestant nations would frequently establish chapels connected with embassies or "factories" (overseas trading communities). Here, seafarers could hear the gospel in their mother tongue. The same happened where emigrant fellow ethnics had established churches in the seaports of a host country. This is not to discount the ministrations of clergy in seaports in general. However, in reality, seafarers ashore were more likely to meet with exploitation than edification.

Only in exceptional cases would the charisma of a specific cleric, and the caliber of Christianity in a given congregation, be such that seafarers would respond in significant numbers. This did happen in the case of three remarkable "Seamen's Preachers." All three were active during the Restoration period of 17th century England and all three suffered persecution for their uncompromising non-conformist faith: *John Flavel* of Dartmouth (Devonshire); *John Ryther* of Wapping (on the north bank of the Thames); and *James Janeway* of Rotherhithe (on the south bank). Their names have already been noted among those whose devotional manuals for seafarers proved amazingly popular,

The 18th century produced no comparable examples of *"Seamen's* Preachers," although there were remarkable instances of *"Seamen* Preachers," seamen who became preachers. Prominent among these were the following three: *John Newton*, the former slave ship captain, who became a clergyman in the Church of England and was one of her greatest hymn-writers; *Torial Joss*, once master of a merchant ship, who won renown as George Whitfield's trusted associate; and S*amuel Medley,* who gave up a promising naval career to become a leading Baptist minister in Liverpool. However, in their cases, the demands of their new vocations left little leeway for specific outreach to seafarers.

If there was little consistency, much less permanency, in ministry among seafarers by both medieval and post-Reformation institutional churches, there was at least one way in which seafarers themselves succeeded in providing a meaningful, church-related ministry. Through *maritime guilds,* many managed to maintain an intimate relationship with the institutional church. "Shipmen's Gilds" became part of the social scene in several British and Continental seaports, especially in the 14th and 15th centuries. Here, they would sponsor mass for endangered or deceased members, chantries and almshouses for mariners and their families, as well as church pageants for the general community.

During the 16th century, few maritime guilds survived the Reformation, at least in England. In France, however, during the 17th century, the maritime guilds' concept of lay-led, mutual support groups resurfaced in the form of "confraternities." As Chaplain-General of the Galleys, *Vincent de Paul* (c. 1580-1660), himself a former slave, founded several "confraternities of charity" to minister to French galley slaves. Alain Cabantous has uncovered fascinating examples of seagoing confraternities, based in the fishing communities of Northwest France, for example the Le Havre-based "Confrèrie du Saint-Sacrement," 1662-1727 (Cabantous 1983; Friend 1992).

During the 18th century, maritime social self-help was, in a few cases, continued by *Marine Societies*. These emerged in both Europe and Britain's American Colonies during the Enlightenment era. Though secular in orientation, and generally limited to merchant shipmasters and naval officers, they would nevertheless frequently support Christian, maritime-related initiatives.

A sporadic, sparsely researched, yet meaningful form of ministry to seafarers over the centuries has been the variety of efforts to alleviate, and eventually eradicate, *maritime slavery*. There were three distinct types of sea-borne human bondage: Galley slavery, naval impressment, and slave trading.

From the time of the Early Church, captives or criminals could be condemned to the systematic torture of *galley slavery*. Over the centuries, even some governments of "Christendom" condoned the practice, despite the protests and charitable endeavors by individual Christians like *St. Vincent de Paul,* with his Sisters of Charity, in 17th century France.

This does not mean that the institutional church was otherwise passive. A well-intentioned yet flawed means of ministry consisted of special offerings by both Catholic and Protestant churches in order to ransom the seafaring victims of corsair piracy. Through intercessory prayer, congregations would also lend spiritual support to the thousands of non-ransomed seafarers, held in slavery in port-cities of the Barbary States. Home congregations gained inspiration from stories of how most of these seafarers steadfastly refused to renounce their Christian faith for a lighter lot.

Several unsung heroes of the faith, who voluntarily cast their lots with the slaves, would work hard for the cause. Among these was *Father Dan* in the port of Algiers during the early 1600s. However, the final elimination of such a profitable, centuries-old source of income as slavery would not happen before the North African naval engagements of the early 1800s.

A second, deeply embedded form of maritime slavery, *naval impressment*, proved equally resistant to change. The policy of "pressing" a people's citizenry into military service was both ancient and almost universal. An island nation like Great Britain would see naval impressment as a necessary evil. During a national emergency, a "hot press" might well whisk away a groom from his bride at the church door, or force homeward bound merchant seafarers into a naval tender before they had a chance to set foot ashore. It took the advocacy of brilliant agitators like *James Edward Oglethorpe* (founder of Georgia) and *Granville Sharpe* ("father" of the British Slave Trade Abolition Movement) to turn the tide of public opinion. Oglethorpe and Sharpe deserve recognition as 18th century precursors of the late 20th century Seafarers' Rights Movement.

They also hold a place of merit in maritime mission history for another reason. Oglethorpe and Sharpe not only denied any need for the "white slavery" of naval impressment for reasons of national security. They also passionately repudiated the notion that "black slavery" was necessary for the national economy. This third form of maritime slavery, the notorious traffic in human flesh, known as the *African Slave Trade,* was in many ways the most horrific.

Jesuit missionary *Peter Claver* (1581-1654) fought for decades to alleviate the lot of surviving slave "cargo" on arrival in the New World. During a lifetime of ministry in the Colombian slave-port of Cartagena, he reportedly cared for and baptized no less than 300,000 victims of white barbarity. Called the patron saint of black people in the Western Hemisphere, Peter Claver actually received canonization (Anson 1948, 30). However, it would require a frontal attack on the trade itself to eradicate such a diabolical system. The launching of that attack relates intimately to the events surrounding the start of organized seafarers' mission.

"THE SET TIME"

Reflecting on the first intentional, broad-based efforts to reach the seafaring world with the gospel, a veteran seafarer is said to have exclaimed, with words borrowed from his day's version of the 102nd Psalm: "Surely, Lord, the time, yea the set time to favour sailors is come!"

In retrospect, after centuries of little more than sporadic efforts by the institutional trustees of the gospel, how did organized maritime mission come about? Why did it begin *when* it did—*where* it did—the *way* it did? In seeking answers to these questions, it is important to consider the following: First, the contemporary climate of change, in church and society, resulting from the religious and humanitarian awakenings that swept through Great Britain and America during the 18th century; second, factors focusing public attention particularly on the plight of seafarers around the turn of the 19th century.

The 18th Century Anglo-American Awakenings

Britain's "Evangelical Revival"

In 1738, a watershed event took place in Britain. A young Anglican clergyman, dedicated but deeply depressed, experienced a dramatic spiritual renewal. At the time, he was listening to Luther's Preface to the Epistle to the Romans, in an Aldersgate Street religious meeting-place in the City of London. During the following 53 years, that same clergyman, *John Wesley* (1703-91), backed by his hymn-writing brother Charles, crisscrossed the nation, praised and pelted, revered and reviled. As a result of his preaching, the horse-riding evangelist became the catalyst of a spiritual revival such as the English-speaking world had never seen.

The effect was not simply spiritual. "The Bible knows nothing of a solitary religion," was one of Wesley's favorite axioms. In 18th century England, those citizens exhibiting upper class elegance appeared undisturbed by the national church establishment. They also saw poverty as an economic necessity, and drunkenness as a legitimate opiate. Wesley, on the other hand, was relentless in rebuking crime and coarseness among both "high" and "low." This included such sea-related social evils as smuggling, wrecking and impressment.

The matrix of Wesley's movement was his "society" structure, subdivided into "class-meetings," the movement's vehicle of change. Although inherited from the renewal group movement within late 17th century German-Lutheran Pietism and Restoration-era Anglicanism, its roots were in the house-churches of the New Testament era. Within decades, Wesley's cell-group movement was able to ground great numbers of working class converts in the Christian faith and thereby, as some saw it, "save England from the excesses of the French Revolution." These renewal groups became nurseries of spiritual and societal change and, eventually, helped develop the British trade union movement. Moreover, Methodism's cell-group system produced the blueprint for the "Bethel Movement" that gave birth to the entire Seafarers' Mission Movement.

The Methodist Revival of mid-eighteenth century England had a revitalizing effect on evangelical-minded members of both the Church of England and the Dissenters, gradually growing into a nationwide "Evangelical Revival." Three basic Reformation principles united those who became known as "Evangelicals": First, the Bible as sole, authoritative norm for faith and life; Second, salvation through the atoning death of Christ, appropriated by grace through faith alone; Third, personal responsibility for witness and service based on the biblical principle of the priesthood of all believers.

Toward the close of the eighteenth century, it was evident that the first flourish of this Methodist-inspired Evangelical Revival in Britain had spent itself. However, signs of a so-called "Second Spring" of that revival were by then already underway. This time the precursor was an event in the life of a Member of Parliament from Hull, *William Wilberforce* (1759-1833). After his self-described conversion in 1785, he was now ready to give leadership to a dedicated group of Church of England lay people in the village of Clapham, southwest of London, derisively known as the "Clapham Sect."

From Clapham, Wilberforce and his friends began a campaign to save the soul and reform the morals of the nation, no less. Due to Wilberforce's rhetoric and close affinity with Britain's "ruling classes," he was able to gain influence where the more marginalized Methodists could not. Despite widespread opposition, the "Claphamites" managed to reinvigorate the Evangelical Party in the established church. With their leadership of the Slave Trade Abolition Movement, they initiated "an industry in doing good." Through that voluntary network, Wilberforce and his Anglican Evangelicals cooperated with Methodists and Dissenters, and formed a British "Evangelical United Front."

America's "Great Awakening"

It was not surprising that the vigor of Britain's Evangelical Revival should soon spread to the mother country's Transatlantic Colonies. However, the scene in America was radically different. A new nation was confronting the dual challenges of forging a national identity while at the same time taming the vast wilderness of the West.

Nevertheless, with the close cultural ties that persisted between both these English-speaking peoples, those revivals would also reveal some remarkable commonalities. By the mid-1700s, the preaching of the "father" of American revivalism, *Jonathan Edwards*, had fueled an American version of Britain's revival that came to be known as the "Great Awakening." *George Whitefield*, Wesley's one-time colleague from "Holy Club" days in Oxford, joined Edwards and reinforced the reach of this colonial counterpart. By the early 1800s, when the American Revolution seemed to have drained off the energy of the original Great Awakening, the latter's after-glow ignited a "Second Great Awakening." This energized a growing network of non-denominational mission and media societies, creating an American-type "United Evangelical Front."

Factors Focusing Public Attention on Seafarers

The "Benevolence Empire," that had now developed on both sides of the Atlantic, provided motivation for a whole series of new missionary endeavors. However, for all this to benefit especially seafarers, it would need powerful motivation. At least five factors eventually contributed to that end.

Captain Cook's Voyages

Within little more than a decade (1768-1779), the epic voyages of Captain James Cook had brought the expanse of the "South Seas," and thereby one third of the earth's surface, within the bounds of the known world. Visions of commercial and political gain gripped much of the Western part of the globe. This accompanied a mounting awareness of public dependence on seafarers, as well as a consciousness of the misery of those seafarers' life situation.

The New Romantic Mood

Toward the turn of the century, a new Romantic Era was fast supplanting the Age of Reason on both sides of the Atlantic. This led to a new fascination with the remote and the bizarre. As a result, interest increased in the proverbial, colorful life of the deep-sea sailor, depicted in contemporary literature as the hapless yet heroic "Jack Tar."

The World Missionary Awakening

After studying the journals of Captain Cook's Pacific voyages, an English shoemaker, *William Carey,* published his renowned missionary manifesto in 1792. This led to the founding of the Baptist Missionary Society that same year and, according to many, the beginning of the "Modern Missionary Movement."

In 1810 came the founding of the American Board of Commissioners for Foreign Missions. A proliferation of mission societies soon followed in Britain and America. For seafarers, the effect would be two-fold. The new mission societies soon realized their dependency and indebtedness in regard to seafarers, as an indispensable means of both transportation and communication. They also saw graphic evidence of how seafarers could compromise the credibility of the gospel in foreign fields—by their own unrestrained behavior when ashore.

The Slave Trade Abolition Movement

Publicity around the Slave Trade Abolition Movement eventually focused on the dire situation of seafarers who provided the crews for the slave ships. This was thanks to meticulous research by *Thomas Clarkson,* an Anglican deacon. He had been seeking evidence for Wilberforce and his colleagues of the reported atrocities of the African Slave Trade. In so doing, he also uncovered proof of a mortality rate of over half the seafarers transporting the slaves. With that, he destroyed endeavors to defend this particular trade as a "nursery for seamen." Instead, he proved it a "graveyard." Small wonder that sailors, under orders to torture, mutilate, even jettison alive their fellow human beings, would stay drunk. They said they simply could not commit such acts if sober. While officials were shocked, those who stood to gain were outraged at the publicity, so much so that Clarkson's life was often in jeopardy. Once, nine infuriated slave-ship captains were within a yard of pushing him over a pier. Charging straight through them, he managed to escape to continue his work. Clarkson, like others who devoted their lives to disclosing the dimensions of the "white man's crime against Africa," also helped to bring before church and public the abuse of one of the most neglected sectors of society—the people of the sea.

Protracted Warfare at Sea

Beginning with the French Revolutionary War (1793-1801) and continuing through the Napoleonic War (1803-1815), Britain was immersed in protracted warfare on land and sea. As an island nation, she was dependent on her sailors in order to keep her overseas lifelines open. She also needed mariners to maintain the "wooden walls" of the navy as her main line of defense. All of this brought the seafarer increasingly into the public eye, at least for the duration of the war.

On the Verge of a New Missionary Enterprise

After centuries of sporadic and inadequate measures by the institutional church, the stage seemed finally set for the intentional inclusion of seafarers in an ongoing outreach ministry. In the worldview of the Medieval and post-Reformation eras, the Western World was seen as "Christendom," a geo-political bloc where church and state were closely interrelated, and where seafarers were simply members of their local parish. With the advent of the Enlightenment and the Industrial Age, together with all their implications for the maritime world, the old structures—such as they were—had broken down. This left the seafarer's situation more precarious than ever. Here was a whole occupation-based "people group" whose human needs were being virtually overlooked by both church and society.

Peter Anson, co-founder of the Catholic Apostleship of the Sea (AOS) that evolved from the year 1920, compares in critical terms the lack of Catholic ministry to seafarers during the 19th century with the "multifarious" activities that had already emerged among the Protestants. However, the overall context faced by 19th century Catholic seafarers was essentially different from that of their Protestant counterparts.

In the predominantly Protestant Anglo-American world that prevailed around the turn of the 19th century, developments had reached the point when one might well ask: Was this at last the "set time" for action?

2

BRITISH FORMATIVE PHASE

(1779-1864)

THE BETHEL MOVEMENT

From the outset of organized seafarers' mission, a maritime emblem known as the *Bethel Flag* played a catalytic role. The Rev. *George Charles Smith* knew which denomination deserved credit for pioneering the movement inspired by that emblem. Smith, himself a Baptist, and widely recognized as "Founder of the Seafarers' Mission Movement," states in a retrospect written in 1828:

> It is notorious that it began, as most good things that require active
> zeal do, among the Wesleyan Methodists, and that three years before
> any member of any other denomination had been permitted to put his
> hand to the work…God was pleased to honour their denomination to
> start this great work (NSM 1828, 385-386).

Floating Hells and Fighting Methodists

There was good reason why the Methodists became the prime movers in the "Sailors' Reformation" that broke out in the early 1800s. In the "Glacial Epoch" into which the National Church of England had sunk during the preceding century, most of her adherents feared any form of "enthusiasm" for the gospel. Followers of Wesley's convictions could hardly expect better treatment than the level of social and physical abuse that their leader had experienced. The seafarer was also still subject to the stigma of a pariah caste at the close of the Napoleonic War. The Methodists, themselves by then frozen out of the Established Church, were therefore the least likely to be deterred by the low, contemporary image of seafarers.

The Wesleyans had more than a reputation for zeal for the gospel and affinity for fellow-humans on the fringes. They had a strategy for effective action. In their "society" system, with its "class-meetings," they had inherited a dynamic model for grassroots, Christian nurture and outreach—with origins going back all the way to the house-church movement in the Book of Acts. That model would also become an effective vehicle for early lay ministry at sea—with the timely reinforcement of the fledgling Bible Society Movement

The Naval and Military Bible Society (1779)

It is a little known fact that the literary media movement, which was soon to change the global history of the church, first served seafarers. It began with the vision of a Methodist lay leader and marble-cutter, *John Davis*, and his friend and fellow lay leader, a furniture-maker called *George Cussons*. They were walking through London's Soho Square, after an evening meeting in nearby West Street Chapel, during the autumn of 1779. What blessings might result, Davis suggested, if they were to distribute some pocket Bibles among men in the armed forces? Cussons liked the idea. The outcome was the founding of the *Naval and Military Bible Society* (NMBS) in November 1779.

At first, the Society called itself only "The Bible Society." There was no other such society nationwide before the founding of the *British and Foreign Bible Society* (BFBS) 25 years later. In that year, The Bible Society added the prefix "Naval and Military." The Society is still active, now as the "Naval, Military & Air Force Bible Society" (NM&AFBS). It holds the distinction of being the *first seafarers' mission-related organization in the world.* Limiting itself to Scripture distribution, it could not qualify as a seafarers' mission organization in the *holistic* sense. Nor was the Society (as its title indicates) concerned with only *maritime* distribution. Nevertheless, its role as the precursor of the Seafarers' Mission Movement remains unchallenged.

Although Methodist-originated, and soon a beneficiary of Wilberforce and his Anglican-Evangelical colleagues, the NMBS has always remained nondenominational. Initiated just as the American War of Independence approached its climax, in a year marked by Captain Paul Jones' dramatic naval victory over the British off Flamborough Head, the Society soon discovered that demands were outstripping supplies. This was especially evident during the latter years of the Napoleonic War. By 1811, with some 150.000 men under sail in the British Navy, contemporary sources confirm the widespread interest in personal possession of the Scriptures. Many sailors would gladly use their meager pay to secure their own copies. Others might lose all in shipwreck, yet make sure they salvaged their Bible.

By then, the NMBS was no longer alone in struggling to meet the increasing demand. The BFBS and others had now also taken up the challenge. Some, like the Society for the Promotion of Christian Knowledge (SPCK), and especially the Religious Tract Society (RTS), founded in 1698 and 1799, respectively, distributed large quantities of Christian literature among ships of war, much of it printed especially for seafarers. By the end of the Napoleonic War, it even made sense to speak of a "Naval Awakening" in the Royal Navy.

The British Naval Awakening

Literary media agencies ashore were dependent on volunteer colleagues afloat who were motivated to promote distribution on board. Methodists (who were the favorite prey of press-gangs of the day) were quick to respond to the challenge. They were also positioned to provide needful lay leadership among their peers. In fact, much of the lay ministry in Britain's wartime navy during these years followed the model of organized Methodism. By the end of the war, there were Scripture-studying cell-groups of both officers and men, actively worshiping and witnessing on board close to one hundred British ships of war.

All of this prompted mixed reactions. These might come in the shape of cannonballs, rolled across the gun-deck in order to break up a Bible-study meeting among shipmates. It could also come from a commander. In one case, a captain complained to his admiral about "psalm-singing Methodists" (by then a derisive term for any committed Christians) who were disturbing the "cohesion" of his crew. After making inquiries about these particular sailors' professional conduct, the presiding admiral heard such superlatives about their skill, their discipline, as well as their courage under fire, that he promptly dismissed the case. Before doing so, he exclaimed that, if such men were Methodists, would to God all his men might become Methodists!

The Naval Awakening was not limited to the lower deck. Admiral (later Lord) *James Gambier,* known during the French Revolutionary War for his courage and consistent walk of faith, became a prominent patron and advocate for the early Seafarers' Mission Movement.

However, among evangelical naval officers, no one made a greater impact than Lieutenant *Richard Marks* (1778-1847). His naval career comprised bouts of early self-described "licentiousness," followed by his dramatic conversion and courageous leadership of a growing Christian community in a British man-of-war. Later, he wrote a popular series of memoirs and "sea tracts" called *The Retrospect* (1816). Despite offers of naval advancement, he rejected these and followed instead a call to ordained ministry among "poor and plain people" ashore. Nevertheless, his parish ministry at Great Missenden, Buckinghamshire, did not prevent him from continuing to serve his fellow seafarers. It was largely Marks' persistent advocacy of the "Seamen's Cause" that prepared the way for the founding of the Church of England *Missions to Seamen (MtS)* in 1856.

From "Nelson Sailor" to "Seamen's Advocate"

Like Richard Marks, *George Charles Smith* (1782-1863) saw service in the British Navy during the French Wars. He, too, could give first-hand evidence of the level of indulgence that would transform a man-of-war into a "floating hell" on arrival in port. However, Smith's relationship to the Naval Awakening would be of a different character than that of Marks.

In 1796, a fatherless Smith left for sea as a fourteen-year-old, bound apprentice to the captain of an American brig. On arriving in Caribbean waters, he became a victim of impressment into a British man-of-war. In 1801, he served with distinction as second captain of the foretop under Nelson at Copenhagen. Shortly afterwards, illness led to his discharge. In 1803, after a wild sailortown spree and renewed illness, he experienced a radical conversion while recuperating in a Reading tavern under the care of a "pious" nurse.

On recovering, the transformed sailor joined the Baptists and began studying for the ministry. This led to a call to a pastorate in the port of Penzance, Cornwall, in 1807. Captivated by his sailor-like directness, seafarers' families joined the many others who flocked to hear him preach. Then, two years later, Smith received what he later saw as his "Macedonia Call." That day, some sailors had just come ashore from a local revenue cutter after surviving a terrible storm. Hearing of the Baptist preacher who was himself a former sailor, they decided to invite him to come and preach a sermon for them on board their ship.

This astounded Smith. Even more so did news of the rising numbers of committed Christian sailors on British ships of war. Sensing their pastoral needs, Smith started a *Naval Correspondence Mission* on their behalf in 1809. His plan was to follow up with personal letters and literature, in order to encourage them and help create a sense of community among them. Soon, soaring postal expenses even began to jeopardize his marital relationship! Smith managed to secure sponsors, however. Among these was *Lady Mary* Grey of Portsmouth, a pioneer promoter of Scripture distribution in the Navy.

With his awareness of publicity needs, Smith combined episodes from the Naval Awakening with his own sea experience to author a series of sailor dialogues, published as *The Boatswain's Mate*. These achieved wide popularity, also in America. During fund-raising campaigns in London, he would include quotes from his correspondence with sailors. This, too, met with a remarkable response. As a result, the religious press became aware of the "Seamen's Cause," and of George Charles Smith as its pioneer advocate. Before long, there was news of amazing developments on the River Thames, as well.

Birth of a Biblical Emblem

The Lord's "set time to favour sailors" appeared to have come at last, as the veteran seafarer had put it. Just as the wider availability of the Bible had already led to spiritual awakening among naval seafarers, the turn had evidently come to merchant seafarers, too. This places in historic context Marine Bible Societies as the *first form of organization to emerge within the Seafarers' Mission Movement* during the early 1800s. The Master had made seafarers the first to whom he once chose to entrust his Word. The seafaring world was now beginning to sense that trust again.

The Marine Bible Society Movement

With the reduction of the naval establishment after the war, many of those reentering the merchant and fishing fleets were veterans of the Naval Awakening. In Britain and America, the Bible Societies, too, began to discover seafarers as one of the most spiritually and materially marginalized sectors of contemporary society. This gave birth to a series of Marine Bible Societies, of which the Naval and Military Bible Society had long been the sole forerunner

The first to emulate the NMBS was the *Thames Union Bible Committee.* Organized in Southwark, London, in 1813, this became the *first form of maritime mission dedicated to serving specifically merchant seafarers in Great Britain.* (The NMBS did not include merchant as well as naval seafarers before 1825.) From 1818, this Thames Union became the *Merchant Seamen's Auxiliary Bible Society*, after which it maintained a steady growth. The key to this was twofold: Ship visitation, rather than relying on seafarers themselves to search out shore-based Bible depositories; and the appointment, in February 1818, of *John Cox*, a naval lieutenant, as full-time agent, visiting the shipping at the Thamesmouth out-port of Gravesend. Cox became, as far as one knows, the *first full-time seafarers' missionary and shipvisitor in the world.*

Not long after its founding in 1804, the BFBS learned to rely on *Agents Afloat* for much of its Bible distribution in foreign ports. These were motivated merchant captains, sometimes also naval commanders, who would offer free transportation and use of their contacts to bring Bibles in different languages to other countries. One of these agents was Captain *Francis Reynalds* of Hull. In 1813, Captain Reynalds made history by initiating the first *ship-based* "Marine Bible Society" on record, enlisting a vessel's own crew as members and active participants in Bible distribution. The port cities of England's North Eastern counties, where Methodism was strong, took the lead in establishing Marine Bible Societies. There were also societies in Scotland, as well as in the Shetlands, the latter including the Greenland fisheries. Nor did the pioneers ignore the barge- and boat-people on inland waterways. The founding of the *Grand Junction and General Sea Canal Bible Association* dates back to 1816.

With the return of peace, the Marine Bible Society Movement in the New World showed even more vigor than in the Old, characterized by a less paternalistic, more participatory approach. First in the field was the "religious capital" of the young nation. Others followed Philadelphia, up and down the Atlantic Seaboard. The next year, in 1820, Rev. *Ward Stafford*, working for the Marine Bible Society of New York, founded no less than 23 Marine Bible Societies in New England. Meanwhile, societies began on Lakes Champlain and Erie and on other "Inland Waters." Most of these elected to become auxiliaries to the new, national *American Bible Society*, founded in New York in 1816.

A remarkable feature of the Marine Bible Society Movement was the formation of several such societies on the mainland continent of Europe, a half-century before any more comprehensive form of seafarers' mission in those parts. Examples include the *Naval Bible Society* at Skeppsholm, Stockholm, in 1815; another at Carlscrona, Sweden's major naval base, in 1819. At Cronstadt, the out-port of St. Petersburg, a Naval Bible Society began as an auxiliary of the newly founded 1816 Russian Bible Society. While these societies were mainly devoted to distribution among naval personnel and their dependents, some started also serving merchant seafarers. This occurred in Hamburg-Altona in

1814, Amsterdam in 1820, and Rotterdam in 1821. A common feature of all these continental versions was the key role played by the BFBS.

Eventually, the regular seafarers' mission societies took over the role of these specialized Marine Bible Societies—except for the NMBS. A champion of the early Movement spoke for many when he wrote of that role:

> Seamen, of all others, should be furnished with the Bible, since, by their profession, they are, a great proportion of the time, deprived of other means of religious instruction (Stafford 1817, 4, 33-34).

Today, seafarers from the former Soviet Union or from other nations with restrictive regimes—whether in Asia or elsewhere—continue to see the possession of a Bible or New Testament in their own language as a personal priority. While the NM&AFBS no longer maintains its own network of ship-visitors, there are some seafarers' mission agencies that still make Scripture distribution, combined with ship visitation, their primary purpose (notably the UK-based Christian Seamen's Friend Society and the South Africa-based Biblia network).

The Thames Revival (1814)

Subsequent events would affirm the historic role played by the Marine Bible Society Movement. First, it helped to jolt the church at large out of its centuries-old inertia in relation to such a mobile vocational group as seafarers, one that was clearly beyond the reach of land-based parish ministry. Second, it helped to channel the energy of the Naval Awakening into what would become the "Thames Revival," also eventually the worldwide "Bethel Movement."

It all began in *Rotherhithe*. This was no coincidence. Located along the south bank of the Lower Pool of London's River Thames, Rotherhithe (Saxon for "Sailor's Haven") had a rich, maritime heritage. The Rotherhithe parish church of St. Mary's was the gravesite of Captain *Christopher Jones* who had set sail from here on his epic voyage with the *Mayflower* in 1620. Here, despite persistent official persecution, *James Janeway*, a Nonconformist clergyman and widely read author of maritime devotionals, ministered faithfully to his flock of seafarers and their families during the 1660s. Here, too, in Rotherhithe's still largely seafaring community, John Wesley could record a "remarkable revival" more than a century later.

Like William Carey before him in the history of *world* mission, *Zebedee Rogers* (d. 1833) was a shoemaker by profession who would come to play a pivotal part in the enfolding history of *maritime* mission. Rogers was an active member of the Wesleyan Methodist Chapel in Silver Street, Rotherhithe. One day, in the summer of 1814, Rogers befriended a collier captain who had attended a service there. After inviting him to his class-meeting, Rogers was in turn invited on board. When Rogers asked the captain whether he thought the crew would come to the captain's cabin and let Rogers lead an informal worship with them, the captain replied, "Go and ask them." Despite their initial surprise, the whole crew came and even witnessed, to their astonishment, their own captain joining in public prayer.

The ship happened to be a brig appropriately named the *Friendship*, one of literally hundreds of North Country collier brigs normally waiting to unload along that particular stretch of the River Thames. The captain, *David Simpson* of Shields, would go on to become a veteran volunteer seafarers' missionary (eventually, as a "Bethel Captain," becoming the first to carry the cause to Archangel in 1831). The date of this first informal gathering, *22 June 1814,* later became the day celebrated as the birth date of the future "Bethel Movement."

When Rogers held another meeting the next time the *Friendship* came to port, the captain of the ship alongside invited him on board his ship, too. "From that time I went on until now," commented Rogers years later. So did the movement of which he was the catalyst. As invitations multiplied, Zebedee Rogers soon needed help from his chapel colleagues ashore.

The crews also received invitations to attend services and class-meetings in Silver Street. Crowds of them came. A key co-worker here was *Samuel Jennings*, a successful Rotherhithe timber merchant who, as class leader, had turned his stable into a subsidiary sanctuary. Here, scores of sailors packed in to take part in *Mr. Jennings' Meetings*—both on Sundays and at mid-week. These combined meetings on board and on shore, however unpretentious, were, as far as one knows, the *first, ongoing program of preaching ever established especially for the benefit of seafarers.*

In 1815, Rogers received a reinforcement for which he was particularly grateful. A young, black seafarer called *Frederick Sanderson* was "awakened by God on board a ship," joined the Wesleyan Methodists, and became a co-worker with Rogers among the collier crews in the Lower Pool. (Later, he left for Jamaica, where he continued a ministry among those of his kinsfolk who had survived the horrors of both slave trade and slave labor.)

Next year, another collier co-worker, this time an enterprising Wesleyan first mate from South Shields, *Anthony Wilkins*, came with suggestions of far-reaching consequence: first, soliciting host-ships for *multiple-crew* meetings, rather than depending only on single-crew gatherings; second, deciding on an appropriate signal to identify such host-ships in good time. Agreement was soon reached to hoist a lantern at the main top-gallant masthead. This led to such an increase in meetings that there was no longer any doubt. On the waters of the Thames, revival had reached the merchant seafarer.

The Bethel Flag (1817)

As the spring of 1817 approached, and the days began to lengthen, there was a need for a *daytime* signal. An easily recognizable flag seemed to be the answer. Three years earlier, Zebedee Rogers had initiated meetings that would grow into the Thames Revival. Again, Rogers was destined to design the emblem that would transform the revival into a movement spanning the globe.

One evening, after much thought and prayer, the word "BETHEL" was, to Roger's surprise, "deeply impressed upon his soul." Later, he learned from his sister that the word signified "House of God" in Hebrew. The delighted shoemaker lost no time in encouraging sailor friends to raise funds for bunting so his sister could sew the word in white letters on a blue ground. On 23 March 1817, Captain *T. Hindhulph*, a Wesleyan Methodist from South Shields, hoisted *the first Bethel flag in history* at the masthead of the *Zephyr*. Over the years, there has been much confusion about the origins and interpretation of the Bethel Flag. The facts cited here build on the most authentic primary resources available (Kverndal 1986, 159-162, with Notes).

Seafarers got the message. They responded in record numbers. Soon after, they had to make a second flag, to meet the mounting demand for signaling simultaneous meetings. Anthony Wilkins (now captain) and his colleagues decided to add a *star* (the five-pointed Bethlehem version) and a *dove* (carrying an olive branch, from the narrative of Noah's Ark). As a result, the flag became a confession of Christ, as commemorated in the three major festivals of the church year: *Christmas,* with the star symbolizing Christ's incarnation; *Easter,* with the dove of peace symbolizing his atonement and resurrection; and *Pentecost,* with BETHEL symbolizing the birth of his church by his Spirit.

As the summer progressed, further flags and "Bethel Meetings" multiplied. Seafarers, first on the Thames and soon across the seven seas, came to recognize the Bethel Flag, with its rich biblical symbolism, as their own. Finally, after centuries of deprivation, they had found a visible means of belonging to the worldwide body of Christ. As such, the Bethel emblem fulfilled a dual purpose: It became a *public profession of faith*, at least on the part of the captain hoisting it. It also functioned as an identifiable *rallying point* for seafarers in port, seeking gospel nurture and a sense of Christian community.

NEW CONFIGURATIONS

Until the summer of 1817, the Bethel Flag and the movement it engendered had been a Methodist enterprise, though never intended as such. At that point, other denominations entered the scene. In the case of George Charles Smith, as a Baptist minister on one of his preaching tours in the Metropolis, his first visit to a shipboard Bethel Meeting on the River Thames made a deep impression. Warmly welcomed as a seafarer among seafarers, he sensed an immediate rapport, and then threw himself into the movement with heart and soul. During his three remaining months in London, he seized every occasion to continue preaching under the Bethel Flag, with seafarers coming by the boatload from up and down the river to hear him.

It became quite commonplace for those who attended such meetings to be pelted by their peers, with both expletives and lumps of coal. After receiving reports of "seditious meetings," even the River Police would sometimes harass them. As he had done during the Naval Awakening, Smith encouraged his "brother sailors" to take negative reactions in stride. Still, as the weeks went by, he had not yet arrived at any specific plan for general mission among seafarers. Before Smith returned to Cornwall, however, this would all change.

From Floating Chapel to Sailors' Palace

That same year (1817), while immersed in impromptu preaching at crowded Bethel Meetings, in the rows of ships on the Rotherhithe side of the Lower Pool, the publicity-conscious preacher from Penzance conceived a plan. He would hold a pre-announced "Seamen's Service" on the deck of a suitable ship, this time near the sailortown district of Wapping. The locally owned *Agenoria*, moored off the shore, proved ideal for the purpose. When the evening arrived, crowds overflowed onto a large lighter lain alongside. Sailors hung in the rigging of adjacent shipping. Ashore, the local population crowded onto the beach, while others filled upper windows of nearby buildings.

The event was a religious sensation. Reportedly, thousands heard Smith's soul-searching sea sermon from Acts 27. The metropolitan press produced headlines about the feasibility of "Aquatic Preaching." It had already recognized George Charles Smith as a gifted public speaker; even the London *Times* had hailed him as the "Prince of Field Preachers." However, it was the *Agenoria* event that now confirmed him as indisputably the "Seamen's Preacher." At the same time, with his burly build and seafaring past, Smith became widely known as "Bosun Smith." (He never sailed as boatswain, but evidently accepted the designation as a token of jovial affection by his fellow seafarers.)

The Port of London Society (1818)

Smith told later that he was watching the seafarers' enthusiastic response from his speaker's platform, made up of three casks and placed on the hatchway of the *Agenonia*. The thought struck him: "What an excellent plan it would be to have a ship converted into a chapel afloat and moored in the Thames for constant preaching to sailors." Convinced that "this was from God," he devoted the rest of his stay to promoting the project of a "permanent pulpit" in the river.

The notion was not entirely new. Under Queen Mary Tudor in the 1550s, a persecuted Protestant congregation had used a ship in the Thames as their clandestine sanctuary. More recently, in 1786, the Marine Society had opened a converted merchant vessel, anchored off Deptford, as a training ship. By now, in 1817, former warships transformed into prison hulks had become a familiar sight on the Thames. However, none of them could provide any precise precedent for the concept of a floating chapel, permanently moored and appropriated for regular public worship services for seafarers. Here was both a national and worldwide innovation.

In the process, Smith enlisted an important ally, *Robert Humphrey Marten.* Marten, a Congregationalist Deacon in the Independent Chapel in Plaistow, was a shipbroker by profession. As such, he was well prepared to head a promotional campaign. To help create the level of interest needed in both business and religious circles, Marten drew up a practical prospectus. Meanwhile, Smith produced a tract entitled *The British Ark;* this included an account of the Thames Revival, and proved widely popular.

Another benevolent initiative earlier that year only helped to enhance these endeavors. The efforts of a group of lay Christians, to relieve the plight of destitute, unemployed sailors, roaming the streets of London during the winter, had resulted in a *Committee for the Relief of Distressed Seamen*. This Committee, founded on 5 January, 1818, acquired seven "Receiving Ships," to be anchored in the river to offer shelter and other support services.

Finally, on 18 March 1818, the *Port of London Society for Promoting Religion among Merchant Seamen* was founded at the City of London Tavern in Bishopsgate Street. The primary purpose would be to supplement care for seafarers' "temporal interests" with "their religious instruction, their moral reformation, and their eternal happiness." A major method was to be "the Ministry of the Gospel, regularly preached on board a floating chapel, on a completely non-sectarian basis." In practice, this would mean mainly Baptists and Congregationalists as active participants, perhaps also Methodists. (Catholic cooperation would have been illegal, and Anglican unfeasible.) Still, here was the *first seafarers' mission organization in the world*, providing a sanctuary set apart for the regular preaching of the gospel for merchant seafarers.

The London "Ark" (1818)

After intense preparations, with both Smith and Marten heavily involved, 4 May 1818 saw the dedication of HMS *Speedy*, a rebuilt sloop-of-war from Nelson's navy, as *The Port of London Society's Chapel for Seamen*. Soon to be known by seafarers everywhere as the *Ark*, she could seat 800. Her permanent place of mooring—by the London Dock Buoy off Wapping New Stairs—was close to the site of the *Agenoria* event the year before. Here was now the *world's first specifically appropriated sanctuary for seafarers*. One of the texts for the day was from Psalm 142:4, "No man cared for my soul." By contrast, as some one later observed, "The Thames, from the first day it began to flow, never witnessed a greater day in its history than this" (Matthews 1911, 187).

Looking back, George Charles Smith, a leading creator and recorder of the Seafarers' Mission Movement's early history, shared the conviction so often expressed by Bethel pioneers: In spite of all the "manifest indifference" of organized Christianity toward seafarers over the years, the Spirit of God had once again "moved upon the face of the waters" and at long last sent revival "through the instrumentality of mariners themselves."

In retrospect, it seems evident that here were two distinct yet closely interrelated phases of one and the same process of "transplantation." The Naval Awakening would only have been an episode, destined to dissolve with the wartime navy itself, had not many thousands of naval seafarers been channeled into the merchant service and thereby into the Thames Revival. Meanwhile, the Thames Revival might never have developed into the dynamism of the Bethel Movement, had it not first been infused with the rugged spirituality of the Naval Awakening. Again, quoting a later seafarers' mission general secretary, the benefits of the whole movement would "without doubt have been extinguished" if not for the prophetic personality of George Charles Smith (Waltari 1925, 71).

There was good reason for Richard Marks to welcome the opening of the *Ark* as "a new era." The only prior form of seafarers' mission had been Christian literary media distribution, as exemplified by the NMBS, the Marine Bible Societies and others. The *Ark* also marked a transition toward the institutionalization of the Bethel Movement. Limited as it was to only one port and only British seafarers, the *Ark* was no more than the first-fruit of that movement. For his part, Smith was sure that the newly born Bethel Movement was destined for greater things—and he was not about to let it die in infancy.

The Bethel Seamen's Union (1819)

George Charles Smith, like his fellow-pioneers, saw the Bethel Movement as global. It represented the literal fulfillment of the prophet's prediction that the Lord's dominion over the seas would extend "from the River to the ends of the earth" (Zech. 9:10). Again, Smith would come to play a decisive role. So, too, would the emblem that had already come to symbolize the Movement. By the summer of 1819, Smith saw that the Port of London Society was too limited in both membership and scope to play any global role. A broader organization would be necessary for the Bethel Flag to become a catalyst for future seafarers' mission expansion. To transform vision into reality, Smith went to work to build a British "United Front" of maritime mission supporters, both Anglicans and Dissenters alike. Among them were numerous seafarers, mostly Bethel veterans and naval officers, as well as merchants and members of the clergy.

On 12 November 1819, at the City of London Tavern, Smith facilitated the founding of *The Bethel Seamen's Union,* to become the *world's first, nationwide seafarers' mission organization.* However, its scope was meant to be worldwide. This "Bethel Union" was to promote a Christian bond of unity among seafarers "round the circumference of the Globe," regardless of denomination or nationality. Seafarer members would commit to worship and witness afloat and ashore under the banner of the Bethel Flag. They would also seek to facilitate further, related efforts, such as the provision of sailors' boarding houses.

It is worthy of note that the first organization in the world presenting itself as a "Seamen's Union" was founded by Christian seafarers—for the spiritual and social welfare of fellow seafarers everywhere. In 1820, Admiral Lord Gambier accepted the presidency of the Society. The same year, the Society expressly recognized its role as global by expanding its name to the *British & Foreign Seamen's Friend Society and Bethel Union* (BFSFSBU). During the following decade, the Bethel Flag continued to unfurl as the symbol of seafarers' mission initiatives in an increasing number of provincial and foreign ports, including across the Atlantic. For several years to come, the story of seafarers' mission would become, in large part, the story of the Bethel Flag.

A major reason for the Bethel Movement's success may have been its vivid *simplicity*—combined with its inherent *mobility*. In London, where it all began, pioneer activists could birth new missions simply by raising their Bethel banner among the most marginalized members of society. First selecting

Rotherhithe's notorious "Screw Bay" district on the south side, and the slums of Stepney on the north, they deliberately took on the very worst of sailortowns.

Among the most active was Zebedee Rogers, the founder of the flag. Rogers would rally "Bethel Press-Gangs" of volunteers from Bethel Meetings on the Thames. With these, he would, for example, hoist Bethel Flags from oars stuck in the windows of a large Wapping pub, whose owner had resolutely refused to "sell liquor on Lord's Day." This improvised press-gang would then hail their comrades in surrounding streets and hunt them up in sailor brothels along "the Highway." They would then cheerfully push and pull their unsuspecting prey into their makeshift mission house, never failing to fill it. Too late, the captive audience would discover another kind of meeting than they had expected in a pub. Nonetheless, no one would normally leave before the close. Auxiliary Bethel Societies would follow in the wake of this concerted campaign to clean up the sailortown environment along both sides of the River Thames.

Another factor in the rapid expansion of the Bethel Movement, both in Britain and abroad, was *The Sailor's Magazine*. Beginning as a literary novelty in 1820 on behalf of the BFSFSBU, this, too, was the brainchild of Smith. He remained its editor, also of its 1827 successor, *The New Sailor's Magazine,* for the rest of his life. Apart from the magazine's success in advocating the cause, it has remained a unique, primary resource for the study of early maritime mission history. (In all, Smith authored some 80 published works in the course of his life; most of them were maritime, many polemic and some poetic.)

Spurred largely by both Smith's authorship and his rousing rhetoric during repeated visits, new provincial Bethel Union Societies sprang up in a growing number of port cities around the British Isles in the course of the early 1820s. Scotland took the lead, in January of 1820, with the *Greenock Seamen's Friend Society* (the first in the world to adopt that increasingly popular self-designation). Leith followed one month later, then Bristol, Hull, and Liverpool, in quick succession.

By the close of 1821, preaching under the Bethel Flag, whether on a ship in port or in some location like a sail-loft ashore, had been initiated in over 60 out-ports. Several did not survive. However, many did, and their immediate goal would be to emulate London by establishing a "permanent pulpit," generally in a rebuilt hulk in the harbor, serving as a floating chapel.

The Bethel Flag Goes Global

At first, the Society's severely limited funds precluded any regular foreign representation. Soon, however, its less structured strategies made it possible to reach out beyond home waters. The Bethel Flag would generally continue to play a pivotal part, especially in cooperation with overseas missionaries stationed in coastal areas. Besides the Bethel banner, they would receive donations of select literature. Some would also be able to benefit by "field training" at Bethel Meetings on the Thames before shipping out, as in the case of William Ward, who left for India in 1821.

William Carey in Calcutta, Robert Morrison in Canton and John Williams in the Pacific were among a long list of world mission pioneers who later became involved in seafarers' mission projects abroad under the Bethel Flag. Missionaries had ample motivation to lend a hand. They would soon see how seafarers from supposedly "Christian" countries could, simply by the nature of their behavior ashore, either reinforce or destroy the credibility of the gospel in the eyes of the native population.

Bethel Captains, too, would play a vital role. As ship's masters, they would lead devotions for their crews at sea. Then, on arrival in port, they would hoist the flag and invite seafarers from other ships to join in worship, often before the astonished eyes of onlookers on shore. Such shipboard meetings frequently became a forerunner of more structured shore-based seafarers' mission. Sometimes local social injustice could become an issue. In the Caribbean, for example, Bethel Captains incurred the hatred of slave-holding merchants by supporting anti-slavery measures ashore, as well as by including native Indians and free Blacks in their shipboard Bethel Meetings.

In British ports, Bethel pioneers would try to reach out also to foreign seafarers. In fact, during the French Wars, Bible and tract distribution among foreign seafarers in prison hulks became one of the earliest forms of maritime ministry. In the course of the 1820s, that concern also extended to foreign-port ministry. Here, the two who became most particularly involved had ties to the BFSFSBU. Both, too, happened to have experienced a wartime conversion.

Northumberland-born *William Henry Angas* (1781-1832) returned to his Baptist faith as a prisoner of war, after reading the remains of a pocket edition of *Dr. Watts' Hymns*. (He had bought it from a French Hussar on guard duty, who was using it to light his pipe!) After serving several years as a merchant navy captain, he left a lucrative shipping career to study theology. In 1822, he became *the first ever to be ordained specifically for seafarers' mission* ("the work and office of a Missionary to Seafaring Men"). Rather than ministering only in home-ports, he sensed a call "to push on to those ports where the message of love and mercy had not yet reached."

Hoisting the Bethel Flag wherever he went, Angas pioneered the work in port cities like Danzig, Hamburg, Rotterdam and Antwerp—while ministering to hard-pressed Mennonite congregations in these areas at the same time. Cut off by cholera at 51, his short life validated what he saw as the Bethel Movement's primary aim: Every Christian on the seven seas must become what none other could be with equal effectiveness—*a missionary among fellow seafarers!*

Danish-born *Carl Gustav Christopher Ditlev von Bülow* (1787-1867) was, like G. C. Smith before him, inspired by the testimony of a Christian nurse, in his case when seriously wounded as a cavalry officer in the Würtemberg army. His vision was—now as a different kind of warrior—to carry the gospel by sailing vessel to the seafaring communities of his fellow-Scandinavians. This he did, with the Bethel Flag aloft, during three major expeditions from 1819 to 1828. The BFSFSBU, both the British and Scottish Bible Societies and, in particular, The Continental Society, all rallied to his support.

Ordained as a Congregational minister (in 1827), von Bülow's revivalist zeal met with a mixed, but mainly positive, reception among the coastal population in Norway. Eventually, however, an expulsion order, procured by Lutheran State Church officialdom, put an end to his "Norway Mission." Nonetheless, he became a precursor of both the Norwegian Mission Society and the Norwegian Seamen's Mission. In addition, his sailing sanctuary strategy became a model for the successful Anglican endeavors launched on the British coast from the mid-1830s, as well as for the North Sea missions to fishers in the 1880s. Von Bülow later continued his missionary labors for foreign seafarers in other ports, including on the Thames.

The British & Foreign Sailors' Society (1833)

In the meantime, maritime ministry in the Metropolis would go through a period of needful realignment. George Charles Smith had long been aware that the *Ark* could not minister to more than a fraction of the thousands of mariners milling around the port of London. The situation clearly called for bolder action.

In 1825, Smith hired the Danish-Norwegian Church in Wellclose Square, capable of holding some 1,000 people. Here, on the north side of the Thames, was, as he bluntly described it, "Satan's undisturbed and favourite kingdom." Here he chose to hoist his Bethel Flag and, for two decades, make this *London Mariners' Church* the metropolitan hub of his many maritime ministries.

Meanwhile, others among the early activists sought to build an organization that could unite the best of the original Port of London Society and the BFSFSBU. After years of struggle, they finally met with success. On 3 July 1833, the *British and Foreign Sailors' Society* (BFSS) formally absorbed both of these forerunners in one common entity. The new Society would have to face hard financial times for many years. However, though soon forced to decommission a decaying *Ark*, in 1834 it acquired an important new asset—the first of a long series of dedicated "Thames Missionaries."

Captain *Benjamin Prynn* (1781-1856), a Cornish-born Wesleyan Methodist, was a veteran of the Bethel Movement and had been active in the Thames Revival. As a respected Bethel Captain, he was the first to hoist the Bethel Flag in numerous ports around the British Isles, as well as in 23 foreign ports. During the 1820s, Captain Prynn developed strong ties with Smith. For the next 22 years, as a Thames Missionary, he now maintained an intensive program of shipboard visitation. Here, he would find good use for his peer ministry experience at sea. With the help of his co-workers, he would lead over 1,000 Bethel Meetings a year.

Captain Prynn also played an active role in the 1829 formation of a *Bethel Covenant*, a fellowship of deep-sea Bethel Captains. Closely identified with the BFSS, it had reached 500 members by the year 1844. They would make up the Society's principal form of overseas ministry at a time when salaried representation abroad was financially impossible. By then, the BFSS had also begun enrolling Christians of other ranks in a corresponding association of "Bethel Men."

In 1845, *Thomas Augustus Fieldwick*, himself a former Junior Thames Missionary, joined the Society as its new leader. His bold vision gave the BFSS the national and global stature it has since enjoyed. By widening the Thames Missionary concept, Fieldwick first facilitated an economically feasible expansion of the Society's foreign work. A precedent had already been set in 1836 when the Society had called *Augustus Kavel*, a Lutheran refugee pastor from Prussia, as a missionary to foreign, especially German, seafarers on the Thames. The sponsor in this case was the treasurer of the BFSS, *George Fife Angas*, younger brother of William Henry Angas, and a long-time friend of the Bethel Movement.

Fieldwick decided to build on the positive results of Kavel's ministry. In 1846, he appointed the pioneer of sailing missions to Scandinavia, Rev. Carl von Bülow, as "Thames Missionary for Foreign Seamen." An increasing number of these were now coming from Northern Europe. When ill health finally forced von Bülow's retirement in 1850, a series of well qualified successors followed him. These included *August Thiemann,* who would play a pivotal role in events leading up to the founding of the Norwegian Seamen's Mission in 1864.

Fieldwick saw the need for a visible rallying point that both seafarers and their friends could view with pride. Finally, benefiting by the public focus on seafarers during the Crimean War, a vigorous fundraising campaign led to the opening, in 1856, of the *Sailors' Institute* in Mercers' Street, Shadwell. With its spacious accommodation for worship, recreation and nautical education, the building soon became known among seafarers worldwide as the "Sailors' Palace." Eventually, it became a model for the "institute" concept worldwide, later also adopted by the "Seamen's Church Institutes" of the American Episcopalians. (In actual fact, it was George Charles Smith who first introduced the *concept*, with its wide range of services, a quarter of a century earlier.)

Combating the Crimp

Just as Marxist propaganda has regarded all religion as "opium for the people," critics of seafarers' mission have painted pioneers of the movement as "sky-pilots," preoccupied with otherworldly concerns rather than seafarers' social welfare. Relevant resources on issues of their day, like impressment, the slave trade, and post-war unemployment, have repeatedly disproved this. Christian *social* concern for seafarers preceded—even paved the way for—concern for their *spiritual* welfare, not vice versa.

Certainly, in the early phase of the Bethel Movement, George Charles Smith and his fellow-workers saw no reason to apologize for prioritizing evangelism. This emphasis was, however, never exclusive, never any narrowed-down "spiritualization" of the gospel. From the early 1820s, one initiative in maritime diaconal ministry succeeded the other. As one seafarer put it, *"We do not have soul-less bodies, nor do we have body-less souls!"*

A Strategy of Substitution

In Great Britain, it was Scottish Bethel Societies that took the lead toward a more balanced, holistic position. Nevertheless, as an individual, no one would play a greater role than George Charles Smith. Just as Smith had already headed early efforts to "reclaim the seafarer's soul," he very soon combined this with a concerted campaign to redeem the seafarer's social status. The 1820s would witness a long list of maritime diaconal initiatives, such as "sailors' reading-rooms," ship's libraries, day schools for seafarers' children, vocational "maritime schools," and societies for the relief of shipwrecked and distressed mariners and their dependents. Smith was either the initiator or at the forefront of virtually every one of them. It was after his move in the mid-1820s, from Penzance to the hub of London's most notorious sailortown, that Smith finally was able to devise a master plan for "Sailor Emancipation," as he called it.

Smith was among the first to raise public awareness for what he saw as the most immediate source of the mariners' miseries—the *Crimping System*. As a member of this international, maritime mafia, a crimp's strategy was to separate the sailor from his hard earned wages. Toward that end, the crimp would focus on building a local monopoly to meet the two most basic needs of any port-bound seafarer—relief from the privation and stress of sea life, and re-employment when no longer willing or able to remain ashore. A successful crimp could command a whole hierarchy of unscrupulous shipvisitors ("runners"), bar and brothel keepers, slop sellers and sea lawyers.

Smith's counter-strategy consisted of a system of "substitution," offering the seafarer positive alternatives at every step, from the very moment a ship arrived. The logical place to commence was the immediate need for boarding and lodging between voyages. In 1827, Smith established a *Destitute Sailors' Asylum* in neighboring Dock Street, in order to provide "soup and straw" for those in the most desperate need. The next year, he initiated the world's first *Sailors' Home* in adjacent Well Street, as a safe haven for seafarers in general. After its completion in 1835, the Anglicans took over the administration. Soon, this would become a model for similar institutions worldwide.

Aware that there were wider needs, Smith went on to introduce a comprehensive *Maritime Establishment,* at least in blueprint. This would incorporate a shipping office and reading-room, a savings bank, slop-chest stores and maritime museum. It would also include legal aid, boys' pre-sea training, maritime lectures, medical help, care for disabled and aging seafarers as well as their dependents, even a sailors' cemetery.

Smith also became a pioneer in combating the "Four Cardinal Maritime Vices"—promiscuity, intemperance, profanity and Sabbath-breaking. In 1830, he founded a *Maritime Penitent Young Women's Refuge* for the rehabilitation of sailortown prostitutes (or "Maritime Magdalenes"). In 1831, he followed up with a *Sailors' and Soldiers' Temperance Union.* In so doing, Smith defied contemporary, anti-Catholic prejudice and developed a warm relationship with Father Theobald Matthew, known as Ireland's "Apostle of Temperance."

Advocating for Systemic Change

In the wake of the French Revolution and its Reign of Terror, the specter of "seditious meetings" was still strong in early 19th century England. This would deter pioneer promoters of seafarers' mission from supporting strikes and collective bargaining to better seafarers' miserable wages. Nevertheless, numerous examples did indicate solidarity with the seafaring community, one that went beyond mitigating suffering to changing the system that created it. They managed to transcend *diaconal* concern, and assumed an intentionally *prophetic* role. Here, too, George Charles Smith was well ahead of his times.

Smith demonstrated the desperate need for a "Maritime Code of Laws" long before there was any question of government or union intervention. Together with others, he protested vehemently (and ultimately successfully) against the "brothelization" of the Navy—Smith's characterization of official condoning of shipboard prostitution while in port. He also fought for justice and social emancipation for that misused class of stevedores called "coal-whippers."

Smith even petitioned the Queen against his own country's role in the Opium Wars, where British seafarers were used as accomplices in crime against the Chinese people. In addition, a whole generation before Samuel Plimsoll, Smith launched a campaign against "sea coffins, or frail ships built cheap, to be lost to gain the insurance." In fact, in his persistent agitation for attitudinal and systemic change, Smith moved well beyond the bounds of maritime philanthropy and became *a forerunner of maritime sociology*.

The Lasting Legacy of George Charles Smith

Many of Smith's plans never came about. Some were premature, left to later generations to implement. Others never survived because they beame casualties of at least two tenacious character traits. Smith's stubborn *belligerency* embroiled him in repeated public controversy. Meanwhile, his tendency toward *eccentricity* led him to refuse to follow convention, causing inevitable problems in Victorian England. Although dishonesty was never at issue, those two characteristics, coupled with a chronic inability to maintain regular accounts, resulted in four terms in debtors' jails between 1836 and 1845.

Finally forced to "give up the ship"—his London Mariners' Church—the Bosun returned to Penzance in 1848. From here, he continued to travel, minister and write, practically until the day he died. On January 10, 1863, he passed away peacefully in his sleep, almost 81 years of age. Only a couple of years previously, as the guest of seafarers' mission societies along the East Coast of the USA, his transatlantic colleagues had feted him as the visionary *Founder of the Seafarers' Mission Movement*.

However embattled "Bosun" Smith became in his day, that legacy has since been widely affirmed. Almost single-handed, George Charles Smith aroused the Christian church from the lethargy into which she had lapsed. In so doing, he helped her to see her responsibility for both the evangelization of the seafarer and the humanization of the maritime world. This was the task of a prophet—with the vision and perseverance of a Maritime John the Baptist.

Anglicans and Methodists

As a convert to the Baptist denomination, Smith was at the same time an ardent advocate for the active participation of other denominations in the Seafarers' Mission Movement—especially "the wealth, the piety, and the influence of the Establishment," referring to the National Church of England.

The Anglican Dilemma

Loyal Evangelicals, committed to their mission-focused agenda within the Church of England, faced a painful dilemma. Should they remain passive, pending the organization of specifically Anglican seafarers' missions, hopefully some time in the future? Or, should they in the meantime support existing nondenominational societies, as far as Anglican Church order would allow?

Like Rev. Richard Marks, most Evangelical clergy chose the latter, as did also a host of recently discharged naval officers of Anglican affiliation. These willingly filled both staff and promotional positions in the nondenominational societies born of the Bethel Movement. Their rationale for joining Dissenters in a "United Front" at this stage was simple. As one Evangelical clergyman expressed it: "The question is not whether our Sailors shall be Churchmen or Dissenters...it is whether they shall be Christians or heathens." An Evangelical admiral put it in more nautical terms, declaring that what the situation now called for was "a long pull, and a strong pull, and a pull altogether!"

Nevertheless, the "irregular" nature of such non-parochial work continued to present problems. Although a concerted, avowedly Anglican enterprise was still decades away, a series of significant local Anglican initiatives did develop in the meantime, some as early as in the 1820s. Among contributing factors were doubtless both G. C. Smith's repeated reminders in his widely circulated *Sailor's Magazine* and the popular authorship of Rev. Richard Marks (including his two series of appeals in *The Christian Guardian,* 1826-27).

The Anglican *Port of Dublin Society* was the first on the scene, as early as 1822. After that came the *Liverpool Mariners' Church Society* in 1825, the *Mariners' Church Society* in Hull in 1828, and an *Anglican Floating Chapel* in Cork in 1830. Even in far off India, an *Anglican Mariners' Church* opened in Calcutta in 1830, also an *Anglican Floating Chapel* in Bombay in 1831. Although in Hull and Calcutta the sanctuaries were both shore-based, the floating sanctuary option was, at this point, still preferred elsewhere.

Early Anglican Initiatives on the Thames

In London, the *Episcopal Floating Church Society* (EFCS), founded in 1825, was the first to promote a national (at first even Empire-wide) Anglican mission among seafarers. Despite a rising awareness of mission within the Church of England at this time, the trend was still not sufficiently strong for the Anglican hierarchy to endorse such plans (Kennerley 1992: 84-85).

None the less, thanks to the support of Lord Melville, then First Lord of the Admiralty, a rebuilt sloop-of-war, HMS *Brazen,* could open in 1829 as a

Sailors' Floating Church, initially moored off Rotherhithe. Since the response of seafarers themselves proved less than expected, the Society removed the vessel to new moorings off the Tower in 1834. However, frustrated by both financial problems and continuing low attendance, the EFCS finally abandoned the failing vessel in the mid-1840s, together with the Society's wider aspirations. Despite this, the Society did fulfill one vital function. It managed to maintain an ongoing Anglican presence on the metropolitan waterfront, transforming it shortly into two somewhat more promising endeavors.

In 1846, committee members of the EFCS decided to launch a *Thames Church Mission* (TCM). The following year, they replaced their former *floating* church with a *sailing* church, buoyed by the reported success of an Anglican initiative of that kind in the Bristol Channel. They commenced with a cutter called the *Swan*, loaned by the Navy and able to accommodate a floating congregation of 120. With a vigorous program of shipvisiting and preaching by Rev. *William Helderness*, the new venture drew an enthusiastic response. Covering all kinds of vessels from London to Gravesend, the TMC eventually came to include fishing craft in the North Sea—thereby becoming a forerunner of the *Royal National Mission to Deep Sea Fishermen* in the 1880s.

In 1847, concerned Anglicans could also consecrate *St. Paul's Church for Seamen* as a shore-based successor to their former Floating Church. Located in Dock Street by Wellclose Square, the chaplain there was at the same time able to serve the nearby Destitute Sailors' Asylum and Sailors' Home.

The Missions to Seamen (1856)

The first successful *national* organization to represent the Church of England followed within a decade after the twin ventures that replaced the EFCS. Apart from the earlier efforts already mentioned, the credit belonged largely to a remarkable Anglican trio—Ashley, Childs and Kingston. Each would make an indispensable contribution toward the creation of the new organization.

Rev. Dr. *John Ashley* was not only the prime mover in developments leading up to the future national society. He also established the mobile method of mission that was to become its original mode of ministry. In 1835, Ashley was between calls while vacationing by the Bristol Channel. One day, he perceived a fleet of some 400 wind-bound sailing ships anchored off the distant coast of Wales, cut off from society. His offer of pastoral service met with such a warm response that he saw this as a call from God. He declined the church already offered him ashore, and devoted the next fifteen years of his life to this form of roadstead ministry. By 1837, his work had become the *Bristol Channel Mission,* in 1845 renamed the *Bristol Channel Seamen's Mission.*

A new era opened up in 1841, with the launching of a mission cutter called the *Eirene,* specifically built for the work. Instead of having to depend on the goodwill of ships' captains to allow services on board their vessels, Ashley could now invite ships' crews to attend his (and their) own sailing sanctuary. Though intended to hold 70, over 100 would often crowd in. In 1850, forced by failing health and financial struggles to bring the *Eirene* to her moorings, the heroic pastor and seafarers' friend finally went ashore for good. The critical question was now: Would it mean also having to abandon this vast, hitherto almost neglected field of maritime ministry?

The answer came in 1855. That year the Society, now reorganized as *The Bristol Mission to Seamen,* made the decision to expand activities to the English Channel. At the same time, it appointed a young vicar in Devonport, Rev. *Thomas Cave Childs,* as "Chaplain to the English Channel." With a cutter similar to the *Eirene,* and with Ryde on the Isle of Wight as his base, Childs maintained an ongoing program of visitation of wind-bound ships for the following two years, all along the south coast from Plymouth to the Downs.

Childs also managed to motivate others to key leadership roles. One of these was a layperson who would very soon be organizing a new national society, unequivocally identified with the Established Church. *William Henry Giles Kingston* was a loyal Anglican with strong evangelical, but by no means bigoted, convictions. Nationally, many already knew him as empire-builder and nautical author. He now came up with a plan for a *Society for Promoting Missions to Seamen Afloat, at Home and Abroad.* The purpose was to combine in one organization all existing and future Anglican seafarers' missions.

Launched in London on 5 April 1856, the new Society united with the Bristol Missions to Seamen as *"The Missions to Seamen"* (MtS). As Secretary, Kingston secured Rev. *Theodore A. Walrond.* Walrond would now lead the new Society through decades of expansion, both nationally and internationally.

Reconciling Diversity in Anglican Maritime Mission

"Anchorage work" by means of sailing sanctuaries remained the primary purpose of the Society for its first few years. During the 1860s, however, the validity of shore-based activities became increasingly apparent. By the end of the century, they had become predominant, given the pace of transition from sail to steam. Finally, in 1964, the Thames Church Mission, with its sole remaining sailing ministry, also formally merged into the MtS.

Another issue claiming early attention was the appropriate role of the laity in operational activities. As Secretary, Walrond campaigned hard for the employment of "Scripture Readers" (later called "Lay Readers") ashore, as well as volunteer "Helpers and Associates" afloat. Both had originated as Anglican counterparts to the many lay workers in the nondenominational Bethel Union. Meanwhile, the Society took care to avoid undue provocation of those with High Church concerns.

Churchmen of Anglo-Catholic persuasion reacted against not only the lay orientation but also the non-parochial organization of The Missions to Seamen. In Rev. *C. E. R. Robinson* they soon found an ardent spokesperson. Renting a riverfront public house as base, Robinson launched a parochial ministry from his own Gravesend church. From here, he reached out to the steady stream of seafarers and emigrants on vessels anchored in that part of the River Thames. This *St. Andrew's Waterside Church Mission* (SAWCM) was, in 1871, able to move into a Mission Church (St. Andrew's) built for that specific purpose, right on the river's wharf-side.

The new Anglo-Catholic enterprise succeeded in mobilizing a new concern for seafarers' ministry among parish clergy in several ports. In the 1890s, SAWCM even sent "Church Ships" out among the North Sea fishing fleets. Subsequent experience, however, affirmed the validity of The Missions to Seamen as a specialized vocational ministry in its own right. In 1939, historic differences were finally reconciled in a merger of both organizations.

Methodist and Other Denominational Initiatives

While all this was going on, British Baptists and Congregationalists, each with their independent church polity, continued to cooperate across denominational divides through the British and Foreign Sailors' Society. Britain's Methodists, on the other hand, like the Anglicans from whom they had derived, decided to form their own denominational mission among seafarers. The *Wesleyan Seamen's Missionary Society*, founded in London in 1843, introduced several significant innovations in the field of maritime mission.

Among such novel features was an informal "Sabbath Afternoon Social Meeting," instituted in the chapel's reading-room. This soon became a popular counter-attraction to the "gin palace." A succession of "Sailors' Bible Women" (usually seafarers' widows) were commissioned to seek seafarers out in their lodgings and elsewhere, in order to "engage them in religious conversation" and provide them with Christian literature. They quickly confirmed seafarers' reputation as "peculiarly susceptible to the influence of a good woman." On shipboard, the Society commissioned crewmembers with a Christian commitment to sail as volunteer "Ship Missionaries," renewing the Methodists' legacy of lay activism back in the original Bethel Movement.

Methodist ministries to seafarers also emerged in Dublin, Hamburg, Gibraltar and, most extensively, in the United States of America. Today, other denominations, too, like the Lutherans, the Reformed and, most conspicuously, the Catholics play a prominent part in maritime mission worldwide. The histories of the respective involvement of these will be the subject of subsequent chapters.

3

AMERICAN FORMATIVE PHASE

(1812-1864)

FROM BOSTON TO SHANGHAI

Earlier historians noted a "divine strategy" during the beginnings of the Bethel Movement—"from the River Thames to the ends of the Earth." Some would see signs of a providential parallel between the start of maritime mission in Britain and America. From a secular standpoint, such conclusions could be dismissed as unscientific. However, from a biblical perspective—of faith in a transcendental God—here was far more than a mere matter of coincidence. As George Charles Smith expressed it as early as in 1820:

> "Here is a sort of simultaneous movement of hearts and hands in the
> Sailors' cause, by brethren in origin, habits, and language, separated
> by the vast Atlantic, and the work must be of God" (SML 1820, 272).

In America, as in Britain, a nationwide *Marine Bible Society Movement* preceded more holistic mission models. Then, with striking similarity, a three-stage expansion of comprehensive maritime mission followed on both sides of the Atlantic: Before 1820, a *metropolitan* port society in America's principal seaport had started taking shape. During the 1820s, a *national* seafarers' mission enterprise came together, accompanied by the proliferation of *provincial* port societies. Finally, the 1830s saw the beginnings of an *international* network. In the meantime, the Bethel Flag achieved a level of popularity that was no less remarkable in the New World than in the Old.

Pioneers of the American "Seamen's Cause"

Joseph Tuckerman and the American Forerunner
Just as the Naval and Military Bible Society of 1779 ushered in the Seafarers' Mission Movement in Britain, so the *Boston Society for the Religious*

and Moral Improvement of Seamen (BSRMIS) became the forerunner in America in 1812. Boston was not only the cradle of the American Revolution. It was the major port city of the largest ship-owning state in the Union. The people of Massachusetts had a heavy stake in her seafarers. Also, an increasing number of Boston's largely Congregational citizenry were moving toward a Unitarian stance, where social progressivism counted for more than theological orthodoxy.

Rev. *Joseph Tuckerman* (1778—1840), the Congregational pastor in the nearby coastal village of Chelsea, proved a catalyst. He was to become a leading Boston Unitarian and a pioneer advocate for the urban poor. The new Society was the result of an appeal by Tuckerman and his colleagues, addressed to the secular Boston Marine Society. The outcome was an alliance of shipmasters, merchants and ministers, with Tuckerman as Secretary. The Society sought primarily to promote the distribution of Christian literature among seafarers and facilitate worship services at sea, conducted by shipmasters themselves.

After only five years, despite a promising start, the Society foundered. A major reason was the outbreak of the War of 1812 between Britain and America. Hostilities began barely six weeks after the launching of the Society, bringing about the blockade of both Boston and other East Coast ports by the overpowering British Navy. An additional reason for the Society's early demise was doubtless its narrow, moralistic focus, reinforced by the lack of any real rapport with seafarers themselves.

Still, at least three positive results did emanate from the endeavor: The young nation's naval personnel could now offer an alternative clientele for the Society's publications. The leaders learned lessons that would prove invaluable for future maritime missions. Finally, the public began to wake up to the plight of the seafaring sector of society's "neglected poor." At all events, the Boston Society for the Religious and Moral Improvement of Seamen did become the *first organization ever devoted to the spiritual welfare of solely seafarers.* In that sense, it distinguished itself from the combined maritime/military character of its British predecessor, the Naval and Military Bible Society of 1779.

Ward Stafford in New York

In America's metropolis, it was not as in Britain, a Methodist-inspired revival movement that resulted in the founding of a port society. In the case of New York it was, as in Boston, an awareness of the misery of the urban poor. Among those concerned were women with a Calvinist affiliation. In 1816, these had formed *The Female Missionary Society for the Poor in the City of New York and its Vicinity.* As their "missionary," they appointed a Presbyterian minister, Rev. *Ward Stafford*, who would play a pioneer role on the New York waterfront.

Although seafarers were not a part of his original assignment, Stafford soon discovered both their social and spiritual "destitution." Before the close of 1816, he had started a regular "Seamen's Meeting" in Lower Manhattan. The next year, he also published a report entitled *New Missionary Field* that presented, in the most graphic terms, the state of the underprivileged in those parts.

Within the body of this study, Stafford offered the *first known public blueprint for multi-service mission among seafarers*—a maritime missiology in miniature. Even antedating the legendary G. C. Smith, he proposed "Marine Schools," "Marine Bible Societies," and "Mariners' Churches" in all major seaports. These would provide accommodation and the regular preaching of the gospel by appointed ministers for seafarers and their families. Stafford argued:

> "When in port they [sailors] . . . have no place of resort, except those which frequently become the grave of their property, their morals, their happiness, and their souls . . . . When they enter a church, they are known and marked as sailors . . . . Most of them would sooner face the cannon's mouth than the [congregations'] thoughtless, supercilious gaze . . . [and be] informed, that there was no room for sailors. Such was not the manner in which they were treated by the Son of God" (Ward Stafford 1817, 1-55).

The Society for Promoting the Gospel among Seamen in the Port of New York or the "New York Port Society," established on 5 June 1818, made Rev. Ward Stafford the *first in history to receive an appointment to a full-time pastoral office among seafarers*. With Stafford at the helm, this non-denominational Society could go ahead with its building plans. On 4 June 1820, at a strategic site on Roosevelt Street, near the East River wharves, they dedicated the New York Mariners' Church as the *first specifically built shore-based seafarers' sanctuary in the world*.

Despite the hopes of the Port Society and its missionary, attendance at the sanctuary was scant. In 1821, G. C. Smith wrote to the New York Port Society urging that they, too, adopt the Bethel emblem for "multiplying the blessings" of the Society, just as on the waterfronts of Great Britain. Smith had already donated a flag the year before, one that became the *first Bethel Flag hoisted on the North American continent,* in the port of St. John, New Brunswick, Canada.

Accordingly, leaders of New York's Port Society and Marine Bible Society formed a *New York Bethel Union* on 4 June 1821. Its purpose was to promote shipboard worship and thereby the ministry of the local Mariners' Church. After all, they reasoned, seafarers had been "so long excluded from the sanctuary" that they could not be expected to respond in significant numbers before the gospel message was "brought to their very cabin doors."

On 22 June 1821, on board the sailing ship *Cadmus* at the Pine Street Wharf, the *Bethel Flag* first flew from the masthead of a vessel in the United States. With that, the Bethel Movement began taking hold on the American side of the Atlantic. By the mid-1820s, the Bethel Union had fulfilled its essential purpose. Though local in name, the New York Bethel Union had introduced a concept with far wider implications—not only for individual American seaports but also for a future American *national* society (see below).

Dr. Jenks in Boston

In 1821, after first flying the flag themselves, the New York Bethel Union presented their colleagues to the north with a replica of it. On the Boston waterfront, shipboard meetings under the Bethel emblem prepared the way for the ministry of Rev. Dr. *William Jenks*, a Congregational pastor. Widely recognized as a biblical scholar, Jenks had also shown great compassion for the oppressed. On 9 August 1818, in response to an appeal by Boston's recently founded "Poor Society," he initiated a "Sabbath Seamen's Meeting" in the sail-loft under the observatory on Central Wharf, soon drawing crowds of up to 400.

In 1823, in order to promote both continuity and community, Jenks organized a core of seafarers and their families into the *world's first, formalized seafarers' congregation.* This Boston-based "Mariners' Church" was located at the Poor Society's Mission House in Butolph Street. Four years later, this led to the founding of the *Boston Seamen's Friend Society,* on 13 December 1827.

Since then, this latter Society has continued to serve the Port of Boston, first led by Congregationalists, later the United Church of Christ. With years, other denominations have also arrived on the scene, such as the Methodists from 1828 and the Baptists from 1843. The Evangelical Covenant Church initiated a ministry from 1880, now known as the New England Seafarers' Mission.

Father Eastburn in Philadelphia

Just as the name "Dr. Jenks" became linked with early maritime mission in Boston, so "Father Eastburn" became synonymous with endeavors on the Delaware waterfront. In some ways, however, they were polar opposites.

Joseph Eastburn (1748–1828) was born in Philadelphia, the youngest of six children. His parents were active in Presbyterian circles coming out of the Great Awakening. Finding assurance in the "all-sufficiency of Christ's atonement on the cross" as a young apprentice, Eastburn sensed an urge to share this discovery with others, and began holding weekly meetings in his home. His Presbyterian pastor, impressed with the young man's gifts as an "exhorter," encouraged him to study for the ministry. Although he was lacking in Latin, he acquired a remarkable degree of basic biblical knowledge.

In high demand as a coffin-maker, Eastburn came to combine carpentry with counseling. In 1805, he received a license from the Presbytery of Philadelphia to serve as chaplain at the city's jail, hospital and almshouse, a position administered by the Quakers. Meanwhile, early urban mission endeavors among the marginalized in Philadelphia soon revealed that seafarers were among the most deprived of all. In Eastburn's case, he was already acquainted with their physical hazards through the tragic loss of a son at sea.

The warm-hearted preacher's response was predictable. On 24 October 1819, Eastburn started a "Mariners' Meeting" in a waterfront sail-loft, two wharves north of Market Street. With that, the 71-year old lay leader had launched into a ministry that would make him a legend. Small of stature, and neatly dressed in a Quaker coat, Eastburn was fervent in the pulpit. Tears would roll down his cheeks as he spoke. The sail-loft, already holding 700, soon became "too confined." Instead, Philadelphia's famous architect, William Strickland, built a stately Mariners' Church for 1,200 on South Water Street.

Joseph Eastburn became the first seafarers' chaplain to be called "Father." Certainly, to many a "prodigal son of the ocean" he was a spiritual father, with sailors' prayer requests constantly coming in, from the Atlantic to the Pacific. His funeral, in 1828, was unparalleled—both in the history of Philadelphia and maritime mission. An estimated 20,000 attended, as twelve seafarers carried his body through crowded streets, preceded by the Bethel Flag. With good reason, George Charles Smith memorialized his friend, Father Eastburn, as "the apostle of sailors in the United States."

On the Delaware, new (now denominational) ministries appeared from the 1830s on. The Baptists entered the scene from 1831, the Methodists from 1845, and the Episcopalians from 1847. A similar pattern would repeat itself in every major seaport along North America's Atlantic, Gulf and, later, Pacific coasts.

Benjamin Parker and the Episcopal Floating Churches

In contrast to the earliest developments in Britain, organized maritime mission in North America was largely land-based. They would use an improvised sail-loft or other building as a seafarers' "Bethel," or a mariners' church built expressly for the purpose. The Episcopalians were the first to introduce floating sanctuaries to the American waterfront, and in a unique version. Their organization can trace its roots back to 1834, with the founding of the *Young Men's Church Missionary Society of New York.* Originally committed to general missionary support, in 1842 the Society resolved to focus especially on seafarers, calling its first missionary for that purpose the following year.

Rev. *Benjamin Clarke Cutler Parker* (1796–1859) first discovered his life's calling in 1841. On a voyage from Boston to New York, his ship became wind-bound off Martha's Vineyard, Massachusetts. Not unlike Dr. John Ashley's experience in the Bristol Channel before him, the hardships facing the crews of the nearly 50 sailing vessels at anchor there made a deep impression on Parker. Shortly afterwards, some 150 sailors gathered in a "public house" to hear him preach. Their hearty response confirmed him in his new vocation.

On behalf of the renamed *Protestant Episcopal Church Missionary Society for Seamen in the City and Port of New York,* Parker could eventually invite his seafaring congregation to their own floating Gothic church. Dedicated on 20 February 1844, and moored at the foot of Pike Street on the East River, this novel form of ecclesiastical marine architecture with its 70 foot steeple was built on top of the divided hull of a former ferry and was capable of seating 500.

It was not always "plain sailing" for the newcomer. Parker found it hard to keep his balance during communion in a high wind. Ships occasionally collided with the structure. Once, under a massive snowfall, it even capsized. Still, this "Floating Church of Our Saviour" proved sufficiently successful to motivate a "sister-ship." In 1846, the "Floating Church of the Holy Comforter" could also welcome people aboard, now on the North River side, at the foot of Dey Street.

Fired with the success of their northern neighbors, Episcopalians in Philadelphia formed a *Churchmen's Missionary Association for Seamen in the Port of Philadelphia* in 1847. Two years later, they dedicated their own, even larger, "Floating Church of the Redeemer." It was these floating churches that laid the foundation for the current-day, shore-based ministries of the Seamen's Church Institutes of both New York/New Jersey and Philadelphia.

Olof Hedstrom and the Scandinavian Bethelship Mission

Some American seafarers' missions followed the less ambitious British model of rebuilding old hulks. In November 1844, the Wesleyan Methodists acquired a former brig. After refitting her as a floating chapel, they anchored her on the North River shore at Pier 11 in New York. In 1845, they transferred her to the Episcopal Methodists, represented by Swedish-born Rev. *Olof Gustaf Hedstrom* and his Norwegian associate, *Ole Peter Petersen*, a former seafarer.

Renamed the *John Wesley*, this Methodist floating chapel—as well as its successor, the *John Wesley II*—served for decades as a floating base for the *Scandinavian Bethelship Mission.* On the North River waterfront, later also in Brooklyn, the Mission ministered to thousands of Nordic sailors and immigrants who kept pouring into the Port of New York during the years ahead.

In 1846 and 1851, the Methodists opened up floating chapels in Baltimore and San Francisco, respectively. In Mobile Bay, they transformed an old hulk into a "Floating Bethel and Hospital" in 1853. Here, a series of Methodist chaplain-physicians would seek to serve sailors in need through a method of ministry unique for their time—that of combining "both Scripture and scalpel."

A National Society with Worldwide Reach

Birth of the American Seamen's Friend Society

It was G. C. Smith who first proposed an American Seamen's Friend Society (ASFS), both in name and concept, in a letter in 1823, addressed to Rev. *John Truair*. The British-born Presbyterian minister had just recently accepted a call as pastor of the New York Mariners' Church.

Having once caught Smith's vision, Truair took on the task with a vigor and resourcefulness worthy of his mentor. Starting with a New York version of Smith's *Sailor's Magazine*, he laid the groundwork for an American equivalent of the British and Foreign Seamen's Friend Society. In 1825, Truair published a plea called *Voice from the Sea,* signed by one hundred masters and fourteen mates. Early the next year, he followed up with a booklet of his own entitled *Call from the Ocean,* setting forth a systematic motivation and methodology for maritime mission. This was widely acclaimed and still ranks as the world's *first known formulation of a basic "maritime missiology."*

Finally, on 13 January 1826, the New York City Hotel became the site of the official founding of the *American Seamen's Friend Society* (ASFS), with the Hon. *Smith Thompson*, Home Secretary of the Navy, as president, and fifteen vice-presidents from Portland, Maine, to New Orleans. In part as a result of

Truair's resignation shortly afterwards, it was not till 1828 that the Society really got under way. Nevertheless, before leaving the helm, John Truair had, to his lasting credit, raised public awareness and seen through to its first fruition an enterprise destined to lead the world in maritime mission for years to come.

The ASFS and the Domestic Scene

The Society was uniquely positioned to offer some degree of coordination among the growing number of American seafarers' missions—from the Eastern Seaboard to the Pacific Coast. Moreover, from the outset, the ASFS intended to embrace not only deep-sea mariners but also "Inland Sailors"—those employed on canals, rivers and lakes. As with saltwater seafarers, the Bethel Flag (first hoisted in the Great Lakes port of Oswego in 1830) rapidly became a rallying point for freshwater mariners, too, and the agencies serving them.

"Boatmen's Friends" would soon find that social reform also had to become a major concern in ministry on the inland waterways, given the level of marginalization there. In that context, they would start Boatmen's Libraries, as well as Sabbath Schools and Free Schools for the impoverished children of inland waterway-workers. They would also speak out against oppressive work conditions, publicly stating that "the very mules on a Kentucky corn plantation" enjoyed better treatment than most boatmen and their families.

The ASFS and International Outreach

With the Christian public showing mounting interest in "foreign" missions, overseas activities would soon become the most distinctive feature of the new society. Meanwhile, since 1828, important changes had taken place in the leadership of the ASFS. A Congregational clergyman, *Joshua Leavitt*, later widely known as an anti-slavery leader, had become "General Agent." Rev. *Charles McIlvaine*, later Episcopal Bishop of Ohio, had taken over as "Corresponding Secretary." With these two at the helm, the Society now identified three strategic world ports to which it planned to send the first in its series of future overseas chaplains.

The foremost choice fell on Canton, the principal port city of Southeastern China. Until then, the only possibility of reaching the inaccessible "Celestial Kingdom" had been by way of tsarist Russia, in order for the gospel to "shine over the Great Wall" of China. However, reports from the British Presbyterian pioneer missionary to China, Dr. *Robert Morrison* (1782–1834), had indicated an alternative solution. A ministry to foreign residents and visiting seafarers at such a strategic port city as Canton could provide an entry point for the gospel into the whole of China, and therefore reach "one fourth of the human race."

For Morrison himself, prospects had looked bleak indeed when he first landed in Canton in 1807. A historic breakthrough took place, however, on 10 November 1822. That day, he would become the *first to hoist the Bethel Flag in Chinese waters,* thereby initiating maritime mission in the world's most populous nation. It happened on board the American merchant ship *Pacific* of Philadelphia, at Canton's deep-sea anchorage off Whampoa. Morrison's sermon that day made a powerful impact, not only on his seafaring congregation, but also on the astonished Chinese onlookers. Prior to this, the local Chinese had only shown scorn for a religion whose supposed adherents, when ashore, behaved with unrestrained indulgence. Suddenly, they saw these sea-going "barbarians" transformed by the Christian gospel before their very eyes.

That same year, in 1822, Morrison produced a *Tract Addressed to Sailors* (the first English-language tract in China). He published proposals for both a "Floating Hospital" and "Floating Chapel," to be stationed at Whampoa. Morrison's reports and repeated appeals for a full-time seafarers' missionary became a call the American Seamen's Friend Society could no longer ignore.

As a result, the Dutch Reformed Church clergyman (later Dr.) *David Abeel* (1804–46) arrived in Canton, in 1830, as the *first full-time foreign-port "sea missionary"* of the ASFS. The event marked a new chapter in maritime mission history. Although the work suffered a severe setback as a result of the First Opium War (1839-42), by mid-century a successor could open a "handsome floating Bethel," built in Whampoa and capable of seating 300.

When this Whampoa Bethel burned down at the outbreak of the Second Opium War (1856-60), the Society launched a new ministry of preaching under the Bethel Flag on the Shanghai waterfront. By 1857, a locally built floating Bethel could open there, too, this time looking like "an abridged Noah's Ark." The work of these American pioneers laid the foundation for major British seafarers' missions that could later commence in Hong Kong and Shanghai.

Meanwhile, in 1833, the ASFS had sent a Presbyterian clergyman from New York, *John Diell*, to Honolulu—the most notorious sailortown in the Pacific. Protecting the population from the undermining image of rum-drunk sailors ashore was again a major factor in the choice of seaport. Diell had shipped his own prefabricated church with him to Hawaii. Later that year, on a site donated by the King himself, the Honolulu Seamen's Chapel could open, with the Bethel Flag flying aloft. Diell's successor, Rev. *Samuel Damon,* would become famous as founder and long-time editor of Hawaii's first newspaper, *The Friend*, originally started as a "mariners' temperance" publication.

The third strategic world port selected by the ASFS was originally Marseilles in largely Catholic France. In 1832, they agreed to postpone that plan and first take over the agency started by G. C. Smith the year before in Le Havre. Here, they built a Mariners' Church, to be served for several years by Presbyterian Rev. (later Dr.) *Eli Newton Sawtell* of New Hampshire. Sawtell launched a public campaign against the blatant forms of cruelty he discovered on shipboard, thus becoming one of the earliest advocates for seafarers' rights.

Having once "cast off," the ASFS expanded its overseas activities by cooperating with missionaries in remote ports like Calcutta, Singapore and Batavia. During the 1840s and into the 1850s, the Society started sending seafarers' chaplains to key ports in South America and the Caribbean, too. These had to contend with rampant disease, constant overwork, and (in those pre-ecumenical days) varying degrees of religious persecution. The Society also entered into joint ventures with its transatlantic counterpart, the British and Foreign Sailors' Society—in Cronstadt, Russia, and Sydney, Australia.

OLD SALTS AND SAILOR MISSIONARIES

Despite important differences, the remarkable similarities between British and North American maritime mission endeavors are a feature of the whole movement's early years. This is also true of the denominational and operational differentiation that evolved during the ensuing formative years. It even applies to the belated American version of a "Naval Awakening."

Anti-Crimping Measures in the New World

Methodist Leadership in America's Maritime Diaconate.
During the 1840s, Methodist missions materialized not only in New York but also in Philadelphia, Baltimore, New Orleans and San Francisco. With the opening up of the Pacific Northwest during the 1870s, a Methodist minister, the British former seafarer and future centenarian, *Robert Sherwood Stubbs* (1823–1925), was indefatigable in seafarers' missions in Portland, Tacoma and Seattle.

In San Francisco, the Methodists had already taken up the work in 1849, the year the gold-hungry "forty-niners" invaded the Bay area. Here, their resourceful chaplain, *William Taylor,* fitted up the sailing ship *Panama* as a "Seamen's Bethel Church"—originally one of the many hundreds of vessels abandoned in the Bay. From this floating sanctuary, Taylor waged sustained warfare against waterfront extortion. It was he who gave the now familiar name of "shanghaiing" to the brazen kidnapping of ships' crews, as practiced by the crimps along San Francisco's Barbary Coast.

Boston's Legendary Father Taylor
No history of seafarers' mission in 19th century America would be complete without due justice to William Taylor's Boston-based namesake, *Edward Thompson Taylor* (1793-1871). Born in Richmond, Virginia, and orphaned at three, he was seven years old when he ran off to sea. Ten years later, while drifting down one of Boston's streets on shore leave, sounds of a revival meeting in the local Methodist church piqued his curiosity. "I crept in through the porthole and stowed myself away upon the gun deck, when a broadside from the pulpit stove me to pieces, and, in a sinking condition, I hauled my colors and cried for quarter." Thus began the colorful odyssey of one of the world's greatest seafarers' preachers.

His ministerial debut was no less dramatic. After capturing him from a Boston privateer at the outbreak of the War of 1812, the British incarcerated him on Melville Island, off Nova Scotia. Here, his fellow prisoners petitioned to have him replace their highly unpopular chaplain—and they got their wish. Although illiterate at the time, the twenty-year-old Taylor captivated his peers with the vivid nautical imagery that filled his preaching.

Although graduated only from the "university of wind and wave," and with practically no formal education, Taylor became a Methodist lay preacher as soon as peace returned. Up and down the New England coastline, seafarers and their families flocked to his pulpit. In 1828, the Methodist-led Boston Port Society called him as their seafarers' chaplain. Supervising the construction of their Bethel, he selected as its site the center of Boston's sailortown, its historic North Square. He had, as he put it, learned to set his net "where the fish ran."

Father Taylor's oratory was always extemporaneous, full of briny wit and pathos. Charles Dickens and Jenny Lind were among the foreign celebrities who came to hear him, while Walt Whitman and Henry Longfellow were among his American admirers. Several of Boston's leading Unitarians remained his faithful financial supporters. He would tell these that they might as well try to heat a furnace with snowballs as seek to save sailors' souls with their "skimmed-milk" sermons. Still, they knew he loved them. They also knew—and respected—that he would leave no sailor standing in his church while land-folks sat in comfort.

There is a story of two Bethel-bound sailors who had lost their bearings in Boston's North End. Seeing the Bethel Flag aloft, one of them, who was able to read at least a little, slowly spelled out the inscription for the benefit of his shipmate: B-E-T, beat. H-E-L, hell. This is where the old man beats hell. That's the place we want." Seafarers knew that Father Taylor's concern for them was always for their total wellbeing—just as with his counterpart, Bosun Smith. Toward waterfront drunks and prostitutes he would show compassion, but battled adamantly against all who exploited them. Single-handedly, he started a boarding house project called "Mariners' House", and a *Bethel Temperance Society*, while continuing to combat the crimp by whatever means he could.

Throughout, Father Taylor's spouse and fellow-worker, *Debora Millett* from Marblehead, stood steadfastly at his side, a woman he openly admired. Sailors dubbed her "Mother Taylor." Her consistent cooperation as the wife of a seafarers' chaplain was no exception. The unpaid and all too often unsung ministry of spouses was the norm—then as later. Mother Taylor had the loyal support of a local group of women called the *Seamen's Aid Society*.

Founded in 1833, this Society was the brainchild of the Christian sociologist, *Sarah Josepha Hale* (1788–1879). The purpose was to reverse prevailing poverty among seafarers' dependents through a strategy of self-help. This was to replace "alms-giving," with all its dependency problems. Through their "Strategy of Wages," they promoted the production of sailors' clothes sewn by sailors' wives. These they would then sell—in direct competition with exploitative sailortown "slop shops." Shortly afterwards, buoyed by their success, the Society opened a *Free School for the Daughters of Seamen,* besides relieving Father Taylor of the management of his "Mariners' House" project.

Charleston, New York and Staten Island

The example of those women in Boston gave an impetus to diaconal ministry among seafarers' families elsewhere. Like their British colleagues, American seafarers' chaplains had already identified the "Crimping System" as the principal inhibitor of lasting improvement in the quality of life of both seafarers and their families. Among the first to point the way in the war against this form of sailortown exploitation on the American waterfront were the leaders of the *Charleston Bethel Union*, founded in 1822.

Although the initial Sailors' Bethel Meetings in this Southern seaport were soon drawing large crowds, their organizers saw further needs. They believed that any sailor, once deprived of proximity to family and friends, would need more than merely spiritual support. Spurred on by their leader, Rev. *Joseph Brown*, they went ahead with what would constitute, in effect, the *first international action for the promotion of seafarers' social welfare*.

In 1823, the Charleston Bethel Union sent out a circular addressed to "all Bethel Unions, Port Societies, and Ship Masters," on both sides of the Atlantic. This sought cooperation in promoting two institutions to counter the crimps: First, *register offices* offering employment opportunities and other incentives to those shipping out. Second, *boarding-houses* providing seafarers with safe lodging and "rational entertainment." The initiatives received endorsements by G. C. Smith and many others, and there were signs of promising beginnings.

Meanwhile, Brown was well aware of the far greater potential of a national society to provide leadership in this regard. In the summer of 1828, the Bethel Union loaned Brown to the recently founded ASFS in New York, pending the arrival later that year of its new leader, Joshua Leavitt. In response, the ASFS pursued plans for a "Sailors' Home" grand enough to dwarf anything the crimps could come up with. By 1842, such a Sailors' Home could finally open its doors at 190 Cherry Street, New York. With accommodation for 300 boarders, it could also offer a chapel and reading room, an employment office, a maritime museum and even a "noble bowling-alley." Following New York's lead, a series of similar ASFS-sponsored, multi-service sailors' homes opened in other American port cities, too, during the first half of the 19th century.

An American Sailors' Home would usually become a base also for the *Temperance Reformation*. In the late 1820s, the ASFS—impressed with the growing numbers of ships' crews volunteering to "sail without grog"—had already begun a campaign against what was seen as the "besetting sin of the sailor." Following the founding of the first *Marine Temperance* Society in 1833, the movement quickly spread through sister societies across the nation, even across the Atlantic. By the mid-1840s, sailors had covered the chapel walls of the New York Sailors' Home with pledges of total abstinence. As thousands continued to join, marine underwriters gladly slashed insurance rates for so-called "cold-water ships."

The ASFS, as a New York-based national society, would set an example for port societies elsewhere in other areas of maritime social concern, too. These could include ship's libraries and educational programs for seafarers, as well as "Sabbath schools" for their children. The Society also initiated a *Savings Bank for Seamen*, and a *Seamen's Cemetery*, providing an alternative to a "pauper's grave" elsewhere—for those who escaped a "watery grave" at sea.

It was nevertheless not New York's crowded Manhattan Island but Staten Island, with its rural environment, which would eventually provide a unique four-dimensional maritime diaconate. By 1833, the *Sailors' Snug Harbor* was finally ready to house almost a thousand of the more fortunate among retired and disabled "old salts"—sailors who were now "decrepit and worn-out." Later, this became a model for a more modest version in Duxbury, Massachusetts, opened in 1852.

On Staten Island, three other institutions were to follow. A *Seamen's Retreat* (or Marine Hospital) was opened in 1837. New York's *Female Bethel Association* followed in 1843, later reorganized as the *Mariners' Family Industrial Society,* in order to provide a "Mariners' Family Asylum" for "Aged Women of the Sea" (ready in 1855). Finally, a *Society for the Relief of Destitute Children of Seamen,* founded in 1846, was able to open a "Sailors' Orphan Home" in 1852.

Discrimination on the American Waterfront

Neither national nor local maritime mission societies were in a position to assume financial responsibility for major diaconal institutions, whether on Staten Island or elsewhere. However, they would advocate for them and, as far as feasible, provide chaplaincy services. Otherwise, proponents of maritime social reform in the New World were generally less limited than their peers in the Old World, who had to contend with the conventions of a more stratified and tradition-bound society. That said, how did conditions on the American waterfront measure up to the basic biblical ethic of *non-discrimination*, as laid out in Galatians 3:28, specifically in relation to gender, rank and race?

Gender Discrimination

In early maritime mission structures in America, male superiority was just as evident as elsewhere. Still, it was not long before women volunteers—organized in *Female Bethel Societies* or *Ladies' Seamen's Friend Societies*—would provide the primary support-base for most maritime mission agencies.

In the Staten Island maritime diaconate, women would soon be doing more than fundraising. They played a leading part in practical operations, too. This would apply to sailors' homes in general, as well as to the shelters for shipwrecked or destitute seafarers frequently affiliated with these institutions.

Socio-Economic Discrimination

American maritime mission pioneers were, like others at that time, prone to paternalistic prejudice. Nevertheless, at least in diaconal ministry, they did show early awareness of the need for diversification. They also saw the need for systemic change if there was to be long-term improvement in the seafarers' overall quality of life. By both pen and pulpit they sought to motivate those in positions of power. This was especially true of the ASFS; it used its national status, national magazine and national connections toward this goal.

Given the dehumanizing conditions of the day, the average life expectancy of a merchant seafarer, after first shipping out, was no more than 12 years. By repeatedly publicizing cases of atrocity committed in the name of "discipline," and the horrific loss of life in frequent "marine disasters," the ASFS sought to stop blatant cruelty and callous disregard for safety at sea. As they confronted miserable wages, abusive hiring practices, and subhuman living conditions under which seafarers suffered in pre-union years, the leaders of the ASFS, in their 1856 Annual Report, even had the courage to call for the conversion of shipowners themselves!

Ethnic and Racial Discrimination

Of some 200,000 sailors in the American merchant fleet at mid-century, four-fifths of them were foreign-born, many from Northern Europe. As a source of cheap maritime labor, foreign seafarers had, by the late 1800s, become even more prevalent. Also by then, resurgent racism had significantly reduced the number of African-American seafarers in America's merchant marine, and virtually eliminated any prospect of their upward mobility.

By contrast, prior to the Civil War (1861-1865), the estimated number of black seafarers (both merchant and naval) reached 35,000, or some 15% of the entire American maritime work force. Jeffrey Bolster's recent research of this period has shed new light on how, during these years, "black sailors were central to African-Americans' collective sense of self, economic survival and freedom struggle." Bolster goes on to say it is an irony of history that the very means that carried ten million Africans to New World slavery "not infrequently became a pipeline to freedom." During the latter part of the 18th and especially the first half of the 19th century, ships provided a unique workplace for African Americans, both slave and free. Here, as blacks and whites shared both perils and hardships equally with one another at sea, color would be "less determinate of daily life and duties than elsewhere" (Bolster 1997).

Nor were career opportunities for black seafarers limited to the North. A significant source of recruitment was the "Underground Seaway" from cotton ports in the South, paralleling the more widely known "Underground Railroad" by land. One favorite nautical escape route passed through Charleston, the busy port of call for whaling fleets on their way north to New Bedford, where Quaker tolerance had long since led to a thriving, black seafaring community.

Given the degree of overall, continued discrimination, the achievements of black seafarers in the pre-Civil War period were remarkable. Some blacks would go on to command their own ships. Otherwise, anti-black prejudice could vary in form and degree, but it was still usually the norm. Particularly notorious was the slaughter that passed for justice on an American ship arriving at Le Havre, France, in 1856. In a report published by the ASFS, their port chaplain, Rev. Eli Sawtell, makes the following statement: "Her papers showed a crew's list of twenty colored men, only seventeen of whom lived to reach port, and eight of them so terribly bruised and mangled, as to be sent at once to the hospital."

Ashore, a black seafarer, whether runaway or "free," always ran the risk of re-enslavement. In the South, maritime racism was even institutionalized—in the form of so-called "Negro Seamen's Acts." These provided for all black sailors to be jailed as long as their ships were in port, to avert unrest among local slaves. (This actually happened with at least 10,000 "free" black sailors.)

By sponsoring special "Prayer Meetings for Colored Seamen," and a series of "Homes for Colored Seamen" in New York's sailortown, the ASFS might seem to be simply complying with contemporary patterns of disguised discrimination. Nevertheless, they did warmly endorse the campaign of a black sailors' activist, *William P. Powell.* For over a quarter of a century leading up to the Civil War, Powell fought for the abolitionist cause, rescuing fugitive slaves from waterfront "man-stealers" and encouraging black seafarers in their struggle for dignity. He combined all this with a well-run "Colored Seamen's Home" in New York, as well as a "Temperance Boarding House" in New Bedford, both of them in the face of the collective fury of competing crimps.

The ASFS also endorsed the 1863 appointment of a black Episcopalian, *Prince Loveridge,* as a "Missionary to Colored Seamen," and Chaplain of the *American Seamen's Protective Union Association* (ASPUA). Founded that same year by blacks on the New York waterfront, the ASPUA seems to have been the *first trade union ever organized by seafarers, black or white, in the United States* (Kverndal 1986, 525-526, 778; cf. Bolster 1997, 181-182).

Finally, no history of maritime mission would do justice to black seafarers without mentioning the name of *Frederick Sanderson.* As a "pious youth of color," he joined the Thames Revival in 1815. While that revival evolved into the worldwide Bethel Movement, Sanderson went on to become a zealous co-worker of Zebedee Rogers of Rotherhithe. He later left for the New World to become a pioneer Methodist missionary in Jamaica (SMNY 1828-29, 228).

American Naval Awakening and Nordic Aftershock

Reform and Revival

Even prior to 1861, while Congress received repeated petitions for the abolition of black slavery, seafarers' friends were also confronting America's leaders with condoning conditions in the United States Navy tantamount to *white* slavery. Since 1831, social reform in the Navy had been a major goal of the American Seamen's Friend Society. This campaign helped promote the renewal of a depleted and demoralized naval chaplaincy. It also led to the prohibition, throughout the navy, of both the official distribution of liquor ("grog") and the practice of public flogging. The activists achieved all this in the face of fierce conservative opposition to tampering with two such historic institutions (Langley 1967; Kverndal 1986, 526-528).

The naval reform campaign of the ASFS culminated in the late 1850s with a belated but remarkable counterpart to the British Naval Awakening of the early 1800s. As in the British version, there were two key factors: contextually relevant media distribution, together with credible peer testimony. The ASFS played a prominent part in both, helping to promote and publicize the lay-led worship and Bible study groups spreading among all ranks throughout the Navy.

It was the U.S. Receiving Ship *North Carolina* at the Brooklyn Navy Yard that became the "cradle" of the growing revival—thanks to the courage of a Scandinavian-American naval seafarer named *John Morris*. On 21 November 1858, Morris had obtained permission to hold a prayer meeting on the ship's lowermost deck. Yet those who came to bawl out this "Big Swede" remained to pray. Within six months, groups of spiritually awakened sailors had spread to scores of US Navy ships. By 1865, Christian cell groups were reported "in all the squadrons of the US Navy." On the flagship of the China Squadron, the commodore himself hoisted the Bethel Flag from the main for public worship every Sabbath. As to the caliber of the thousands who responded, these were, commented officers not necessarily professing the faith, "the best men in the Navy."

Rev. *Charles J. Jones,* a British-born former seafarer and Presbyterian senior chaplain of the New York Mariner's Church, became a central figure in the revival. Cooperating closely with Morris, Jones provided a crucial level of cohesion—very similar to that of G. C. Smith's Naval Correspondence Mission nearly 50 years earlier (Jones 1884; Kverndal 1986, 526-533).

Vikings in Reverse

Jones had, as his associate at the Mariners' Church, a Norwegian Methodist and Lay Chaplain, *Ole Helland.* Helland developed a special rapport with the many Scandinavian recruits coming through the Brooklyn Navy Yard at that time. He was also involved with the local Scandinavian Bethelship Mission.

Seafarers who responded to this outreach would join with fellow converts from the other New York-based Methodist or Baptist maritime missions—as well as those from ships of the US Navy—in a joint endeavor. Together, they formed a band of "Sailor Missionaries"—also called "Vikings in Reverse"— who would "re-migrate" with their newfound faith to their Nordic homelands.

Sponsored by the American Seamen's Friend Society, these became the workforce of that Society's *Scandinavian Missions.* Led by pioneers like Swedish *Fredrick O. Nilsson* (or Nelson) and Danish *Fredrick L. Rymker*, they continued their respective missions in key port cities in Norway, Denmark, Sweden and Finland. In contrast to grassroots folk, reactions by church officials were predictable—even if the long-term consequences were not. Branded as heretics by the Lutheran state church hierarchy, the returnees encountered harassment, imprisonment, even banishment from their native lands.

It is nevertheless a fact of history that current-day Methodist and Baptist church bodies—in each of the Nordic nations—owe their origins largely to the fearless witness of those 19th century Sailor Missionaries. This would prove no less true of today's Lutheran-affiliated Nordic Seafarers' Churches (see below).

4

TRANSITIONAL PHASE

(1864-1920)

CONTINENTAL EXPANSION

The mid-1860s opened up a new era in maritime mission history. By then, there was international consensus on the need for a holistic methodology.
This meant that the first "Formative Phase" of the movement was over. At the same time, various initiatives on the mainland of Europe indicated the end of what had hitherto been a virtual Anglo-American monopoly.

The Nordics Launch Forth

The Father of Nordic Seafarers' Missions

The earliest roots of organized Nordic seafarers' mission go back to the Medieval Church and the sporadic work that preceded Anglo-American ministries. Following the Reformation, a distinctive feature of this work was the Lutheran emphasis on Scripture as the "primary means of grace." This took the form of maritime devotional aids (from the late 1500s), the preaching of the gospel in embassy chapels, and later the ministry of Nordic emigrant churches.

With the arrival of the organized Seafarers' Mission Movement in the early 1800s, Nordic seafarers, with their basic knowledge of nautical English, would often be able to benefit from the ministries of major British and American societies. Impressed with the large numbers and relative receptivity of Nordic mariners, some agencies introduced native language initiatives among them, not only on British and American waterfronts, but also in their own home ports.

For that purpose, the British and Foreign Sailors' Society appointed a German-born evangelist, *August Thiemann*, who became their foreign-language "Thames Missionary." Thiemann spent the winter of 1860-61 in Norway to improve his Scandinavian language skills. While there, he publicized broadly both the BFSS and the Bethel Flag among the maritime oriented Norwegians.

During a return visit next winter, he even helped to found Norway's first seafarers' mission society in the port of Stavanger, in November 1861.

Meanwhile, the local church hierarchy had begun to question "un-Lutheran doctrine" in Thiemann's preaching. He did not receive another invitation. Still, his efforts had not been in vain. Half a century after the founding of the first Anglo-American maritime mission societies, the Nordic national scene had changed. Their merchant fleets had reached a level that had made both the need more pressing and a potential support base more viable. In addition, religious revivals had led to greater lay activity within the Nordic state churches. By the early 1860s, the winds of change were evident everywhere.

The situation now called for a caliber of leadership capable of generating a truly *national* initiative. Thiemann's 1861 visit became the crucial catalyst. Following the founding of that "Seamen's Society" in Stavanger, he left for nearby Bergen. Though failing to establish any port society there, too, he did succeed in convincing a recently graduated theologian called Storjohann of the acute need for mission outreach to Norwegian seafarers. That young theologian would go on to become the recognized "Father of Nordic Seafarers' Missions."

Johan Cordt Harmens Storjohann (1832-1914) arrived shortly afterwards in Scotland in order to pursue further theological research. Here he encountered Scandinavian seafarers milling around in the docklands of Leith, and felt prompted to hold an improvised worship service for them. His sermon spurred the chief officer of a Norwegian sailing ship to seek out the preacher in neighboring Edinburgh the next day. That episode finally convinced Storjohann: "Our seafarers must have their own pastors!" In the end, as with G. C. Smith, it would be seafarers themselves who conveyed the decisive call.

In Bergen the following year, he set to with determination. First, he formed a committee of clergy, merchants and sea officers who, on 31 August 1864, founded "The Society for the Proclamation of the Gospel to Scandinavian Seamen in Foreign Ports," later known as the *Norwegian Seamen's Mission.* Though established as an independent voluntary society, the new organization maintained an affiliation with the Lutheran Church of Norway. The Society immediately began building a network of Norwegian "seamen's churches" in major seaports around the globe—in all 35 in the course of the first 50 years.

Like his British predecessor, G. C. Smith, Storjohann was not primarily an administrator and did not continue to lead the mission. With his charisma and rhetorical skills, however, he was one of the most powerful preachers of the day. These gifts, combined with his forceful personality, were needed in order to overcome the prevailing ecclesiastical inertia. All this also enabled him to play a pivotal role in founding similar organizations in the other Nordic countries.

Emergence of a Nordic Paradigm

A common Lutheran national heritage had long existed between the three Scandinavian kingdoms, Norway, Denmark and Sweden. Finland, although then under Russian rule, shared that bond. In each of these countries, seafarers made up a substantial part of the population. With the situation now ripe for national maritime mission initiatives there, too, Storjohann was anxious and prepared to share his vision with all four Nordic nations.

In Denmark, a tireless advocate of global missions, Rev. *Jens Vahl*, had already made an appeal on behalf of seafarers, but failed due to the outbreak of war with Prussia in 1864. Storjohann encouraged Vahl and his fellow Danes to persevere. The result was the founding of the "Danish Society for the Proclamation of the Gospel for Scandinavian Seamen in Foreign Ports," in Copenhagen in 1867. Like Storjohann's own model, it established close ties with the national Church from the start. The Society has since continued to grow worldwide, eventually as the "Danish Seamen's Church in Foreign Ports."

In the case of Sweden, Storjohann became even more involved. In 1869, after an abortive attempt three years earlier, he managed to persuade the new Evangelical National Missionary Society to adopt mission among seafarers as an integral part of their world mission outreach. Following an unsuccessful attempt to combine seafarers' mission with mission among Muslims in ports like Constantinople and Alexandria, the Society instructed its maritime missionaries to focus exclusively on seafarers. In 1876, the General Synod of the Church of Sweden initiated its own seafarers' chaplaincy in foreign ports. This "Church of Sweden's Board for the Pastoral Care of Seamen" was then able to take over the facilities of its predecessor and full responsibility for Swedish seafarers abroad.

With the inclusion of Finland in the Nordic family of seafarers' missions, Storjohann was no less involved than in the case of Sweden. After a five-year series of appeals to the Finnish Missionary Society and its Director, Rev. *K. J. G. Sirelius*, he visited Helsinki in 1874 and finally won the whole-hearted support of the Finnish clergy. He then traveled the length of the land, taking the laity by storm. The outcome was the "Society for the Provision of Pastoral Care for Finnish Seamen in Foreign Ports"—founded in 1875, with parliamentary approval. Like the freedom-loving Finnish people itself, the Finnish Seamen's Mission would subsequently survive both the nation's heroic struggle for independence, from 1917 to 1920, and its even costlier campaign to *maintain* that independence against the might of Stalin's armies, from 1939 to 1945.

It is noteworthy how involved *global mission* advocates were in the historic origins of all four Nordic foreign-port seafarers' missions. Nevertheless, it seemed unsound, both psychologically and in principle, to identify Nordic seafarers with those who had never heard the gospel. However nominal their personal commitment might be, they would none the less have been both baptized and confirmed (at one time even as a prerequisite for shipping out).

As indicated, each of the four Nordic seafarers' missions would present strong similarities, linked by the bonds of history and culture, as well as by the powerful personality of Storjohann. Although the current Global Era has caused considerable change, a common core legacy has led to a level of cooperation that amounts to a veritable "Nordic Bloc," with a corresponding *Nordic Paradigm*. This has been characterized by the following four features:

Strong National and Denominational Ties*:* Just as each of their national flags portrays the Christian cross, all four organizations share a basic allegiance to their respective national churches. While only Sweden's maritime ministry is fully integrated into the national Lutheran church structure, with each of the others the state has at least accepted some level of financial responsibility.

Holistic Approach to Ministry: The Nordic seafarers' missions have traditionally prioritized worship and specialized pastoral care, yet always with a holistic diaconal concern for all the seafarer's human needs. Emphasizing a "home-like" rather than "institutional" atmosphere, they usually refer to their facilities as seafarers' *churches,* not *centers.* Moreover, in their official titles, all four have now adopted the self-designation "Church" rather than "Mission."

Differentiation between Foreign and Domestic Port Ministry: With the involvement of each of the four countries in international shipping and carrier trade, most of their seafarers' missions have focused on foreign-port ministry. Only the Finnish Seamen's Mission has also assumed responsibility for home-port ministry. In Norway, Sweden and Denmark, other organizations have taken over the latter, usually in combination with fishers' ministry.

Combined Seafaring and Residential Target Groups: While Nordic seafarers have always been the primary target group, the work has also always embraced the needs of resident compatriots abroad. In fact, several seafarers' churches started thanks to concerned emigrants within Nordic "diaspora" communities around the world (Kverndal 1978, 103–134; 1986, 591–610).

Toward German National Maritime Mission

Hanseatic Initiatives

Although, like their Nordic neighbors, the Germans and Dutch shared a rich, maritime heritage over the centuries, they were not quite ready to organize indigenous maritime mission as early as the Nordics. There were historical reasons for this. Compared with the Lutheran state church homogeneity of the Nordic nations, the Germans and Dutch displayed a more *multi-denominational* church landscape. Each featured a large Catholic presence and (at least in pre-Bismark Germany) extensive political disunity. Still, a number of sporadic, pre-organizational maritime mission initiatives did surface in both countries.

In Germany, as in Britain, the beginnings of indigenous Christian ministry among seafarers go back several centuries, to home-grown maritime guilds or confraternities. It was the medieval merchants' confederation, the Hanseatic League, which took the initiative. In Hansa strongholds like Lübeck, Hamburg and Bremen, a Shipmasters' *Society* would sponsor prayers for fellow seafarers in peril or lost at sea. Such guilds would also provide help for their dependents.

The Reformation resulted in the discontinuation of mass for the dead in Germany's Protestant states. Social-diaconal guild activity would nevertheless continue. It even expanded, for example in the form of anti-slavery measures to counter the attacks of the Muslim Barbary States. The guilds sponsored a *Slave Chest* to redeem enslaved hostages and support their needy families. In addition, *Convoy Escorts* would protect merchantmen in pirate-infested waters, with each carrying a lay preacher. After the Hansa dissolved, one vessel remained at anchor in Hamburg as a *Guard Ship*. From 1715 on, the city's Senate replaced the vessel's lay preacher with an ordained pastor—to minister to the floating population. This unique, city-sponsored, *ship-based chaplaincy* continued for almost a century, until Napoleon's forces seized the Guard Ship in 1811.

Another guild-sponsored maritime welfare initiative, known as *Seamen's Houses,* fared somewhat better. Such institutions continued to meet the needs of disabled and impoverished seafarers and their families in several German port-cities. Before organized indigenous maritime mission materialized, the general impact of British-American maritime missions also helped prepare the way.

The British Forerunner: William Henry Angas

Hamburg, second only to London among Europe's port cities at the time, witnessed its *first recorded shipboard services under the Bethel Flag* in 1821. This was thanks to pioneering Bethel Captains and public interest. Although the meetings were usually in English, German residents and seafarers joined in. In October 1822, the British Baptist and former sea captain, Rev. *William Henry Angas,* also arrived on the Hamburg waterfront. Affiliated with the BFSFSBU, he had studied German expressly for this purpose, seeing Hamburg as a key base for future indigenous maritime mission on the continent of Europe..

In his ministry, Angas made full use of the Bethel Flag. He also translated, printed and distributed many "sea tracts" in German, and founded a Sunday School for seafarers' children. This inspired *Johann Gerhard Onken* to carry on Angas's work, in cooperation with the pastor of the local Evangelical English Reformed Church. Onken held the *first public sermon under the Bethel Flag in German* (and actually on board a German ship) in March 1824.

Angas went on to focus on German seafarers in British ports, wherever possible in cooperation with resident German nationals. Unwittingly, he thus prepared for their role in pioneering a national German maritime mission 50 years later. Before his premature death in 1832, Angas had thereby become a British forerunner of the German Seamen's Mission (Kverndal 1986, 255–260).

The German Forerunner: Johann Hinrich Wichern

The early efforts of Angas and Onken were not sufficient to "contex-tualize" the Bethel Movement on Germany's waterfronts. They were, however, a model for others. Foremost among these was *Johann Hinrich Wichern* (1808–1881), later recognized as Germany's "Father of the Home Mission Movement." Born in Hamburg, Wichern was aware of the marginalization of people of the sea and, in the mid-1840s, wrote about the urgent need for a German "Ministry to Sailors." At the time, he was also involved in the renewal of the former city-funded waterfront chaplaincy, based on Hamburg's historic "Guard Ship."

In his well-known *Memorandum* ("Denkschrift") of 1849, Wichern calls for a church-wide, holistic implementation of Christ's love, specifically including seafarers. Here, he compares their neglect by his own church with the accomplishments of British and American agencies during recent decades, and challenges his church to integrate seafarers' mission into its future home mission structure. During a visit to England in 1851, he gained grassroots ideas by personally witnessing the work of seafarers' mission facilities there.

Given the complicated bureaucracy of church and state in mid-century Germany, no immediate organization resulted from Wichern's early advocacy. Germany's Protestant "Evangelical Church" had become an amorphous mix of Lutheran and United Lutheran-Reformed state churches. Moreover, the political unification of Germany's individual states also lay in the future. By the 1880s, when the Protestant churches were ready to act, it was, however, Wichern's initial endeavors within those churches that would give the final impetus.

The Founding Father: Friedrich Martin Harms.

It was routine practice for early maritime missions in British port-cities to include German seafarers in their outreach activities. It began with foreign Scripture and tract distribution during the Napoleonic War years, 1803–15. Besides Rev. William Henry Angas, several others were active over the years. Rev. *C. F. A. Steinkopff*, Pastor of the German Lutheran Chapel of the Savoy, London, was especially involved, as "Foreign Secretary" of the British and Foreign Bible Society. Rev. *Carl von Bülow* expanded his early Scandinavian outreach to include German seafarers, completing his lifework with a four-year term as "Thames Missionary to Foreign Seamen" for the BFSS, 1846–1850.

In 1836, as already noted, Rev. *Augustus Kavel,* a Lutheran pastor from Prussia, sought asylum in England from religious persecution in his homeland. Here he served for the next two and a half years as a missionary of the British and Foreign Sailors' Society to German seafarers on the Thames. Before leaving Britain with a party of fellow refugees to help found the colony of South Australia, he formed "an auxiliary to an intended German Sailors' Society to be established in Germany itself" (Kverndal 1986, 372, 746).

Although Kavel's goal of a national seafarers' mission society in Germany was not immediately realized, his and similar efforts eventually bore fruit. German-ethnic congregations in British port-cities became so impressed that they began taking active part themselves. In 1856, Rev. *D. A. Herschell*, a German Christian Jew, provided a powerful further impulse by founding an *Association for Supplying Scripture to Foreign Sailors.* For decades, Herschell's organization supported German-ethnic waterfront workers, both in London and in other British port-cities. Among Herschell's beneficiaries was one who would one day become the *Founding Father of the German Seamen's Mission.*

In 1869, Rev. *Friedrich Martin Harms* (1844–1919), born in the Baltic seaport of Rostock, arrived as a 25-year-old in Sunderland in order to take over the recently formed German congregation there. Soon, he also found himself immersed in ministry among the many German seafarers roaming around both there and in neighboring port-cities. Unable to cope with volunteer help alone, Harms turned to his homeland. It was the Central Board of the Wichern-initiated Inner Mission that first responded. With their support, he returned to Sunderland and conducted a broad survey of needs among German seafarers in British ports.

Back in Germany, the Protestant institutional church finally appeared ready to act, with the Lutheran state churches leading the way. On 29 September 1886, a Lutheran Inner Mission Conference in Hannover decided to form a *Committee for Church Ministry to German Seafarers Abroad.* This in turn resulted in a *German Lutheran Seamen's Ministry Association.* That day, in 1886, has since been the official "birth date" of the German Seamen's Mission.

The next year, this Hannover-based "Lutheran Association" sent Rev. *Julius Jungeclaussen* to Cardiff, as their first, full-time chaplain to the Bristol Channel. This led to a *General Committee for German Evangelical Seamen's Mission in Great Britain,* established in 1889 as a result of extensive travels by Harms. Within a quarter-century, the Lutheran Association had initiated centers worldwide, from the German homeland to America, Africa and Australia.

Despite an initial rebuff by Bismark himself, Harms helped facilitate a *Committee for German Seamen's Mission in Berlin* in 1895, representing Germany's Evangelical state churches. Like the Lutheran Association before them, this new "Berlin Committee" began working in close cooperation with German congregations abroad. Soon they, too, could open stations worldwide, in their case from the Baltic to South America and the Far East. By 1914, this threefold configuration of UK-, Hannover- and Berlin-based associations, which Harms had finally forged, embraced 55 stations at home and abroad, employing 27 clergy and 63 lay workers (Münchmeyer 1912; Thun 1959; Freese 1991).

Origins of a Network in the Netherlands

Pre-History

The Netherlands experienced the 17th century as a golden age. With more than one third of their low-lying homeland seized from the sea, the Dutch had long been a sea-minded nation. As Dutch sea power reached its peak in the late 1600s, the spiritual welfare of Dutch seafarers became a national priority.

The archives of Holland's maritime museums reveal an abundance of self-help manuals for mariners from the early 1600s. Foremost was the principal work by the Dutch lawyer-theologian, *Hugo Grotius, in 1627.* In his *De veritate Religionis Christianae* ("On the Truth of the Christian Religion"), he tried to help seafarers protect themselves from "evil-disposed persons" in port cities. Instead, he suggested they help refute the claims of "pagans" by becoming voluntary "foreign missionaries." In 1635, *Adam Westerman* published his *Groote Christelycke Zeevaart* ("Great Christian Navigation"), a popular collection of sea-related sermons, songs and prayers, which went through numerous editions. Similar devotional aids for Dutch merchant seafarers and fishers would follow over the next two hundred years.

Another significant form of maritime ministry during this period was the chaplaincy service of the Dutch East India Company. Established in 1602, the Company soon became the largest trading organization in the world, with outposts from South Africa to the China Sea. Over the centuries, the Company sent out almost five thousand ships. Most of them carried an ordained ship's chaplain or lay "sick comforter" of the established Dutch Reformed Church.

As in Germany, Anglo-American maritime mission would help prepare the way for indigenous Dutch maritime mission. The United Netherlands Bible Society, cooperating with the BFBS, helped form an *Amsterdam Marine Bible Society* as early as in 1820, with "retired Captains of pious character" as directors. Its success led to a similar agency in Rotterdam the following year.

In the mid-1820s, Rev. *William Henry Angas,* fresh from his pioneer ministry on the Hamburg waterfront, focused on the Dutch. During previous studies, he had already acquired fluency in the language. As he now toured Dutch ports from Rotterdam to Flushing, he found a willing co-worker in Captain *Van Zeuglan Nyevelt* of the Netherlands Navy. Angas drew up a *Memorial to the Dutch Nation* on behalf of their seafarers, intended for circulation "in all the sea-ports of Holland." On his return to England, he used every opportunity to continue ministering to Dutch and other foreign seafarers.

In the New World, immigrant members of the Dutch Reformed Church, both in New York and other Atlantic Coast cities, joined in ministering to Dutch seafarers through existing seafarers' mission agencies. Dr. *David Abeel,* a descendant of immigrants from Amsterdam and graduate of the Dutch Reformed Church New Brunswick Seminary, arrived in Canton, China, in 1830. He would become the first in a long list of foreign-port seafarers' missionaries sent out by the American Seamen's Friend Society in the course of the nineteenth century. In 1842, the English Reformed Church of Amsterdam helped launch an *Amsterdam British and American Seamen's Friend Society.* For several years, this continued to receive support from both the BFSS and the ASFS.

Delayed Birth

A combination of circumstances continued to delay the development of indigenous Dutch maritime mission. Rev. *Jacob Leij,* a chaplain and historian involved with post-World War II Dutch seafarers' mission leadership, identified at least one relevant factor in the course of an interview with the Author in the 1990s. During the 19th century, when widespread revivals were generating a range of mission initiatives on both sides of the Atlantic, nothing similar ever evolved in the Netherlands. Most of the Calvinist churches there seemed preoccupied with "divisive doctrinal concerns," resulting in major schisms..

Prospects finally changed during the 1890s, with the help of the chaplain of the Norwegian Seamen's Mission in Rotterdam, Rev. *Thorvald Egidius Isachsen* and, not least, his Dutch-born wife, *Dudock van Heel.* In October 1892, this Dutch-Norwegian couple rented a building near the waterfront for use as a reading room by Dutch seafarers. There was also overnight accommodation, as well as a chaplain's residence. In cooperation with the Maritime Manning Director ("Waterschout") in Rotterdam, *S. B. Ortt,* the couple then organized a Christian-based, indigenous *Dutch Seamen's Union* ("De Zeemansbond"). This group succeeded in opening a Seafarers' Home, with Ortt's daughter, *Freide*

Ortt, in charge. That day, 23 February 1893, would later become the official birth-date of indigenous Dutch maritime mission.

Shortly afterwards, the Seamen's Union managed to establish a similar institution in Amsterdam. Laywomen of "high social standing" were to play a key role in this early Dutch seafarers' mission enterprise. Details of how that organization would eventually merge with others in 1934, to form a broader, national network known as the *Netherlands Seamen's Center* ("Nederlandse Zeemanscentrale"), belong to the 20th century (NZC Archives).

PROGRAMMATIC CHANGE

As the formative years of organized maritime mission drew to a close in the mid-1860s, maritime transportation, too, was entering a time of transition. During the first half of the 19th century, innovations in the design of sailing ships had brought the balance between speed and cargo-carrying capacity to the very peak of perfection. Nowhere was that more striking than in the sleek structure of the famous Baltimore Clippers. Meanwhile, alternatives to wood and sail had also moved ahead: "By 1865 steamships had at last developed to a point at which they could successfully compete with sailing vessels" (Greenhill 1980, 6).

The implications for maritime mission of this transition from sail to steam would continue to increase during the decades ahead, with the development of new docklands and faster turnaround time in port. Another issue was the "climate change" in contemporary culture and theology. When the Bethel Movement found organizational expression in the 1820s, it evolved as an offspring of the evangelical awakenings on both sides of the Atlantic. From the mid-1800s, secularization, spurred by advancing scientific discoveries, had begun to make its mark in maritime mission, too. By that time, a reorientation or "paradigm shift" in maritime mission and ministry was well underway.

Most apparent were two major areas of change—providing multi-faceted service through shore-based "Institutes" and promoting advocacy for systemic change within the industry. The dominant players on the global scene were still the British and the Americans. Among these, by far the most conspicuous were "The Big Three"—the British and Foreign Sailors' Society (BFSS), The Missions to Seamen (MtS), and the American Seamen's Friend Society (ASFS).

From Bethels to Institutes

The British and Foreign Sailors' Society

By the mid-1860s, the early Bethel Movement's principle of seafarer-centered "mission from below" had all but given way to the agency-centered delivery of wide-ranging human services by means of purpose-built facilities ashore. In fact, the public introduction of the "Institute" concept had already taken place a decade earlier. In 1856, the *British and Foreign Sailors' Society,* as the oldest of the three major organizations, had opened their multi-service "Sailors' Palace" in Shadwell, London. As the century progressed, the service-oriented Institute model rapidly gained ground, not only in each of the three leading maritime mission organizations but also beyond.

Meanwhile, the BFSS continued to expand, both in home-ports and overseas, under the leadership of Rev. *Edward W. Matthew* ("Father Neptune," as the generously bearded Secretary came to be called). In 1863, as a headstrong 17 year-old seafarer, he went through a dramatic conversion on board a floating chapel in the Bay of Alexandria, Egypt. The chapel was an iron ship, donated to the Society by the "Pasha" (the regional ruler).in person. At the time, he had stated: "It is true that I am a Mohammedan, but still I am no bigot, and am ready to help forward anything that is likely to do good." (Matthew 1911).

During his long turn at the helm (1878–1916), Matthew led the Society through a time of remarkable renewal that reached its peak in the 1890s. Most striking were all the new stations overseas, in the Mediterranean, South America, South Africa and Australasia. By the outbreak of World War I, the BFSS was operating over 100 stations at home and abroad, with a corresponding number of chaplains and lay missionaries. Whether referred to as "Sailors' Institutes" or still "Bethels," the Institute model of holistic service was by now the norm.

British and American Anglicans

The Anglican *Missions to Seamen,* founded in 1856, also went through a remarkable expansion, benefiting by its identification with the National Church. However, the gathering momentums of change from sail to steam, and therefore from anchorages to docklands, could easily have rendered the MtS irrelevant. After all, visiting vessels at anchor in roadsteads was its original purpose. Fortunately, the infant Society could draw on the gifts of two talented leaders during its critical years: its Secretary, Rev. *Theodore Augustus Walrond,* and its Bristol Channel Chaplain, Rev. *Robert Buckley Boyer.*

Within five years, the first rudimentary "Institute" opened in Deal. In 1863, Boyer—already well known on the Cardiff waterfront as an indefatigable foe of the crimping system—followed up with a former frigate, moored there as a "Church and Institute." Soon similar floating facilities had opened elsewhere. By the 1890s, however, church ships had seen their day and the MtS, like the BFSS, went over to shore-based institutes. By World War I, the number of MtS churches and institutes had surpassed that of the BFSS and reached close to 150. In addition to some 150 chaplains and missionaries, or "lay readers," the MtS could also count on more than 80 "honorary chaplains" worldwide.

Overseas, the Anglican MtS had its largest growth in ports connected with the Commonwealth. In the USA, however, the situation was unique. There, under the auspices of the Protestant Episcopal Church of America, they had already established Anglican-affiliated maritime ministries in New York (1842) and Philadelphia (1847), well before the Missions to Seamen in England. In 1920, the work culminated with the incorporation of a national organization called the *Seamen's Church Institute of America* (Kelley 1940, 349–367).

A notable exception was the wild waterfront of San Francisco. Here, Rev. *James Fell,* a trained boxer, had arrived from Liverpool in 1893. Soon widely known as "Fell of 'Frisco," he had reputedly fought and beaten every crimp on the waterfront. That included a notorious Irish prizefighter who, impressed by being "knocked out by a padre," promptly joined Fell's team! This unlikely ally helped Fell lay the foundations for the *Seamen's Church Institute of San Francisco*—to be transferred in 1914 to the American Episcopalians.

The American Seamen's Friend Society

In the pluralistic context of the United States, only the American Seamen's Friend Society, with its denominational diversity, was able to fill the role of a national maritime mission organization. As such, the ASFS followed the same model of de-centralized flexibility as the BFSS. Robert Miller has borrowed from modern market terminology and characterized this as a "franchise" model, with a common "brand" identity (in this case the Bethel Flag emblem), combined with a high degree of local autonomy. The Anglicans, on the other hand, would represent a "chain store" model, with a common, denominational legacy and a relatively centralized structure (Miller 1995, 192). Both models would continue to co-exist toward the close of the 19th century and into the 20th.

Coffin Ships and Sailors' Rights

Winds of Change on the Theological Waterfront

In his research on the maritime aspect of Victorian working class religion, Stephen Friend links growing public support for seafarers' and fishers' missions to their evident success—compared with other forms of home mission at the time. That success he attributes partly to the inherent folk religiosity of Britain's seafaring communities, partly to the fact that maritime mission staff came largely from the ranks of seafarers themselves. At a time when middle class Victorian evangelicals were horrified by working class alienation from the institutional church, seafarers' missions—with their more relaxed ministry— appeared to be a far more promising charity investment (Friend 1994, 2003).

In exploring further the relevance of seafarers' missions to the lives of their clientele, Friend focuses on the theological paradigm shift during the 19th century in the perception of poverty. Instead of seeing sin as the root cause, and personal salvation as the cure-all, there was a growing recognition that churches must join in the struggle against poverty itself "before expecting the working classes to respond to evangelism." This meant moving from a unique emphasis on Christ's *atonement*—and sacrifice for human sin, toward a greater acceptance of his *incarnation*— and solidarity with all who are marginalized and hurting.

In maritime mission, this translated into a reorientation from a salvation-centered or *soteriological,* to a more "Kingdom"-centered or *holistic* approach. The Bethel Era's emphasis on redemption of the individual soul was giving way to a more comprehensive vision of the reign of God, integrating evangelism with healing and justice (in harmony with Jesus' programmatic declaration in Luke

4:16-21). This development owed much to 19th century Anglo-Catholic activists and Christian Socialists, but not least to the publicity given by evangelical Christians to the abuse of the underprivileged in contemporary society.

Alston Kennerley has documented how both the BFSS and the MtS had begun to integrate lodging facilities into their Institute model by the late 1800s (Kennerley 1989). *Agnes Weston* (1840-1918) was among the independent activists in the field—with her "Sailors' Rests," a combination of Sailors' Institutes and Sailors' Homes, built during the 1870s and 1880s, principally in the naval ports of Plymouth and Portsmouth. Beloved by beneficiaries of her ministry worldwide, "Mother Weston" paralleled the ministry of her Swedish namesake, *Agnes Welin* (1844–1928). In 1887, "Mother Welin"—in the face of strong male prejudice—successfully raised a five-story *Sailors' Temperance Home* for seafarers in the heart of London's West India Docklands. (See entries on both Weston and Welin in *Oxford DNB,* 2004, by Kennerley and Kverndal.)

From the late 1800s, all the "Big Three" (the BFSS, the MTS and the ASFS) broadened their social engagement to include not just diaconal services but also proactive systemic change in the seafaring world. The BISS and ASFS were among the first to hail Richard Henry Dana's classic exposé of abuse at sea, in *Two Years before the Mast* (1840). Later, they strongly endorsed a sorely needed regulatory system in the maritime industry. Rev. Edward Matthews, of the BFSS, created a sensation in 1885, when he published a scathing indictment of shipboard cruelty in his *Belaying-Pin Gospel.* The results reverberated far beyond the Society's constituency. Besides the "Big Three," four individuals would make a unique contribution to advocacy for maritime systemic change.

Mansfield: The Man who Outcrimped the Crimps

On the New York waterfront, an Anglican, Rev. (later Dr.) *Archibald Romaine Mansfield* (1871–1934), brought the Institute concept quite literally to a new height. In 1913, he opened the thirteen-story multi-service facility of the Seamen's Church Institute at 25 South Street. Here, he could combine lodging for 2,000 seafaring guests with a restaurant, bank, post office, laundry, chapel, shipping office, store, even a navigation and marine engineering school, later also a gymnasium, medical clinic and more. With that, "Twenty-five" became the largest and best-equipped facility of its kind the world had ever seen.

Contrary to critics' claims, the gigantic project was no reckless gamble. Rather, it represented the cornerstone in a calculated social strategy. Here was far more than a mere multiplication of diaconal ministry. The goal was no less than *radical systemic change* in the structure that sustained the crimp's stranglehold on the waterfront. From the start, Mansfield had decided on a bold, twofold plan: On a practical level, he would "do for the sailor just what the crimps did, but do it right," outdoing them with his multi-faceted Institute. On a legal level, he would take up the fight to free ships' crews from their centuries-old status of condoned bondage while under contract.

At sea, a sailor's life was at the mercy of the captain. If seafarers sought escape ashore, they were "deserters" and authorities hounded them like runaway slaves, imprisoned them and returned them to their masters on board ship. As one of Mansfield's modern-day successors, Dr. James Whittemore, put it: "Slaves had been freed by the 13th Amendment to the US Constitution, *but not seamen.*" To change the slave status of the seafarer, the law itself had to be changed. Toward that end, Mansfield established a *Seamen's Branch of the Legal Aid Society*, thereby initiating the Institute's legal assistance to seafarers.

Mansfield also mounted a protracted lobbying campaign in Congress. Here, he could count on the cooperation of his Board Manager, *J. Augustus Johnson,* a former US Consul General in Beirut and committed advocate of maritime legal reform. In 1898, Johnson pushed through the *White Bill* in Congress, seen as "the first minimal civil rights bill for seamen." Against his critics, whether in unions or missions, Mansfield maintained it was integral to the gospel mandate to secure not only seafarers' "compensation in the next world," but also to meet their legitimate "secular needs" in this.

Mansfield died in 1934. (By that time the curse of crimping had also died.) In port, flags flew at half-mast, and 2000 seafarers attended his funeral. The *New York Times* eulogized him as one who not only preached and prayed for sailors but fought for them—against vicious forces that had once made New York "the worst seaport for seamen in the world." Now, he "left it the best" (Whittemore1985, 113-118).

Furuseth: The Father of the Seafarers' Rights Movement

Mansfield and Johnson had received invaluable help with the passage of the White Bill from a unique ally in Washington. While immersed in close combat with the crimping community in New York, they knew they had a fearless friend in Congress called *Andrew Furuseth* (1854–1938). Furuseth seemed born for the task. A native of Norway, he had gone to sea at sixteen and sailed before the mast under seven flags. After ten years, he had seen enough of abuse. He went ashore in San Francisco in 1885 and committed the rest of his life to ending legalized slavery at sea. An avid reader, gifted with an analytical mind, he became a nationally known expert in seafarer-related maritime law.

Furuseth saw brutality on board as "*the serfdom of the sailor,*" while desertion laws mandated imprisonment and forced return to ship. With cool logic, he developed a twofold strategy to abolish this practice. First, he provided leadership for the struggling maritime union movement. From 1886, he served as Secretary of the new *Sailors' Union of the Pacific* and, from 1908, also as President of the *International Seamen's Union*. Second, he moved from San Francisco to Washington DC in 1894. Here, during his incessant, twenty-year lobbying campaign in Congress, he never tired of repeating that fundamental principle of international law—enshrined in the medieval maritime code of Oléron: *Sailors are not to be treated as slaves!*

Furuseth's efforts culminated in 1915 with the signing of the Seamen's Act, abolishing imprisonment for desertion—whether by any seafarer in U.S. ports or by American seafarers abroad. Though named after its official sponsor,

Senator La Follette, it soon became known as "The Seafarer's Magna Carta"—
and earned for Furuseth the title of "Abraham Lincoln of the Sea."

Furuseth devoted the remainder of his life to enforcing these reforms while
expanding their substance and scope, including through the new *International
Labor Organization* in Geneva. The opposition could sometimes be brutal.
Furuseth's hardy physique and courage, however, proved equal to every
challenge. He once remarked that they could throw him in jail but they could not
give him narrower space, coarser food or a lonelier life than he had had as a
seaman. Confronted with Communist infiltration in the unions he led, he flatly
refused to allow their "maddened desperation" to compromise free association.

In the final analysis, it was Furuseth's faith—his Christ-centered (though
often unorthodox) piety—that nurtured both his moral authority and his tenacity.
He affirmed the Benedictine monastic maxim, *Work is Worship* ("laborare est
orare"). In the Mediterranean world of Jesus of Nazareth, he noted, there were
nine slaves to every free person. As Furuseth saw it, a major purpose of Christ's
coming was to abolish slavery and restore to all human beings both *dignity* as
"created in the image of God," and *freedom* to "exercise their creative faculty."
Humane conditions of life and work are therefore not a matter of charity but
justice, and not to be undermined by cheap labor, whatever the source. As such,
Andrew Furuseth was a true forerunner of Liberation Theology (Axtell 1948;
Nelson 1990).

Plimsoll: The Politician who Made his Mark

Known nationwide as "the Sailor's Friend," *Samuel Plimsoll* (1824–1898)
literally made his mark in history with "Plimsoll's Mark"—the load-line
required on ships' sides throughout the world. The mark would indicate the
depth to which any given ship could legally be loaded. Like Wilberforce and his
friends in the Slave Trade Abolition Movement at the close of the preceding
century, Plimsoll was a genius in arousing public outcry through the printed
word. In *Our Seamen*, published in 1872, he unmasked the greed of those who
sent unseaworthy, heavily insured vessels to sea. Known as "Coffin Ships," their
sole purpose was to sink, thereby securing "blood money" for their owners.

When Plimsoll entered Parliament as a Liberal member for Derby in 1868,
his earlier experience of destitution, as a bankrupt coal merchant in London, had
already given him a sense of solidarity with the poor. Since then, he had become
aware of the plight of *seafarers*, together with the need for universal load-line
provisions. Like his transatlantic counterpart, Andrew Furuseth, he fought for
the rest of his life with one aim in view—justice in the seafaring world. Also
like Furuseth, Plimsoll saw the national legislature as the decisive battlefront.

For five years, Plimsoll experienced repeated reversals due to dogged
resistance by the ship-owning lobby. By then, however, he had become a
national hero that politicians could no longer withstand. In 1876, a humbled
Prime Minister Disraeli had to pass a Merchant Shipping Act enacting load-line
provisions and a range of other reforms. Still, opposition continued for years to

come. He even witnessed one overloaded ship leave port with the Plimsoll Mark painted on her funnel, simply to show the captain's contempt for the new law!

Like Furuseth, Plimsoll found his strongest support in the relatively young maritime union movement. In 1887, *J. Havelock Wilson*, the embattled British Union pioneer, was delighted when his hero agreed to become President of Wilson's new *National Amalgamated Sailors' and Firemen's Union* (a forerunner of the *National Union of Seamen*). Yet in personal demeanor, Plimsoll, the consummate, extrovert publicist, could hardly have been more different from the frugal, self-effacing Furuseth. Although human failings might surface in the heat of battle, Plimsoll's saving grace was a willingness to admit his shortcomings. At all events, he was instrumental in bringing about "one of the greatest shipping reforms in the history of the world" (Masters 1955).

Hopkins: The Priest who Promoted Maritime Unions

In contrast to Plimsoll, *Charles Plomer Hopkins* (1861–1922) has remained relatively unknown until recently. Yet his contributions to maritime mission and maritime union history are both unique and enduring. Born in Massachusetts, USA, to an American master mariner and his Cornish wife, he grew up partly in Burma, where his father was a river pilot. Educated in England and majoring in music, he returned to Burma as Cathedral Organist in the port of Rangoon. It was soon apparent that Hopkins had a remarkable rapport with seafarers. In 1885, he was ordained as Anglican Port Chaplain there. Later, he also served in Calcutta. As chaplain, he found fulfillment in both of his life's passions—maritime religious communities and justice in the seafaring world.

In Calcutta, Father Hopkins gathered a group of seafaring believers into an Anglican community, the *Order of St. Paul*. Members committed themselves to a religious life based on the Benedictine rule, living in a port priory. The Order's strategy was to offer new workers for the different seafarers' missions worldwide. Visiting seafarers were welcomed with a mix of colorful Anglo-Catholic liturgy and recreational attractions. Also, they could join a "Seamen's Guild" affiliated with the Order—the *Seamen's Friendly Society of St. Paul.* Seafarer communicants increased rapidly, "from tens to thousands" in Calcutta alone. Meanwhile, similar work sprang up in several other Indian port cities, too.

Shipowners, on the other hand, attacked the Order as nothing but "a trade union in disguise." Certainly, his magazine highlighted news of Plimsoll's campaign. Also, he became involved in some thirty court cases on behalf of seafarers—and won nearly all of them. Shipowners tried again, unsuccessfully, to blacken his name. Finally, his health undermined by malaria, Hopkins returned to the United Kingdom in 1894. His colonial ordination now no longer recognized by his church authorities, he threw himself into helping Havelock Wilson consolidate his struggling National Seamen's and Firemen's Union.

As documented in recent research by Robert Miller, the success of the landmark 1911 Seamen's Strike was largely thanks to Hopkins. However, his health never fully recovered. He died in 1922 of complications related to malaria. Nor was his promising Order of St. Paul ever the same, once its founder had left the scene. Nevertheless, Peter Anson acknowledged it was Hopkins' "seafarer-centered" model of maritime mission that inspired his founding of the Apostleship of the Sea. Hopkins' concept of seafarers as partners in maritime mission would again find affirmation toward the dawn of the Third Millennium.

As a champion of seafarers' rights, Hopkins could be forceful, even fierce. Yet he was fair. While rejecting authorities' admonitions to "stick to his spiritual ministry," he stated that the goal was "not only to *demand* rights, but also to show seamen how to *do* right." Though Hopkins' own church withheld official affirmation, the state made him a Commander of the British Empire, in recognition of his conciliatory role between unions and shipowners on the National Maritime Board during World War I.

There was a synthesis between the twin passions in Hopkins' life—his campaign against seafarers' *social* abuse by profit-hungry employers, and his intolerance of seafarers' *spiritual* abuse by those he saw as religious zealots. Both converged in his lifelong commitment to the calling and dignity the Master once accorded his first seafaring followers (Miller 1989, 1992 and 1995b).

Focus on Fishers

Before the late 1800s, there still existed no maritime mission organization solely dedicated to ministry among fishing communities, even though these made up by far the greatest proportion of seafarers worldwide. This does not mean they were totally overlooked. They had been included in general maritime mission endeavors since early Christian media distribution. Later, in the 1830s, the ASFS initiated a special outreach to *whalers* in the "South Sea Fisheries." In Britain, fishing communities would benefit from the coastal activities of the BFSS. From the 1850s, they formed a part of the tireless ministry of *Thomas Rosie* and his *Scottish Coast Missions* (later merged with the BFSS). Combined missions to coastal and fishing communities also spread to the New World, including Canada's Atlantic Northeast, the Pacific Northwest, as well as Alaska.

Mather: The Fishers' Friend

It was the late 19th century rise of North Sea fishing which was to provide the catalyst for change. Around 1880, there was a public outcry over reports of appalling conditions in the vast population on board the North Sea fishing smacks. Reactions even rivaled the "coffin ship" uproar. This time the target was the "Copers"—notorious as "floating grog shops" that offered cheap liquor, tobacco, gambling and prostitution. Graphic accounts of atrocities affecting not least young apprentices filled the press and shocked the public.

When one concerned fishing vessel owner offered to facilitate an on-site study of the situation, the newly appointed Secretary of the Thames Church Mission, *Ebenezer Joseph Mather* (1849–1927), needed no second invitation. On 27 August 1881, Mather went to visit Samuel Hewett's "Short Blue Fishing Fleet" in the North Sea. That day became the official birth date of the *Royal National Mission to Deep Sea Fishermen* (RNMDSF), with Mather as founder.

Mather was at first a member of the Plymouth Brethren; later, he became an Anglican. Together with his business background, he brought both creativity and perseverance to the task. There were also strong similarities between him and George Charles Smith, as Stephen Friend's research shows. Mather capitalized on widespread concern to introduce a new mission ship concept, combining commercial enterprise with evangelistic outreach. His strategy was simple. Copers were essentially "floating crimps." Therefore, when the crimp went offshore, missions must also go offshore—so as to deny him a monopoly.

As the number of mission ships increased, so too did financial pressures. In 1885, after first cutting his ties with the TCM, Mather made what one journalist called a "Napoleonic stroke." He decided to let all five mission ships start selling duty-free tobacco to grateful fishers—but at a price that soon sounded a death-knell for the copers. In 1886, Mather also masterminded a "Hospital Ship" that combined spiritual with sorely needed medical care. These new "Bethel Ships" would continue with considerable success for many years.

Escalating financial commitments eventually led to a crisis, resulting in Mather's resignation in 1889. Nevertheless, he had by then contributed more than anyone toward international recognition of fishers as a distinct class of seafarers, deserving of a dedicated form of outreach. Mather also unwittingly helped keep alive the early Bethel Era concept of "ship-based" ministry— pending its renewal in a very different context (Friend 1994, 1995 and 2003).

The Royal National Mission to Deep Sea Fishermen

In 1897, Queen Victoria recognized the significance of the work of the RNMDSF by according it the prefix "Royal." Others would willingly emulate the Mission's model. Among these was *Wilfred Thomason Grenfell* (1865– 1940), a medical doctor and convert of Moody. It was he who had successfully tested the hospital ship model for Mather in the North Sea in 1888. In 1892, he crossed the Atlantic to head the Mission's new hospital ship ministry among the fishing and coastal communities of Labrador and Newfoundland

Here, Grenfell's ingenuity led to a series of social reforms and new institutions. These have inspired succeeding generations in both Britain and North America with ideals of social service in Christ's name. His work was eventually integrated into the *International Grenfell Association,* founded in 1912. The Association has, since 1926, continued independently of the RNMDSF (Rompkey 1991, Friend 1991).

The accomplishments of the RNMDSF, which was now essentially nondenominational, even spurred some competition. This was especially evident with the Anglicans' *St. Andrew's Waterside Church Mission.* This group's leadership reacted strongly against what they saw as a sectarian "Salvation Army kind" of strategy. In cooperation with an affiliated East Anglian-based *North Sea Church Mission* (f. 1895), SAWCM did attempt a "Church Ship" alternative to the RNMDSF "Bethel Ships," but gave up after mixed results.

Among those who followed the RNMDSF model were the Salvationists themselves, with a so-called *Salvation Navy.* From its origins in 1885, this novel enterprise managed to include both coastal and deep-sea fishers in its "Naval Brigade" until it fell victim to the effects of World War I. From 1891 to 1897, Canon Hawkins maintained a Catholic ministry among fishing apprentices, *St. Joseph's Confraternity*, based at his church, St. Mary's, in Grimsby.

On the European mainland, the Norwegians were again first among the Nordics with a fishers' mission. In early 1880, preceding the RNMDSF by over a year, the *Norwegian Home-Port Seamen's Mission* was organized in Bergen in response to a lay-led initiative by fishers themselves. When they decided to supplement their land-based facilities with a series of Bethel Ships, they made use of the RNMDSF model.

In Denmark, a *Danish Home-Port Seamen's Mission* started up in 1905. This was largely the result of the Copenhagen "Bethel Ship" ministry, initiated in 1881 by a Danish ASFS "Sailor Missionary," *Andreas ("Andrew") Wollesen*. Corresponding initiatives followed in the other Nordic nations, as well as in Germany and the Netherlands. After the year 1900, as the fishing industry went through a period of structural change, the RNMDSF gradually phased out its Bethel Ship fleet in favor of a growing network of shore-based facilities.

A French Catholic initiative in the 1890s was also attributable to the early international impact of the RNMDSF. Since the late 1850s, the two mission priests, Abbé Bernard and Abbé Beaudouin, had aroused public awareness of the outreach of the "confraternities" of Northwest France in Icelandic fisheries. A French naval officer, *Bernard Bailly*, took the initiative toward a national, ongoing ministry. During the early 1890s, he repeatedly visited England to study first hand the work of the RNMDSF. Back in Paris, he enlisted the aid of his two brothers in the Augustinians of the Assumption. With their help, he founded a *Société des Oeuvres de Mer* ("Society for Maritime Ministry") in December 1894—as a kind of Catholic counterpart to the Protestant fishers' mission in Britain.

From 1895 on, the new Society developed an expanding hospital ship ministry, seeking to meet the physical and spiritual needs of both French and other fishers in the waters off Newfoundland, Labrador, Iceland and the Faeroes, later also in the North Sea. From 1920, the Society played a key role in the prelude to the church-wide Catholic maritime mission enterprise that became the *Apostleship of the Sea*. As the latter got under way, the Société des Oeuvres de Mer gradually merged into it. This process would become part of the subsequent Ecumenical Era of maritime mission history (Anson 1948; Miller 1995a).

Section
2

Ecumenical/Modern Era
(1920-1974)

5

CATHOLIC REGENERATION

AOS (1920)

PRE-HISTORY OF A NEW APOSTOLATE

By the early 20th century, a new era was already under way in the maritime world. In maritime *industry*, the transition from sail to steam was nearing completion. In maritime *ministry*, the transition from a Bethel-based ministry to an institute-based model had also become apparent. Within the church at large, the overriding issue was the scandal of entrenched denominational division and the quest for Christian unity. That need was now as urgent in maritime mission as in other areas of Christian outreach.

Evidence of a New Era

The Quest for Ecumenical Collaboration

Well before 1920, there had been several cooperative initiatives in both maritime and world mission. Chaplain *Robert Stubbs*, later known as the "Seamen's Apostle of the Pacific Northwest," proposed a "Christian Alliance of the Seamen's Friend Societies of the World" in 1884. His plan did not materialize, although its purpose was as relevant as ever—to combat the crimp, the common enemy of seafarers on every waterfront.

The first attempt at facilitating structured, multi-denominational cooperation in international maritime mission took place in Boston, Massachusetts, in October 1899. Sixty-three delegates converged from Canada and the United States for a meeting billed as an "International Conference of Sailor Workers." Dr. Archibald Mansfield of New York became Secretary of the "International Committee," charged with promoting "seamen's missions and agencies for legal aid to seamen" in every major seaport. In 1908, the New York-based American Seamen's Friend Society also sponsored a multi-denominational "International

Conference of Chaplains, Missionaries and Workers," representing "six different nationalities."

Two years later, the first "World Missionary Conference," held in Edinburgh in 1910, called for Christian cooperation and unity as a key condition for the fulfillment of the Great Commission. The Edinburgh Conference, though rooted in a 19th century context of Western-world self-confidence, would none the less be seen later as a landmark event in church history, credited with giving birth to the ensuing "Ecumenical Movement."

Still, neither these early maritime mission conferences, nor the Edinburgh Conference of 1910, were strictly speaking ecumenical, since they were still *Protestant* events. Furthermore, the devastation unleashed by World War I stalled whatever ecumenical momentum might have developed, whether in the church at large or in the seafaring world.

Despite many decades of Christian maritime welfare, it was not Christian maritime ministry but *secular maritime industry* that would take the first steps toward international cooperation for the wellbeing of seafarers. In 1896, the solidarity shown by British seafarers toward striking dock-workers in Rotterdam resulted in the founding of the *International Transport Workers' Federation* (ITF), an organization that would have a profound impact on seafarers' social welfare in the century ahead.

In the wake of World War I, the *International Labour Organisation* (IL0) originated in 1919, in affiliation with the new "League of Nations" (from 1945, the "United Nations"). Headquartered in Geneva, the ILO introduced a unique formula for *tripartite decision-making* by governments, employers and trade unions, working together to promote world peace through worldwide social justice. From 1920 on, the ILO's "Maritime Sessions" have adopted a series of Conventions, many of key significance for conditions of life and work at sea.

In 1928, the Geneva-based *International Social Christian Institute,* an offshoot of the post-1910 Ecumenical Movement, initiated communication between major Christian seafarers' mission agencies and the ILO. The goal was to share past experiences and establish cooperation in areas of common concern. Among those actively engaged were *J. Havelock Wilson*, the British maritime union leader, and *T. Salvesen*, a Norwegian shipowner known for his dual engagement in both seafarers' mission and social justice. The attempt proved premature, however. In the 1920s, there was still no firm framework for even *inter-Protestant* maritime mission, let alone Protestant-*Catholic* cooperation.

The Ecumenical Era in maritime mission is the history of how, despite all odds, the two major confessional configurations, Protestants and Catholics, did eventually converge. First, there was the primary impediment to overcoming the "Denominational Great Divide," that the Church of Rome had no maritime mission structure even remotely comparable to those of the Protestants. Second, prior to 1932, Protestants had still not consolidated over a century of organized maritime mission endeavors into any kind of cooperative structure, capable of bridging their own denominational demarcations. Only against this background can one comprehend the miracle that materialized in the second half of the 20th century.

The Prelude to a Dramatic Decade

A variety of Catholic maritime ministry initiatives did surface—both before and after the Reformation. Nevertheless, powerful factors inhibited any coordinated Catholic approach on an international level.

First, there was the pervasive anti-Catholic bias that prevailed in much of the United States and throughout the United Kingdom around the turn of the 19th century. This excluded Catholics from meaningful participation during the entire start-up period of organized seafarers' mission. Later too, although the Catholic Emancipation Act of 1829 removed many humiliating disabilities for British Catholics, discrimination persisted, inhibiting Catholic maritime mission initiatives well into the second half-century.

Then there was France. In the wake of the Revolution of 1789, secularism, rooted in anti-clericalism, ran deep during the whole following century. Also, the defeat of the French at Trafalgar, in 1805, set back the nation's sea-power, as well as public awareness of people of the sea, for years to come.

In spite of all this, exceptions did occur in 19th century Europe, and they did so first in France. Toward mid-century, Christian concern began to surface in the French navy. There were officers who engaged in shipboard peer ministry, before going on to serve in Catholic missions overseas. From the late 1850s, as already noted, *Abbé Bernard* and *Abbé Beaudouin* launched a ministry to fishers from Brittany and Normandy in Icelandic waters. From 1860 to 1870, other French priests, as well as some Dutch, engaged in similar missions in the Orkneys and Shetlands region. In Britain, too, there were modest beginnings, like the occasional appointment of Catholic chaplains to the Royal Navy. Even so, until 1887, it was still illegal for Catholic naval chaplains to serve at sea.

In contrast to such sporadic events, a series of Catholic maritime mission initiatives did materialize during the last decade of the century. A contributing factor may have been the relational "climate change" resulting from the Catholic Archbishop Manning's successful arbitration in the London Dock Strike of 1889, followed by Pope Leo XIII's historic encyclical *Rerum Novarum* in 1891. The latter landmark proclamation encouraged Catholics to involve themselves openly in outreach to the marginalized in contemporary secular society.

Robert Miller, in his research of the "Catholic Sea Apostolate," has identified a similarity between the sequence of events in the 1890s and the beginning of organized Protestant maritime mission in the early 1800s. First, there was a focus on furnishing Christian literature—with naval rather than merchant seafarers as the primary beneficiaries. Also, the confraternity concept was initially central, featuring seafarers as "apostles among their shipmates."

Besides Miller's research, major resources on the pre-history and early history of Catholic maritime mission include the writings of Peter Anson, Arthur Gannon, Alain Cabantous and Vincent Yzermans, as well as the archives of Apostolatus Maris in the Vatican. The Author's 1986 reference work, which

traces seafarers' mission history up to the 1860s, also includes an overview of
early Catholic work up to that point.

The First of the Forerunners

The Sailor who "Started it All"

There is general agreement that the upsurge of concern for Catholic
seafarers' mission is linked to an incident in a small seaport on Scotland's Firth
of Forth in the fall of 1889. Just as a Baptist minister received his wake-up call
from seafarers themselves in 1809, so too did a Catholic clergyman 80 years
later. As Rev. Lord *Archibald Douglas* himself recalled the event, he was just
removing his vestments after Mass in his church of St. Margaret's at South
Queensferry. Suddenly, "a sailor opened the door, and launched out there and
then with the zeal of an apostle into the subject—the need for action, if the
Catholic bluejackets are not to go to the dogs...."

Douglas saw this as a reminder he could not ignore. He first convened an
impromptu committee of colleagues to brainstorm. He then sent an appeal for
prayers and practical help to the readers of the *Messenger of the Sacred Heart.*
The piece was published in the January 1890 issue, entitled "Jack Wrecked at
Sea" (alluding to Paul's words about spiritual shipwreck in 1 Tim. 1:19).

The *Messenger* was the popular English-language magazine of the
Apostleship of Prayer (AOP), an international Jesuit association. Founded in
France in 1844, as a confraternity for the promotion of prayer "in union with the
Sacred Heart of Jesus," the British chapter had chosen Wimbledon as its base.
Referring to the events that led to the 20th century *Apostleship of the Sea*,
Douglas would say, "It was the sailor at South Queensferry who started it all."

Simultaneously, Pope Leo XIII had selected "Sailors" as the particular
prayer theme ("General Intention") for AOP members during the month of May,
1890. Fr. *Augustus Dignam* SJ (1833–94), Director of the AOP and Editor of the
Messenger, made the most of what seemed a providential affirmation. He wrote
a rousing editorial, highlighting the plight of neglected Catholic seafarers as
contrasted with the proliferation of Protestant maritime missions.

Dignam repeatedly reminded his readers to rally around the cause in
prayer. In January 1891, he published a letter from a Catholic naval seafarer
appealing for religious reading matter for lonely Catholic sailors on overseas
naval service. It was simply signed "Bluejacket." The same year, leaders of the
London-based *Catholic Truth Society* (CTS) formed a *CTS Seamen's Sub-
Committee* to coordinate Catholic maritime literature distribution. (The CTS had
already begun supplying libraries for troopships and emigrant ships two years
previously.)

From then on, the AOP and the CTS would partner with each other,
working toward a worldwide maritime mission structure. Catholic women
activists, several of them "society ladies," would also play a key role. Among
these were the Hon. *Georgina Fraser,* as Secretary of the CTS Seamen's Sub-
Committee, and *Mary Scott-Murray,* as the primary "Promoter" of the maritime

sector of the AOP. This partnership was called "Work for Catholic Bluejackets" (WCB), promoting prayer life and literature distribution within the Royal Navy.

Father Francis Goldie who Laid the Foundation

However central the role of the AOP and CTS, no less was the contribution of three major Catholic religious orders—the Society of Jesus, the Society of St. Vincent de Paul, and the Augustinians of the Assumption. Among these three, the Jesuits played a dominant role. The person who galvanized the whole disparate movement was Fr. *Francis Goldie,* SJ (1836-1913). As ship's chaplain on troopships to India in the 1880s, he already had a personal affinity with people of the sea. As a Jesuit priest, his gifts as coordinator and publicist helped him network with each of the other two religious orders.

In 1892, while engaged by his Order as a lecturer, Goldie gave a significant maritime-related paper at a CTS conference in Liverpool. In a broad-ranging review, Goldie was actually the first to envisage a *worldwide bonding of Catholic seafarers.* Inspired by the lay Society of St. Vincent de Paul (SVP), he proposed a non-parochial "confraternity." He was also indebted to Hopkins' Anglo-Catholic model, the Order of St. Paul. Thirty years later, Peter Anson would affirm Goldie's ideas in his blueprint for a new Apostleship of the Sea.

That same year, Goldie gave out a *Guide to Heaven for the Use of those at Sea* on behalf of the CTS. This became an official prayer book in the Royal Navy. Goldie also made efforts, through his writings and public appearances, to expand Catholic outreach beyond the navy to merchant seafarers and fishers.

On 18 May 1893, the opening of a *Catholic Sailors' Club in Montreal* marked the first of such facilities in the "modern" era of the Catholic maritime apostolate. Here, Goldie's influence, together with that of the CTS Seamen's Sub-Committee, was a contributing factor. He encouraged the SVP to expand the shipvisiting activity they had already begun in port cities on either side of the Atlantic. There is also reason to link his name to the shore-based seafarers' facilities built by the SVP and the Jesuits in several port cities in the USA.

In the United Kingdom, the SVP took the lead in London four months after Montreal. It began in Wellclose Square, the scene of Bosun Smith's heyday two generations earlier. By the turn of the century, there was some form of facility in a few ports in North England, too, also with SVP help. The same happened on the Continent, with AOP involvement. In France, as already noted, the third religious order, the *Augustinians of the Assumption,* founded the *Société des Oeuvres de Mer,* in 1894, emulating the British RNMDSF. The Assumptionists would later play an important role in today's *Apostleship of the Sea.*

The 1895 Precursor

The Seamen's Branch of the AOP

Although both Father Goldie and the Catholic Truth Society would stay actively engaged, other Jesuits would now become the lead players, in close collaboration with the Apostleship of Prayer. Following the anonymous Bluejacket's appeal in the *Messenger* in January 1891, the confraternity's Wimbledon-based Editor/Director, Father Dignam, had continued integrating Catholic seafarers (mainly from the Royal Navy) into the general membership of the AOP community. However, membership enlistment was at best modest.

Partly because of correspondence with sailors themselves, Father Dignam reached the conclusion that rigid devotional commitment to the AOP Rule was not compatible with the realities of a seafarer's life. Instead, he developed a simpler version for use in a "Seamen's Branch" of the AOP, to be called the *Apostleship of the Sea.* Because Father Dignam died in September 1894, the task of actually starting up this revised version of the Seamen's Branch fell to his successor, Father *Gretton* SJ, the event taking place on 23 April 1895.

The "Apostleship of the Sea" of 1895 was essentially a *precursor* of the modern-day organization by the same name. It was, in fact, a maritime segment of what was still a broad-based *Apostleship of Prayer,* dedicated to "devotion to the Sacred Heart of Jesus." This new maritime branch of the AOP would lead to impressive results—at least on the Glasgow waterfront.

The Glasgow Connection

In 1892, a Swiss Jesuit priest, Fr. *Joseph Egger,* SJ (1843–1910), had joined the staff at the Clydeside church of St. Aloysius, Garnethill, Glasgow. Here, he accepted the AOP as one of his parish responsibilities, also promoting the "Seamen's Branch" of that confraternity. The ensuing events were linked to a future "foremother" of Catholic ministry to merchant seafarers, both on the Glasgow waterfront and far beyond, *Catherine ("Kate") Howden.*

As the daughter of one merchant sea captain and the young widow of another, Howden was well motivated for the work at hand. Already familiar with the Catholic initiatives in the docklands of London, she wrote a letter to the *Glasgow Observer* in January 1898 under the heading, "Spiritual Destitution of the Catholic Seaman." Her concern was specifically for *merchant* seafarers. Here, she made readers aware that a local "Ladies' Committee" was already organized for literature distribution on the Clyde waterfront. What they now needed was a number of *males* who could actually visit the ships.

Recent research indicates that Howden had a direct influence on the course of events that now unfolded at St. Aloysius (Miller 1995, 83-88). An Irish immigrant, *Daniel Shields* (1877–1940), who was working as a streetcar driver, had already proved invaluable in the parish youth ministry. From 1899, in response to Howden's challenge, Father Egger enlisted him as a "Promoter," to provide leadership for a shipvisiting team from the church's recently organized youth group.

Known as the "Working Boys," these were, like their leader, young working class men with few funds but great enthusiasm. While Howden used her home in Glasgow as a repository for collecting Catholic reading matter, rosaries and other devotional aids, Shields and his Working Boys would fan out—two by two—distributing them on their weekend forays. They would then refer interested seafarers to a modest, new Catholic Sailors' Institute, to nearby Catholic churches, or to recommendable lodging facilities.

A major purpose was to enroll seafaring members into the worldwide, devotional fellowship of the Apostleship of Prayer via its new maritime arm. For the benefit of foreign seafarers, multi-language membership leaflets were also available. Very soon, new members were joining by the thousands.

On the Eve of World War I

There is no record of any Catholic port ministry comparable to the level of activity in Glasgow at the turn of the 20th century. Here, Catherine Howden would faithfully continue her work, including distributing Sacred Heart badges, and sending supplies to contacts elsewhere, like London and New York.

At the same time, however, the ultimate dependency of the enterprise on Shields would eventually lead to its undoing. In 1905, Shields left to join the Jesuits as a Lay Brother, and now found a new avenue for his missionary vocation in the Zambesi Mission in Africa. Without its tireless original leader, the once vibrant Catholic shipvisiting program on the Glasgow waterfront eventually expired. In 1919, the ministry's courageous catalyst, Catherine Howden, died—a casualty of the post-war influenza epidemic—at the age of 61.

Despite the demise of the Glasgow initiative, the experience gained there would prove invaluable. Through local SVP branches elsewhere, Catholic concern for maritime mission began to increase from England to Australia. Until he passed away in 1913, Father Goldie continued to encourage SVP involvement. By then, Catholic ministry had commenced in more than 20 ports worldwide. There was also the ongoing French mission to deep-sea fishers maintained by the Société des Oeuvres de Mer. In 1905, a Vatican Instruction entitled *Jam Inde* had given a degree of international recognition to this Assumptionist-affiliated organization. The document anticipated the advent of a more comprehensive "pan-Catholic" maritime mission structure. The turmoil of World War I, however, would prevent this until after 1918.

THE ANSON ERA (1920—1924)

From Oblate Brother to Founding Father

Anson's Early Years

Despite the destruction and carnage caused by four years of global conflict, several pre-war Catholic port ministries survived. Meanwhile, during the heat of World War I, a young man made an important decision. The outcome meant that he would play a pivotal part in the birth of a new *Apostleship of the Sea* as the maritime arm of the Catholic Church.

Peter F. Anson (1889–1975) was born the year an anonymous sailor delivered his historic wake-up call at Queensferry in Scotland.. Anson's mother was Scottish and his English father was an Admiral in the Royal Navy. Endowed with a restless curiosity, Anson was, according to a Catholic colleague, "a true renaissance man" (Oubre 1998, 9). From his mother he inherited his artistic talent and his life-long love of the sea.

For two years, Anson studied architecture in London. Meanwhile, in 1906, he became familiar with an Anglican Benedictine community on Caldey Island. For Anson, that teenage contact with Caldey forged a link that would last all his life. Located near the shipping lanes off Tenby, on the south-west coast of Wales, the Caldey community kept their bond with the sea through nightly prayers, on behalf of those plowing the waters. The community even ran its own "monastic fleet" of small craft to maintain communication with shore

After moving there in 1910, Anson would make Caldey his principal base while he continued to feel torn between a monastic and a maritime-related lifework. In 1913, the Anglican community on Caldey became collectively "reconciled to Rome." As for Anson, he never wavered in his allegiance to the Catholic Church. However, by becoming an "Oblate Brother," he did not have to commit to the community's religious vows, yet could still associate with its prayers and work. In Anson's case, that work would vary, related as it was to the community's library and publications, interspersed with extended travels. Over the years, Anson produced a rich legacy of personal memoirs and research.

"A Plea for Catholic Seamen"

An event in the summer of 1917 helped "Brother Richard" to clarify his course in life. *Mary Scott-Murray* of Bournemouth invited Anson to be her Assistant Secretary. For over 25 years, she had been leader of the Apostleship of Prayer's literature and correspondence ministry among Catholic naval personnel (the "Work for Catholic Bluejackets"). His first task was to prepare an updated version of the AOP "List of Catholic Naval Officers." Anson took this on with enthusiasm. He later even referred to it as his "initiation" into the Catholic sea apostolate. By 1920, he had not only agreed to take over Scott-Murray's remaining responsibilities. He had also expanded them with the task of Honorary Secretary of a "Sailors' Branch" of the *Catholic Reading Guild*.

Anson reminisced later that it was during this work, "about 1919," that he visualized what the Apostleship of the Sea could become (Anson 1948, 98). His access to library resources at Caldey, as well as those at Fort Augustus Abbey in North Scotland, resulted in a pioneering project of maritime missiological research. The purpose was to explore the history and current status of both Catholic and Protestant maritime mission, particularly among merchant seafarers and deep-sea fishers. In the spring of 1920, he "boiled it down" to an article presented in *The Universe* of 30 April 1920 as "A Plea for Catholic Seamen: Catholic and Protestant Activities—A Contrast."

Anson quoted the recent statistics from "the multifarious activities of the chief Protestant societies," and compared these with how "strangely neglectful" the Catholics had become of their own fellow-Catholic seafarers. Stressing the need for a worldwide *Catholic* organization, Anson's conclusion was to the point: "The greater the activity of Protestant missions, the greater the dangers to which Catholic sailors are exposed."

Half a century later, in the light of a very different ecumenical climate, Anson expressed that he was "almost ashamed" of the adversarial tone of his "Plea." Still, understandable as it was in the context of the day, it actually was (as he later recalled) "the spark that kindled the fire." The publication of the "Plea" generated spirited discussions in Catholic media, both in Britain and abroad, especially in France and even in Rome.

The New Apostleship of the Sea

The First Meeting (1920)

In May 1920, Anson set off on a fact-finding tour of a series of port cities. High on his agenda was Glasgow. Among the many letters pouring in before he left was one from Brother Daniel Shields, SJ, back from his mission assignment in Africa and again immersed in ministry in Glasgow. Shields shared how, while in Africa, he had learned with sorrow of the demise of his former shipvisiting ministry. From then on, he had never ceased to pray that it would one day come to life again.

During his five-day visit in Glasgow, Anson plunged into a hectic field-study along the Clyde under the mentorship of Shields. This was when he was, in his own words, "first initiated into the ways of shipvisiting." As they covered the waterfront together, Shields discussed his dream of "a great revival" of the shipvisiting work in Glasgow that had lain "defunct" since before the war. The bonding between the two Brothers—one Jesuit, the other Oblate—would form the first link in *a unique trio of laypersons.*

The second link was forged in August that same year—with *Arthur Gannon* (1890–1979), an active member of St. John's in Portugal Street. He, too, had written to Anson in response to the "Plea." Disturbed by the current plight of neglected Catholic seafarers, Gannon had been wondering whether the parish branch of the *Catholic Young Men's Society* that he led might be able to help. In his response, Anson advised him to "get in touch with Br. Shields."

From then on, matters moved swiftly. While Anson continued his traveling, Gannon and Shields agreed to call a meeting, with Shields enlisting "the few laymen who had taken part in the earlier enterprise," and with Gannon recruiting colleagues from his Young Men's Society. The outcome was a letter to the *Glasgow Observer,* signed by Gannon, announcing a small committee "to reorganise the work which was carried on for so many years in Glasgow under the direction of the late Fr. Egger, SJ."

A meeting convened on 4 October 1920, at Glasgow's Catholic Institute, resulted in a "Central Committee" which elected Gannon as Honorary Acting Secretary. The primary task would be visitation of ships in the docks. Catholic priests would help form parochial committees and invite volunteers and subscribers. Although (as recorded by Gannon) "less than a dozen men attended," the local press produced headlines like "Active Work Commenced."

Within weeks, a vigorous program, headed by young Catholic lay people, was well under way—from the Broomielaw to Clydebank. Soon "seafaring men of all nations were making a real difference in the statistics of dockside Catholic churches." Four decades later, Gannon affirmed the significance of it all in the opening sentence of his official history: *"The first meeting of the Apostleship of the Sea was held on October 4th 1920 at Glasgow"* (Gannon 1965, 1).

Anson himself was not present at that meeting. Instead, he was acquiring first-hand sea experience on a series of deep-sea fishing vessels. Between voyages, he continued to promote Catholic port ministry wherever he could. In Glasgow the next year, he praised the zeal of the local "lay apostles," now like 20 years ago, faithfully visiting every ship they could reach along the Clyde.

The Provisional Constitution (1921)

At sunrise, on 6 July 1921, Anson was at the helm of the steam-drifter *Morning Star* in Moray Firth. As with Paul, the dim vision he had had two years before was now "finally christallised." He would "scrap" the concept of a revived Seamen's Branch of the Apostleship of Prayer and "replace" it with "a new organization of a much more comprehensive character." This organization's distinctive features would be threefold: It would be *international*—reflecting global catholic unity, while also allowing for local diversity. It should be *participatory,* including not only members ashore but also seafarers themselves—as fellow-missionaries and not just beneficiaries of ministry. Finally, it would need to be *holistic*—promoting not only seafarers' spiritual needs but also their other human welfare needs.

Returning a few weeks later, Anson found his proposals resisted by "a few conservative spirits" on the local committee, notably Daniel Shields. He saw any departure from the 1890s model as disloyalty to the memory of his mentor, Fr. Egger, fearing a wider scope would jeopardize "the definite spiritual nature" of the original Glasgow shipvisiting work. "Unconvinced by friendly warnings," Anson went to work on what he called his "jig-saw puzzle," a "Provisional Constitution" that could provide reassurance yet still embody his new vision.

The final draft included input by both Shields and Gannon. Based on a grassroots "Parochial Committee" structure, the new organization would be *for* and *by* seafarers, made up of not only shore-based members but also an "International Union of Catholic Seafarers" as its seagoing arm. The concept of seafarers themselves as the primary promoters of mission echoed the "Catholic Action" principle of "like to like" lay activism, promulgated by Pope Pius XI. It also resembled the notion of "Sailor Promoters" in the 1890s Apostleship of Prayer. Anson himself stated he had actually acquired the concept from the Bethel Union-linked International Sailors' Brotherhood of the BFSS, as well as from Father Hopkins' Order of St. Paul. After having obtained prior permission from the National Director of the Apostleship of Prayer, Fr. Bliss SJ, the Committee adopted the same name as the Seamen's Branch of the AOP—the *Apostleship of the Sea* (AOS).

At Gannon's request, Anson designed a distinctive badge for the new organization. This he did on Michaelmas Day, 29 September 1921, sitting by the lighthouse on Caldey Island, as he recalled later. With its lifebuoy, anchor and heart symbolizing faith, hope and love, the emblem embodied, like the Bethel Flag before it, biblical meaning—here based on 1 Corinthians 13:13. It also symbolized the centrality of the "Sacred Heart of Jesus" in the spirit of the 1895 forerunner of the AOS. Since then, the emblem has gained global recognition, identifying the AOS as the maritime arm of the Catholic Church everywhere.

Shortly after Bishop Toner of Glasgow had conveyed the approval of the Provisional Constitution, the first Annual Meeting took place in Glasgow, on 11 October 1921. Although Gannon could only report eleven Catholic "seamen's institutes" worldwide compared with over 500 Protestant ones, the nucleus of a Catholic international organization was finally in place. For Anson's part, he now received a "roving commission" as Honorary Organizing Secretary, an official recognition he would use well during the following two years.

The Papal Blessing (1922)

Carrying with him a letter of recommendation from Cardinal Bourne in November 1921, Anson embarked on a promotional tour that would include Belgium, France and Italy. His primary goal was Rome, to secure what he saw as a precondition for internationalization—papal recognition of the new organization. An important contact for Anson was *Donald Mackintosh,* Rector of the Scots College in Rome, who was shortly to become both Archbishop of Glasgow and, for the next two decades, the proactive President of the new AOS.

After this meeting, Cardinal Gaspari, as Secretary of State, sent an official letter to Anson, dated 17 April 1922, bestowing the blessing of Pope Pius XI on "so noble an enterprise," adding the prophetic assertion that it would one day "spread more and more along the sea-coasts of both hemispheres." Since then, this document has been the de facto "charter" of the AOS (Anson 1948, 104).

Anson now immersed himself in forging international connections between already existing Catholic maritime mission centers, while at the same time contending with mounting health problems. In 1924, as a result of the latter, he found he had to resign as Secretary, leaving the position in the hands of Arthur Gannon. For many years to come, Anson was nevertheless able to serve seafarers in other ways, both as maritime mission historian and marine artist. In 1966, in recognition of his unique role in the founding of the AOS, Peter Anson received the papal Knighthood of Saint Gregory.

In Retrospect—a "Birth Process"

Historical Analysis

What Anson and Gannon had in mind was different from the maritime branch of a Jesuit-led confraternity of prayer. They were looking toward an organization in its own right—not an appendage of another. The Vatican has consistently affirmed this position. It has repeatedly referred to the embryonic 1895 (AOP-linked) version of the AOS as having "died" during World War I. At the same time, it has stressed the "historical continuity" between the 1920 meeting in Glasgow and the present Apostleship of the Sea.

There is still the question as to whether 1920, 1921 or 1922 was *the exact year of foundation of the AOS.* Rather than struggle to identify a definitive yet arbitrary founding date, the analogy of a "gestation period" and a threefold birth process might perhaps permit a more dynamic view of the historical facts. If the year 1920 brought the actual "birthday" of the new AOS, then the year 1921 signified the initial "post-natal care," with the year 1922 marking the "official blessing" of the newcomer. At all events, this approach to the issue of origins certainly allows for the appropriation of a pre-existing "family name" by a new entity—with its own unique identity—25 years later.

Consistent with this view of the events of 1920-22, it has become customary to refer to that original "lay trio"—Anson, Shields and Gannon—as "Co-founders of the Apostleship of the Sea." Indisputably, all three were, in their way, actively involved in the founding process. However, just as Francis Goldie became the forerunner among his Jesuit colleagues in the 1890s, so Peter Anson was the key co-founder among his lay colleagues in the early 1920s. In fact, his vision of a "reborn" Catholic sea apostolate and his persistent pursuit of that vision, were so basic that it might well be argued: What George Charles Smith was for Protestant maritime mission in the early 19th century, Peter Anson was for its Catholic counterpart in the early 20th century.

Source Materials

Peter Anson found it wise to integrate into his 1921 draft constitution certain elements of the original 1895 model of the AOS, as revived in Glasgow in 1920. However, in his subsequent authorship, he insists that the AOS, as it ultimately took shape after 1920, was essentially "a new organisation" (Anson 1944, 102-109).

By contrast, *Robert Miller,* in his M.Phil. Thesis *Ship of Peter,* gives an appraisal of Anson that becomes, at times, severely critical. In terms of the origin of the Apostleship of the Sea, Miller seeks instead to make a case for *continuity* between the original, AOP-linked 1895 AOS and the post-1920 version of the AOS. He offers the AOS Congress of 1930 in Liverpool as a more appropriate founding date for the AOS in what he calls its "international guise" (Miller 1995, 175).

On the other hand, *Giovanni Cheli* and *Gérard Tronche,* on behalf of the AOS International Secretariat in Rome, have reiterated the traditional Vatican view of discontinuity between the limited AOP-linked 1895 AOS and the international modern-day AOS. They continue to trace the origin of the latter to "a group of lay people in Glasgow (Scotland) in 1920" (*Apostolatus Maris* No. 58, 1997, 12; *IASMM Newsletter,* Spring 1998, 8).

THE GANNON ERA (1924—1961)

International Participation

The French Connection

One way in which Peter Anson departed from the example of his Protestant predecessor from Penzance was in knowing when to withdraw. He could not have left the helm in more capable hands than those of Arthur Gannon. Daniel Shields had provided an invaluable link with the past. In order to meet the challenges of the new organization's formative years, the situation now called for wise, faithful guidance. Arthur Gannon's administrative and networking skills, combined with his Catholic loyalty, made him well qualified.

Gannon had already proved himself an excellent Honorary Secretary of the original 1920 Glasgow Committee. He had also taken over as Honorary Organizing Secretary of the de facto "AOS Headquarters Council" of 1921 during Anson's repeated absences. Gannon's goals were now twofold: *1) Internationalization: C*reating a coherent global structure compatible with the diversified mix of existing and future Catholic maritime ministries, to ensure the universal scope or "catholicity" of the work. *2) Supranationalization:* Integrating the international work under the *"*supranational" authority of the mother church in Rome, to ensure its distinctive, Roman Catholic identity and credibility (Gannon 1965, 58).

With papal recognition of at least the concept of the new enterprise now secured, Gannon could focus on the organization's international future. Just as a "Glasgow Connection" had helped set the stage for the birth of the new AOS in 1920, so it would now fall to a "French Connection" to facilitate the *internationalization* of the AOS during its formative period up to 1930. In that process, besides the groundwork already laid by Anson, the most prominent part would be played by the *Augustinians of the Assumption,* sponsors of the French fishers' mission, founded in 1894 as the "Société des Oeuvres de Mer."

In 1925, the *Fédération des Oeuvres Maritimes Catholiques Françaises* was formed in Paris, to combine Catholic maritime ministries throughout France in one and the same loose-knit structure. Gannon now reasoned: If the concept of a federation could work nationally, why not internationally? As a result, with the cooperation of one of Anson's Assumptionist friends, Canon Alfred Bernard, the first *AOS International Congress* could take place at Port-en-Bassin in Normandy in 1927. Miller credits the French with thereby acting as "midwives" of today's largely "horizontal" AOS structure (Miller 1995, 195).

Gannon's Greatest Asset

The second AOS International Congress also took place in France, in Boulogne-sur-Mer. Delegates converged from the USA, Britain, Belgium, Holland, Spain and Germany. Among them was the Catholics' pioneer port chaplain in Germany, Father *Hans Ansgar Reinhold* (1897-1968*).* From now on, Reinhold would become Gannon's key co-worker during a time of decisive developments. In maritime mission history worldwide, the significance of Reinhold's role has only recently become recognized (Kverndal 2004, 29-30).

Born in 1897 to a devout Catholic family in Hamburg, Reinhold grew up in an ecumenical environment. He attended a Lutheran school and made close Protestant and Jewish friends. Like his later friend Anson, after testing himself among the Benedictines, he realized that monastic life was not for him. However, the liturgy he learned to love did lead him into the priesthood, to which he was ordained in 1925. Like Father Hopkins before him, besides church liturgy his other life-long passion would be social justice advocacy.

Selected for continuing studies in Rome, he remained there until the winter of 1928-29. At that point, the German Bishops' Conference called him to return to Germany in order to organize a Catholic Maritime Apostolate there, with centers in the nation's major seaports. Reinhold was already familiar with sea-life. As a young man, he had served on a freighter in Asian waters. Now, with his genius for languages and empathy with the marginalized, Reinhold was considered well qualified for such an assignment.

Peter Anson visited Reinhold at his new "Seemansheim" in Bremerhaven. Later, he recorded how he recognized Reinhold as a kindred spirit and a ground-breaking maritime missiologist. Gannon, too, discovered Reinhold's skills and would come to rely on him to mastermind the restructuring of the AOS during the early 1930s. The following interpretation of Reinhold's life and work builds mainly on his own biography, as supplemented by other sources (Reinhold 1968; Anson 1944 & 1948; Gannon 1965; Maguire 1994; Kverndal 2004).

Reinhold helped solidify the horizontal dimension of the young organization into a global network. In that regard, the next AOS Congress would prove pivotal. It was held in Liverpool in 1930. Here, the delegates agreed to establish an "International Council," representing the various countries so far involved. Reinhold suggested the name *Apostolatus Maris Internationale Concilium* or "AMIC" ("International Council of the Apostleship of the Sea"). Under AMIC and its new constitution, the AOS would grow steadily through the next two decades, with Gannon at the helm at its UK headquarters.

The next AOS Congress, held in Amsterdam in 1932, also made history, in this case by inaugurating an *International Section of the AOS for Women Seafarers,* not least for those employed on passenger liners or in the fishing industry. Reinhold's advocacy for these and other victims of discrimination had already brought him into trouble with shipowners who complained they "had not expected a chaplain who would represent the just demands of their men."

When Hitler came to power in 1933, Reinhold also had problems with the new Nazi authorities. He interceded on behalf of a Hungarian seafarer who had been imprisoned for disparaging remarks about the Führer. From then on, he was a marked man, and his bishop whisked him away from Bremerhaven to Hamburg, in order to start a seafarers' center there.

"HAR" (the nickname his colleagues gave him) quickly developed his Hamburg facility into a model seafarers' center. In 1934, he organized an AOS International Congress in that city which drew more than two thousand participants. The Congress was remarkable on at least two counts. First, it was "a milestone on the road to Rome." By officially adopting a revised version of the AMIC Constitution, the internationalization process was completed, a prerequisite for the organization's integration in the Vatican. Second, Reinhold cast the Congress as an act of open defiance to the Nazi regime. Regardless of the two uniformed SS men stationed in front of the platform, Reinhold omitted the obligatory "Heil Hitler" salute and exchanged the prescribed "Horst Wessel" chant with a hymn. Neither of these affronts would be forgotten—or forgiven.

The Nazis were at the time trying to gain control of the nation's maritime unions, whether by infiltration or intimidation. They were aware that Christian seafarers, as well as Communist-leaning leftists, were a significant source of resistance. Given Reinhold's unique standing in the seafaring community, and the popularity of his group discussions with visiting ships' crews, government spies had already identified his center as "a hotbed of anti-Nazi activity." In less than a year, the Gestapo arrested Reinhold following a raid at the center.

Alerted that the Gestapo had now marked him for concentration camp, Reinhold managed to outwit the Gestapo and, with the help of intrepid Jesuit colleagues, escaped across the Dutch border in 1935. Catholic historian Vincent Yzermans speculates that the Gestapo had also targeted him "for a reason that most people did not know at that time"—Reinhold's partial Jewish ethnicity (Yzermans 1995, 86). From Holland, he sailed for England where he helped organize the International AOS Congress in London in October that year.

Reinhold in America

From 1932 to 1933, while he was still port chaplain in Hamburg, Reinhold had made five trips to New York as ship's chaplain on North German Lloyd liners. He records his disgust at the disparity between the quality of life of the crewmembers compared with the luxurious lifestyle of pampered passengers. He also recalls his instant fascination with New York and how this was the beginning of his "love for America." With the door to Germany now effectively closed, Reinhold would focus on serving seafarers from across the Atlantic. Leaving the Old World behind him, he stepped ashore in New York in August 1936 for good, "penniless, but with a great deal of ambition and hope."

On the New York waterfront, Reinhold was soon supporting seafarers on strike, cooperating with the Catholic social activist Dorothy Day. His attempt to found a Catholic maritime union failed in the face of Communist tactics. By association, however, Reinhold was for a while labeled a Communist radical himself by pro-Franco colleagues. After some seminary teaching engagements, he felt free to accept an offer by the Bishop of Seattle to launch a Catholic seafarers' ministry in that Pacific Northwest port city, arriving there in 1939. Ironically, after the outbreak of World War II, he then became the victim of a rising anti-German sentiment. Some even accused him of being a Nazi spy who was serving as a seafarers' chaplain in order to pass on information about British and American ship movements!

In spite of such charges, Reinhold was still able to found an AOS center in Seattle that has served the port ever since. So as not to compromise that work at the time, he reluctantly agreed to a transfer to parish ministry in Central Washington State in October 1941. His access to the sea now severed, Reinhold devoted himself to that other great interest in his life—spiritual renewal through involvement of the laity in liturgical reform. For this, he received a doctorate of divinity from Benedictine-affiliated St. John's University in Collegeville, Minnesota. Eventually, Hans Ansgar Reinhold also received belated recognition as leader of the Liturgical Movement in America, as well as pioneer advocate for "everything that led up to the reforms of Vatican II." He died in 1968, after a long battle with Parkinson's disease.

Reinhold's Legacy

It remains a tragedy that bigoted charges of Nazi sympathies should prevail in America, while in Europe equally false accusations of Communist complicity would fail. Nevertheless, in Europe Reinhold did leave a lasting legacy as a pioneer in maritime missiology. This achievement transcends both his denomination and his lifespan.

As the unique maritime missiologist Reinhold was, he rejected the formulation "for the spiritual welfare of all seafarers" as the *objective* of maritime mission. This was "too vague," especially at a time when totalitarian ideologies were vying with one another for the soul of the mariner. For guidance, Reinhold referred to Scripture, specifically Jesus' programmatic declaration in John 17:3: *"This is eternal life: that they may know you, the only true God, and Jesus Christ, whom you have sent."* Since nothing can be more vital than eternal life and, since knowing Jesus Christ is the key to that life, to reveal Jesus to the seafarer has to be the overriding concern of the maritime apostolate, he insisted.

How is this to happen in the context of a seafarer's life? Again, Reinhold advocated a *Scripture-based strategy*—Christ's own methodology as presented by the Sea of Galilee. Just as Christ elected not to "make the masses his helpers," focusing rather on "picking a few fishermen and training them" as his first *Apostles* of the Sea, today's *Apostleship* of the Sea must do likewise. They must "select and train an elite." Through a leaven-like spirituality and professionalism, they can become an "ecclesiola" (a miniature church) on every ship, "proud of being a member, nay a limb, of the Mystical Body of Christ," reflecting the kind of "inner revolution" which can "reveal Christ" to those who do not yet know him.

In that context, Reinhold called for a new public image of the average seafarer. Seafarers are not "weaklings and parasites," and therefore "objects of charity, primarily in need of benevolence and preventive care." They are neither better nor worse than people ashore, but equally deserving of respect and dignity. This meant meeting both their natural and "supernatural" needs through a holistic and stimulating ministry of education and edification. To provide that quality of ministry, Reinhold argued for new standards of excellence for personnel and facilities. Shipvisitors and other workers would need screening and training. This would require a comprehensive knowledge of seafarers' lives. Seafarers' facilities must never descend to serving simply as a front for religious purposes. Instead, they were to offer the very best in hospitality, recreation and educational opportunities.

Prior to Reinhold, Anson—who had himself coined the term "maritime missiology"—had been the sole pioneer in the field. Although they were now fellow pioneers, their respective roles were very different. Whereas Anson, who had no formal theological training, focused mainly on the *history* of maritime mission, Reinhold, as a well schooled theologian, was to be the first to formulate an intentional *theology* of maritime mission. Given the realities of pre-Vatican II Roman Catholic-Protestant relations, Reinhold's maritime missiology might have seemed specifically addressed to fellow Roman Catholics. Much of it nevertheless transcends denominational boundaries. As such, it has never been more relevant to the whole world of seafarers than at the present time.

With Reinhold's "seafarer-centered" approach and rejection of "objectification" in maritime mission, he raised a concern that would re-emerge as a major issue in the subsequent Global Era of Maritime Mission. Judged by both the *adversity* he had to overcome and by the *catholicity* of the timeless truths he stood for, this humble, prophetic figure called Hans Ansgar Reinhold—hated by Hitler and beloved by seafarers—certainly had no peer (Kverndal 2004).

Supranational Identity

The Move to Rome

With Reinhold's removal from the European scene in 1936, it left Arthur Gannon to pursue the second of the dual goals that Reinhold had helped to initiate—the transfer of AMIC and AOS International Headquarters from Glasgow to Rome. That process had to wait for several years, due to World War II (1939–45). Nevertheless, as the clouds of conflict were gathering, AOS statistics for 1938 showed impressive global growth: 22 full-time and over 300 part-time Catholic Port Chaplains in 317 seaports worldwide.

Thanks not least to the perseverance of Gannon, the organization somehow survived the upheavals of the war. Five years later, the AOS had recovered sufficiently to convene an International Congress in Rome. Like the Liverpool Congress in 1930, the Rome Congress in 1950 would also prove decisive for the future shape of the AOS. Complementing the federated "horizontal" dimension of *internationalization* secured in 1930, the 1950 Congress put in place the "vertical" dimension of *supranationalization,* setting the stage for the organization's move to Rome. Gannon would later characterize this Congress as "AMIC's finest hour." At the same time, in recognition of Gannon's personal role in reaching that goal, the Vatican made him a Knight Commander of the Order of St. Gregory.

Apart from Gannon, there were two other vital players involved in the implementation of the move to Rome. In 1852, *Pope Pius XII* (who served from

1939 to 1958) issued the Apostolic Constitution *Exul Familia* "On the Spiritual
Care of Migrants." For the AOS, this document had particular relevance. First,
it affirmed placing the administration of AMIC under the Sacred Consistorial
Congregation at the Vatican—the cardinals making up the Pope's closest body
of advisors. At the same time, it finally found an official location for the pastoral
care of seafarers within the Church of Rome—among the different categories of
"People on the Move." In the words of one observer, the Pope had now "given a
new face to the Apostleship of the Sea." In Catholic ecclesiastical terminology,
this meant the AOS had at last gained a secure "canonical status" (Frayne 1965;
Oubre 1998).

The other key player at this point was *Jean-Marie Butel,* a French Jesuit
priest and already well known as leader of the AOS in France. Since 1944,
Father Butel had served as founder/director of the *Mission de la Mer* ("Mission
of the Sea"), a seagoing arm of the "Priest Worker Movement." From 1946, he
had played a major role in helping Gannon organize the 1950 Congress. Gannon
quickly recognized Butel's special gifts and lobbied hard for him to lead the new
AOS headquarters in Rome. In March 1953, the Consistorial Congregation did
appoint Butel as the first Executive Secretary of the new AOS International
Secretariat. At the same time, Father *Bernard Haanen,* leader of the Dutch AOS,
became Field Secretary, while Gannon served as Lay Member of the
International Secretariat.

Reaching "Adulthood"

Father Butel's tenure was brief but intense. Added to the daily pressures of
the AOS transition task, Butel also bore the burden of directing and supporting
his seagoing colleagues in the Mission de la Mer. Meanwhile, that mission's
well-intentioned purpose—to provide priests who could work in solidarity with
seafarers in their everyday lives—came into conflict with the Vatican's
endorsement of the "Catholic Action" model of *lay activism.* In that plan,
seafarers themselves would become the primary "promoters" of Christian
witness at sea. For Butel, the ensuing stress seems to have been a factor in his
premature death due to heart failure in July 1955.

Despite this, prospects for the relocated AOS had never been more
promising. Where Butel left off, others would carry on. As relevant structures
and church laws ("canons") developed, the work now entered a period of
unparalleled expansion. Meanwhile Gannon, relieved after years of "operating
on a shoe-string," was able to contribute continuity to it all, until failing health
forced him to retire in 1961.

By then, Daniel Shields, the senior member of the "Lay Trio" of founding
figures, had passed away in 1940. Peter Anson returned to Caldey, and then
went on to Scotland where he died in 1975. Arthur Gannon, the only married
member of the three, moved to the outskirts of Southampton. In his memoirs, he
maintains that *Alice Pearce*, his wife and constant fellow-worker from the
1920s, was no less a co-founder of the AOS than he. Gannon died in 1979.

When Gannon had "cleared his desk" in 1961, this marked more than the end of a "Gannon Era." By the beginning of the 1960s, the Apostleship of the Sea, born on the Clyde in 1920, had now reached "adulthood." Although conceived later than its Protestant predecessors, the AOS was in no way "cloned." In contrast to both the horizontal model of the now renamed British Sailors' Society (BSS) and the more vertical model of the MtS, the AOS was able to integrate both dimensions—contextual *diversity* through nationally-based dispersed authority, combined with Roman Catholic *unity* ensuring universal commonality.

At last, Catholics who ministered among people of the sea had found a common voice for their own distinctive identity. This had been a precondition for entering into meaningful relations with other Christians—as an equal player in a spirit of authentic ecumenicity.

6

PROTESTANT CONSOLIDATION

NAMMA (1932)

THE NORTH AMERICAN SCENE

It fell to the United States to introduce the *world's first structured form of collaboration in multi-denominational maritime mission.* With a national constitution built on the separation of church and state, the multi-cultural nature of America's immigrant society had resulted in an inherently multi-denominational landscape. The maritime mission agencies that covered the waterfronts from Maine to the Pacific Northwest by the early 20th century reflected that same untroubled multi-denominational coexistence. Many of them originated from outreach initiatives by immigrant congregations in port areas. Others might still have ties with the only nondenominational national organization—the American Seamen's Friend Society (ASFS).

Birth of a New Network

Generated by Crisis: The Great Depression

As early as in 1832, the ASFS initiated the *first known attempt at organized port-level cooperation* in maritime mission. That year they held an "Annual meeting of all ministers of the gospel laboring among seamen" in the port of New York. By 1859, the concept had reached a *national* level, with "friends of seamen from all parts of the United States" meeting that year, again in New York. Subsequent attempts followed, both in Boston in 1899 and in New York in 1908, to initiate multi-denominational, multi-agency cooperation on an *international* level. None of these initiatives generated any permanent framework, however. After the disruption of World War I, it would take the social upheavals of the Great Depression of 1929-30 to reach that point.

In America, as elsewhere in the world, the 1920s post-World War I slump in shipping led to lean years for seafarers. By the end of the decade, in the wake of the Wall Street stock market crash, the situation had become desperate.

Thousands of unemployed seafarers roamed the nation's waterfronts. In New York, the line of destitute seafarers frequently snaked around the whole city block occupied by the South Street Seamen's Church Institute. The new, eight-story Seamen's House YMCA on 20th Street, opened in cooperation with the ASFS in 1931, was likewise overwhelmed by seafarers thrown out of work.

Against this grim background, a determined group of port chaplains from the United States and Canada decided to "pull together" in a structured form of partnership. Meeting in May 1932 in Philadelphia, they adopted the name *National Group of Seamen's Agencies* (NGSA), and agreed on two fundamental functions that have characterized the organization ever since: Internally promoting "closer cooperation" between its own members, while externally presenting a "common front" in matters pertaining to seafarers' welfare.

Although Catholic maritime ministries in the USA and Canada were not included, the Protestant agencies did represent different denominations. Evidently, they also took their *advocacy* role seriously. During the organization's early years, its representatives focused primarily on social needs of the day, and their efforts produced important results. After persistent lobbying in Washington DC, the NGSA received credit "in large measure" for both the Seamen's Relief Bill of 1933-34 and other legislation on seafarers' behalf.

Tested by Fire: The New Global War

The world had barely recovered from the Great Depression when World War II (1939-45) embroiled the nations in global slaughter on a scale unparalleled in human history. Since the sea-lanes served as lifelines for the belligerents, merchant seafarers again found themselves in the front-line of world conflict. With the availability, and therefore welfare, of competent crews suddenly seen as a matter of national security, the stress level experienced by seafarers' centers soared. In his research on British Seamen's Missions up to 1970, Alston Kennerley has identified three distinct sources of such stress: (1) the quality of physical facilities, (2) the need for spiritual support, and (3) the degree of secular control (Kennerley 1989, 155-247). All three presented similar challenges for American agencies, too, after the USA entered the war in 1941.

Although enemy action never affected American centers directly, demands on them for quality services, accommodation and enhanced programming had never been higher. As a result, American agencies found it necessary to carry out a series of significant renovations that would not have been possible without substantial public funding.

In addition, the American merchant marine was soon suffering a higher rate of casualties than any of the nation's armed services. This contributed to an increased need for counseling and spiritual support, a situation which would stretch staff resources to their limit and often beyond. The logic of governmental concern was indisputable. If seaworthy *ships* were indispensable to national security, so too was the supply and support of *seafarers* qualified to run them, including their welfare needs.

Confronting Two Major Issues

Secular Welfare: A Complementary Relationship

At this point, seafarers' welfare provision was almost entirely in the hands of the Christian voluntary sector. The dialogue initiated in the late 1920s, between the major Christian-based agencies and the ILO in Geneva had, at least so far, been inconclusive. There also remained the long-standing misgivings of many maritime union leaders. As their historic hero, Andrew Furuseth, had long since insisted, any paternalistic dependency on charity undermined a seafarer's healthy sense of self-reliance. It was also a matter of simple justice. A seafarer was entitled to the same freedom of choice as any fellow citizen ashore, including access to recreation and accommodation options.

Christian seafarers' agencies closed ranks and argued that "temporal" and "spiritual" aspects of welfare were inseparable and integral to an authentic, holistic concept of the gospel. At the same time, participation in religious observances at Christian-based facilities was entirely voluntary. The US government's War Shipping Administration worked out a compromise that both unions and voluntary agencies could accept. The outcome was the launching of the semi-official *United Seamen's Service* (USS) in September 1942.

Based on complementing, rather than competing with, existing voluntary agencies, the USS opened combined club and hotel accommodations in 16 ports worldwide within the first year, subsequently also seven convalescent rest centers. With industry and public support, the USS has, since then, continued to provide maritime welfare services, especially in ports connected with US overseas military bases. In 1973, the American Merchant Marine Library Association (AMMLA), founded in 1921 as a "Public Library of the High Seas," affiliated itself with the USS.

Theological Consensus: A Holistic Approach

The end of WWII allowed the membership of the National Group of Seamen's Agencies to reorganize and, in 1951, incorporate in the State of New York as the *National Council of Seamen's Agencies* (NCOSA). In 1967, they changed the name to the *International Council of Seamen's Agencies* (ICOSA). As ICOSA, the organization would now continue until 1991, when it assumed the name *North American Maritime Ministry Association* (NAMMA).

After 1945, the Association experienced two decades of calmer times. The social implications of the Great Depression and the war years had meant prioritizing practical issues. The post-war period of peace, however, opened new opportunities for theological reflection. In a revised constitution, the organization gave more direct expression to a distinctively Christian identity. Although the original organizers had recorded that they were "Co-workers with Him, who dwelt in Capernaum, a City by the Sea," a clearly Christian identity was not obvious in the organization's neutral-sounding name.

By now, the relationship between "social" and "spiritual" aspects of maritime mission had also become an issue of concern in the organization. The

Nordic seafarers' missions' representative on the Board of Directors, Rev. *Johannes Aardal* (then Chaplain-Director of the Norwegian Seamen's Church in Brooklyn), acknowledged that there were those who now believed that "social welfare work" should be left to secular agencies, allowing the churches to limit themselves to "Christian spiritual work." Aardal himself saw "no dividing line" between the two. In fact, he emphasized, in no field was this more obvious than in ministry among seafarers. At the same time, he could in no way condone the neglect of spiritual needs out of one-sided concern for social necessities. That would amount to offering "stones in the place of bread."

In 1958, Aardal moved from New York to Bergen, Norway, to his new position as General Secretary of the Norwegian Seamen's Mission. As such, he would play a crucial part in bringing the Nordic Seafarers' Mission Bloc on board ICOSA's future global offspring—the International Christian Maritime Association (ICMA).

NATIONALLY ORIENTED MARITIME MINISTRY

Of the national seafarers' mission organizations that emerged on the mainland continent of Europe in the second half of the 19th century, the Norwegian, Danish, Swedish and Finnish were first in the field. The bonds of cultural commonality within this "Nordic Bloc" would become even stronger through the challenges of the 20th century. For national maritime mission in Germany and the Netherlands, internal consolidation would need more time.

The Nordics: Toward Structured Solidarity

Pre-1945 Challenges

During the 1920s, international freight rates plummeted and ships were laid up by the thousands. Like others, Nordic seafarers' missions, too, became immersed in emergency aid to unemployed compatriots, cast "on the beach" in port-cities around the world. After that, no sooner had the tide begun to turn, when a world war would once again take its toll on the lives of Nordic as well as other seafarers.

The ordeal would affect each of the Nordic nations in different ways. The Finns found themselves locked in a six-year struggle for survival against Stalin's Soviet armies. The Swedes, though also affected, managed to maintain cautious, freedom-friendly neutrality. Although Hitler's occupation forces cut off many Danish merchant seafarers from their homeland, the Norwegians—with more merchant ships and seafarers' mission centers than their Nordic neighbors combined—were in a particularly precarious position.

For five years of self-imposed exile (1940-45), Norwegian merchant seafarers fought side by side with the Allies, from the Battle of the Atlantic to the beachheads of Normandy and beyond. According to a spokesperson for the British Government, their contribution amounted to the military equivalent of a million men in the field. The global network of Norwegian seafarers' centers, now coordinated from the Norwegian Seamen's Church in blitz-battered London, strove to provide pastoral care and a home away from home for those in the front-line of war at sea. Cut off from a Nazi-occupied home country, the Norwegian Seamen's Mission rose to the challenge.

Post-War Priorities

When the Norwegian government in exile returned in 1945, a nucleus of the first Nordic state-sponsored seafarers' welfare network was already functioning. During the renewal of their decimated merchant fleets, all four Nordic nations built up similar structures. In line with the prevailing political ideology of the "welfare state," their goal was to provide seafarers with the same social status and services at sea as their fellow citizens enjoyed ashore. They opened seafarers' hotels and sports stadiums in several world ports, while also initiating a range of educational and recreational programs for seafarers.

The resulting challenge confronting Nordic seafarers' missions, during and after World War II, was the same as that facing their American and British colleagues. The nightmare of war had spurred societal secularization on both sides of the Atlantic. Here and there, a few voices within Nordic maritime unions might call for Christian-based agencies to leave all but strictly "spiritual" welfare to the new, state-sponsored secular services. However, a mutual sense of fairness did eventually prevail, doubtless reinforced by the massive goodwill that seafarers' missions had accumulated. The mission agencies readily accepted the invitation to join with government officials, unions and shipowners in overseeing the new state-sponsored seafarers' services.

Simultaneously, the Nordic seafarers' missions embarked on ambitious programs of rebuilding and expansion. In pastoral ministry, the Norwegians led the way with support for pre-sea and peer ministry programs for seafarers. In 1955, on the initiative of the Swedes, the four organizations, together with the Danish Home-port Seamen's Mission, established a *Nordic Council of Seamen's Missions*. The members agreed to meet at regular intervals to exchange views and resources. A further purpose was to present a common Nordic voice vis-à-vis civic authorities and the maritime community. Later, in 1979, the nucleus of an Icelandic Seafarers Mission joined their Nordic colleagues.

The 1960s stand out as a "Golden Age" in Nordic National Seafarers' Mission collaboration. Now, the overriding issue looming on the horizon was the "outsourcing" of the maritime labor force. Until now, the Nordic seafarers' missions had had their hands full, reaching out on behalf of their respective nationally established churches to their *own* members who still made up the crews of their burgeoning national merchant fleets. Within a couple of decades, all of that would change.

The Germans: A National Network

Thun's Twin Goals

A different challenge confronted the maritime mission movement in Germany in the beginning of the 20th century. With a far greater Catholic presence, there was also wide denominational diversity within the Protestant majority. Would it be possible for the three existing Protestant organizations to converge into one national network in the years ahead?

Friedrich Harms, the founding figure of the Protestant German maritime mission, passed away in 1919. Before that, a promising young colleague—again from the German diaspora—was fortunately ready to take over. Since 1903, Rev. *Wilhelm Thun* had served in Leith, Scotland, the oldest branch of the General Committee for German Evangelical Seamen's Mission in Great Britain. Three years later, in response to repeated requests from German-American pastors, the Hannover-based "Lutheran Association" appointed Thun to start a German seafarers' mission in New York harbor.

Thun set up a combined mission and home in Hoboken, New Jersey, the hub of German ship arrivals in the area. German seafarers responded well. He also established a framework for the *German Seamen's Mission of New York,* later based in Manhattan. Rev. *Hermann Brueckner* succeeded Thun in 1909 and would remain at this post for most of the next half-century.

Back in Hamburg-Altona, Thun would face four fearsome national crises. First there was the ruination of World War I (1914-18), with its aftermath of secularization and demoralization during the Weimar Republic of the 1920s. After that came the Great Depression of 1929-30, with the increasing risk of revolution by a Communist-infiltrated labor force. From 1933 on, the nightmare of Nazism, with Hitler's master race megalomania, would engulf the nation. Finally, from 1939 to 1945, it all culminated with World War II.

Throughout, Thun held on to two main goals: to affirm the Christian identity of seafarers' mission as an integral outreach ministry of the Protestant Church in Germany; to achieve some sense of organizational unity among such maritime mission as had by then begun, both at home and abroad.

In trying to preserve the Christian identity of Protestant German seafarers' mission, Thun had courageous allies. Foremost among these was a group of pastors that included the former u-boat commander, *Martin Niemöller*, and the young theologian, *Dietrich Bonhoeffer*. These had joined Germany's "Confessing Church" in taking a prophetic stand against the Nazi theology of the so-called "German Christians." The latter's credo was simple: "The Swastika on our breasts, the Cross in our hearts." For Niemöller, resistance led to concentration camp, for Bonhoeffer execution. Hitler finally failed to compel complete compliance by the churches, whether Protestant or Catholic. Nor did his henchmen succeed in "nazifying" their maritime outreach ministries.

In endeavoring to forge a unified German seafarers' mission, Thun tried every avenue. In 1923, he helped form a Federation of the Hannover-based Lutheran Association and the Berlin-based United Church Association, now known as the *German Evangelical Seamen's Mission.* Other seafarers' mission associations joined them in 1925, among them the British "General Committee."

Over the years, entrenched denominational and territorial loyalties would continue to dog the efforts of the new Federation's director. Nevertheless, Thun integrated the *German Seamen's Mission in Bremen* as a member, and enabled the organization to survive Hitler's abortive attempt at general church "unification" under a bogus "Reich Bishop." Then, in 1941, Thun linked the Federation, for its own protection, closer to the Central Board of the Inner Mission of the Evangelical Church in Berlin, and gave it the shorter name of the *German Seamen's Mission* ("Deutsche Seemannsmission").

Dr. Maas and a Mission Milestone

With the collapse of Hitler's Third Reich in 1945 and the daunting challenges ahead, Thun found it was time to pass the torch to two younger colleagues, Rev. *Kieseritzky* and Rev. *Haarmann* who now took over his responsibilities in Hamburg and Bremen. From 1956, Dr. *Heinrich Maas* of Bremen, Senate Director and Chairperson of the German Seamen's Mission, would provide powerful leadership during two decades of expansion. This led to advances in domestic ports as well as in a series of foreign ports, with new initiatives in West Africa, Iran and Indonesia. Maas also made advances within the shipping industry and paved the way for his mission's role in the future International Christian Maritime Association.

In 1974, the leadership agreed on a revamped structure for the overall organization. Continuing as the *German Seamen's Mission,* it would henceforth operate from Bremen, with one President, one General Secretary (a theologian), and one Director. With that, German maritime mission had reached a milestone, and the German Seamen's Mission could continue to develop its own distinctive identity in the global community during the last quarter of the 20th century.

In the relationship between Protestant and Roman Catholic seafarers' missions in Germany, there had been frequent cases of practical cooperation between individuals in the face of joint Nazi oppression. Still, bridging the gulf between the Protestant and Catholic maritime missions as such would take a miracle—in both Rome and Rotterdam.

The Dutch: In Quest of Cooperation

Early advocates of Dutch maritime mission had to contend with the same situation that confronted their German counterparts—the long-standing disunity among Christians, especially between the different Protestant church bodies. In the early 1920s, the *Seamen's Union* ("Zeemansbond"), which had somehow survived World War I, was still the sole Christian-based agency for indigenous Dutch outreach to seafarers.

It took until 1927 before a "union for the spiritual and moral benefit of seafarers" was founded in Amsterdam under the name *Netherlands Seamen's Center* ("Nederlandse Zeemanscentrale"). In 1934, the Rotterdam-based

Seamen's Union merged with this Amsterdam-based Netherlands Seamen's Center under the joint name of the latter, with its Dutch acronym "NZC." The organization managed to come through World War II and has continued up to the present, currently based at the "Zeemanshuis" in Rotterdam. The *Netherlands Christian Seafarers' Association* ("Nederlandse Christen Zeelieden Vereniging"), founded in 1930, would also merge with the NZC in 1987, bringing with it the Association's quarterly publication, *Quo Vadis.*

During World War II, Dutch naval chaplains found themselves ministering to many merchant navy fellow nationals cut off from home. With the advent of peace, this prompted the "Reformed Churches in the Netherlands" to send seafarers' chaplains to several port-cities overseas. Due to changes in the international shipping industry, Dutch maritime mission expansion abroad would be short-lived, while domestic port ministry continued to lack cohesion. None the less, in the field of international maritime ecumenism, the Dutch would, by the late 1960s, be playing a unique and vital role.

BRITISH MARITIME MINISTRY

The Challenges of Depression and Global War

Common Cause with Colleagues

In the United Kingdom, the question of cooperative maritime mission was more complex than in the case of North America or the rest of Europe. After the First World War, many of the independent, local societies did not survive. This left the two major Protestant networks (MtS and BSS) and their young, fast-growing, Catholic counterpart (AOS) to dominate the scene. Each of them was pre-occupied with developing their own priorities and structures. Nevertheless, all of them faced common challenges, as they prepared for a new day in inter-organizational and interdenominational relationships.

The Great Depression also affected UK-based maritime missions through the early 1930s. They, too, had to focus all available resources on alleviating the plight of so many seafarers now losing their livelihood. The situation had barely begun to improve when World War II broke loose with all its repercussions. Overall, a very similar dynamic developed in wartime Britain as in the USA, in terms of the stress factors identified in Alston Kennerley's research.

Given Britain's geographic location well within the war zone, domestic recreational and lodging facilities sustained inordinate damages. Staff resources were stretched even further by the never-ending need for counseling and spiritual support services. As to the third stress factor—of mounting secular control, British maritime mission agencies, like their American counterparts, soon found themselves making common cause in defense of their institutional autonomy and religious identity.

Compromise with Government

The British Government did not want to pay the political price of any coercive approach. Still, in 1938, it had committed itself to action by accepting Recommendation No. 48 of the International Labour Conference of 1936, on the Promotion of Seamen's Welfare in Ports. In order to implement this instrument, the Government appointed a *Seamen's Welfare Board* in 1940, bringing together representation by both maritime unions and shipowners.

A survey by this Board found an acute need for improved amenities among voluntary-owned (usually Christian-based facilities. At the same time, it also established the need for building secular-based, well equipped Merchant Navy Houses and Clubs. In order to secure sufficient public funding to remain viable, the respective voluntary agencies arrived at a compromise. While upgrading to more uniform standards, they agreed to live with a limited level of control by secular authority, at any rate for the duration of the war.

Post-War Reorientation and Reconstruction

Ideological Paradigm Shift

In wartime Britain, the acceptance of Government control in all areas of social life set the stage for a new socio-political paradigm in the post-war era. With the introduction of a national network for social security and health care, the "Welfare State" now became a reality in British everyday life. (It had already arrived in Scandinavia and, in modified form, with the New Deal in America). Consequently, many began to wonder if there would be any future for the voluntary sector at all, whether maritime or otherwise.

Such fears would prove unfounded. The year 1948 saw the establishment of a semi-official *Merchant Navy Welfare Board,* taking over the role of the wartime Seafarers' Welfare Board. With state and industry respecting the autonomy of the voluntary sector (still by far the major provider of seafarers' welfare services), the new Board would include representatives of the voluntary agencies, too. In succeeding years, the Board would allocate national insurance grants as a significant source of funding for the various maritime mission agencies. At the same time, these latter would continue to receive substantial annual grants from the *King George's Fund for Sailors,* founded already in 1920 as a means of coordinating national funding appeals.

A consequence of societal secularization in post-war British maritime mission was the transition from a century-old "institute" model to a modern-day "club" model. This would replace a range of maritime social welfare services with an emphasis on relaxed, unstructured hospitality. In effect, maritime mission agencies were responding to a growing awareness of justice and solidarity, rather than privilege and charity. Finally, the social forces of change, unleashed during World War II, appeared to have promoted a new sense of self-reliance among seafarers of the world.

What might seem like surrendering to secular welfare would again instead become a blessing in disguise. With the welfare state assuming responsibility for basic social services, the voluntary agencies were now free to focus on a more personalized, relational ministry of pastoral care, offering rich opportunities for individual counseling and Christian discipleship. The crucial challenge soon facing those agencies would be to move from the *paternalistic* paradigm of the past—with its agency-centered "top-down mission," and into the *partnership* paradigm of the future—with its seafarer-centered "mission from below."

Technological Innovation

World War II became a catalyst for more than ideological transformation. It generated a surge of *technological* change, including in the field of maritime transportation. That change would be the beginning of a "Maritime Industrial Revolution." In marine propulsion, the 1930s had already seen the substitution of coal with oil in steam-driven vessels. They also saw the advent of diesel powered motor vessels. Following World War II, a host of innovations arrived—from the size and design of ships to new technologies in automation, navigation and loading systems. All of this would have drastic implications for maritime industry and therefore also for maritime ministry.

The full impact would not be apparent for some years, however. In the meantime, the shipping industry not only recovered from wartime losses; it also entered a period of mounting prosperity through the 1950s and 1960s. Likewise, maritime mission agencies, in Britain led by the MtS, BSS and AOS, experienced a corresponding time of reconstruction and expansion.

In spite of this promising picture, a key conference in Oslo, Norway, in 1948, had already sounded a note of urgency, alerting to the prospect of turbulent times ahead. Shipowners, confronted with soaring capital costs, were in some cases already resorting to registering their ships under "Flags of Convenience" (FOCs) with nations notorious for their lack of enforcement resources. The purpose was plain: to escape the dual burden of home-state taxation and regulation and to cut crew costs by hiring low-paid non-union maritime labor. The Oslo Conference, convened by the International Transport Workers' Federation (ITF), would make its mark in maritime history as the opening salvo of the *ITF Anti-FOC Campaign.*

For global maritime ministry, the question was: Were the world's maritime mission agencies prepared to take on the kind of complex challenges they would now need to face? In hindsight, they were clearly not, and for at least two important reasons.

First, through the 1960s and well into the 1970s, those agencies were, with very few exceptions, a Western-world monopoly, operated on a monocultural basis. The typical crew composition of the future, however, would be very different. Drawn from the low-cost international maritime labor force, it would rapidly become largely non-Western and multicultural, with profound implications for maritime mission and ministry.

Second, until the end of the 1960s, the existing Western maritime mission establishment was still seriously fragmented. In terms of intra-Protestant denominational consolidation, the North Americans and the Nordics had taken the lead and made noteworthy progress. Yet so far nothing comparable had developed among British Protestants. In 1929, the Prince of Wales publicly urged the MtS and BSS to merge. This did not happen, although the two did set up a type of "Seafarers' Trust" for future joint undertakings. As for the wider ecumenical scene, in Great Britain of the 1960s, the deep divide between Protestants and Catholics seemed as entrenched as ever.

Here, too, change was on the immediate horizon. Both the degree and nature of that change would prove to be astonishing. Just before the full impact of the Maritime Industrial Revolution began making itself felt during the mid-1970s, a "Maritime Ecumenical Revolution" would signify the spiritual equivalent of a global climate-change—for not only *Intra-Protestant* but also *Catholic-Protestant* relations. The prelude to that revolution would this time play out in the Roman Catholic Church.

7

ECUMENICAL COLLABORATION

ICMA (1969)

RENEWAL IN ROME

In spite of all the horrors of World War II, or perhaps because of them, a rediscovered sense of human interdependence, together with the wartime dilution of discrimination in gender, race and religion, contributed to a common yearning for international justice and peace. Following the founding of the United Nations in San Francisco, in 1945, that body passed a historic "Universal Declaration of Human Rights" in 1948. At the same time, a renewed spirit of ecumenical idealism gave fresh impetus to the quest for worldwide inter-church cooperation. This resulted in the inauguration in Geneva of a World Council of Churches (WCC), also in 1948. Most of the major Protestant denominations joined the WCC, as did also the Orthodox. The gulf in relation to the Church of Rome, however, remained as real as ever.

The Pope who turned the Tide

From Sharecropper's Son to Papal Nuncio

Among church historians, there is general agreement that the watershed event in the evolution of the Ecumenical Movement was the Second Vatican Council ("Vatican II"). There is equally broad consensus that the concept and course of that Council were inseparably associated with one person—namely Pope John XXIII. Who was he? What prepared him to play such an important role? More specifically, what aspects of his life might have connected him with maritime mission?

Angelo Giuseppe Roncalli (1881-1963) was the son of a sharecropper and the third of 13 children. He was born in a remote village near Bergamo in the Alpine foothills of northern Italy. Angelo was eleven years of age when his devout, hardworking parents managed to send him off to prepare for the priesthood. At the diocesan seminary in Bergamo, he came under the influence of leaders in Catholic social activism. Ordained in 1904, he went on to earn a doctorate in theology. For several years he then served as both Seminary Professor and Diocesan Secretary under the Bishop of Bergamo. Bishop *Camillo Guindan* was an unabashed advocate of social justice, and controversial as "the most progressive prelate in Italy."

On his return from serving as military chaplain during World War I, his superiors saw Roncalli's relational gifts as a potential asset in Vatican diplomacy. This led to his consecration as archbishop in 1925, and assignments in Bulgaria, Greece and Turkey. Subsequently, he became Papal Nuncio to President Charles de Gaulle's newly liberated France in 1944. Here, Roncalli's efforts to identify with "radical" Catholic clergy, who were struggling to relate to alienated, secularized society, earned him wide respect. That struggle would one day help motivate key reforms in the future Vatican Council which was to become his crowning lifework.

From Patriarch to Pope

In 1953, Pius XII appointed Roncalli a cardinal. He also named him Patriarch of Venice, the Adriatic home port of Marco Polo, and the city that, for centuries, had served as the center of a medieval maritime republic. On his arrival, a procession of gondolas and other vessels greeted the new Patriarch and escorted his official launch up the Grand Canal to the Piazza San Marco. From that first day, Roncalli won the hearts of the people. For the five years he was there, Roncalli affirmed his reputation as "the People's Prelate"—accessible to all. With disarming simplicity, he could characterize Marxism as a "negation of Christianity," reject Communism's political manipulation, and yet bestow genuine love on any of its adherents.

A former principal chaplain of the British and International Sailors' Society has provided an example of the warm personality of the future Pope. When a British warship called at the port of Venice, during a cruise in the Mediterranean in the mid-1950s, David Harries, then a young chaplain in the Royal Navy, received orders from his commander to pay his respects to the local Catholic leader. He did so with no small trepidation—as a loyal son of the Presbyterian Church of Scotland. However, the Cardinal immediately put him at his ease, spoke with him as a brother in Christ, and offered him a blessing that would follow him ever since: *The Savior bless you! The Savior's love go with you! The Savior's light lead you and all seafarers home!*

Little could the young naval chaplain have known that, a decade later, this unpretentious prelate would create a climate change in Catholic-Protestant relations—not least in the seafaring world. Even less could the cardinal himself have suspected that outcome, when he hurriedly left for Rome in early October 1955, in order to elect a new pope on the death of Pius XII. By the 12th ballot, the Patriarch of Venice had become Pope John XXIII. At 77 years of age, the new pontiff was not expected to introduce any major changes, pending a more long-term successor. However, the election of John XXIII was not the only surprise. His agenda would usher in a new era—in the church and in the world.

The Council and its Implications

The Church at Large

Unprepared as he was to become pontiff, John XXIII came with no preconceived plan for his papacy. When, not quite three months after his election, the new Pope announced to a stunned gathering of cardinals his decision to convene an "Ecumenical Council" of all the bishops of the Church, he had no hesitancy in attributing it to "a sudden inspiration of the Holy Spirit." By naming this 21st assembly the "Second Vatican Council," he intentionally inferred significance comparable to that of the historic First Vatican Council convened by Pius IX in 1869.

Pope John XXIII was equally unequivocal in defining the dual objectives of the Council as both the renewal and the reunion of the entire church. In pursuit of these closely connected aims, a key concept was that of *aggiornamento*, or "bringing up to date." For the church to meet the modern world with a witness that was credible and relevant there would have to be profound reforms.

The work of the ensuing Council continued through four "Sessions" during the fall months of 1962 to 1965. Resolutely carrying on his work, despite debilitating illness, John XXIII would only live to see the First 1962 Session. He died in June 1963. His successor, Paul VI, would continue the process already in place, without interruption and in the same spirit.

The Church Maritime

Although there were less than five years for John XXIII to make any substantial difference in the maritime world, that is precisely what he did. He may not have served among seafarers directly. Yet he had a remarkable rapport with the water-borne workforce in Venice, the gondoliers, and he would fondly refer to the city as the "Queen of the Sea." Many of the traits of character that won for John XXIII a special place in history would be equally indispensable in ministry among seafarers. These included not least his transparent humanity and integrity. Later, in an address to the International Conference of the AOS in Rome in 1961, he seized the opportunity, as one who was "now at the helm of the vessel of St. Peter," to express his solidarity with seafarers, deprived as they were of "the daily support of family and of the spiritual help of the parish."

The reorganization of the church and its hierarchy in a democratic direction was an initiative of Vatican II that would have far-reaching, internal ramifications. For example, it removed bureaucratic barriers to allow the use of the vernacular in liturgy, thereby revitalizing worship and congregational participation—on shipboard as well as on shore. Together with this came a new emphasis on promoting the missionary role of the laity. The Pope, in his 1961 address, had already spoken of Christ's "singular love" for seafarers as "his closest collaborators." On that occasion, he had portrayed the seafarer as one whose soul "looks naturally upward towards heaven," joining his peers in making Christ known at sea and being "proactive in this environment to be gained for Christ Jesus." Within a generation, this concept would become a dominant feature of maritime mission strategy among both Catholics and others.

For many, including those in the maritime world, the most significant sign of change was the recognition of non-Catholic Christians as no longer "heretics" but fellow-believers, no longer objects of mission but partners in dialogue. Redefined as "estranged brethren," they could now be in communication, if not yet in communion. In maritime mission, this development cleared the way for a hitherto unthinkable degree of Catholic-Protestant interrelationship—even multi-level partnership—in meeting the overall human needs of seafarers.

In relating to those of non-Christian faiths, Vatican II found itself confronting a resurgence of other world religions. These had revived, in the wake of post-World War II, de-colonization and the influx of migrant workers in the West. A Catholic missiology evolved that more clearly recognized the positive spiritual values evident in many non-Christian religions. It also reflected the need for inter-religious dialogue and cultural flexibility. At the same time, it emphasized the necessity of salvation through Christ, and therefore continuing witness—though without coercion and in the context of freedom of religion. All of this had particular relevance to the religious pluralism in the non-Western maritime labor force soon to dominate the seafaring world scene.

Vatican II not only broke new ground relating to concerns common to fellow-humans everywhere, regardless of faith. John XXIII, with his lifelong commitment to social justice and peace, was personally dedicated to defusing the Cold War between the Communist and Capitalistic Blocs. He even received credit from Nikita Khruschev for helping avert World War III during the Cuban Missile Crisis of 1962. That dual commitment to both human rights and reconciliation was evident in documents from Vatican II. Both would also become major issues in the maritime sector in the last quarter of the 20th century.

Before he died, the Pope expressed the hope that the Second Vatican Council would result in the world witnessing an outpouring of the Holy Spirit equivalent to a "New Pentecost." In the wake of the winds of change released as a result of the papacy of John XXIII, not only the Church of Rome but also the Church Universal has never been the same since. The way that change would affect the Church Maritime, too, and most especially the integrity of its unity, would soon become apparent as the 1960s progressed.

REPERCUSSIONS IN ROTTERDAM

"Here are some unknown Americans who are coming to Europe to tell us how we should run our seamen's work..." It was in late 1968. The remark came from a European port chaplain working on the Rotterdam waterfront. It formed part of a candid report on an American-initiated "International Consultation on Services to Seafarers," to be held in the port of Rotterdam, 24-28 August, 1969.

In hindsight, everyone agreed that it was fortunate that these "unknown Americans" persevered. On the face of it, some skepticism was understandable. If the stage was set for a new era in maritime mission cooperation—as the world woke up to the ecumenical implications of Vatican II—why should the largely Europe-based maritime mission establishment look across the Atlantic for leadership? The short answer is simply that the situation still called for a viable catalyst. A most unlikely pope had first played that role in the *prelude* to global collaboration in maritime mission. Now only North America had any structural entity reasonably ready for the *realization* of such a development. The crucial question was whether it would rise to the occasion.

How ICMA Was Born

The North American Catalyst

In 1966, one year after the Council in Rome, the North Americans adopted a far-reaching resolution at their annual assembly, held that year in Savannah, Georgia. Serving as President from 1964 to 1968 was a Presbyterian attorney of Swiss background based in New Orleans, Dr. *Emile Dieth* (1911-2002). Dieth was a man of vision. He was aware that his was the only organization in the world providing multi-denominational collaboration in maritime mission, as yet only among Protestants and only in North America. In 1967, Dieth headed his organization's change of name—from a *National* to an *International* Council of Seamen's Agencies (ICOSA), including Canada and the Caribbean.

Was this basically North American entity now planning to incorporate the whole world? For some, it might have seemed so, especially when the organization now elected, as its Vice-President, Dieth's friend, Rev. *Jan Willem Schokking,* Port Chaplain of the Netherlands Seamen's Center in Rotterdam. However, the facts clearly contradict any such conclusion. At its annual meeting that same year, Dr. Dieth led his organization to explore the possibilities for creating a totally separate structure, one that could promote both fraternization and cooperation, on a truly worldwide scale. Not only was there an urgent *need* for such an organization—in light of the changes already beginning to impact international shipping. Now, in the wake of Vatican II, it was finally also *possible*—across all denominational boundaries.

In early 1967, still under Dr. Dieth's leadership, the North American association made a second significant move toward the same purpose. As a board member, Rev. *Bernard Spong,* Executive Director of the Lutheran-affiliated Seafarers' and International House of New York, was delegated to make contact with the WCC in Geneva. Given the theological climate of the day, one might well ask, why bring in the World Council of Churches? The WCC was a vortex of controversy. With the onslaught of the "Secular Theology" of the 1960s, some WCC members saw all institutional churches as "irrelevant" and mission as an "imposition." As a result, polarization was widespread throughout the membership. Yet, leaders of the North American association saw two good reasons for such a connection. First, the WCC still represented the only viable, global framework for inter-confessional collaboration in mission. Second, the North American association was in itself based on the acceptance of theological and denominational diversity.

The Catholics' doctrine of the absolute authority of the papacy had hitherto prevented them from joining the World Council of Churches. Might the Church Maritime afford an exception? In December 1968, Rev. Bernard Spong, now the new President of the North American association, took the plunge. With his own organization and the WCC as co-signatories, he issued an invitation to Catholics and Protestants alike to an *International Consultation on Services to Seafarers,* to be held in Rotterdam, 24-28 August 1969. The Apostleship of the Sea, now with its International Secretariat lodged in the Vatican, accepted the invitation. With that, the worldwide maritime mission community had entered a new era.

Historic Days in Rotterdam

By March 1969, the original co-signatories had enlisted five fellow sponsors. Besides the Apostleship of the Sea, they comprised The Missions to Seamen, the British Sailors' Society, the Nordic Seamen's Missions, and the Dutch Seamen's Mission. In securing such broad endorsement, Dieth and Spong, President and Chairperson, respectively, of an overall "Steering Committee," could count on their Dutch colleague as a key coordinator. Chaplain Schokking headed a local Organizing Committee, with M. Feikema, Director of the Netherlands Seamen's Center, as Secretary. For bringing all the Nordics on board, Rev. Johannes Aardal, General Secretary of the Norwegian Seamen's Mission, deserves major credit.

More than one hundred delegates from 52 Christian-based voluntary organizations, representing some 400 centers in 66 countries worldwide, took part in the Consultation. Among those invited to send representatives were the Israel Maritime League, as well as several secular agencies, including the International Labour Organization, the Rotterdam Port Authorities, and both Norwegian and Dutch governmental seafarers' welfare organizations. In his history of the Rotterdam Consultation and the organization to which it gave birth, Bishop Bill Down characterizes many of the delegates as "strong personalities...involved in their particular tradition and area of maritime ministry for a long time. They were not the sort of people who could be pushed around" (Down 1989, 125).

The opening ecumenical worship service of the Consultation was described as "momentous." Rev. Schokking made use of First Corinthians 13:13 to set the stage. Dr. Emile Dieth, as the original driving force behind the whole enterprise, spoke on behalf of the seven sponsoring agencies. He challenged fellow delegates to respond to change in the seafarer's world by pursuing the dual purpose of the Consultation: To study the nature of the seafarer's needs; then, to strategize as to the most appropriate action to meet those needs, while seeing both tasks in the light of God's promises in Romans 8:28-39.

Guided by Spong, as Chairperson of the Steering Committee, the Consultation continued with a series of presentations and workshops on a range of subjects relating to the life, work and welfare of seafarers. In the meantime, delegates experienced "a growing sense of excitement and expectation," regardless of past rifts and rivalries. As one observer remarked, "The Holy Spirit was at work among us . . . moving us forward and away from our own small circles." When the Consultation culminated with a Statement of "Conclusions and Resolutions," it passed unanimously.

The most decisive event took place on the last day, with the assembly's unanimous agreement to form "an international association of Christian voluntary organisations." As to the nature of this association, they agreed that it should be "a consultative and representative body." They also decided that the overall purpose should be both internal and external:

> (a) to foster collaboration and mutual aid amongst constituent bodies and to further common interests; (b) to be the collective and respected voice of the association within the industry and outside it; which can offer counsel and be heard within the councils of those bodies whose deliberations in any way affect or influence the lives and welfare of seafarers (*International Consultation Papers 1969*, ICMA Archives).

Finally, the delegates mandated a "Working Committee" to implement the resolutions of the Consultation. A plenary resolution directed that this Working Committee should include "a representative of the German Seamen's Societies," in addition to the members of the Consultation's original Steering Committee. (The German Seamen's Mission was represented by a strong 10-member deputation under the leadership of Dr. Maas and Rev. Kieseritzky.)

With that, five historic days came to a close in Visser't Hooft House in Rotterdam. The participants, aware that they had just witnessed a historic ecumenical breakthrough, found themselves singing the Doxology: "Praise God, from whom all blessings flow!" In effect, if not yet in name, the *International Christian Maritime Association* (ICMA) had been born.

Toward Organizational Structure

Dr. Daisuke Kitagawa: ICMA's First Secretary

The euphoria of the Rotterdam Consultation's final day, Thursday, August 28th, 1969, had hardly subsided when the Steering Committee met next morning. Having fulfilled the catalytic role of convening the Consultation, the North Americans—contrary to the earlier apprehensions of some—were glad to be able to hand over the leadership to their European counterparts.

With the current President of the North American association, Bernard Spong, still in the chair, the Steering Committee became the new "Working Committee." Rev. Prebendary *Thomas P. Kerfoot* and Rev. Monsignor *Francis S. Frayne* accepted appointments as Co-Chairpersons. Kerfoot was long-time Secretary General of the London-based (Anglican) Missions to Seamen. Frayne, formerly from Liverpool, was now serving with the Apostleship of the Sea in Rome and slated to become International Secretary of the Seafaring Sector of the Vatican's new "Pontifical Commission for the Pastoral Care of Migrants and Itinerant Peoples."

For the important position of combined Secretary and Treasurer, the World Council of Churches offered the part-time services of the Japanese-American Secretary for Urban and Industrial Ministry in its Department of World Mission and Evangelism. Born and raised in Taihoke, Japan, Rev. Dr. *Daisuke Kitagawa* (1910-1970) was the son of a Japanese Anglican priest. Sensing a call to follow his father's vocation, he studied first in Japan, graduating from St. Paul's University, Tokyo. After continuing his theological education in the United States, he was ordained an Episcopal deacon there in 1939 and assigned to a Japanese mission congregation in the outskirts of Seattle, Washington. His country's attack on Pearl Harbor, on 7 December 1941, prevented him from returning to Japan to continue in ministry there.

From then on, Kitagawa found himself swept up in the paranoid persecution of the Pacific Coast Japanese-American community, resulting in their internment under concentration camp conditions for most of the war. Kitagawa personally experienced the entire tragedy, first as chaplain to fellow-internees, later as government and church representative for resettlement issues. Widely respected for his integrity in advocating for the social claims of the gospel, Kitagawa became an American citizen in the 1950s and received a Doctorate of Divinity from his alma mater in Japan. Through the 1960s, he continued to serve in key roles in racial/ethnic relations, both for the Episcopal Church in America and for the WCC on the world scene.

Such was the man the WCC had assigned to represent it as co-sponsor of the Consultation in Rotterdam in the summer of 1969. Characterized by fellow-participants as a "real godly man," Dr. Kitagawa had already given a presentation on the third day of the Consultation. His keynote address had the heading, *Seafarers as an International Community.* Among some of those present he might have brought to mind that world-renowned Japanese "Prophet of the Poor"—*Toyohiko Kagawa* (1888-1960). Yet few could have foreseen the long-term implications of this solitary Asian voice in their midst.

According to Kitagawa, despite evidence of important changes in an increasingly global maritime industry, society's prevailing perception of people of the sea continued to be paternalistic. Seafarers were still "handicapped juveniles." They continued to be a marginalized sector of society, in need of "protection" by welfare agencies—not adult citizens, "endowed with a right to *participation* in decisions pertaining to their own welfare."

What Kitagawa called for was a "re-visioning" of the seafarer's social status worldwide. In an era of globalization, our developing one-world society must, he maintained, accept the seafarer as a *world citizen.* The international community could no longer condone a concept of seafarers as "little short of being disenfranchised," roaming aimlessly around like people belonging to no country—including their own. He concluded:

On the contrary, in terms of the contribution they make to society at large through their occupation they should belong to the whole world...as if they were citizens of *every country* they visit in the course of their duty. Some people may think that this is much too visionary, but to accept the sovereignty of nation-states as forever unalterable is to keep on dreaming the past that is no more. Economically and technologically, one-world is an accomplished fact, and it is the existing structure of the international community that needs to adjust itself to the reality of the contemporary world (*International Consultation Papers 1969*, ICMA Archives).

Kitagawa saw the two most important functions of "any new ecumenical agency specializing in services to seafarers" as: (1) Providing a *forum*—to "help all the national agencies become more internationally oriented;" (2) Creating *instrumentalities*—to "enable seafarers to participate responsibly in the decision-making process in matters which will affect their own welfare and that of their families." With that, the first executive leader of ICMA had prefigured the characteristics of the new paradigm of maritime mission that would emerge during the final decade of the 20th century. This would see the seafarer as the primary participant—or *subject*—of maritime mission, rather than solely as the passive recipient—or *object*—of such activity.

Dr. Kitagawa's tenure was tragically brief. After only seven short but intensely active months, he succumbed to a heart attack and died on 27 March 1970, a severe setback for the work. Like Reinhold, three decades earlier, Daisuke Kitagawa's personal involvement in maritime mission proved short. However, in foreseeing the future shape of seafarers' mission and pointing to the need for fundamental change, both must rank as prophetic voices in any history of 20th century maritime mission (Kitagawa 1964; Kverndal 2004).

ICMA's Title and Constitution

Besides appointing a slate of leaders on 29 August 1969, the Working Committee had to confront the issue of an appropriate title for the new entity. They agreed on *The International Christian Maritime Association,* together with an interpretive sub-title to be included in all future publications. After a slight modification, the final wording would read: "A free association of Christian organisations engaged in welfare work for seafarers." During the weeks that followed, member agencies affirmed both the title and its acronym "ICMA," as well as the sub-title.

During its first formative years, from 1969 to the mid-1970s, ICMA faced major challenges. The first of these was a viable organizational structure. In this regard, the Working Committee certainly lived up to its name. Armed by the Consultation with a 3-year mandate, the Committee was to prepare for an International Conference in 1972. Within that time, they would need to provide the blueprint of a Constitution, together with a selection of studies and proposals in matters of major concern for the welfare of seafarers.

After the sudden demise of Dr. Kitagawa, the WCC found a successor who was both a layperson and former seafarer. Norwegian Captain *Jan Örner* had seen active service on merchant and naval vessels during World War II. He was currently Deputy Director of the WCC's Department for Inter-Church Aid, Refugee and World Service. From the office in Geneva, already made available by the WCC as ICMA's first Secretariat, Captain Örner piloted the work through a critical stage of the organization's first formative phase.

By October 1970, Örner had secured an important observer status for ICMA at the International Labour Organization (ILO). Alert to the notorious lack of awareness regarding maritime mission in church and mission circles worldwide, Captain Örner introduced the concept of ICMA to the global readership of the WCC's *International Review of Mission,* through a paper on "Missions to Seamen" (July 1971). He was also an advocate for academic study and research in the field of maritime mission. As such, he negotiated grant funds essential for the Author's dissertation research on maritime mission history.

On Captain Örner's retirement in December 1971, his successor, Dr. Kitagawa's former Secretary, *Machteld van Vredenburch,* broke new ground in gender inclusiveness by becoming the first woman to hold that kind of executive responsibility in maritime mission. It fell to her to coordinate final preparations for ICMA's First Plenary Conference in London in July-August 1972.

Close to 200 attended the Conference, including Dr. *Eugene Carson Blake*, General Secretary of the WCC, and Archbishop *Emmanuele Clarizio*, Pro-President of the Vatican's Pontifical Commission for the Pastoral Care of Migrants and Itinerant Peoples. The success of the Conference was largely due to the leadership of ICMA's Co-Chairpersons, Kerfoot and Frayne. In the words of Bill Down, as "firm friends and men of charisma, intelligence and the ability to put visionary thoughts into practical terms," Kerfoot and Frayne made the event a "tour de force" (Down 1989, 127).

A major accomplishment was the acceptance of ICMA's Constitution, as proposed by the Working Committee. After first affirming both ICMA's name and its Christian identity, the document elaborated on the dual functions of ICMA as established in 1969, namely to provide mutual collaboration within its own membership and a collective voice beyond. It also defined ICMA's membership as consisting of the founding agencies represented in Rotterdam, plus any similar societies subsequently invited by ICMA's "Standing Committee." The latter seven-member successor body to the existing Working Committee would manage the affairs of the organization and hold future Plenary International Conferences, initially on a triennial basis.

Toward Institutional Identity

International or National?

In 1969, ICMA's founders had agreed unanimously that the organization should be "consultative" as well as "representative" in nature. From the start, staffing and funding constraints confirmed the necessity for the *consultative* nature of the organization. More debatable would be whether ICMA was truly *representative*. Whom did this "international" organization intend to represent? Also, with accelerating change in the global maritime industry, was it enough to refer to the wide-ranging purpose in ICMA's self-identification as: "A free association of Christian organizations engaged in welfare work for seafarers"?

The first test of identity came early, in the form of the following question: *How could "nationally-oriented" societies be included in a cooperative organization that purported to be "international"?* A leading member of the American deputation at the Rotterdam Consultation in 1969, speaking from the perspective of proliferating pluralism within his own culture, blasted all nationally-oriented agencies—especially the Nordics—as "illegitimate" in today's maritime world. "In an industrial mission, that our work really is," he said, "we should not be guilty of preserving the last vestiges of colonialism...." The four Nordic agencies delegated the senior among them, Rev Johannes Aardal, to deliver a response on their behalf at ICMA's First Plenary Conference, in London in 1972 (Kverndal 1978, 103-104).

In a paper entitled *Ethnic and Religious Groups and their Special Needs,* Aardal presented a well-researched rationale for the historic evolution of the Nordic national agencies, coupled with a detailed justification for the need they continued to fill. The climate of a Nordic home-away-from-home would enhance the traditional receptivity of Nordic seafarers to indigenous pastoral ministry. At the same time, Aardal did recognize the reality of increasing multi-cultural pluralism at sea. The outcome was a carefully crafted bridge-building resolution that sought to "encourage multi-denominational, multi-ethnic and multi-national centres," out of which qualified chaplains could operate. However, this should create "no conflict" with the relevance of nationally oriented centers in serving the needs of "particular groups."

Christian or Non-Christian?

When national crews on Nordic-owned ships decreased abruptly during the early 1980s, the issue of nationally oriented maritime mission would resurface. Well before that, however, a second major test of ICMA's chosen identity had appeared—almost as soon as the first. Whereas the first examined the level of *inclusiveness* in the word "International" in ICMA's title, the second would test the level of *integrity* in the word "Christian" in that same title. *Was it the intent of the organization to exclude non-Christians from its membership?*

For the founding members of ICMA's 1969 Steering Committee in Rotterdam, agreeing on a clear Christian identity for the new organization was their first order of business on the morning of August 29, even before agreeing on a name. The presence of *Moshé Pomrock,* an observer representing the Haifa-based *Israel Maritime League,* had brought the matter up. Together with him were other agency representatives who did not identify themselves as Christian observers, yet shared a common concern for the welfare of seafarers. Unlike the secular agencies, this agency was affiliated with a non-Christian religion, one with which the Christian community shared a common legacy. The question arose as to the eligibility of the Israel Maritime League for "full membership."

The issue was especially sensitive since it was only 21 years after the birth of the embattled state of Israel, and two years since it had been on the verge of annihilation. The Steering Committee was well aware that the Christian identity of the organization had so far not been at issue. Moreover, the document entitled "Conclusions and Resolutions," passed unanimously by the Consultation on August 28, was consistent with that identity. The new association was to consist of *Christian* organizations. Its ministry approach would be *holistic* ("directed toward the seafarer as a whole person"). Its scope would be *inclusive* (reaching out without discrimination to seafarers everywhere, regardless of "nation, race or creed"). Also—in accord with Dr. Kitagawa's visionary *seafarer-centered* model of ministry—a specific goal would be "the creation of Christian communities aboard ship." The outcome was categorical, yet conciliatory:

> It was decided that a letter be sent to Mr. Pomrock stating that while the body which was established and agreed was an association of Christian voluntary organisations engaged in welfare work for seafarers, he and his organisation would be welcomed as collaborators, would be kept informed of progress, and would receive invitations to attend any future world wide consultations (*Minutes of ICMA Steering Committee,* 29 August 1969).

The Committee was determined to do justice to *both* sides. It sought to safeguard the concern of any organization—to maintain the integrity of its own chosen identity. It could not simply open up its decision-making membership to a party unable or unwilling to commit to the primary mission inherent in its identity. Yet the Committee also wanted to respect the integrity of others (in this case non-Christians) by not imposing any commitment alien to them. Rather, they would welcome open communication and collaboration with all interested parties in areas of common human concern. (By the late 1960s, this was already happening elsewhere, in interfaith dialogue and cooperation between Christians and non-Christians in the areas of social justice, peace and the environment.)

Having affirmed the Christian identity of the new entity, the Committee Members could now devote themselves to the organizational implications. As they began preparing a Constitution to present at ICMA's First Plenary Conference in 1972, the Committee decided to reinforce ICMA's Christian identity. They did so by prefacing the Constitution with a proviso stipulating the following criterion: To qualify as "Christian," a member organization would need to be "connected with any Christian Church or Christian community recognized by the World Council of Churches or the Vatican."

The definition for WCC membership was, "Churches which confess the Lord Jesus Christ as God and Saviour according to the Scriptures and therefore seek to fulfill together their common calling to the glory of the one God, Father, Son and Holy Spirit." Even this wording could not avoid the confrontation ICMA would experience at its Second Plenary Conference in 1975. Moreover, the WCC's wording, "common calling," could not fill the need for a statement of mission specifying the missiological nature of such an organization as ICMA.

Other Unresolved Issues

In response to this latter need, the Author provided a "Research Progress Report" to ICMA/1972 in London. This offered an update on the first academic study of the history of the Seafarers' Mission Movement. It went on to state the case for ICMA itself to organize a section on "Maritime Mission Study and Research." It would take 18 years before that vision came to fruition—then as an independent entity, though with ICMA linkage: The International Association for the Study of Maritime Mission (see *Perspective* by Stephen Friend).

Other significant issues surfaced at ICMA's First Plenary Conference in London, though without any possibility of resolving them at that time. This applied to a range of topics, from seafarers' families to maritime training. However, two of these would become core issues in the decades ahead, relating to lay leaders (or "animators") aboard ship, as well as exploitive conditions on ships flying "Flags of Convenience" (FOCs).

. Unaddressed issues also included the question of a more adequate level of executive leadership. To assist between the 1972 and 1975 Plenary Conferences, Prebendary Tom Kerfoot of the Missions to Seamen and Rev. Johannes Aardal of the Nordic Council of Seamen's Missions agreed to serve as Co-Chairpersons. They also handled ICMA's ongoing affairs with the assistance of individual members of ICMA's Standing Committee.

As the workload continued to escalate, the need for a permanent secretariat became increasingly critical. Nevertheless, with the successful conclusion of ICMA's First Plenary Conference in 1972, it was clear that a historic breakthrough had occurred. A structured network for the global maritime ministry community—or "maritime ecumene," as it came to be called—was at last a reality. ICMA was in itself evidence that the 20th century "Ecumenical Era" of maritime mission had arrived.

At the same time, by the mid-1970s, there were unmistakable signs that a new "Global Era" in maritime mission history was under way. This did not imply the abrupt ending of one era and the equally sudden beginning of another. On the contrary, maritime ecumenism would need to continue taking hold, as a precondition for viable maritime mission during a time of radical change in global maritime industry. In that sense, the "Ecumenical Era" would be an essential, ongoing undercurrent—accompanying the evolution of the new "Global Era" into the 21st century.

Section
3

Global/Postmodern Era
(From 1974)

8

THE SHIPPING REVOLUTION

TECHNOLOGY AND TRADE

Globalization and Maritime Mission

The Phenomenon of Globalization

"We must all hang together, or assuredly we shall all hang separately." So said Benjamin Franklin of Philadelphia, as he and his colleagues signed the American Colonies' Declaration of Independence from the British Crown in July 1776. All were aware that they were signing their potential death warrants for high treason. In today's context of commonality of destiny, the same might be said of the whole human race, as we look back at the 20th century and face the future of the planet we share.

The past century has seen a rising urgency in the quest for worldwide unity and solidarity, fueled by a series of monumental, mainly preventable global tragedies. Prominent have been global conflict, even genocide, proliferation of weapons of mass destruction, the rampant spread of AIDS, the suicidal pollution of the world's natural resources and, since 11 September 2001, the eruption of international terrorism on an unparalleled scale.

Apart from such overwhelming negative factors, the last quarter of the 20th century also saw the mass marketing of the microchip, followed by the surge in universal computer use and internet access during the 1990s. Not only did the political border between the Communist Eastern Bloc and the Free World disappear. With the benefits of information technology (IT) within universal reach, this would demolish the dividing walls in global communication and usher in a borderless human society. An Information Age has taken over from Western civilization's three-century-old Industrial Age. In a world no longer solely divided between the "haves" and the "have-nots," but also the "knows" and the "know-nots," this "Digital Gap" is presenting new challenges.

During the 1990s, motivated not only by the fear of self-annihilation, but also by the unifying potential of this virtual Information Revolution, it became common to speak of a process of *globalization*. There is consensus around a general definition of globalization as "the growing impact of worldwide interconnectedness" (Held 2001, 324-327). However, the exact nature of that impact has become controversial. The concentration of resources and power in transnational corporations, as well as other borderless organizations, opens up vast possibilities for both good and evil. One thing seems certain: globalization itself—with its transcendence of traditional nation-state borders ("transnationalism")—is here to stay.

Implications for Church and Mission

Especially relevant in our context is the impact of globalization on the Christian church and its mission. Despite its positive potentials, once free from all restraint it might well promote two troubling tendencies: (1) *Polarization of society*—as unelected transnational organizations in the developed world impose a deregulated market economy on the developing world, resulting in a growing gulf of disparity between rich and poor. (2) *Pulverization of culture*—as an indifferent "postmodern" mindset threatens to undermine both public solidarity and individual identity. (See Kjell Nordstokke's *Perspective* below.)

Postmodernism—the culture emerging in the wake of globalization at the turn of the 21st century—also holds both negative and positive potential. Missiologist David Bosch, quoting from his Japanese counterpart *Kosuke Koyama*, reminds his readers about the Oriental character for "crisis," meaning not only "danger" but also "opportunity" (Bosch 1991, 3).

Foremost among postmodernism's negative implications is its rejection of things conventional or universal. Fueled by all the choices opened up by the Information Revolution, a kind of consumerist "market mentality" has evolved in both an economic and ideological sense. In postmodern parlance, nearly everything is "up for grabs," or "okay if it works for you." This translates into a subjectivity and relativity that appears to place postmodernism on a collision course with Christian mission. Where objective truth is nonexistent, and choices have equal value, mission may end up being seen as an intolerable imposition, and even labeled as "religious imperialism."

In that encounter, however, there are reasons to believe that Christian mission may not be so easily dismissed. Postmodernism alone may risk promoting economic disparity and societal fragmentation. Meanwhile, at the very core of the postmodern mindset is openness to the equal validity of every conceivable option—therefore also that of the Christian gospel. Many leading physicists now concede that science is too narrow in its methods to explain all reality, and is "not inherently inimical to the Christian faith" (Bosch 1991, 350-355). According to Dr. *Francis Collins*, the world famous former atheist and evolutionary biologist who now heads the Human Genome Project, "Science is not threatened by God; it is enhanced. He made it all possible" (Collins 2006).

How would globalization and postmodernism impact maritime ministry? It was the *maritime* world that would witness the phenomenon of "history's first globalized industry" (Tony Lane in SIRC 1998-99 A.R.). No sooner was a worldwide maritime ecumene under way, under the banner of ICMA, when it would face challenges that no one could have foreseen. The following seeks to trace the contours of that new maritime industrial environment—as a logical precondition for exploring its implications for maritime mission and ministry.

The Shape of the Shipping Revolution

D-Day on the Beaches

It is safe to say that few, if any, of the Allied troops that waded through withering enemy fire onto the beaches of Normandy, in the early hours of 6 June 1944, took time to reflect on the technological triumphs that had made it all feasible in the first place. They had other matters on their minds, as they struggled to secure beachheads amidst the carnage and confusion of that fateful day in the final campaign to liberate Nazi-occupied Europe.

Still, as maritime historians have since pointed out, the technological breakthroughs behind "Operation Overlord" and "Mulberry Harbour," forged under the pressures of total war, would resurface in the postwar revolution in the shipping industry. This applies to artificial harbors, containerization, roll-on/roll-off equipment, lighters carried on board ships, floating dock ships and mobile landing ramps. Other features resulting from wartime research were gas turbine propulsion, radar and other navigational means, above all the invention that would herald a new era of history—the digital computer (Corlett 1981, 5-8).

When identifying the origins of change in postwar shipping, there is consensus on both timing and terminology. In terms of *timing,* the return to peace in 1945 led to massive reconstruction programs. Yet in both ship and port design there was mostly a return to improved versions of pre-war patterns. Not until into the 1960s would change become revolutionary. As for *terminology,* the concept of "revolutionary change" was far from new in the annals of maritime history. The late 19th century transition from wind to steam power was clearly already a "Maritime Industrial Revolution." The post-World War II phenomenon, however, went way beyond just ships, affecting both port infrastructures and non-maritime methods of transportation. Ships would be only one link in an era of integrated transportation systems. Two authoritative publications on the topic both highlight the concept of a "revolution" in *shipping*—not just ships (Corlett 1981; Gardiner 1992).

The Consultant Editor of Robert Gardiner's 1992 volume, *The Shipping Revolution*, Dr. *Alastair D. Couper*, is a Professor of Maritime Studies, a former Master Mariner, and a Founding Director of the Cardiff-based Seafarers' International Research Centre (SIRC). In his Introduction, Couper links the principal factors contributing to the postwar shipping revolution to the two main functions of merchant ships of any age:

> Merchant ships have two main functions. They are the servants of trade and relate in their designs and patterns of movement to the commodity supply and demand needs of the world. Merchant ships are also business ventures and reflect the financial decisions of

owners and managers. The first objective influences the second but does not dictate it. Owners will order ships, accept cargoes and follow routes to the extent that they are profitable and safe. The background to their financial decisions is the operational environment (Gardiner 1992, Introduction).

Couper goes on to characterize this post-war "operational environment" as especially volatile. Among the many variables affecting supply and demand, he lists shifts in conventional trade patterns resulting from several major geo-political events. In addition, there is the effect of international conventions dealing with the safety of ships, the living and working conditions of ship's crews, and the protection of the marine environment.

Automation and Specialization

Technological breakthroughs combined with the volatility of the shipping environment led to a remarkable variety of vessels, in order to fill the mounting needs in postwar maritime transportation. Perhaps the most conspicuous features of that process were the dual concepts of "automation" and "specialization." Both were associated with the need for saving time, labor, resources and expenses, in the face of immense international competition.

As to *automation*, wartime innovations meant that machinery could become self-operating, incorporating automatic control by means of electronic sensors, monitors and consoles, all facilitated by digital computer technology. In shipbuilding, this led to decreased costs and increased capabilities. It revolutionized cargo-handling, navigation and engine room routines, resulting in increased reliability and reduced crew size. Finally, in port development, automated systems of cargo handling radically changed the location, construction and operation of modern-day port terminals throughout the world.

Specialization emerged as the other major feature giving shape to the postwar shipping revolution. There seemed no end in sight to the long list of ship types designed to meet the market needs of an increasingly globalized world—many reflecting "revolution" rather than "evolution." The following four categories of ship types focus on specific cargoes or purposes, largely based on the model adopted by the British National Maritime Museum in *The Ship*.

CURRENT-DAY SHIP TYPES

General Cargo Ships

The Container Revolution

The most far-reaching feature of postwar shipping resulted in a total transformation of the general cargo sector, now generally referred to as the "Container Revolution." The catalyst was the pressure of prohibitive expense—both in time and money—in handling general cargo in seaports of the postwar Western world. The conventional "break-bulk" method meant that a costly cargo liner, built as a fast, modern-day transport machine, was "for more than half of [its] life constrained to be a very inefficient warehouse" (Corlett 1981, 8). There was an obvious need for some form of standardization, a system of "unitization" that could eliminate the labor intensive process of placing all shipments first into crates or packages—each prone to pilferage, breakage or weather damage.

Instead, "containerization" facilitates streamlined transportation of cargo, virtually from door to door, in huge, standard-sized, specially constructed metal containers. They are then moved by "inter-modal" means—via interconnecting "modes" of transportation (trailer, train and ship) and lifted by special gantry-cranes from shore to ship and ship to shore at ports of departure and arrival.

Modern-day containerization was originally the brainchild of an American trucker, *Malcolm MacLean,* as he tried to bypass bottlenecks of break-bulk congestion in port after port. After years of frustration, he bought his own ship-owning company. He could then make container-carrying ships serve as "mobile bridges" along one and the same free-flowing roadway or railway. In April 1956, he first tested the concept in coastal trade, beginning with a converted post-war T-2 tanker called *Ideal-X* between Newark, New Jersey, and Houston, Texas. In 1957, he converted a cargo vessel, the *Gateway City,* for this purpose, integrating the "Lo-Lo" (lift-on/lift-off) principle. In so doing, MacLean had created a completely new kind of cargo-ship—the *world's first container ship.*

In 1961, MacLean renamed his company "Sea-Land" and went on to pioneer the use of shore-based gantry-cranes in deep-sea container ports. Very soon, one major international liner company after the other went over to these "box ships." By the turn of the century, Sea-Land had merged into Denmark's Maersk concern, which has since assumed world dominance as "Maersk Line."

In 1965, shipping companies reached international agreement on a standard container size of 20x8x8 feet, known as "Twenty-foot Equivalent Units" (TEUs). Over the years, container ship design has so far moved through a series of five "generations." By late 1980s, a new "Post-Panamax" generation of container ships had already surpassed the maximum imposed by the size of the Panama Canal. By 2006, the industry was even planning "Malaccamax" box ships of 18,000 TEUs—enough to stretch 75 miles!

Other Combinations

Given the cost of container-port infrastructure, many seaports, especially in the developing world, still depend on the old break-bulk method of cargo handling, using conventional cargo liners, or "combination" ships. Foremost among the latter are *roll-on/roll-off (Ro-Ro) ships.* Inspired by World War II tank landing ships (LSTs), Ro-Ro ships allow for driving wheeled vehicles on board—and eventually off again at destination. There are now several variations of multi-purpose *semi-container ships,* with a range of possibilities. For temperature-sensitive cargoes like food and fruit, there have, ever since prewar years, been specialized *refrigerated ships.*

Bulk Cargo Ships

Oil Tankers

An excavated Viking ship has provided the remains of what must have been an early form of navigable water barrel. The real breakthrough in waterborne transport of liquids in bulk, however, only came in the 1870s. In 1878, the brothers of peace activist Alfred Nobel were the first to transport kerosene from the Caspian Sea via the Volga and through Russia's waterways. They used a small Swedish-built steam tanker, the *Zoroaster,* of 400 deadweight tons. One hundred years later, the size of her gigantic successors peaked with the 1976 launching of the French-built turbine tanker *Batillus.* With a length of a quarter of a mile, and capable of carrying over half a million tons of crude oil, she was, at the time, by far the largest ship in the world.

Two factors appear to have played a major role in the "quantum jump" that culminated with the construction of such a colossus. The "economics of scale" dictate that building and operating costs decrease dramatically with the increased size of any given ship. As the proportion of tankers reached 50% of the world's total tonnage in the early 1950s, shipowners had the added incentive of the public demand for oil. Second, there was the recurring impact of Middle Eastern geopolitics. The closure of the Suez Canal in the wake of armed conflicts in 1956 and 1967 spurred construction of larger tankers in order to offset the longer alternative route round the Cape of Good Hope. This led to a frenzied building of supertankers, reaching over 300,000 dwt by the early 1970s.

In retrospect, most industry observers came to see this explosive rate as a recipe for disaster. The situation deteriorated with the December 1973 oil embargo. The Organization of Petroleum Exporting Countries (OPEC), made up of mainly Middle Eastern oil producing states, was founded in 1960 to assert local control of indigenous oil resources vis-à-vis the oil corporations of the West. In the fall of 1973, OPEC stunned the world market with the first in a series of crude oil price hikes, resulting in a four-fold increase in one year. Then, following the indecisive Arab-Israeli War of October 1973, OPEC attempted to pressure policy makers in the United States and other Western nations with a selective embargo on oil shipments to them, starting in December 1973. All this had a drastic domino effect throughout the global economy, sending it into a recession from which it would only begin to recover in the early 1990s.

No sector of the global economy suffered a more severe slump than shipping. The cutbacks created an oversupply of tankers, which, in turn, led to bankruptcies, large-scale scrapping, and widespread unemployment. Still, there remained a steady demand for the crude carrier's predecessor, the smaller-sized *products tanker,* able to carry different petroleum types simultaneously. Special "niche" trades generated a range of other *specialized tankers,* such as an assortment of highly liquefied natural gas (LNG) carriers, liquefied petroleum gas (LPG) carriers, chemical carriers, edible oil carriers, molasses tankers, wine and alcohol tankers, even orange juice tankers.

Bulk Carriers

Other bulk trades, too, would undergo change. For the carriage of dry cargoes in bulk, like grain, coal, ore, logs and wood products, dry bulk carriers would never rival the size of their nearest "relative"—the very large crude carriers (VLCCs). However, they were still vast by prewar standards. There also emerged multi-purpose *"combination carriers,"* like ore/bulk/oil carriers and flexible short-sea "mini-bulkers." All these eventually ousted that humble veteran workhorse since prewar years, the all-purpose traditional "tramp-ship."

Passenger Ships

Cruise Ships

As in any revolution, not only are new creations born, but some of the old may die. This was poignantly true of passenger ships. No sooner had those majestic state-of-the-art transatlantic passenger liners of the 1960s reached their pinnacle, when they received their death-blow—from the modern jet-propelled airliner. Ironically, in little more than a decade, the passenger liner would stage a remarkable comeback, with cruise ships soon becoming the world's fastest growing ship-type. The fate of the traditional passenger liner parallels that of the pre-1970s cargo liner, which eventually re-emerged as container ships.

As a concept, cruise ships have existed since Cleopatra used a lavish barge to "cruise" down the Nile. Closer to our own era, Mark Twain was a pioneer on the first-ever cruise trip from the United States—traveling as a journalist with the paddle-wheeler *Quaker City* to the Mediterranean in 1868. By the year 2000, the industry had moved from a few converted passenger liners into a "mega-ship" generation of purpose-built floating resorts, with a total of ten million passengers. Despite a massive disruption due to the September 11 terrorist attack, the cruise industry still seemed poised for further growth. In fact, an elite market has surfaced, offering passengers the ultimate in luxury living, whether on smaller vessels or so-called "apartment ships."

. While others, too, have remained involved over the years, the Americans, British and Norwegians have come to dominate the market. Americans have made up the largest proportion of passengers, with Miami-area ports as a popular departure point. The number of cruise ships registered under "Flags of Convenience" has also continued to grow. Meanwhile, conditions of life and work for the multi-cultural crews, making such a luxurious lifestyle of "sea, sun, sand and service" possible, have frequently stood in stark contrast. As the ITF quotes one rueful former crewmember, "There are two realities on a cruise ship: that of the passengers which is paradise, and that of the crew which can be hell."

Passenger Ferries

Though more modest in size, passenger ferries have also undergone explosive developments in recent decades. Defined as vessels specially built to carry passengers and/or vehicles for road and rail on a regular, relatively short run, modern ferries display great diversity in design as well as size. Since the mid-1960s, when the first *Ro-Ro ferries* appeared on the English Channel and Scandinavian routes, the Ro-Ro principle has become standard almost everywhere. Construction varies from relatively big "super-ferries" offering cruise ship facilities, to smaller-sized "fast ferries"—like the high-speed catamarans made in Mandal, Norway. As with tankers and bulkers, modern ferries, too, have foundered from time to time, in their case with particularly shocking loss of life. This has resulted in many revisions of safety requirements.

Specialized Ships

The list of different types of specialized ships continues to grow in pace with new needs and technologies. This applies not only to familiar categories like coastal vessels, fishing vessels, tugs, icebreakers, cable ships and dredgers. It is also true of newcomers like car carriers (with over 30 miles of cars!), semi-submersible heavy lift ships, and support vessels for the offshore oil industry.

In *marine propulsion,* there has been no comparable revolution but there has certainly been evolution. In *steam* propulsion, steam turbines had surpassed the time-honored triple-expansion engine by the early postwar period. After the 1973 oil embargo, *diesel*—a slow starter in prewar ship propulsion—eventually became the preferred choice. This was attributable to its relative fuel economy, especially with the additional boost of turbo-charging technology. As to any *nuclear-powered* alternative, although found to be feasible in limited fields like submarines and certain other naval craft, as well as specialized icebreakers, its dangers and disadvantages have so far obviated any "maritime atomic age."

THE DOWNSIDE OF DEREGULATION

The Structural Impact of Globalization

Positive Possibilities

There were a number of benefits for the human race from the Shipping Revolution that were quite beyond dispute. In 1987, the British Maritime League reminded the House of Commons Transport Committee:

> "All trade depends on transportation…Over ninety-nine and a half per cent by weight of all trans-ocean cargo is carried in ships, under half a per cent in aircraft; and there is no viable alternative mode for most of it" (Down 1989, 63).

Given the global community's dependence on sea transportation, together with its own growing interdependence, the more efficiently and economically ships are able to deliver their cargo, and thereby promote mutual international intercourse, the greater the overall human benefit. In that sense, the Shipping Revolution—with its gigantic strides in both automation and specialization of ships—was obviously beneficial.

Negative Realities

Despite the potential benefits of globalization for humankind, certain patterns of ownership and operation resulting from escalating change would prove increasingly problematic. Shipping had always been an international business ever since the origins of organized commerce, and prior to the 1970s it had been characterized by an overall semblance of stability. Since the 18th century, when half of all international seaborne trade was carried by British ships, much of the structure of shipping—the "regulatory system" of international law, institutions and practices—had been British in origin. Even after World War II, when most trades were still under the control of the Western maritime states, regulation remained in the hands of relatively few but reasonably reputable organizations. There had developed a kind of workable balance between national interest and a regulatory system essential to the international operational environment.

In *Voyages of Abuse,* a penetrating analysis of the scenario surrounding the current-day exploitation of seafarers, the lead author, Professor Alastair Couper, contrasts past conditions in the world of shipping with the "near chaos" that has since developed. Given the increasing volatility of the operational environment since 1973, coupled with increased mobility of capital and labor, the structure of shipping has "moved from international to global," thus becoming not only the *first* globalized economic activity, but also the *most* globalized such activity.

With the opening of previously Marxist economies from 1989 on, the international maritime structure became even more global. Couper characterizes this shift as not simply a "continuation of trends" but a "qualitative change." The traditional, international system, together with its accompanying strategies, would now be "irrelevant" and in acute need of replacement by a truly effective regulatory configuration (Couper 1999, 8-10). It was this profound paradigm shift in maritime *industry* that would now confront the new maritime ecumene with the urgency of creating a relevant strategy for maritime *ministry.*

Flags of Convenience—or Necessity?

The Cause

According to a cardinal principle of international law, going back to customs and codes way before the 19th century, a ship must always carry some kind of identification of nationality in order to facilitate the safe and orderly conduct of ocean traffic. Failure to do so would mean risking seizure. Both literally and figuratively, that mark of identification is referred to as a ship's flag, symbolizing the sovereign state under whose body of laws and regulations any given ship operates wherever she sails. Some have likened ships to pieces of floating sovereign territory.

Prior to the 1970s, shipowners would mostly operate their ships under the flag of their own citizenship. The owners and their ships would normally be subject to the same legal regime. In most cases, however, shipowners have long

been free to "flag out" and "re-flag" at will, by choosing for their fleet the flag—
or "register"—of any nation state willing to provide that option. Even before
World War II, a small number of shipowners had begun exercising that right by
transferring tonnage to an alternative register run by the state of Panama. The
problem was that the purpose of this register was totally different—namely
neither sovereignty nor seaworthiness but simply financial gain. Shortly after the
war, first Liberia and Honduras, later others too, joined Panama in offering this
maritime type of outsourcing to so-called "open registers."

As defined by the United Kingdom Committee on Shipping, an
international open register is one which allows for both ownership and crewing
of its merchant vessels by non-citizens. It requires no income tax—only a low
annual fee—and has no means of enforcing regulations regarding ship's safety
or crew conditions. For shipowners, faced with soaring postwar operating and
capital costs in a climate of "cut-throat" competition, open registers offered an
attractive opportunity to avoid both income tax and burdensome regulations,
while at the same time being free to hire ship's crews from the world's cheapest
labor markets.

The post-1973 shipping slump further increased cost-cutting pressures on
shipowners, forcing many into bankruptcy. Some survived by entering into
international mergers; more and more resorted to open registers. The 1980s
witnessed a virtual explosion of the latter as dozens of developing nations,
especially small island states from the Caribbean to the Pacific, saw this as a
welcome source of foreign currency.

The Cost

Maritime unions saw matters differently. As early as in 1948, the Congress
of the *International Transport Workers' Federation* (ITF), meeting in Oslo,
Norway, collectively denounced the dehumanizing results of the open registry
system and launched an international campaign that has continued ever since.
While documenting the descent into substandard shipping and abusive crew
conditions, the ITF has made one non-negotiable criterion the cornerstone of its
campaign: To avoid being considered an open registry ship, there must be a
"genuine link." *The nationality of the flag a ship flies must be the same as the
nationality of that ship's beneficial owner* (ITF 1999, 14).

By "beneficial owner" is meant the owner who stands to gain special
benefits. Since the primary purpose of the open registry system is to evade
responsibility for both income taxes and regulatory requirements, maritime
unions, as early as in the 1950s, adopted the designation "Runaway Flags"—
also to be known as "Flags of Convenience." Shortly afterwards, shipowners
responded by adopting the equally emotionally charged term "Flags of
Necessity," claiming they had no other choice if they were to remain
competitive. Eventually, American shipowners (the major beneficiaries of the
system) settled for the more neutral concept "effective control" and, in 1974,
founded the Federation of American-Controlled Shipping (FACS).

None the less, by the mid-1970s, the term "Flags of Convenience" had gained wide usage. Indeed, it would be futile to deny that such registers exist for the "convenience" of states and shipowners whose common concern is to maximize profits in an intensely competitive global market. It would be equally futile to deny that the FOC system can only carry on at tremendous cost—both to the maritime industry as such and to seafarers in particular. As to the negative impact on the industry itself, the verdict is unequivocal. Companies condoning the system have never succeeded in preventing accusations of exploitation and unfair competition. In fact, in "the stormy seventies" the prospect of easy profits for the industry's more ruthless risk-takers led to what Alastair Couper calls a whole new brand of "buccaneering entrepreneurs."

Although some of these soon went bankrupt, others managed to exercise a dysfunctional downward pressure on the industry, leading to depersonalization and non-transparency throughout the shipping world. By manipulating costs on a global scale, it was now possible to finance, build, register, manage, insure and charter one and the same ship—all in different countries, with the actual owner becoming virtually invisible and without accountability.

A Compromise?

During the late 1980s, some states sought to mitigate the negative effects of the FOC system while salvaging certain financial advantages. Norway, for long a leader in traditional ship ownership, launched the first of these "Second Registers"—also called International or Off-shore Registers—in 1987. Other traditional maritime states soon sought to emulate the Norwegians' initiative. By flying the national flag of the genuine owners, the system removed the stigma of a regular FOC register, while at the same time allowing those owners to hire cheaper non-national maritime labor under certain conditions. Still, critics see these as essentially "Quasi-FOC" ships, and the ITF has continued to monitor them closely.

Second Registers have had little or no impact on the mounting proportion of the world's merchant fleet flying regular Flags of Convenience. By the end of the 20th century, FOC ships had risen from about 15 per cent in 1960 to over 50 per cent of the world fleet, in terms of total tonnage (ITF 1999, 8; SIRC 2001, 91ff.). Given the detrimental effect of the system on the maritime world, the situation confronted the Christian maritime community with a challenge that left no other choice but to mount a broad, forceful response. Before addressing this, we will need to explore the consequences of not only the FOC system as such, but the whole Shipping Revolution, in relation to the overall quality of life of people of the sea.

WHATEVER HAPPENED TO THE SEAFARER?

Superships: A Mixed Blessing

Social Isolation

Just as the Shipping Revolution resulted in a depersonalization of those who owned and operated the ships, it became obvious that it could lead to a dehumanization of those who sailed them. In 1962, it took Rachel Carson, with her book *Silent Spring,* to raise public awareness of modern civilization's pollution of our planet. In 1974, it took Noel Mostert, with his *Supership,* to sound the alarm about the potentially disastrous effect of modern ship types both on the people who operate them and on the marine environment. In a riveting first-hand account of life aboard a 200,000 ton crude carrier, he describes "the debasing effect" of these giant ships on seafaring—not least "the strange psychological pressures such a life places on officers and men" (Mostert 1974).

Those pressures related directly to the restructuring of the maritime industry, resulting from increasing automation and specialization during the post-World War II period. The most sophisticated technology could only be as reliable as the people who operated it. As the Shipping Revolution ran its course, the cost of ignoring the consequences in terms of the human factor began to raise concern. All this became evident in the dramatically reduced size of crews. With new labor-saving equipment, computerized navigation, un-staffed engine-rooms, multi-skilled crew training and revolutionized cargo-handling, combined with specialized port terminals, the number of crew on ever larger vessels fell from approximately 40 to 20 per ship, sometimes even less.

For shipowners, faced with escalating costs, cutting crew expenses could be a matter of economic survival. For the remaining crew members, however, it meant jeopardizing a level of social interaction already constrained by the harsh sub-culture of a floating "total institution." Often compared sociologically to a prison, sea life could now qualify as "solitary confinement." To social isolation could be added boredom bred by repetitive action or by simply staring at consoles. This easily eliminated any sense of job satisfaction. As one veteran mariner put it, "Now we are no more than cogs in a big machine."

Other Implications

Port terminal innovations, contributing to less turn-around time in port, could mean crucial savings for shipowners. For the crew, it meant less relief from tensions built up during longer periods of social deprivation at sea. Specialization of ship types and trades could also mean a reduced range of ports of call. As a result, "a package holiday might offer more opportunity of seeing foreign places than a seafaring life" (Hope 2001, 343). Also, in order to safeguard such enormous capital investments, the responsibilities of a burgeoning "bureaucratization" were now being shared by far fewer officers and crew. This could easily push stress and fatigue levels to breaking point. The lethal combination of such factors, and the family problems resulting from them, has led to a disturbing rate of suicides at sea.

The shipping revolution also had far-reaching repercussions on a spiritual level. Organized maritime mission of the 1970s, however committed to a comprehensive range of Christian welfare provision, was still based on a model of *shore-based* hospitality centers. Crew reductions and faster turn-around meant that fewer and fewer seafarers could go ashore at all. More terminals were now too remote to make it possible. All of this resulted in reduced possibilities for human service delivery by maritime mission shore staff.

The technological revolution did see a wide range of improvements in shipboard crew facilities—from single cabins to swimming pools. Moreover, longer periods of home leave helped relieve the strains of family separation. A series of studies in maritime sociology appeared during the 1960s and 1970s, many of them in Scandinavia. These would offer information and support in matters ranging from seafarers' family dynamics to addictions, health hazards, and high mortality among seafarers. Nevertheless, some things are still simply inherent to seafaring life—even in an age of superships. As one participant put it at a USS Symposium on *The Maritime Industrial Revolution and the Modern Seafarer* in 1972, you can look aft on one of these ships and "see nothing but rows of door knobs [with] not a human being in sight."

This was a time when a majority of active seafarers still came from the traditional Western maritime nations. By the end of the 1970s, the ethnic composition of the world's merchant ship crews would begin to look very different. Some of the recent improvements in crew conditions might well have come to stay, but others quickly proved irrelevant. Moreover, for many of the newcomers, the ongoing impact of globalization in the maritime world would mean not just more marginalization, but also a level of abuse amounting to dehumanization.

Substandard Ships: A Litany of Abuse

Reining in Runaway Registers

In 1992, an impartial panel of experts, convened by an Australian Parliamentary Inquiry, published a report entitled *Ships of Shame*. The report created an international sensation way beyond the shipping community. In his preface the Chairperson, Peter Morris MHR, states:

> At the onset of the inquiry committee members were generally aware that there were problems associated with some ships calling at Australian ports. They were not prepared for the sickening state of affairs associated with the operation of sub-standard ships that was revealed as the inquiry proceeded (*Ships of Shame* 1992, Preface).

A "substandard" ship is generally one that fails to conform to official, minimum standards of safety and crew conditions. These standards have developed over the years and now constitute a crucial component of "the maritime regulatory system." By far the most significant are those contained in a number of instruments ("conventions") developed by two intergovernmental agencies of the United Nations—the International Labour Organisation and the International Maritime Organisation. A number of non-governmental organizations (NGOs) also play an active role in the formulation of UN regulations. Apart from primary participants like the International Transport Workers' Federation and the International Shipping Federation, these include the Seafarers' International Research Centre, as well as the International Christian Maritime Association and its associated Centers for Seafarers' Rights.

Given the level of expertise represented by both UN agencies and NGOs, the real problem is one of *enforcement*. Standards are only as good as the system that ensures accountability. Neither the ILO nor the IMO have any mechanisms to secure compliance. Under current international law that authority rests squarely with each participating sovereign state. Any international convention requires ratification by a flag state in order to apply to ships flying that state's flag. Even after such ratification, flag states are still free to flout their responsibilities, as routinely happens with states that operate FOC registers.

For such "Runaway Registers," this does not mean there are no restraints whatever. For example, in the wake of its 1948 Congress in Oslo, the International Transport Workers' Federation instituted a system of "ITF Collective Agreements" concerning salary, union membership and other social benefits. The system offers FOC owners a hard choice: meeting certain social criteria or facing an international port worker boycott. The establishment of a worldwide watchdog network of ITF-FOC Inspectors in 1971 has resulted in a kind of "selective truce" on the world's waterfronts. This has certainly managed to rein in some of the worst cases of abuse.

Also, when ILO Convention No. 147 introduced the concept of *Port State Control* (PSC) in 1976, it carried the potential for a promising breakthrough. Coastal states that have ratified the convention can now, in case of need, exercise the right to arrest any visiting foreign flag vessel, in order to enforce compliance with minimum standards affecting the ship's safety, pollution hazards or the social welfare of the crew. Based on a region-by-region agreement (a so-called "Memorandum of Understanding" or MOU), these PSC inspections, although they have so far proved to be of limited value, do represent at the very least a significant step in the right direction.

Still, the day has yet to come when runaway flags have nowhere to run. As to the ITF, its leaders have no illusions. They have served clear notice that their long-term objective remains the same—not just improvement but "total elimination of the FOC system." True, ships can become "substandard" without necessarily being FOC-registered. As Dr. Couper points out, however, notoriously substandard ships all too often prove to be precisely those operated by the "substandard sector of ship-owning"—as represented by the FOC system (Couper 1999, 1).

The Dehumanizing Nature of Crew Abuse

During the 1970s, the ethnicity of the world's merchant seafarers went through a revolutionary shift, from traditional Western seafaring nations to low-cost labor-supplying nations of the developing (mainly Asian) world. Less scrupulous shipowners and labor-exporting governments both had a stake in preventing this new category of seafarers from belonging to effective maritime unions. The powerlessness of maritime unions to represent such seafarers, and the lack of enforceable laws to protect them, could only increase their vulnerability.

For present purposes, the following represents only selective examples of the long litany of abuse still practiced under the FOC system. They come from a series of published exposés that began appearing in the 1990s:

* *Operating unseaworthy ships,* ranging from "rust buckets" to aging ships with major but carefully disguised defects, all in disregard for human life, property and the environment, in clear violation of SOLAS and international maritime safety regulations.

* *"Class-hopping,"* by fraudulently transferring tonnage to less accountable classification societies, willing to certify vessels already rejected by more reputable societies.

* *Providing subhuman crew quarters,* with cramped cabins, unacceptable toilet and sanitary facilities, and non-functioning heating and cooling systems, not only on many FOC ships but also on a certain sector of national-flag shipping.

* *Making seafarers accomplices in pollution* by instructing captains and crews to follow cargo-cleaning and dumping procedures in clear violation of MARPOL and other anti-pollution regulations.

* *Condoning rogue recruiters,* unscrupulous "manning agents" who fleece unemployed seafarers by issuing questionable contracts for illegal recruitment fees to be deducted from future pay.

* *Conniving in "Black Lists,"* often maintained by "manning agents;" alerting both colleagues and prospective employers about seafarers considered "troublemakers" (for having defended their rights or contacted the ITF or a union). Repressive regimes also keep records, threatening non-submissive seafarers and their families with reprisals.

* *Fostering financial fraud,* by cheating crewmembers with "double book-keeping" methods, denial of earned overtime, and non-payment of family allotments.

* *Jeopardizing safety at sea,* by ignoring fraudulent certification of officers and inadequate training of other ranks, as well as by means of under-manning and overworking, all in violation of the IMO International Convention of 1978 (STCW).

* *Practicing deliberate malnutrition* in relation to ILO standards, in some cases cutting back catering costs to the point of serious sickness and semi-starvation with rotten food and polluted drinking water.

* *Tolerating physical abuse by officers,* as a means of intimidating crewmembers who claim their just rights under international law—in extreme cases leading to maiming, even murder. (One seafarer in ten allegedly experienced physical abuse according to the ITF-sponsored MORI Report.)

* *Allowing the continuation of sexual harassment,* even rape, of women seafarers, through discriminatory and oppressive practices, especially on cruise ships.

* *Denying essential medical care* by colluding with agents in preventing responsible treatment and offering "attractive" waivers of the right to sue in cases of serious injury or

death, etc., all in spite of seafarers' centuries-old right to adequate care when taken ill or injured while under contract.

* ***Refusing repatriation of seafarers*** on completion of their contract, or for other reasons recognized by long-standing international law, but all too frequently disregarded for frivolous or fraudulent reasons.

* ***Abandoning the crew****,* seen by seafarers themselves as the ultimate abuse, in defiance of both international law and public morality. Whether a ship's owners, in an ironic reversal of the mutiny on the *Bounty,* would simply leave their crew stranded in a faraway port, or themselves literally run away from a run-down ship and a crew with a huge back-log of wages, such scandals were occurring, according to *Lloyd's List*, at least once a week by the turn of the 21st century.

In the face of such overwhelming evidence of the dehumanizing downside of deregulation in the maritime industry, some might regard the phenomenon of "floating sweatshops" as inevitable and simply allow "market forces" to play out. That option was not open to a maritime mission community unwilling to see seafarers themselves reduced to mere objects—without inherent human worth.

At New Year 1997, the German Seamen's Mission's newsletter *Lass Fallen Anker* printed answers from international colleagues to a questionnaire quoting the challenge Jesus poses in Luke 9:25: What would it profit a person to win the whole world, yet lose one's own soul? How could this relate to today's maritime world? Among the different responses, a former seafarer and later lawyer offered the following, under the heading "Bankrupted Humanity":

> From humble beginnings, he had climbed to the top of the shipping world. After years of hard work, shrewd business deals and tough cost-cutting, he now owned a large fleet of ships that provided him with wealth and possessions beyond the wildest dreams of his impoverished youth. He had bought old ships, searched out the cheapest labor, and cut all operating costs to the bone. Investments in training and crew retention made no sense to him. Crewmembers, like his ships, could be replaced when they wore out. Anyway, in his mind, his crews were better off working on his ships than starving at home. What had he gained? His short-sighted business practices not only jeopardized his investments. One major casualty—a real possibility with his untrained, demoralized and fatigued crews—could undo his entire financial empire. But he had also bankrupted his humanity. He had become separated from the people whose toils made his wealth possible—and also from God (Douglas Stevenson).

9

THE PROPHETIC CHALLENGE

ETHNIC REVOLUTION AT SEA

"Can women do *this* mission?" The question came from a Chinese missionary. She was ministering among the poor, the prostitutes and the prison inmates in the port of Bangkok. The year was 1990. The context was a maritime mission consultation, challenging Christians to get involved in outreach to fellow-Asian seafarers on a waterfront notorious for illicit drugs and prostitution. The convener's response was: Of course a woman can do this kind of mission—and often a whole lot better than a man, especially when she shares the same cultural background as most modern-day seafarers.

The Maritime Face of Globalization

Changing Features: Non-Western Seafarers

The incident in Bangkok serves to highlight two forms of change, both of them well under way in the maritime world of 1990. The one, based on gender, will be a subject for later. The other, based on ethnicity, is a key concept in the current context. "Outsourcing" to mainly Asians in the global maritime work-force had become an "Ethnic Revolution." In the wake of the geo-political upheavals of 1989, its rapidity astonished many even within the industry. In *The History of the Ship*, in a chapter aptly headed "Boxes, Bulkers and Babel," Richard Woodman discusses the connection between radical change in ship types and the Babel-like mix of the crews now sailing them (Woodman 1997, 313-315). As transnational corporations sprang up everywhere, sweeping aside traditional national borders, nowhere was the situation more volatile than in the maritime world. Here, free market forces, combined with the FOC system, brought about both windfall and havoc.

Commenting on the fate of British shipping resulting from those market forces, Prime Minister Margaret Thatcher bluntly called it "a sunset industry." Certainly, the result for British seafarers was devastating. From a prewar position of dominance, British seafarers were, by the 1990s, almost extinct, at least in terms of the lower ranks. In varying degrees, the picture was grim for seafarers of other Western maritime nations, too. From the 1960s, the situation had deteriorated to "a few shrinking enclaves," as Bruce Nelson noted (Nelson 1990; Hope 2001). The picture would become only somewhat less catastrophic for officers, especially in the topmost ranks. Even there, an eroding recruitment base would inevitably generate problems.

Seafarers from traditional, Western-world maritime communities found themselves unprepared for these implications of the mounting global inequities in standards of living. Escalating unemployment led to a host of hardships in this maritime version of industrial "outsourcing." Conversely, many nations of the developing world stood to benefit by the new, relatively speaking lucrative, employment opportunities that now opened up to them.

For owners and operators in the industrialized world, there were two major incentives for hiring ship's crews from developing nations: (1) *Cost-cutting* weighed most; developing world seafarers would willingly work for a fraction compared with hard-won Western levels of wages and social benefits. (2) *Compliancy* would be attractive to less scrupulous owners, anxious to evade international regulations; non-unionized (or weakly unionized) developing world seafarers ("Crews of Convenience") would be less likely to protest in cases of abuse, for fear of dismissal or other forms of reprisal.

There was nothing new about hiring foreign crews to sail nationally owned ships. This had happened for hundreds of years. The difference was that now it had become the norm. In the late 19th century, American owners had hired large numbers of Norwegian and other Nordic seafarers. By the late 20th century, the numbers of Norwegian seafarers on national-flag ships had dropped dramatically, as Norwegian shipowners were hiring foreign, often Filipino, crews for their expanding Second Register fleet.

By the final two decades of the 20th century, the Philippines had become the world's foremost supplier of maritime labor, with Manila recognized as the "Manning Capital of the World." An island nation, with an ancient seafaring heritage, the country was, by the turn of the 21st century, supplying at least 200,000 active merchant seafarers of an estimated total of 1,250,000 worldwide. China, Indonesia, India and Burma had by then also become major suppliers. The post-1989 collapse of the Communist Bloc brought Russia, the Ukraine, and Eastern Europe into prominence, too. Still, after the year 2000, Asians of various nationalities continued to constitute a clear majority of the world's merchant seafarers. By contrast, Western maritime countries now accounted for only 13 per cent of them, according to SIRC statistics.

Changing Challenges: Multi-Cultural Crews

Globalization not only changed the appearance of the maritime workforce. Ethnic and cultural pluralism carried with it a whole range of other challenges as well. In the past, mono-cultural ship's crews might all come from the same home community. Now, there could be over half a dozen nationalities on board any given merchant ship, with thirty or more on large cruise ships. Among the negative consequences of this degree of diversity, two factors could cause special concern: *Ship's safety* could be compromised by miscommunication (a repeated recipe for marine disasters). *Human stress,* always a problem in any "total institution," could reach uncontrollable levels where exacerbated by perceived offense. This could lead to violence, even murder or suicide. Some crewing agents were reportedly "mixing" crews in order to protect shipowners from "problems," prompted by collective action in response to cases of abuse.

Despite such potential scenarios, there was wide consensus in the industry that multi-nationality in crew composition had come to stay. Professor *Tony Lane*, Director of the Seafarers' International Research Centre, went even further. At a SIRC Symposium in 2001, he not only anticipated that multi-national crewing would increase as maritime states continued to reduce nationality restrictions. Lane also predicted that wisely practiced multi-national crewing could lead to "an upward leveling of conditions among the various nationalities." It could even be a way for the global shipping industry to "do its bit for international relations":

> Merely by observing the standards of best practice industrial employment, but doing it with an international workforce, gives us a wonderful opportunity to present the shipping industry as a working example of the advantages of globalism. In a world where everyone hungers for peace and stability, it would be hard to exaggerate the commercial and human benefits to be had from being the world's role model (SIRC 2001, 114).

Lane's optimistic conclusion received corroboration by research results from a three-year *Shipboard Based Study of Mixed Nationality Crews,* presented at the same symposium. The study came up with several quite unexpected benefits of responsible multi-ethnic crewing for operators and seafarers alike.

The real root of the problem was, therefore, not globalization as such. It lay less in the *ethnicity* of the new maritime work force than in the systematic exploitation of its *vulnerability*. Confronting this exploitation, as well as empowering its potential victims, would be among the most daunting challenges facing the Christian maritime ecumene into the new millennium.

Exploitation or Empowerment?

"No Less than an Insult to God!"

In the run-up to the Apostleship of the Sea's XXI World Congress in 2002, on "The Mission of the Church to the People of the Sea in the New Globalised World," the AOS quarterly featured the reflections of a ship's master. Under the title "Seafarers as Global Victims," the captain responds to the recent pronouncement of a prominent public figure who asserted that the seafarer is "a vital element of globalisation, not one of its victims":

> Unfortunately the seaman is also the first one to "have his head cut off" [according to] the trade unions and professional associations

concerned. They remind that the seafarer has always been an *expendable object,* something to be used and thrown away. [Seafarers are only remembered as] a human factor when it is a question of charging them with 85% of the troubles that happen on or to ships. This is globalization, a nebulous business phenomenon in which lusting greed for profit is justified on the grounds of commercial competition and which allows all involved except the seafarers to make themselves scarce, hide away and withdraw from sight whenever there is a question of assigning responsibility. (*Apostolatus Maris* 2002/1, 4).

An expendable object—those three words go to the core of the problem. If people accept depriving seafarers of their dignity as fellow humans, and consider them as no more than disposable commodities, the whole issue of "dehumanization" becomes irrelevant. History has shown that it was this kind of objectification (or "reification"—from the Latin word "res," meaning "thing") that opened the way for every form of human exploitation over the centuries. Not only that, all human beings—without exception—are created "in the image of God," as uniquely portrayed by Jesus Christ (Gen. 1:26-27; John 14:9). Therefore, defacing that image is no less than an insult to God the Creator and Jesus Christ, his incarnate Son (John Paul II 1981; Bosch 1991, 355-358).

A consistent commitment to social justice and healthy relationships (or "shalom") in every sphere of human life runs right through the Scriptures, from Genesis to Revelation. The prophetic call as voiced in Micah 6:8 and Jesus' own Messianic Manifesto in Luke 4:18-19 are just two examples among many. The history of the Christian Church tragically includes events that have been utterly at odds with gospel values. At its best, however, it also reveals a legacy of loyalty to concern for "restorative justice," one that goes beyond retribution to the restoration and empowerment of fellow humans who are oppressed by unjust societal structures (Sider 1997; Wallis 2005).

By the late 20th century, that legacy could still cause critical reactions in some quarters. There was, for example, a strongly worded article in a professional shipping journal about "political bias" in maritime mission circles, exemplified by the recently founded New York-based Center for Seafarers' Rights. In a July 1985 editorial, NAMMA's newsletter offered a response that included a reminder headed "Who's Going Overboard?"

It is a fact of history that the first measures to improve the incredibly harsh social and physical conditions of the seafarer's life were initiated by men and women motivated by a clear Christian commitment, and only achieved in the face of the most bitter opposition by defenders of the status quo. Those who decried the interference of "do-gooders and sky-pilots," insisted that the Church must "keep its nose out of politics and labor relations."

It would seem relevant to remember one thing Hitler and Stalin did have in common: an intense intolerance of genuine Christianity (or any other faith) loyal to an authority higher than that of their own

Nazi or Communist credos. But a church which, when confronted with human need in any shape or form, simply "passes by on the other side," has parted company with Him who held forth the way of the Good Samaritan. Because it has then, precisely as Karl Marx contended, become an opiate for the people, a peddler of pies in the sky, and hence no "earthly" good.

Colleagues in the *Seamen's Church Institute's Center for Seafarers' Rights* simply stand in a direct line of biblical prophetic tradition, which cannot remain silent where the fundamental rights and human dignity of fellow men and women are under attack. In so doing, fellow workers in maritime mission the world over stand shoulder to shoulder with them, regardless of denomination. If this be "political bias," then would to God there were more of it!

Toward Specialized Counter-Measures

By 1985, the SCI Center for Seafarers' Rights was already a reality. Its impact, on both maritime industry and maritime ministry in the new Global Era, would mark the beginning of a *Seafarers' Rights Movement.* In that light, the events leading up to the launching of this New York-based agency merits a special place in any history of late 20 century maritime mission.

As early as in 1969, ICMA's first Secretary, Dr. Daisuke Kitagawa, had fearlessly indicted contemporary society for tolerating the alienation of international seafarers from the global community. At ICMA's First Plenary Conference in 1972, delegates added their own growing concern, in a resolution deploring the "exploitive conditions of life and work experienced by some seafarers sailing under flags of convenience." ICMA's Plenary Conferences in 1975 and 1978 reiterated that concern, as evidence of abuse—especially under FOC registers—continued to escalate.

Simultaneously, there was an increasing sense of frustration rooted in the realization that resolutions alone, however vigorous, could not suffice to resolve the plight of abused seafarers. Eventually, just as North America had been the primary player in the proliferation of the FOC system, North America would also provide the first coordinated effort by maritime mission activists toward its repudiation. As early as in 1977, Rev. *Dale Umbreit,* port chaplain in Savannah, Georgia, and a director of NAMMA, proposed a preliminary blueprint for such action in a paper highlighted later that year by ICMA. Here, he characterized the level of abuse he had witnessed on the waterfront as part of a growing "world crisis." Specifically, he called for colleagues to compile facts and raise a "united moral voice," in order to arouse world consciousness and insist on remedial action through international agencies like ICMA, ILO and the UN (*ICMA News,* No. 2, 1977, 2-3).

Through the late 1970s, Umbreit's North American colleagues continued to confront ever-increasing exploitation. In the port of New York, for example, the Senior Chaplain of the Seamen's Church Institute there, Rev. *George Dawson*, became his agency's primary "labor trouble-shooter." The daily load of abuse cases he found himself struggling with on a regular basis resulted in more than 30 ship arrests over the years. In 1979, North American chaplains invited *Eugene Spector*, Research Director of the National Maritime Union, to address the issue in a keynote address at their Annual Conference held that year in Pensacola. *Watermarks* subsequently highlighted his scathing attack on current-day substandard shipping—with its "slave-trade" crew conditions and "rust-bucket" level of seaworthiness.

The crucial question was how to enlist the specialized skills and comprehensive resources needed for a viable, coordinated strategy. For most observers, it probably came as no surprise that it was the Seamen's Church Institute of New York/New Jersey, with its record of Christian social concern, which would now take the lead in shaping such a strategy.

THE SEAFARERS' RIGHTS MOVEMENT

The SCI Center for Seafarers' Rights, and Sister Agencies

The Instigator: James R. Whittemore

When Rev. Dr. *James R. Whittemore* became Executive Director of the Institute, in 1977, he came with a solid record of pastoral ministry in the Episcopal (Anglican) Church. He had also developed close ties to the sea and social justice. He served as a naval officer in World War II. He was deeply involved in the post-war Civil Rights Movement. When he took over leadership of the world's most prestigious seafarers' center—with its 23-story skyscraper at 15 State Street—shipping was in its deepest depression in decades. Whittemore took "cross bearings" and ordered a thorough fiscal review. This revealed that the whole Institute enterprise was "headed for the shoals of financial disaster." His next step, therefore, was to call a "ship's council" of staff colleagues and management consultants in order to explore options.

The outcome was a needs assessment highlighting two major priorities. The first was to assure survival by selling the Institute's State Street skyscraper. This had replaced Mansfield's massive 25 South Street structure in 1968. However, it had become under-utilized and a source of soaring deficits, largely due to the rapid change in the maritime and airline industries. After overseeing the sale and move to temporary facilities in 1985, Whittemore supervised the building of the SCI's current state-of-the-art center of operations at 241 Water Street, opened in 1991, in the heart of historic South Street Seaport.

The second priority indicated by the needs assessment was a focus on seafarers' human rights, the result of a new look at the Institute's basic raison d'être. Whittemore stressed that the "bottom line" was not survival, but faithfulness to the Institute's identity in a new context. From his earlier years of volunteer service on the SCI Board of Managers, he was already aware of Mansfield's campaign to make social justice for seafarers a core commitment of the Institute. Now, as Whittemore put it, that commitment meant moving out of the "housing business" and competition with the crimps of yesteryear, in order to fulfill the Institute's mission in an era of new forms of abuse at sea.

Whittemore also initiated a new SCI "Statement of Purpose," articulating the Institute's dedication to "the safety, well-being, dignity and professional competence of seafarers and those who work in international transportation and commerce." He was especially concerned with expanding the Institute's purpose to include "the larger maritime industry." He saw this as a precondition for achieving the systemic, industry-wide social change necessary to impact the quality of life of seafarers. More importantly, it was a key to catching "a glimpse of the *Imago Dei* ("image of God") in the face of seafarers, upon whom international trade and commerce are so dependent" (Whittemore 1982).

A specific strategy to implement such a vision, at least in embryonic form, was launched. The following narrative of events leading up to that point is based primarily on the Doctor of Ministry Projects of the two persons most immediately involved, James Whittemore and Paul Chapman, supplemented by the Author's personal contact with both, as Executive Secretary of NAMMA at that time (Whittemore 1985; Chapman 1983).

The Implementor: Paul K. Chapman

Rev. Dr. *Paul K. Chapman* shared with Whittemore a personal history of involvement in the American Civil Rights Movement. An ordained American Baptist minister, he was the grandson of the one-time Director of the Boston Baptist Seamen's Bethel. He had lived for 13 years in an "intentional community" with roots in the 19th century Separatist Community Movement, before deciding to relocate to the city of New York. Here, in 1979, Whittemore hired him to "promote ecumenical cooperation in the Port of New York and New Jersey."

As a member of the SCI staff, Chapman very soon became familiar with not only Whittemore's thinking in regard to justice issues in the maritime world, but also concrete cases of abuse with which colleagues on the waterfront chaplaincy team were contending on a daily basis. He was appalled by what he heard and saw. Shortly after joining the SCI, Chapman had agreed with Whittemore that they would both take advantage of a Doctor of Ministry program at New York Theological Seminary that might enhance their respective ministries among seafarers. Chapman recalls having heard Whittemore use the term *Seafarers' Rights* frequently in connection with these plans. When Chapman was to select a project for presentation, he chose this topic, with Whittemore's encouragement.

Once freed from other tasks, Chapman threw himself into his project in a flurry of research and networking. By early 1981, he had drawn up his project proposal, obtained the approval of the Seminary and had it endorsed by the Institute. Entitled *Human Rights for Seafarers,* its main substance appeared as a regular "SCI Project" in the form of a 22-page booklet the same year. This awoke widespread interest and rapidly went through three printings. Whittemore was, according to Chapman, "supportive of the project at every juncture."

As Chapman saw it, the International Transport Workers' Federation, dominated by "primarily Western unions," could have presented a problem in "protecting their own power in the process of seeking justice for Third World seafarers." Instead, he soon found them to be "an authentic and indispensable ally in a Herculean task." Another matter was SCI's Board of Managers, which included shipowners among its members. It was therefore essential to convince these members that "the enemy was not so much open registry per se as it was substandard shipping." If this were indeed the specific target, they would all be dealing with a common enemy.

Finally, there were Chapman's own colleagues in the North American Maritime Ministry Association. Their active participation would be crucial to any strategy for change. In February 1981, NAMMA's Board did endorse the overall purpose of the project. Still, some of its members feared at first that any involvement of ship visitors in the process of data gathering for the project would inhibit future freedom of access on board. This motivated Chapman to "switch strategies" and focus on personally cataloging individual cases of abuse—which were ongoing and plentiful. By July 1981, any lingering reservations had finally evaporated. After an impassioned appeal by Chapman at ICMA's Plenary Conference in Berlin that summer, that body unanimously endorsed the SCI's Project for Seafarers' Rights.

ICMA/Berlin was the breakthrough that set the issue of Seafarers' Rights on course as a core concern of the worldwide maritime ecumene. Six months later, in January 1982, the SCI brought together lawyers, union and government officials, as well as port chaplains, for a first-ever "Workshop on the Rights of Foreign Seafarers in United States Ports." This would have strategic significance in terms of two crucial needs—awareness-raising and coalition-building. That same month, NAMMA's Board passed a resolution to endorse and actively sponsor the SCI Project. With that, Whittemore was able to justify a new level of commitment and upgrade the Project to a *Center for Seafarers' Rights* (CSR). This meant that the CSR was now an official "Division" of the Institute, on a par with its Divisions for Seafarers' Services and Maritime Education. Paul Chapman became the Center's first Director.

The CSR initiated several parallel programs—conferences, workshops, research and legal projects, including the publication of a series of educational booklets. In close collaboration with NAMMA and ICMA, the following special events were among CSR highlights in the course of the next decade:

* ***Cruise Ship Workshop in Miami,*** "Cruise Capital of the World," in 1984, culminating in a consumer boycott threat against marginal "fun ship" operators with the most notorious records of crew abuse.
* ***Port State Control (PSC) Conference in New York***, in 1986, bringing together, for the first time, representatives of maritime industry and maritime ministry to consult for that purpose. It called on the US Senate to follow Europe's example and apply PSC to foreign flag ships visiting American ports by ratifying ILO Convention No. 147 (on minimum safety and social standards on merchant ships). In support of the CSR, NAMMA conducted a successful follow-up campaign to secure ratification in 1988.

* A Maritime Manning Conference in Manila, "Crewing Capital of the World," in 1987, to expose and counter the fraudulent practices foisted on Filipino seafarers by marginal manning agents. Close cooperation between the CSR and ICMA, as well as Filipino officials and bona fide manning agents, resulted in agreeing on a groundbreaking "Code of Good Practice for Manning Agents."

* A Chaplains' Seafarers' Advocacy Training Program in New York, in 1990, jointly sponsored as a pioneer project by the CSR and NAMMA, eventually becoming part of the Center's regular program.

As awareness-raising and networking progressed, sister agencies of the New York CSR were also started overseas. In 1986, the London-based (Anglican) Missions to Seamen called Rev. *Chris Collison* to head a unit that would, by the 1990s, become a Department for Justice and Welfare under Rev. Canon *Ken Peters*. In 1987, the (Roman Catholic) Stella Maris Center in Barcelona initiated a justice ministry that developed into an AOS-affiliated "Centro de los Derechos del Marino," under the directorship of Dr. *Ricardo Rodriguez-Martos Dauer*.

When Chapman stepped down as director of the original New York CSR, in September 1990, it signaled the end of the formative phase of the new movement. When questioned about his interpretation of the purpose of maritime ministry, Chapman responded: "Some may well see me as one-sided in my commitment to justice in the maritime world. But until the issue of seafarers' rights is recognized as an essential part of the church's maritime ministry agenda—so be it!" By 1990, that goal had been reached. Cooperation in questions of seafarers' human rights had become a shared responsibility, transcending denominational diversity in maritime mission worldwide.

Who was the actual "founder" of the first Center for Seafarers' Rights? Without question, *Whittemore* had the basic vision before ever hiring Chapman, after which he went on providing the means to implement it. For his part, *Chapman* seized the opportunity offered him, and ran with it—for a whole decade. In light of these facts, it would seem that James Whittemore and Paul Chapman together can both be considered "co-founders" of the first Center for Seafarers' Rights. It took the combination of a *visionary* with Whittemore's leadership skills, as well as a *missionary* with Chapman's persistence, to create the synergy needed to counter systemic injustice in the maritime world at this "kairos" moment in history.

Consolidation: Douglas B. Stevenson

Eventually, both NAMMA and ICMA became beneficiaries of Whittemore's vision and leadership during his respective tenures as President and Chairperson of each of these organizations. Finally, in 1992, Rev. (later Canon) *Peter Larom*, a former seafarer and overseas missionary, succeeded Whittemore at the Seamen's Church Institute. For the decade that followed, Larom continued to build on his predecessor's legacy with zest and creativity.

Meanwhile, two years earlier, Whittemore had also secured the services of Commander *Douglas B. Stevenson* to head the Institute's Center for Seafarers' Rights as Chapman's successor. As a 20-year veteran of the U.S. Coast Guard and a practicing attorney-at-law, Stevenson had engaged in strategic planning for the Coast Guard. He had also negotiated U.S. positions at the United Nations on such issues as the International Law of the Sea, arms control and the marine environment. A conciliator by nature, Stevenson believed that, instead of making decisions affecting the welfare of seafarers "purely on economic grounds," it was important that the Center for Seafarers' Rights should, as he put it, "help bring to the 'marketplace' the influence of the church" (*Lookout* Spring/Summer 1991, 4).

Whereas Chapman's affinity with organized labor was particularly relevant during the startup struggles of the CSR, the subsequent need for consolidation now called for the broader background in the shipping industry that Stevenson could contribute. Maximizing his "ombudsman" role, Stevenson set about enlisting the cooperation of socially responsible shipowners who were committed to good management practices. Stevenson placed a priority on reinforcing CSR cooperation with the worldwide port chaplaincy network. He not only expanded seafarers' rights workshops for port chaplains nationwide. He also launched these on an international level. In so doing, he worked in cooperation with the SCI's International Training Center for Workplace Ministry under Rev. Dr. *Jean R. Smith*—from 1990 the new Director of the Institute's Seafarers' Services Division.

Stevenson's tenure coincided with the 1990s decade of far-reaching change on the world scene, spurred by the collapse of Communism and growth of globalization. Meanwhile, pressing advocacy challenges continued to emerge or re-emerge, for example: the abandonment of ships' crews, piracy, stowaways, people-smuggling, maritime refugees ("boat people"), crisis preparedness, seafarers' medical care, safety at sea, ecology concerns, fishers' rights, and much more, including post-9/11 issues relating to port security.

In confronting these challenges, Stevenson chose to allocate them to three main program areas: *Legal assistance*—for both seafarers and port chaplains worldwide; *Education*—also for both seafarers and port chaplains; *Advocacy*—for seafarers' human rights, both nationally and internationally, within governmental and non-governmental organizations. There were also other forums connected with maritime industry and maritime ministry.

By the Turn of the Century: Failure or Success?

Reasons for Optimism

Larom's leadership and ongoing support would prove crucial to the success of Stevenson's sector of ministry. As the maritime ecumene faced the future at the turn of the century, was it justifiable to characterize the new Seafarers' Rights Movement a "success story"? Had two decades of sustained effort made an impact on the level of exploitation in the seafaring world? By the close of the 20th century a majority of the world fleet had re-flagged to FOC registers (52.6% by 2000), and the percentage was likely to continue to rise. Nevertheless, there were at least two reasons for optimism.

First, at its 1998 Congress in New Delhi, the ITF decided to revisit the *target* of its anti-FOC Campaign. It was time to recognize that crew conditions on some nationally flagged ships were now even worse than on many FOC ships. The focus would therefore need to be more on *substandard shipping as such—irrespective of flag.* A growing number of owners felt they had to flag out to FOC registry in order to stay competitive. Yet they saw it made sense to comply with minimum international crew and safety standards. Meanwhile, the ITF's move did not mean diluting their efforts to eliminate the FOC system. Rather, it merely meant making the methods more fair and effective—by expressly including non-FOC substandard ships in the campaign.

Second, in terms of *strategy,* by the turn of the century there was evidence of a more intentional focus on the enforcement of an international regulatory system. The goal was not more regulation as such, but rather (as the ITF put it) *more intelligent regulation.* Among indicators of this already happening were developments like the following:

* ***Port State Control:*** Adopted by more and more states, resulting in region-by-region "Memorandums of Understanding" (MOUs) in order to enforce minimum safety and social standards on foreign ships visiting their respective ports.
* ***Flag State Audit:*** Commissioned by the ITF and completed in 2001, measuring the level of conformance with criteria for "maritime best practice" in 70% of the world fleet.
* ***Geneva Accord:*** Adopted in 2001, in order to initiate the consolidation of all previous maritime-related ILO instruments in one single ILO Convention.

The Christian-based Seafarers' Rights Movement could not, of course, take sole credit for these developments. None the less, by the year 2000, that movement had already proved its potential for making a difference—and therefore being to some extent "transformational"—at least in the following two important respects:

First, in terms of *empowerment,* abused seafarers had received help toward self-help, rather than just top-down paternalistic charity. Often caught in a dilemma of abuse afloat, or blacklisting ashore, only seafarers could decide whether to stand up for themselves. By the year 2000, however, those who did would at least know that, in every port with a Christian seafarers' agency, they would find a friend—one who would help them know their rights, obtain justice in that port, and stand by them come what may.

Second, in terms of *advocacy, e*veryday maritime ministry practitioners could make no claim to exhaustive legal expertise. However, by the year 2000, more governmental and non-governmental agencies than ever before were working with ICMA's specialized seafarers' rights ministries in New York,

London and Barcelona, toward the common goal of equitable global governance in shipping.

A Plimsoll Line for Seafarers' Rights?

At ICMA's first Plenary Conference in Asia, held in the Philippines in 1985, the Author, then Executive Secretary of NAMMA, introduced a proposal for a *Plimsoll-line for Seafarers' Rights:*

> A hundred years ago it became possible at last to agree on an international convention preventing the clearance of ships in or out of port anywhere in the world without complete compliance with certain basic *load-line* requirements. Why should it not now be possible to obtain a corresponding global enforcement of requirements affecting their crews' basic *quality of life*? This would make international freight competition dependent *not on how low* crew conditions and benefits could be brought down, *but on how high* seamanship and service could be raised up (*Watermarks* 1-2/1985, 8).

The Author had already advanced the gist of that proposal during a panel program at the General Assembly of the Norwegian Seamen's Mission, in Trondheim in 1961. At that time, representatives of both shipowners and unions alike had, in unmistakable terms, dismissed it—as well as the whole notion that maritime mission had "any business in maritime industrial relations." Judging by the level of momentum that was beginning to build at the turn of the 21st century, global consensus on a "Plimsoll-line for Seafarers' Rights" looked like a realistic possibility after all. Certainly, the ILO's adoption of the *Consolidated Maritime Labour Convention,* in February 2006, represented a historic development, already hailed as a "Seafarers' Bill of Rights." If duly ratified and effectively enforced, it could even reverse the notorious downward social spiral of FOCs and finally make the whole system irrelevant (Couper 1999, 166-179).

Such was the status on Seafarers' Human Rights, in general, at the turn of the century. Another matter was the prospects for what could be considered "Seafarers' *Ultimate* Human Right." Would the worldwide maritime ecumene see a corresponding kind of unanimity, as it continued to grapple with the implications of the Shipping Revolution—this time in terms of the new context of religious pluralism at sea?

10

THE DISCIPLESHIP CHALLENGE

RELIGIOUS PLURALISM AND HUMAN RIGHTS

As seen, the worldwide maritime community responded with remarkable unanimity to threats against seafarers' social welfare in the wake of the post-World War II "Ethnic Revolution." Achieving a corresponding consensus on seafarers' *spiritual* welfare would prove to be a very different matter.

Mission—A Human Right?

A Chinese Case Story

It was in the mid-1950s, shortly after Mao Tse-tung's takeover of Mainland China. A teenager from Canton had swum through shark-infested waters and Communist patrols to freedom in Hong Kong. Now he was planning to major in physics at Taiwan's leading university. His ambition was to be a Buddhist monk and eventually control natural phenomena—with the help of science and ancient formulas he had learned from his grandfather. One day all that changed. During a student excursion to a lake area, he was in danger of drowning. When all looked hopeless, rescue came at the very last moment.

Next day, he learned that a campus pastor (*Sally Jones*, a veteran China missionary) had sensed a sudden uneasiness on his behalf at precisely the time he was drowning, and had immediately prayed for his deliverance. The aspiring monk then knew he had a problem. He found the only way he could now "save face" was at least to read the Chinese New Testament the missionary had given him earlier, but which he had not yet opened. He could later relate how amazed he was to discover that Jesus Christ had already secured his salvation two thousand years ago, without any need for reincarnation. He started wondering why no one had told him about this earlier. After all, here was a matter of his ultimate destiny. Yet he had been unaware of any alternative; he had not been able to exercise that most basic human right, the freedom to choose.

The outcome was that *Joel Hui Tsu Shen* not only sought baptism but completed a Christian theological education, eventually becoming a district president in the indigenous Chinese-Lutheran Church in Taiwan. In 1976, he

accepted "promotion" to the position of port chaplain at Tacoma Seafarers'
Center in the Pacific Northwest of America. Here, for the next two decades, he
would continue to offer the gospel alternative to visiting seafarers—regardless
of race or religion.

A Logic often Missed

None of the ship's crews Chaplain Shen would visit were more receptive
than the increasing numbers of fellow-Chinese, whether Buddhist or atheist. Nor
could anyone have been more careful than he to avoid coercion. In his own
experience, no one had tried to pressure him or "proselytize" him. His case
speaks of a logic missed by some who simply oppose sharing the Christian
gospel in any form—whether on the waterfront or elsewhere.

The massive influx of low-cost labor from the Non-Western world since
the 1970s meant that merchant seafarers would now be mostly adherents of non-
Christian faith communities. With the notable exception of Filipino seafarers
(most of them Roman Catholics), merchant seafarers might be Muslim, Hindu,
Buddhist, Shintoist, Animist, as well as Communist. Meanwhile, seafarers from
the traditional maritime nations of the West, with at least a nominal Christian
affiliation, had become an endangered species. The international labor force now
presented a picture of multi-racial religious pluralism. As a result, many of those
engaged in maritime mission came to realize that a traditional *home* mission
task had now become a *world* mission challenge.

Dealing with Objections

In the context of continuing secularization in Western society, it is hardly
surprising that some would draw the line at hospitality and justice advocacy, and
see anything beyond that as unacceptable. Before exploring mission strategies
appropriate to the new religious scene at sea, we will first examine the validity
of *maritime mission as such*. Late 20th century advocates of biblically based
mission among seafarers found themselves dealing with objections very similar
to those facing the first pioneers of such mission (Kverndal 1986, 531-541).
These objections have continued to follow three general lines of argument:

Was Maritime Mission "Impossible"?

Given the rising statistics and religious fervor of non-Christian religions,
was not mission among the seafaring followers of such faiths now virtually
impossible—and an exercise in futility? Already in the early 1980s, an editorial
in NAMMA's Newsletter (*Watermarks* April 1981, 1-2) set the stage for a
theological rebuttal on that score: Opposition to mission, persecution and
spiritual conflict were considered quite "normal" for the Christian church from
its very infancy (Eph. 6:11-113). The forces of evil had failed to prevent
Christ's atoning death from ever happening. Since that first Easter it seems
logical that those same forces would confuse the issue, rendering it seemingly

impossible or too costly to make the good news of that unique event available for all—whether on land or sea.

A later editorial found reason to follow up with a *historical* refutation of that same "impossibility" argument: The "new reality of religious pluralism" at sea was nothing "new" in the history of the Christian church. On the contrary—as attested by the biblical record in the Book of Acts—that church was never more engulfed by a whole host of other faiths than at its very outset. Yet never did the number of Christian believers multiply more rapidly. Nor was that contagious growth only due to the courage or charisma of those early Christians themselves. Rather (as Roland Allen underscores), it was then, and has since remained, a result of that unique feature of Christianity: the persuasive power of Christ's own Spirit, reinforcing the faithful witness of his followers wherever they "raise him up," by word or deed, as attested in John 12:32, 16:8-10; Acts 1:8 (*Watermarks* Dec. 1987, 1; Allen 1962).

Was Maritime Mission "Immoral"?

ICMA was only three years under way when chaplains, meeting at an East Asian Regional Conference in Hong Kong, in November 1972, were already discussing the "neglect" of the rising proportion of Asian seafarers, and the "problem" of communicating the gospel to people of a non-Christian tradition. It was not until 1985 that ICMA held its own first Plenary Conference in Asia. Here, they passed important resolutions on human rights, especially as these affected seafarers of the leading provider country, the Philippines (also the host of the Conference). However, no formal resolutions resulted from challenges raised by the mounting religious pluralism at sea.

For many Western participants, however, this Conference was the first time they had heard about two recently established, indigenous Korean maritime mission agencies, and the remarkable receptivity they had already encountered in their evangelization of fellow-Asian seafarers. This did not prevent a warning from a Western delegate that such activity could be "counter-productive." As time would tell, similar misgivings continued surfacing toward the end of the century, evidenced at ICMA and NAMMA conferences in 1999 and 2000.

In the contemporary climate of religious pluralism on shipboard, many equated the term "evangelism," even "mission" itself, with coercive "proselytism." They portrayed it as an intolerable "imposition," in conflict with a Christian ethic of neighbor love and respect for the convictions of others. Ironically, such arguments peaked toward the close of the 1990s, a period proclaimed by the primates of both the Catholic and Anglican Communions to be a "Decade of Evangelism."

In its original sense, the word "evangelism" simply means communicating good news—in this case the Christian gospel—making it freely available to all. Surprisingly perhaps, free access to the gospel alternative is also in harmony with a basic "postmodern" principle—to make things a matter of freedom of choice. Even more importantly, it constitutes a principle affirmed as fundamental to "the dignity and worth of the human person" in the *Universal Declaration of Human Rights,* passed by the General Assembly of the United Nations 10 December 1948. In the words of that document's Article 18:

> Everyone has the right to freedom of thought, conscience and religion; this right includes freedom to change his (her) religion or belief, and freedom, either alone or in community with others and in public or private, to manifest his (her) religion or belief in teaching, practice, worship and observance.

The subsequent Article goes on to protect *propagation* as a prerequisite to changing one's religion. It expressly includes the "freedom to seek, receive and impart information and ideas through any media and regardless of frontiers."

No one has been able to refute the sheer logic of that principle, just as that aspiring young Buddhist monk also came to see it. Moreover, the principle has to apply equally to all religions—Christian and non-Christian. Wherever a mission agenda is inherent to the core identity of any religious faith, its adherents must have equal freedom to pursue it—always provided they do so in a non-coercive manner and within the bounds of mutual respect for the basic human rights of others. Practice would be another matter, however. Two examples from NAMMA's newsletter, both quoting Asian voices, must suffice.

In 1985, *Watermarks* carried the keynote address at ICMA's Plenary Conference in the Philippines. Here, Rev. *Michael Chin,* at that time the Chinese-ethnic chaplain-director of the Anglicans' seafarers' center in Melbourne, Australia, made an impassioned plea for intentional evangelism in the context of holistic mission among his seafaring fellow-Asians:

> Change we must. And listen we must. But as we seek ways in which to bring the word and love of our Lord Jesus Christ to the world of the seafarer, let us not short-change them. That word must be declared and not just demonstrated. I hear them saying: 'Don't come on too strong. But don't be so fearful of affronting us that you don't confront us at all. You can give us all the affluence in the world. You can give us all the rights in the world. But if you don't give us the Gospel, you have given us nothing (*Watermarks* July 1985, 13).

In November 1989, *Watermarks* editorialized on the ICMA Conference held in Lagonissi, Greece, the first to focus primarily on "Christian Ministry in a Pluralistic World." Taking part was Rev. *Segundo Big-asan,* a Filipino and former Lutheran District President in Manila, now port chaplain there. Asked what he, once an animist, had found in Christ that animism could not give him, he replied with one word: "Forgiveness!" He then came with a counter-question that would remain unanswered: "Why should I withhold from my fellow-Asians what I've discovered only Christ can offer—forgiveness and new life, here and forever?" Maybe, the editorial continued, some of us could sense the Lord saying once again, as he did in ancient times: "*Let my people go!* My seafaring people, too. Let them go—without infringing on any of the human rights I have given them; above all, the right to choose the Gospel freely—and share it with others."

The keynote speaker at the same ICMA Conference, *Dr. D. G. Muldner,* a widely known Dutch Professor of Comparative Religion, reinforced that point further. Asked by one workshop leader if proliferating religious pluralism now meant the time had come for Christian seafarers' centers to include on staff emissaries of *non-Christian* religions, Muldner spoke plainly: "The person of Jesus Christ and the message of the Gospel are unique. We cannot help anyone by giving a mixed message." His conclusion was clear: the greater the religious *diversity,* the greater the need to present Christianity's *distinctiveness.* Anything less would be "basically immoral" (*Watermarks* Nov. 1989, 1).

Was Maritime Mission "Immaterial"?

If maritime mission is seen as not only possible but also manifestly moral, then to withhold the gospel from visiting seafarers would be a double betrayal—both of those seafarers and the author of that gospel. Nonetheless, there were, by the mid-1970s, still many who maintained that mission in the traditional sense was no longer relevant to the needs of the world, and therefore at best "unnecessary."

Understandably, concern generated by the WCC Assembly in Uppsala in 1968—for the "humanization" of society as the overriding objective of Christian mission—continued to find ready followers in a world replete with injustice and inequity. As a result, many joined the adherents of contemporary "Secular Theology," and plunged into "projects which might just as well—and more efficiently—be undertaken by secular agencies." Meanwhile, others still remained mired in the morass of missionary malaise that led to such "a terrible failure of nerve about the missionary enterprise" itself (Bosch 1991, 6-7).

In spite of this, the late 1960s were already showing signs of renewed concern for evangelism. These were partly a result of the "first love" of fast-growing churches in the non-Western world. Their participants made up a half of the 4,000 who met in 1974 in Lausanne, Switzerland, for the first "International Congress for World Evangelization" (Berentsen 1994, 146-150). Convened by the world's leading evangelist, Dr. *Billy Graham,* the "Lausanne Congress" would be the second of the 20th century's two most important events in the context of global mission. Vatican II, as the first of the two, had already marked the culmination of decades of struggle toward a rebirth of ecumenism in the Church Universal during the 1970s.

The climax of the Lausanne Congress was the unanimous adoption of the closing statement of commitment known as the *Lausanne Covenant.* The document's fifteen affirmations make up a theology of mission focused on the implementation, in today's world, of Christ's Great Commission to go make disciples of all nations (Mt. 28:18-20). As such, the Covenant would become a global rallying cry for biblically based mission into the new millennium. To quote the Chinese world mission leader, *Thomas Wang,* "The church scene at that time was like still water—without stirring. God threw a rock into the water and the spiritual ripple has been ever widening—until today it touches all the shores of the world."

That ripple effect left its mark on each of the three major manifestations of the Christian church. First, it led to a second such International Congress, this time held in Manila in the Philippines, in 1989. Second, many of the participants at Lausanne I came from churches affiliated with the WCC, leading to a revived WCC emphasis on the role of evangelism in world mission. Third, a similar dynamic developed in the Roman Catholic Church. Catholic delegates were warmly welcomed as observers at the 1974 Congress. This resulted in a joint document, *The Evangelical-Roman Catholic Dialogue on Mission 1977-1984* (ERCDOM). Here, "in a world of rising religious pluralism," they confessed together "the necessity of proclaiming the Gospel's call to repentance, faith and gathering of the people of God."

Making the Case for Authentic Maritime Mission

Only in the wider context of the Lausanne Covenant of 1974, as well as its aftermath, is it possible to interpret the renewed response to mission in the *maritime* world of the late 20th century. Of particular relevance to that response would prove to be the publication of two documents: *The Seafarers' Covenant* (1989) and *NAMMA's Statement of Mission* (1990).

The Seafarers' Covenant (1989)

The *Seafarers' Covenant* came about during the "Second International Congress for World Evangelization" ("Lausanne II") in Manila, July 10-20, 1989. This was the first major international global mission event at which the maritime dimension of that mission was part of the program. Participants originally agreed on the Seafarers' Covenant at workshops on "Seafarers' Mission" that formed a part of Program Track 690 on "Migrants." The text derived from a draft by the Author, who led the workshops together with his colleague, Rev. *Ray Eckhoff*, Chaplain-Director of Tacoma Seafarers' Center in the Pacific Northwest (*Watermarks* Nov. 1989, 6-8; Douglas 1990, 453-456).

Conceived as a maritime adaptation of the Lausanne Covenant of 1974, this document consists of an Introduction, followed by seven Affirmations and a Conclusion. Whereas the complete text of the Covenant appears as an Appendix (below), the parts dealing with two missiological implications of globalization are especially relevant in the present context: (1) Evangelism and Social Concern; (2) Evangelism and Other Faiths.

Evangelism and Social Concern: The document asserts in Affirmation #3 that Christian witness on the waterfront, in order to be credible, has to be *holistic*. Affirmation #5 goes on to address the gospel's "Social Imperative," in solidarity with the modern-day Seafarers' Rights Movement. It repudiates any form of polarization that may threaten a healthy balance between both evangelism and social responsibility.

Evangelism and Other Faiths: The arrival of religious pluralism in the globalized maritime workforce confronted the maritime mission community with a very different form of polarization: the dichotomy between *fundamentalism's* problem with unconditional love for those of other convictions, and *universalism's* apparent rejection of the need for the Christian gospel. The Covenant's text in Affirmations #3 and #5 focuses particularly on the latter of these two extremes. Fundamentalism's intolerance of other views runs so counter to a spirit of shipboard solidarity, that it has never gained ascendancy at sea. Nonetheless, one cannot discount it—least of all in today's globalized world. See Per Lönning's *Perspective* on the phenomenon (below).

In contrast to fundamentalism's intolerance of a rich *diversity* and universalism's intolerance of a distinctive *identity*, the *Seafarers' Covenant* sought to strike a biblical balance. In so doing, it reflected both the *inclusive universality* of the Gospel's offer of salvation for all, and the *exclusive uniqueness* of Jesus Christ as the source of that salvation. Dr. *Visser't Hooft* had a word for it. Asked what would be the major issue in missiology in the new millennium, he replied without hesitation: "The uniqueness of Christ. If Jesus is not unique, there is no gospel!" (IBMR April 1989, 1).

NAMMA's Statement of Mission (1990)

By 1990, a climate of convergence around the relationship between ecumenism and evangelism was apparent in North American maritime mission, much as it had been at Lausanne II in 1989. Following a comprehensive canvas of members' views, NAMMA unanimously adopted the resulting document at the 1990 North American Maritime Ministry Conference in New Orleans. Soon to be known as *NAMMA's Statement of Mission (NASOM)*, the wording was primarily the product of its principle promoter, NAMMA's President (later Monsignor) *James Dillenburg* and his Catholic consultant-theologian, in cooperation with the Author (a Lutheran) as NAMMA's Executive Secretary.

Five years earlier, the organization had prepared the way by agreeing on a statement entitled *Purposes and Responsibilities of ICOSA.* Authored by Dr. James Whittemore, Dillenburg's Anglican-affiliated predecessor as President, that document represented the first time any cooperative agency for maritime mission had encoded an unequivocal commitment to social justice for seafarers—in terms of their "welfare, dignity, safety and wellbeing."

In its 1990 Statement of Mission, NAMMA not only reinforced that affirmation. It paralleled it with a corresponding commitment to credible evangelism. The document called for the implementation of a biblically balanced, ecumenical and holistic understanding of *Christ's Great Commission* in Matthew 28:18-20, as the core of authentic maritime mission and ministry. It affirmed the Great Commission as "Jesus' own Statement of Mission." It endorsed "a human solidarity that respects plurality of cultures and peoples, and which can be enriched by dialogue with persons of other faiths." For the full text of NASOM 1990, see *Appendices* (below).

NAMMA's 1990 manifesto ends with the following words: "Agreement in essentials, freedom in non-essentials, love in everything!" Certainly, in comparing the *Seafarers' Covenant* with *NASOM*, it was difficult to find anything but agreement in essentials. In effect, these two documents together made up a vindication of maritime mission on each of the three counts where it had been called into question. As a Lutheran professor of systematic theology, Dr. *Carl Braaten*, puts it: "If the Christian church does not evangelize the billions who have not yet heard the Good News, there is no one else in the world to do it" (Braaten 1992). This was, of course, equally true of the Church Maritime. Mission as such—including maritime mission—remains integral to the very identity of the Christian faith.

The principal challenge would now be to develop an effective *strategy*—for maritime mission at this point in history. The final decade of the 20th century would mean even more turmoil and change. Internally, NAMMA, a major participant in global maritime mission, would come close to foundering from lack of an effective code of collegial ethics. Externally, factors like increasing exploitation of seafarers, massive geo-political upheavals, as well as mounting militancy among major world religions, all would now take center stage, thereby profoundly affecting both the status and outlook for maritime mission by the beginning of the new millennium.

A PARTNERSHIP PARADIGM FROM BELOW

"I want baptize to Jesus!" The Chinese seafarer from a freighter in port was clearly in a hurry; but he knew what he wanted, as he entered the local seafarers' center. "Wonderful," said the chaplain, "but first I shall have to make sure you have the necessary instruction." Pointing urgently to his watch, the seafarer responded, "But ship leave in half hour!" He then explained how he had picked up a Christian radio station during the passage across the Pacific. Here he had heard to his astonishment of a Jesus who had paid with his life on a cruel cross for the sins of not only him but everybody else. Now he wanted to make sure he could qualify. The chaplain, to his relief, remembered how the Apostle Philip had confronted a corresponding question from another stranger on the move many centuries ago, in that case an Ethiopian court official (Acts 8:26-41).

After baptizing the sailor, the chaplain sent with him a New Testament and some beginner's Bible study correspondence materials, all in Chinese, with spare copies for others on board who might also be interested. A few months later the ship was back. No less than nine seafarers had completed the course, and four of these now wanted to be baptized. In effect, a genuine cell church, or "Small Christian Community," had been born on that ship.

This was no isolated incident. It revealed certain salient features characteristic of the kind of seafarer-centered paradigm of mission "from below," emerging as the most viable evangelism strategy in this new Global Era. Tracing the evolution of that paradigm calls for a two-stage approach: first, the historic role of "Small Christian Communities" in the church at large; second, the development of "Maritime Christian Communities" as a corresponding seafarer-centered paradigm of ministry.

Small Christian Communities

Early Church "Sodalities"

James O'Halloran, an Irish, ordained member of the Salesian order, traces the origins of "Small Christian Communities" to Christ himself:

> They have their origins in the itinerant community that trod the dusty roads of Palestine with Jesus in the gathering of the early Christians which formed in Jerusalem after the first Pentecost (cf. Acts 2:42-47; 4:32-37), and in all those groups that sprang up in the gentile world largely as a result of Paul's work (O'Halloran 1996, 13).

O'Halloran agrees with most historians that a "sea-change" came about with the conversion of Constantine who, in 313 AD, decreed Christianity to be the state religion of the Roman Empire. From then on, O'Halloran points out, the Christian church changed from a "communitarian" model to a predominantly "hierarchical" one. The earlier model, based on grassroots communities meeting in house churches, came "from below" amidst the pressures of pluralism and persecution. The Book of Acts is full of evidence of how those cell groups provided the power needed for the proliferation of the New Testament Church. With the coming of a hierarchical model of "top-down" church leadership, Christianity became the fashionable religion of the Empire—and much of its vitality vanished. Membership was now nominal, witnessing became blunted, "and the Church has never been quite the same" (O'Halloran 2002, 166-172).

Nevertheless, the vision of the church as a community was never lost. The American missiologist, Dr. *Ralph Winter,* distinguishes between "two redemptive structures of God's mission"—sodalities and modalities—both of them evident even in the very earliest New Testament Church. The term *sodality* (a "companionship") is used for the successor to Jesus' original itinerant community—Paul's "Missionary Band" structure. This intimate form of fellowship would come to include committed Christians like Barnabas, Mark, Silas, Luke, Lydia, Priscilla, Aquila, and many more. The term *modality* (a method "laid down") is used of the inclusive "New Testament Church" structure, as this evolved from institutional forms such as those glimpsed in the earliest congregations in Jerusalem, Antioch and elsewhere in the Book of Acts.

Winter emphasizes the interdependence between the two structures, despite their mutual tension. In the post-Constantine Medieval Church, it was the sodality-type monastic orders, led by Irish Celtic mission pioneers, which "more than any other force" would contribute to the evangelization of Europe during its Dark Ages. Following the Reformation's dissolution of the monastic movement, the 18th century saw the revival of the communitarian concept— through the "small churches" of the German-Lutheran Pietist Movement and the "class" network of Britain's Methodist Revival. The ensuing upsurge of Protestant sodality-like voluntary mission societies resulted in the 19th century missionary advance known as "The Great Century" (Winter 1999, 220-230).

Modern-Day "House Churches"

In the latter half of the 20th century, there was a remarkable renewal of communitarian Christianity—this time in predominantly Catholic Latin America. Hundreds of thousands of *Base Ecclesial Communities* (BECs) had emerged by the 1980s. These grassroots groups sought to relate the Bible to "basic" human needs. They were "ecclesial" because they functioned as an alternative church within the institutional Catholic Church. They were "communities" in a common commitment to the "kingdom" priorities of Christ, especially his "preferential option for the poor" (Mt. 6:33, Lk. 4:18-19).

The movement spread quickly among marginalized people polarized by glaring social inequities. *Gustave Guiterrez,* a Peruvian priest, provided the theological rationale for the movement with his Liberation Theology. Though more conservative-leaning members of the Catholic hierarchy initially branded this theology as Marxist-influenced, the movement had come to stay. As BECs became a catalyst for church renewal throughout Latin America, they eventually won conditional Vatican approval. Soon they also spread to other continents and other denominations through *Ecumenical Base Communities* (EBCs). In many ways, these cell churches would parallel the explosive growth of "house churches" in Communist China.

David Bosch sums up the social dynamic of Liberation Theology, and its various models of small "intentional" communities, as promoting the empowerment of mission from below. As such, it represents a reversal of the Enlightenment legacy of "objectification*,"* seeing certain categories of fellow-humans as objects or mere means toward a perceived purpose. Historian and futurist, Dr. *Riane Eisler* elaborates on the wider, sociological context in her recent book on *The Power of Partnership.* She shows how, in all human relationships, a "top-down" model of domination inevitably leads to discrimination and exploitation. By contrast, a team-based partnership paradigm "from below" allows for both a free flow of communication and maximum participation (Eisler 2002).

In harnessing that "power of partnership" in the cause of Christian mission, nothing can compare with the role of Small Christian Communities through the first two millennia of the Church Universal. Nowhere does that apply more conspicuously than in the itinerant context of the seafaring world and the ongoing history of the *Church Maritime.* The most recent research in the field of maritime missiology clearly confirms this conclusion.

Maritime Christian Communities (MCCs)

Their Relevance

Around 1820, during the heyday of the early Bethel Movement, a recently converted sailor, questioned about his irrepressible enthusiasm for sharing the gospel, had this explanation: *"I just cannot go to heaven alone!"* Those words reflect the compelling concern for others generated by discovering the depth of Christ's love on the cross, as depicted in 2 Corinthians 5:14-15. That level of spirituality constitutes the very core of Christian discipleship characteristic of Small Christian Communities everywhere, and not least at sea.

By the mid-1970s, a dual gravitational shift within the seafaring world was making *Maritime Christian Communities* not only relevant but indispensable. As "Asianization" of the maritime workforce gathered momentum, so did the new phenomenon of religious pluralism at sea. Meanwhile, reduced turn-around times for ships in port, coupled with the frequent relocation of port terminals to remote areas, were already resulting in a loss of contact opportunities ashore, between ship's crews and shore-based maritime ministry personnel.

Both of these trends enhanced the relevance of MCC-based seafaring partners in ministry. ICMA's early leadership could confirm that conclusion: MtS General Secretary *Tom Kerfoot* emphasized that the new context of port logistics called for a combined seafarer/agency partnership paradigm—"with by far the greater part of the effective pastoral and missionary work done by seafarers themselves at sea." Kerfoot's counterpart in the AOS at the Vatican, *Francis Frayne*, emphasized that the current "startling shift" toward religious pluralism at sea meant that Christian seafarers must now be encouraged to recognize their own responsibility as "heralds of Christ in their journeyings across the oceans of the world."

A paper published later by IASMM summarized a dual sea-based strategy for fulfilling those inseparable functions of mission anywhere—holistic outreach and spiritual nurture, both built on the biblical principle of "the priesthood of all believers":

> In the current context of maritime mission, each of them take on a particular note of urgency: (1) *Shipboard peer ministry,* with seafarers witnessing to fellow-seafarers through their daily walk of life is the only means by which most of today's non-Christian Two Thirds World seafarers can be reached with a contextualized offer of the Gospel. (2) *Shipboard fellowship groups,* as an expression of Christian community at sea is an absolute necessity, if any new-born Christian is to find the strength to be an effective witness, or even survive—in the sub-culture of the 'total institution' known as a ship (Kverndal 1994, 11).

Their History

Nothing can quite compare with the growth of Maritime Christian Communities at the height of the Bethel Movement in the 1820s. Without those intrepid trailblazers and the Bethel emblem they rallied around, available resources in funds and personnel would have been unequal to the daunting task of maritime evangelism and follow-up on such a global scale.

What had begun as a sodality-like, spontaneous movement gradually evolved into institutions. Ship captains, with their status of absolute authority, led the way in forming their own organized associations. These were nondenominational and affiliated with the BFSS and ASFS. By the year 1900, more than one thousand shipmasters were active members on the British side alone. Often the words "Bethel" and "Brotherhood" would form part of an association's name. In addition to adopting a Bethel-linked emblem, they would subscribe to a "rule of life," committing to a consistent walk of faith and witness in relation to both fellow seafarers and others.

The latter part of the 19th century also saw the development of denominational associations—among the Anglicans, the Scandinavian Lutherans and later also the Catholics. By the turn of the century, such associations would include other ranks as well. Nonetheless, the combined effect of devastation and secularization in the wake of World War I took its toll. After half a century of regression, the whole MCC movement lapsed into a state of dormancy, with only few exceptions.

Finally, beginning in the 1960s, sporadic signs of new life began to appear. In 1968, what was now the British Sailors' Society (BSS) merged its fellowship with that of the Anglican MtS, into one multi-denominational organization called *The Seafarers' Fellowship.* The hope was that the resulting synergism would ignite new energy. Meanwhile, a nondenominational, British-based *Merchant Navy Christian Fellowship,* inaugurated in 1959, merged with an earlier officers' fellowship in 1962. Also during the 1960s, the Norwegian Seamen's Mission made a concerted effort to promote a renewal of the Norwegian version of the seafarers' fellowship movement (a work with which the Author was personally involved).

The global maritime scene was, however, about to change. While non-Western seafarers were already more numerous, existing (Western-world) maritime Christian associations seemed unable to see, much less adjust to, the ethnic revolution that was now well under way. There were also signs of an over-dependence on shore-based chaplaincy. By 1988, after 20 years of struggle, the MtS and BSS found it was time for their joint Seafarers' Fellowship project to be "respectfully laid to rest," as their last newsletter put it. In 1989, the remaining network of the Merchant Navy Christian Fellowship merged into the Seamen's Christian Friend Society. In Norway, veterans of the national-ethnic "Brotherhood of the Sea" decided to make Christian-based, preliminary maritime education the focus of their efforts.

The New Bethel Movement

The Korea-Tacoma Connection

By the 1980s, prospects of any renewed seagoing Christian fellowship movement might have seemed bleak. Yet, it was simply darkest before dawn. Significantly, the first light to appear was in the East, as a spontaneous seagoing cell-group movement took shape—at first mostly among Korean seafarers.

The fact that the Koreans led the way was no accident. By the 1970s, the growing Christian minority movement in South Korea was already breaking out of its nationalistic, mono-cultural mindset. In 1974, Korean Christians sent a strong delegation to the First International Congress on World Evangelization in Lausanne. In Seoul that same year, a group of church leaders formed what would become the *Korea Harbor Evangelism* (KHE), the first indigenous maritime mission agency in the non-Western world, founded as a joint maritime and world mission venture. It is the confluence of these two mission events—the Lausanne Congress and the founding of the KHE—that point out the year 1974 as a distinctive starting-point for the new Global Era of Maritime Mission.

By this time, Korean seafarers' openness to the gospel—and their enthusiasm for spreading it—had begun to impress seafarers' chaplains everywhere. By the late 1970s, noticeable numbers of small groups of Korean Christian crewmembers were already making a practice of meeting each in their own designated "holy place" on board—set apart for Bible study, fellowship and prayer. One of those on whom this phenomenon made a deep impression was a newly appointed Lutheran port chaplain in the Pacific Northwest.

Rev. *Ray Eckhoff* (1930-2000) had become Chaplain-Director of the Tacoma Seafarers' Center in 1976. Like so many of his colleagues before him, he felt at first frustrated by the constant rupture of promising pastoral contacts every time a ship cast off again. Not finding any Bible correspondence course especially written with seafarers in mind, Eckhoff set about preparing one. It consisted of a series of ten bible-based booklets, presenting a primer in the Christian faith, translated into the principal languages of non-Western seafarers of the day. By checking it first with a wide range of colleagues, including Catholics, he tried to make the manuscript as nondenominational as possible.

Eckhoff went on to make the series the center-piece of a *Ministering Seafarers' Program* (MSP). Launched in 1977, the MSP was in many ways reminiscent of G. C. Smith's "Naval Correspondence Mission" in the early 1800s. Essentially a strategy for pastoral follow-up and discipleship training among seafarers—through individualized counseling by mail—the stated objective was two-fold: first, to promote their own spiritual growth; second, to equip them to minister to their peers and, where possible, initiate an onboard fellowship group. The resulting Maritime Christian Community would then elect one of their own to the role of coordinator and Bible study/worship leader.

Eckhoff emphasized the program as a *Multiplication Ministry,* following Paul's plan in 2. Timothy 2:2. This biblical principle of "spiritual reproduction" was already the cornerstone of an international Bible study movement, the

Navigators. Its founder, *Dawson Trotman,* had coached one single sailor on a US battleship on how to share the faith with his shipmates, one at a time, and then obtain a commitment to go and do likewise. By the time she went down at Pearl Harbor in 1941, 125 had made such a commitment on board that ship, while many more would follow suit on others (Skinner 1974).

Another component of the Ministering Seafarers' Program was enlisting *inter-agency cooperation.* As colleagues began seeing the benefits of the whole concept, Eckhoff would coordinate reports of seafarers willing to serve. He would then distribute the resulting "Ship Lists" online to hundreds of colleagues worldwide, regardless of denomination. This he did for almost two decades, receiving constant confirmation, from Catholics to Southern Baptists, about their value as a shipvisiting tool.

As for the Korean scene, the KHE continued with its primary focus— outreach to *international* seafarers. Meanwhile, another indigenous Korean nondenominational agency came on the scene, in this case oriented toward fellow-ethnic *Korean* seafarers. The *Korean Seamen's Mission* (KSM) commenced in 1982, based in the nation's premier port city of Pusan. After developing a worldwide network of affiliates known as "Branches," the agency changed its name in 1996 to *Korea International Maritime Mission* (KIMM).

Most active among the latter agency's founders was a group of dedicated young Christians who had intentionally trained as merchant navy officers in order to serve as "Sea Missionaries," maintaining their daily vocations as maritime "tentmakers." Having themselves been involved in the MCC Movement among Korean seafarers, they continued to make contact with Korea's maritime colleges and other training facilities a major priority. Their leader was a former fisher and converted Buddhist, *Jonah Won Jong Choi,* now an ordained Presbyterian pastor and eventually Doctor of Ministry.

Results were remarkable. By the mid-1980s, KIMM (then still known as KSM) could report over 2,000 committed seafaring members, with active fellowship groups on over 500 ships. Not surprisingly, a special cooperative relationship resulted between KIMM and Tacoma Seafarers' Center. After working out of that center as its North American base of operations from the mid-1980s, KIMM was, in 2003, able to acquire its own "Mission Home" in Edmonds, near Seattle, for this purpose.

Meanwhile, other Asian seafarers, too, were responding to the Tacoma-based Ministering Seafarers' Program, not least Filipinos, who now represented the largest group in the international maritime workforce. By the late 1980s, Asian-ethnic MCCs had convincingly proved their viability as a source of spiritual renewal and self-multiplication at sea.

International and Interdenominational Coordination
Among the different denominations that were showing renewed interest in lay ministry at sea during the 1980s were not least the Catholics. In 1982, the Vatican endorsed a program for training and commissioning active seafarers as *Extraordinary Ministers of the Eucharist Aboard Ship* (EMEs). Largely the

brainchild of Msgr. *James Dillenburg,* then National Director of the AOS/USA, it built on the renewed emphasis on lay ministry engendered by Vatican II. The designation derived from the unique doctrine of the Eucharist in the Catholic Church. Following a pilot project on the Great Lakes, prospects for wider acceptance increased with a *Fellowship Ministry Program* started by *Karen Lai* in Galveston, Texas, in 1992. Lai would become the first Catholic laywoman publicly appointed a "Port Chaplain." (See her *Perspective* below.)

Also during the 1980s, the Southern Baptist Seafarers' Ministers' Fellowship endorsed a program of *Christian Seafarers' Bible Fellowships.* Originally developed during the 1970s by a Chinese-ethnic port chaplain, Rev. *Yun Young* of Philadelphia, it focused especially on Filipino seafarers. Several hundred such Bible-studying fellowship groups developed, thanks in large measure to Yong's personal commitment to the project.

It was obvious that ethnic change was now opening up the possibility for a renewal of maritime ecumenicity—or a major missed opportunity. Capitalizing on the situation, Ray Eckhoff took the initiative, in 1984, to establish an *International Coordinating Committee for Maritime Follow-up Ministry* (ICCMFM). Besides providing a forum for shared concerns, ICCMFM also made it a priority to advocate for ICMA to take over this responsibility.

THE QUEST FOR IMPLEMENTATION

In December 1988, an editorial in NAMMA's newsletter *Watermarks* carried the following headline: "Seafarers' Fellowship—No Goodbye but a New Beginning!" After contrasting the virtual demise of Western-world seafarers' fellowships with the current spontaneous upsurge of their Asian-ethnic counterparts, the editorial summarized the situation with this challenge:

> Yes, we may have to say goodbye to forms of fellowship no longer relevant to the changing context of seafaring. But never to the concept! If we are serious about *Christian ministry in a pluralistic world* (the theme of ICMA's Plenary Conference next year), we will have to intentionally focus at future conferences on how to promote witnessing and worshiping fellowship at sea. That is, if we claim (with the Apostles' Creed) to believe in "the communion of saints." Both shore-based ones—and the seafaring kind.

Time for Reappraisal

The opportunity for ICMA to rise to the challenge did, in fact, present itself, at ICMA's 6th Plenary Conference in Lagonissi, Greece, in 1989. Here, a multi-denominational group of ICCMFM-affiliated chaplains from the Pacific Northwest, with the assistance of MtS General Secretary Bill Down, presented a resolution worded as follows: "To establish a multi-lingual, ecumenically-based fellowship of Christian seafarers under the auspices of ICMA."

The text made reference to the agreement originally reached in 1978 at ICMA/New York. There, Bill Down had underscored the need for ICMA, as"the most appropriate body" to organize an ecumenical Seafarers' Fellowship, since there was "no more effective instrument of evangelization than a dedicated Christian life." The resolution passed unanimously. Nonetheless, even though ICMA's plenary had now endorsed the concept of an ICMA-linked fellowship structure *in principle,* there was not yet agreement in ICMA's executive leadership on its details *in practice.*

For their part, chaplains affiliated with ICCMFM re-committed themselves to keeping the concept alive until the right formula could be found. The *Apostleship of the Sea* (AOS) and the new maritime mission research agency, the *International Association for the Study of Maritime Mission* (IASMM), founded in 1990, would soon be joining them in this process of reappraisal.

The Role of AOS/1992 in Houston, Texas

Peter Anson, as co-founder of the AOS in 1920, was unequivocal about its initial intent: The Apostleship of the Sea is not primarily an organization *for seafarers*, but essentially *of seafarers*, where every seafaring member is trained to become "an Apostle among his shipmates." In the post-Vatican II context of greater ecumenical awareness, there was growing recognition of the bond between believers in Christ *beyond* denominational boundaries—at sea just as ashore. In 1988, the Vatican-based *AOS Information Bulletin* (No. 20) addressed the need to train "apostolically activated Christian animators" on board ship, promoting "Christian community at sea," internationally.

The AOS showed it was undeterred by current ICMA inaction, making Christian peer ministry and fellowship at sea the central emphasis of its upcoming AOS XIX World Congress in Houston, Texas, in 1992. With the theme "Christian Living Aboard Ship," the AOS invited a wide spectrum of observers from other denominations. Archbishop *Giovanni Cheli,* President of the AOS, concluded the Congress with the following challenge, in a paper on the relationship between the Apostleship of the Sea and the Church Universal:

> "Is it sufficient for ICMA to bring together the officials of organ-
> izations responsible for the pastoral ministry of seafarers from
> different churches? Or should one not think in terms of *establishing
> concrete bonds of fellowship between all seafarers who desire it?"*

At the Congress, Msgr. *Francois Le Gall* of the AOS Secretariat shared with the Author (as a delegate of the Lutheran World Federation) his personal perspective on the issue: "Sometimes," he said, "the Lord seems to use extraordinary circumstances as a kind of *locomotive* for the challenges of change. Just as on a battlefield in war, so too in the context of a ship at sea, witness is not ultimately a matter of denomination. You do what you need to do as a Christian. Without denying our denominational identity, we can see how the

Lord is trying to 'pull' us like a locomotive to the higher loyalty we share as followers of Christ."

The Role of IASMM's 1994 Research Papers

The origins and current implications of both "Maritime Christian Fellowship" and "Maritime Follow-up Ministry" became the first research project of the 1990 newcomer, the *International Association for the Study of Maritime Mission* (IASMM). The first issue of IASMM's journal, *Maritime Mission Studies,* carried papers on those two closely interrelated topics—an area never previously the subject of comprehensive academic research (Kverndal 1994; Eckhoff 1994).

The first of these studies identified possible reasons for an often recurring reluctance against actual involvement. Given the widely recognized validity of sea-borne Christian community in *principle,* it seemed likely there had to be certain inhibitive factors in *practice.* The study suggests a series of six possible factors—theological, ecclesiological, psychological, sociological, historical and practical.

Despite any such inhibitive dynamic, the study pointed out that, by the mid-1990s, the ongoing process of reappraisal was resulting in a new consensus and the possibility of a two-fold fellowship structure. The proposed concept consisted of primary membership in a specific *confessional* fellowship, coupled with simultaneous membership in a general *multi-confessional* fellowship.

No one faced a deeper dilemma in this issue than the Roman Catholics. On the one hand, they would be bound by the centrality of the mass and the integrity of the "magisterium" (teaching authority) of the church. On the other hand, in the spirit of post-Vatican II ecumenism, they would want to affirm authentic fellowship with non-Catholic fellow believers in Christ as both Savior and Lord. At the same time, there was a growing recognition within their own ranks that Catholic Lay Eucharistic Ministers could never alone meet the urgent need for inclusive, supra-denominational Christian communities on shipboard in today's multi-cultural context at sea.

As early as in 1990, Dillenburg's predecessor at the Vatican AOS Secretariat, Msgr. *John O'Shea,* in a letter to the Author, had predicted the formation of an *International Seafarers' Christian Fellowship* as a future umbrella organization. With this, he suggested, an *International AOS Fellowship* organization could then be affiliated, "provided care be taken not to infringe on the Catholic character" of such an AOS entity.

Two Major Distractions

There was general agreement that ICMA would inevitably have to play a crucial, coordinative role. In the course of the 1990s, however, two distracting factors would surface—the first associated with seafarers' human rights, the second with NAMMA. As for the former, while cases of flagrant injustice continued to multiply into the 1990s, the Christian maritime ecumene had no option but to close ranks in a concerted campaign of solidarity with abused seafarers anywhere and everywhere. This called for the prioritization of industry-wide systemic change.

At the same time, NAMMA found itself embroiled in two debilitating crises in the mid-1990s. No sooner had a collegial ethics conflict erupted when serious electoral irregularities further threatened the organization's integrity. The incident that precipitated the first of these crises took place in December 1993, and resulted in an eight month period of unparalleled "internal conflict and strife." According to the subsequent official report, a letter severely critical of a fellow-member of NAMMA's board had been circulated by "certain officers and members of the board." The gravity of the allegations eventually became public and led to legal action. The Board left it to NAMMA's Vice President at the time, Rev. *Theodore E. Mall*, to promote a process of disclosure and reconciliation. This he did, with firmness and fairness (*IASMM Newsletter* Autumn 1995, 10-11).

As for NAMMA's electoral crisis, this resulted from alleged improprieties during the 1994 NAMMA Annual Assembly in New York. Once more, Mall's negotiating skills were enlisted to chart a course of action. This resulted in an impartial investigation and recommendation for change by the New York Center for Seafarers' Rights. NAMMA deserves credit for fairness in its journey toward self-healing from both crises. One who helped promote that journey was also Bishop *Bill Down*. At NAMMA's 1995 Conference in Toronto, hosted by Rev. *David Mulholland*, Down shared invaluable insights on conflict resolution and personal renewal (see Appendix #4 below).

Despite these delays, as the year 2000 approached, there were signs of renewed concern for peer ministry and Christian community-building at sea. Central would be those fundamental issues for maritime mission in any age, the *identity issue* (integrity of purpose) and the *strategy issue* (efficacy of practice). Here, ICMA, NAMMA and IASMM would each come to play important roles.

Reaffirming Christian Identity

ICMA/1999 in South Africa

By the year 1999, the identity and basic purpose of maritime mission itself had become the most pressing issue in the maritime ministry community. This was apparent at ICMA's 8th Plenary Conference in Durban/Drakensberg, South Africa, that year. A keynote speaker, Chaplain *Jurie Van Zyl,* affiliated with the post-apartheid South African Navy, confronted the issue head-on:

> "As a Christian," he asked, "am I flying a *Religious Flag of Convenience?* This is actually what I'm doing when I try to 'cross over' to another culture, in a well-meant attempt to inculturate the gospel without first 'lashing down' who I am—in other words [revealing my] *identity*. I will then be most likely 'washed over-board,' and lose everything in the process. The same goes for an organization like ICMA. It will be self-defeating if ICMA assumes it has fulfilled its obligation to Christ's Great Commission in Matthew

28 simply by calling itself 'Christian.' Unless ICMA confirms its
self-understanding in terms of a clear Bible-based *identity,* backed by
an authentic *spirituality,* it will confuse or even alienate exactly those
who have a right to know. Still more tragically, it will 'miss the boat'
in a post-modern age with boundless opportunities for the gospel"
(*IASMM Newsletter* Winter 1999/2000, 10-11).

In the lively discussion that followed, no-one could directly deny the logic
of that line of argument. One delegate nevertheless alleged that if ICMA became
involved with *evangelism,* this would inhibit *ecumenism* and "that would be the
end of ICMA." To this another delegate countered that non-coercive evangelism
does not *negate* ecumenism, but *necessitates* it—as confirmed by Christ himself
in John 17:21. Others, too, expressed strong views, making it quite evident that
ICMA as such was not at this point prepared to take up the issue of a
comprehensive mission statement comparable to the one that NAMMA had
produced in 1990.

What ICMA/1999 did achieve was to provide a prelude for the dramatic
developments that would unfold through the next three annual conferences of
ICMA's North American co-founder NAMMA. Here, participants would
witness an apparent attempt to resurrect the familiar "Immoral Argument"
against the very concept of evangelism, one which had never been conclusively
laid to rest since it first began to reassert itself in the mid-1980s.

NAMMA Debates and IASMM Research Papers

NAMMAC/2000 in Port Everglades, Florida, set the stage and
determined the shape of the ensuing debate. With the current "new" level of
religious diversity, some participants in Florida maintained that *multi-
denominational* cooperation (i.e. with other Christians) must now give way to
multi-faith cooperation (i.e. with non-Christian religions). This would mean
departing from the historic understanding of "ecumenism." More importantly,
for individual agencies it would have two further far-reaching implications: (1)
For the agency's ministry staff, it would mean the inclusion of *non-Christian co-
workers* (Muslim, Buddhist, Hindu, etc.). (2) For the agency's agenda, it would
mean the elimination of *evangelism.*

In the fall of 2000, IASMM published a paper entitled *Time for Clarity.*
Taking the Florida "multi-faith" initiative seriously, it identified the polarizing
effect of the "new" dichotomy now emerging between anti-ecumenism and anti-
evangelism. Instead, it concluded with an appeal for *convergence,* through "a
combined commitment to *both* ecumenism and evangelism—in a context of
biblically balanced holism, with Christ's Great Commission as "the core
distinctive of Christian identity."

The next Spring, IASSM published a "Position Paper" that reinforced that
conclusion. Put together by a broad ad hoc group of 45 co-signatories
identifying themselves as "members or friends of NAMMA," it carried the title
Historical Background, Analysis and Proposals. It referred to a NAMMA
Committee's "Proposed New Constitution and Bylaws," scheduled to be voted

on at NAMMAC/2001 in June that year. The Position Paper focused on the proposal's two most sweeping innovations, both based on the Florida "multi-faith" initiative: (1) Removing any distinctively *Christian identity* from its current Constitution and Statement of Mission. (2) Expressly opening NAMMA's *voting membership* to those of any faith—or no faith.

The Position Paper documented how these two proposed changes would violate both "the substance and the spirit" of the organization's historic identity. The document was, on request, coordinated by Rev. Theodore Mall, and posted on the "Maritime World" web-site of Mall Publishing's Maritime Library Division. Shortly afterwards, the paper was distributed at NAMMAC/2001 in Corpus Christi, Texas. As a result, participants requested withdrawing the original draft of the new Constitution and Bylaws for revision and re-presentation the following year.

NAMMAC/2002 in Quebec, Canada, finally saw sufficient convergence to pass a new NAMMA Constitution and Bylaws. From now on, an abbreviated version of the organization's "Statement of Mission" would read as follows:

> NAMMA is an ecumenical Christian association of individuals and organizations in maritime ministry. NAMMA assists with spiritual, moral, justice, and physical concerns of seafarers and all others in the maritime community. NAMMA is open to inter-religious cooperation and dialog.   .

This version constituted a compromise between widely divergent views. It neither reiterated nor rejected key components of NAMMA's Statement of Mission of 1990. Nevertheless, it did clearly affirm that most fundamental factor—an unconditionally Christian identity. Also, it expressly included references to justice issues and inter-religious dialogue—two concerns both strongly emphasized in the 1990 version.

The passing of NAMMA's new organizational framework was in large part attributable to the perseverance of the association's new Executive Secretary, Rev. Dr. *Peter R. Michaelson.* After his nine-year turn at the helm of NAMMA (1991-2000), Dr. Paul Chapman stepped down at NAMMAC/2000 in Florida, where he was recognized for his pioneer role in the field of Seafarers' Human Rights. When Michaelson (an Anglican) came on board from the beginning of 2001, he brought with him expertise in another important field— ecumenical relations. After NAMMAC/2002, he made the following observation on the outcome of the protracted reorganization process he had inherited:

> This was hammered out by many people . . . . Perhaps the only remaining disagreement in NAMMA about it results from tension between evangelism and mutual respect of tradition [or ecumenism]. If we must have tension among us, that is a good one to have, since Christ commands us to do both (*Waterlines* Fall 2002, 6).

Michaelson predicted that this would "not be the end" of NAMMA's process of change. Among issues as yet unresolved was that of *membership eligibility.* Participants at NAMMAC/2002 let the issue of non-Christian membership eligibility remain unchanged for the present. As noted above, ICMA once had to confront a very similar dilemma. It chose to maintain the integrity of its Christian identity by not opening up decision-making membership to those unable or unwilling to commit to that identity. At the same time, ICMA invited participation and collaboration in regard to all parties engaged in welfare work among seafarers (*ICMA and Other Faiths,* IASMM Occasional Papers, No. 3). How NAMMA, as a cofounder and member of ICMA, will eventually resolve this matter remains to be seen.

Meanwhile, in light of NAMMA's constitutional reaffirmation of "inter-religious cooperation and dialogue" in 2002, it was noteworthy that the very next year, NAMMAC/2003 in Oakland, California, would convene under the theme "Biblical Dialogue with Other Faiths." Approaching inter-religious dialogue from an intentionally *biblical* perspective met a warm welcome by many, who saw it as evidence of a new trend toward convergence.

Recommitting to Sea-Based Strategies

If convergence around the issue of identity was giving ground for hope, even more so were indications of resurgence in promoting crew-based peer ministry and Christian community at sea. For many, NAMMAC/1999 in Seattle/Tacoma in the Pacific Northwest had been a "wake-up call" about the significance of ship-based ministry. This conference was the first opportunity for the wider maritime ministry community to connect first-hand with the Tacoma home base of Chaplain-Director *Ray Eckhoff* and his Ministering Seafarers' Program. The following year, this pioneer figure in the revival of modern-day maritime follow-up ministry passed away, leaving others to build on his legacy.

At ICMA/1999 in South Africa, *Peter McEwen,* Deputy General Secretary of the British merchant navy officers' union NUMAST, concluded his keynote address on "the shipping industry" with some candid comments on the future shape of maritime ministry. With dramatically less turn-around time in port, he could foresee "a sharp reduction" in *center* usage. This trend would "force Missions back to their original purpose," focusing less on *center-based* welfare delivery and more on facilitating *ship-based* services. These latter could consist of either appointing *professional ship's chaplains*—for seagoing (on-board) welfare ministry, or training *lay crew-members*—to be available as "conduits" for welfare services among their fellow seafarers (*ICMA Plenary Conference Report 1999,* 67).

The Professional "Sailing Chaplains" Model
The model mentioned first by McEwen was also the subject of a 1999 ICMA Conference paper on *Sailing Chaplains,* offered by Rev. *Kurt Edlund* of

the Finnish Seamen's Mission. Since his personal pioneering of the concept in 1983, the workforce had now grown to two full-time employees plus a roster of 60 parish pastors serving as part-time sailing chaplains on practically half the Finnish flag fleet. According to Edlund, their task was to serve as a kind of ambulating *welfare officer,* each living and working "side by side" with a particular ship's crew in their own daily environment.

Among seafarers themselves and their unions, the response had been consistently positive. Shipping companies, too, had begun contributing substantially toward this documented enhancement of their own corporate quality of service. This Finnish initiative would constitute a key component in a comprehensive study by the Cardiff-based Seafarers' International Research Centre (SIRC). Known as the *Sailing Chaplains Project,* and commissioned in 1998 by the ITF Seafarers' Trust, it was coordinated by Dr. *Erol Kahveci.*

Finally published in November 2002, the project included not only Finnish but also multi-national crews, thanks to the cooperation of sailing chaplains affiliated with the German Seamen's Mission and the Apostleship of the Sea in the Philippines. The general conclusion was that sailing chaplains do provide "services of quality to seafarers which cannot be provided from shore-based maritime ministries and welfare agencies." It was significant that 97% of the seafaring respondents felt the sailing chaplains' Christian identity did not hinder this positive assessment, rather the opposite.

The report also examined two further, yet very different, models of ship-based welfare service delivery, one religious the other secular. Both bore some resemblance to the Sailing Chaplains Model and were therefore included in the study: Catholic Seafarer Priests of France, and Sailing Political Commissars of the People's Republic of China (SIRC 2002).

ICMA lost no time in following up on the Report's positive evaluation. The Executive Committee endorsed an *International Sailing Chaplains Training* program (ISCT) as a new ICMA activity—parallel to its 6-year old "Seafarers' Ministry Training" (SMT) for regular port chaplaincy. Developed under the leadership of ICMA's Chairperson, Rev. *Sakari Lehmuskallio,* General Secretary of the Finnish Seamen's Mission, a 4-year ISCT pilot program would run from 2004-2008. The aim would be to build a growing worldwide network of ICMA-certified, professional sailing chaplains. An ISCT Supervisor, directly responsible to ICMA's General Secretary, would coordinate the program.

The Peer-based "Ministering Seafarers" Model

Crewmember "conduits" for welfare services among fellow seafarers would also see a significant breakthrough at the turn of the century. Like its institutionalized sailing chaplaincy counterpart, the grassroots model of maritime peer ministry—increasingly referred to as *Ministering Seafarers*—was the subject of a special paper presented at the 1999 Conference. The author was Rev.*Werner Strauss,* a port chaplain serving the indigenous Lutheran Church in Singapore and Malaysia. Here, he presented a personal adaptation of the original Tacoma-based "Ministering Seafarers' Program." This model, he maintained, maximized "the most valuable asset on the ship"—seafarers themselves—as not only "recipients" but also potential "messengers" of the gospel.

.   The professional "Sailing Chaplaincy" concept had lent itself well to the rigorous statistics-based research of a specialized secular agency like SIRC. The sodality-like "Ministering Seafarer" concept, however, would more appropriately be the object of *missiological* research, in this case in close collaboration with IASMM. As a result, papers relating to three relevant doctoral dissertations made up the nucleus of the program at IASMM's Sixth International Conference in the port of New Ross, South East Ireland, in the summer of 2002 (*IASMM Maritime Mission Studies Supplement,* Spring 2004).

The first doctorate in the world to focus primarily on Maritime Missiology was by Rev. Dr. *Jonah Won Jong Choi* of Korea International Maritime Mission. His Doctor of Ministry dissertation, defended at New York Theological Seminary in 1996, dealt with *Shalom and the Church Maritime: A Korean Perspective on Maritime Missiology.* Choi's central thesis presents the need for a more "sea-based ministry," specifically in the shape of "Maritime Shalom Communities." These he defines as shipboard Christian communities incarnating a *maritime* application of the holistic biblical concept of shalom. In this context he places emphasis on the recruitment and training of crew-based lay "Sea Missionaries" as future fellowship coordinators on shipboard, a strategy already well tested in his own organization.

Rev. Dr. *David Chul Han Jun* of Korea Harbor Evangelism earned the next doctorate in the field. He received a Doctor of Missiology degree in 2001, from Fuller School of World Mission, based on *An Historical and Contextual Mission Approach to Seafarers by Korean Churches with Special Reference to Muslim Seafarers.* Jun, too, argues here for a new ship-based paradigm, prioritizing the role of seafarers themselves, ministering in solidarity with fellow seafarers as primary agents of contextual ministry among their peers.

In relation to specifically Muslim seafarers, Dr. Jun agrees with those who see Islam as both the greatest challenge and the greatest opportunity facing Christian global mission in the 21st century. This applies especially to modern-day maritime mission—in an environment normally unconstrained by severe apostasy laws. Because of Korea's own experience of colonial exploitation and cultural isolation, Jun argues that Korean-ethnic chaplains have a natural feel for the mindset of Muslim seafarers. In building bridges of witness among these, Jun disavows any hint of negative confrontation. Instead, he advocates an incarnational approach in the form of "friendship evangelism"—in sync with the gospel's own core of non-coercive, unconditional love.

While both these Korean colleagues were able to contribute an *experiential,* Asian perspective, their Irish counterpart, Rev. Dr. *Paul G. Mooney* of the (Anglican) Mission to Seafarers, could provide a comprehensive *theological* foundation for this seafarer-centered strategy. At the 2002 IASMM Conference in Ireland, Mooney shared a "preview" of his thesis. Then, in December 2002, at the Faculty of Protestant Theology of the University of Brussels, he successfully defended his ThD dissertation on *Maritime Mission in the New Millennium: A Participative Pastoral Paradigm for Ministry and Mission in a Globalised Industry.* Published in 2005, it now bears the title: *Maritime Mission: History, Developments, A New Perspective.*

A Watershed Dissertation

In a review of Paul Mooney's dissertation in 2004, the Author maintains that this represents no less than "a watershed event in maritime missiology." Mooney himself summarizes the overall purpose of his work with the following observation on the two interrelated "revolutions" involved:

> There has been a major revolution in the transport of cargo by sea and in the commercial and crewing practices affecting seafarers in the latter part of the twentieth century. This revolution in the maritime industry has been so profound that it demands a revolution in the practice of mission and ministry among seafarers....The purpose of the study is to identify an emerging paradigm that is capable of responding to the challenges that are posed to mission and ministry among seafarers by the contemporary developments in the seafaring world (*IASMM Newsletter* Spring 2004, 4-5).

In a world where the phenomenon of globalization has come to stay, shipping—as the main means of global transportation—is a vital part of that process. Meanwhile, its transient off-shore work force has become dehumanized as a "commodity," vulnerable to abuse of human rights and prone to social, even spiritual, alienation. In response, Mooney calls for an *alternative globalization* in the shape of an *alternative form of humanity,* rooted in Jesus' programmatic proclamation in Luke 4:18-19. Here, good news is preached to the poor, sight restored to the blind, debts are remitted and captives released. Those are the characteristics of the Kingdom of God that Jesus made the core of his message—an alternative Jesus embodied both in his own person and through all who would sincerely seek to follow him (Mark 1:15).

The Shape of a New Paradigm

This understanding of biblical anthropology demands unwavering solidarity with seafarers against any form of abuse or injustice in their work environment. Mooney reminds that commitment to Kingdom values also entails discarding any *paternalistic pastoral practices,* however well intentioned, that end up objectifying seafarers. "Objectification" results whenever seafarers are treated as *objects* or passive recipients of care, instead of empowering them as *co-subjects* or active partners in mission. Having confronted objectification of seafarers in terms of abusive conditions in the maritime *industry,* how could the maritime ecumene possibly justify objectification in the form of continued "top-down" methodology in maritime *ministry?*

Nowhere is the New Testament record more specific in affirming seafarers as co-subjects in mission than in Jesus' "Great Commission," as expressed in Matthew 28:18-20. As Jesus sends his disciples forth into the world, Mooney underscores that his central charge for them is to "make disciples. "Nor is this solely an issue of seafarers' inherent God-given dignity. It is also a matter of biblical *ecclesiology*. In today's world, Mooney maintains, maritime mission agencies can only carry out the fundamental task of "disciple-making" *effectively* if they will accept the challenge to "take on board" the biblical principle of the priesthood of all believers. As Mooney puts it:

> No matter how empathetic, meetings with seafarers in the course of ship visiting and duties in the seafarers' centre cannot be but occasional and almost random elements in an overall strategy of pastoral care. Sustained and empowering pastoral care can only be primarily exercised by ministering seafarers working among their peers.

As seagoing disciples, themselves making "disciples of all nations," lay crewmembers serving as ministering seafarers are simply obeying the Great Commission—"to continue the mission of Jesus." Still, Mooney makes reference to two important reasons for caution. First, in authentic, maritime mission, there is no room for a coercive kind of evangelism—no "hard-sell" approach; genuine witness has to be both sensitive and respectful. Second, solidarity with seafarers must be both unconditional and transparent, with no "hidden agenda." Although maritime mission will result in making disciples out of more people, mentally reducing seafarers themselves to a mere *means* to that end would be just another form of "objectification," and therefore immoral.

Mooney agrees in principle with the position of the AOS, that seafarers who make up a Christian community on board embody *A New Way of Being Church*. Such is the title of a 1997 paper by Archbishop *Francesco Gioia*. As "God's People of the Sea," these are not "exiles." On the contrary, as a specific "social stratum" of human mobility, they are an integral part of "the ecclesial reality" that makes up "the universal church" (*Apostolatus Maris Bulletin* No. 58/1997, 14-16). That assertion affirms Mooney's own contention—that "the prime aim of maritime mission has to be the expression of Christian community at sea." Only then can an authentic Church Maritime become a visible reality in today's seafaring world.

Practical Implications for Maritime Mission Agencies

Is contemporary maritime mission prepared to embrace the above view? Given the irreversible fact that in the seafaring world of the new century nothing will ever be the same, Mooney sees the resulting challenge as a fundamental "re-visioning" of maritime mission, entailing two distinct yet interrelated tasks:

First, "re-orientation" of maritime mission, moving from a uniquely *agency-centered* to a primarily *seafarer-centered* approach, will entail a "paradigm shift in thought as well as organizational structure." This kind of mental adjustment translates into replacing an essentially "top down" model of mission with mission "from below"—in solidarity with the deprived. Such radical empowerment of seafarers can only come at the cost of a Christ-like *kenosi* ("self-emptying") by established seafarers' agencies (Philippians 2:5-11).

Second, the resulting "re-structuring" of maritime mission means seeing seafarers now as the primary agents of mission, yet "does not dispense with the need for seafarers' agencies, but rather redefines their role." If it is to be valid, maritime mission in the future can no longer be "agency-centered." However, if it is to be functional and maintain sustainable structures, such mission will certainly have to be *agency-supported.*

As a result, in an emerging "integrated" paradigm of maritime mission, one that is *both seafarer-centered and agency-supported,* seafarers and seafarers' agencies will complement each other as "coworkers" in a partnership of participation, Only this kind of combination can ensure the degree of "joint ownership" that will be crucial to success. For seafarers themselves, a "seafarer-centered" paradigm secures a sense of ownership, by empowering them to play a primary role in shipboard discipleship and decision-making affecting their own welfare. For seafarers' agencies, an "agency-supported" paradigm gives these, too, a sense of ownership, specifically through their indispensable facilitative role in equipping "God's people of the sea" for ministry (Ephesians 4:11).

Mooney commends the Tacoma-based *Ministering Seafarers' Program* for having provided a pioneer model for such a pivotal area of ministry. Nevertheless, the MSP, like the other individual programs that were to follow, still lacked that key condition for sustained engagement by seafarers' agencies across the ecumenical spectrum—cross-denominational or cross-organizational ownership and recognition. Mooney argues that *only ICMA* can fulfill that condition – by enabling seafarers to become *mission partners,* "fully integrated" into the very ministries and structures of the organizations making up this global maritime mission network.

Paul Mooney has provided an ICMA-affiliated discipleship training proposal as an Appendix to his dissertation, entitled *Programme for Training Seafarer Lay Ministers, Fellowship Coordinators, Shipboard Animators.* For ICMA/2004 in New Orleans, Mooney received a formal invitation to present his program proposal in this strategic forum. Responsibility for its implementation now rests where it has to—with ICMA, the organizational embodiment of the maritime ecumene.

Such a programmatic role on the part of ICMA has the potential for being completely compatible with the new ICMA-affiliated *International Sailing Chaplains Training Program.* True, as Mooney mentions, the Sailing Chaplaincy concept does imply certain inherent limitations. No agency-operated "professional" chaplaincy can possibly fill the pressing need for a truly indigenous seafarer-centered peer ministry, nor reach more than a fraction of the total workforce. Still, the Sailing Chaplaincy concept does demonstrate a visible symbol of solidarity with seafarers. Sailing chaplains might also serve (even unknowingly) as "animators" of ministering seafarers and fellowship groups before moving on to other ships.

It is far too early to predict precisely the place of Mooney's research in the ongoing saga of maritime mission history. Nevertheless, the successful defense of his dissertation in 2002 opens a new chapter in that history, with this *first scholarly researched comprehensive theology of maritime mission.*

Will Modern-day Maritime Mission "Put Out Into the Deep"?

IASMM/2002 marked a major transition. For the Association itself, it represented a handing over of the helm after its first 12 years, as the Author left the presidency to the conference host, Paul Mooney. It also marked a "kairos" opportunity replete with possibilities—both in terms of the Christian world community and the wider human community.

First, in the Christian world community, shipboard/maritime Christian communities have—in today's context of religious pluralism at sea—unique openings for positive witness with global ramifications. It is as indigenous peer ministry among fellow seafarers that such witness "from below" gains grassroots relevance as *contextualized.* As the world mission community has yet to realize, the "ripple effect" can be astonishing—not least in seafarers' home countries, many now closed to conventional mission. A Singapore-based missiologist, Dr. *Daniel Bloomquist,* observed in an interview with the Author:

> Seaports have become gateways through which seafaring strangers from all over the world come to us by *centripetal* movement, after which they are 'spun back' to all parts of the world again by *centrifugal* movement. What a unique, God-given opportunity to give away the gospel – just where these two movements intersect!

In the wider world community, the borderless globalized society of a "world without walls" needs the "church without walls" that the *cell-church* model is uniquely able to offer—whether on land or sea. As Dr. *Raymond Fung* has found in the Bible's "Isaiah Vision," any local Christian community can promote a potential multi-faith partnership with neighboring non-Christians anywhere, based on a "shared agenda" like Isaiah 65:20-23 (Fung 1992, 2). Indeed, on shipboard too, a Christian "Fellowship Coordinator" is often the one that crewmembers, regardless of faith, will look to as their natural spokesperson in case of justice- or welfare-related concerns.

At the same time, a small Christian community can offer the wider human community on any given ship an inclusive climate of *spiritual hospitality.* Without diluting distinctiveness, but with mutual tolerance and respect, such shipboard cell groups can encourage open dialogue in a spirit of acceptance akin to the amazing attraction the Early Church held for inquirers of other faiths (John 12:32; Ephesians 2:14). In these and other ways, particularly in a post-September 11 context, Christian shipboard communities can mirror a model of coexistence and hope for civic society, so sorely needed in today's troubled and fractured world

When the Master called his first seafaring followers to a new life of discipleship, he challenged them to "put out into the deep."(Luke 5:4). Will modern-day maritime mission respond to that same challenge by literally shifting its primary focus seaward? Will it recognize ministering seafarers as a "new way of being church"—embodying the Church Maritime as the people of God among the people of the sea? IASMM's Conference in Ireland, in 2002, witnessed the breakthrough in theory of a paradigm expressing precisely this new reality. Still pending is that paradigm's breakthrough *in practice*. Paul Mooney makes the urgency of that challenge clear. This chapter concludes with an Asian colleague's excerpt of Mooney's message (Jun 2001, 86):

> Shore-side facilities will still be necessary as centers of hospitality, resource and facilitation. At the same time, the central charge of Christ's Great Commission is to make disciples (Matthew 28:18-20). If seafarers' missions fail to train and empower *seafaring disciples* to minister on board *seagoing ships,* then those missions will not only have failed to respond to the challenge posed by the contemporary maritime context. They will also have failed as Christian missions obedient to the way of Jesus.

11

OTHER CURRENT CHALLENGES

INDIGENIZATION: NEW PARTNERS

In May 1991, in what was then still Leningrad, just three months before the hard-liners' last desperate attempt to salvage the Soviet regime, the Author was visiting the mansion that for years had served as an "Interclub" highlighting Communist culture for foreign seafarers. Above the magnificent marble staircase hung a huge picture of Lenin. The escorting senior staff person hastily assured, "It's coming down." Then, as an afterthought, he added, "I suppose the question is—what's going up?"

That would indeed be the decisive question, also for thousands of Eastern-Bloc seafarers as they now began their search—not only for jobs on flag-of-convenience ships but also for a new meaning for their lives. In seeking to fill the void left by the bankruptcy of Marxist materialism, would they only find a *Western* brand of materialism—consumerism? Would they discover an alternative—an authentic portrayal of Christ and a different kind of revolution?

The Geo-Political Scene

The Post-1989 Collapse of Communism

Pope John Paul II visited his native Poland in 1979. Poland was then still a satellite state of the Soviet Union, under totalitarian oppression ever since World War II. His dramatic visit ignited the Solidarity Movement of free trade unions—from 1980 led by *Lech Walesa*, a devout Catholic, and his fellow-workers from the Lenin Shipyard in Gdansk. As the movement swelled to a symbol of Eastern Europe's struggle for freedom from Communist rule, *Mikhail Gorbachev* threatened to send in Soviet tanks. The Polish-born Pope promptly responded that, in that case, he would be among the first to man the barricades.

With those words, one man, *Karol Wojtyla*, pope, poet and playwright, turned the tide of history. As the pragmatic politician he was, Gorbachev realized that the military might of the Red Army had met its match. In November 1989, emboldened by the Pope's fearless stand and message of hope, millions of beleaguered East Europeans breached the Berlin Wall and peaceably tore down the misanthropic Marxist-Leninist regimes that for decades had held them hostage. By the end of 1991, the Soviet Union itself had dissolved. Instead, while most former Soviet Republics merged together with Russia to form a Commonwealth of Independent States (CIS), some elected autonomy.

In China, following the student uprising in Tiananmen Square in June 1989, a Communist dictatorship has continued. This is also the case with North Korea, Laos, Vietnam and Cuba, although with varying levels of economic reform. Nevertheless, the fall of the Berlin Wall on 9 November 1989, with the consequent collapse of Communism elsewhere, has since stood out as the defining geo-political event of the late 20th century.

The Post-9/11 War on Terrorism

Shortly after the turn of the century came what will likewise remain a defining event, this time for the early 21st century—the terrorist attack on America on September 11, 2001. When organized militants commandeered and crashed loaded passenger planes against those symbols of America's economic and military power, the World Trade Center in New York and the Pentagon in Washington DC, it marked the beginning of a very different kind of global warfare.

First, this "War on Terrorism" signaled the start of a borderless, *globalized* conflict, waged by adversaries no longer limited by the boundaries of nation states. Second, this war was not against some godless ideology, but rather religious extremism—combined with factors such as economic inequity and cultural insensitivity.

A paper published by IASMM in the aftermath of 9/11 reminded readers of the awesome responsibility of first finding "the right response to such demonic deeds":

> We [especially in America] shall never forget how, only three days after the attacks, the Dean of our National Cathedral, one whose own foremothers and forefathers arrived on these shores on the bottom of a slave-ship, prayed publicly: "Lord, give our leaders wisdom—that as we act we not become the evil we deplore." We have good reason to continue praying that prayer (*IASMM Newsletter* Spring/Summer 2002, 12).

Both the 1989 fall of the Berlin Wall and now the 9/11 terrorist attack would inevitably have—each in their own way—a profound impact on the current context of maritime mission. However, the fundamental factor affecting the shape of mission everywhere was the geographic shift in the global growth of the Christian faith itself.

A Shifting Center of Gravity

Asian Bishops in the Lead

Japanese-born *John Watanabe* was deeply disappointed when World War II came to a sudden end. He had just completed his training as a one-man submarine torpedo—so as to fulfill his dream of giving his life for the Emperor, by single-handedly sinking an American battleship. Then, as a prisoner of war, he made an amazing discovery in a New Testament he had received from an American navy chaplain. The Son of God had given *his* life for *him*! Watanabe eventually became Bishop Primate of the Anglican Church of Japan. In the 1980s, he chose to become a seafarers' chaplain on the East Coast of Africa.

Korean-born *William Choi* narrowly survived a bloodbath in his youth when Communists overran his homeland. While seeking refuge in a Buddhist monastery, he discovered the gospel of Christ. His new faith led to seminary, eventually becoming Founding Bishop of the Anglican Diocese of Pusan, South Korea. In the 1980s, he too moved on to be a seafarers' chaplain, in his case on the Pacific Coast of the USA. (See Choi's *Perspective* below.)

It was no coincidence that two such prominent Asian church leaders should each sense a call to port chaplaincy at that time. In the context of maritime mission, the 1980s were—in two very different ways—witnessing a kind of "gravitational shift." First, the ethnic composition of the worldwide maritime workforce was becoming more non-Western and increasingly Asian, and this at an accelerating rate. Second, statistical studies showed that, by the year 2000, there would, for the first time in history, be more Christians who were native to the Eastern and Southern Hemispheres than the Western and Northern. The same would apply to indigenous missionaries sent out by the younger Christian churches in those parts. The title of a book by Philip Jenkins, *The Next Christendom: The Coming of Global Christianity* (2002), aptly summarizes the nature of this remarkable worldwide shift.

The Urgency of Indigenization

On the background of this dual shift, those two Asian church leaders were sending an unmistakable message, underscoring the urgency of indigenization in contemporary maritime mission. "Indigenization" signifies the process of promoting an "indigenous" ministry, one that originates with the felt needs of those native to a certain society or ethnic group. As a ministry "from below," it stands in contrast to "top down" models, paternalistically imposed from above.

With few exceptions, the prevailing maritime ministry establishment was still conspicuously Caucasian and Western-dominated. There has long been wide recognition, however, that communication of the gospel would be more effective if entrusted to people of a similar culture. This underscores the strategic significance of a peer-based, *seafarer-centered* paradigm—of worshipping and witnessing communities at sea. In the final analysis, indigenization must primarily mean endorsing seafarers themselves to be church among their peers (Mooney 2005, 162-168; Kverndal 1992, 9).

The supportive role of shore-based agencies would still be indispensable. Here, Westerners could continue to make important contributions in cross-cultural ministry, including in special "niche" ministries such as education, research and justice advocacy. Meanwhile, the need for integrating a greater proportion of non-Western agency staff was becoming increasingly acute. No less significant was the need to establish non-Western, indigenous agencies wherever possible.

A key case in point would be the founding of *Korea Harbor Evangelism* (KHE) in 1974—the world's *first non-Western indigenous maritime mission agency*. This event also provides a point of demarcation for the ongoing "Global Era" of maritime mission. By the late 1980s, indigenous agencies had commenced in a few other Asian port-cities. In these cases, there could initially be a varying degree of Western (generally ICMA-related) involvement—as happened in Japan, Taiwan and the Philippines.

Post-1989 Indigenization

The Former Soviet Bloc

Nowhere did change arrive more dramatically than in the former Soviet Union and its satellites. Although part of that vast land mass lay within the West, oppressive regimes had reduced them to a Developing World status. These countries' seafarers had soon boosted the ranks of the global maritime labor force by "One Sixth More" (in the words of the theme of the next ICMA Conference). Gone was now the Red rhetoric—about Western "bourgeois" seafarers' chaplains, operating as "Land Based Pirates." By 1990, Western centers were reporting a "huge demand" for Russian Bibles.

Meanwhile, the 33 former Communist-built Russian "Interclubs," with no viable indigenous welfare structure to sponsor or replace them any more, were fast falling into disarray. ICMA responded with a series of exploratory exchange visits from December 1990 on, initiated by ICMA's General Secretary, Rev. *Bernard Krug*. Despite four years as a German prisoner-of-war in Soviet Siberia, Krug had learned to love the Russian people and also become a passionate peace activist. On the Russian side, the visits were led by Krug's friend, Deputy Director *Roald Aliakrinsky,* of the International Federation of Water Transport Workers' Unions. Aliakrinsky was a former Soviet merchant navy officer, in his case, too, a peace activist.

In the decades that followed, ICMA members sponsored indigenous initiatives in many former Eastern Bloc port-cities: first in the Baltic, with the Catholics and Lutherans in the lead; then in the Black Sea, often sponsored by BISS; in Vladivostok, KIMM initiated an indigenous venture. From Montgomery, Wales, Rev. *Jack Jones* helped launch, in 1990, an indigenous agency called *LIFE International Seafarers' Centers,* in Albania, Romania and Bulgaria. Pending greater involvement by the Orthodox Church, indigenous Baptists have been particularly active in this whole region. In neighboring Greece, the *Greek Free Evangelical Church of Lipasmata* in Piraeus has maintained a faithful, pioneering ministry among seafarers in these parts ever since the 1960s, headed by Brother *Spyros Portinos* and British-born Sister *Jennifer Jack.*

The Peoples' Republic of China

Like its fellow-Communist Soviet neighbor, the People's Republic of China (PRC) had long demonstrated a concern for seafarers' social welfare—through a similar combination of Political Commissars at sea and Interclubs ashore. In post-1989 Mainland China, prospects for indigenous maritime ministry were far more complex. The Communist take-over in 1949 led to years of persecution of Christians, culminating in the Red Guard rampage of the Cultural Revolution (1966-76). Despite this, China had experienced more church growth than any other nation in modern history. This was largely due to the combined effect of both the official "Three-Self Patriotic Movement" (self-support, self-governance and self-propagation) and its underground counterpart, China's "House Church Movement."

In recent years, indigenous Chinese Christians had met with increasing public respect. Nevertheless, the popular image of Christianity in China was still that of a "foreign" religion. Apart from earlier Catholic initiatives, the Christian faith had gained a foothold in China in the wake of "gunboat diplomacy," unleashed on this ancient Asian civilization by "barbarians" from the West during the 19th century Opium Wars. True, Christian outreach among seafarers did have a history going back to 1822, when pioneer missionary Robert Morrison first hoisted the Bethel Flag on board ships in the anchorage of Canton. Still, since then, maritime ministry in China's port-cities had never been anything other than an essentially *Western* enterprise.

On the other hand, China's growing socio-economic liberalization, during the 1980s and 1990s, did open up new opportunities for international contact, also in the area of seafarers' welfare. From their century-old vantage point in the Mariners' Club of Hong Kong, the Anglican Missions to Seamen came to play a leading role on behalf of ICMA. As early as in January 1986, MtS Secretary General, Bill Down, and Hong Kong Senior Chaplain, *Wally Andrews*, paved the way with a three-day visit to China's No. 1 port city, Shanghai. In 1987, Dr. James Whittemore of New York, then chairperson of ICMA, joined these two on an expanded fact-finding visit, to Beijing and Nanjing as well as Shanghai. Here, all three found a warm welcome as they discussed future relations between Western maritime ministry agencies and PRC maritime unions, port authorities and Interclubs. They also met with leaders of the China Christian Council and the Three-Self Patriotic Movement.

It seemed providential that ICMA's incoming General Secretary, Rev. *Michael Shoon Chion Chin,* was an embodiment of East/West biculturalism. Born and raised in the Chinese diaspora of Malaysia and Singapore, having also lived in Hong Kong and the PRC, he was now a citizen of Australia and, most recently, Senior Chaplain of the Missions to Seamen in Melbourne, Victoria. Now, in 1991, Chin was well qualified to reinforce relations with maritime and church officials in the PRC, in cooperation with Andrews' successor, Rev. *Peter*

Ellis. One visible result of Chin's repeated visits to the PRC was a first-ever Chinese delegation to ICMA's Plenary Conference in Helsinki in 1994.

By 1997, the door was open for the International Association for the Study of Maritime Mission (IASMM) to help carry the process one step further. As President of IASMM, the Author received an invitation to give guest lectures on the history and status of maritime mission, at leading theological seminaries in the PRC (Nanjing, Shanghai and Guangzhou), as well as in Hong Kong. This offered an opportunity to bring the Bethel Flag back to China, by presenting a replica to each of those seminaries, precisely 175 years after the first hoisting of that emblem in Chinese waters. More importantly, the visits also raised the issue of "self-theologizing" by Chinese Christians in this "new" area of ministry. Given the prevailing realities, could an embryonic, indigenous maritime ministry somehow emerge in a fast changing China?

During his seminary visit in Nanjing, the Author asked Bishop *K. H. Ting,* the long-time leader of the nondenominational Chinese Church, himself a survivor of years of persecution, whether he was an optimist about the future of the Christian Church in China. "Yes, I have to be," he answered, "after the foreign missionaries were forced to leave, China's Christians learnt self-reliance—through the irresistible power of prayer in Jesus' name." On receiving a copy of the history of the Seafarers' Mission Movement, the Bishop bestowed his blessing on the cause of worldwide maritime mission in our own day, voicing the same optimism about the future of an authentically *Chinese* contribution to such ministry. Considering the growing proportion of seafarers from a nation representing practically one fourth of the human race, such consequences could be incalculable (Kverndal 1997-1998, 10-12).

Examples of post-1989 indigenization in maritime ministry were not all directly related to the former USSR or the PRC. The Lutheran World Federation established the *Lutheran Maritime Ministry Consultancy* in 1984, for the specific purpose of promoting indigenous, non-Western participation in maritime ministry. During the late 1980s and early 1990s, this Consultancy became—through seminary lectures and on-site seminars—directly instrumental in a series of indigenous initiatives in port cities in Oceania, South-East Asia and Africa. At the same time, the Catholic, Anglican and BISS networks also initiated indigenous maritime ministries, not only in Asia and Africa but also in Latin America (in Brazil especially in cooperation with local Baptists).

Post-9/11 Maritime Ministry and the Muslim World

Religious Fundamentalism

The immediate impact of 9/11 on indigenization in maritime ministry was a heightened sense of urgency, to help build a better one-world human community. This would mean not just understanding and relating positively to other faiths, but also facing up to the factors fueling fundamentalist extremism— whether in non-Christian or Christian guise.

The 1990 NAMMA Statement of Mission concludes : *Cooperation where we can agree, respect where we cannot, love in everything!* In matters of faith, where minds are not completely closed and there seems to be some willingness to communicate, two tremendous blessings may well result from open, honest dialogue: first, *active cooperation*—in areas of common concern as fellow-humans, such as social justice, peace and the human environment; second, *peaceful coexistence*—with mutual respect for the freedom to follow different understandings of absolute truth and inherent mission agendas, as stipulated in the Universal Declaration of Human Rights.

By the year 2000, out of a world population of over six billion, there were 2,015 million (33%) defining themselves as Christian; 1,215 million (19.6%) as Muslim; 900 million (15%) as Hindu; 360 million (6%) as Buddhist; and 18 million (1%) as Judaic (Barrett 2001). Islam was therefore already the leading non-Christian global religion. Given that the principal perpetrators on 9/11 were members of Osama Bin Laden's Islamic terrorist network, it was inevitable that Muslims would now become a focus of attention. Founded in 1989, the network was known as *Al-Qaeda* ("The Base"). The 9/11 attacks would reinforce a rising global awareness of radical Islam, already resulting from the anti-modernist tyranny of the *Taliban* (or "Student") regime in Afghanistan during 1996-2001.

Not all who identify themselves as Islamic are "Islamists." It would be just as unfair for Westerners to consider all Muslims as militant fanatics, as for Muslims to equate consumerist decadence in the West with authentic Christianity. As one Middle-Eastern American cleric put it in the aftermath of the 9/11 attack, speaking for moderate Muslims everywhere, "It's not a question of where we come from. We share a common humanity."

After 9/11, there was still enough prejudice against Muslims in Western society, and still sufficient resentment in the world of Islam, to present seemingly insurmountable impediments to indigenized Christian maritime ministry among Muslim seafarers. There has been mutual rivalry—often open hostility and persecution—between these two most numerous world religions ever since the seventh-century origin of Islam. Despite a joint Abrahamic heritage, each continues to have distinctly different truth claims and mission agendas.

That said, there are still countries that openly identify themselves as "Islamic States," run by clergy-controlled theocratic governments. Here, the harsh blasphemy and apostasy codes of *Shariah* ("Islamic Law"), although in violation of UN provisions, continue to make conventional Christian ministry in such ports practically speaking impossible.

Building Bridges with Muslim Mariners

In spite of such challenges, there can be no justification for depriving Muslim seafarers—representing the religion of over a fifth of the human race—of any access to the Christian gospel. It would be impossible to reconcile such a conclusion—either with the word of the Founder of that gospel, or with those seafarers' own ultimate human rights. Among various opportunities still available, would be the recruitment of Christians with a personal linkage to Islam as shore-based staff at existing seafarers' centers.

A case in point is that of Rev. *Peter Ibrahim*. Born in the Sudan as the son of a Muslim sheik, he was entrusted to an Anglican missionary doctor in order to gain a good education. Eventually he experienced a call to the ministry as a missionary himself. Thanks to the vision of General Secretary Carl Osterwald of the German Seamen's Mission, a Lutheran missionary society agreed to sponsor Ibrahim as a GSM port chaplain among the many non-Western mariners arriving in the docklands of Hamburg in the early 1980s. Asked how Muslim crewmembers responded to Christian ministry by one of their own, he replied:

> "Fine! You see, because I'm from the Sudan I speak Arabic. And Muslims get so surprised to hear that someone who speaks Arabic is a Christian. Does this anger them? On the contrary! It gives me instant respect and rapport. For example, Egyptian seamen will spontaneously bring me to any Coptic Christian shipmates on board" (*Lutheran Maritime News,* September 1985, 1-2).

Whereas Chaplain Ibrahim exemplified a form of *shore-based,* indigenous Muslim-oriented ministry worth emulating, he saw this as first and foremost supportive of *ship-based* ministry. By that he meant enlisting and empowering seafarers as ministers among their own, in sync with the Tacoma Model which he warmly endorsed. It would later fall to Dr. *David Chul-Han Jun* to elaborate on this approach with particular reference to Muslim seafarers.

Dr. Jun sees peer ministry, by seafarers with a personal Muslim affinity, as a major opportunity to reach Muslim seafarers of today with an indigenous offer of the gospel. In his groundbreaking dissertation, he states that promoting such an affinity confronts maritime ministry with a twofold challenge: to develop not only an *understanding* of Muslim thinking, but also an unconditional *solidarity* with Muslim seafarers "at their level of human need." He argues that nowhere can this form of incarnational, non-coercive "Friendship Evangelism" be more effective than through the peer ministry and grassroots fellowship of shipboard Christian communities (Jun 2001, 116 ff.).

Such a strategy calls for a sincere spirit of apology for discrimination or other offenses in the past, combined with a robust reliance on the persuasive power of the Spirit of Christ (John 16:8). Only then will there be reason for optimism—despite arguments to the contrary. A Christian fellowship group would, within the wider shipboard community, offer a forum for both inter-religious dialogue and cooperation in common welfare concerns. In this way, it would promote the cause of human community—at any rate at sea. Moreover, for Muslim seafarers drawn to the Christian gospel, a Christian cell group in their midst could provide at least some sense of Christian community, as a preliminary alternative to their previous sense of worldwide Muslim community, or "Ummah." (See also William Choi's *Perspective* below).

As Christian mission among people of the sea confronted the challenges of the Third Millennium, indigenization would continue to constitute a compelling need, related to respect for identity. Quoting ICMA General Secretary Michael Chin in 1994, would maritime ministry in the Developing World, including the former USSR and the PRC, be able to develop in ways which seafarers indigenous to these cultures could discern as "distinctively their own"? Despite promising beginnings, the outcome would largely depend on the corresponding level of *transformation* that the worldwide Western maritime ministry establishment would be willing to undergo.

TRANSFORMATION: A CHANGING WEST

It was the final day of ICMA's 4th Plenary Conference, held in the Allied zone of beleaguered Berlin in July 1981—over eight years before the fall of the Wall. Participants were gathered in the historic chapel of the "Johannesstift," the diaconal compound founded by the mid-19th century pioneer of both German home mission and German seafarers' mission, Johann Hinrich Wichern. In the pulpit stood Rev. *Carl Osterwald,* General Secretary of the German Seamen's Mission and at that time Chairperson of ICMA. His text was Christ's challenge to all who claim his name: "You are the light of the world!" (Matthew 5:14). What followed took the form of a public confession:

> He asked if we realized what a miracle it was that we had, each with our own particular background, been meeting here in Berlin. Because—40 years ago we would have killed one another, and been decorated for it into the bargain! In a moving personal testimony, he told how he too, as a youth, had fallen under the spell of Hitlerism. He really believed the inscription on the banner he then marched under: 'Better dead than slave!' Because he was in the dark, he had no idea of the liberating power of the Gospel of Christ. But where Christ becomes Lord of people's lives, there is light. Now, as he thought of all who lived without that light on *both* sides of the Iron Curtain, as well as on board the ships of the world, he wanted to remind each one of us once more "You are the light of the world*!* If not you—who else?" (*Watermarks* Sept. 1981, 9-14).

Here, one who was himself a survivor of the Nazi nightmare put his finger on the crux of the matter: Would Western-world maritime mission rise to the level of transformation called for—by both the challenge of indigenization and other pressing needs? In 2002, in a world forever changed by the events of 1989 and 9/11, Carl Osterwald came out of retirement to deliver a paper pointing to both the shape and the source of such transformation (Osterwald 2004). He gives the substance of that paper in his Perspective (below).

The Global Network: ICMA

Toward Indigenization

To what extent did the maritime ecumene reflect the hope held by Osterwald during the last quarter of the 20th century? How far had the biblical call to transform rather than conform (Romans 12:2) led to the transfer of power, personnel and other resources in actual *practice*? The degree of global transformation had approached the miraculous in terms of ecumenical cooperation. Overt denominational "turfism" now belonged to the past. In terms of indigenization and related issues, significant change was less evident, yet on the way.

Rev. *Bernard Krug,* who took over as ICMA's General Secretary from Prebendary *Tom Kerfoot* in 1982, was, during his nine-year tenure, untiring in his advocacy of justice for oppressed seafarers everywhere. In 1991, ICMA appointed, for the first time, an Asian-ethnic General Secretary, Rev. *Michael Chin.* Five years later, he was followed by Rev. *Jacques Harel,* a French-ethnic native of the Indian Ocean nation of Mauritius.

At ICMA's 1985 Plenary Conference in the Philippines—the first in the Southern Hemisphere—topics showed growing concern for issues relating to ethnic, cultural and religious pluralism at sea. In the area of Seafarers' Rights, ICMA initiated a groundbreaking "Maritime Manning Conference" that led to a "Code of Good Practice for Manning Agents." This signaled a new beginning in the global combat against corrupt crewing patterns.

During the 1990s, ICMA helped launch a number of important projects, in "niche" areas of ministry, with the support of the ITF Seafarers' Trust. Each of these had some bearing on indigenization and related issues. They included a Seafarers Ministry Training (SMT), an International Sailing Chaplains Training (ISCT), a Crisis Preparedness Committee (CPC), as well as an International Seafarers' Assistance Network (ISAN).

Structural Change

Beyond this kind of coordinative role, ICMA could only operate within its own self-imposed, financial and constitutional limitations. In 2002, under Rev. *Sakari Lehmuskallio* as Chair and Rev. *Berend van Dijken* as General Secretary, ICMA initiated a professional *Development Study* to propose possible change in policy and structure. Without eroding the decision-making status of ICMA's Executive Committee member agencies, the study did motivate structural change toward regionalization and grassroots participation.

In 2003, with Dr. *Jürgen Kanz* as its new General Secretary, the organization resumed a cooperative relationship with its co-founder, the WCC's Department of World Mission and Evangelism. Also, with Canon *Bill Christianson* of the MtS as Chair from 2004, ICMA had, by 2006, increased its membership to 27 organizations and its regions to nine, each with a Regional Coordinator. In 2007, Rev. *Hendrik F. la Grange*, Durban-based Mission

Director of the Christian Seaman's Organisation, came aboard as General Secretary.

"The Big Three"

The Mission to Seafarers (MtS)

"The Big Three" (BFSS, ASFS and MtS) had dominated the 19th century scene in Anglo-American maritime mission. During the late 20th century, it was *The Missions to Seamen* that would lead the way in confronting the challenges of industry-wide change. When Canon *Bill Down* took over from Tom Kerfoot as Secretary General in 1976, he sent a questionnaire to colleagues, calling for feedback on charting a course for the future. One chaplain summed up their collective response: "It is the industry which writes the agenda." With British seafarers fast vanishing from the great sea-lanes, this Society might well have chosen to retrench. Instead, the MtS elected to redirect its resources and reach out proactively to the international workforce—in all its diversity and complexity.

In his book *On Course Together,* Down describes how the MtS did, in fact, "reset" its agenda in order to meet the requirement of relevancy amidst radical change. Factors like increasing automation, faster turnarounds, smaller crews, and relocation to remote terminals, led to less need for conventional shore facilities. The focus was instead on shipvisiting and a ministry of comprehensive pastoral care, based in more modest facilities and—wherever possible—operating ecumenically under one roof. The MtS also responded to the mounting need for advocacy on behalf of exploited seafarers from the Developing World. In 1986, the MtS appointed Rev. *Christopher Collison* to a staff position that ultimately became a Secretariat for Justice and Welfare under Rev. Canon *Ken Peters.*

Down was committed to the principle of *partnership* (as opposed to paternalism) at all levels of maritime ministry. Under Down's leadership the Society functioned "no longer simply as a missionary society of the Church of England, but rather as the international organisation of the Anglican Communion ministering to the seafarers of the world." From now on, the MtS "Head Office" in London would become a "Central Office," acting in a coordinative rather than directive capacity, with "National Councils" and "Liaison Bishops" around the world (Down 1989). After Down became Bishop of Bermuda in 1990, his successor, Canon *Glyn Jones,* carried the process of restructuring an important step further with the creation of a "Consultative Forum." In the year 2000, the Society changed its name to *The Mission to Seafarers*, to reflect gender-inclusiveness.

Jones' incoming successor, Canon *Bill Christianson,* gave a glimpse of this "one mission of God" at ICMA's 1999 Plenary Conference in South Africa. In a keynote address entitled "Preparing for Change—A Theological Perspective," he suggested that such a theology, to be truly transformational, would need to be grounded in Scripture, focused on Jesus, and following the

Spirit—in ways which must be "sought out in every generation." One example of this would be the MtS i-church initiative in 2006, offering seafarers a computer connection with the worship, fellowship and counseling services of the wider church. In 2007, also on Christianson's watch, the MtS launched a new mission ship in Dubai, named the *Flying Angel*, a modern-day version of the Society's original method of mission afloat, complete with ecumenical chaplaincy, internet café, medical clinic and a Muslim welfare officer.

The British & International Sailors' Society (BISS)

The other major—and older—British-based Protestant agency, then called the *British Sailors' Society*, responded to late 20th century contextual change in largely similar ways. By contrast, however, this Society had, both in leadership and chaplaincy staff, always embraced a broad diversity of denominations. These included Baptists, Reformed, Methodists, Lutherans, as well as Anglicans. This left the Society free to sponsor indigenous maritime ministry initiatives around the world—regardless of denominational affiliation. In this way, the Society furthered the cause of indigenization during the 1990s, supporting such initiatives in a series of port-cities in Asia, Africa, South America and, eventually, the former Soviet Union.

Deeply involved in this process was the Society's Presbyterian Principal Chaplain, Rev. *James W. MacDonald*. He also produced a widely distributed audiotape entitled *2000 Reasons for Believing,* to mark the New Millennium among today's multi-cultural crews. In various ways, the Society sought out new strategies to meet changing needs. In 1986, for example, the Society that had begun in 1818, with the former warship *Speedy* on the Thames, launched its first motor-home type "Mobile Seafarers' Center"—aptly called *Speedy II.*

Under the leadership of *Graham Chambers*, the Society's Australian-born General Secretary during the 1980s and 1990s, the BSS responded to the need for structural change as well. As shipping moved down-river, and the Port of London had to close its traditional docks to ocean-going shipping, the Society decided to leave London, for the first time in its long history. It relocated to the fast-growing container and passenger port of Southampton.

In 1995, the British Sailors' Society changed its name to the *British & International Sailors' Society* (BISS), to reflect the multi-national identity of the seafarers it now served in a globalized industry. At the same time, in a shift toward a more decentralized structure, it transformed itself into a network of autonomous sister societies, each called an "International Sailors' Society" (ISS). Besides BISS, there were now an *ISS Canada,* an *ISS Southern Africa,* an *ISS Australia* and an *ISS New Zealand.* By 2002, the Society's engagement in the Ukraine had developed into an indigenous *ISS-Odessa Region* (ISSOS).

After 20 eventful years as General Secretary, Graham Chambers left the helm, in 2000, to *Alan B. Smith,* who came from a long career in the Royal Navy. In 2006, he was in turn succeeded by *Robert Adams,* a leader with extensive experience both at sea and in shipping. Since 2002, MacDonald's successor as Principal Chaplain, Baptist-affiliated Rev. *David Potterton,* has vigorously continued the Society's long history of indigenous port chaplaincies worldwide. In October 2004, Potterton—in cooperation with the Author—led a commemoration of Rev. George Charles ("Bosun") Smith at the gravesite in Penzance. The occasion marked the 200th anniversary of Smith's personal call to the ministry, later to become the founder of not only BISS but the entire Seafarers' Mission Movement.

The American Seamen's Friend Society (ASFS)

For much of the 19th century, the Americans played a leading role among "The Big Three" on the maritime ministry world scene. Following "the glory days of American sail," however, American-flag merchant shipping went through a period of drastic decline. In the course of the 20th century, NAMMA and ICMA would assume the role of the ASFS as both catalyst and coordinator of maritime ministries, in North America and worldwide, respectively.

It fell to the Society's last Executive Secretary, Rev. *William A. Hallen*, to lead the ASFS from its New York "Flatiron Building" offices during the 1960s and through the 1970s. While Hallen was still there, the Society was able to maintain certain ship's library and Bible distribution services, and continue making meaningful grants to both NAMMA and individual agencies. On Hallen's retirement in 1979, however, the Board of the ASFS decided it was time to transfer the Society's funds and archives to the maritime museum and library of Mystic Seaport in Connecticut. When widely beloved "Chaplain Bill" passed away in 1990, it meant farewell to the last living link with the leading agency from the "heroic age" of maritime mission.

The Apostleship of the Sea (AOS)

The Gracida-Dillenburg Decade of 1980-90

The largest Christian denomination, the Roman Catholic Church, had its own unique historic identity. The Apostleship of the Sea, as the maritime arm of that church would respond to the challenges of industry-wide change in a likewise unique way. In his 50-year history of the *American Catholic Seafarers' Church* (1995), Msgr. *Vincent Yzermans* describes how the AOS sought to address the tensions generated by the late 20th century's whirlwind of change (Yzermans 1995). The Second Vatican Council had pointed the way with its renewed emphasis on ecumenical cooperation and the ministry of the laity. Yet Yzermans saw a church and a ministry still "mired in the very impediments which the Council had attempted to shed." As in the case of ICMA, it so happened that the catalyst for global change would once again come from North America.

René H. Gracida was a Benedictine-affiliated bishop of Mexican parentage. Besides having grown up close to the sea, his interest in the AOS derived partly from discovering the writings of his fellow-Benedictine, Peter Anson. In 1975, as the first Bishop of Pensacola-Tallahassee, Florida, Gracida was appointed "Episcopal Promoter" of the Apostleship of the Sea in the USA

(AOS/USA). As such, and for fourteen years, he demonstrated decisive leadership in the organization, according to Yzermans. Committed to what he saw as the primary purpose of Vatican II—"the updating of the Church"—Bishop Gracida lost no time in laying out a blueprint for also updating its maritime apostolate.

In 1976, at an Inter-American Conference of the AOS in Oakland, California, Bishop Gracida publicly shared his vision. To achieve "greater participation," the AOS needed not only a more democratic process with shared decision-making but also a broader base, involving lay and not least seafaring membership. He proposed a restructuring, replacing the existing AOS/USA with "a new entity," the *National Catholic Conference for Seafarers* (NCCS). As a discussion forum, the new NCCS would be distinct, yet still "vitally linked" with the official AOS structure. In the process, Gracida enlisted several gifted young co-workers. Two of them, Port Chaplains James Dillenburg and Rivers Patout, of Green Bay, Wisconsin, and Houston, Texas, respectively, helped draft a Constitution and Bylaws for the new organization.

As its first President, the NCCS chose Rev. (later Msgr.) *James E. Dillenburg* (1976-78). He would go on to become "the most prominent among many exceptional leaders that now emerged in the American maritime apostolate" (Yzermans 1995, 182-184). In 1980, Dillenburg succeeded Rev. *James Keating* of Chicago as National Director of the AOS. In that position, working closely with Gracida, as well as activist colleagues in the AOS in the USA such as Rev. *Rivers Patout* and Rev. Dr. *Thomas Snyderwine*, Dillenburg prepared a series of core concerns for the agenda of the NCCS.

Among these concerns were: (1) Empowering *seafarers themselves* to be "the Church on board," through Christian education and the commissioning of lay "Extraordinary Ministers of the Eucharist" (a faculty that received papal approval in 1982). (2) Enlisting deacons and qualified lay persons (of both genders) as *port chaplains,* and establishing professional standards for *all* AOS port chaplains, ordained and lay. (3) Enhancing *ecumenical cooperation,* including (from 1979) integrating the NCCS into NAMMA's (at that time ICOSA's) annual conferences. (In the late 1980s, the NCCS even hired this Lutheran-affiliated Author to assist Yzermans with the research needed for his history of the AOS in the USA.)

After Dillenburg became President of NAMMA (1988-90), he was instrumental in creating that organization's groundbreaking "Statement of Mission" of 1990. That accomplishment formed a fitting finale to a *Gracida-Dillenburg Decade* of remarkable progress for the AOS in the USA.

Meanwhile, all this had not gone unnoticed in the Vatican. In the turbulent time of transition following Vatican II, Msgr. *Francis Frayne* had worked untiringly at the International Secretariat of the AOS in Rome, to enhance both the visibility and viability of the global maritime apostolate. Frayne's untimely death in 1986 prevented him from seeing the AOS become an *Opus* ("special work") of the Church in 1988, with its own identity and office—albeit within the wider mandate of what became a *Pontifical Council for the Pastoral Care of*

Migrants and Itinerant People. Despite this and other evidence of progress, the new President of the Council, Archbishop (later Cardinal) *Giovanni Cheli,* soon realized that a reorganization of the worldwide AOS was essential—if this were to meet the demands of a new Millennium. Cheli found he now needed the skills that Dillenburg had already shown on a national level.

In response, Dillenburg threw his heart into the preparation of a pivotal event—the *XIX AOS World Congress in Houston, Texas, 1992.* With the theme "Christian Living Aboard Ship," the Congress focused on the role of seafarers as fellow-workers in the maritime apostolate. Since today's seafarers were "spending up to 90% of their time at sea, with no chance of contact with the Church ashore," the Congress confirmed that the emphasis must now be on "preparing seafarers *to be* the Church on board," as Dillenburg put it. The Congress served to highlight the urgency of creating structures that could "promote seafarers evangelizing one another" and build "faith communities at sea." Dillenburg would now devote all his energies toward facilitating those new structures for the AOS. This meant four years of intense teamwork, both with his French-language Fellow Secretary at the Vatican, Msgr. *François LeGalle,* and with colleagues worldwide.

In 1996, Dillenburg could return to parochial ministry in Green Bay, Wisconsin, leaving the resulting draft of a new AOS Constitution to his successor, Fr. *Raymond Maher,* as well as to Fr. *Gérard Tronche,* who had succeeded LeGalle two years earlier. Finally, on 31 January 1997, Pope John Paul II signed what he chose to call an *Apostolic Letter Motu Proprio "Stella Maris."* By inserting the words "motu proprio" (by own volition), the Pope underscored his personal identification with the contents of this first judicial document issued by any Pope uniquely devoted to the Apostleship of the Sea (Oubre 1998, 54).

First, the Apostolic Letter expands the pastoral responsibility of the AOS to encompass three categories of sea-related persons collectively called "People of the Sea": (1) *Seafarers as such*—those who actually serve or voyage on merchant ships or fishing vessels. (2) *Other "Maritime Personnel"*—like port- and offshore workers, maritime students and retired seafarers. (3) *Sea-related persons*—dependents of the above, as well as maritime ministry/AOS workers. In 1997, the Vatican operated with a global aggregate of over 300 million such people of the sea (*Apostolatus Maris* 1997/II).

Second, the document endorses *mission from below,* by committed Christian seafarers serving as "God's people of the sea." In his comments, Archbishop Cheli underscores this point. By beginning at grassroots—with seafarers themselves as primary agents of ministry, rather than with the hierarchy at the top—the Apostolic Letter is in harmony with the "genesis" of the AOS as "the initiative of a group of lay people in Glasgow (Scotland) in 1920." It is therefore the responsibility of AOS chaplains to identify and train (1) seafaring lay leaders capable of "creating and guiding a Christian community on board," as well as (2) those with the special devotion needed to serve as "extraordinary ministers of the Eucharist" among their peers at sea.

This validates both the wider *Christian* (supra-denominational) and the specifically *Roman Catholic* (denominational) forms of shipboard fellowship that emerged at the XIX AOS Congress in 1992. The document further reinforces the *role of the laity at large* in the current AOS, by authorizing the appointment of deacons, lay persons and members of religious orders as Co-Workers—to assist or substitute for chaplains "in matters which do not require the ministerial priesthood."

The document then goes on to spell out organizational structures—at local, national, regional and international levels. True, the Vatican Curia's Pontifical Council still provides direction and coordination through a "General Secretariat." The basic model of organization, however, is "federated" by broadening local involvement through deliberately "dispersed authority." The later introduction of 9 "AOS Regional Coordinators" has reinforced this trend.

With that, the NCCS in America had seen its major goals become a model for the 1997 reorganization of the AOS worldwide. In 2001, after 25 years, members of the NCCS agreed to give their organization a new constitution and a new name: *The Apostleship of the Sea of the United States of America* (AOSUSA). Fr. *Sinclair Oubre,* Port Chaplain of Port Arthur, Texas, and recently graduated Licenciate in Canon Law, became President. As for the "official" arm of the work, the National Director of the AOS in the USA, Deacon *Robert Balderas,* resigned in 2000, after a decade of dedicated service through the 1990s as the first deacon ever to serve in that position. His successor, Fr. *John Jamnicky,* helped facilitate a permanent secretariat for the AOSUSA in Port Arthur, with *Doreen Badeaux* as Secretary General.

At the start of the New Millennium, it now appeared that the maritime arm of this generally hierarchical church body was moving more proactively than any other toward a lay *seafarer-centered* paradigm of ministry. In that sense, concludes Oubre, the AOS was now "more akin" to what Anson, Gannon and Shields had originally—in 1920—hoped it would one day be (Oubre 1998, 60).

The National Maritime Ministries

Nordic Seafarers' Missions

Rev. *Johan Storjohann* reportedly looked like a loaded cannon, "all primed and ready to go off," as he waited in vain to bring up the needs of Nordic seafarers at the annual meeting of the Norwegian Missionary Society in 1864. That rebuff was later seen as a blessing in disguise, since it forced him to focus on founding a separate society for that purpose. As noted earlier, he then went on to become the founding figure of the whole family of Lutheran-affiliated Nordic seafarers' missions. It was no coincidence that in each case there emerged an initial connection with world mission. However, all four national churches soon recognized the valid theological and psychological reasons for distinguishing between the world mission task of primary evangelism among strangers to the gospel, and the home mission strategies needed to re-evangelize and/or nurture fellow nationals.

Then, as globalization began to gather momentum during the 1980s, a dramatic dilemma would confront Western nationally-oriented maritime ministries. As unprecedented numbers of (largely Asian) seafarers began to take over, these would represent a *world mission* rather than *home mission* challenge. For the Nordic seafarers' missions, choices were limited: (1) simply close down, (2) transform existing centers to serve multi-national needs, or, (3) minister to remaining Nordic seafarers jointly with other categories of fellow nationals abroad.

For none was that dilemma more difficult than for the *Norwegian Seamen's Mission* (NSM). From 1977 to 1987, the Norwegian-flag merchant marine declined by almost 80 per cent (Tenold 2006). With the opening of a Norwegian International Ship Register (NIS) in 1987, the transition to non-Norwegian crews on Norwegian-flag shipping seemed irreversible. Given the need for church-related outreach among escalating numbers of fellow Norwegians temporarily abroad, the NSM opted for the third of the above alternatives—ministering to the needs of all fellow nationals abroad, seafaring and resident, as did also the other Nordic seafarers' missions.

These developments served to revive doubts among ICMA colleagues about the justification for any nationally oriented maritime ministry whatever, in the context of globalization. This prompted a mediatory role by the Author—in his dual capacity of having been with NSM headquarters staff before serving in executive positions in international maritime ministry. By the 1990s, there did emerge a new recognition of complementary roles, rather than polarization, between the internationally and nationally oriented components of the maritime ecumene. There were at least two areas, where Nordic national maritime ministries were now promoting a new sense of solidarity within the maritime ministry world community.

First, in terms of *ecclesiology,* retiring General Secretary Michael Chin acknowledged, in his 1996 farewell address, the need to share "the rich Nordic heritage" of making seafarers' mission a priority in the life of the institutional church. The continuing centrality of corporate worship in the very design of their centers testified to this. Also, each of the major Nordic overseas seafarers' ministry organizations had replaced "mission" with "church" by the beginning of the 21st century. Doubtless important was their increased focus on the respective diaspora communities and fellow-nationals on the move—students, business people, tourists and other overseas workers. This change became evident in the new name of the Council of Nordic Seafarers' Missions: *The Nordic Council of Seafarers' and Other Churches Abroad* (1998).

Second, in terms of *specialization,* the Nordics confirmed their basic solidarity with the wider community by the readiness with which they shared the early expertise they gained in "niche" sectors of current-day maritime ministry. This would include: outreach ministries to both *truckers* in dock areas and *off-shore personnel* on maritime oil rigs; responding to increased disaster threats by *crisis-preparedness* planning; also sharing computer technology to offer pastoral counseling and build a virtual *net church,* an initiative since 2006 emulated by the MtS. In many cases it fell to the Norwegians to take the lead, while the Finns initiated a modern-day *ship's chaplaincy* program. That program's prime mover, General Secretary *Sakari Lehmuskallio,* did much to reinforce a positive image of Nordic international engagement during his tenure as ICMA's Chairperson from the year 2000.

As for the respective Nordic *domestic-port agencies,* although founded for the primary benefit of *fellow-national* seafarers (frequently fishers), these found themselves increasingly serving *international* (often developing world) seafarers. While the Finnish Seamen's Mission had always embraced both, several new initiatives now emerged also elsewhere. In close affiliation with the Danes, an independent *Iceland Seafarers' Church* evolved in 1979, and a *Faeroes Seafarers' Church* followed in 1980. In 1996, twelve Swedish domestic-port agencies formed an Association that became an independent member of ICMA. In the Arctic Norwegian port of Kirkenes, the local Lutheran parish opened a seafarers' center in 1997, launching a successful outreach especially to merchant seafarers and fishers from neighboring Russia.

Meanwhile, world mission agencies continued to be virtually unaware of the global mission challenge—and potential partnership—represented by today's multi-religious maritime workforce. By the late 1980s, this had become a major concern in the Author's role as a roving Lutheran Maritime Ministry Consultant. Some modest beginnings in resource sharing did surface, such as: the Danish Santal and Home Port Missions helping out on the waterfront of Manila; also, two major German Lutheran global mission agencies funding port chaplaincies in Hamburg and Singapore.

German Seafarers' Mission

By the beginning of the 1970s, a process of transformation toward more intentional, international engagement was well under way in Germany's national network for seafarers' mission. The German Seamen's Mission continued promoting global, ecumenical partnership, as staked out under the robust leadership of Dr. *Heinrich Maas.* So much so, that it has never wavered since.

The onset of the Shipping Revolution did lead to the closure of some centers now rendered redundant. Still, Dr. Maas's vision of an indigenous Christian "hub" center in Jakarta, Indonesia, the land with the largest Muslim population in the world, would become a fitting memorial to his tenacity. Dr. Maas made sure to entrust the implementation of this project to Rev. *Carl Osterwald,* since 1973 "Senior Pastor" of the German Seamen's Mission. Despite a series of obstacles, and thanks to Osterwald's dogged perseverance during the years that followed, the dedication of the campus could take place in 1986, with the Indonesian Community of Churches finally taking over.

Following the reorganization of the German Seamen's Mission in 1974, Carl Osterwald became the Mission's first General Secretary under its new constitution in 1976. In a programmatic address in 1975, Osterwald had called on his colleagues to claim their self-identity as a *mission*—sent to serve seafarers in a spirit of ecumenical, holistic hospitality, yet also always remembering that "The love of Christ—like all love—needs to be declared!" (Freese 1991).

For almost a decade, both as GSM General Secretary and, for part of the time, as ICMA Chairperson, Osterwald lived out his commitment to holistic mission and ecumenism. The task of building on that legacy fell first to Rev. *Ulrich Wahl* from 1984 and then, from 1996, to Dr. *Jürgen Kanz*. Despite cutbacks in public financing, Kanz—a former missionary in Tanzania— managed to expand the Mission's indigenous involvement globally. He also introduced a new official logo for the German Seamen's Mission, highlighting the Mission's advocacy role with a Christian anchor-cross, together with the words "Support of Seafarers' Dignity." After "retiring" in 2003, and leaving the leadership to Rev. *Hero Feenders,* Dr. Kanz went on to succeed Rev. Berend van Dijken as General Secretary of ICMA (2003-2007).

Dutch Seafarers' Mission

As in Germany, Protestant maritime ministries in the Netherlands adopted a similar international-ecumenical orientation. For the Dutch, however, retrench-ment during the 1970s would prove even more severe, notably overseas. By the mid-1990s, no Dutch Protestant port chaplaincies abroad had survived.

On the domestic scene, in 1977, *A. M. Harissa,* an Indonesian Reformed Church elder and former seafarer, was called to provide indigenous ministry among the many non-Western seafarers then entering Rotterdam, especially from South-East Asia. In recent years, the *Netherlands Seamen's Center* (NZC) has led efforts to coordinate a national network of Dutch Protestant maritime ministry. Participants include the *Protestant Merchant Marine Ministry,* the *Maritime Ministries of the Dutch Reformed Churches*, and the *Diaconal Harbor Project* of Rotterdam.

At the same time, Dutch Protestant agencies have maintained close relations with their Catholic colleagues in the Netherlands Apostleship of the Sea (including in the Dutch dredging ship ministry). In recent years, both have—together with the Filipino Seafarers' welfare network—shared space at the Rotterdam "Zeemanshuis."

On the international level, the Dutch have kept up a consistent commitment to ecumenism through ICMA—ever since Rev. *Jan W. Schokking's* key role in Rotterdam in 1969. In 2000, Rotterdam became the site of ICMA's Secretariat, when Rev. *Berend van Dijken* took over as General Secretary. Van Dijken had, for some years, served as Superintendent Chaplain for the NZC, a position formerly held by Rev. *Jacob Leij* when Chairperson of ICMA.

Over the years, Dutch seafarers' mission has exercised considerable influence by extension—through fellow-ethnic expatriate communities. Among *Dutch-ethnic North Americans*, especially those affiliated with the Christian Reformed Church (CRC) rose to the challenge, headed by their mentor, Rev. *Jan Wristers*. Arriving in the New World in the aftermath of World War II, Wristers, together with his wife and constant colleague, *Ada Wristers*, entered on a lifelong ministry of pastoral care among seafarers, finally based in New

Orleans. On his death in 1980, several North American chaplains of different denominations could say that they owed their initial involvement directly to the example and encouragement of this "chaplain to chaplains."

One of those whom Wristers mentored became the CRC's first official "Harbor Chaplain." Rev. *Hans Uittenbosch* began his Montreal-based ministry along the St. Lawrence Seaway in 1965, and went on to become President of NAMMA in 1976-1980. Another was Rev. *J.E.F. Dresselhuis,* who from 1970 and for 23 years pioneered a CRC port ministry in Vancouver BC. "Jeff" went on to render a unique service to NAMMA colleagues over the years, with his well- researched listings of sources for Christian media for seafarers.

Like their compatriots in North America, the Dutch-ethnic expatriate community in *South Africa* has roots going back to 17th century Dutch emigration. In response to the "dire need" that local Reformed churches in Cape Town discovered on their waterfront during World War II, they formed a *Dutch Afrikaans Seamen's Committee* in 1944. This eventually grew to become a nation-wide *Christian Seaman's Organisation* (CSO), still headquartered in Cape Town, but now an active member of ICMA, ministering in seven South African port cities. Through its chaplains, all of them ordained Reformed clergy, the CSO continues to focus mainly on Christian media and pastoral care, while working in daily ecumenical cooperation with local multi-service seafarers' centers. According to Rev. Hennie la Grange, CSO Mission Director in Durban and ICMA General Secretary from 2007, the CSO sees its ministry as "not stand-alone, but complementary to the other essential services that make up holistic maritime mission"—in the spirit of Acts 6:1-4 and 1 Cor. 12:12.

The North American Network: NAMMA

NAMMA's Ecumenical Journey

How did NAMMA respond to the call for transformation? Around the turn of the century, the Association was served by four executive secretaries, ordained clergy of Lutheran, Baptist, Anglican and Christian Reformed Church affiliation, respectively: Dr. Roald Kverndal (1979-1991), Dr. Paul Chapman (1991-2000), Dr. Peter Michaelson (2001-2005), and Rev. Lloyd Burghart (from 2006)—the first in NAMMA history to be based in Canada., where he had served for several years as CRC port chaplain in Montreal. While the presidency alternated more frequently, it was significant that Rev. *Rivers Patout* became NAMMA's first Catholic in that position in 1980, while *Maggie Whittingham-Lamont* (an Anglican) became its first woman president in 2006.

No development could have been more transformational during these years than NAMMA's ecumenical journey. It really began in 1968. That was the year the New York-based Lutheran President of NAMMA, then still known as ICOSA, together with his 100% Protestant board, "took the plunge" and invited the Catholics to join in launching ICMA. That year, too, three Houston clergy, a Catholic, a Presbyterian and a Methodist, introduced the first phase of a new concept. In 1973, after the founding of ICMA four years earlier, an integrated, ecumenical enterprise called *Houston International Seafarers' Center* became a reality, a model many would later emulate.

Although Protestants and Catholics were both on board at global level in 1969, they had still been sailing their separate ways in North American waters. Then, in 1971, the "Houston Trio," led by Catholic chaplain Rivers Patout, came up with an idea, together with an Anglican board member of ICOSA, Rev. *Arthur Bartlett*. That year, ICOSA and the AOS in the USA would be holding their respective annual conferences simultaneously in the San Francisco area. Patout and Bartlett scheduled a joint boat trip in the Bay as a break. It would turn out a positive experience for all. Even more time would be required, however.

Finally, in 1979, what was by then the National Catholic Conference for Seafarers (NCCS) and ICOSA agreed for the first time to combine their programs in a joint conference in Pensacola—thanks not least to the efforts of Bishop René Gracida. From then on, that formula would become a yearly event. Soon the effect began to show at grassroots level. For example, in one port a couple of years later, at a first-time informal breakfast meeting, ICOSA's (Lutheran) Executive Secretary witnessed the local Catholic port chaplain exclaim to his Southern Baptist counterpart: "We've worked this waterfront for years without exchanging a word. Here we are—eating, even praying together!"

During the early 1980s, ICOSA was enriched by the advent of further "Denominational Associations." Emulating the Catholics with their NCCS, the Anglicans and Lutherans followed suit in 1981 with the *Missions to Seamen in North America and the Caribbean* (MSNAC), and the *Lutheran Association for Maritime Ministry* (LAMM). In 1983, a *Southern Baptist Seafarers' Ministers' Fellowship* (SBSMF) evolved. Rather than leading to divisiveness, such associations have since reinforced NAMMA and the cause of ecumenicity, by raising awareness and resources within each of the denominations concerned.

Beyond ecumenical relations between different Christian denominations, how did NAMMA respond to the issue of *interfaith relations*—interacting with other (non-Christian) religions? NAMMA placed this issue squarely on the agenda at its 2003 Annual Conference in Oakland, California. With "Biblical Dialogue with Other Faiths" as the theme, there were presentations by eminent spokespersons for all the major non-Christian world religions—Muslims, Buddhists and Hindus. As a result, virtually all those present affirmed the need to combine cooperation in areas of *common humanity* with mutual respect for each religion's *distinctive identity*. In that sense, NAMMAC/2003 in Oakland became a "New Breakthrough in the Bay."

Two Transforming NAMMA Agencies

Among NAMMA's members, none could quite compare with the North American Anglicans' "flagship" agency, the *Seamen's Church Institute of New York and New Jersey*. As the numbers of American seafarers plummeted during the 1950s, it fell to a Norwegian-born sea captain, *Jörgen Björge,* then an SCI lay chaplain, to play a unique role in assuring that agency's continued relevancy.

"Captain George" (as seafarers called him) persistently called for, and then went on to lead, the SCI's expansion to incorporate the rapidly growing container-hub at Port Newark, New Jersey.

Still by far the most comprehensive maritime mission agency of its kind in the world, the SCI of NY/NJ comprised three components at the turn of the 21st century: The Center for Seafarers' Services, the Center for Seafarers' Rights, and the Center for Maritime Education (currently operating at three locations: New York NY, Paducah KY, and Houston TX). Although also a charter member of NAMMA, the SCI of NY/NJ had, by 2003, become such a major player on the world scene that ICMA could welcome the agency as a member in its own right. That same year, the agency's Executive Director, Rev. Canon *Peter Larom,* after handing over the leadership to Rev. Dr. *Jean Smith,* went on to launch and lead a promotional partner of MSNAC, known as the *Alliance of Episcopal Maritime Ministries* (AEMM).

It marked a major ecumenical breakthrough when the Southern Baptist Seafarers' Ministers' Fellowship accepted an invitation to join NAMMA's Board of Directors. Credit for bringing his traditionally independent denomination on board belongs to Rev. *John Vandercook.* A seasoned WWII navy veteran, he had already brought the Southern Baptists on board in the field of maritime ministry. Back in 1963, together with his wife *Catherine Vandercook,* the couple opened a seafarers' center in their own living room near the New Orleans waterfront. In 1983, he led his fellow Baptists to participate in NAMMA's Annual Conference, that year held in New Orleans.

John Vandercook's son, Rev. *Philip Vandercook,* currently heads what has grown into a major Mississippi river-port operation, now known as *Global Maritime Ministries* (GMM). Based in New Orleans with satellite ministries beyond, the agency also reaches out to countless numbers of port personnel. In the mid-1990s, the younger Vandercook transformed the original SBSMF into *Port Ministries International* (PMI). PMI helped NAMMA co-host ICMA/2004, and has continued to cooperate with NAMMA and enrich its fellowship.

Independent Maritime Ministries

Past Developments
By the beginning of the 21st century, the majority of Christian-based maritime mission agencies worldwide were in some way affiliated with ICMA. A small minority continued to take a different stance. These agencies appear to have two principal characteristics in common: (1) *Emphasizing evangelism strongly*—over and above social implications of the gospel. (2) *Promoting partnership selectively*—leaving less room for cooperation with others who may claim Christ as Savior and Lord, but differ theologically.

Perhaps the best characterization of these agencies might be "Independent Evangelicals"—in contrast to the many that see themselves as "Ecumenical Evangelicals." The most prominent among them is currently the non-denominational, UK-based *Seamen's Christian Friend Society* (SCFS). It is also by far the oldest. Founded in London in 1846, in cooperation with Rev. George Charles Smith, the SCFS can therefore claim personal ties back to the early Bethel Movement. After focusing on a ministry of evangelism in UK ports up to the 1980s, the SCFS then decided to "go global." Beginning by taking over a non-denominational port ministry, initiated by Tacoma Seafarers' Center in Manila, the Society has built up a worldwide network of SCFS-linked port ministries in the Philippines and elsewhere since the 1990s. The SCFS has also engaged itself in a vigorous pastoral follow-up and fellowship program.

A number of like-minded maritime ministries emerging in recent years have hitherto concentrated on specific major world ports. This has been the case with *Lighthouse Harbour Ministries* in Vancouver BC and vicinity, Canada, *Het Havenlicht* in Amsterdam, Netherlands, and *Freunde für Seeleute* in Hamburg, Germany. Two recent books by Martin Otto give striking examples of the latter Hamburg-based agency's participation in current-day follow-up and "church planting" ministry at sea (Otto 2002 and 2007).

Future Prospects

In September 2000, a diverse group of some 75 port missionaries from around the world convened at Lake Yale, north of Port Everglades, Florida. Here, with Rev. Dr. *Paul Peterson* of Tacoma as coordinator, they agreed to establish a networking relationship, eventually known as *Harbour International Ministries* (HIM). Its principal purpose would be to express and nurture the kind of independent, distinctively evangelical identity its membership held in common—despite their mutual diversity. This was the culmination of three earlier "International Conferences of Evangelical Port Missionaries," in Vancouver BC (1991), Manila (1994) and Cape Town (1997). Following a fifth international conference in Hong Kong in 2004, it remains to be seen whether a more structured umbrella organization may emerge.

More importantly, does the future hold out any prospect of change—in terms of a more united witness within the worldwide Church Maritime? By the 1990s, there were already signs that this might well be happening. Some HIM participants were already involved with NAMMA, thereby facilitating communication on a personal, if not yet organizational, level. One example was *Seward Seamen's Mission,* a robust cruise-ship outreach established in 1993 by the (non-denominational) "Alaska Christian Ministry to Seafarers." In 2005, *Biblia Harbour Mission,* a South Africa-based founding member of HIM and a lay-staffed, independent, sister-organization of CSO, decided to become a member of ICMA. Shortly before, work began on an ITF-funded seafarers' center in the busy West African port of Tema, Ghana, run by the SCFS and BISS in cooperation. (This Author believes that would have made old Bosun Smith, the hero of both societies, very happy.)

In the final analysis, the outcome will doubtless depend on the willingness of both the ecumenical majority and the independent minority to face up to one and the same biblically mandated challenge: *To commit to respecting the others' chosen identity—in a spirit of reconciled diversity for the sake of the gospel.*

12

OTHER CURRENT CHALLENGES
(Continued)

INTEGRATION: ALL PEOPLE OF THE SEA

An important way in which Western-world maritime ministry would manifest transformation during the last quarter of the 20th century was through the integration of relatively un-reached categories of sea people. In the past, these might have been victims of discrimination or oversight. Now, there were also those who were newcomers on the maritime scene of a rapidly globalizing world. By the turn of the century, most modern-day maritime ministry agencies were, in varying degrees, struggling to address unmet needs within each of the three categories which John Paul II, in his 1997 Apostolic Letter *Stella Maris*, collectively calls "People of the Sea": (1) Seafarers as Such, (2) Maritime Personnel, and (3) Sea-related Dependents.

Seafarers as Such

Women: At Sea and on the Waterfront

For years, people have discounted women in sea-related vocations by using the male designation *seamen,* which—in effect—takes women for granted. Only comparatively recently has there been an effort to adopt the more gender-inclusive designation *seafarers* in generic usage, while reserving the word "seamen" for more gender-specific purposes.

True, prior to World War II, seafaring was an overwhelmingly male-dominated vocation. Seldom, if ever, would women be working at sea, except at the very bottom of the ship's hierarchy—in the catering or cabin departments of mainly passenger vessels. In the wake of gender emancipation due to the need for total mobilization of human resources during World War II, it became apparent that women were capable of "manning" any position—also at sea. First, they proved themselves as radio operators, notably on Norwegian ships. Then, there were women serving as navigating officers. As technology continued to replace muscle-power, female engineer officers began to appear, too. As women even outperformed their male counterparts, the days were finally over when Russian cargo ships crewed entirely by women would shock the industry.

With the late-20th century boom in ferries and cruise-ships, the proportion of women at sea in that sector had, by the mid-1990s, risen to 9%, according to an ITF survey. Although that figure would not be representative of the overall picture, the trend has been unmistakable. More women continue to ship out. As they do, committed Christians among them will, with their distinctive gifts, reinforce the fellowship and witness of Christian communities at sea.

Meanwhile, ITF surveys were also able to disclose the scandalous level of continued gender discrimination at sea. Coordinated by *Sarah Fincke,* the Women's Officer heading the ITF's "Women's Network," the surveys showed how women seafarers still had to face formidable sexist barriers to recruitment, training and advancement, as well as pervasive pregnancy-related prejudice. Even more troubling was evidence of "overt sexual harassment" at sea—in a "macho," male-dominated environment, bereft of normal support systems. The ITF also pinpointed proven resistance to equal employment opportunities for women as long-shore workers—with the conspicuous exception of Russian waterfronts (*ITF Women* 1996; Zhao 2003).

In terms of women who *minister* among those who sail, IASMM has cooperated with NAMMA in researching endemic inequity there, too. A research paper from the year 2000, entitled *Women on the Waterfront,* traces for the first time the long, ignoble history of male discrimination against women in mission and ministry among seafarers. The study first recognizes "the unostentatious efforts of countless and usually nameless women," faithfully serving through the centuries in vital *supportive* roles in maritime ministry. It then focuses on how certain exceptional women have, during these last 200 years, managed to challenge and break those two male monopolies—executive leadership and pastoral ministry in seafarers' mission (Kverndal 2000).

In terms of *executive leadership,* even in the early 1800s and through the 19th century, there were some among the "Christian fair" who boldly defied contemporary norms of "domesticity and decorum" by launching a series of new measures to ameliorate the lot of marginalized mariners. Nevertheless, it was not until the final quarter of the 20th century that sexist ceilings in maritime ministry leadership began to break in a broader sense. First, in the course of the 1980s, came a number of both Baptist and Catholic female founders and directors of seafarers' agencies. Finally, by the mid-1990s, women also gained access to presidency-level leadership, first in denominational associations (NCCS and LAMM). Then, in 1996, Chaplain *Karen Lai* and Rev. Dr. *Jean Smith* became joint vice-presidents of NAMMA. In 2006, NAMMA went on to elect *Maggie Whittingham-Lamont* of Halifax, Canada, as its first woman president.

In terms of *pastoral ministry,* female participation in the key function of *shipvisiting* had for long presented a seemingly insurmountable barrier—at any rate in male eyes. After all, this entailed entering on a regular basis into a predominantly male environment—a "floating total institution." Yet, women who had come to know the chivalrous characteristics of the average seafarer felt far from intimidated. Among these, American women of Catholic religious orders were first in the field, in the 1970s. Eventually, others would follow suit. In 1979, American Anglicans, affiliated with the Seamen's Church Institute of NY/NJ, broke an even more controversial barrier by appointing a woman, Rev. *Victoria Sanborn,* to an ordained port chaplaincy position. Nordic Lutheran seafarers' churches soon began doing the same.

In the wake of Vatican II, with its expanded opportunities for ministry by women within the Catholic Church, *Karen Lai,* chaplain-director of Galveston Seafarers' Center, emerged as a passionate advocate for greater participation by women in chaplaincy and leadership, both in North America and worldwide. In 1992, she started a network of "Women in Maritime Ministry" (WIMM). While President of the NCCS in the mid-1990s, she used that platform well, as she continued campaigning for the unique, nurturing role of women—especially in the role of seafarers' "surrogate family," as she put it. By the turn of the century, she had gained even more visibility for the cause, through her authorship (Lai 1999 & 2002). See also the Perspective by Karen Lai (below).

The world's first full-time non-Western woman seafarers' chaplain, *Irette Ramoelinina,* is also worthy of special mention. Since 1991, she has served on the waterfront of Madagascar's premier port city, Toamasina (formerly Tamatave). Here, heading the indigenous maritime ministry of the Malagasy Lutheran Church, she has written maritime mission history in ecumenism through her ground-breaking cooperation with the local Catholic AOS agency. No less remarkable has been her innovative outreach to sea-related women who have been systematically abused for centuries—port prostitutes. During the mid-1990s, in a port notorious for its large numbers of these women, one of their own sex and race started a ministry of rehabilitation and job training that is now a prototype. See also Irette Ramoelinina's Perspective (below).

Progress in this field was particularly remarkable in a non-Western context, where the subordination of women is not only more common, but often dictated by both religion and society. Despite gains in recent years, the status of sea-related women, also in the West, still leaves much to be desired.

> Worldwide maritime mission without God's self-revelation through half the human race would result in an utterly *amputated* witness on the waterfront. Only as the distinctive contribution of women is adequately enlisted can there be an authentically holistic witness to the shalom of Christ in the maritime world—and therefore the *whole* world—in the new millennium (Kverndal 2000).

Fishers and Fisherfolk

"If seafarers are the forgotten people of the world, then fishers are the forgotten of the forgotten," declared Douglas Stevenson. He was speaking on behalf of the New York-based SCI's Center for Seafarers' Rights, at the AOS

World Congress in 1992. Three years earlier, in 1989, the SCI had resolved to confront the issue by launching a comprehensive "Commercial Fishers' Project." Prepared by Research Associate *Sarah Bittleman,* the resulting report, published the following year, was to the point: To explore why not only society, but even the religious community that ministers to seafarers, had "generally neglected fishers. *"* While this particular study focused particularly on the plight of North American fishers, its findings contributed to a new level of awareness in wider circles during the 1990s.

That awareness-raising called for agreement on appropriate *terminology.* In fairness to the many women also employed in the fishing industry, the terms "fishers," "fisherfolk" and "fishworkers" were now increasingly used in preference to the gender-exclusive "fishermen." However, was it correct to consider fishers as *seafarers?* Despite acknowledged neglect, there was agreement—at least in the maritime ministry community—that fishers were indeed seafarers; they followed a vocation entailing sea-going vessels. The UN reported a total of some 35 million fishers worldwide in the year 2003 (*Apostolatus Maris* 79/2003, 15). If families were included, the figure would reach 200 million, and further still in order to embrace all people dependent on fishing and fish-processing for their livelihood.

Not only were fishers many times more numerous than merchant seafarers. They were far more vulnerable in their living and working conditions. Consultations and workshops through the 1990s helped raise awareness of the dire need among fishing communities worldwide. With a mortality rate 12 times greater than in other high risk vocations, the physical danger in fishing was only one aspect threatening their quality of life. In 1994, a report by the Lutheran World Federation's Maritime Ministry Consultancy put it this way:

> Authorities have been anxious to update the supply of fish, but have largely neglected the fate of fishers. Factors like rampant over-fishing, mounting pollution of the marine environment, and diminishing fish-stocks, coupled with a glaring lack of unionization and advocacy, have led to fierce competition, widespread abuse, and pervasive poverty throughout the global fishing community. An acute need to "de-stress" during brief spells ashore has all too often destroyed whole families and reinforced alienation from a Church that simply does not seem to understand—or even care.

A consensus developed that the Christian church could not wait for fishers to contact the church. The church must reach out to them, proactively integrating fishers into its overall outreach to seafarers through both pastoral and prophetic ministry. It was important to distinguish between the two categories within the worldwide workforce of fishers: (1) *Artisinal* (small scale or coastal) fishers, who make up the vast majority of fisher-folk, operating small boats in coastal or inland waters. (2) *Industrial* (large-scale or deep-sea) fishers, operating modern, motorized vessels with crews of up to 50, often in waters half a world away.

In pastoral ministry: Those reaching out to merchant seafarers have come to recognize their responsibility to include local *artisinal* fishers and their families, too. Also, Christian congregations in the vicinity of a center have launched particular programs offering pastoral/diaconal care as well as Bible-study and fellowship groups. (Several recent initiatives in Indian, Indonesian and African coastal waters have proved the viability of such efforts.)

In prophetic ministry: Mounting numbers of *industrial* fishing companies have in recent years taken advantage of the FOC option. This has led to rampant abuse among especially Asian "crews of convenience" in the fishing sector. Due to the notorious lack of regulation and unionization among them, industrial fishers have become even easier prey than merchant seafarers. Following up on the SCI's 1989 initiative, the specialized Christian justice ministries in New York, London and Barcelona continued, during the 1990s, the momentous task of advocating for systemic change in the fishing industry—in cooperation with other concerned agencies like the ILO, IMO, ITF, SIRC and ICSW.

Meanwhile, the British, French and Nordic fishers' missions have continued their historic involvement in all aspects of fishers' welfare. The AOS maintains an active International Fishing Committee. On the North American scene, NAMMA has also had a special Fishers' Committee. Long led by Rev. *Andrew Krey* and, more recently, by Fr. *Sinclair Oubre,* this has promoted networking to support social integration and self-empowerment among fishers and their families. See also the Perspective by Gérard Tronche (below).

Inland Waterway Mariners

"The very *mules* on a Kentucky corn plantation" were treated better than people employed on the navigable rivers, lakes and canals known as America's "Western Waters." Such was the opinion of one of their early 19th century advocates in the New World. There, as in the Old World, these "Inland Sailors" seemed to share the same, if not even greater, social marginalization. Known variously as boatmen, watermen, lightermen and bargemen, these mariners and their families were first "discovered" by the pioneers of the early Marine Bible Society Movement in Britain and America. These were in the forefront of establishing Sabbath and Free Schools for the children of this category of nomadic families, many of whom also needed food and clothing.

The world's first organized inland waterway ministry appears to have been the *Grand Junction and General Sea Canal Bible Association,* founded in England in 1816. Christian-based agencies for the spiritual and social betterment of this impoverished people group eventually emerged on both sides of the Atlantic, also on the inland waterways of the Netherlands and Germany. In Germany, there developed an *Association of Evangelical Inland Waterway Missions* ("Verband der Evangelischen Binnenschiffermission"), with origins in the 1870s. Now headquartered in Stuttgart, this national network maintains close links with the German Seamen's Mission.

The linkage between "brown-water" and "blue water" ministry would become especially apparent in coastal areas. Typical examples have been the

Scottish Coast Missions of the mid-1800s, and the subsequent Canadian missions among the remote coastal communities of Newfoundland, Labrador and British Columbia. Today, the Seamen's Church Institute of NY/NJ represents a unique combination of both forms of ministry. In 1997, the Institute branched into brown-water ministry with its innovative "Paducah Project." Paducah, Kentucky, at the confluence of four major river systems, is today the hub of inland waterway traffic nationwide. The program has since expanded to two state-of-the-art Centers for Maritime Education at both Paducah and Houston, supplemented by an extensive pastoral network of river chaplaincy known as "Ministry on the River" (Smith 1998/99).

Mission Ship Crews

There have been many mission-related watercraft (both stationary and mobile) since the early formative phase of organized maritime mission. By contrast, "mission ships" in the present context refer to vessels acquired or employed in the service of specifically *global mission*. There are those who maintain that the first authentic "mission ship" was therefore none other than *Noah's Ark*. After all, with her divinely ordained shipwright and captain, the purpose of this amazing vessel was to fulfill God's global plan of mission (Genesis 6:8-22). Be that as it may, in terms of modern-day maritime mission history, it was the Bible society "Agents Afloat," and Bethel Captains of the early 1800s, who really pioneered the concept.

At the same time, the (London) Missionary Society launched a series of vessels bought or built to serve as dedicated mission ships. Following in the wake of the first of these, the ss *Duff*, as early as in the late 1790s, their purpose was to transport missionaries, their families and mission supplies to their future fields among the South Sea Islands, eventually also elsewhere. As the world mission movement gathered momentum, other mission societies followed suit. To crew their vessels, they would call committed Christians. Also, in order to offset expenses, they would search for commercial cargoes as well.

There was soon a need for a smaller, shallow-draft vessel, meant for more local inter-island communication and new mission ventures in the area. Shortly after his arrival in Tahiti in 1817, the Congregational missionary martyr, Rev. *John Williams,* personally built the pioneer model for this type of vessel. By the end of the 1820s, indigenous Tahitian, Tongan and Fijian missionaries had begun making their own key contribution, by transforming their traditional, former war canoes into what became a *Deep Sea Canoe Mission,* reaching across much of that part of the Pacific.

By the mid-1900s, over 30 world mission agencies employed several hundred sea-going mission ships. Together, these made up what one researcher has called a "Gospel Navy" (Livingston 2002/3). By the 1970s, most of these had also been phased out, due to air travel and other factors.

Then the unexpected happened. It began with a band of American college students who shared a common goal, winning the unreached millions in the post-World War II generation for the gospel—especially those in nations most economically and spiritually deprived. Pointing to a world map, their leader, *George Verwer*, said that since it was *the sea* that covered most of the planet, the most effective means of making the message known must be *by ship*—thereby reaching huge numbers of people in port cities around the world.

The outcome of Verwer's vision was that he and his fellow workers formed a non-denominational mission organization, *Operation Mobilization* (OM) which, in 1970, bought a 30-year old Danish passenger ship. Renaming her *Logos* ("Word"), they transformed her into a floating book fair. The next year, she sailed off on her "maiden mission" to Asian port-cities. Since then, the OM mission ship saga has steadily expanded. By 2007, the *Logos Hope,* another (far larger) former Danish passenger ship, would complete rebuilding and join the other current OM ship, the *Doulos* ("Servant"), a former Italian floating casino. With crews totaling 500 multinational volunteers (professional seafarers and students), the OM ships have had over a million visitors annually, welcomed in countries often inaccessible to conventional Christian mission. Here they have provided millions of educational and Christian books, as well as discipleship training where possible—including among seafarers in port.

Since the early 1980s, Y*outh with a Mission* (YWAM) has operated a corresponding *medical* mission outreach with its *Mercy Ships*. After rebuilding a former Italian luxury liner as a modern hospital ship and medical school, they renamed her *Anastasia (*"Resurrection"), crewed her with 450 volunteers, and sent her on year-round medical missions, to impoverished population groups worldwide. By 1994, *YWAM* had added three smaller Mercy Ships to their fleet. As ship-based agents of mission, both crew and staff of these modern-day mission ships form an integral part of the people of the sea. In that sense, they represent a renewal of the connection with global mission that was so characteristic of the first era of organized maritime mission.

Maritime Personnel

Offshore Workers

From the mid-1970s, a few veteran chaplains of the Norwegian Seamen's Mission began bringing Christmas gifts to offshore workers on the storm-swept oil rigs based on the Norwegian North Sea Continental Shelf. Then, in 1982, the Norwegian Seamen's Mission responded to the express invitation of both oil companies and unions by appointing Rev. *Knut Mölbach* (formerly Norwegian Port Chaplain in New York) to pioneer a specialized form of full-time industrial chaplaincy. For thousands of Norwegian seafarers who had lost jobs, due to the effect of globalization on the Norwegian merchant fleet, offshore installations offered an alternative—and for the Norwegian Seamen's Mission a chance to continue contact with many of their former "floating congregation."

Two decades later, six offshore chaplains were regularly rotating on 38 oil rigs, while a seventh served with the supply fleet. Here, in another type of "total institution," they shared everyday privations and perils in incarnational solidarity with the general workforce. Management and workers alike now see offshore chaplains—living literally "on the same platform" as their flock—as indispensable to both morale and safety. In this stressful environment, offshore ministry demands a form of specialized counseling that has made such chaplains a natural resource also in modern-day maritime "crisis preparedness." Other maritime missions have sought to adapt the Norwegian model to meet their own regional needs. See also Perspective by Anita Tronsen Spilling (below).

Port Workers

The New Orleans-based *Global Maritime Ministries,* the "flagship agency" of the Southern Baptists, have integrated into their overall ministry a specific outreach to their local port workers, offering them hospitality, welfare services and counseling. The awareness of this need may account for the increasing use of terms like "port chaplaincy" and "port ministry."

In one sense, all staff members at port-based seafarers' centers are "port workers," given that they normally work within a certain port area. At all events, it is mandatory today to maintain positive relations with local port authorities, not only if a center is to operate on actual port property, but also in order to obtain access to terminals and ships in port. Port chaplains normally nurture positive relations also with other shipvisitors—representing immigration, quarantine, ships' agents and unions. As to port prostitutes, promising outreach initiatives have surfaced in recent years, such as in Toamasina and Bangkok.

Truckers

Not all seafarers' centers have become involved in ministry among drivers of the tractor-trailers that haul cargoes to and from port loading areas. Still, trucking as a mobile profession has many similarities with seafaring. Some seafarers' centers have integrated a special outreach to truckers as part of their regular ministry. In Europe, for example, the Norwegian Seamen's Mission has launched such ministries in megaports like Rotterdam, Antwerp and Hamburg, thereby—as with offshore ministry—offsetting some of their loss of national seafarers. In North America, seafarers' centers in Port Newark, New Jersey, and Gulfport, Mississippi, have been especially proactive in trucker ministry.

Shipping Personnel

Many members of the shipping profession have been seafarers themselves. Those engaged in the shore-based operation of merchant ships (shipowners, ship operators, shipbrokers, ship's agents, etc.) constitute an integral category of "maritime personnel." Recognizing this, maritime mission agencies have sought to cultivate positive relationships with their local shipping community. Some have integrated them into their stated sphere of ministry by instituting special programs for shipping personnel. One example is the professional shipping-related courses offered by the New York-based Seamen's Church Institute. Another is the Korean-language *Galilee* quarterly, distributed to both seafarers and the shipping community by Korea International Maritime Mission (KIMM).

Maritime Students

Even before the beginnings of organized seafarers' mission, there were those who saw it important to provide prospective students with the best possible vocational training for a seafaring career, in combination with guidance in Christian faith and ethics. Both Jonas Hanway and G. C. Smith engaged in pioneer ventures in this field. Even within the more secularized society of the post-World War II Western world, some maritime mission societies were still able to provide chaplaincy services at public maritime educational institutions, notably the MtS and BISS in Britain. The Norwegians and Danes even ran Christian-based maritime colleges that are continuing today. In Asia, too, the AOS in the Philippines could provide "Christian Formation" classes at maritime educational institutions, while KIMM was able to initiate comprehensive chaplaincy and training programs at similar institutions in Korea.

Sea-related Dependents

Seafarers' Families

Seafarers' families have for centuries been a subject of concern for Christian ministry, from the widows and children of members of medieval mariners' guilds to desperate dependents of modern-day crews of convenience, cheated of their hard-earned allotments by unscrupulous operators. Belonging to the most numerous as well as the most vulnerable category of people of the sea, distressed and bereaved families of shipwrecked or otherwise missing seafarers became a vital focus of ministry from the very first years of organized maritime mission on both sides of the Atlantic.

More recently, the founding of ICMA opened new networking possibilities for promoting the welfare of seafarers' families, struggling with separation-related concerns. The theme of ICMA's Second Conference in Denmark in 1975 was, in fact, specifically: "The Personal and Family Implications of Being a Seafarer." ICMA's 1985 Conference in the Philippines developed this theme, especially in regard to *Asian* seafarers' families. During the 1980s, KIMM introduced a series of remarkably popular *Christian Family Retreats,* available for seafarers on furlough in Korea.

In the meantime, also secular-based advocacy agencies for seafarers' families' common concerns emerged in many parts, especially in Northern Europe. Here, the ILO and SIRC have taken up both the global coordination of welfare provisions for seafarers' families, and the research of seafarers' family life issues, respectively.

Retired or Unemployed Seafarers

Over the centuries, elderly or invalid seafarers—once for good reason called "decayed and decrepit"—would have been the responsibility of their own nuclear family, if they had one. Where this was not possible, prospects would be grim indeed. Only a few of the more fortunate benefited by sporadic measures— from medieval almshouses to the homes for "old salts" that opened in the wake of the 19th century Seafarers' Mission Movement. In the latter category, nothing has ever surpassed the monumental buildings that made up the original "Sailors' Snug Harbor" on Staten Island from the 1830s.

The most pressing problem for *retired* seafarers, at least in the Western world at the end of the 20th century, would be very different from the situation of their predecessors. Suddenly thrown into unemployment in today's globalized maritime labor market, many have found themselves too young to retire and too old to re-train. As a result, advocacy on behalf of unemployed seafarers has become an important maritime ministry concern in recent years. That concern is one of the many shared with the modern-day maritime union movement.

COOPERATION: OTHER ORGANIZATIONS

Among important issues confronting Christian maritime mission during the late 20th century was not only the challenge of *integration*—of all who belong among "People of the Sea." There was also the challenge of proactive *cooperation*—with those promoting the wellbeing of seafarers from motives other than expressly Christian, such as civic or humanitarian. In addition, it was possible that some might become involved from non-Christian yet none the less faith-based motives. How should maritime missions relate to different categories such as these, and what were the individual identities involved?

Toward a Double Breakthrough

From Mutual Suspicion

As already seen, early Christian maritime mission agencies were involved in a range of social welfare activities—including justice and advocacy issues. This was several decades before the advent of modern-day maritime unions. Once these came on the scene with their own social justice agendas, tension began building between missions and unions. For seafarers to take charge of issues affecting their own welfare was, in the eyes of these struggling maritime unions, a matter of self-respect and simple justice. For established missions, the unions seemed to symbolize a single-minded "secularizing" emphasis on physical concerns—to the exclusion of spiritual needs.

With time, that mutual suspicion subsided to a kind of uneasy co-existence that continued into the Global Era and the early 1980s. This was not only the case with maritime labor unions. It was also largely characteristic of relations with other (governmental and non-governmental) secular agencies that had some connection with seafarers' welfare. Complicating the picture was the fact that, by the early 1980s, Christian missions were still delivering an estimated 90% of maritime welfare services worldwide.

To Proactive Partnership

It was only as the dehumanizing downside of the Shipping Revolution began to take its toll that matters changed. Maritime unions discovered that seafarers' chaplains—committed to a balanced, "holistic" understanding of ministry—were in reality indispensable partners in a common cause, confronting the escalating abuse of seafarers' human rights. Simultaneously, Christian missions came to appreciate the crucial role of maritime unions—especially where represented by the International Transport Workers' Federation, with the professional expertise of their labor negotiators and inspection personnel. This mutual discovery resulted in a historic breakthrough in the mutual relations between Christian and secular welfare providers.

Then, at the start of the 21st century, there were signs of a second breakthrough in that relationship. This time it referred to the other of those two major mission challenges of the Shipping Revolution—the new level of religious pluralism in the globalized, multi-ethnic maritime workforce. One effect of the 9/11 tragedy was to add a new note of urgency to the need for Christian maritime missions, to relate positively to those of other faiths—by building human community, while respecting religious distinctiveness..

It was important to recognize the same basic human right for seafarers of all religions (including Muslims, Hindus and Buddhists) to freedom of choice and mutual respect in the exercise of their faith—not only at sea but also on the waterfront. There were already signs of such a breakthrough at NAMMA's Conference in 2003—around the theme "Biblical Dialogue with Other Faiths." For secular maritime welfare providers, too, such signs of breakthrough on the part of Christian agencies would be welcome. As a result, the overall history of relations between Christian and other maritime welfare providers is one of gradual maturation toward a more "adult" partnership—in a joint search for commonality, while accepting individuality.

Other Major Organizations

The International Transport Workers' Federation (ITF)

Founded in 1896, as a coordinating body and collective voice for transportation-related trade unions worldwide, the London-based ITF has always been the undisputed world leader in the campaign against the FOC system. In this regard, it has repeatedly recognized the importance of the grassroots cooperation offered by port chaplains everywhere. In order to help offset the loss of traditional welfare funding, hurt by the growth of FOC shipping, the ITF established, in 1981, an auxiliary source of sponsorship called the *ITF Seafarers' Trust*. This would, in the words of the Trust, be "dedicated to the spiritual, moral and physical welfare of seafarers, irrespective of nationality, race, or creed."

The annual allocations of the ITF Seafarers' Trust have been of crucial importance in funding Christian maritime welfare facilities worldwide—increasingly for the particular benefit of new or struggling centers in the port-cities of developing nations. Although others, too, have benefited on an equal level, Christian-based agencies have hitherto been the primary beneficiaries, given their continued proportionate role in maritime welfare provision globally.

See also the Perspectives by the ITF's General Secretary, *David Cockroft*, and the Trust's Senior Administrative Officer, *Tom Holmer* (below).

The International Labour Organization (ILO)

Due to the international nature of both the sea and seafaring, the founding of the *International Labour Organization (ILO),* in 1919, was of momentous significance for seafarers' welfare worldwide. Headquartered in Geneva, as a specialized United Nations inter-governmental agency for the promotion of global social justice, the ILO brings together representatives of governments, employers and trade unions in a unique tripartite decision-making formula. Together, these seek to improve, and subsequently monitor, labor conditions everywhere—through "Conventions" and "Recommendations."

The ILO has devoted more Conventions to the social welfare of seafarers than to any other vocational group. Following a historic "Geneva Accord" in 2001, shipowners and maritime unions instituted a process that had, by the year 2006, produced a *Consolidated Maritime Labour Standards Convention.* Intended to include all 60-plus maritime-related instruments in one simplified document, this may well, when duly ratified, serve as a long overdue global "Seafarers' Bill of Rights." For the promotion of a comprehensive, holistic concept of seafarers' welfare, the ongoing observer status of ICMA at the ILO continues to be of vital importance.

The International Maritime Organization (IMO)

In order to cope with the escalating rate of technological change in post-World War II shipping, the London-based *International Maritime Organization* (IMO) was established in 1958, as a second specialized inter-governmental UN agency. The IMO's mandate is more narrowly focused than the ILO's. Whereas the ILO deals with socio-economic issues, the IMO concentrates on technical issues, primarily maritime safety (including relevant crew training standards) and pollution prevention. Quoting its own slogan, the IMO seeks "safer shipping and cleaner seas." In these technical areas, IMO Conventions can inform and effectively supplement the ILO. Though not based on the ILO's "tripartite" system, practically all its many member states have ratified its Conventions.

Among the IMO's achievements are International Conventions on Safety of Life at Sea (SOLAS), Standards of Training, Certification and Watchkeeping for Seafarers (STCW), and the Prevention of Pollution from Ships (MARPOL). Here too, ICMA's observer status continues to be important. In 1983, the IMO founded a *World Maritime University* (WMO) in Malmö, Sweden, to promote professional, global expertise in advanced maritime training, with special emphasis on the implementation of the IMO's own Conventions. See the *Perspective* contributed by General Secretary *Epthimios Mitropoulos* (below).

The International Shipping Federation (ISF)

Apart from altruistic motives, it is now widely recognized that running "a happy ship" is simply good business. The level of competency and morale of the crew is crucial to any given ship's reliability and efficiency. The London-based *International Shipping Federation* (ISF*)* is the "Employers' Association," for shipowners operating more than half the world's merchant fleet. The ISF coordinates concerns regarding labor relations ("human resource issues") for both regional and national shipowners' associations worldwide. It holds consultative status in the ILO, as well as other UN regulatory bodies.

Although the ISF shares considerable common ground with the ITF in the elimination of sub-standard ships in general, they differ on certain aspects of FOC shipping. The ISF cooperates closely with its likewise London-based sister organization, the *International Chamber of Shipping* (ICS). The ICS is the corresponding "Trade Association" for ship operators in the various trade sectors such as container ships, tankers, passenger ships, etc.

The International Committee on Seafarers' Welfare (ICSW)

Historically, it was Christian maritime welfare that, in the 1920s, took the initiative toward a forum for communication and coordination with secular maritime welfare. This was in the early years of the ILO in Geneva. The attempt proved premature, because Christian agencies were still without any structured linkage among themselves. It was not till half a century later that a fresh initiative materialized—this time from the secular side, represented by the ITF.

In 1976, thanks largely to the vision and tenacity of the Assistant General Secretary of the ITF, Swedish-born *Ake Selander,* an *International Committee on Seafarers' Welfare* (ICSW) came together in London as a "Working Group." Ten years later, the ICSW formally organized—with the ITF, ILO, ISF, USS and ICMA as principal co-founders. A growing number of governmental and other maritime welfare agencies have since joined. In 1992, the *International Sports Committee for Seafarers* (ISS) became an ICSW Sub-committee.

Lieutenant Commander *Andrew Elliott* RN took over as Secretary from Selander in 1999. Relocating to Watford, Hertfordshire, in 2002, the ICSW has vigorously pursued its mission—"To promote the practical implementation of the ILO Instruments on Seafarers' Welfare." With major funding by the ITF Seafarers' Trust, and in active cooperation with ICMA, ICSW projects have included: Regional ICSW Seminars—coordinated by Regional Seafarers' Welfare Committees, Ship Welfare Visitor Training courses, Global "Twinning" of Seafarers' Centers, an Information Technology Service Pack, a Seafarers' Health Information Programme (SHIP), a Port Directory of Welfare Services, and an International Seafarers' Assistance Network (ISAN), a "freephone" referral service launched with SIRC assistance in 2003.

The Seafarers International Research Centre (SIRC)

In the international maritime community of the early 1990s, it was recognized that up to 80% of accidents at sea were the result of *human error,* while research had so far focused largely on *technological* factors. It was important to redress that imbalance by now giving priority to the industry's "human factor." In January 1995, members of the ITF Seafarers' Trust convened a broad-based conference of representatives from maritime industry and welfare institutions at Cardiff University, in Wales. The outcome was the establishment of a *Seafarers International Research Centre* (SIRC).

With initial funding from the ITF/ST, the Center would affiliate with the prestigious Maritime Studies Department of Cardiff University, but otherwise be completely independent. There was consensus that the primary area of research would be seafarers' safety and occupational health. The Center's overall purpose would be to help formulate policy on such issues for the shipping industry's decision-makers. One of the Center's principal architects, Professor *Alastair Couper* of Cardiff University, became its first Director. With its series of professionally produced projects by an exceptionally qualified research team, the Center has since won worldwide acclaim for the reliability of its studies. See also the *Perspective* by the current Director, Dr. *Helen Sampson* (below).

From the outset, the maritime ministry community responded positively to the Center's holistic concept of welfare. Of relevance to Christian missions have not only been scientifically researched projects on topics like FOCs, globalization, fatigue, isolation, AIDS, mortality, multicultural crews, women seafarers, and family life. SIRC has also provided professional expertise for *ministry-related* projects, like the roles of maritime welfare organizations, sailing chaplains, and enhanced use of the Internet. In this context, ICMA continues to serve on SIRC's Management Board and Advisory Panel. Since 1998, communication has also evolved between SIRC and its Christian-based counterpart, the International Association for the Study of Maritime Mission.

Faith-based Non-Christian Maritime Ministries

Apart from sporadic instances, the possibility of cooperation with faith-based maritime ministries other than Christian has yet to materialize in a general sense. Nevertheless, NAMMAC/2003 in Oakland, California, did represent an important first step. It prepared the ground for dialogue and future cooperation in areas of common humanity with those of other faiths who may, in the future, engage in outreach on the waterfront. Certainly, if and when Muslims, Buddhists, Hindus or those of other non-Christian religions so decide, they would—according to the United Nations' Universal Declaration of Human Rights—have a perfectly equal right to do so.

EDUCATION: TOOLS FOR MARITIME MINISTRY

"Jesus wove education into the fabric of the Great Commission by sending forth his church to make disciples of all nations" (Coleman 1989). With that reminder from Matthew 28:18-20, a veteran seminary professor highlights the fundamental role of education in the fulfillment of the Lord's mission—also its maritime dimension. As his disciples (literally "students"), Christ's followers are not only to follow his message in their own lives. In so doing, they are also called to reach and teach others (2 Timothy 2:2), thereby fulfilling their Master's global strategy of multiplication ministry on both land and sea.

Ever since the early 1800s, Christian maritime missions have taken a series of educational initiatives. In recent years, enhanced possibilities for such endeavors have opened up in the wake of the current Information Revolution and its resulting "knowledge explosion." ICSW Chairperson *Robert T. Korner* characterized the situation in the year 2000: "Information Technology will alter how seafarers remain connected to family and society, how seafarers learn, and how spiritual and health needs are met." The following explores the response of Christian maritime mission to education-related challenges from the perspective of three categories of tools: Training – Resources – Research.

Training

For Seafarers Themselves

Faced with a desperate level of educational need in the early 1800s, pioneer maritime missions in Britain and America found they had to start "Sabbath Schools" and "Free Schools" for illiterate seafarers and their families. At the latter, "sea boys" and adult seafarers could, in addition to help with navigating "the sea of life," also obtain rudimentary nautical skills. As elementary education became more available toward the mid-1800s, a few Christian-based British agencies started operating residential nautical schools (Kennerley 1997). In Europe, both Norway and Denmark still maintain their own version of such schools. On the American scene, the Center for Maritime Education of the New York-based Seamen's Church Institute remains unique in its field, with three locations in New York, Paducah and Houston.

Meanwhile, a different opportunity for Christian maritime vocational education has presented itself. At both pre-sea and officer-level nautical schools and training ships, from Britain and Norway to South Korea and the Philippines, port chaplains have offered courses in "Christian Formation," i.e. basic ethics and faith orientation

For Practitioners of Seafarers' Mission

From the early 1800s, there was never any formalized method of professional training for seafarers' mission personnel. Many considered sea experience at the "University of the Sea" to be an advantage, though by no means a necessity. Likewise, theological education and ordination were not necessarily a prerequisite. Bible knowledge certainly was, as most notably in the case of Father Taylor of Boston. Otherwise, it was essentially a question of "learning by doing," interacting over time with seafarers themselves in their particular conditions of life and work.

It was only during the Global Era of the movement, beginning in the last quarter of the 20th century, that more structured options could be offered in basic, and eventually also advanced, education in the field of maritime mission and ministry. Apart from "in-house" denominational or organizational orientation seminars, the historic inter-confessional "first" happened in North America. The ecumenical "Houston Trio," led by AOS Port Chaplain Rivers Patout, started the *Houston Port Chaplaincy Training School* in 1974. Consisting of a two-week program of Field Study and Clinical Pastoral Education, with twelve candidates drawn from different denominations, the school met a valid need, received warm endorsement by NAMMA, and has continued ever since as an annual event.

Following the Houston initiative, other models have commenced elsewhere. In 1979, the SCI of NY/NJ introduced a pilot program which, under Rev. Barbara Crafton and later Rev. Dr. Jean Smith, became the non-denominational *International Training Center for Workplace Ministry* (ITC), prioritizing participation from the non-Western world. Still the most comprehensive model in the field, the ITC has, since 1992, offered from 10-week to 10-month Internship Programs. The ITC has included a *World Haven Program*, from 1999 operated in collaboration with the SCI's Center for Seafarers' Rights (CSR). This has sought to provide an advocacy network for ITC graduates worldwide. Meanwhile, the CSR has continued to offer its own highly-rated *Port Chaplains' Seafarers' Rights Workshops,* in North America and overseas.

From the mid-1980s, indigenous candidates were also the focus of Lutheran training initiatives: *Seminars on Maritime Follow-up Ministry* given by Tacoma Seafarers' Center, and *Maritime Ministry Training Seminars* offered in a number of Asian and African port cities, run by the LWF Maritime Ministry Consultancy. In 1996, the Korea International Maritime Mission (KIMM) established its *International Maritime Mission Training Institute* (IMMTI), now led by KIMM's Mission Director, Dr. *Byeong-Eun Lee.*

With the worldwide demand for more training options far outstripping the supply, there was no problem finding ready candidates for an ICMA-sponsored *Seafarers' Ministry Training* (SMT) program. Rev. Berend van Dijken was the first Coordinator in Rotterdam in 1997. Like the original Houston model, it offered a two-week intense immersion in maritime ministry skills for recently appointed chaplains. In this case, participants were principally of non-Western origin. With SMT/Hong Kong in 2001, Asia provided the site for the first time, and Rev. *Martina Platte,* GSM Chaplain in Hong Kong, took over as Coordinator. With SMT/Durban in 2006, Africa also joined in hosting the event. At the same time, ICMA sponsored the concept of a three- to four-day *Maritime Ministry Introduction* (MMI) course, designed for chaplains new to the work, floating it first in the Odessa region.

Given its declared purpose, the *International Association for the Study of Maritime Mission* (IASMM) kept in close touch with ICMA about issues relevant to ICMA's educational role. IASMM offered off-campus continuing education ("distance learning") opportunities, for both SMT graduates and other maritime chaplains. By the turn of the century, a Lutheran North American IASMM member, Dr. *Serge Castigliano,* could supplement this with a *first-ever*

Maritime Clinical Pastoral Education (MCPE) program, offered at the New York-based Seafarers' and International House.

IASMM also gave publicity to Dr. Paul Mooney's 2002 dissertation, with its *Seafarer Discipleship Training* (SDT) program. Presented as an official proposal at ICMA/2004, this could provide a core curriculum for preparing seafarers to minister among their peers at sea. ICMA-certified seafaring graduates from this kind of ecumenical discipleship program could then receive supplementary preparation, for licensing as lay ministers by their respective denominations or organizations. The proposal has potential to help implement a seafarer-centered paradigm for maritime mission in the 21st century.

Whether ICMA and the maritime ministry world community will respond to this kairos opportunity remains to be seen. Meanwhile, thanks primarily to an initiative by the Anglican MtS Secretariat for Justice and Welfare (headed by Canon Ken Peters), an exploratory *Education & Training Forum* took place in November 2002 in London, with broad participation by both Christian and secular seafarers' welfare providers. The outcome gave good ground for optimism about such a solution as suggested at ICMA/2004. (Regarding ICSW-coordinated *Ship Welfare Visitor Training* courses, see chapter 14 below.)

Resources

Maritime Devotional Resources

"Mariners' Manuals," intended to nurture faith and help seafarers "navigate the ocean of life," began to appear as early as in the late 1500s. The upsurge in distribution of Scriptures and seafarers' homilies, prayer books and manuals, during the early 19th century Bethel Movement, is now recurring in the New Bethel Movement of the Global Era. Since the geo-political upheavals of 1989 and after, many seafarers' centers have found it hard to keep up with demands for Bibles and New Testaments, especially in Russian, Chinese, and—increasingly—also Arabic. The world's first maritime mission-related agency, now known as the Naval, Military & Air Force Bible Society (NM&AFBS), has seen its distribution of Scripture portions proliferate both globally and ecumenically—with cooperating agencies ranging from the SCFS to the AOS.

With the advent of electronic media, seafarers can now benefit from not only Christian radio programs but also audio- and video-tapes, CDs, DVDs, etc., including the popular *Jesus Video.* By 2002, the number of viewings of this authentic reproduction of St. Luke's Gospel had already reached many millions worldwide—in hundreds of languages. By 2003, the Mission to Seafarers could report that the *Alpha Course,* a basic introduction to Christianity, was being well received, also among seafarers.

In the field of Bible study materials, the Ministering Seafarers' Program designed by Ray Eckhoff has inspired a LAMM-sponsored amplification entitled the *WaterWords* series (2002), edited by Dr. *Robin Dale Mattison* and published by Mall Maritime Library. From 2006, the MtS i-church initiative has brought the worship and teaching resources of the wider church within reach also for those at sea.

Promotional Resources

Media produced in order to promote awareness, interpretation, and ongoing support for seafarers' missions also have a long history, going back to the very first organizations formed for that purpose. Here too, IT has greatly expanded the possibilities. Agency web-sites now offer easy access to viewing or downloading of organizational literature like reports, newsletters, etc. Several organizations have produced promotional videos and guidelines for developing new maritime ministries. Also, the celebration of a specific "Sea Sunday" has become an annual tradition in many seafaring nations, with the distribution of special resources to inform both churches and the general public about the indispensable role and human needs of modern-day mariners.

Port Security Resources

Almost overnight the 9/11 terrorist attacks on America made "Port Security" a dominant factor fueling the continued marginalization of seafarers. In September 2001, Canon Peter Larom had already, together with his successor Dr. Jean Smith, led the SCI's response to the *literal* fallout from those attacks. Only a few blocks from Ground Zero, the SCI's New York head office and its staff, together with hundreds of volunteers, were within hours playing a crucial role as a round-the-clock rescue station. The next July, Larom laid out the *long-term* implications of 9/11 in a paper for IASMM/2002 entitled *Future of Maritime Ministry: The New Port Security and the Marginalization of the Seafarer* (Larom 2004).

In charting a viable course through those implications, Larom's colleague, Douglas Stevenson, was—as attorney and US Coast Guard Commander—uniquely qualified. He lost no time in seeking to counter the consequences of overzealous anti-terrorist security restrictions. These had started seriously impeding both shore leave by seafarers and access to ships by seafarers' chaplains. In response, Stevenson launched a concerted campaign, first obtaining feedback from port chaplains far and wide, after that confronting both government and industry with hard, irrefutable evidence. He showed such measures to be not only unfair and even inhumane, but also counterproductive. They were, in fact, diverting valuable resources from real risk factors, including the countless containers still crisscrossing the oceans with their contents in most cases unchecked, at least until recently.

Since port security was a global problem, the sustained engagement of all three New York, London and Barcelona-based maritime justice ministries would prove vital. This applied not least to the implementation of the ILO's 2003 "Seafarers' Identity Documents Convention" and the IMO's "International Ship and Port Facility Security Code" (ISPS). By 2007, it was hoped that a new "Transportation Worker Identification Credential" (TWIC) Program would help overcome the many security problems in port areas of the USA.

In this protracted process of balancing legitimate port security concerns with the human rights of the maritime workforce, there was an unforeseen side-benefit, however. As ITF General Secretary David Cockroft pointed out, there is now a growing awareness by governments about "the ease with which flags of convenience can be used, not just by bad employers but also criminals and even terrorists." This has made effective enforcement of international regulations an urgent global priority, one that might even spell the overdue end of the entire FOC system. Nevertheless, it bears repeating that anti-terrorist measures alone can never prevent terrorism without addressing its root causes, not least the global inequities that continue to feed the despair of the dispossessed.

In addition to taking the lead in educating the maritime ministry community, as well as public policy-makers, about the human consequences of 9/11-related port security measures, the NY Center for Seafarers' Rights has produced a battery of brochures, consultation reports, seminar materials, newsletters and e-mail updates on other justice-related issues, too. These include the 1999 publication of an informative 365-page *Seafarers' Handbook* on shipboard life and the marine environment.

Piracy and Stowaway Resources

The Christian maritime justice ministries in New York, London and Barcelona have also joined hands with other agencies in addressing the late 20th century resurgence of one of the oldest forms of marine terrorism—international *piracy*. Already prior to the 9/11 attacks, reports of piracy on the high seas (and even in port areas) were escalating in frequency and viciousness. The perpetrators were mostly organized gangs using speedboats and deadly weaponry, from machetes to machine-guns. In 1981, the London-based International Chamber of Commerce established an *International Maritime Bureau* (IMB) as a global maritime detective agency, dedicated to combating piracy and shipping fraud. In 1992, in response to the alarming increase in brazen attacks, the IMB opened a *Piracy Reporting Centre* (PRC) in Kuala Lumpur, Malaysia, to track such attacks globally.

PRC reports have long pinpointed Indonesian waters and the Malacca Straits as the most notorious of the world's piracy "hotspots," closely followed by India, the Caribbean and increasingly the coast of Northeast Africa. Deep-sea fishing vessels are especially vulnerable, sometimes completely vanishing following a "hijacking." In 2005, pirates off Somalia even attacked a regular cruise vessel with rocket fire! The lack of political will among regional authorities to enforce anti-piracy policies has, in the past, proved particularly frustrating. But here, too, it seems that 9/11 has made a difference. The IMB has identified a linkage with "political piracy"—perpetrated to fund militant fundamentalist groups. As *Michael Grey* of *Lloyd's List* comments, seafarers who are used to official indifference to previous attacks might be "forgiven some cynicism over the way in which everyone is becoming enthusiastic about security" (*The Sea*, Jan-Feb 2004).

The good news is that piracy attacks have now often failed, thanks to increasingly well-informed and vigilant ship's crews. In recent years, however, a kind of kindred covert activity at sea, in the shape of *stowaways* and organized human trafficking, has been on the increase, driven by the disparities of global economics. As with piracy, maritime missions have helped raise awareness here too. In the case of human beings hidden on board, however, circumstances may well call for advocacy. Cruelty and revenge run completely counter to the Christian gospel. So, too, does punitive pressure on ship's crews in order to prevent people-smuggling in the first place.

Crisis Preparedness Resources

The sinking of the passenger ferry *Estonia,* off the coast of Finland in 1994, cost 852 lives. As the worst post-World War II marine disaster, it prompted ICMA to organize a response in the shape of a *Crisis Preparedness Program.* Launched in the year 2000, this offered a series of regional training courses to provide coping skills in crisis situations, including associated trauma. As leader of the project, Rev. *Terje Bjerkholt* was an experienced oil rig chaplain with the Norwegian Seamen's Mission. The General Secretary of the Swedish Church Abroad, Rev. *Jan Madestam,* summed up the basic rationale: "The Church cannot provide an answer to the why of every catastrophe, but she can bring God's presence—where people are met with unconditional love."

In 2003, a project originated in Britain to help prevent crisis situations at sea from developing in the first place. The *Confidential Hazardous Incident Reporting Programme* (CHIRP) encourages concerned seafarers to report any maritime safety-related issues, so as to generate effective remedies without revealing the identity of the reporter. With The Mission to Seafarers distributing the program's newsletter, *Maritime Feedback,* the scheme seeks to counter the current blame culture—leveled at seafarers as automatic scapegoats.

Health-Related Resources

Issues relating to health and hygiene for seafarers have engaged maritime missions from the very beginning. This applies not only to the curbing of alcohol abuse and the spread of sexually transmitted diseases (STDs), but also the provision of hospital services and medical care, specifically for seafarers and their dependents. With the recent increase of research and resources, not least in terms of HIV/AIDS, as well as stress-related ailments, seafarers' missions have continued to work closely with other agencies in disseminating information. In 2003, the ICSW and its member organizations started a *Seafarers' Health Information Programme* (SHIP) in collaboration with the International Maritime Health Association (IMHA). Meanwhile, the missions have also continued to partner with the ICSW in promoting health and fitness at sea through the latter's *International Sports Sub-Committee* (ISS) and "Sportsweeks." See also relevant *Perspectives* by *Darrell Schoen* and *Ruth Kverndal* (below).

Information Technology Resources

No factor has in recent years had such a profound impact on issues affecting maritime welfare in general as increased access to Information Technology—whether for seafarers, their dependents or those who serve them. It has become a priority for all maritime welfare agencies, church-affiliated or otherwise, to make advances in telecommunication more readily available for seafarers. To that end, the ICSW has issued a comprehensive *IT Service Pack*.

While many ships' crews have yet to gain general access to phone, fax and internet while at sea, for those visiting seafarers' centers ashore, dedicated space for both telephone and computer usage has become standard service. With opportunities for shore leave becoming increasingly limited, cell phones and cost-effective calling cards are already a normal part of shipvisiting kits for port chaplains everywhere. Meanwhile, the International Seafarers' Assistance Network (ISAN) continues to alleviate the lack of physical proximity to loved ones at home.

Research

Rationale for a Specialized Entity

Ongoing research remains a primary precondition for the provision of effective training and resources in maritime mission. Prior to the 1970s, maritime mission decision-makers had to rely on "ad hoc" measures for securing and processing information. Such forms of research would make do with conference papers and special reports. It had always been difficult to find the time and focus necessary for reflection—in a vocation notorious for overextension. In addition, there was the inherent challenge of objectivity—amidst the conflicting demands of institutional loyalty and image consciousness.

With the advent of globalization in the maritime world, the need for an agency with expertise in maritime mission research became increasingly evident. At ICMA's First Plenary Conference in London in 1972, the Author presented a *Research Progress Report* on the first academic study of the history of the Seafarers' Mission Movement. It ended with the following plea:

> In waging his long and lonely battle for the recognition of missionary research, Dr. Kenneth Scott Latourette spoke in the 1930s of the 'criminal waste' of neglecting the fruits of past experience. With the tremendous challenge of change confronting the maritime ministry of the 1970s, the issue is not whether we can afford to pursue systematic research, but—whether we can afford *not* to (Kverndal 1995, 7).

Despite expressed interest on the part of several individuals, notably ICMA's future General Secretary, Prebendary Tom Kerfoot, ICMA was at that time not prepared to accommodate a specific research unit within its own organizational structure. Of course, this did not invalidate the need. After the

Author's fifteen-year research odyssey, such an entity did materialize—formally independent, yet strongly supportive of ICMA

The International Association for the Study of Maritime Mission

Finally, the year 1990 saw the founding of the *International Association for the Study of Maritime Mission* (IASMM). The Association's Secretary and Co-founder, *Stephen Friend*, details the subsequent history and current role of IASMM in his Perspective (below). The Author, as the Association's first President, would later elaborate on the dual characteristics of the fledgling organization: On the one hand, it had to embody *inclusiveness*—in terms of ecumenicity, ethnicity and relevancy, in order to relate to the contemporary multi-religious maritime world. On the other hand, it would need to emphasize *distinctiveness*—in terms of a clear, Christian identity, so as to fulfill its unique servant role in the global maritime mission community (Kverndal 1995, 1-9).

In 1998, on IASMM's invitation, ICMA's Executive Committee appointed a representative of ICMA to serve ex officio on IASMM's General Committee. The move affirmed the commonality of concern between the two organizations. By then, IASMM had already established a connection with its secular counterpart, the Seafarers International Research Centre, as well as with the ITF Seafarers' Trust (a major sponsor of both SIRC and ICMA).

In essence, IASMM seeks to respond to the requirements of an indispensable "niche" ministry in the maritime ecumene—to study both the past history and present scene of maritime mission, so as better to serve the holistic human needs of seafarers in a fast changing postmodern world. In that context, David Bosch summarizes the creative tension inherent in all authentic mission studies—also in the field of maritime missiology:

> "Missiology, as a branch of the discipline of Christian theology, is not a disinterested or neutral enterprise; rather, it seeks to look at the world from the perspective of commitment to the Christian faith. Such an approach does not suggest an absence of critical examination; as a matter of fact, precisely for the sake of the Christian mission, it will be necessary" (Bosch 1991, 9).

THE END OF THE BEGINNING

During World War II, as favorable news began to break at last, Churchill told his embattled people that this was not the end of their struggle. Nor was it even the beginning of the end. But perhaps it was *the end of the beginning!* The same might possibly be said of the most recent years in the ongoing history of maritime mission. Following the long delay after the Master's first call by the shores of Galilee, the Bethel Movement of the early 1800s did not mark the end of the quest for a viable, sustainable strategy of seafarers' mission. Nor has the emergence of a New Bethel Movement two centuries later. However, perhaps this latter development does signal the end of the beginning of that quest.

If this is true, it affirms that the global maritime mission enterprise, as portrayed in the preceding Historical Part of the book, is now well under way into the third stage of its continuing saga. After a *formational* (or premodern) era, and a *transitional* (or modern) era, maritime mission has now entered a *transformational* (or postmodern) era. In the search for an authentic paradigm of maritime mission for the 21st century, it remains to trace the evolving shape of such a paradigm in the subsequent Systematic Part of this book.

PART II

OVERVIEW
OF MARITIME MISSION

13

THEORETICAL FOUNDATIONS

MOTIVES FOR MARITIME MISSION

"Why do you do this for us?" The question came from a Soviet sea-woman. She was speaking for a group of seafarers returning from a sightseeing trip in the center's van. The chaplain-chauffeur responded, "It is because people in churches around here have discovered the limitless love of Jesus Christ and want to share that love with strangers who come to our port cities." After a long pause, the woman replied through her interpreter, "Tell your friends in the churches—thanks for being *our* friends."

This happened in the late 1980s, shortly before the Berlin Wall came down. The Communist-indoctrinated seafarers were puzzled. According to still current stereotypes, all Americans were supposed to hate all Russians, and vice versa. Yet, before the ship left, several of those same seafarers had asked the chaplain for a Bible in Russian. The episode gave evidence of a crack already appearing in that infamous wall between East and West—with seafarers as potential peacemakers in a polarized, postmodern world.

As those familiar with port ministry well know, many others have raised the same question as those Soviet seafarers, over the years. Ultimately, it addresses the "why" of maritime mission and ministry. The issue of motivation constitutes the very heart of any missionary endeavor and needs to come first in a systematic overview of the theology of maritime mission.

Refutation: Taking Objections Seriously

As early as in New Testament times, Paul prepared Christians for the need to "demolish strongholds" of anti-missionary argumentation (2 Corinthians 10: 4-5; Ephesians 6:12). Similarly, the early pioneers of organized mission among seafarers found that the refutation of objections *against* maritime mission had to form an integral part of advocacy in *support* of such mission. Despite the very different context of modern-day maritime mission, current negative arguments have proved remarkably similar to those of the early 1800s. These follow the same lines as then, representing maritime mission as (1) *impossible,* if not (2) *immoral,* and at all events (3) *immaterial.* The corresponding counter-arguments continue to form the nucleus of a *Maritime Mission Apologetics.*

The "Impossible" Argument

To the suggestion that the "new" reality of religious pluralism at sea has made maritime mission "impossible," the most effective response has been to refer to *reality itself.* Never were professing Christians engulfed by a more aggressive host of other faiths than in the original New Testament Church. Yet, never did the number of believers multiply more rapidly than then. To maintain otherwise would be a denial of history, as recorded in both the Book of Acts and elsewhere. It would also fly in the face of the proliferating shipboard Christian communities in the modern-day maritime workforce.

The "Immoral" Argument

As to the allegation that maritime mission has, in today's context, become "immoral," evangelization is, on the contrary, an issue of *fundamental human rights.* Christians, too, have committed terrible abuse toward those of other faiths over the centuries; and much remains in terms of frank apology and meaningful amends. Still, the *principle* stands firm. As stated in Articles 18 and 19 of the UN's Universal Declaration of Human Rights: every human being has the right to choose, to change and, within the bounds of mutual respect for the human rights of others, to express and propagate his or her "religion or belief." No one is free to choose, however, without knowing what there is to choose between. Therefore, every faith must also have an equal human right to follow a *mission agenda* inherent to that particular faith—always provided one concedes that same right and respect to other faiths, with mission agendas of their own. There is urgent need for change, if this is to hold true on every waterfront.

The "Immaterial" Argument

To the assertion that maritime mission has become immaterial in this post-modern and post-9/11 world, a biblically balanced understanding of holistic mission has, instead, made verbalization of the gospel more necessary than ever. A "holistic" approach recognizes that *the gospel* of Christ—just like *the cross* of Christ—has a vertical and horizontal dimension, relating to God and fellow-humans, respectively. To a *fundamentalist* kind of extremism (or "verticalism") that downplays the plight of others, Jesus responds that the way we relate to "the least of these" is how we relate to him as the Son of God (Matthew 25:31-46). To a *universalist* kind of extremism (or "horizontalism") that discounts salvation through Christ, he asks how the greatest success in the world would help, if it comes at the cost of one's eternal soul (Matthew 13:26). Toward the end of the 20th century, it was no longer spiritualistic *verticalism,* but universalistic *horizontalism* that posed the greater challenge in the maritime mission community. That trend resulted from an understandable disgust with both human rights abuse at sea, and the blind fanaticism of religious fundamentalism.

All of this combined to make *justice-related* issues the overriding concern and the *evangelism* component of holistic mission seemingly "irrelevant."

Freedom of choice—so highly prized by the post-modern mindset— logically necessitates evangelism, in order to make the gospel alternative freely available for everyone. At the same time, after 9/11 there is a heightened awareness of the need to promote a one-world sense of global, civil community. Increasingly, people now recognize that this can only happen if (1) proactive cooperation in matters of human common concern combines with (2) mutual respect for the distinctive beliefs and mission agendas of others.

Motivation: Proactively Making the Case

When William Carey, the future "Father of Modern Missions," was well on board and bound for India, the owners abruptly turned him off the ship as soon as they discovered the object of his journey. According to the policy of the (British) East India Company, any disturbance of the religious status quo in the "native" population at that time could spell "trouble" governing them. As it happened, Carey succeeded shortly afterwards in booking passage with a Danish ship instead, arriving in Calcutta in 1793.

Before encountering such *politically* motivated objections, Carey also had to face down the *theological* rebuke of a senior colleague at a ministerial meeting. When Carey took up the question of global mission, his colleague's immediate response was, "Young man, sit down!" He added that God would manage perfectly well without human help. The reason why Carey could carry on undeterred was because he was already motivated to refute such objections. Before 1792, William Carey had found his anchor in the Bible's own basis for mission.

By the mid-1820s, after the initial upsurge of the Bethel Movement, the onset of institutionalization underscored the need for a presentation of a rationale for mission among seafarers. Prominent among spokespersons for such motivation was the "Sailor's Advocate," Rev. George Charles Smith. Some of the motives advanced by both Smith and others could be both complex and subjective. Supporting the spiritual and moral welfare of seafarers would be to the benefit of national security, transport safety, public health and commercial prosperity. This served the human instinct of self-interest within the community at large. Yet for some, it would also serve the altruistic incentive of indebtedness. Anything to improve the wellbeing of seafarers was, in light of their indispensable contributions to society, only a repayment. To quote Albert Schweitzer, this was "not benevolence, but atonement."

In the following, however, the focus will be on the Bible's "objective" motive for mission—the so-called "Great Commission." It derives its name from the command of the Lord of Mission to his followers after his resurrection. According to the New Testament record, he gave it in varying versions. It is the one from Matthew, chapter 28, verses 18-20, which most people associate with this concept. The finale of the first Gospel is the basis for the following analysis.

With his opening statement, "All authority in heaven and on earth is given to me" (28:18), the risen Christ sets the stage for the culminating purpose of his three-year public ministry—to inaugurate a missionary movement with no less than global and eternal implications. Such an enterprise was now essential in order to make the fruits of his incarnation, atonement and resurrection available—to all of humankind, for all time to come. Endowed as he was with ultimate power, Christ was at last ready to empower his followers also, as he sent them off on their new, epoch-making assignment: "Therefore, go and make disciples of all nations" (28:19). Those words contain answers to three crucial questions—each of them vital to the Christian missionary enterprise.

From Whom Does the Missionary Mandate Originate?

In *Transforming Mission,* the most widely recognized compendium of missiology in this post-modern era, David Bosch describes how, since the 1950s, virtually all Christian persuasions—Protestant, Orthodox and (since Vatican II) Roman Catholic—have embraced an understanding of mission as *Missio Dei* ("the Mission of God"). Earlier, one saw mission as an activity of *the Christian Church*—"introducing people from the East and the South to the blessings and privileges of the Christian West." Finally, it has become clear that:

> Neither the church nor any other human agency can ever be considered the author or bearer of mission. Mission is, primarily and ultimately, the work of the Triune God, Creator, Redeemer, and Sanctifier, for the sake of the world, a ministry in which the church is privileged to participate. Mission has its origin in the heart of God (Bosch 1991, 389-393).

The Latin word *mission* means "sending." Because God persists in loving the created world, the spreading of love belongs to the very nature of God. God is a "sending" God. According to Matthew, it is as *the Son of the Father,* the second person in the Triune Godhead, that Jesus Christ now sends his followers on this mission to all nations. Each of Matthew's fellow-evangelists affirms this in their respective versions of the Great Commission: Mark 16:14-18; Luke 24:45-49, continued in Acts 1:8; John 20:21-23.

Whom Does the Missionary Mandate Address?

In a preceding verse, Matthew makes particular mention of "the eleven disciples,"—the remaining apostles, following the defection of Judas. Throughout his gospel Matthew also uses the term "disciple" *generically*, about both male and female followers of Jesus. However, these are not just "students" seeking to learn from their Master. They are members of an "alternative community," committed to being his fellow-workers, eventually recognizing him as their Savior and Lord. As such, "the first disciples are prototypes for the church"—now about to emerge (Bosch). They are not primarily persons gifted for a special vocation as preachers. They are witnessing members of the wider,

Christian community. Jesus' first seafaring followers are therefore models for his seafaring disciples among today's people of the sea.

Among the four versions of the Great Commission it is Luke's, as continued in Acts 1:8, that most distinctly depicts the missionary nature of the third person in the Trinity, the *Holy Spirit:* "But you will receive power when the Holy Spirit comes on you; and you will be my witnesses . . . to the ends of the earth." Since the day of Pentecost, personal empowerment by the Holy Spirit has remained the precondition for becoming an effective witness, whether on land or sea. It is the Spirit-born love of Christ that has always provided the compelling motive to persevere (2 Corinthians 5:14-15). This raises the question: For what specific assignment are such witnesses to be equipped?

What Purpose Does the Missionary Mandate Seek?

Matthew's version spells out, in 28:14, the over-arching purpose of the Master's charge—*to make disciples* ("mathetenein"). Three years earlier, when Jesus first called those disciples, his original commission had been to become "fishers of people" (Matthew 4:19). Far from trying to "entrap" anyone, the intention was clearly to "attract" (John 12:32). To make disciples signifies in this context not to coerce, but to make freely available the means to become disciples of Jesus. In modern mission terminology, Jesus has initiated a form of "multiplication ministry." Toward that end, he spells out a concise, two-fold strategy: "baptizing them in the name of the Father and of the Son and of the Holy Spirit, and teaching them to obey everything I have commanded you" (28:19-20).

Since then, Christians have interpreted the significance of such *baptizing* in very different ways—as sacrament or symbol, by pouring or immersion, at infancy or maturity. None the less, about baptism's *intent,* as a rite of initiation into the Christian community, there continues to be relatively wide agreement.

By contrast, the assignment of *teaching*—to obey the Lord Jesus in "everything"—entails a continued, life-long commitment: "As the Father has sent me, I am sending you" (John 20:21). In John's version, Jesus is making his own life of dedicated service a *holistic* model of mission for his disciples of every age (Stott 1975, 23-25). It is known in its most condensed form as Jesus' "Great Commandment"—of unconditional love for God and neighbor (Luke 10:27). In his "Nazareth Manifesto" (Luke 4:18-19), Jesus begins his own ministry with a proclamation of forgiveness, healing and liberation, manifesting the arrival of the *Kingdom of God* (Matthew 10:7). To teach that same "kingdom agenda" still constitutes the core of the Master's missionary mandate.

That mandate entails both universal and timeless dimensions. Jesus begins by calling his first followers to go and make disciples of "all nations," in other words—*all of humankind* (v. 19). Without including all those who have their livelihood on the sea, how else could world mission embrace the whole world? Furthermore, the final words of Matthew's version promise Jesus' empowering presence *for all time*: "And surely I am with you always, to the very end of the age" (v. 20). Without Jesus' empowerment of constantly new generations of *seafaring disciples*, how else could the task of reaching the whole world continue in a sustainable manner—as predicted in Matthew 24:14?

If modern-day maritime mission is not going to lose its authentic, biblical bearings amidst the turbulent seas of globalization or—as Paul Mooney puts it— become irrelevant, even obsolete, it needs to shift to a new, agency-facilitated, seafarer-centered mission paradigm. That means one that takes seriously, also in the maritime world, "that the central charge of the Great Commission is to make disciples" (Mooney 2005). Charting the course of maritime mission—toward this primary goal of the Lord of Mission—will be the focus of the following section on the "Dimensions" of maritime mission.

DIMENSIONS OF MARITIME MISSION

Quoting Rev. Jan Wristers, mentor of Dutch-American port chaplains, it was certainly not the Apostle Paul's plan to preach to seafarers from the pulpit of a sinking ship. As with global mission, it was the Lord himself who "invented" maritime mission. In Acts 27, Luke actually provides us with

> two remarkable reminders of the two sacraments which Christ himself ordained. On the instructions of an angel of the Lord, Paul 'took bread, and giving thanks to God,' led in a meal reminiscent of the Eucharist. Finally, as the ship broke up on the shores of Malta, they jumped overboard and were all "saved through the water"—I Peter 3:20 (*Watermarks* 3/1980, 10-11).

Not only was maritime mission, like all mission, *initiated* by the Lord, the New Testament offers several examples of how he also indicated ways by which his followers could *participate* in that mission. The immediate task is now to explore the nature of such mission, characterized here as "Dimensions" rather than "Objectives," following the example of Bosch (1991, 8-11, 367, 511-519).

Proclamation: The Evangelistic Dimension

Of the six dimensions of maritime mission under consideration in this overview, *evangelism* merits first place. As seen by both leading Protestant missiologists and Catholic sources, evangelism represents the very "heart" of mission, "If you cut the heart out of a body, that body becomes a corpse. With evangelism cut out mission dies; it ceases to be mission" (Bosch 1987, 100; *Ad Gentes* 1965, 13). As another professor put it, "If the Christian church does not evangelize the billions who have not heard—or no longer heed—the Good News, there is no one else in the world to do it" (Braaten). This applies no less to evangelism in the mission of the Church *Maritime* (*Watermarks* 2/1990, 1).

The word "evangelism" derives from the Greek verb meaning literally "to announce good news." In the New Testament, it signifies the proclamation (or spreading) of the Gospel of Jesus Christ. Over time, the term has also acquired a *negative* meaning. Repeated abuse of the term has led many to equate "evangelism" with "proselytism," seeking to convert others at all costs—whether by coercion or seduction. A veteran seafarers' chaplain in Seattle, *Norris Stoa*, used to say that "evangelism" is in itself a beautiful word, for at its center there is the word "angel." This reminds us that it was, in fact, an angel of God who, according to Luke 2:10-11, first proclaimed the gospel of Jesus Christ as Savior of the world..

The Nature of Evangelism in Maritime Mission

The following is an example of evangelism in action on the Pacific Northwest waterfront. It was at a time when Soviet ships still carried a commissar in charge of their crews' ideological welfare. As soon as the chaplain introduced himself and offered hospitality and help, he encountered a curt rebuff: "You have no business on board this ship. Since our revolution in 1917, Russia is a Communist state. So, here we are all atheists." "I was once an atheist myself," said the chaplain, "at least in a practical sense." His curiosity piqued, the commissar demanded to know more. "I always knew there had to be a God," the chaplain responded, "because you can't get the whole of creation out of nothing. Only, I did not want anything to do with him. I was a practical atheist. You are presumably a theoretical one." "So what happened?" asked the commissar. "I'm here because of a revolution launched over 1900 years before yours—and it's still going on," said the chaplain.

Then, assuming a commissar would have to know at least something about the "competition," the chaplain continued: "It hit home when I discovered that God's own Son had himself paid for all my failings. So, why should I have to? And why should you?" Taken aback, the commissar found himself letting the chaplain come aboard anyway, with consequences neither of them could have foreseen—a vanload of his fellow crew-members, only too anxious to accept an invitation to shop and sightsee and make new friends.

This shipvisiting episode illustrates the unstructured nature and unpredictable outcome of evangelism opportunities during the brief encounters typical of today's waterfront. In terms of *methodology*, Paul the pioneer missionary put it plainly: he was willing to become all things for all people, so that "by all possible means" at least some might be saved (1 Cor. 9:22). In maritime ministry, too, the means of evangelism are virtually limitless, whether that witness may be by word (spoken or written) or by deed (works of love or the testimony of a transformed life).

Since evangelism is basically an announcement, some degree of *verbalization* is indispensable, at least if the good news is to come across with sufficient clarity. There is one fact that distinguishes the Christian gospel from every other religion—that Jesus Christ, as the Son of God, gave his life on the cross to wipe away the guilt of every single human being (Eph. 2:8-9; Gal. 2:21; 1 John 2:2). One cannot comprehend the unconditional love of the crucified and risen Christ from either nature or any form of human endeavor alone. Quoting

Bosch (1987, 101): "Our lives are not sufficiently transparent . . . we must name the Name of him in whom we believe" (John 14:6; Acts 4:12; Phil. 2:6-11).

No less vital is the need for personal appropriation of the forgiveness and kingship of Christ through faith (Mark 1:15; John 1:1-12, 3:16; Acts 2:38). Yet the purpose of evangelism is not to "convert." It simply means to *bear witness to Jesus Christ,* by word and deed, in obedience to his commission (Mt. 28:18-20), leaving the outcome (such as conversion and its consequences) to the only effective source of persuasive power—his Spirit (John 16:8).

Likewise, with the commissar caught off his guard, the point was not the outcome. Least of all was it about securing another "decision-for-Christ" for promotional purposes. It did exemplify some key components in a strategy of non-coercive, yet intentional, *friendship evangelism* on the waterfront. This means refusing to be confrontational, but being ready to offer a testimony, centered in the core of the gospel (1 Peter 3:15), while blending verbal witness with diaconal hospitality. In many cases it also means cooperating in follow-up ministry with colleagues in subsequent ports of call.

The Need for Evangelism in Maritime Mission

An enthusiastic young student-chaplain, taking part in a shipvisiting training session in an East African port city, felt confused. The son of a sorcerer in an outlying village, he had experienced the power of the gospel during an evangelistic meeting there in his youth. Recently, he had encountered a spokesperson for the "pluralist" position in relation to inter-religious dialogue. To him, it just made no sense: "If I'm supposed to make a Buddhist seafarer a better Buddhist, or a Muslim seafarer a better Muslim, am I to make a Communist seafarer a better Communist? Or make a seafarer who practices sorcery a better sorcerer?" The incident gave the seminar leader an opportunity to discuss alternative approaches to witnessing among those of other faiths or no faith. Those approaches may vary all the way from zero justification for evangelism in any shape—to evangelism as an ultimate human right for all.

In the relatively young discipline of "Theology of Religions," it has become customary to distinguish between three ways of relating to other faiths—pluralism, inclusivism and exclusivism. *Pluralists* argue that religious pluralism in today's society cannot allow a monopoly on divine revelation or absolute truth claims by any religion, including Christianity. *Inclusivists* see Christianity as the culmination of all religions, while "including," as the name implies, the revelation of sufficient truth and "salvific value" in other religions to secure salvation for their adherents, too. While both positions support interfaith dialogue, pluralists see evangelism as intolerant and inclusivists see it as unnecessary.

The *exclusivist* view derives its name from the fact that it "excludes" any source of salvation other than the gospel of Christ as uniquely revealed in the Holy Bible (John 14:6, Acts 4:12). In its extreme form, exclusivism assumes the unconditional "lostness" of all who do not have a personal and explicit faith in Jesus Christ as Savior and Lord.

Many are committed to the biblical uniqueness of Christ, yet see this latter conclusion as unduly harsh. Instead, they choose a combined *inclusive-exclusivist* position. This growing group recognizes God's "general" self-revelation to all human beings as Creator, through nature, history and conscience, in accordance with the First Article of the Apostles' Creed. They therefore see dialogue with other religions as vital, in order to promote (1) *solidarity,* by seeking out common ground as fellow-humans; (2) *witness,* by word and deed, to God's "special" self-revelation as Redeemer, through the biblical record of the life and work of his Son, Jesus Christ. Although the *love* of God is unconditional (1 Tim. 2:4), the *salvation* of God is conditional—on a response of faith (John 3:16; Rom. 10:11-15).

"Inclusive-exclusivists" hold that it would be both unloving and unjust to maintain that faith in Christ is the *only source* of salvation, without making that knowledge *universally available*—through non-coercive missionary outreach. (See Section 3 of the *Seafarers' Covenant,* also António Barbosa da Silva's *Perspective* below.) Christ himself (in John 4:1-42) and his Apostle Paul (in Acts 17:16-34) both highlight a positive posture of proactive witness as an essential ingredient in interfaith dialogue. Meanwhile, the need for such "dialogical witness" does not negate the heart-wrenching possibility of ultimate lostness. Rather, it leaves the fate of those who have not had a chance to hear the gospel (or have only heard a distorted version) to the only One in a position to judge with justice and mercy. Bill Down, then as General Secretary of the MtS, put it this way in 1987:

> We can't opt out of interfaith discussion and relationships....Be humble: It is arrogant and false to believe there is no truth and nothing of value in other faiths. And be loyal: Never think that you must water down your Christian commitment. Dialogue with people of other faiths does not involve you in compromising your beliefs— rather it broadens, deepens and strengthens the faith (*Flying Angel News* May-June 1987, 4).

Dialogue, most often in the shape of unstructured conversation, will likely remain the dominant form of verbal communication of the gospel in the future, among people of the sea, too. It is nevertheless far from alone. In maritime mission, as in other areas of mission, dialogue as verbal communication remains inseparable from *living the word,* in the form of diaconal ministry, now sometimes called "diapraxis." Indeed, the relationship between evangelism and incarnational witness constitutes a key issue in the following section.

Incarnation: The Diaconal Dimension

The scene could hardly have been more dramatic. The year was 1999. Here were two newly commissioned, white South African navy chaplains, once raised under the nation's notorious apartheid regime. They were participating in the closing communion service at a national conference of naval chaplains. The others were all black—at this previously all-white event. Then, in a spontaneous act of reconciliation, the two formerly privileged whites went round the room washing the feet of each of their black colleagues. The event ended with unrehearsed embraces (as recorded by the Author, in an interview with Chaplain *Jurie Van Zyl* at ICMA's 1999 Plenary Conference).

The incident became a remarkable reenactment of the historic record of Jesus washing the feet of his disciples the last evening before he went to the cross (John 13). For the Christian Church, as well as for individual Christians, that record has since served to portray two issues surrounding Christ's diaconal call, whether on land or sea: its distinctive *identity* and its compelling *necessity*.

The Identity of Diaconal Service in Maritime Mission

In the New Testament Greek, the term *diaconia*, like its Latin equivalent *ministry*, occasionally occurs in the broader sense of "service." More often, however, it conveys the meaning of service in a Christian connection. Correspondingly, the term *diaconos* signifies the role of "servant" in a similar context. This is also how Jesus and his early followers used the term.

Throughout his public ministry, Jesus rejected the role of a socio-political messianic emancipator, identifying himself instead with Isaiah in his prophesies of the Messianic Servant (Mark 10:45; Isaiah 42: 1-4; 52:13-53:12). Nowhere did Jesus assume that identity more graphically than when he inaugurated his Last Supper by first washing the feet of his followers. With that gesture of self-humiliation, he made this "the connecting link between Jesus' diaconal ministry and the new messianic community" into which he now called his disciples (Nordstokke 1999, 38). For Jesus, his servant role culminated shortly afterwards with his ultimate "self-emptying" (*kenosis*) on the cross, as portrayed by Paul in Philippians 2:5-8. In making that supreme sacrifice for all, Jesus' diaconal ministry was, of course, unique.

By his act of foot washing, Jesus was demonstrating a *transformational* model of discipleship—with diaconal ministry at its core (John 13:15). With his declaration in Luke 4:18-19, Jesus had, from the beginning, placed all those on the periphery—the marginalized, the poor, the sick and those in greatest human need—right at the center of his messianic kingdom. That last evening, he now calls his messianic community to multiply the implementation of that diaconal program. He calls them to start fulfilling the third petition of the prayer he had taught them, and bring at least a *foretaste* of God's kingdom to this earth, as it already exists in its fullness in heaven (Mt. 6:10).

As for the marginalized mariners of the seafaring world, maritime missiology has benefited in recent years from the research of two Nordic theologians: Dr. *Kjell Nordstokke,* former President of the Norwegian Diaconal Institute, and Rev. *Kaarlo Kalliala,* Dean of the Finnish Archdiocese of Turku, himself a former seafarers' chaplain ((Nordstokke, 1999; Kalliala 1997). Both affirm two cardinal conditions for social action to qualify as diaconal ministry.

Motivation needs to be transparent, unconditional love: There must be "no strings attached," in terms of the beneficiary's identity or desired response.

Such is God's love. Such must the Christian's be (Mt. 5:43-48). Otherwise, manipulation may all too easily be the outcome.

The ministry must be empowered by the indwelling Spirit of Christ: (2 Cor. 5:14). It is this Christological dimension that gives diaconal ministry its specific "ecclesiological" identity as "a special way of being church." Others may, and do, perform acts of selfless love. However, to translate "diaconia" into simply "church social work" would, in the words of Kalliala, be as appalling as to call baptism "church child wash"!

Given the vulnerability of seafarers to both isolation and exploitation, both these researchers focus on *hospitality* as central, not only to the concept of diaconia, but to the very core identity of maritime mission (see also Koenig 1985). With the scourge of "xenophobia" (fear of strangers) still widespread, the Church Maritime, as part of the Church Universal, belongs to a global institution that exists solely for the sake of others. Maritime mission at its best creates a mutual sharing between host and guest. This reciprocal relationship is just as real when seafarers visit mission centers ashore, as when mission workers visit seafarers in their own combined home and workplace on board.

Kalliala has coined the concept of *strangership* in order to highlight the sacred bond made by the brief encounters typical of a mobile ministry like maritime mission. This kind of encounter creates an inclusive community, one that Kalliala characterizes as "strangerhood." He goes on to compare this kind of community with the term *paroikia* (or "sojourning") that Peter uses to describe the New Testament Church (1 Peter 1:1,17). As sojourners (or "those of the Way"), Christians are "resident aliens"—with no "enduring city" on this earth (Hebrews 13:14; John 17:13-18). Through a ministry of mutual hospitality, Christian seafarers' centers may serve as a timely reminder for today's parish-based, institutionalized church ashore, of its essentially nomadic calling (Hebrews 13:14). See *Perspective* by Paul Hiebert (below).

The Necessity of Diaconal Service in Maritime Mission

When seafaring strangers voice their astonishment as to why workers at local missions do what they do, it underscores the necessity of the diaconal dimension in this type of ministry. Unless maritime mission is "incarnational," it cannot meet the test of *credibility*. Unless such mission is also biblically "holistic," its different components cannot receive appropriate *priority*.

Credibility: The necessity of *incarnation* ("embodiment") in mission is clear from John's portrayal of the birth of Jesus Christ: "The Word became flesh" (John 1:14). As Jesus himself affirmed throughout his ministry, in order to be believable the gospel would need to be *seen* as well as *heard* (John 1:46). Just as "the deed without the word is dumb, the word without the deed is empty" (Leslie Newbigin). If unconditional love is to become the "body language" of the church of Christ, his followers must make that love both visible and tangible for those in need (James 2:14-18). Just as it was said of early Christians that they were "turning the world upside down" (Acts 17:6), the postmodern world needs that same uncompromising solidarity with the world's most needy, not least on the waterfront. Chaplain Ray Eckhoff's comment bears repeating: "They won't care what we know till they know that we care".

Priority: This is not the place to rehearse the perennial problem of the "primacy" issue between evangelism and social concern, or between "spiritual" and "physical" welfare. In the pioneer period of organized seafarers' mission, spiritual welfare did seem to be of "primary" importance, evident in the priority given to promoting the preached or printed *Word*. Still, despite stubborn stereotypes to the contrary, those same pioneers did also involve themselves in an ever widening range of diaconal ministry, from seafarers' lodging to the rehabilitation of port prostitutes, simply as a natural response to the claims of the gospel. For them, the Great Commandment (Mt. 22: 36-39) was no less valid than the Great Commission (Mt. 28:18-20). They intended no narrow spiritualization of the faith, no downgrading of life *before* death. They readily agreed with the words of one newly converted tar in the early Bethel era: "We sailors don't have soul-less bodies—but neither do we have body-less souls!"

A clearer understanding of biblical *holism,* as an interdependence of body, mind and spirit, has made the concept of "primacy" a relative non-issue. In practice, unconditional love requires a first response to urgent need. In Jesus' own example of the Good Samaritan, the immediate need was not for the *proclamation* of the gospel, but for its *demonstration*—in the shape of first aid, food and shelter (Luke 10:25-37). For most modern-day seafarers' chaplains, it is the diaconal task, of meeting seafarers' most pressing physical, social and emotional needs, that fills most of his or her workweek—and rightly so. To quote St. Francis of Assisi, "Preach the gospel at all times—if necessary use words."

Even though God's love in Christ is unconditional, regardless of result, diaconal care nevertheless does open doors of opportunity for pastoral counseling. An alert shipvisitor will discover how a conversation about a material concern may uncover a deeper spiritual need. Such was the case in Jesus' encounter with the "other Samaritan," the woman at the well (John 4:4-42). The sensitive way in which Jesus deliberately leads her, not only to conversion but also to effective witness among her own people, is the perfect paradigm for pastoral counseling in a cross-cultural context—with special relevance on today's waterfront.

The story of those two Samaritans, male and female, reveal Christ's own view of the relationship between social concern and evangelism—as two complementary components in holistic ministry. Both are indispensable. Or, as *John Stott* puts it, good news and good works belong inextricably together. Which component will have "practical" priority must depend on immediate needs in any given situation (Stott 1975, 22-23). That does not negate the "ultimate" priority of eternal salvation, as Jesus himself explicitly states in Mt. 16:26. He is also the one who, at the last judgment, links personal faith in Christ to his or her diaconal concern for the most marginalized of this world (Mt. 25:31-46). For more concerning the issue of ultimate destiny, see the

"Eschatological Dimension" below. Meanwhile, Rev. *Christopher Collison,* then on staff with the MtS, summed up the situation as follows:

> The first Christians had the balance. We, too, are not in the business of saving souls and ignoring poverty. But nor must we stand by the exploited and stay silent on spiritual riches in Christ . . . Evangelism is the bedrock business of the Church. Without it, caring will be hollow (Collison 1987, 35-37).

Transformation: The Prophetic Dimension

A former seafarer once sounded off on the catastrophic consequences of keeping silent in the face of gross violations of human rights. First decorated as a u-boat commander, eventually becoming a bishop of the Evangelical Church of Germany, *Martin Niemöller* (1892-1984) landed in a concentration camp during World War II, for his fearless resistance to Hitler and his henchmen. Reflecting later on lessons learned from that harrowing experience, he wrote:

> When Hitler attacked the Jews, I was not a Jew, and therefore I was not concerned. When Hitler attacked the Catholics, I was not a Catholic, and therefore I was not concerned. And when Hitler attacked the unions, I was not a member of the unions, and therefore I was not concerned. Then, Hitler attacked the Protestants, including myself—and there was nobody left to be concerned (*Congressional Record* 14 Oct. 1968, 31636).

Could a comparable catastrophe erupt among victims of injustice in the globalized modern-day maritime workforce? Why is a transformational, prophetic ministry more imperative now than ever before?

In Principle—an Insult to God

The seafaring vocation has always been rife with danger and deprivation. Where due to circumstances inherent in seafaring itself, the focus of diaconal ministry has been to mitigate—wherever it has proved impossible to eradicate. Meanwhile, for centuries, seafarers have been victims of *preventable* suffering, notably injustice and exploitation. Holistic diaconal ministry cannot elect only to alleviate a *symptom* of suffering. It also has to address the underlying *system,* the situation that sustains victimization. Seeking "systemic" change in any society has always provoked resistance among those with a stake in conserving the status quo—like the religious elite who executed the "radical" Jesus. It takes compassion and courage to overcome the temptation to condone the conspiracy of silence that allows abuse to continue. Yet such is the calling of the prophet— also among victims of injustice at sea.

The history of organized maritime mission provides examples of prophetic confrontation of injustice from the very earliest pioneer period. G. C. Smith launched the first systematic campaign against the "Crimping System"—the favorite form of maritime exploitation in his day. He roundly rejected any piecemeal solutions or "social atomism." It also took courage and perseverance for his successors, like Elizabeth Fry, Sarah Hale, Eli Sawtell, Samuel Plimsoll, James Fell, Archibald Mansfield and Hans Ansgar Reinhold, to challenge the entrenched inequities of the age. In 1856, in a bold blueprint for maritime social reform, the American Seamen's Friend Society challenged shipowners to provide livable wages, better food and decent quarters for their crews. They even went on to call for the conversion of shipowners themselves, not just those who sailed their ships (ASFS *Annual Report* 1850, 5-12).

When the maritime union movement eventually came into its own toward the turn of the 20th century, several of its pioneers, like Andrew Furuseth and Charles Hopkins, were motivated by Christian convictions. At first, tensions occasionally emerged between *maritime unions* (understandably sensitive to paternalism in any form) and *maritime missions*. For unions, the watchword was straightforward: "Humane conditions of life and work for seafarers—an issue of social justice, not benevolence!"

The free market forces of globalization resulted in increased vulnerability to exploitation within the international maritime workforce. The consequent dehumanizing effect on the lives of seafarers and their families found maritime unions and maritime missions making common cause in a widening range of justice and welfare issues. Details of this development belong in the history of the "New Seafarers' Rights Movement" (above). For maritime mission, a commitment to justice for people of the sea is non-negotiable. The ultimate accountability of seafarers' chaplains is toward neither unions nor owners, but (as the name implies) to seafarers themselves—under God.

A world that reduces persons to things will also raise things to gods, so the saying goes. Certainly, *objectification*—treating human beings like objects of profit or gratification—becomes, in biblical terms, more than indignity or injustice. Since every single human being is created "in the image of God," whatever defaces that image becomes tantamount to blasphemy and therefore an insult to God. Ever since biblical times, the messianic message of heralds of justice has remained the same—from Amos in the Old Testament (5:24) to the Master himself in the New (Luke 4:18-19): *to restore the divine image of all humankind—on land and sea!*

In Practice—a Two-Part Strategy

In the ongoing struggle against dehumanization at sea, a two-part strategy has gradually evolved. There, as in other fields of mission, there is an ongoing need for both *empowerment* on the one hand, and *advocacy* on the other.

Empowerment of the potential victims of injustice: Seafarers frequently have to deal with a desperate dilemma, either to suffer in silence in the face of blatant abuse, or to bear the consequences of bringing up complaints—from physical violence to blacklisting, even arrest and incarceration. Only each individual seafarer can make the decision to stand up for his or her legitimate rights. Nevertheless, today's worldwide support network, from front-line seafarers' chaplains to regional ITF inspectors, can provide the resources and sense of solidarity to make all the difference. In partnership with seafarers as potential "change agents," the various church and secular agencies can promote a new "seafarer-centered" paradigm in a meaningful way. In recent years, it has, in fact, become common for multi-cultural crews to look to the coordinator of a shipboard Christian cell group to be their joint spokesperson in issues of both human rights and general welfare at sea.

Advocacy among those in a position to make systemic change: If seafarers are to stand up for their rights, they need to know those rights and have reason to believe they will be enforced. Much remains on both scores. Here too, the level of cooperation, between mission-related and other maritime agencies, promises well for the future. In this post-9/11 world, building "civic community"—together with members of other faiths or no faith—has become a matter of urgency. Promoting this *Isaiah Vision* of joint action for human welfare (Isaiah 65:20-23) has given added significance to the prophetic pursuit of justice as a prerequisite for peace.

As emphasized earlier, that advocacy role has to include the "Ultimate Human Right"—the freedom to choose and share one's faith in a way that does not violate the Universal Declaration of Human Rights. Holistic mission in the name of Christ holds special promise. It can count on a unique resource: Christ's Spirit in the role of the Divine Advocate, reinforcing any word or act of witness in his name—any time and anywhere (John 14:16, 26; 15:26; 16:7-8).

Specific Categories of Concern

One of the most meaningful justice-related words is the biblical concept of *shalom.* In the sense of reconciliation, healing and wholeness between God and humankind, shalom presupposes both apology and reparation. In the world of the seafarer, action designed to achieve the restoration of God's shalom in the wake of abuse may mean confronting any of the following five challenges, all of them interrelated:

Discrimination—due to skin, status or sex: The notion of willfully discriminating against fellow-human beings—whatever the reason—flies in the face of the God who loves the whole world, both so-called "righteous" and "unrighteous," without favoritism (John 3:16; Matthew 5:45; Rom. 2:11). No one has expressed this more categorically than the Apostle Paul, himself once a bigoted Pharisee. In his letter to the Galatians (3:28), he lists three examples of discrimination, each of which are incompatible with the Christian faith: (1) *Intolerance* regarding race or ethnicity ("Jew or Greek"). (2) *Prejudice* in terms of socio-economic status ("slave or free"). (3) *Inequity* related to gender ("male or female"). The list is far from exhaustive. Discrimination due to age, physical condition or sexual orientation is no less reprehensible.

Impoverishment—through unfair labor practices: "Speak up for those who cannot speak for themselves! Defend the rights of the poor and needy!" Those inspired words of wisdom from Proverbs 31:8-9 summarize God's "preferential option for the poor," those whom society has left out. The Bible is clear on the obligation of the whole human community to redress the injustice that creates poverty and marginalization (e.g.: Jeremiah 22:13-17; Amos 5:11-24; Matthew 25:40; Luke 14:13, 21; James 5:1-6). *Nelson Mandela* is on firm scriptural ground when he declares, "The greatest single challenge facing our globalized world is to combat and eradicate its disparities." Among seafarers of the world, as a nomadic people group, marginalization has long been widespread. Here, maritime mission agencies and maritime unions have found common cause. Responsible shipowners, too, show support for fairer labor practices at sea, including through the ILO, the IMO and the ICSW.

Jeopardizing—in matters of safety and health: As late as 1874, a report of the American Marine Hospital Service estimated the average length of a sailor's life, after going to sea, to be no more than twelve years. Since then, that statistic has greatly improved. Yet, despite large strides in safety at sea, service in merchant and fishing vessels continues to be among the world's most hazardous vocations. Although often attributable to perils inherent to travel by sea, this situation is still in large measure due to human factors. These may relate to stress, fatigue, or criminal reasons such as piracy, other forms of terror and, most particularly, substandard shipping associated with flags of convenience. For two major reasons, Christian ministry among seafarers cannot remain neutral about safety at sea—plain neighborly love and a holistic understanding of human welfare. That legacy has continued from the Apostle Paul's practical help in saving the lives of all aboard a storm-tossed grain-ship long ago (Acts 27:27-44) to the current-day SCI Centers for Seafarers' Rights and Maritime Education, as well as ICMA's active participation in the ILO, the IMO and the ICSW. The same is true of maritime ministry agencies' concern for seafarers' health issues, not least in such areas as recreational activity, crisis counseling and AIDS prevention.

Degradation—of the marine environment: The publication of Rachel Carson's *Silent Spring* in 1962 resulted in the modern-day environmental protection movement. In stark and scientific terms, Carson portrayed the catastrophic consequences of ignoring the delicate balance between sustainable development and the natural ecosystem on which all life depends. More recently, the AOS highlighted the results of rampant pollution and depletion of marine resources at its XXth World Congress in 1997, in Davao in the Philippines. Here, participants explored the theme: "People of the Sea— Collaborators in God's Creation," in light of the mandate in Genesis 1:28-30. Meanwhile, ICMA has continued to work with the IMO on the implementation of its Convention on the Prevention of Pollution from Ships (MARPOL). Ships' crews can also impact the global environment, by modeling multi-cultural community and peace in a world where modern warfare represents the ultimate degradation of the environment.

Intimidation—regarding seafarers' ultimate human rights: Articles 18 and 19 in the UN Universal Declaration of Human Rights of 1948 stipulate the fundamental freedom of every human being to choose, change or share any religious conviction. "Theocratic" states (those that maintain a state monopoly regarding religion) are, by definition, in conflict with these provisions. It appears unacceptable that states that condone and even instigate religious persecution are co-signatories of the very UN instrument forbidding such action. Global watchdog organizations regularly document how millions of people of faith—both Christian and non-Christian—continue to suffer arrest and even death for their belief. Where does this leave seafarers' missions and current-day multi-religious ship's crews? (1) These missions can help bring the proven power of public opinion to bear on officials and states that are in non-compliance. (2) They can make sure they themselves meet all seafarers—regardless of religion—with unconditional love. In so doing, they will be respecting the human right of freedom of choice for all, while relying on the reinforcing power of Christ's own Spirit (John 16:8). This is in sync with the Latin root of *religion* ("binding together"), and will help make ship's crews mobile models of tolerance and peace-making for the conflicted, wider communities ashore.

Contextualization: The Cultural Dimension

The silence was palpable. It was in the summer of 1997. A congregation of over one thousand in Shanghai's major Protestant church had just heard the Author (as Maritime Ministry Consultant to the Lutheran World Federation) begin his sermon with a personal apology. He acknowledged his co-responsibility, as a Westerner, for the continuing consequences of the notorious Opium Wars, inflicted on an ancient sovereign nation by seaborne invaders from the West. After a long pause, he added, "Since the Lord's Prayer makes your own forgiveness dependent on your willingness to forgive others, judging by your silence it seems you have a problem." No sooner had their senior pastor translated that reminder than the whole congregation came back in Chinese with a thunderous "We forgive you! We forgive you!"

During a thirty-minute message that day, the preacher encouraged this Chinese congregation to launch indigenous maritime mission, as opportunities emerged on their own waterfront. Following this, their senior pastor twice protested the guest preacher's attempts to close, saying: "But you cannot stop preaching now!" (For the Author this was certainly a novel experience.) The episode can illustrate the importance of a spirit of repentance and reconciliation as a precondition for communication—especially in a context of cross-cultural mission.

Following the Opium Wars, Westerners carved out a series of enclaves along the coast, from Canton to Shanghai, and gained access for missionaries to China's vast interior. This came, however, at disastrous cost. The inevitable linkage between Christian mission and Western imperialism has ever since remained an open wound, reinforcing the perception of Christianity as a "foreign," imperialist religion (*IASMM Newsletter* Winter 1997-98, 10-11).

The history of Western imperialism, whether in military, economic or cultural form, continues to present a formidable impediment to communication of the Christian gospel throughout most of the non-Western world. This will continue to call for a spirit of repentance and humility—not least on the part of those engaged in the current multi-cultural context of maritime mission. The very diversity of cultures among modern-day mariners highlights the need for "cultural bridge-building." Two factors enhance that need: (1) The spiritual receptivity typical of mobile people groups, far removed from the conforming pressures of a home environment; (2) The fact that those who return home, wanting to share their new-found faith, will be coming to countries frequently closed to conventional missionary activities.

By the term *culture*, anthropologists imply "structured customs and underlying worldview assumptions" that have come to govern the lives of any given group of people. The New Testament offers examples of how the Early Church sought to make an originally Jewish Christianity culturally relevant to the surrounding Greek-speaking Gentile world (e.g.: Acts 10, 15 and 17). Today, the Church Maritime faces the corresponding need for a "contextualized" mission strategy and an "indigenized" personnel policy (Bosch 1991, 420-32).

A Contextualized Maritime Mission Strategy

In the 1970s, missiologists coined the concept of "contextualization" to signify the process by which the authentic message and ministry of the Christian faith can become relevant ("inculturated") in the lives of people living in another culture. Today's multi-cultural maritime workforce represents a dual contextualization challenge: (1) Ethnically, given the multicultural composition of most ship's crews. (2) Vocationally, given the unique nature of the seafaring subculture.

As Paul Mooney maintains in his recent research results, only a *seafarer-centered* strategy—one that recognizes ministering seafarers as the primary agents of mission among their own—can adequately meet the challenges of the new, globalized context of maritime mission, while also doing justice to Christ's Great Commission to make disciples in the maritime world. This was the formula for the extraordinary success of the original Bethel Movement in the early 1800s. There still exists no other methodology more relevant to the seafarer's context of life and work on the current scene (Mooney 2005, 162-7).

An Indigenized Maritime Mission Personnel Policy

The term "indigenization" signifies the process whereby a church or ministry becomes free to develop, under the guidance of the Holy Spirit, an identity native to its own culture. The concept has roots in missiology, as far back as the mid-1800s. In today's new mission context on the world's waterfronts, the white Western-dominated maritime mission power structure faces a particularly urgent need for indigenization. Past experience and logic indicate that mission is most effective when the main responsibility for it is entrusted to people of a culture similar to those to whom they minister.

Already in the 1980s, as the Ethnic Revolution in crew composition gathered momentum, there were calls for *Asianization* in seafarers' mission strategy. For the Western-world maritime mission establishment, this would require a deliberate disavowal of "paternalistic" practices, evidenced by change in both personnel policy and the transfer of resources. It would also entail foreswearing tendencies toward "turfism," as well as actively cooperating with indigenous non-Western initiatives. All this calls for a Christ-like attitude of self-emptying ("kenosis") as in Philippians 2:5-8 (*Watermarks* Dec. 1986, 8-9).

Nevertheless, as Mooney points out, this will not mean the eclipse of Western-world maritime mission. Their agencies will continue to play a crucial role in co-ordinating and in providing resources. There will also still be a need for Western personnel as bridge-building partners, provided all involved are well qualified in cross-cultural skills and sensitivity. In that context, personal sea-experience can be an additional asset (Mooney 2005, 158-169).

Cooperation: The Communal Dimension

It is sometimes said: "We must not fracture the face of Christ on the waterfront!" The rationale seems self-evident. If seafarers see different ship-visitors, each claiming to represent the same deity, yet clearly competing with one another, the effect is bound to undermine the credibility of both messengers and their message. The issue of promoting unity among professed Christians is essentially a question of loyalty to Christ's Great Commission—and ultimately to Christ himself. In his last prayer in John 17:21, Jesus pleads for those who will come to believe in him "that all of them may be one . . . so that the world will believe." With those words, he highlights how *ecumenism* can be an essential precondition for *evangelism*. So much for the argument by opponents of mission that ecumenism and evangelism are somehow "incompatible."

Two extremes can easily sabotage ecumenical cooperation: (1) Reducing it to a superficial form of camaraderie; (2) Preventing it altogether by an arrogant lack of respect for reconciled diversity. NAMMA's 1990 Statement of Mission concludes with the following feasible balance: "Agreement in essentials, freedom in non-essentials, love in everything!"

In a Christian context, one often refers to this "communal" dimension of the faith as *fellowship*. This term can have two distinct yet interrelated meanings—either "communion" or "community." In the sense of *communion* (in Greek "koinonia"), fellowship is at its core far more than just the "horizontal" dimension between fellow human beings coming together in a common cause. It entails above all the "vertical" or *divine* dimension of relating to God—the relationship which Christ gave his very life to restore (I John 1:3-7). In the sense of *community,* fellowship connotes the visible embodiment of that communion—in the shape of those "two or three" (or more) who have the promise of Jesus' personal presence wherever they come together in his name (Matthew 18:20).

How the concept of Christian fellowship has historically manifested itself in the seafaring world has already been the subject of detailed examination, specifically: (1) At the inter-organizational level—with the emergence of ICMA and its regional affiliates; (2) At "sea-level"—with the history of Maritime

Christian Communities. The following, however, focuses on two interrelated functions that both form part of a viable, contextualized way of "being church" in today's mobile maritime workforce—*follow-up* and *fellowship*.

Providing Ecumenical Maritime Follow-up Ministry

As the title of this book implies, the principle purpose of maritime mission is to invite seafarers everywhere to become God's people of the "Way of the Sea," thereby embodying the Church Maritime. Like the church at large, that church is not only a "pilgrim church" in a figurative sense (Hebrews 13:14). The Church Maritime is, by its very nature, quite literally mobile. As in all forms of mobile ministry, this means making the most of only the briefest encounters. With fast turn-arounds and post-9/11 security restrictions, such is now more than ever the case, as today's shipvisitors well know. Since Christ calls not just to decision but to discipleship, and since discipleship takes time, the key issue in maritime discipleship translates into a question of systematic and caring *follow-up*. Engaging in evangelism without proactive follow-up makes about as much sense as leaving a new-born baby on the sidewalk to fend for itself. How are agencies to provide for effective pastoral follow-up in terms of its two basic ingredients: *training* and *resources*?

Dr. Paul Mooney (like many others) foresees that a future seafarer-centered mission paradigm will still call for ongoing support by shore-based ministries—not least in the area of *training*. In that regard, ICMA's 9th Plenary Conference in New Orleans, in 2004, signaled a historic breakthrough. Following Mooney's workshops on "Elements of a Seafarer-Centered Paradigm for Maritime Missions," ICMA's plenary received, for the first time, a proposal for action toward that end (reported in *IASMM Newsletter* Winter 2004/5, 5):

> *To expand the maritime mission network*—to include ministering seafarers, as an integral part of mission and ministry among seafarers.

> *To train ministering seafarers*—according to a common core program, certified and commissioned by church or denomination to be ministering members of their own mission agencies.

> *To initiate a study of existing lay programs*—and then operate a pilot program coordinated by ICMA through participating missions for five to seven years.

The significance of this proposal is that it meets the need for *denominational/organizational "ownership."* It revives the twofold approach that first emerged at the AOS World Congress in 1992, one that combines (1) *denominational* primary loyalty, with (2) *supra-denominational* ecumenical solidarity. Compared with the ICMA-coordinated "Seafarers' Ministry Training" (SMT), launched in 1997 to promote *professional* maritime chaplaincy, this type of *peer-based* "Seafarers' Discipleship Training" (SDT) presupposes a vastly wider involvement of both instructors and participants, with ICMA here too playing a central role.

Training also requires relevant *resources*. The same "dual-level dynamic" applies to resources relating to the SDT model, as in the case of the SMT model. The need for Christian follow-up materials, Bible-study aids, as well as pastoral follow-up correspondence, now also by e-mail, shows no sign of diminishing. Doctrinal, devotional and worship materials specific to Roman Catholics or Protestants will likewise be relevant as long as denominational boundaries remain a reality in this life. (They will fortunately *not* be in the next!)

Meanwhile, both training and resources in maritime follow-up ministry presuppose a level of *coordination*. Paul Mooney expressly includes this need in his proposal to ICMA, quoted above. No one has underscored this need more consistently than Ray Eckhoff. His pioneer "Ministering Seafarers' Program," with its inter-agency communication system and "ship-lists," will provide a rich resource for research in the study project Mooney has now publicly proposed.

In the January 2007 issue of *The Sea,* Rev. *Tom Heffer* (MtS Director of Chaplaincy) announced the launching of a new *Online Christian Community for Seafarers,* as a maritime component of the "i-church," currently sponsored by the Anglican diocese of Oxford, England. Coordinated by the MtS port chaplain in Singapore, Rev. *Mervyn Moore*, the new MtS website link (via www.missiontoseafarers.org) can now give seafarers immediate global access to e-mail counseling, chat-room fellowship with other seafarers, as well as a wide range of worship and study materials.

Empowering Christian Communities at Sea

Follow-up ministry is intimately linked with the promotion of fellowship—whether in the sense of "communion" or "community." Indeed, fellowship is no less than a major purpose of follow-up. If the more *immediate* need for follow-up ministry is to reinforce the positive impact of Christian witness, then the *long-term* purpose needs to be the promotion of spiritual growth toward mature discipleship (Ephesians 4:13). Healthy, self-multiplying discipleship cannot result without the nurturing and empowering effect of Christian fellowship. An embattled *Martin Luther* even went so far as to liken Christian fellowship ("mutual conversation and consolation" with other Christians) to Scripture and the Sacraments—as an additional "means of grace."

Is it possible to create and sustain biblical fellowship at sea, given the peer pressures of a total institution like a ship, as well as the multi-cultural nature of today's maritime workforce? History has proved how the organized Seafarers' Mission Movement did, in fact, begin as a worldwide proliferation of worshipping, and witnessing, Christian shipboard communities under the Bethel banner. During the current Global Era, signs have already surfaced of an incipient "New Bethel Movement," with sporadic initiatives by different denominations to provide encouragement and support services.

In the late 1980s, the same "dual-level" dynamic emerged in the modern-day version of Maritime Christian Fellowship, as noted above. Ray Eckhoff's

Tacoma-based "Ministering Seafarers' Program" placed a major emphasis on identifying, nurturing and (with their permission) sharing information on seafarers with leadership potential to serve as "Fellowship Coordinators." Jonah Choi's Pusan-based organization (KIMM) trained many maritime "tentmaker" missionaries among future career officers at Korean nautical education institutions. Leadership training as Fellowship Coordinators will also need to be part of any future crew-based, ICMA-affiliated, training program.

Given the fact that mariners in general already sense a bond of non-sectarian kinship with fellow-mariners everywhere, there is good reason to believe that the majority of interested seafarers will identify with a future global Maritime Christian Fellowship network *without* denominational demarcations. The typical seafarer's soul simply has, like God's mercy, something of "the wideness of the sea." At the same time, given the central role of the clergy-consecrated Eucharist in Roman Catholic doctrine and piety, there is equally good reason to respect the need of Catholic seafarers to affiliate additionally with their own denominational fellowship, as manifested by the Apostleship of the Sea. To that end, the AOS continues to commission lay seafarers as "Eucharistic Ministers" at sea. On the other hand, there need not be any practical conflict in belonging to *both* levels of fellowship—denominational and supra-denominational—in one and the same ship's crew.

How does all this relate to crewmembers who profess a *non-Christian faith or no faith at all?* In today's context of multi-religious crews, an inclusively "communal" dimension of maritime mission has to embrace more than "ecumenical," (i.e. inter-Christian), relations. Jesus has told his followers never to place their light under a bowl. They are there to share (Matthew 5:14-16; 2 Corinthians 5:15). Many of today's seafarers come from countries where Christians are still not granted "religious reciprocity"—equal civic status under the Universal Declaration of Human Rights. The test of a Christian seafarers' fellowship has to be that non-Christian shipmates, too, wherever they come from, can sense a spirit of hospitality reflecting Jesus' own unconditional love. They need to know they are respected and, if they so wish, will be warmly welcome—just as the persons they are (John 10:16; 12:32).

In other ways, too, a shipboard Christian community can show it is no self-complacent, spiritual "cozy-club." Its members, if alert, will often find opportunities to show solidarity with their crewmates at large, in the *wider* human community of a ship. This can, for example, happen through diaconal care or advocacy initiatives in whatever welfare and justice issues may come up. As Bosch underscores, nothing can compare with "the very *being*" of a Christian community to impact skeptical onlookers (Bosch 1991, 414). In that sense, *diapraxis* (living and working together) can prove even more effective than *dialogue* (merely talking together).

Building on Bosch, modern-day missiologists (like Alan Kreider, Wilbur Shenk, Stephan Bevans and Roger Schroeder) are now applying his "paradigm" approach to the *post-Christendom* conditions confronting today's global church. In the pre-Christendom era that prevailed prior to the fourth century paradigm shift introduced by the Emperor Constantine, religious pluralism was the order of the day. Christians were surrounded by active adherents of other faiths. Frequently, the raw power of the state itself was unleashed against them in open persecution. This was a world where Christians really saw themselves as "resident aliens" (1.Peter 1:1). They were keenly conscious of their Lord's commission to continue his witness in the world in the power of his Spirit alone. Undaunted, they made *mission* the central focus of both life and worship.

From the middle of the fourth century, all that changed with the advent of "Christendom," and its "marriage of convenience" between Christianity and state power. In territories where all were considered "Christians," mission was no longer an issue—except on the "fringes." There it became an "extra," largely left to religious professionals or "enthusiasts." Not till the present era of globalization has the world witnessed a definitive shift, notably in the West, as "Christendom's institutions and assumptions stagger on or disintegrate." Will Western Christians now become less dependent on external sources of power, and enable the "post-Christendom" global church to recapture the vibrant sense of mission of the Early Church? If so, there is reason to believe the proliferation of Christian communities at sea may play a relevant and important role (Kreider 2005, 59-68; Bevans & Schroeder 2005, 69-72; Shenk 2005, 73-79).

Consummation: The Eschatological Dimension

During a tremendous storm in the days of sail, it looked as if the ship was about to founder. "This is the time to pray!" exclaimed one of the passengers. "This is the time to *pump!*" roared back a fellow-passenger, who was lending a hand as best he could. As the saying goes, there are times to pray as if it were no use to work, and there are times to work as if it were no use to pray.

The Bible predicts that the present universe will one day end with widespread disasters. This is especially the case in its last book, *Revelation* (also known by its Greek name, the "Apocalypse"). These end-time events will accompany the return (or "Parousia" in Greek) of the resurrected and glorified Jesus Christ who will then judge both the living and the dead. Ironically, despite the volume of Scripture devoted to this theme, Christ's followers have disagreed about the subject throughout the ages. Even the majority of those who profess to accept the *certainty* of his return differ dramatically in the nature of their *response*. Those differences also have significant implications for maritime mission. They translate into a choice between extremist views on the one hand and a biblically balanced tension on the other.

End-time Extremism—Fixation or Negation

Over the centuries, there have been countless Christians, even church bodies, which have adopted a literal understanding of Revelation 20:1-6. Here, the apostle John recounts his vision of Christ returning to earth at the end of this age, in order to reign for one thousand years over a perfect world order, prior to the final judgment. The precise time and nature of that "Millennium" has long been the subject of dispute—between so-called "Pre-millennialists" and "Post-millennialists."

Pre-millennialists see the return of Christ as taking place *prior* to the Millennium, during which his followers will share in his reign. Although Christ himself has, in fact, listed a series of so-called "signs," or convulsive events in nature and society that will precede his return, he has expressly warned against any human attempts to predict the precise timing of this climax of history (Matthew 24:1-25:13). Despite this, ever since the Early Church, many have done just that (2 Thessalonians 2:1-4). This kind of fixation on end-time scenarios has, in the past, all too easily led to either alarmism or escapism, more recently resulting in a billion-dollar end-time media market.

Post-millennialists, on the other hand, have seen the return of Christ as taking place *subsequent* to the Millennium. It will, they maintain, only come as the climax of a thousand-year golden age of earthly prosperity produced by Christians themselves—the evolutionary effect of the spread of the gospel in society. Critics object that this theory—by logical implication—leads to *negation*, by simply eliminating any need for Christ's physical return to earth.

Biblical Tension—between the Already and the Not Yet

After the trauma of two World Wars, post-millennial optimism in human potential has all but lost support in favor of the pre-millennial position—pinning all expectations on God's sovereign intervention alone. Meanwhile, ever since St. Augustine in the fifth century, Bible scholars have increasingly come to identify with a third alternative, the so-called *Amillennial* position. This sees the one-thousand-year reign of Christ as symbolic language—like so much of the Book of Revelation. Accordingly, the Millennium is equal to the whole of the present "interim period" between the First and Second Advent of Christ—from his incarnation to his return at the end of the present era. This period is usually characterized as the "Era of the Gospel"—with all its opportunities for mission throughout the world.

This Amillennial interpretation avoids the pitfalls of the extremist attitudes so often associated with a literalist understanding of the Millennium. At the same time, it makes room for a balanced biblical alternative: Living in the present, in the light of eternity ("sub specie aeternitatis"). As David Bosch sees it (1991, 498-510), the key to this lies in *the third petition of the Lord's Prayer.* "Christians can never be people of the status quo." They are to proclaim and demonstrate God's coming kingdom—"on earth as it [already] is in heaven." Secondly, Christians are never *identical* with that kingdom, however committed they may be to the kingdom's values. They are a part of a struggling pilgrim church. In the present era, Christians can at best be a tentative "in-breaking," a foretaste of the eschatological fullness of the reign of God at the end of this era. The ultimate triumph of good over evil remains uniquely God's own gift—in God's own time (Revelation 21:1-5).

In this current "in-between" era, Christians are called to live in the creative tension between the "already" and the "not yet." In this tension, Christ has made *mission* the overarching agenda of his church. First, the gospel of the kingdom will be preached throughout the world as a testimony to all nations. "Then," he declares, "the end will come" (Matthew 24:14). The church is not "a sect composed of a few souls rescued from the tumultuous sea of history," as René Padilla reminds us. The church is the "cosmic manifestation of God"—moving it to *Mission Between the Times* (Padilla 1985, 196-8). This applies in a very special sense to his church among the People of the Sea, with their proven potential for reaching areas in the world otherwise closed to conventional missionaries.

Perhaps the Author can be forgiven for ending this dimension of maritime mission on a personal note. His five-year-old daughter was with him, visiting ships in port one day. As they passed a particularly sleazy joint near the harborfront, she remarked, "Dad, the Devil is terribly strong, isn't he?" Then, as though to reassure him as well as herself, she added, "But you know, Dad, Jesus is stronger!"

When Christ gave his first hesitant followers their marching orders, he prefaced his Great Commission with the reminder that it was he who had ultimate power—in heaven as well as on earth (Matthew 28:18). Ever since, that assurance—together with his parting promise that he would be with them to the end—has meant more than mere words. For embattled believers everywhere, that pledge continues to be a beacon of hope, reminding them that in Jesus Christ they are not only on the *same* side, but also ultimately on the *victorious* side—in spite of the failings of his followers. For his whole church on land and sea, those words of unfailing love will continue to reinforce the sense of urgency inherent in the impending return of the Lord of Mission—at the consummation of human history.

14

PRACTICAL ASPECTS

IMPEDIMENTS TO MARITIME MISSION

The history of the navy in the British Napoleonic War era includes many examples of the opposition that "new believers" had to be prepared for from fellow mariners on board. For example, records show how a captain complained vigorously to his admiral that a number of his men had become "Methodists," at that time a disparaging term for any committed Christian. He charged that their Bible study meetings when off duty were disturbing to the rest of his ship's company. When the admiral inquired about these particular men's professional conduct, however, such were the reports of their skill, discipline and courage under fire that he finally exclaimed, "If such men be 'Methodists,' then I wish to God *all* my men were Methodists. Case dismissed!"

As soon as the war was over, and thousands began re-entering the merchant service, it was clear that prejudice persisted there too. One merchant navy captain, evidently typical of many, on hearing about plans to minister among seafarers in general, declared dryly, "You might as well preach to the mainmast as to sailors." Shortly afterwards, the Bethel Movement would rebuff the stereotype that the daily demands of seafaring life were somehow incompatible with living as a dedicated Christian at sea. Still, this does not alter the fact that the typical sub-culture at sea would—and likely always will—pose challenges to the norms and values of a Christian lifestyle.

Addressing this tension constitutes one important issue among several in the following survey of impediments to maritime mission. Given the fallible nature of Christians everywhere, including the Church Maritime, a seafarer-centered paradigm of maritime mission, however "successful" in some respects, will still be vulnerable in others. "Impediments" mean more than just "problems"—like the theoretical objections dealt with above under "Maritime Apologetics." This book uses the term "impediments" about obstacles sufficiently severe to be capable of frustrating the basic objectives of maritime mission. The challenge is therefore to identify such impediments in order to develop strategies that can either eliminate them where possible, or mitigate them where inevitable.

Seafarer-related Impediments

Ever since humans dared cast off from the relative safety of their land habitat, they have recognized seafaring as a particularly hostile environment. Even today, with all the latest in safety measures and navigational aids, statistics show that seafaring remains one of the most hazardous vocations in the world. Its most distinctive characteristic is that of *mobility*. Tied for months to an ever-wandering workplace, one that is also their home, seafarers are mobile—and therefore essentially "transients"—by their very vocation.

A ship conveys not only the challenges of mobility. It also implies *totality*. Building on the breakthrough research of Goffman in the early 1960s, maritime sociologists have focused on the nature of the modern-day merchant-ship as a mobile form of "total institution." In common with prisons, boarding schools, barracks, mental hospitals and monasteries, it confines a ship's crew in a self-contained society-in-miniature. This carries with it radical implications, by nature both disruptive and corruptive.

Disruptive Implications for Seafaring Life

Putting to sea inevitably leads to a degree of "depersonalization." The seafarer regularly forfeits such "primary relationships" as close family and friends. Normally already "homeless," the seafarer's social isolation may increase further, due to both the ethnic and linguistic barriers of a multi-cultural crew and today's diminished crew size. Furthermore, the seafarer's maladjustment to society will frequently fuel a negative public image—with natural consequences for the seafarer's own self-image. Recent research has demonstrated the negative impact of this social alienation on mental health. (SIRC estimates that three seafarers currently commit suicide every week.)

Despite studies on seafarers' *social* isolation, however, relatively little research has so far focused on their *spiritual* isolation. Physically removed from fellowship, and other familiar sources of spiritual nurture and support, seafarers become doubly deprived. In this way, they belong to one of the most uprooted vocations in the world. In the days of sail, an old saying illustrated how seafarers could adjust to spiritual starvation, and even see it as self-imposed. Outward-bound sailors would simply lay their conscience behind on a certain imaginary island, where it would quietly remain until they could pick it up again on their journey back home! Even after the advent of organized seafarers' missions, and the availability of more credible coping strategies, seafarers still routinely face spiritual privation.

Corruptive Implications for Seafaring Life

The predicament facing seafarers is not limited to their isolation. The fact that *disruptive* forces constantly deprive them from meeting their legitimate human needs, both social and spiritual, make them all the more vulnerable to the many *corruptive* factors to which they are exposed, both at sea and on shore.

Seen from three perspectives, these factors may threaten the seafarer with not only depersonalization but, in some cases, outright dehumanization:

Unconditional Crew Solidarity: From a sociological standpoint, a "total institution" can confront the crew with "group cohesion." Rigid rules regulate the behavior of every member of the ship's company, covering virtually every situation of life or leisure. Hallowed by centuries of tradition, these norms relate to the crew's acute awareness of interdependence—compressed into a common space, joined in a common enterprise, and exposed to common perils. In order to ensure unquestioning conformity with this subculture of solidarity, a series of sanctions have emerged, ranging from ridicule to blatant physical abuse. The resulting climate of coercion could present impediments to an individual's commitment to the Christian faith. Loyalty to a higher authority, often requiring a different lifestyle, may well seem incompatible with a demand for unconditional crew cohesion (John 17:15; Acts 4:19).

Exploitation of the Seafarer's Recreational Needs: For most of the 19th century, sailors arriving ashore, and yearning for relief from prison-like conditions afloat, would encounter the mafia-like monopoly of sailor-town extortion known as the "Crimping System." Although crimping in its most blatant forms has long since crumbled, shore-based profiteers still promote pornography and prostitution, as well as the abuse of alcohol and other drugs. Given, for example, the growing proliferation of AIDS and other sexually transmitted diseases, the cost in ruined lives for both seafarers and their families continue to be devastating.

Dehumanization of the Seafarer's Vocation: Since the early 1800s, there have been vast improvements in key aspects of seafarers' conditions of life and work. Nevertheless, certain industry-wide developments during the current Global Era have led to both devaluation of seafarers themselves and dehumanization of their vocation (detailed in chapters 8 and 9 above). As early as in 1981, NAMMA's newsletter joined in raising awareness of this scandal with a provocative headline: "Still Slavery at Sea?" (*Watermarks,* Dec. 1981, 1-2). In addition to the erosion of seafarers' human rights in general, there has been an alarming increase in cases of brazen abuse by certain "rogue" ship operators. Examples include: *smuggling* of drugs and other cargoes, even human beings; *piracy* with the use of more sophisticated weapons; *plundering* of endangered marine resources; *pollution* of the marine environment; and since 9/11, the rising risk of *terrorism,* using containers or whole ships to perpetrate acts of carnage. In recent years, there has also been a disturbing tendency on the part of the authorities of sea-bordered nations toward *scapegoating* of ship's officers and crews, in cases of marine mishaps within their respective waters.

Agency-related Impediments

"For too long the Western church has tended toward an *intellectual* expression of its faith, failing to face realistically the *supernatural* manifestations it must confront." So says a leading Latin-American missiologist,

Dr. *Samuel Escobar*, about current-day global mission (Escobar 1993, 134). His words ring no less true in modern-day *maritime* mission.

The Bible indicates the ultimate reason behind the obstacles opposing the missionary enterprise—the spiritual conflict between God's mission and "the forces of evil in this world" (Eph. 6:10-18). It is difficult, also for Christians in this post-modern age, to see this world as "enemy-occupied territory," needing to be reclaimed for Christ. Yet Christ and his apostles are unequivocal about the ultimate origin of evil everywhere (John 11:31, 16:33; 1 John 4:4, 5:19).

Many human failings are linked to inter-personal relations, also between fellow-Christians. Vulnerability in this regard may relate to a low level of spiritual health. On the waterfront as elsewhere, such impediments can surface not only on a corporate level, but also on an individual level, among mission staff and other personnel.

Policy Issues

Hurdles hindering healthy maritime ministry may stem from policy decisions or from the general climate of leadership. A breakdown in either case can seriously impede both ecumenism and evangelism in any agency.

Violation of Christian Unity: The following real-life example highlights the debilitating effect of disunity among Christians on today's waterfront. A shipvisitor from one of the many seafarers' missions in a major North American port-city was making his rounds. He had just posted his agency's handout on the ship's bulletin board, next to a number of similar materials from other Christian agencies. A Chinese officer passed by. He stopped, looked incredulously at the crowded collection of competing invitations, and commented dryly: "Too many!" That incident began a new era of inter-agency cooperation in that particular port-city.

Obstruction of authentic evangelism: Disunity among Christians is not alone in undermining the credibility of the Christian gospel among those of other faiths or no faith. The shipvisitor of one fundamentalist-leaning mission was quite forthright about following his agency's narrow, one-dimensional agenda: "When I go on board, as soon as I'm one on one, I zoom in on 'The Four Spiritual Laws' and ask for a decision for Christ. If that seafarer is not willing to make a commitment there and then, I cannot devote precious time to anything other than 'the one thing needful.' So, I just move on to another, and another, and so on." Such extremism, however well meant, violates biblical truth by being anti-ecumenical. It also flies in the face of both the Great Commission and the Great Commandment by ignoring Christ's own clearly stated holistic agenda—of loving, unconditional care for body, mind and spirit.

Such fundamentalist *perversion* of biblical evangelism is no better than the opposite extreme—universalist *aversion* to evangelism altogether, seeing anything beyond advocacy and hospitality as an intolerable "imposition." Both extremes deny the non-Christian seafarer's human right to freedom of choice in matters of faith and conscience.

Personnel Issues

Normally, both officers and crew will greet any shipvisitor from a seafarers' center with a warm welcome that others, whose business takes them on board ship, can only envy. The reason is the accumulated goodwill built up by their predecessors, ever since the early 1800s. To gain goodwill was, from the very beginning, a primary policy goal of seafarers' missions everywhere. This was already evident in the name they frequently adopted—"Seamen's *Friend* Societies," seeking to serve the friendless, exploited mariner. Still, chaplains and other seafarers' center staff are also subject to the fallibility of human nature. Moreover, they have to deal with challenges common to their particular profession, be they psychological, educational or spiritual.

Psychological Impediments: Daily demands encountered by modern-day port chaplains call for higher, not lower qualifications than for their parish-based counterparts. They require robust health, physically and psychologically— together with empathy, creativity and integrity. All too often unrecognized by the wider church ashore, seafarers' chaplains are often isolated from oversight and support that colleagues in congregational ministry can take for granted. Unless an agency's leadership maintains high standards for not only the screening of candidates, but also monitoring and support systems, the consequences can be a formidable impediment to effective ministry. These may range from individual burnout to the breakdown of an entire agency.

Educational Impediments: "Learning by Doing" was the only available, educational tool during the pioneer period of seafarers' missions. Of course, prior sea experience could prove an invaluable asset, as in the case of the movement's founding figure, Bosun Smith of Penzance and Boston's Father Taylor, both of them trained in the "University of the Ocean." Nor was the absence of formal academic education necessarily a barrier to effective maritime ministry. Although sailors were certainly no simpletons, they wanted no "long-winded" preaching, with "jaw-cracking dictionary words," according to Philadelphia's Father Eastburn in the 1820s. In modern-day maritime ministry, recognized certification and continuing education have both become important. Opting out of available training opportunities in this field would present a real impediment to the professional credibility of such ministry in the future.

Spiritual Impediments: Maritime missions everywhere have obviously been affected by varying levels of Christian spirituality among their own regular personnel. In contrast to the more general understanding of "spiritualities," the term "spiritual" refers here to a personal relationship with Christ. The Apostle John's use of the dual concepts of "light" and "life" can provide a relevant biblical basis. Reborn and indwelt by the Spirit of Christ, through personal trust in his death on their behalf (John 3:3-21), Christians sense the call to a daily walk of faith, guided by the *light* of his truth, as they share a new quality of *life* empowered by his Spirit (1 John 1:5-10).

Such is the norm. Nowhere is there a more vivid illustration of this than in the earliest days of the New Testament Church, as portrayed in Acts 2:42-47. United and nurtured by the Spirit of Christ in *fellowship* and *prayer* around both the *Word* and the *Eucharist,* its first members were already embarked on the core commitment that has defined disciples of Christ in every age—his *Great Commission.* The biblical record is just as forthright about how soon that first spiritual wellbeing became marred by the fallibility of human nature (Acts 5:1-11; Philippians 1:15-18).

The history of maritime mission and ministry provides a similar scenario, from the unspoiled spontaneity of the early Bethel Movement to the fluctuating levels of spirituality after that. As a result, theological positions have spanned the whole spectrum—from fundamentalism's fixation on other-worldly priorities to universalism's preoccupation with this world alone. Meanwhile, on an individual level, hypocrisy, belligerence, abuse, lack of zeal, prayerlessness and other forms of spiritual self-starvation or toxic faith, have all been within the bounds of possibility for every level of agency personnel. This can have disastrous implications for an agency's internal morale and external image, illustrated in Romans 2:24 and 1 Corinthians 12:26. For a modern-day analysis of spiritual pathology, see Arterburn 1992.

STRATEGIES FOR MARITIME MISSION

The Asian captain of a newly arrived cargo vessel was obviously busy. He seemed glad, however, to meet with the local port chaplain, who requested permission to visit his ship. The captain was familiar with the many practical services offered by Christian seafarers' centers and knew what these meant for his crew. He also wanted the chaplain to know that he was an active adherent of another faith. The chaplain, sensing that the captain really wanted to talk, assured him of his respect. "Captain," he ventured, "I may not know much else about you. But I do happen to know your best friend." His interest piqued, the captain countered, "How come?" That gave the chaplain an opportunity to explain: "If some one had given his life for you and me and the whole world, could you find a better friend?" "Tell me more," said the captain, and invited the chaplain to sit down.

The outcome of the encounter was that the captain gladly accepted the offer of a New Testament in his own language. Another potential seafaring disciple had taken a first step. Of added significance was the fact that the captain's home country was now closed to conventional Christian mission. The incident, which is far from unique, highlights the rich range of opportunities that maritime mission still affords on the world's waterfronts, perhaps none more so than shipvisiting by chaplaincy staff. This and other strategies make up the following three-part analysis of issues relating to personnel, operations and models in current-day maritime ministry.

Personnel

In the fourth century AD, a compassionate young "pagan" named Martin, then serving with the Roman army in France, tore off half his cloak and gave it to a beggar in need. Little could he have known that he would ultimately become canonized as St. Martin of Tours and a worldwide model for future chaplaincy ministry. The diminutive for "cappa" (Latin for "cloak") is *cappela,* the origin of the term "chaplain." St. Martin's spontaneous act has spawned several legends about the "Holy Covering," as his torn-off cloak came to be called. Since then, a ministry of care for body, mind and spirit of all in need has become the bedrock characteristic of chaplaincy everywhere.

Within the Christian Church at large, at least in the West, the realities of a pluralistic, postmodern era have made mainstream congregational or territorial structures increasingly irrelevant. This has left entire sectors of society a mission field, virtually untouched by the gospel and the institutional church. *Sector ministry* is the name for the specialized, non-parochial ministry with which modern-day chaplaincy seeks to fill this "ecclesial vacuum" (Legood 1999). Compared with other settings such as hospitals, prisons, universities, or industry, the need for such ministry is nowhere more pressing than at sea, given the level of marginalization resulting from the seafarer's vocational mobility.

Liminal space (from *limen,* Latin for "threshold") has also become a key concept in current ecclesiological research. The threshold areas of society are where worlds meet and where sector ministry can penetrate. In his recent dissertation, Paul Mooney emphasizes this concept's relevance to the seafarer-centered paradigm shift in maritime mission. Both seafarers themselves and seafarers' mission personnel are "liminal people," living and working at the margins of settled society and the traditional church (Mooney 2004, 162-3). This marginality affords both ministering seafarers on board and seafarers' chaplains on shore a common identity as *resident aliens.* They are to be "in" and yet not "of" this world (John 17:13-19; Hebrews 13:14).

Shore-based Seafarers' Ministry Practitioners

Seafarers' chaplains who are newcomers to the waterfront may, like their colleagues in other areas of sector ministry, experience an initial "culture shock." Coupled with this may be the sense of being suspects, at all events "outsiders," in relation to the church at large, according to Australian theologian *Gerald Arbuckle* (Legood 1999, 162). At the same time, while their marginal status leaves chaplains free to serve the special needs of seafarers, both pastorally and prophetically, they also experience community—in two distinct spheres: first, in solidarity with seafarers themselves, not least those partnering in peer ministry at sea; second, in fellowship with others involved in shore-based chaplaincy at every level.

Chaplains in maritime sector ministry can also become catalysts for creativity in the wider church. Here, their ministry at the margins can challenge their colleagues in mainstream ministry to break attachments to irrelevant methods and unnecessary barriers "for the sake of the mission of Jesus Christ" (Arbuckle). It is of utmost importance to integrate maritime mission studies into the curricula of all seminaries, mission schools and other relevant educational institutions. For two good reasons such action has long been a goal of IASMM:

It will raise wider awareness and support for this sector of mission. It will also provide vital opportunities for the recruitment of qualified personnel.

A veteran, who was asked what he considered most important among *psychological qualifications* for this work, responded briefly and to the point: "You need to be a king-sized individualist." Certainly, a healthy level of self-reliance must rank high, at least in a ministry defined by unpredictable challenges and an exceptionally isolated work environment. Other personality traits, such as cooperation and communication skills, are also paramount, as noted above under "Personnel Issues as Impediments to Maritime Mission."

As to *educational qualifications,* the above section on "Education: Training, Resources and Research" lists options available in the current post-1974 Global Era. In addition, one of the most promising methods of acquiring a practical grasp on maritime ministry is field study. In the early 1820s, it was already standard practice for future missionaries to obtain "schooling" in the Bethel Meetings on the Thames. In recent years, maritime ministry *internship programs* have become available at seafarers' centers, as a contextual education option for seminary students. For active seafarers' chaplains, the need for *continuing education* has resulted in training options by major maritime mission agencies, with IASMM continuing to offer advanced opportunities.

As for *spiritual qualifications,* the self-sabotaging effect of neglecting the spiritual well-being of maritime ministry practitioners has already been discussed under "Personnel Issues as Impediments to Maritime Mission." Whether one sees seafarers' chaplaincy solely as a professional vocation or primarily as a divine call must be a matter of personal choice. The same applies to methods of Bible reading, meditation and prayer. Given the daily demands of chaplaincy on the waterfront, fellowship with colleagues in port ministry, as well as participation in programs of the wider church, can be important sources of spiritual nurture and renewal.

Ship-based Seafarers' Ministry Practitioners

The first seafarers' ministry practitioners were, as a fact of history, *ship-based.* As the Bethel Movement took hold in the early 1800s, seafarers were ministering to fellow-seafarers both on board ships at sea and in ports around the world. No human agencies had recruited, trained or commissioned them. As they got together with their shipmates, those who had learnt to read would share from the Scriptures as best they could. Prompted by the Spirit and trusted by their peers, their numbers rapidly multiplied, as they unwittingly wrote the opening chapter of the history of organized seafarers' mission.

As to professional ship's chaplains, although there were various versions of them over the centuries, their effectiveness proved to be mixed, and they were at all events few and far between. By contrast, today's *Sailing Chaplain's* offer quite different prospects. They can, as noted earlier, contribute toward a viable, *ship-based* alternative in an era of drastically decreasing opportunities for *shore-based* maritime ministry. Meanwhile, non-professional, peer-based *Ministering Seafarers'* represent another ship-based alternative. For further on both the

Sailing Chaplains and Ministering Seafarers Models, see "Ship-based Models of Maritime Mission" below.

Whereas Sailing Chaplains of the future will need to fulfill *qualification criteria* comparable to those of their professional shore-based colleagues, the nature of the challenge is somewhat different for non-professional crew-based Ministering Seafarers. In the past, the recruitment and monitoring of Ministering Seafarers have been on an unstructured ad hoc basis. Following Paul Mooney's proposal at ICMA/2004, there is now the prospect of an ICMA-coordinated, agency-supported process of training, commissioning and monitoring for future Ministering Seafarers. That will be a sound investment indeed—for both maritime ministry and maritime industry.

Operations

In a Pacific Coast seaport, in the wake of harsh 9/11 port security restrictions, it had been a busy day for the local seafarers' chaplain. He had finally obtained leave for the Muslim crew to accompany him ashore to the center's bus. Some wanted to be taken to a shopping mall, others to the local mosque, the rest simply wanted to get away for some sightseeing. As they returned to their ship, they expressed curiosity about their benefactor's faith, and gladly accepted the offer of a *Jesus Video* in Arabic. When the ship shortly afterwards returned to the same port, they all wanted Bibles in Arabic. After exhausting the center's own stock, the chaplain contacted his colleagues in the ship's next port of call to supply the remaining needs. Meanwhile, one more ship sailed on, its crew a spiritual "work in progress"—under the impact of probably a very different Jesus than the one they had previously heard of.

This episode highlights the unpredictability of maritime ministry in practice. There is no limit to how widely details of daily activities may vary from port to port. Nevertheless, the kind of operations that engage maritime mission practitioners everywhere fall into three general categories: (1) Outreach -related activities; (2) Service-related activities; (3) Advocacy- and promotion-related activities.

Outreach-related Activities and Shipvisiting

Like all forms of "liminal" or "sector" ministry, maritime chaplaincy is by definition *outreach-oriented.* This sector of society simply mandates that kind of strategy, since it is normally beyond the reach of the static structures of a residential parish or congregation. Proactively reaching out with the good news of the gospel, by word and deed, to fellow-humans who would otherwise be without its blessings, that is how organized seafarers' mission began in the early 1800s. That is also the way it can remain relevant in the future.

In one sense, the term "outreach" conveys the wider meaning of "mission" as such, comprising not only proclamation but also service and advocacy. In the present context, it refers to the classic core of all mission—evangelism. As already noted, there is nothing "narrow" about the scope of biblically defined evangelism. If the gospel is to be universally available, *the means of evangelism* need to be unlimited in range—"all things for all people" (1.Cor. 9:22; Phil. 2:5-8). Meanwhile, the ultimate goal of evangelism remains quite specific—personal participation in the blessings of the gospel by as many as possible (1.Cor. 9:22; 2.Cor. 5:20; Phil. 2:11; 1.Tim. 2:4). This dialectic tension, between the limitless means and unique goal of biblical evangelism, must define the shape of outreach activities in maritime mission just as in global mission. In practice, the primary context of maritime evangelistic outreach is the visitation of ships in port.

The Limitless Means of Maritime Evangelism: The bishop who was about to ordain the Author into ministry with seafarers had one piece of practical advice for him, based on his personal experience: "Don't be afraid to get your hands dirty!" (This would inevitably result from faithfully visiting all "hands" on deck and in the engine room.) As a child in the Norwegian expatriate community in London, the Author had already seen the positive rapport resulting from such a "dirty hands" policy. He had witnessed literally dozens of stalwart seafarers, on any given Sunday, line up in the church aisle to take part in Holy Communion. Later, that former seafarers' chaplain, Bishop *Johannes Smidt,* went on to become one of Norway's great 20th century preachers.

Any shipvisitor, ordained or lay, male or female, needs to bear two vital matters in mind, from the moment of stepping on board: (1) In contrast to other forms of industrial chaplaincy, the shipvisitor is *strictly a guest,* entering not just the workplace but also the home of the crew; (2) The shipvisitor represents a faith whose God is committed to *unconditional love* toward every single human being (Rom. 3:23, 5:8). Both factors make it eseential to listen to and prioritize *the immediate felt needs of preferably every seafarer on board.*

In this kind of "deck-plate ministry," such needs appear to be practically infinite. They may range from one-on-one pastoral counseling to the most mundane matters, like obtaining a recent newspaper in Mandarin Chinese, fixing a broken denture, or shopping for underwear on behalf of a ship-bound crew member—to send as a birthday gift for his wife half a world away. In one case, the Author's wife saved the day, when she placed our newborn baby daughter in the arms of a second officer, who was visibly overcome after just receiving news over the phone about the safe arrival of his own first baby back home.

The Unique Goal of Maritime Evangelism: The General Secretary of a major maritime mission organization once wrote to his colleagues on the waterfront, "Every time you climb up a ship's gangway, make sure you breathe a prayer for guidance and blessing." An experienced seafarers' chaplain himself, he went on, "And even though you may not actually find a natural *opportunity,* let it at least be your heart's *desire* to leave a greeting from God about Jesus with every seafarer you meet on board." With that, he was certainly not advocating any coercive approach. Even a cup of cold water, given in Jesus' name, can qualify as an authentic act of evangelism (Matthew 10:42). The veteran chaplain, Dr. *Kaare Stöylen*, was simply suggesting *a healthy self- test in spiritual alertness and caring,* in the midst of overwhelming practical demands (*Watermarks* 3-4, 1985, 1).

Both Peter and Paul admonish their followers to be prepared "in season and out of season," so they can answer every one who asks about the reason for their faith (2 Tim. 4:2; 1 Pet. 3:15). Relationship-starved crewmembers certainly *ask;* this applies especially to seafarers from the non-Western world, with their more overt spiritual awareness. For the shipvisitor, it all depends on everyday preparedness, nurtured by a healthy level of personal spirituality. He or she will soon discover opportunities for *explicit* sharing of the faith to be just as abundant as the many *implicit* ways of witnessing while on shipboard.

Opportunities may present themselves during casual conversations around the ship, or in the course of sharing a meal at the mess-room table. They may also take the shape of an invitation to the cabin of a seafarer burdened by bad news from home, unresolved guilt or plain loneliness. The scenarios are endless. During travels in Asia, the Author will not easily forget the look of sheer helplessness of his escorts from the local Communist Interclub. A group of crewmembers on a ship from those parts requested—and at once received, right there on deck—an impromptu public prayer for the ship's safety and their families' welfare. Another time, there was a passionate plea for a last-minute shipboard service by a desperate ship's captain, himself a self-professed non-believer. His Asian-ethnic crew refused point blank to take his ship to sea, after surviving a near-fatal storm, without first a service of thanksgiving on board.

Given the increasingly limited opportunities for shore leave, shipboard worship service or informal Bible study gatherings have, in recent years, become more frequent in many ports. Where (as in the case of Catholic Filipino seafarers) there is a need for ministry by a particular denomination, a shipvisitor needs to make every effort to secure such cooperation. Of course, identifying, enlisting and equipping potential "Ministering Seafarers" will always rank as an important priority for any shipvisitor alert to the crucial need for pastoral follow-up. Besides supplying the known needs of a fellowship group on board, ship-visitors normally have, as part of their shipvisiting pack, not only newspapers, news magazines, issues of *National Geographic*, etc., but also Christian litera-ture, scripture, worship aids like inspirational CDs, DVDs, and not least *Jesus videos*, as far as possible in relevant languages.

Various organizations have promoted guidelines and training courses for shipvisitors over the years. Since 9/11, Christian and secular maritime welfare agencies have initiated a partnership in this area. In 2004, BISS Senior Chaplain *Bill McCrae* helped the UK Merchant Navy Welfare Board launch a *Foundational Course for UK Shipvisitors.* In 2006, the ICSW published plans for a *Ship Welfare Visitors' Training Course* in Singapore, in cooperation with ICMA. Meanwhile, Dr Jean Smith of SCI NY/NJ headed the compilation of a comprehensive *ICMA Ship Visiting Handbook,* electronically published from the year 2005. Given the central significance of shipvisiting in maritime mission, a summarized version of well-tested, Christian-based *Shipvisiting Guidelines* is included as an Appendix below.

Service-related Activities and Seafarers' Centers

A ministry of faithful shipvisiting in any given port city—even without being based in any local seafarers' center—may well qualify as an authentic seafarers' mission. By contrast, no authentic seafarers' center, once established, can expect to function without a viable shipvisiting program. This intimate connection has never changed, and probably never will. Over time, however, the role of seafarers' centers as such has changed radically.

The Changing Role of Seafarers' Centers: Historically, organized maritime mission began as a seafarer-centered, ship-based operation, with the origins of the Bethel Movement. As shore-based "Bethels" emerged in British and American seaports during the 1820s, these were still predominantly *outreach-oriented,* and continued to work in close partnership with seagoing Bethel captains and crews. The paradigm shift from the mid-1800s to an agency-centered, shore-based delivery of comprehensive *welfare services* was to continue until the advent of the late 20th century "Shipping Revolution." With mounting automation, reduced size of crews, shorter turn-around time and drastically decreased opportunities for shore leave, large, multi-service shore facilities no longer hold unchallenged sway.

As the current shift to a more seafarer-centered, ship-based emphasis gathers momentum, the resulting *partnership paradigm* will doubtless still mean a continuing need for shore-based facilities. Nevertheless, such centers will need to be more specialized—focusing primarily on the provision of coordination and resources for maintaining an effective *shipvisiting* program, together with related *follow-up* activity.

The Nature of Center-based Activities: A hundred or so homeless men were waiting in line for a meal, at a church shelter on America's Eastern Seaboard. Before the volunteers began serving them, the local pastor invited an elderly African-American woman to offer a prayer. Her response was short and hands-on: "Jesus! We know you are in this food-line. Help us to serve you well. Amen." The Lord did say that whatever his followers did for any of "the least of these" they did it for him (Matthew 25:40). The gist of that prayer is worth bearing in mind when offering hospitality of any kind on the waterfront.

As emphasized under the "Diaconal Dimension of Maritime Mission," hospitality represents "the core identity of maritime mission as such." Even though genuine, shared hospitality may also be a regular feature of everyday shipvisiting, there is no question that a well-appointed seafarers' center can offer a far wider range of hospitality. In that sense, the Seamen's Church Institute of NY/NJ leads the world in both size and scope of maritime center-based ministry. Meanwhile, other agencies will normally offer at least some combination of center-based service in areas like transportation, communication, visitation, edification, recreation and education.

Advocacy- and Promotion-related Activities

Promoting the struggle for seafarers' rights and a robust system of agency support merit separate treatment among maritime mission operations:

Advocacy for Seafarers' Human Rights: All three Christian-based advocacy centers for seafarers' human rights—in New York, London and Barcelona—affirm the indispensable role routinely performed by seafarers' chaplains on the world's waterfronts. ITF inspectors endorse that conclusion. Given their goal of being among the first on board, coupled with the level of trust in which they are traditionally held by seafarers, chaplains have become the foremost "eyes and ears" of advocacy for seafarers' justice everywhere. Seafarers serving as leaders of Christian fellowship groups at sea have also often become spokespersons for their shipmates about justice and welfare issues on shipboard. As a result, seafarers' rights will need to be part of any future core curriculum for training "Ministering Seafarers."

Promotion of Seafarers' Mission Agencies: Modern-day maritime mission is based on a network of voluntary Christian organizations. Securing promotional support is therefore of fundamental importance for every maritime mission agency. In practice, that translates into matching *motivation* with the intended *target group.* The latter may be any one of the following three: the general public, the maritime industry or the Christian community.

(1) In relation to the *public,* reminding of its "moral indebtedness" is especially relevant, given the many deprivations inherent in one of the most dangerous but essential vocations—transporting 95% of all world trade. Far from just "charity," the issue here is society's debt of honor. Such arguments are particularly pertinent when launching public appeals, observing national "Sea Sunday " events, collecting Christmas gifts for seafarers, or applying for grants from public foundations. Recognized human welfare needs, rather than "sectarian" concerns, are likely to draw wider public support. For example, an agency may elect to publish an abbreviated version of its mission statement, like "Meeting the physical, emotional and spiritual needs of seafarers," or simply "Caring for Seafarers of the World."

(2) In relation to the *maritime industry,* positive personal relations with the local port authorities will always be vital. In many cases, not least in North America, port authorities provide the site, even the physical facilities, for church-related seafarers' centers. In several port cities, authorities now sanction "port levies" on ship arrivals—voluntary donations paid through the respective ship's agents, in support of the human service delivery of local seafarers' centers. The rationale should be self-evident. Caring for the crews who care for the cargoes is central to the image of any well-functioning seaport. During his 2002-2006 tenure as NAMMA's President, Rev. *James Von Dreele* of SCI Philadelphia broke new ground by initiating an "Industry Advisory Board" (IAB) to promote maritime ministry awareness and support within the wider maritime industry, not least among its many responsibile-minded shipowners.

(3) In relation to the *Christian community,* it is disconcerting that not only the institutional church, but also even the global mission community continue to be largely oblivious to the nature and significance of the maritime mission enterprise. There is an urgent need for proactive and effective awareness for the sake of mission consciousness and mission strategy within the wider Christian

community. At the same time, such awareness-raising continues to be crucial for maritime mission itself, since the Christian community will always be the primary base of supply in terms of funding, recruitment and prayer support. One positive factor in this context, however difficult to define, is the magnetic "pull" that this ministry exerts on so many practitioners, as confirmed by a remarkably high retention rate. In the Pacific Northwest, for example, following in the footsteps of that centenarian pioneer chaplain on the Seattle-Tacoma waterfront, Rev. *Robert Stubbs* (1823-1925), octogenarian and nonagenarian chaplains have continued serving in maritime ministry right into the 21st century.

Models

Ship-based Models of Maritime Mission

As indicated earlier, there are currently two main models of ship-based ministry: Ministering Seafarers and Sailing Chaplains.

Ministering Seafarers' Model: When organized maritime mission began with the early Bethel Movement, Christian seafarers ministered to fellow seafarers on board ship, as well as wherever they went. This was also how ship-based maritime mission re-ignited as a New Bethel Movement in the late 1970s. Besides being based on peer witness, inherently contextualized as "mission from below," the model has two further advantages. In terms of sheer numbers, it is capable of multiplication on every ship on the seven seas. Also, Ministering Seafarers returning to their home communities have consistently been a powerful means of reaching areas of the world now closed to conventional methods of Christian mission.

Sailing Chaplains' Model: Launched by ICMA in 2003, as a current-day version of the historic "ship's chaplaincy" concept, this model, too, has a long record of service behind it, from the Middle Ages to modern-day naval vessels and cruise ships. As ICMA-trained, agency-appointed professionals, Sailing Chaplains work alongside crewmembers at sea for agreed periods of time, contributing an important alternative model of ship-based ministry. In so doing they symbolize a strong sense of solidarity with seafarers. Also, Sailing Chaplains can reinforce the role of potential Ministering Seafarers by serving as "animators" for emerging Christian shipboard communities before moving on to other ships.

Shore-Based Models of Maritime Mission

The emerging seafarer-centered paradigm shift toward ship-based models still presupposes an indispensable role for shore-based support ministry. Such ministry may or may not work out of a local center facility (Kahveci 2007).

Seafarers' Center Model: An effective, well-run seafarers' center, strategically located in or near a major dock area, will normally enhance both the scope and quality of service available to visiting seafarers. With the new paradigm shift toward more seafarer-centered ministry, agencies running shore-based facilities share dual challenges: To prioritize support services for ship-based ministry, through shipvisiting, resource-provision and follow-up. Yet also, to reach out, wherever possible, to fishers, seafarers' dependents, pre-sea trainees, retirees, dockers, truckers and others in the wider maritime community.

Extended Ministry Model: Four maritime-related ministries by extension have more recently emerged, mostly as a result of Nordic initiatives, specifically: "Ambulating Chaplaincy" to visit ships and expatriates in widely dispersed regions; "Off-shore Ministry" on oil- and other ocean-drilling platforms; "Crisis Preparedness Ministry" to provide intervention in connection with marine or other human disasters; and "I-Church" counseling, worship and study opportunities for seafarers via the Internet.

On-Call Model: This low-key model has become the most widely used form of maritime mission worldwide. It builds on one or more concerned clergy persons in any given port area being available "on call" for visiting seafarers who require the voluntary services of an ordained minister. Such services may include ship, home, hospital or prison visitation, as well as pastoral and crisis counseling, ministerial acts and worship services, often on board.. The *ICMA Directory* lists hundreds of these "volunteer" or "honorary chaplains," usually with their denominational or organizational affiliation. Sometimes they share responsibilities on a mutually agreed "roster" basis. In these ways, an on-call model may provide a measure of ministry where available resources are minimal, or where the level of shipping does not justify full-time chaplaincy.

The Appendices below include a recent, real-life example of how a volunteer port chap-laincy can develop into a viable center-based seafarers' mission. In this case, the original catalyst was the volunteer training of the Southern New England Lutheran Seafarers' Ministry headed by Rev. *Andrew Krey*, at that time Director of Chaplaincy at Seafarers' and International House, New York.

SUMMARY

THE WAVE OF THE FUTURE

"Every branch of theology—including missiology—remains piecework, fragile, and preliminary. There is no such thing as missiology, period." So says David Bosch, as he brings his masterwork on modern-day missiology to a conclusion (1991, 498). If mission is to be faithful to its ever evolving character, there can never be more than an *interim* definition. First, the *study* of mission has to be subject to change, because so is the overall *context* of mission. Second, because mission is ultimately *God's* mission *(Missio Dei),* and therefore infinite, mission simply defies defining in finite, *human* terms.

Precisely the same applies to *maritime* mission. After exploring the historical and systematic evolution of the maritime missionary enterprise, a comprehensive definition might seem appropriate. However, because the pace of change in the world of seafarers, too, continues to escalate, no definition of maritime mission can claim finality. Like the people of the sea, it must itself be "on the move." It can at best be only a work in progress.

The Author's 1986 volume on *Seamen's Missions* does include a tentative, historically limited, definition of organized maritime mission (Kverndal 1986, 560-561). It summarizes the nature and purpose of the work as reflected in primary source materials up to the mid-1800s—the end of the movement's first formative years. How would a definition of maritime mission look like at the beginning of the 21st century? Such a definition needs first and foremost to be as objective as possible, seeking common ground by building on a biblical basis that transcends differences. At the same time, that formulation needs to reflect the actual historical evolution of maritime mission up to the present. This project calls for a two-stage approach: The first need is to identify the basic biblical and contextual *preconditions* for the task in hand. The second will then be to determine the *components* of such an interim definition.

Biblical and Contextual Preconditions

As to *biblical preconditions* for such a definition, maritime mission derives its missionary nature from the very character of the Triune God, as revealed in both the Old and New Testaments. Just as mission in general is

Missio Dei ("God's Mission"), so too *maritime* mission is *Missio Maritima Dei* ("God's Maritime Mission"). The purpose of maritime mission is to incorporate all whose occupations relate to the sea in the overall purpose of Christian mission. The Lord of Mission himself spells out that assignment in the principal biblical texts making up the "Great Commission": (1) To make the unique message of salvation through Jesus Christ universally available—as per his *mandate* in Matthew 28:18-20. (2) To implement that charge through holistic witness—as per his *model* in John 20:21. (3) To fulfill that task through the empowerment of his Spirit—as per the *means* laid out in Acts 1:8.

As to *contextual preconditions* for a relevant definition of maritime mission, the pace of global change during the latter half of the 20th century has been unparalleled. In *scientific* terms, the explosive development of information technology has promoted the phenomenon of globalization, and in the maritime world fueled a veritable Shipping Revolution. In *geo-political* terms, a borderless war against terrorism, impelled by ideological and religious extremism, has followed on the end of the Cold War against Communism. In *religious* terms, the resurgence of non-Christian religions has brought new urgency to inter-religious relation. In *ecclesial* terms, the end of Western superiority in the global Christian church has coincided with a dramatic shift to non-Western predominance in both membership and mission engagement.

As a result, in order to be both biblically faithful and contextually relevant, an interim definition of maritime mission needs to consist of two distinct yet complementary components: (1) A biblical core foundation of ongoing validity; (2) A synopsis of aspects of maritime mission which are relevant to the context of seafaring at this particular point in history. This concept of a dual-component interim definition coincides with current post-Bosch thinking about the church's mission, as an ongoing interaction between certain *constants* on the one hand, and continually emerging *contexts* on the other (Bevans and Schroeder, 2004).

An Interim Definition

(1) Christian maritime mission incorporates extending to people of the sea everywhere the call of Christ to make disciples of all people; sharing his unconditional love through a ministry of witness, service and advocacy, in order to promote their holistic welfare in body, mind and spirit; above all, providing every seafarer with a viable opportunity to become, by faith, a new creation in Christ, integrated into his global church, and empowered to live under his reign as his witness in the world. If the Christian church is to be loyal to her Lord, it is primarily those who claim the name of Christ that are called to implement that core assignment, in the unity of his Spirit and in the changing context of every generation—to the end of the age.

(2) At the dawn of the third millennium, radical change in the wake of growing globalization has made an impact on the maritime industry that mandates a profound paradigm shift also in maritime ministry:

- *The continuing dehumanization that undermines the quality of life in the maritime workforce constitutes a clear prophetic challenge: this calls for constant countermeasures in cooperation with all concerned.*
- *The new level of religious pluralism among today's multi-cultural crews, combined with reduced turn-around time in port, constitutes a compelling discipleship challenge; this necessitates moving to a ship-based, seafarer-centered peer ministry at sea, with an equally vital shore-based support system to provide resources and coordination.*
- *Rising religious pluralism also underscores the urgent need for interfaith dialogue and diapraxis, seeking to learn from one another and cooperate in all areas of common humanity—like justice, peace, health and the environment; this needs to be coupled with mutual respect for truth claims and mission agendas inherent to the identity and dignity of others, as required by the Universal Declaration of Human Rights.*

Today's Challenge

If the picture at this point in history is indeed as portrayed above, how will the worldwide maritime mission community respond in the decades ahead? Will the Western-world maritime ministry establishment embrace the challenge of change and throw its support behind a new beginning of ship-based peer ministry at sea, as well as partnership opportunities with indigenous non-Western ministry initiatives ashore? Will the worldwide maritime mission community raise new and needful awareness of these possibilities within the wider Christian church, especially within its world mission community?

In the world of today, there are prophets of doom who predict the rapid demise of Christianity itself in what they already call a "post-Christian" era. Contrary to that view, an increasing number of modern-day missiologists recognize an emerging parallel to the "pre-Christendom" Early Church—with its uncompromising commitment to mission. Primarily, they see signs of renewed dependency on the Spirit rather than the state as the church's source of power. They are also aware that modern information technology can provide resources for mission hitherto never imagined.

Nowhere is the potential prospect for such renewal greater than through the continued spread of today's global network of seagoing Christian communities, those who make up the body of Christ among the people of the sea—the Church Maritime. By far the greater part of the earth's surface is covered by water, as of now 71%. Therefore, the glory of the Lord can never fulfill the vision of Habakkuk 2:14, and "cover the earth as the waters cover the sea," without those to whom he first entrusted his gospel, and who, when once given the opportunity, have consistently proved his most faithful followers: Those of the Way of the Sea!

PART III

PERSPECTIVES
ON MARITIME MISSION

1

DANCING WITH THE ELEPHANT
Multi-Ethnicity and Maritime Ministry
Miriam Adeney

MIRIAM ADENEY is Associate Professor at Seattle Pacific University and Research Professor of Mission at Regent College, Vancouver, British Columbia. She teaches regularly in Southeast Asia and Latin America. She holds a PhD in cultural anthropology from Washington State University. She has authored numerous books including God's Foreign Policy: Practical Ways to Help the World's Poor, *and* Daughters of Islam: Building Bridges with Muslim Women. *At the North American Maritime Ministry Conference in Seattle in 1984, Miriam Adeney gave a paper entitled* Communicating Christ to the Asian Seafarer's Mind.

The Problem

When the elephant and the mouse gave a party, friends came from far and near. They ate and drank and sang and danced. And no one celebrated more exuberantly than the elephant. "What a party, Mouse! Wasn't that something!" he exclaimed when it was over. But there was no answer. "Mouse? . . . Mouse?" called the elephant. Then he found his friend—smashed under his feet, crushed by his enthusiasm. An African told this story to point out one of the dangers of inter-ethnic ministry. Powerful partners can crush you.

Certainly no true minister *wants* to stomp on those of another race. Nevertheless, in the world of the sea, race remains an issue. There is exploitation of cheap labor on "flag of convenience" ships by shipowners from stronger nations. There is continuing conflict in multi-ethnic crews, especially between officers and other ranks. There is the inhuman treatment of stowaways and political/economic refugees. Westerners may dominate in resources, policies and personnel, with the best will in the world. However, sometimes we act like elephants.

Lessons from the Past

We have a long history of distinction between "us" and "them" (Hiebert 1996, 63-82). In the Middle Ages, a non-European was often seen as a "monster," an "infidel," or a "heretic." During the Age of Exploration, such others were seen as "pagans." Commercial interests viewed them as potential "slaves." Enlightenment thinkers called them "savages," "primal" and "primitive." Early twentieth-century anthropologists classed others as "natives." For the average American today, others may be "exotic" or "problems" or "good business contacts."

As long as the slave trade was taken for granted, Americans considered slaves fully human. Everybody could see that some Africans were smarter than some Caucasians. But "when voices were raised against this inhuman traffic, particularly by influential men and representatives of powerful organizations, the slave holding interests were driven to find moral justification for enslaving human beings" (Montagu 1964, 39). Citations from the Bible, evolutionary theory, psychological intelligence testing and cultural anthropology's early race classifications provided "proof" of some races' inferiority.

Earlier, when European explorers first encountered local people on other continents and islands, a similar question had arisen: Were these creatures human? If not, they could be treated like animals. That was tempting. What a labor pool! However, in 1537, Pope Paul III made a ringing proclamation in his encyclical, *Sublimis Deus:* "The Indians are true [human beings]." What did he mean? He spoke as a Christian. Others, like ourselves, are created in the image of God. This is classic Christian theology. Others, too, are sinners. Others are invited to eternal salvation by putting their faith in the atoning work of Jesus Christ. Others are called to full membership in Christ's Church, his "one body," with full rights and obligations in liturgy, government, ministry and mission. As fellow members of the body, we are to hurt when others hurt and rejoice when they rejoice. Our gifts and callings are complementary.

Practical Implications

How would such a theology shape seafarers' ministry? At the most elementary level, it would incline us to *honor seafarers' mother tongue.* Nothing brings more joy than hearing your own language in a strange port. This happens where visiting seafarers are met by shipvisitors and center staff familiar with at least some words in their respective languages. Also important are, of course, Bibles, booklets, cassettes and videos in all the commonly-used languages. Thus can a Mauritanian seaman far from home run the *Jesus video* in his own language. Today that video is available in hundreds of languages.

Language and culture, gifts of God, help a person remember who he or she is in space and time. Seafarers are not just cheap labor. People raised them, and cared for them. They have a heritage. Undoubtedly some of the elements of this culture are exploitative and evil. Nevertheless, patterns of wisdom and beauty and truth also reverberate throughout their culture. These are not neutral. They are from God who has endowed every people in his image with creativity.

Using seafarers' native languages is only the first step in ethnic ministry. *Cook their food! Play their music!* While food and music, and also gathered photos and posters from their home places, can stab them with sensory delight, they still remain surface matters. Ethnicity penetrates deeper—to different ambitions, family patterns, spending habits, and political goals. It is not so easy to maintain empathy in these areas. Yet, as counselors and advocates for seafarers generally, and especially as mentors to those growing in faith, we must try to appreciate how their cultures shape their behavior.

Such sensitivity might transform our teaching and preaching; also our music, administration and organization style, counseling, evangelism, and community service. Not least in counseling, it may lead to listening more carefully to the indirect nuances.

Theological Reflections

Many maritime ministers have struggled for justice and humaneness. A pioneer model in this regard is *George Charles Smith*. He ministered to marginalized seafarers and their families throughout his long life, 1782-1863 (Kverndal 1986, passim). In 1815, Smith learned of an impending "Fishermen's Famine" among the Scilly Islanders. Twenty-five miles from Land's End, these people had supported themselves by transporting contraband to and from France. Fast coastguard cutters recently had stamped out their livelihood. Crop failures on the islands had left them destitute. Smith researched the reports, procured and sent food, clothes, blankets and medicine, and founded a local micro-enterprise project through which the Scilly women could generate some income. Although authorities had wanted to hush up the impending catastrophe in order to avoid any possible scandal, Smith noised it about. This got the attention of sympathetic naval officers and the slave trade abolitionist William Wilberforce, and eventually secured royal patronage. A national relief committee for Scilly was the result (Kverndal 1986, 168-69).

Years later, Smith entered the fray on behalf of another group of "outsiders," the Chinese. In the 1840s and 1850s, Britain pushed opium into China while China's pagan rulers struggled to keep it out. Smith asked, how will God judge "purportedly Christian peoples, who would permit poison to be thrust down the throats of a non-Christian nation at the point of the bayonet?" (Kverndal 1986, 570). Not before 1997 could Hong Kong, which traced its roots back to that shabby start, finally celebrate its freedom from the British. Sailors were tools in those dark deeds; Smith would not be quiet about it. Neither can we ignore seafarers' socio-economic realities today.

Other religions must receive attention. The great themes of these faiths have structured seafarers' worldviews. In these religions, a crucial element is missing—God visiting this planet in Christ, God entering our pain in Christ's death, and God generating the power for new beginnings in Christ's resurrection. Nevertheless, they may have glimpses of truth, wisdom, and justice. Buddhism sensitizes us to the paradox and suffering that pervade our world. Confucianism reminds us of our roots, and of the need for courtesy in the family and in society. Muslims emphasize the greatness of God, the naturalness of prayer, and the centrality of community. We can value such qualities in these heritages. To do so is to learn to think alongside our friends who come from these backgrounds.

Toward a New Ethnic Sensitivity

To appreciate our seafaring friends' thought patterns, to hear their questions and their wisdom, this is our call. Just because people look a certain way, or do not speak our language, is no excuse to bypass their culture. Every culture is the life-way of people made in the image of God, regardless of their standard of living. Most people with whom God has communicated throughout history have lived in cultures far different from the West at the beginning of the 21st century. Was Noah literate? Did David believe in democracy? Did Mary have indoor plumbing? Yet their lives were as valid as ours are. They experienced friendship, love, parenthood, creativity, learning, responsibility, choice, dignity, adventure, and relationship to God. Every seafarer has a similar heritage.

The challenge remains daunting. The job will be too big for any of us if we truly open our arms to embrace Chinese and Bahamians, Norwegians and Costa Ricans, Russians and Koreans. We need to link forces with churches and agencies across the board. We will find out what Bible societies, radio ministries, publishers and international student services are doing in our seafarers' languages. Through e-mail we will make introductions and referrals. In this way we can tap into existing resources, both media and human. Where resources are lacking, we can make common cause to get appropriate literature developed.

Seafarers are not projects, but people. Not objects, but subjects. Their mystery deserves not trumpeting elephants but quiet followers of the One who "became flesh and lived among us." As he adapted to an alien culture, we too must try to see through other eyes and stand in other shoes. With the changing ethnic composition of ships' crews, and with diverse nationalities of fishers in port as a result of changing times, seafarers' mission needs new ethnic sensitivity. Then, as seafarers travel on to bless the nations, "from the rising of the sun to the going down of the same, the Lord's name will be praised" (Ps. 113:3).

2

RELIGIOUS PLURALISM AT SEA
Relating to Those of Other Faiths
António Barbosa da Silva

ANTONIO BARBOSA DA SILVA was born and raised in the Cape Verde Islands, off the northwest coast of Africa, a former Portuguese colony with a Creole culture and seafaring heritage. As an 18 year old, he enlisted in the Portuguese air force. Unhappy about fighting to preserve Portugal's colonies, he finally found sanctuary in Scandinavia. In 1969, contact with Christian students in Oslo, Norway, led to a renewal of faith and a commitment to theological training. He earned his ThD degree in 1982 in Sweden, with a dissertation on The Phenomenology of Religion as a Philosophical Problem. *He has served profess-orates in Comparative Religion, Ethics and Systematic Theology in Sweden and, after 1995, in Norway.*

Navigating Today's Multi-Religious Waters

This postmodern era has raised awareness of a "pluralistic" world of multiple religions. Many see relating to those of other faiths as the central theological issue now facing the worldwide Christian church. At theological seminaries, the study of Christianity's relationship to other faiths has evolved into a relatively new discipline called "Theology of Religions." Meanwhile, Christians are wondering how they can be loyal to their call, to witness to their faith in Jesus Christ, without showing disrespect for people with different beliefs or no belief at all (Barbosa da Silva, 1986).

The term "pluralism" has at least two meanings. One is *sociological,* referring to the many religions in the world. In this sense, the world has always been pluralistic, with some areas becoming even more so due to increasing emigration and inter-communication. The second meaning is *theological*. It not only recognizes the variety or plurality of religions in the world but presupposes the equal validity of their respective truth claims.

One can recognize the existence of pluralism in the first (sociological) sense, while not identifying in any way with the second (theological) sense.

There is wide consensus that there are at least three ways in which one can respond theologically to the religious pluralism of our age. These are known as pluralism, inclusivism, and exclusivism. In exploring the significance of each, the principal focus will be on the differences between (1) Presuppositions regarding *divine revelation*, and (2) Implications regarding *mission and dialogue.*

Religious pluralism, both as a sociological fact and a subject of theological debate, is as prevalent in the maritime world as it is ashore. In the wake of globalization, multi-cultural crews have become commonplace in today's international maritime workforce; the following analysis is no less relevant to maritime mission than it is to world mission in general.

Pluralism: A Universalistic Approach

The pluralist insists that the right of every person of faith to be respected must begin with accepting another's view of divine revelation as equivalent. Pluralism holds that there is no distinction between the validity of *general* and *special* revelation. "General" revelation affirms God's self-manifestation through nature, history, conscience and the various world religions. "Special" revelation concerns God's self-disclosure through the Christian Holy Scriptures. To the pluralist, both categories are essentially equal in validity.

Pluralists maintain that every religion offers an alternative, yet equally authentic, way of salvation, since each conveys sufficient saving truth about God, as "Ultimate Reality." For that reason, pluralism endorses the doctrine of "universalism," a belief in the ultimate salvation of all human beings everywhere. There is therefore no need for mission. In fact, pluralist theologians, like *John Hick*, *Paul Knitter* and *Wilfred Cantwell Smith*, portray the concept of Christian world mission as morally offensive, imperialistic, insulting to sincere believers of other faiths, even "blasphemous."

As a result, pluralists preach *dialogue*—instead of the gospel of Jesus Christ. The purpose of such inter-religious dialogue is not to compete but to complete—through mutual understanding and enrichment. The goal is not to convert the other, but to make the Christian a better Christian, the Buddhist a better Buddhist, the Muslim a better Muslim, and so on. This will, pluralists claim, contribute to global peace as well as a greater grasp of the truth and God's overall purpose in today's world (Netland, 2001).

Inclusivism: A Compromise Approach

Those who hold to an inclusivist view assert that Christianity represents the culmination of all religions, and as such is "superior" to every other faith. However, even though God has revealed Jesus Christ as the Savior *par excellence,* non-Christian religions can nevertheless provide sufficient revelation of "light" and "truth" to ensure salvation. In this way, inclusivists seek to reconcile the all-embracing, saving will of God (1 Tim. 2:4) with the reality that many have still not heard the gospel of Jesus Christ, or have not heard it in a valid way. As biblical justification for their stance, inclusivist theologians frequently quote the Old Testament prophet Malachi (1:11) and refer to God's unconditional love.

Despite good intentions, because of such selective Bible reading, inclusivism ends up making mission unnecessary—if not (like pluralism) even counterproductive. According to *Tormod Engelsviken*, Professor of Missiology at the Lutheran School of Theology in Oslo, the bottom line for any theology of mission claiming to be Christian has to be whether or not it promotes Christian mission (Engelsviken 1994 & 1995). If salvation were possible without the atonement of Christ, then he died for no purpose (Gal. 2:21). This would render the core content of the gospel superfluous. With such "reductionism," both the Christian church and its mission would lose their very *raison d'être*.

Since inclusivism assumes that all people will gain ultimate salvation, regardless of faith in Christ, the practical outcome becomes universalism—just as with pluralism. Also like pluralism, inclusivism ends up with a form of interfaith dialogue that might well enhance mutual relations but nevertheless would reject the Bible's own mission agenda.

Exclusivism: An Intentional Biblical Approach

The exclusivist view derives from the exclusive claims of both Jesus Christ himself and his apostles in the New Testament. Among the most categorical of these is the statement of Jesus in John 14:6: "No one comes to the Father except through me." Another example is the assertion of Peter in Acts 4:12: "Salvation is found in no one else, for there is no other name given under heaven by which we must be saved." Exclusivism, like inclusivism, accepts both general and special revelation. Contrary to both pluralism and inclusivism, however, exclusivism denies that God's revelation outside Christianity is sufficient for the salvation or redemption of humankind.

Exclusivism does not imply lack of compassion or respect for others. Pluralism denies Christ as Savior, while inclusivism denies the need for explicit faith in him. Given the Bible's own emphasis, exclusivism intentionally affirms not only the unique role of Christ as Savior, but also the need for personal faith in him as equally crucial. Precisely because the Word of God so powerfully portrays Christ as the sole source of salvation, the very uniqueness of this truth requires making it universally available by means of *mission*. If salvation comes by grace through *Christ alone*, everyone needs to know and appropriate that fact through *faith alone*. Global access to salvation would be impossible without global mission, as Paul puts it in Romans 10:13-15. Withholding mission would therefore be not only immoral, but a betrayal of the human right to freedom of choice in all matters of faith and conscience.

This still leaves many unanswered questions. One of the most troubling of these is the ultimate fate of those who, through no fault of theirs, have never received any valid offer of the Christian gospel. The Bible does not dwell on this particular issue. Rather than resort to speculation, biblical exclusivism can only entrust to the God of all justice and mercy what has not as yet become manifest through biblical revelation (Deut. 29:29).

Exclusivists do not rule out the role of inter-religious dialogue. Rather than dispensing with it, classic Christianity has always seen dialogue as promoting at least two positive purposes—human solidarity and gospel witness. As Professor *Jan Martin Berentsen*, my colleague at the University School of Mission in Stavanger, Norway, underscores, each of these purposes is "indispensable" from a biblical view of mission (Berentsen 1993 & 1994).

First, dialogue with other faiths is essential to peaceful coexistence, social justice and the protection of the environment. Such "humanitarian" dialogue for the sake of the global community is relatively non-controversial—on the common basis of God as Creator, as in the first article of the Apostles' Creed.

Second, inter-faith dialogue is a precondition for witness to the gospel of Jesus Christ. As Paul proved so masterfully at the Areopagus in Athens (Acts 17:16-23), that kind of "theological" dialogue conveys a challenge that is inevitably controversial. Still, the New Testament is full of it! In fact, the Bible and the history of the Church both strongly support the need for dialogue in mission. By contrast, dialogue and mission as understood by both pluralism and inclusivism are an invention of postmodernism and its influence on theology.

Relevance to Religious Pluralism at Sea

Mission among seafarers is preeminently holistic, with a major emphasis on both diaconal and prophetic ministry. Yet here too, some degree of verbalized witness is indispensable. All of the above has a potential bearing on mission among today's many mariners of non-Christian faith. This includes both the possibilities and limitations of inter-religious dialogue. My vocation has so far not included personal experience in ministry among seafarers. Consequently, I choose to end by quoting the following three-fold approach to effective witness on the waterfront by a veteran Dutch-Canadian port chaplain:

Without coercion! True, mission is a matter of urgency. Yet our witness must not take on the character of force or railroading. It is the love of Jesus Christ that must motivate us. We are called to go only as his ambassadors.

Without arrogance! We ourselves have received salvation only by pure grace—as a free and unmerited gift. Each of us has to admit we are not one whit better than our Hindu, Muslim or Buddhist neighbor. The gospel is not the product of any human brain or moral superiority, but the good news of Jesus Christ.

Without fear! It is the Son of God who has given us the Great Commission—to go make disciples of all nations. We are only called to obey. It is he who has the power to persuade and change the lives of individual people or nations, whether on ship or on shore. So we can go without fear, knowing that Christ has, according to Matthew 28:18-20, personally promised every one of us: "I will be with you—to the end of the age!"

(J.E.F. Dresselhuis, "Seafarers and Non-Christian Religions,"in *Watermarks,* June 1987.)

3

MARITIME MINISTRY
AND MARITIME ECOLOGY
From a Developing World Perspective
Thomas P. Batong

THOMAS P. BATONG was born and raised in the Philippines. He completed theological studies there, as well as in the USA, with a Doctorate of Ministry in 1980 at Concordia Theological Seminary, Indiana. He then became Seminary Dean, subsequently President, of the Lutheran Church in the Philippines (1980-1991). In 1992, the Geneva-based Lutheran World Federation (LWF) called him to become Asia Secretary of its Department of Mission and Development. Here, he helped promote Lutheran engagement in ecumenical maritime mission in the non-Western world. Since returning to the Philippines in 1997, he has continued to cooperate in that endeavor.

The Current Ecological Crisis

During recent decades, the Christian church has had to confront a mounting number of critical issues. There is wide consensus that one of the most urgent of these is the worldwide ecological crisis. Science sounded the first global wake-up call through Dr. *Rachel Carson's* sensational findings in her 1963 best-seller, *Silent Spring*. By highlighting the interconnectedness of the whole of creation, she made millions aware of the impending ecological catastrophe resulting from unrestrained degradation of the global environment.

In 1996, the Lutheran World Federation sponsored an ecological conference in Singapore, focusing on the negative impact of globalization upon the environment. Here, *Rita Miscal* of India commented on how it was possible to ignore the effect of human activity upon the earth's environment in the early stages of the Industrial Revolution (LWF 1996). This could only happen when such activity was relatively restricted in scope. Today, modern science and technology have acquired a speed and scale that threaten to destroy the biosphere that sustains the very existence of the human species.

However, there is a clear distinction between the environmental concerns of the developed and the developing nations. The industrialized nations can prioritize pollution control and resource conservation if they so choose. Caring about aesthetic surroundings, clean air or pure water, cannot be the immediate concerns of developing nations, where multitudes of poor are simply looking for their next bowl of rice, a roof over their heads and fuel for cooking their meals.

In this gathering global crisis, the marine environment is especially vulnerable. Today's world is experiencing not only health hazards but a depleted marine habitat, resulting from oil spills, toxic wastes and chemicals dumped in oceans, lakes and rivers. Added to these are the effects of nuclear waste products and nuclear explosions that have contaminated both fishing grounds and human life, thereby threatening the entire ecosystem. In 1997, the Apostleship of the Sea made this menace to the marine environment the focus of its 20th World Congress, held in Davao City, Philippines, under the title: "People of the Sea: God's Collaborators in Creation." Here, several papers pointed to the excesses of today's global market economy, and how unsustainable fishing leads to the exhaustion of marine resources, as well as the exploitation of laborers of the sea.

One speaker at the 1997 gathering, Fr. *John Leyden*, an Irish Columbian missionary working in the Philippines, delivered the following challenge:

> *Future generations, if they survive, will look back on our times and ask, "Were there any voices that proclaimed the truth in that time of crisis? Did anyone take a stand for life? Did the Christian tradition have anything to say?"*

The Biblical Basis for Eco-theology

Indeed, Christian tradition, as rooted in the Bible, has much to say about both God's creation and the role of human beings in relation to that creation. The departure point for a biblical "eco-theology" is the Genesis record of God as Creator of heaven and earth, declaring it all to be "good." All creation—both human and non-human—was the work of the same holy hands. God then entrusted to humans the stewardship (not ownership!) of all non-human creation.

Although humans betrayed God's trust, the New Testament reveals that God still so loved the world that he gave his own Son to rescue it from the disastrous consequences of that betrayal (John 3:16). In the original Greek, the word for "world" is *cosmos,* meaning not just human beings but the whole universe—as sociology professor, Dr. *Tony Campolo*, reminds us in *How to Rescue the Earth without Worshiping Nature* (1992). In rescuing the earth, it is relevant to remember that water covers the greater part of that earth's surface.

Accountability to God for stewardship of his creation also entails responsibility *horizontally,* to fellow human beings. The greatest of God's commandments—solidarity and love for our neighbors—requires no less. Those who are most vulnerable to the consequences of environmental irresponsibility are the poor. Faithful stewardship of God's creation is therefore essentially a justice issue, in other words one of "eco-justice." As citizens of the world and therefore trustees, not mere consumers, we have a God-given calling to counter a culture that condones the mismanagement of our planet. This responsibility, shared by all human beings, has to include the universal ratification of international instruments like the Kyoto Protocol of 1997, intended to combat the catastrophic effects of global warming. Among these effects is the potential obliteration of coastal communities throughout the world, with disastrous implications not least for fishers and their families.

Ecological Implications for Maritime Mission

The Gospels portray a close linkage between Jesus' teachings that touched on the spiritual and material needs of people by the Sea of Galilee. Just as at the time of the disciples, so also today, millions depend on marine life for their livelihood and daily needs. A holistic understanding of mission, one that seeks to address all the human needs of fishers and other seafarers, has to consider the negative impact of the whole range of activities capable of depleting the marine environment and its vital resources.

At the Singapore Conference of the Lutheran World Federation in 1996, Dr. *Sun Hoi Kim* of Korea called for a bold, broad program of environmental education, to combat the arrogance of today's technology-driven society (LWF 1996). Such a program needs to include both practitioners of seafarers' mission and seafarers themselves, given the global consequences of littering at sea, oil spillage and the dumping of toxic wastes. At the same time, through a prophetic ministry of advocacy, maritime mission also needs to reach the decision-makers in government and industry who can help safeguard the marine environment from their perspective, and rein in those involved in the many forms of abuse.

In that regard, seafarers' missions have consistently supported IMO's 1973 International Convention for the Prevention of Pollution from Ships (MARPOL). This apportions responsibility for marine pollution between both ships and sea-ports. In general, seafarers themselves are well aware of these and similar regulations. In their own interest, they have excellent motivation to abide by them. However, there is a continuing need to defend visiting seafarers. Regrettably, overzealous port authorities have, in the past, routinely and unfairly charged them with complicity in almost all cases of local pollution—even where these may be generated from land or by a port's lack of contingency provisions.

Finally, the care of creation is a common human concern, one with which most of us can identify, regardless of religion. We all have a worldview and the need to try to make sense of our environment. We are all tenants who share, as a sacred trust, the care of this our only planetary home. Ecological concern can therefore become an indispensable factor in reaching the many non-Christians among today's seafarers with the gospel of God's love for all creation.

To quote Dr. Kim again, for today's "groaning creation," the gospel is "a message of hope, as the children of God cooperate in the redeeming work of Christ and the healing of creation." There is indeed hope, because ultimately it is Christ himself who will make all things new, as he fulfills his promise of a new heaven and a new earth (Rom. 8:22; 2 Pet. 3:13; Rev. 21:1-6). It is also Christ who, according to Matthew 6:10, calls us to work and pray that this earth shall, in the meantime, look at least a little more like heaven.

4

MULTI-CULTURAL COMMUNICATION
In Ministry among Asian Seafarers
William Choi

WILLIAM CHOI was born in Korea and raised in a multi-religious mix of traditional Asian religions. In 1950, caught in a bloody battle between North and South during the Korean War, he found refuge in a Buddhist monastery at the summit of a nearby mountain. While the monks there meditated on Buddha, he himself came to a commitment to Christ. This led him to ordination in the Anglican Church of Korea, and graduate studies in Australia, Japan and the USA. From1974, he served as Bishop of the Diocese of Pusan. In 1987, he took early retirement in order to serve as Anglican Port Chaplain, first in San Pedro, California, finally in Seattle, Washington, where he now pursues theological research and authorship.

The majority of Asian seafarers—except for Filipinos—are non-Christians. They are widely diverse in culture, language, and values. Their religions are principally the following: Animism, Shamanism, Confucianism, Taoism, Buddhism and Shintoism in the East-Asian world, Hinduism in India, as well as mainly Islam in Indonesia, Malaysia, Bangladesh and Pakistan. Besides these traditional religious backgrounds, there have been Communist regimes in China, North Korea and Vietnam since World War II. In recent decades, secularism and Western culture have also spread into Asian societies.

In seeking to build bridges toward effective Christian ministry among today's many Asian-ethnic seafarers, we need to know: Who would Asian seafarers of non-Christian background say Jesus Christ is—the one whom we see as both the foundation and goal of authentic seafarers' mission?

While *Animism* is the belief that all natural objects and phenomena possess individual spirits, *Shamanism* is the belief that only certain individuals—or "Shamans"—possess the power to influence such spirits. Seafarers influenced by Shamanism might therefore see Jesus as a spirit or a great shaman, one who can communicate with various spirits and demons. However, they would not know that Jesus Christ is one with the almighty God who has sovereign power over all spirits and demons, as demonstrated in Matthew 8:32, for example.

Confucian seafarers would see Jesus Christ in a moral light, as one of many exemplary "Gentlemen" (*Jun-Zi* in Chinese, *Gun-Ja* in Korean, *Kun-Shi* in Japanese). This would be due to Jesus' teaching about morality, such as in the "Beatitudes," and in his preaching of unconditional love. Confucius (552-479 BC) taught about benevolence and heaven-sent virtue. He said, "As long as we show benevolence toward others, there will be no evil." (Chapter *Li-Ren-Pian*, Analects). However, according to the Christian Scriptures, human moral conduct is neither the condition nor the goal for becoming a Christian, as we see in the conflict between the Pharisees and Jesus on this issue (Luke 18:9-14). Rather, it is to live the life of a Christian in the will of God.

Who would *Taoist*-oriented seafarers think Jesus might be? Cultic Taoists might regard Jesus as if he were either one of many deities or the supreme god (*Yu-huang-shang-di*, Respected Sovereign/Supreme Being). To a philosophical Taoist, Jesus Christ would be seen as "the way" (*Tao* or *Dao*), "the lifeless reality." Lao-zi (c. the 6th century BC) wrote, "There are ways, but the Way is uncharted" (Chapter 1, Book of *Lao-zi).* For Christians, however, Jesus himself is the Redeemer, the one who brings people not simply to some natural destination, but to God, the Father, who is the source of life eternal (John 14:6).

Buddhist seafarers might accept Jesus as one of the "enlightened" ones who became a Buddha, one who is awakened through an enlightenment, just as a man named Gautama was in the 6th century BC, in India. They believe that Gautama became Buddha through "the Middle Way" (renouncing both secular and ascetic lives, but focusing on contemplation). Buddha taught people about doing good works, the cycle of life as a form of "resurrection," and enlightenment for "paradise" (*nirvana*) as a form of eternal life. However, it is the mission of Jesus Christ to reveal the truth and love of the Living God the Father and, by the power of the Holy Spirit, to draw all of humankind to himself—for time and eternity (John 8:12; 11:25; 12:32-33).

Japanese *Shintoists* might see Jesus Christ as a parallel to one of their Shinto gods. Jesus, to them, would be a Jewish national hero, rejected by his own people. Japanese heroes, however, have become deities, such as by "divine wind" suicide bombing in World War II. As a result, they are the objects of worship in national shrines, especially the *Yasu-Kuni-Jin-Ja* in Tokyo. The stories of Jesus in the gospels might seem like fabricated myths, which Western culture has developed into theology through an institutionalized organization called the Church. Contrary to Shintoism, which is a Japanese racial cult, Christianity is universal. Jesus Christ is beyond both Eastern intuitional culture and Western intellectual metaphysics. In reality, Jesus Christ is "The Good Shepherd" who lays down his life for his sheep, a flock that potentially extends to the whole human race (John 10:11-16).

To atheistic *Communists*, Jesus Christ is the enemy. They promote Stalin, Mao and Kim Il Sung as their saviors, not in a spiritual but in a material sense. "Modern communism is specifically linked to the ideas of Karl Marx and the concept of a classless society based on common ownership of the means of production" (Bullock, 1977). In 1952, during the Korean War, I noticed an atheist soldier outside St. Nicholas Church in Sangu-Ju, South Korea. He was striking a bronze crucifix repeatedly until it broke up in pieces. Meanwhile, he shouted loudly, "It's because of this guy that I am in this war!" The original concept of Communist ideology, to seek bread and human equality for all, appears lost in spiritual blindness. This modern superstition is blind to the truth that Jesus Christ is "The Bread of Life." They have yet to discover him as the Divine Victim, crucified on the cross on our behalf in order to liberate us from the despair of our human condition (John 6:47-51; 8:36).

Hinduism, with its broad integration of alternative faiths, is the majority religion of India. As such, it is therefore frequently the religious background of Indian seafarers. Some time ago, on a ship at Pier 5 in the port of Seattle, an Indian seaman asked me for a picture of Saint Mary. "Are you a Christian?" I asked him. He replied, "Yes," and said, "I believe in every god of all kinds of world religions. And I collect pictures of these gods." He took me into his cabin on the ship and proudly showed me pictures of gods and spirits of different religions on the wall. It reminded me of the Apostle Paul saying: "Men of Athens! I see that in every way you are very religious. For, as I walked around and looked carefully at your objects of worship, I even found an altar with this inscription: To an Unknown God" (Acts 17:22-34). What my Indian friend had not yet recognized, the apostle Peter summarizes in Acts 4:12. Here, he categorically states that one can find salvation in "no one else" but Jesus Christ.

Islam has now become the world's second largest religion, and many Muslims are among today's multi-religious maritime workforce. How would the average Muslim mariner, as a sincere follower of the Prophet Muhammad, see Jesus Christ, the central figure of the Christian faith? First, he would certainly be very well aware of him. The person of Jesus ("Isa") appears in no less than 90 verses of Islam's own Holy Scriptures, the Qur'an. Second, most Muslims would see Jesus in a very positive light. The Qur'an openly recognizes Jesus' supernatural birth by the Virgin Mary ("Miriam"), his sinless life and his role as a great prophet, one who performed many miracles, who showed great compassion, and who one day will return to judge the whole human race.

However, the core of the Muslim faith is its basic creed (*kalima*): "There is no God but Allah, and Muhammad is his prophet." Compared with all others, Muhammad is, without parallel, "the seal of the prophets." At the same time, the Qur'an expressly rejects the divinity of Jesus Christ as the Son of God, along with both his atoning death on the cross and his bodily resurrection. The average Muslim seafarer would not, therefore, see Jesus as the self-giving Savior that the Bible portrays as paying with his life for the wrongdoings of the whole human race. Nor would he sense the assurance of salvation this alone can provide. Nevertheless, the universal language of love and respect can go a long way to opening the hearts and minds of Muslims, too. It can even motivate toward checking out the primary source of Christian faith—the words of Christ himself, as recorded in the New Testament.

Jesus Christ went to Galilee from the very beginning of his mission. The region of Galilee had long been in spiritual darkness. There had been "heathen" gods there since the Assyrians, in 721 BC, virtually wiped out the country of Galilee. The prophet Isaiah had, with good reason, referred to this marginalized region as the "Galilee of the Gentiles" (Isa. 9:1-2). Today's "gentiles" are the multi-ethnic seafarers of the world, whether they are from the East or the West. In culture, values and beliefs, they seem to represent a prescription for polarization. The logical methodology, contractual relationships, individualism, and transcendence of the West, all stand in stark contrast to the intuitive cognition, natural harmony, collective cooperation, and immanence of the East. For example, how would a Westerner react to this popular prank among modern Japanese youth? "Even on a red light, we are not scared if all of us cross together!"

Rudyard Kipling has said, "East is east and West is west, and never the twain shall meet." However, Isaiah—in verse 2 of his prophecy—points to a reason for hope. With the coming of the Messiah, "a great light has dawned"— for modern-day, marginalized mariners, too. For my part, I strongly believe that, on both land and sea, East and West can come together and merge in Jesus Christ! As he himself has promised, "Abide in me, and I will abide in you" (John 15:1-11). Then, indeed, "People will come from the east and the west, from the north and the south, and sit down at the feast in the Kingdom of God" (Luke 13:29).

5

MARITIME INDUSTRY
AND MARITIME MINISTRY

An ITF Perspective

David Cockroft

DAVID COCKROFT was born in England and educated in Politics and Economics at Oxford University. Since then, he has devoted his entire professional life to the British and, eventually, also the international trade union movements. In 1985, he joined the London-based International Transport Workers' Federation (ITF). Here, he began as Research and Publications Secretary. In 1991, he became the Federation's Assistant General Secretary, and in 1993 its General Secretary.

Some people may find the alliance of trade union and church hard to swallow. Although few, I hope, will go as far as one of our Cypriot shipowner friends. He wrote to the Archbishop of Canterbury to complain that the Mission to Seafarers was in league with the devil for accepting money from the ITF Seafarers' Trust! The simple fact is that, despite our very different starting points, the ITF and Christian maritime ministry have been thrown together by force of circumstances. We share many of the same values and we pursue many of the same goals. Together, we are striving in our different ways to protect and advance the interests of one of the most exploited groups of workers in the world.

The focus of maritime ministry has been (and I assume still is) primarily, though far from solely, the spiritual and moral welfare of seafarers. By contrast, the ITF's focus has always been their material well-being—jobs, incomes, working conditions. We both started out dealing mainly with seafarers from North America and Europe. Now we find ourselves spending the majority of our time and energy dealing with the needs of Asians, Latin Americans, Africans and, more recently, Europeans from countries such as Russia, the Ukraine and Georgia.

The ITF is, and has always been, an organization led by its members. The majority of those members come from the traditional maritime countries—the shipowning countries. However, an increasing number now come from developing countries that supply labor to developed country shipowners. The ITF's Flag of Convenience (FOC) Campaign is led primarily by the desire of our unions to defend and maintain their jobs and working conditions.

The ITF came into existence almost 100 years ago when maritime unions (seafarers and dockers) realized they were powerless against international ship-owners, unless they acted on an international basis. Even before the term "globalization" was in general use, the ITF was dealing with it. The principle of international solidarity, of mutual defense of the weak against the strong, is not so very different from much of the teaching of the church. Of course, our prime aim has been—and still is—to defend the interests of the workers who belong to our member unions. Yet every day, with the assistance of the church and its port chaplains, we find ourselves extending a helping hand to seafarers who have no connection at all with trade unions.

The reasons for our ever closer cooperation, despite the very real differences, are not difficult to spot. It is not the result of careful foresight and long term planning. Rather, it is a natural reaction to the tide of human misery brought upon the maritime industry by the flag of convenience system—appallingly, the world's first global deregulated labor market.

Of course, the church and the ITF do have a lot in common. We both insist that labor is not a commodity and that workers have rights, including the right to fair treatment and dignity in their work. We both do what we do in this industry because there was no one else to do it. However, international organizations such as the IMO and ILO, which have long been much better at adopting standards than seeing them enforced, have recently begun to take their responsibilities more seriously. Maritime security is now a major IMO concern in the aftermath of the tragic events of 9/11, and the ILO adopted very rapidly a new standard regarding seafarers' identity documents. We are glad that the year 2006 has finally seen the adoption of the first ever comprehensive, consolidated ILO maritime labor convention. This instrument now replaces the many previously existing, yet often ignored, standards. Also, for the first time, port states will enforce it in practice, whatever the flag states may or may not do.

Nevertheless, the maritime industry still includes some disreputable and unsavory characters. The International Commission on Shipping (ICONS) Report, entitled *Ships, Slaves and Competition*, which was produced in 2001 by former Australian transport minister Peter Morris and his team, makes this quite clear. Some people are evidently attracted to the bottom end of the shipping industry by its potential for turning a quick profit, and its guarantee of anonymity. Meanwhile, the seafarers are the ones who suffer.

For better or for worse, circumstances have thrown us together. I am sure that it is for better. My staff, the ITF's more than 130 inspectors, and I all gain enormously from the contact and the experience that we have with port chaplains. We provide complementary, and not competing, service to seafarers.

Not only can chaplains deal with the many complex human problems that are beyond our competence, but they can also "boldly go" where ITF inspectors would normally get thrown off the ship.

There have been many changes to get where we are today, and the process of change is continuous. As unions in many parts of the world came under political attack in the 1980s, so the industrial power of the ITF in many countries declined. In its place, we have been forced to devise new and more sophisticated strategies to make life difficult for the FOC shipowner.

We now have an impressive inspectorate around the globe, and not just in Europe and Australia where we have had our traditional strength. We also have an equally tough bunch of inspectors in North America, Asia, Latin America and, increasingly, Africa. Our objective, which we believe missions share with us, is that there should be "no place to hide" for bad shipowners. Almost as important has been the changing perception of the ITF and its activities within the maritime industry. I am a firm believer in the principle that one newspaper article is worth a thousand press releases. Hence, I was quite pleased to see a Lloyd's List editorial state that "a significant number of shipowners privately agree with the ITF arguments against FOCs and would shed few tears if the ITF were ever to reach its stated aim of driving ships back to their national flag."

The ITF has a day-to-day job to provide help and assistance to seafarers in distress. We also have a much bigger job to perform in the maritime labor market as a whole. There we need to maintain discipline in the supply of labor, and to establish and enforce minimum labor standards on those ships whose owners deliberately decide to take on a false nationality.

Most industry commentators are worried about what is happening to the shipping industry. This applies to even some of those used to defending the FOC system and trying to persuade people to call them "flags of opportunity" or "free flags." Following the 1986 UN convention, FOC tonnage has grown. Second and parallel registers have also grown. As traditional maritime nations adopt the philosophy of "if you can't beat them, join them," there has been a flood of seafarers and rust-bucket ships from former Communist countries, where being paid even a small wage in dollars can be worth a fortune in national currency.

All these factors have contributed to an industry in which any shipowner who looks after his workers can risk undercutting by a less scrupulous competitor. Another result is that the seas are now filling with aging ships, many of which should have seen the scrap heap years ago. FOCs currently account for more than half of the world's merchant tonnage. Forcing those ships back to genuine national flags is going to be a desperately difficult task. To mix a metaphor, the tide has turned but the horse has bolted.

The ITF's affiliates have changed and the ITF-FOC campaign is changing too. However, its twin objectives remain the same: to drive ships back to their genuine flag and to maintain and raise minimum labor standards in the shipping industry. I would be dishonest not to admit that we have failed—spectacularly—so far to achieve the first of these aims. It will never happen without widespread political support. In the second, I believe we have had significant success.

ITF agreements now cover around 7000 FOC ships, and the number is growing every year. For a large and growing number of these ships we are engaged in direct negotiations with shipowner representatives to reach the world's first global wage agreement. Industrial action against non-ITF ships and, more importantly, the number of ports in which such action takes place, are both growing. Dockworkers in many countries realize that they too need support from the ITF and from seafarers' unions. They are prepared to deliver solidarity in return.

We have always had a good story to tell. Our files in London overflow with cases of outrageous exploitation. However, we have not always been very good at telling the public about them. In my former capacity as head of the ITF's Research & Publications Department, I was able to assist in changing this. We now produce the *Seafarers' Bulletin* and numerous other publications, many of which we distribute with the assistance of port chaplains.

We have to devote much more attention to the law. I am married to a lawyer; I know well that it is not the world's most popular occupation. However, we need to use the law in a more creative way in defense of seafarers' rights. We have now built up a trained network of ITF-experienced lawyers to assist our inspectors and others, like port chaplains, who have an interest in seafarers' rights.

We do, in fact, devote a lot of time to proactively building coalitions with other interest groups that share our goals, and particularly with the port chaplains and missions. This is something which has to be done locally by our inspectors and affiliates, and internationally through the medium of ICMA and its constituent organizations.

I have mentioned that many things are changing in the trade union movement. One of the most drastic is the balance of power between the national and international levels. National seafarers' unions are getting weaker while the relative importance of the ITF itself continues to grow. This is not something that we planned, but the alternative would be far worse.

The main reason for the ITF being able to take on this role in the maritime industry is our financial resources. The reason we have the financial resources is that my predecessors, many years ago, realized the need to make those shipowners who benefit from the FOC system pay something for the privilege. Thus, for every crewmember on a ship with an ITF approved collective agreement, we collect a contribution currently set at $250 per year. The income is spent partly on financing the infrastructure of the ITF-FOC campaign. Through the Seafarers' Trust, this income also finances a wide range of seafarers' welfare projects. True, the behavior of the capital markets over the past few years has made life considerably more difficult. However, for reputable ship-owners, having the ITF making life difficult for their less scrupulous rivals is not such a bad thing.

While we have reluctantly been taking over many of the traditional functions of national maritime unions, we are also taking on the role of financing much of the maritime welfare work that, in the past, has belonged to national governments and religious bodies. Once again, the reasons are not hard to find.

Among politicians and the general public in the traditional seafaring nations of the Western world, interest in the maritime industry is at an all time low, as fewer and fewer of their people are able to seek a seagoing career. For example, no member of Congress will lose his or her seat because of seafarers' votes. Western governments are withdrawing their support for welfare activities, and governments of labor-supplying nations do not have the money or the will to replace them.

Given the global nature of the churches' commitment to social justice and welfare, the situation is different for maritime ministry. But for the missions, too, radical change in the maritime industry has made it increasingly difficult to sustain support. Hence, the ITF is becoming a major factor in church-related seafarers' welfare through the Seafarers' Trust. Since support by the Trust requires the involvement of local ITF affiliates, this is also a practical way of improving cooperation between unions and port chaplains.

While not in any way retreating from the basic principles for which the ITF has stood since 1896, we are constantly seeking new ideas to advance the interests of seafarers and to make the maritime industry a safer, more humane place. I hope and trust that our cooperation with Christian maritime ministry worldwide will continue to grow in the years to come.

6

HOLDING ONTO JUSTICE AND HOPE

Toward a Spirituality of Maritime Ministry

Barbara Cawthorne Crafton

BARBARA CAWTHORNE CRAFTON, an ordained Episcopal priest, has served 11 years as chaplain to merchant mariners, in affiliation with the Seamen's Church Institute (SCI) of New York & New Jersey. In 1983, she became the first woman director of the International Seafarers' Center in Port Newark, NJ, and, from 1991, she was Vicar of SCI's Seaport Chapel. She has also served at historic Trinity Church, Wall Street, and as Rector of St. Clement's Church in Manhattan's Theater District. Since 2002, she has led the New Jersey-based Geranium Farm, an institute for spiritual formation. As an actor and producer, she has received many awards in the field of faith and the arts, including the Gabriel Award for religious broadcasting. Barbara Crafton's essay collection The Sewing Room *was the first of her many books on meditation themes, now reaching a worldwide readership.*

Not so very many years ago, there was a chasm in maritime ministry—between ministry as spirituality and ministry as advocacy. This was early in the history of the Center for Seafarers' Rights (CSR), begun in 1982 at the Seamen's Church Institute of New York as a resource for port chaplains, as they confronted seafarers' rights abuses in the course of their work.

Today it is difficult to imagine our work without the CSR. But those of us who were in this work in those days remember that some of our colleagues viewed its advent with alarm. Did it not encourage a dangerously secular focus on politics and the law at the expense of the more traditional forms of witness and compassionate service in maritime chaplaincy? Might it not encourage chaplains to confuse their role with that of union organizers or maritime lawyers? In fact, would they not be assuming a false level of competency in an area better left to secular professionals, while at the same time neglecting the pastoral ministry for which they had been both called and trained?

Advocates for seafarers' rights articulated the same misgivings in reverse. Was not a ministry that shrank from involvement in anything controversial an abdication of prophecy in favor of a spirituality safely insulated from hands-on involvement with a major, often frightening part of a seafarer's life? Did not a focus on prayer, confession, corporate worship, and daily reading of scripture, encourage chaplains and seafarers *not* to work for justice? Instead, would not this kind of spirituality simply lessen the pain caused by injustice without joining the struggle to alleviate *injustice itself*?

Put succinctly, many chaplains perceived our work in reductive terms. If you were an advocate for seafarers' rights, you would not spend time in prayer that might be better employed in advocacy. And if you were a minister of the gospel, too much focus on advocacy would endanger your actual calling, in other words the explicit preaching of the Good News for the world. These two roles seemed mutually exclusive to many. Few thought a port chaplain could be both. Mutual suspicion dogged ecumenical maritime ministry for the better part of a decade.

The waterfront was not the only venue for this mutual suspicion. All justice activity in America since the 1960s has assumed that those who pray will not picket, and those who picket will not pray. Civil rights advocates were often embarrassed, for instance, by the intense hope of heaven in virtually all black spirituals. To them, it sounded like "pie in the sky when you die," a cowardly way of referring this world's sorrows to the tribunal of the next world. To them, utter reliance upon the power of God seemed to discount the power of men and women. That enslaved people should hope for heaven seemed like acquiescence in evil on earth, refusing to engage in the struggle for equality. Advocates wished the enslaved had sung *other* songs, brave songs about power in this world instead of comfort in the next.

But the attitude in these early spirituals has proven to be the result of a clearer understanding of what courage is, and what power is. To cling to the hope of heaven through four centuries of chattel slavery was not a sign of cowardice or weakness. It was evidence of tremendous strength and courage. To place all one's trust in God is not to deny human power; it is merely to state whence human power comes. To pray for God's deliverance is not to acquiesce in one's own oppression. Rather, it is to gather strength for any adversity that may still come to pass.

This reflects my own spiritual journey. As a young theological student I looked askance at heaven as a kind of escape hatch, a denial of personal responsibility for the here and now. But compared to the "immortality" of my twenties, the hope of heaven now only strengthens the resolve to do something about it in this life. That connection between *time and eternity* is also a vital part of holding onto a vision of both *justice and hope*.

What was true for the American victims of the African Slave Trade is no less true for the victims of modern-day maritime bondage. The assumed split, or bifurcation, between spirituality and advocacy in the early 1980s was a heresy. Today it is recognized as such by virtually everyone in maritime ministry. Advocacy does not *oppose* spirituality; it *arises* from it. So now we are free to move naturally between the sacred and the secular, to see all human experience as resting in the hand of the God who is never absent from any aspect of it. We are not split human beings, doomed to cordon off our souls from the rest of ourselves. We are on our way to a spiritual adulthood that joins them both together.

Just as chaplains have to deal with their specific bifurcation challenges, so the seafarers we serve have to deal with theirs. I can no longer remember how many seafarers have told me that, on board ship they are "not the same person" as they are at home. They even dramatize this self-inflicted split, this "self-bifurcation," in a most curious way; many seafarers simply "change faces" when they are at sea. They grow a mustache, or else they shave one off. They grow muttonchop whiskers, or a full beard. Often I have been warmly greeted by a young man I cannot recall ever having met. I literally do not recognize him. He notes my confusion and laughs, "I changed my face!" In this way, he is documenting his two selves, the split between his *on board self,* the guarded self who is cut off from everything at home, and his *shore-side self,* the loving husband and father he left behind and who still lives there. Some kinds of loneliness are just too much for him to endure, and so he creates a new, tough self that *can* endure. And then he makes a new face to fit this tough, new person.

That the seafarer does this is spiritually dangerous to him. It is a survival mechanism, of course, enabling him not to face the fact of having done things he knows would jeopardize what he has at home, things of which he even disapproves on genuine principle. "I am a devoted husband and father," it enables him to say, "I don't know *who* this bearded Lothario is." At home he does not get drunk, nor does he use amphetamines. Who is this mustached, badly behaved *bandito* anyway? It is as if he needs to say: The guy who fell off the fidelity wagon was not the *real* me....

But we cannot split ourselves in two. Two selves cannot both inhabit the same body. The project of growing into what Paul calls "the full stature of Christ" really means: the complete reconciliation within us of that which is hidden with that which is visible. As fully as can be realized this side of heaven, we struggle for integrity, for that purity of heart which *Sören Kierkegaard* describes as "willing one thing." The world is complex, and the human spirit intricate. Spiritual adulthood will allow *all* parts of us to stand the light of day without shame. At least, all growth in Christ ultimately *aims* at this.

If we are to help the seafarer gather the courage to overcome his self-bifurcation, we cannot maintain the heresy of our own. If we had to choose our number one job as seafarers' chaplains, this would be it: to bring together the two selves—in both our own lives and theirs, *spiritual unity within the self.*

In a sense we are all of us on temporary "shore-leave" here in this life. Meanwhile, in the still largely masculine world of the sea, a male minister can provide a model of how it is possible to combine courage with trust in God. For women seafarers, a female minister can of course provide a model too, of integrity and God-given self-respect. Seafarers do not have to be something their own mothers would not recognize, just because they move closer to Jesus. The stakes are high. The seafarer endangers his very life if he cannot allow his two selves to meet. In this age of rampant AIDS and other sexually transmitted diseases, he may also be endangering the lives of his loved ones. How wonderful when we see bifurcation overcome and healing happen—before others are hurt.

In the final analysis, the ministry of a chaplain is a struggle for justice and compassion arising directly from, and leading back to, *a life of prayer*. Maritime ministry may mean connecting seafarers with home and family by phone or computer. But it also means more. The word "religion" comes from the Latin for "re-tying" or "re-connecting." Christian spirituality is about connecting with Christ, and therefore leads to prayer in Christ's name. That's when things start happening.

It was Easter Sunday. Chaplain *Francis Cho* was already on board, and he heard that an ailing seafarer was being sent home without maintenance and care before his contract was up. The crew knew that this was illegal and wanted the chaplain's help. He prayed with them and with the sick man. However, the captain had already summoned the agent to take the man directly to the airport, and the agent was on his way. On shore, Father Cho saw the agent in a phone booth, making the airline reservation. As soon as he hung up, the chaplain introduced himself and began to make his case: Today was Easter Sunday. It was unthinkable to endanger a man's life on the feast of Christ's victory over death. This was the day that Jesus arose, the day on which our great human tragedy became, instead, the story of our salvation. The agent stared at the priest in bewilderment. But Father Cho was just warming up. He went on to remind his surprised listener about the longing of Israel for deliverance from oppression, about the hope of heaven, about Christ's work in overcoming sin and error. No, Easter Sunday simply could not be the day to deliberately hurt another human being.

None more surprised than he, the agent saw the logic of this argument and assented to it. The chaplain returned to the crew with the good news. The agent called the company and negotiated maintenance and care for the sick man. The captain heard the news and just knew: that day something stronger than any of them had touched them all.

7

THE APOSTLESHIP OF THE SEA
Historic Emergence and Current Direction
James E. Dillenburg

 *JAMES E. DILLENBURG has roots in the port of Green Bay, Wisconsin, where he served as port chaplain from 1969. As co-founder of the NCCS, he became its first President 1976-78, then National Director of the AOS/US 1980-1985. In 1988, he was elected President of NAMMA (then known as ICOSA). In 1990, the Vatican called him to serve as International Secretary of the worldwide AOS in Rome. In 1992, Pope John Paul II appointed him a personal chaplain with the title of Monsignor. In 1996, he returned to Green Bay to pastor St. Elizabeth Ann Seton Parish, while continuing to serve as AOS Consultant to the Pontifical Council for the Pastoral Care of Migrants and Itinerant People.*

Origin and Early History

As an organization, the Apostleship of the Sea (*Apostolatus Maris*) is a relative newcomer in the family of church-affiliated maritime welfare agencies, officially founded in the early part of the twentieth century. Before that, from 1895, the name "Apostleship of the Sea" (AOS) was already in use in reference to a Seamen's Branch of the Apostleship of Prayer. However, there was at that time no notion of any Catholic organization dedicated to maritime mission as such.

Following World War I, a Benedictine brother, Peter Anson, a member of the Apostleship of Prayer, became aware that Catholic seafarers were not being ministered to in a systematic and comprehensive manner by their own church. Furthermore, he realized that they needed to live and share their faith at sea as well as at home. In 1920, Anson—together with two likewise lay associates, Brother *Daniel Shields*, SJ, and *Arthur Gannon*—initiated an organized ministry to Catholic seafarers, originally based in Glasgow, Scotland. For this, they requested and received permission to adopt the title of the Apostleship of the Sea.

Two years later, they submitted their plan to Pope Pius XI, asking for his blessing on this emerging enterprise. In so doing, the Holy Father urged that the new organization be implemented world-wide. As the AOS grew over the years, so did its presence in the Church. Its first international meeting took place in Port-en-Bessin, France, in 1927. In 1930, an International Council of the Apostleship of the Sea ("Apostolatus Maris Internationale Concilium") was organized "to unite and coordinate the action in favor of the spiritual, social and moral welfare of seafarers in the world." When it set up shop only 16 years later, the AMIC, as it was then known, could count 183 Catholic port ministries in 30 countries.

Except for a brief period in London, the AOS continued to be headquartered in Glasgow, Scotland. In 1950, a petition was made to Rome, asking that the AMIC be housed there, "where all the Catholic world converges." Space was quickly made available at the Sacred Consistorial Congregation where it remained until 1970. After that, all ministries dedicated to "people on the move" were incorporated into the Vatican's Pontifical Commission (later Council) for the Pastoral Care of Migrants and Itinerant People.

Subsequent Developments

At the time when the AOS was founded, seafarers frequently needed an inexpensive place to stay while looking for a new berth aboard ship. Wages were low. Various unsavory waterfront characters were quite willing to separate the sailor from his meager salary. Church-supported facilities would therefore seek to provide a safe and wholesome environment in which seafarers could live while waiting to ship out again.

However, as a result of revolutionary change in the maritime industry during the last quarter of the twentieth century, hotel facilities are no longer needed in most ports. Shipping companies can fly in crews to meet ships which now arrive on schedule. Moreover, the turn-around time for ships in port—and therefore for seafarers ashore—has been drastically reduced. In many ports, Stella Maris Clubs and other church–operated welfare agencies continue to offer seafarers, who are able to make use of them, a safe place to meet local people. Still, the fact remains—many seafarers now spend almost all their time at sea. As a result of globalization, ship's crews consist increasingly of low-cost maritime labor from a pluralistic world of different ethnicities and religions. This, too, is having a profound impact on current-day maritime ministry.

As important as welfare, justice and social concerns are, spiritual welfare has always been the central motivating force behind the AOS. Without that, the soul of the ministry would be missing. At the XIX AOS World Congress in Houston, Texas, in October 1992, it was the resulting need—to provide pastoral care in light of the new realities of the contemporary maritime world—that formed the focus of intentional study. In consequence of these realities, what was now the role of Catholic seafarers as members of their Church?

Reflecting on the Congress theme, "Christian Living Aboard Ship," participants agreed that, with modern-day seafarers spending over 90% of their time at sea, a shore-based church ministering only "to" seafarers would be virtually irrelevant. But even more importantly, participants agreed that the God-given dignity of every seafaring person needed to be reaffirmed. To do everything for others is to deny them that fundamental dignity. Children of God, at sea as on land, are called to live out their faith and share it with others, rather than be considered as mere *recipients* of their Church's services. For both reasons, the emphasis would therefore need to be on preparing seafarers *themselves* to be the Church at sea, and on building their own communities of faith on board.

Here were clearly shades of Peter Anson's original vision. Although actually originating as a "band of lay apostles," the AOS had gradually evolved into what came to be perceived as a maritime ministry bureaucracy directed from above by priests and bishops. It was this perception that had to be challenged at the Congress. The Vatican office would still need to play a vital coordinating role. But seafaring lay people must again become "apostles" wherever they might be, on board or at home.

Since then, some seafarers have been trained as "Extraordinary Ministers of the Eucharist" (EMEs). These have been prepared and commissioned to bring the Holy Communion with them and hold Eucharistic services aboard ship when away from port, especially on Sundays and holy days. In addition, both lay men and lay women have been specifically hired to do ministry. While there may at first have been some skepticism about lay people serving in this role, lay ship visitors have actually seen doors opened to them which might otherwise have been closed to those wearing Roman clergy collars. This is especially true for women whose femininity tends to soften a hard and masculine world—made even harder by the steel cocoons where seafarers live and work.

Contemporary Goals and Strategies

What is happening in the AOS today? In January 1997, Pope John Paul II published a historic Apostolic Letter named "Stella Maris," setting forth the text of a new Apostolic Constitution for the AOS. This has now opened the door for a worldwide membership organization. This sees all seafarers, including fishers, together with their families, as well as port and shipping personnel, as "People of the Sea." As such, they may all become members of a revamped AOS where local membership now entails both national and world levels. To some extent this had already been the case in previous years, but not in any well defined way. In 1997, the XX AOS World Congress in Davao, Philippines, was able to develop the concept in comprehensive form.

Significantly, the new Apostolic Constitution of 1997 expressly affirms seafarers themselves in the role of primary agents of ministry among their own, as they engage in "creating and guiding a Christian community on board." The document also reinforces the role of the laity *ashore* by authorizing the appointment of "Co-Workers" to assist ordained Catholic port chaplains. Furthermore, the document includes a powerful affirmation of the need for ecumenical cooperation with other Christian maritime mission organizations.

The AOS did discover long ago some of the problems with such cooperation. Since 1969, however, the heads of the various agencies have sought new ways to cooperate through the auspices of the International Christian Maritime Association (ICMA), of which the AOS was a co-founder. Where difficulties sometimes still arise, these may be due to personality clashes, misunderstandings, or lack of appreciation for doctrinal differences. Understandably, the AOS is unwilling to surrender to others its inherent responsibility for ministry to Catholic seafarers, least of all in its sacramental theology. Overall, however, doctrinal differences do not keep ICMA members apart. On the contrary, maritime ministry already practices much of the cooperation still only talked about by ecumenists.

As in the infancy of the Church, Christians in modern-day maritime ministry do not need consensus before living and acting out their faith. The "new evangelization" that Pope John Paul II called for in the Third Millennium is no less essential in the maritime world. This requires an "audacity of faith" from us all. The Gospel is *Good News* for the modern world—not only on land but also at sea!

Therefore, the Apostleship of the Sea must not just be another institution promoting seafarers' welfare or defending their human rights. In helping to bring God's plan to the maritime world, the AOS also seeks to make seafarers themselves conscious of their liberation in Christ—so that they will get on their feet, share their faith in him, and participate in building a maritime world which refuses to resemble a convict ship!

8

A MARINER'S VOICE

Chaplains and the Challenge of Change

William R. Douglas

 *WILLIAM R. DOUGLAS is a Master Mariner with over 25 years of sea experience. Originally from Cape Town, South Africa, he gained a post-graduate degree in education there. In 1994, he joined the Center for Maritime Education at the Seamen's Church Institute of New York & New Jersey. From 1997, he became the pioneer Director of that Institute's two successful satellite ventures in maritime education—first in Paducah, Kentucky, then in Houston, Texas.*

"They that go down to the sea in ships, that do business in great waters; these see the works of the Lord, and his wonders in the deep" (Ps. 107:23). Based on personal observation and memories from life at sea, this Perspective endeavors to examine problems and needs encountered by the merchant mariner that chaplains around the world might possibly face. Many of these have been experienced by seafarers throughout the ages. However, modern technology and other new conditions have also presented other kinds of challenges, such as:
- Ships are now more than 80 times larger than in the 16th century
- While a ship of 160 tons in 1550 had about 25 crew, a modern ship of 250,000 tons employs a complement of 25 to 30 crew
- The trend toward reduced manning increases the individual work load
- Schedules are awkward and hours are long
- Break-bulk cargoes are now containerized, and bulk cargoes the norm
- Turn-around times are shorter
- Many cargoes are highly dangerous and require great care and skill
- MARPOL and OPA90 regulations threaten job security
- Crews are diverse in nationality, language, culture and religion
- Threats of piracy and terrorism present serious security problems
- Suspicion against members of certain nations tend to brand mariners as potential criminals, preventing shore leave in many ports

Mariners do not view themselves as objects of charity; nor do they consider themselves needy. Typically, mariners are proud of their profession and take pride in their job, their ship and their unique skills. Nevertheless, sadly, the social standing of mariners has declined in recent decades. During the two world wars, nations honored merchant mariners for their role. Now, a generation that never saw those wars tends to forget them. Radical change in the working environment of mariners, driven by modern-day market forces, has seen the demise of the great merchant fleets of traditional seafaring nations. The practice of "flagging out" has led to multi-national crews that have little loyalty to either their ship or its owner. The ship has become merely a place of work. All this has undermined both the mariner's self-esteem and his social status.

A mariner leads two separate lives. His life on board is very different from the one at home. He takes a little of his own identity to sea with him, but behaves under a different individuality with respect to his duties and his shipmates. He faces a situation that those who work ashore and commute daily from home rarely share.

The first and most noticeable challenge to a seafarer is one of *loneliness*. It is a loneliness born out of distance from loved ones. He is not alone, but being away from familiar faces and places makes him aware that he is a stranger. Loneliness among strangers is always one of constant incompleteness. One can share a joke with a stranger, but not one's innermost emotions, experiences and problems. Gradually, friendships build but these can never replace the family.

Associated with loneliness is a sense of *remoteness*. One is inevitably far from one's own familiar surroundings. More importantly, one is apart from home and one's nuclear family. One cannot share birthdays, bad days, great days, sickness, sadness or achievement. Things can go wrong at home and the mariner feels powerless. They are also remote from their belongings, hobbies, favorite radio and TV programs, current affairs, meeting places, and places of worship and fellowship.

Although an increasing number of women are seeking a life at sea, sadly the overwhelming preponderance of mariners are male. This is the reason for the use of the masculine gender in this paper. In the absence of female personnel in a world of men, the social structure takes on a very different tone. In an all-male society, there is a tendency for courtesy and gentleness to suffer first.

Monotony and tedium tend to be a part of life on board ship. And yet, one is always looking forward—to leaving port, to being at sea, to arriving at the next port, to transiting the Suez or Panama canal, and finally to getting home again. One wishes one's life away. Social life suffers further stress because, at any given time of day and night, some personnel will be on duty while others will be asleep. The net result is that the average mariner is constantly working, eating or sleeping, frequently tired, and not up to socializing.

In a way, the ship's company becomes the *de facto* family unit. Personalities are different, and inevitably lead to situations found in any family. There is much laughing and sharing but then clashes of personality can occur. The mariner does not choose his "family," and has to get along. Over-familiarity with others might become onerous. There is little privacy and no escape. Nevertheless, one generally manages to maintain an orderly shipboard lifestyle.

Mariners tend to self-eliminate themselves if they cannot cope. Thus, they are usually perceived to be easy-going and enjoying the company of others.

A mariner works strange hours. This is not unique. Nurses, police, emergency teams and others also experience this. However, a mariner does not go home while off duty. He is on call at any time, so he is virtually always on duty. Occupational stresses (especially for officers) include heavy responsibilities for lives, the vessel, equipment, cargo (not least dangerous ones), the environment, hazards in transit, and a highly regulated vocation.

One burden to mariners is the behavior of visitors from shore while the ship is in port. A vessel is constantly the object of visits by personnel whose duties are essential to the running of that vessel: the pilot, immigration officials, customs officers, local authorities, agents, ship-chandlers and others. To these people, the ship is just a place of work. They do not regard their visits as any intrusion. They often fail to recognize that the ship is home to a typically exhausted crew who need privacy and quiet, and have to catch up on sleep.

Many seafarers are religious. They observe their own religious traditions and readings of sacred scripture while at sea. However, this can suffer due to work hours and other shipboard issues mentioned above, in addition to being away from any home place of worship. As chaplains reach out to these and other seafarers, they provide a unique service that few others understand. In their pastoral role, they are not only dealing with people of diverse nationalities and backgrounds, but also those of other religions or no religion at all.

Given this overall context, and viewing it from the standpoint of a lay Christian, what is therefore the essential calling of a chaplain to seafarers? I personally believe that a devoted chaplain will take to heart the core of the Apostle Paul's charge to Titus—never to shrink from delivering the message of God's Word, but uphold its doctrine fearlessly, showing incorruptness, gravity, sincerity, and sound speech (Titus 2:7-8).

Life for the mariner can be hectic and dangerous. It can also be fulfilling and challenging. Nothing beats the peace of a midnight watch at sea under a clear, dark tropical sky; or steaming quietly through the Mediterranean on a sunny day, the water unbelievably blue, while playful porpoises frolic in the bow waves. One can almost be amazed that one should be paid for that kind of pleasure!

As a young man, I was very familiar with the description in Revelations 21 of heaven. However, part of that description surprised me: "*And I saw a new heaven and a new earth: for the first heaven and the first earth were passed away; and there was no more sea.*" Why would there be no more sea? I loved the sea. I loved ships and everything about the sea. What would heaven be like without a sea? As I grew to maturity, I realized at least one thing that passage must mean: There will be no more parting.

9

ROLE OF RESEARCH IN
MARITIME MISSION

With Particular Reference to IASMM

Stephen Friend

STEPHEN FRIEND, born and raised in the town of Grimsby, England, served as Assistant Superintendent with the Royal National Mission to Deep Sea Fishermen from 1967 to 1973, working in fishing ports in Scotland and England. He then left the waterfront to pursue a teaching vocation, combining inner-city social justice advocacy with academic studies in Leeds. From 1988, he joined the faculty of the Anglican-affiliated College of Ripon and York St. John (now York St. John University), eventually becoming Senior Lecturer in Theology. In 2007, he plans to defend a PhD dissertation entitled "A Sense of Belonging: Religion and Identity in Fishing Communities 1815-1914." Since co-founding the International Association for the Study of Maritime Mission (IASMM) in 1990, Stephen Friend has continued to serve as that Association's Secretary and Editor.

Earlier Research Endeavors

Prior to the 1980s, the study of maritime mission was conspicuous, not only by its absence from church histories but also by the many folk-tales and legends that passed as history. During the 19th century, *George C. Smith* and his son, *Theophilus Smith*, provided a record of significant events in the history of maritime mission and in the first half of the 20th century *Peter Anson* provided an immeasurable service, not only by recording much of the data available to him, but by collecting copious archive materials for posterity.

However, with the exception of the work of G. C. Smith and Peter Anson, there was—until the 1980s—little published material about the work of the Christian Church among seafarers. Exceptions were the various publications on behalf of particular maritime missions—predominantly for publicity purposes. True, much of this work can be extremely useful to the researcher. Still, it needs analyzing, organizing and indexing, in order to allow for the publication of more objective and comparative studies.

This does not mean that there were no source materials of real relevance to the wider work of maritime mission. On the contrary, the mass of published material in this area is staggering: letters, diaries, minutes, accounts, reports, photographs, magazines, etc. Recent researchers into the history of maritime mission constantly express their surprise at the vast array of primary source materials available. Yet this surprise applies no less to the lack of care taken over these same materials. Documents often appear in damp, unsuitable environments, packed in cardboard boxes, and left to suffer the ravages of time and the environment. Any attempts at organization of these materials tend to depend on the interest of individual employees.

It was only after a 15-year worldwide research odyssey that *Roald Kverndal*, in 1984, could complete a breakthrough ThD thesis in this field. Entitled *Seamen's Missions: Their Origin and Early Growth,* and published two years later, this mammoth overview became the first academic-level study of the origins of the Seafarers' Mission Movement. In 1989, *Alston Kennerley* followed with the first PhD thesis on the topic *British Seamen's Missions and Sailors' Homes, 1815-1970.*

By 1990, these two were still the only doctoral dissertations on the subject of seafarers' mission. Nevertheless, by then it had already become apparent that others, too, were engaged in scholarly studies in the general field of maritime mission and ministry. As early as in 1980, *Richard Blake* had defended his MPh thesis on *Aspects of Religion in the Royal Navy c. 1770—c. 1870.* In 1989, *Robert Miller* published *From Shore to Shore: A History of the Church and the Merchant Seafarer.* That same year, *Bill Down* published *On Course Together: The Churches' Ministry in the Maritime World Today.*

A Specialized Research Organization

It was perhaps inevitable that the small band of researchers in this area should meet up. On 3 June 1990, three researchers of maritime mission, each of whom had been struggling alone in the field for several years, agreed to meet in Leeds, North England. The outcome was the founding of an organization soon to be known as the *International Association for the Study of Maritime Mission* (IASMM). The new association would thereby come to have Yorkshire as heritage—in common with George Charles Smith, the founder of the movement itself. (For further details, see "The Origins of IASMM" in *Maritime Mission Studies,* No. 2, Autumn 1995, pp. 1-9.)

The following year, a number of others interested in the field joined the co-founders for the fledgling association's First International Conference, held at the "Stella Maris" Seafarers' Center in Tilbury, England. Here, the participants agreed on a basic organizational structure. In order to promote the overall purpose implicit in its name, the association's stated aims would be to preserve, analyze, and make accessible, sources relevant to this area of study. As Secretary, the association elected one of its co-founders, Stephen Friend. Formerly with the Royal National Mission to Deep Sea Fishermen (RNMDSF), he was now a lecturer in theology at York St. John University. The willingness of this well-established, church-related institution to accommodate the association's secretariat would prove an important, stabilizing factor in its future growth.

For the position of President, the organizing conference elected another co-founder, Roald Kverndal. As a maritime missiologist who was also engaged in maritime mission development on the world scene, he had his home base in Seattle, USA. At IASMM's Second International Conference, held in New York in 1993, Kverndal identified three principles he saw as fundamental to the association's *"raison d'être"*: First, *inclusiveness,* in both its denominational and ethnic diversity; second, *distinctiveness,* in its servant role within the Christian maritime mission community; third, *comprehensiveness* in its orientation toward not only the past but also the present and the future.

Research Concerning Current and Future Needs

After a series of successful international conferences and numerous publications, the work of the association has continued to expand. Although it is still relatively small, IASMM currently has members in 15 countries worldwide. ICMA holds ex officio membership on IASMM's General Committee. IASMM has also established cooperative relationships with both the Seafarers International Research Centre, and the ITF Seafarers' Trust. IASMM cordially welcomes new members.

Given the growing interest in IASMM so far, what value might people place on the specialized study and research of maritime mission in the long term? Experience during the association's first fifteen years has already revealed its relevance in relation to each of its original aims—preserving, analyzing and publicizing resources for maritime mission.

In 1996, IASMM sponsored a first time "Conference on Maritime Mission Archives," chaired by Bishop Bill Down. This confirmed the need for retrieving, and safely storing, unique materials that would otherwise be lost forever. Here, all maritime mission organizations have a common interest, together with all future individual researchers. Meanwhile, IASMM continues to take the lead in promoting such preservation at accessible locations.

One example that underscores the urgency of this concern is the situation in British fishing communities. In 1994, Stephen Friend completed an MPhil thesis on *The Churches' Work Amongst British Fishing Communities during the 19th Century.* His PhD thesis in 2007 also relates to this subject area: *A sense of Belonging; Religion and Identity in Fishing Communities 1815-1914.* This research has uncovered ample evidence confirming the true extent and depth of religiosity among this sector of Victorian working class society—contrary to previous assumptions. However, this research has also confirmed the incalculable cost to both maritime and other areas of academic research when archives of primary and secondary sources are in jeopardy.

IASMM's second stated aim of promoting analysis and reflection is, of course, crucial to the association's fundamental usefulness. In a mission with such overwhelming practical pressures, a "niche" ministry that motivates proactive reflection can become virtually indispensable. In this context, the denominational and ethnic diversity of IASMM's membership has created a cross-fertilizing research environment that has already produced rich results.

An example of this is the wide-ranging research leading up to the MPhil and PhD theses (in 1995 and 2002, respectively) by the association's third co-founder, Robert Miller. These focus on the historic emergence of the Catholic Apostleship of the Sea and the faith and practice of the medieval seafarer. Another example, from an Asian view, is the series of maritime mission-related doctoral theses produced by affiliated Korean colleagues: *Young-Hwan Kim* (1990), *Jonah Wonjong Choi* (1996), *David Chul-han Jun* (2001), and *Byeong-Eun Lee* (2005).

The association's third aim, namely making the results of study and research available where needed, is only a logical consequence of the previous two. In seeking to communicate such results, IASMM has three target groups in view: first, the maritime mission community; second, the church (including seminaries and mission schools); third, the public (including educational and maritime institutions).

Just as many archive materials can now become widely available electronically, the same applies to the results of ongoing research. Besides its own web site, the association has developed a series of publications in the form of a biennial IASMM Newsletter, a refereed journal (*Maritime Mission Studies),* and Occasional Papers. As far as feasible, IASMM also provides consultative services in the field of continuing education for port chaplains and basic training for seafaring lay ministers, as well as papers and workshops for maritime mission conferences.

A no less important channel of communication is the ongoing published works of individual members of IASMM. For example, IASMM's first Vice-President, Dr. Alston Kennerley has, as Professor of Marine Studies at the University of Plymouth, as well as through various publications, promoted the linkage between maritime mission and maritime education. Dr. Paul Mooney, the current President of IASMM, has, with his PhD thesis, *Maritime Mission: History, Developments, a New Perspective* (2005), produced the first academic-level theology of maritime mission, which offers a new "seafarer-centered" paradigm of maritime ministry for the 21st century. Dr. Kverndal has, with his current book, *The Way of the Sea,* contributed the first comprehensive maritime missiology, one that seeks to reach a wide readership, both within and beyond academic circles.

In the final analysis, the task of the International Association for the Study of Maritime Mission is the scholarly study of the past and present scene, in order to serve as effectively as possible the current and future research needs of maritime mission and ministry. As awareness of those needs continues to grow, there is good reason to believe that the current limited level of resources will also increase to allow a response more commensurate with the importance of this ministry.

ECUMENICITY IN THE MARITIME WORLD
With Special Reference to the Role of ICMA
Jacques Harel

JACQUES HAREL, born and educated in the island republic of Mauritius, comes from a French ethnic background. After theological studies in Rome and ordination in France, he returned to serve his native diocese in Port-Louis, Mauritius. Here, he became Dean of the Cathedral in 1979, and from 1986 National Director of the AOS in Mauritius. In 1996, he moved to Southampton, England, to serve as ICMA's first Catholic-affiliated General Secretary. After returning to the AOS in Mauritius in 2000, Monsignor Harel became General Secretary of the worldwide AOS at the Vatican in 2004.

Ecumenism as ICMA's Raison d'Etre

One of the most significant events in the history of modern ecumenism may well have been the founding of the International Christian Maritime Association (ICMA). This is not surprising. When the modern ecumenical movement emerged early in this century, it was originally motivated by a desire for greater effectiveness in global mission. Missionaries who had preached a gospel of love and reconciliation, while competing and fighting with each other, finally found they were contradicting the words of Christ in John 13:35: "By this all will know that you are my disciples, if you love one another." The same holds true in maritime mission, too.

The founding of ICMA dates from 1969, as a Christian association of charitable, non-profit organizations. All of these relate to Christian communities recognized by the World Council of Churches, or by the Vatican. All of them are engaged in promoting the well-being of seafarers and their families, irrespective of creed, color, nationality or political opinion. As such, ICMA is an active "player," not just a "discussion forum."

Among ICMA members today, ecumenical cooperation and mutual respect for one another's ecclesiastical discipline and tradition is a given. Not so very long ago, one would see a chaplain of another denomination or society as a rival, if not an outright adversary. Recently, a chaplain told me that a few years back, when he saw another chaplain boarding a ship, his first reaction would be to think, "What is this man doing on my quay?" Today, in many parts of the world, for missionary, theological and practical reasons, chaplains form teams, share resources, and often work together out of jointly operated centers.

Ecumenism, as we live it on a daily basis, can be a long and painful process. It may still involve misunderstanding and confrontation. However, it must always reject jealousy, pettiness or a spirit of mistrust. Fortunately, more often than not, it then becomes a source of genuine joy and satisfaction. "I have told you this so that you will be filled with my joy" (John 15:11). The purpose of this paper is to share some of the convictions and ideals that motivate ICMA's ecumenical journey.

Ecumenism and Evangelism

One of the greatest challenges facing all Christian ministry today is our capacity to speak of Jesus in a way that connects with people's daily experience. To most seafarers we encounter, Christian values and traditions are strange or alien. This may be because they themselves are not Christians, but it may also be because of living in a secular or materialistic environment.

In these circumstances, it is important that we learn to tread humbly among the seafarers we meet, learn to listen to them, and merit their trust. While we need to respect the beliefs and values of others, however much they may differ from our own, we still have an obligation to proclaim to all the Good News that Jesus is "The Way, the Truth and the Life" (John 14:6).

I feel that the best way to express our faith is to position ourselves more as witnesses than as teachers and masters. That is also how Jesus himself puts it in Acts 1:8: "You shall be my witnesses to the uttermost parts of the world." These last words of our Lord, before he ascended to heaven, are a constant reminder to us in ICMA of the international nature of our vocation. Both our members and those among whom we minister come from all over the world. The ecumenical basis of our association is inherent to the international nature of our network of solidarity between chaplains and social workers worldwide.

We Christians believe that it is in Jesus that God has most fully revealed his love and his plan for the redemption of humanity. The mission of the church, of ICMA and of all Christian ministry, is to continue together this work of Jesus Christ. In ICMA, we believe that it is important to carry out this task of evangelism in partnership with local churches and communities. I have been a port chaplain myself and know how important it is for a chaplain or co-worker to gain acceptance by the local churches. Testifying to the love of Jesus Christ in the maritime world is a shared responsibility of the whole Christian community.

The originality of maritime chaplains is that we minister right in the work place. However, ship-visiting cannot only be a social occasion. One of the more delicate areas we have to cope with is how to bring on board the Good News of Jesus Christ in today's context of religious pluralism at sea. Developing nations are now the major labor supplying countries, bringing to ports all over the world large numbers of seafarers of non-Christian faiths. As we try to meet this challenge, we need to understand and respect the creeds of others. In so doing, we also need the support and assistance of the local Christian communities. In relation to fellow-Christians on board, we refer each person to their respective pastors and priests for the administration of sacraments.

Ecumenism and Advocacy

Social justice and the prophetic dimension of our work is also an important aspect of our cooperative ministry. Our credibility depends greatly on our willingness and capacity to be prophetic. The Bible teaches us that we cannot separate the love of God from love of our neighbor. The love of God demands of us no less than total commitment to the service of our brothers and sisters, as fellow human beings..

We all know there is a sector of the shipping industry that exploits labor and worries only about material profit and gain.. It is not the chaplain or ship-visitor's role to organize trade unions or get directly involved in labor negotiations. However, when faced with exploitation, injustice and the violation of basic human rights, we cannot sit back and do nothing. If we are only interested in the welfare of the soul and close our eyes and ears to social concerns, we run the risk of being completely irrelevant and losing all credibility. If our centers are merely places of recreation and worship, how can we possibly be faithful to the trust placed in us by God and by seafarers?

As we are reminded in Isaiah 58:6-10, the poor, the defenseless, the marginalized, are the special focus of the love of God and his church. This option for the poor excludes nobody from God's love. It seeks to eliminate whatever imbalance that may exist in favor of the rich and powerful. We in ICMA rejoice in the work for social justice and seafarers' rights by our membership. This applies to both countless chaplains individually and specialized centers and ministries set up by some of our member agencies.

Some may object that, by being prophetic, we are being partisan, political and unfaithful to the Church's primary role of preaching the gospel. However, the gospel speaks of the whole person, of human rights and dignity, of justice and freedom of conscience. If by defending the needs of the whole person our action has political repercussions, then in that sense we have a political role. We need to remind ourselves that our Lord's ministry had political repercussions, too. In short, ICMA must never shirk its calling to be, as Bishop Bill Down puts it, "the conscience of the industry" (*On Course Together,* 1989).

Ecumenism and Worship

Has the ecumenical character of ICMA run out of steam? Certainly, we cannot underestimate the theological, psychological and cultural differences that still separate us. We live in a world where intolerance is not politically correct. However, it is a world where it is possible to disguise intolerance—behind words like "identity" or "tradition." These may be well-meaning concepts per se, but in practice they may well run counter to authentic ecumenism.

The soul of ecumenism is prayer. To those who were opposed to the ecumenical movement, Pope John XXIII, paraphrasing Saint Augustine, once commented that—whether we like it or not—all Christians are brothers and sisters; and we will stop being brothers and sisters when we stop saying "Our Father."

ICMA conferences and meetings provide great opportunities for praying and worshipping together. They emphasize what we have in common, not what may still divide us. Christian prayer is participation in Christ's prayer to the Father. In prayer, we all take part in the love of Jesus for his Father. Worship is corporate prayer, and a powerful reminder that we are of the same family. The Lord's Prayer is the ecumenical prayer par excellence, uniting us in the celebration of our common faith and baptism.

In this world, we are all pilgrims. As we pray together, plan and work together, we give witness that Christ's body, the church, is communion and not division (1 Cor. 12:27). It is a communion where there is neither Jew nor Greek, neither slave nor free, neither male nor female, for we are all one in Jesus Christ (Galatians 3:28). We pray for the realization of this unity—*when* Christ wills it to come and in the *way* in which he wills it to come!

11

ART, THE GOSPEL AND THE SEA
In the Wake of China's Cultural Revolution
He Qi

HE QI, a native of the ancient inland port city of Nanjing in Mainland China, grew up in the atheist convulsions of his country's Communist Cultural Revolution of 1966-76. Below, he recounts his odyssey of faith, eventually becoming the first in his nation to earn a PhD in Religious Art and, subsequently, a Professor of Christian Art at Nanjing Theological Seminary, gaining world renown in his field. Here, he shares his passion for indigenous art as a bridge, bringing the gospel of Christ to our world's post-modern people—both on land and sea.

My Discovery

Chinese people have this tradition: You come to know principle through image. This is how we communicate when we write—by picture-based script. This was how I came to the faith—through the medium of art.

During the Cultural Revolution (1966-1976), I was sent away to do physical labor in the countryside together with other middle-school students. One day, I discovered a book on European art which had escaped destruction. There, for the first time, I saw a picture of Raphael's *Madonna and Child*. The painting moved me so much that I had to copy it. I worked by candlelight and then shared it with friends for inspiration. This was a time when art meant mostly making portraits of Mao Tse-tung. So, while others were doing Maos, I did Madonnas.

The softness of the Virgin's smile touched me so much. Everywhere people claimed to be seeking truth. Yet at the same time they had their knives out. Raphael's art did not convert me. However, it became a bridge for the gospel. In China, there are two ways for a person to become a Christian. One is by the influence of your family background. Another way is by your own choice. For me, it was the latter—under the influence of Christian art.

In the unrest after Mao's death in 1976, I went through a period of personal unrest, too. I had to battle with the two largest obstacles to Christianity in China—the one historical, the other cultural. Just as Muslims cannot forget the Crusades, Chinese people cannot forget the Opium Wars. When Western cannons came, Christian missionaries came as well. So, in Chinese history Christianity is closely connected with colonialism. Besides that, in Chinese culture Christianity has always felt foreign. Why? Buddhism became so enmeshed with traditional Chinese culture that people forgot that originally it came from the outside. By contrast, the Christian gospel came wrapped in a Western package. Soon people would even say: "One more Christian, one less Chinese...."

In spite of this, when I got the chance to study the history of Christian art, I found the living Christ and the meaning of his gospel. Both Buddhism and Christianity confront the phenomenon of ugliness and evil in the world. But where Buddhism looks for a way of escape, Christianity looks for what love can do. This last century of conflict and bloodshed in China has shown that our people do not lack a spirit of struggle and combat. But we have lacked love. I discovered that nothing is more radical and revolutionary than the message of God's love—shown above all in the images of the crucifixion and resurrection of his Son. Through art, I want to share with others that unique message of divine love.

My Dream

Thanks to the Nanjing-based Christian social service agency, Amity Foundation, I was eventually given the opportunity to study medieval art in Europe. This made it possible for me to complete a PhD at the Nanjing College of Arts, the first ever in the field of religious art in Mainland China. After that, at the invitation of Bishop K.H. Ting, then president of the recently re-opened Nanjing Theological Seminary, I joined the faculty as Professor of Christian Art.

It was strange to think that, not many years earlier, Red Guards had occupied the campus of that seminary, made a big bonfire with classic books from the library, and floated a banner with quotes from Chairman Mao from the Academic Tower. Now Bishop Ting wanted all theological students to see art as a way to enter into dialogue with China's contemporary culture, spread the gospel, and let it be a source of light and salt in society.

This is also my own vision. Life is so short. I want to grasp every moment of my own lifespan to do one thing—fight for the contextualization of Chinese Christian art! Art is the window of the heart. Through our eyes the love of God can reach our hearts. I want to help people to use art as a bridge into the Kingdom of God. In China, not only do many see Christianity as a Western, non-Chinese religion. They see Jesus as an ancient man who is long gone. They need to change this wrong idea of Christianity. They need to see a Chinese Jesus, one they can all relate to in the context of their everyday lives.

Does any of this have anything to do with the sea and the lives of seafarers? After all, in contrast to a number of nations in the West, the Chinese have not traditionally seen themselves as a maritime people, or one primarily preoccupied with sea-related activities.

It is, of course, true that China is bordered by no less than four seas. There are several major port cities and countless fishing communities along a coastline stretching from Russia to Vietnam. At the same time, China's vast national network of rivers and canals employs more waterway workers than any other nation in the world. It is also true that, under the Ming dynasty, Admiral Zheng set sail from my home port of Nanjing with a huge fleet in July, 1405, on the first of several bold overseas voyages halfway around the world.

However, that kind of involvement in a big international maritime venture was an exception. For ages, Chinese tradition was predominantly agricultural, and therefore land-based. The very name "China" means the "Middle Kingdom." All beyond its borders were barbarians by comparison. Like the original idea of the Great Wall, Chinese culture kept a closed door to the rest of the world. As Confucius put it, "Do not go far away while your parents are still alive."

In spite of this, because of globalization and economic reformation, China has, in recent years, begun to open its doors to the outside world. This has meant mounting numbers of Chinese ships and seafarers presently engaged in international trade. The Beijing-based, state-owned China Ocean Shipping Company (COSCO) has now become one of the world's largest shipowning corporations. By 2004, China's merchant fleet, including that of Hong Kong, had reached third place globally. Thousands of ships currently carry China's flag into port-cities all over the world. At the same time, China has become one of the leading suppliers of international maritime labor. As a result, Chinese seafarers serving on foreign-flag ships have become a common sight.

There are many ways for Christian seafarers' mission agencies to make use of art in their ministry to both Chinese and other international seafarers in ports around the world. Examples include beautiful illustrations in worship aids and other media for use at sea, videos with an engaging Christian content (competing with the perversion of art through pornography), and tasteful decorations in seafarers' centers (including their worship space).

The multi-purpose architecture of a typical seafarers' center can itself be a powerful witness to the gospel, by simply being there for everyone. Such centers try to meet the whole range of seafarers' human needs. No less importantly, they do so not only on special days, but every day of the week. Instead of the sort of sanctuaries that create fear through a cold, top-down disconnect between church and society, here all are welcome—all the time.

In Confucian culture, people are not equal. When Jesus called simple seafarers as his first followers, he strongly stated that all are equal before God. Like seafarers, we all need the beacon light of the gospel of Christ to find both our bearings and the bravery we need to face the storms of life. Art is like the sea—universal. I believe the more art becomes indigenous, the more international it will be. I want to see Christian art—not least the folk art of China—convey to everyone the limitless love and mercy of God through his Son Jesus. This is my dream.

12

WORLDVIEWS AND NOMADS OF THE SEA

An Anthropological Perspective on Maritime Mission

Paul G. Hiebert

PAUL G. HIEBERT was raised in India in a Mennonite missionary family and served there as a missionary himself for seven years. Trained as an anthropologist, and with a PhD in that field from the University of Minnesota, he has taught at Kansas State University, the University of Washington, the School of World Mission at Fuller Theological Seminary, Pasadena, California, and (from 1990) Trinity Evangelical Divinity School, Deerfield, Illinois, where he has chaired the Department of World Mission and Evangelism. Dr. Hiebert has authored many publications in anthropology and missiology.

The Significance of Worldviews

Culture shapes seafarers, as it shapes us. Yet differences between people of the sea and the land run deeper than behavior and beliefs. Underlying every culture is a worldview that shapes how its people see and relate to the world.

People perceive the world differently because they make different assumptions about reality. Taken together, the basic assumptions about reality that lie behind the beliefs and behavior of a culture are called a "worldview." Worldviews are the "eyeglasses" with which people look at reality, not what is actually there. Because people take these assumptions for granted, they generally reinforce them with deep feeling. Anyone who challenges them can become the object of vehement behavior.

Traditional (Tribal) Worldviews

The worldviews of tribal people around the world vary greatly. However, a few general themes are common to many of them. First, the world itself is seen in animistic terms, as inhabited by gods, spirits, ancestors, and other beings that share in the same life force. These interconnect with each other in complex webs of relationships that people must maintain by means of magic or placating.

Second, traditional worldviews center on the tribe and its members who alone qualify as fully human. Outsiders are subhuman, so to cheat or kill them is not a sin. Third, such worldviews concern primarily questions having to do with this life—health, children and prosperity, and with the evils that threaten it—sickness, barrenness and disaster.

In the wake of the Enlightenment, the modern missionary movement of the early 19th century equated Christianity with Western civilization. This had two fateful consequences: First, Christianity acquired a *foreignness* that became a big barrier to the spread of the gospel. Second, the old beliefs and customs did not die out, but simply went underground, leading to the very *syncretism* the missionaries had so eagerly sought to prevent.

In a sense, the gospel is foreign to *every* culture, for the gospel is God's prophetic voice to sinners and the cultures they create. This includes the West where earlier missionaries were blind to how "pagan" flaws, like materialism and secularism, would eventually seduce their own Western Christianity. All cultures are, as such, morally neutral—equally capable of receiving or negating the gospel. All missionaries have to grapple with the challenge of "contextualization"—making the gospel relevant in any given cultural context.

The Modern Worldview

The modern worldview, which is characteristic of us in the West, is radically different from the traditional type. It divides reality into two domains. Most of us assume that we live in a real or *natural* world. This operates according to natural laws which human reason can discover by using the methods of science. Meanwhile, there is also the *supernatural* realm of religion. This has to do with heaven and hell where God, angels and demons dwell. Given our growing emphasis on the material world and the sciences, we compete for power and possessions, resulting in mounting materialism and secularism.

The basic problem with this modern worldview is the sharp distinction it draws between the supernatural and the natural. The former has to do with other-worldly, ultimate concerns, the latter with this-worldly, existential issues, in a world subject to natural laws, with little need for any God. This modern form of dualism marginalizes the gospel, relegating all religion to the private sphere.

Meanwhile, despite the physical wellbeing made possible by science, there is today growing doubt that the modern worldview alone can make sense out of life. There are now calls for a "postmodern" (or "late modern") worldview. Here the challenge to Christian faith is not so much secularism as *relativism* ("anything goes"). To the postmodern mind, experiences are no longer denied; they are all affirmed. The basic criterion is simply pragmatic ("does it work?"). What, then, is an authentically Christian response?

The Biblical Worldview

The biblical worldview is different from, and challenges, both the traditional and modern worldviews. It sees all humans as eternal beings, created in the image of God, and of infinite value. It also recognizes that we are sinners in rebellion against God, individually and corporately. Yet no matter how flawed we may be, there is redemption and perfection through Christ. At the heart of this gospel message is the concept of "shalom." This begins with a right relationship with God, involving forgiveness and obedience. It also involves right relationships with humans, characterized by love and care for one another. Total shalom is the goal of history, when God and God's people will share in an eternal fellowship of perfect love, joy and peace.

In the West, which still sees science as public truth, authentic Christian witness is to proclaim publicly a holistic gospel. That means a gospel that brings all of life under the lordship of Christ, integrating both existential needs and ultimate concerns. The biblical worldview calls those who claim it to identify with the world—yet as a prophetic *counter-cultural community* in the world. As such, it stands against what is evil in every culture, while calling all people into the kingdom of God, to share in the salvation which is for every one.

Sociological Factors that Impact the Worldview of Seafarers

The worldview of seafarers on any given ship will vary widely. However, there are certain sociological factors that impact the basic worldview that all seafarers share as a vocational group—regardless of cultural particularities. As we minister among seafarers, the following four common characteristics can perhaps help us understand something of the specific subculture of the sea:

Nomadism

Seafarers are nomads and, over time, they develop a transient mentality. Many have no permanent residence they can call "home." Periodically, they may return to a family and community, but soon they must be ready to move on. At sea, they live in temporary quarters. Companions and surroundings are constantly changing. By contrast, we land people look for permanence. We like to settle, and develop stable communities of people familiar to us. This contrast makes it difficult for land people to minister to sea people. Most churches have grown among people who live in one place for relatively long periods of time. Land people have little idea of how to plant churches among nomads.

Living in the Present

As land people, we work hard to control our lives. We plan our futures, and live by calendars and schedules. Sea people must learn to live in a world often beyond their control. At sea, they suffer long times of hardship and loneliness. In port, they gather with other sailors to break the tedium of life at sea. Their past is the stories they tell and retell among other sailors. Their future is unpredictable. So, they must make decisions based on living in the present. For them, there is little point in long-term planning.

Self-reliance

To survive, seafarers must be self-reliant. They put a strong emphasis on the freedom of the individual and on fair play. Each must stand up for him- or herself. They live in small groups. To organize their lives, they depend on personal interaction, rather than on large institutions. In today's multi-ethnic crews, disputes are always a possibility, compounded by seafaring being still a mainly male-centered world. For *women* seafarers, the ship as a floating "total institution" continues to present a real risk of gender-based harassment and sexual abuse. For them, sea life calls for even greater vigilance and self-reliance.

Culture Brokers

Every seafarer brings along his or her own cultural heritage, but they meet and live with people from other cultures. In that sense, seafarers become "culture brokers," simultaneously members of two or more different cultures, without fully identifying with any of them. As such, they are often lonely and caught between worlds. Most people expect others to be loyal to them and their agendas; otherwise, they become suspicious. That is why our warring world needs natural culture brokers—like seafarers.

Implications for Ministry with Seafarers

Given these deep differences, to minister effectively, as people of the land among people of the sea, we must come to terms with *marginality*. Jesus himself was a marginal person, on the move and out of tune with what the Jewish leaders wanted and expected of him. He related to people on the fringes of society—like lepers, tax gatherers and prostitutes. Christians, too, are to be marginal people. They live in the world, yet as citizens of the Kingdom of God, no longer fully at home there.

Next, we must find the most effective *strategies of ministry* with these nomads of the sea. We need to develop modular multi-media devotional materials relevant to their tough, lonely, nomadic lifestyle. Christian seafarers need systematic training to form nurturing, Bible-studying cell groups on board ship. Too often, we continue to see seafarers as objects of ministry, not as potentially key ministers themselves. Centuries ago, Muslim sea traders took Islam to the West Coast of India, Indonesia and the Philippines. But ever since the Early Church, Christian seafarers had already crisscrossed the oceans with the gospel. Today, they are again taking it to countries around the world closed to conventional Christian missions. They deserve the encouragement, logistic support and prayers of the global mission community.

Finally, there is a *prophetic aspect*. The church ashore has invaluable lessons to learn from the reemerging church at sea. Ever since the Israelites settled in Egypt, God's people have been a sedentary people. The church in general knows little of how to reach people who are constantly on the move. Migrants, refugees, students, tourists and other mobile people groups form no natural cohesive communities of mutual support. In a sense, Christian seafarers, as nomads of the sea, are prophets, people who can speak from the outside. They provide us with a broader perspective and critique that can help us in our culturally parochial churches—as we struggle with our role in the postmodern settings of this increasingly mobile world.

13

THE SEAFARERS' TRUST

Its History and Future Directions

Tom Holmer

TOM HOLMER was born in Oxford, England. Due to his parents being in the foreign service, however, he grew up on the international scene—in places as far apart as Germany, Singapore and the Ivory Coast. He joined the International Transport Workers' Federation in 1994, working first with their Actions Unit and then their Flag of Convenience Campaign, before beginning, in 2003, as Assistant Administrative Officer with the ITF Seafarers' Trust. From early 2005, he became Administrative Officer of the Trust.

Historical Developments

The Seafarers' Trust belongs to the International Transport Workers' Federation (ITF). The ITF is a global federation of some 600 trade unions within the transport industry. The ITF has separate sections for road, rail, civil aviation, fisheries, inland navigation, tourism services and seafarers. Among these, the ITF collectively represents well over half the world's merchant seafarers.

In 1981, the ITF established the Seafarers' Trust as a registered UK-based charity. As such, the Trust is "dedicated to the spiritual, moral and physical welfare of seafarers, irrespective of nationality, race or creed." The Trust originated due to the ITF Flag of Convenience (FOC) campaign. This has been fighting for more than 50 years to improve conditions on FOC ships and ultimately end the whole FOC system. The Trust's income derives principally from the investments of the ITF's International Seafarers' Welfare Assistance and Protection Fund. This fund consists of contributions collected from ship-owners who stand to benefit from the FOC system.

In the early years of the Trust's work, by far the largest proportion of grants was for buildings. The second largest was for vehicles, most often in countries where seafarers' welfare organizations were already well established. Over the last few years, however, there has been an effort by Trustees to take a more proactive approach. This has led to the recent emphasis of the Trust on reducing the proportion of grants for buildings and increasing the proportion for projects like the International Seafarers' Assistance Network and, more recently, the Seafarers' Health Information Programme, which started in 2004.

The Trust is also continuing to support scholarships for students from developing countries at the World Maritime University in Malmö, Sweden, as well as the work of research bodies such as the Seafarers International Research Centre in Cardiff, UK. The hope is that any one of these large projects may have the capacity to improve the lives of a large number of working seafarers and their families because of their global reach.

A serious limitation in the ability of the Trust to help seafarers has been the reduction in its annual income, due to the fall in capital markets since 2002. This has brought down the annual Trust budget from a recent high of almost US$ 18 million in 2000 to less than one third of this amount for 2004 and 2005. Luckily, a new Trust strategy, including some major regional projects, began before capital markets declined. As capital returns continue to recover, we hope that there will be a modest expansion in the Trust's annual expenditure.

In earlier years, it was the ITF General Secretary, *Harold Lewis*, who directly operated the Trust. When *David Cockroft* took over as General Secretary in 1992, while remaining Trust Secretary, he transferred responsibility for administering the Trust to a specialist officer, *Mark Dickinson* (later ITF Assistant General Secretary, before joining the UK ship's officers' union NUMAST). In 1996, *Timo Lappalainen*, Finnish Port Chaplain in Antwerp, became the Trust's first full time Administrative Officer. In March 2005, I replaced Timo, who went back to his native Finland to work with international aid projects. Later, in September 2005, *Roy Paul*, Mersey Mission to Seafarers Chaplain in Liverpool, joined me as Assistant Administrative Officer.

From Timo Lappalainen's term at the helm began an expansion of welfare funding through regional programs. These could more closely target the areas of particular need, where seafarers' welfare facilities were non-existent or underdeveloped. During this time, the majority of Trust spending switched from the developed to the developing world. This has seen the Trust financing projects at a time of economic upheaval in Indonesia, Russia and former Soviet bloc countries, Africa, and parts of Central and Latin America. The ports concerned are usually in places where the local community is too poor to be able to build a structure for seafarers' welfare work without external support.

Future Directions

The Trust may be able to provide funds, target resources for training, and finance the setting up of a welfare structure. However, we are always aware that work with seafarers on a personal level goes on, thanks to the efforts and dedication of a relatively small group of people. The overwhelming majority of these are from various denominations of the Christian Church who want to reach out to seafarers and offer them support, as they and their families face a life with many difficulties. These people provide human contact between those on shore and those on ship, something that seems increasingly hard to achieve with mounting security restrictions and time constraints. For seafarers, these people can make a vital difference. Unlike most people in the port, they are not there for commercial reasons, but as friends.

Still, the number of seafarers who get to meet welfare workers and benefit from their services is relatively few. There remains a need to see that the services offered meet the most pressing requirements and become available to the greatest possible number of seafarers. The financial sustainability of the work with seafarers is therefore a great concern for all the agencies dealing with seafarers' welfare. The goal is to develop a structure for welfare facilities that the entire port community will widely recognize and support. In that regard, the ICSW is doing great work in bringing together people from all sides of the shipping community. Its aim is to put an effective network in place. Hopefully, this will bring the financing of seafarers' welfare work, as intended by ILO Convention 163, onto a more secure basis in any given country or port.

Bringing seafarers' welfare to the notice of the people running ports is an uphill struggle.. However, it is important to see services, such as telephones and email, readily available to port users. In these days, when the ISPS code has made it so difficult for seafarers to enter and leave port areas, it is essential to pay particular attention to their legitimate human needs once they arrive.

While all this is going on, there is consensus that life is becoming progressively harder for seafarers. The clientele of seafarers' welfare workers is often those who have little money to spend. Most of the seafarers' centers that have served seafarers for years now have to look for sources of income beyond the seafarers themselves. Centers that have to close do not necessarily do so for lack of need, but for lack of finances. Sources of finance that were reliable for years suddenly dry up, and a center that has been marginally viable suddenly goes into loss and has to close. Today's challenge is to adapt to change—while maintaining and, where necessary, expanding existing welfare structures.

Through regional programs, the Trust is continuing to try to address the imbalances of the giving in previous years, and thereby raise the profile of seafarers' welfare. The aim is to get as many partners as possible involved in this work. As we assist with providing services in one place, we hear of their withdrawal elsewhere. It seems to the Trust that everyone in the maritime industry, whether governments, port authorities, agency companies or ship-owners, should recognize, and therefore support, the good work of so many people. One of the aims of the Trust and the ICSW is to bring welfare providers together in associations that can exercise a meaningful role in the support and coordination of efforts to assist seafarers.

It is a continuing frustration that the Trust has many good applications for funds, of which it can accommodate only a small proportion. There is a great need for additional funding on behalf of this marginalized and largely forgotten group of skilled people. On the other side, many people continue to work selflessly for the wellbeing of seafarers, whether they are from churches or unions, or have other motivations. The Trust looks forward to working with them all for many years to come.

14

OUT OF AFRICA
Discovering Maritime Ministry
Peter Ibrahim

PETER IBRAHIM, shortly after he was born into the family of a Sudanese Sheik, was adopted and raised by a Christian missionary doctor. As a refugee from his war-torn native Sudan, he eventually settled in Antwerp, Belgium. In 1980, he graduated with a Licentiate in Theology from the University of Brussels. After ordination by the Lutheran Church in Tanzania, the North Elbian Mission Center in Hamburg, Germany, called him to minister among the many non-Western seafarers arriving there, in cooperation with the German Seamen's Mission. In the late 1990s, he returned to his original "home port" of Antwerp to serve with the British & International Sailors' Society there. Since then, he has also promoted indigenous maritime ministry in Tanzania and elsewhere, as International Coordinator with the Lutheran Association for Maritime Ministry.

From Sudan to the Docklands of Hamburg

Born into the large family of a Sheik in Sudan, I became an orphan at birth, since my father had died just before. My ailing mother placed me with two more of her twelve children in the care of an English medical missionary. In this way, I received a Christian upbringing within the context of an Arabic Islamic culture. For my baptism at the age of five, I asked if I could have the name Peter, because I had already heard such wonderful things about him from the Bible. Little did I then know that I, too, would one day be closely connected with the sea.

In the mid-1960s, I graduated from the American Mission School in Omdurman, the Sudanese capital, and left for Belgium with a scholarship to study linguistics. Due to the escalating civil war in Sudan, I was able to obtain political refugee status in 1973 and remained in Belgium. Meanwhile, as an expatriate myself, I became active in a German-Lutheran diaspora congregation in Antwerp. That same year, I followed a call to commence theological studies.

Before I could graduate from the Protestant Seminary in Brussels, *Carl Osterwald*, the General Secretary of the German Seamen's Mission, had contacted me and challenged me to consider the acute need for indigenous mission among Africans and Asians on Western world waterfronts. Soon he had lined up funding support from the World Mission Department of the North Elbian Church. That is how, by the 1980s, my unlikely odyssey from the interior of Africa landed me in the docklands of Hamburg.

Biblical Foundations for Maritime Mission

When I took up my assignment as seafarers' chaplain on the Hamburg waterfront, I had only recently begun to realize that there is already solid foundation for such ministry in the Bible. Given my personal background, this delayed discovery was understandable. It certainly is a fact that motivation and methodology for maritime mission are both deeply rooted in Scripture.

Already in the Old Testament, we read in Psalm 107 about the wondering and wavering faith of those who sail the ocean in ships to earn their living. They see at first hand not only the wonder of the Lord's creation, but also his mighty power to command it. In the midst of mountainous seas, when they call in their distress on the Lord to save them, he stills the storm. The waves become quiet, the men become glad, and the Lord guides them to their desired haven. The writer reminds them they have ample reason to thank the Lord for his unfailing love. This passage also reminds us all of the special spiritual receptivity typical of people of the sea.

Turning to the New Testament, we read in Matthew 4 about those whom Jesus once called to be his first followers. As he was walking along the shore by the Sea of Galilee, he saw two fishers, Simon called Peter and his brother Andrew. They were busy casting their net into the lake to catch fish. Jesus called to them, "Come with me, and I will teach you to catch people!" At once, they left their nets and followed him. Shortly afterwards, the same happened with two other brothers, James and John, fishers too. Maritime mission is more than merely ministering to the needs of people of the sea. It sees them as potential partners in the mission of the Lord.

After his resurrection, Jesus makes it clear that the scope of that mission is no less than global. In the final chapter of his gospel, Matthew quotes the Master telling his seafaring followers to go and make disciples of all nations, baptizing them and teaching them to obey all he has commanded them (28: 18-20). From the very beginning, people of the sea belonged to this worldwide mission of Christ—not only among its beneficiaries but as key carriers of that mission.

Nowhere in the New Testament is there any command that Christians are actually to *convert* anyone. Genuine conversion can only come about by the action of the Spirit of Christ (John 15: 26; 16:8). The command is to bear witness to Jesus Christ, as also underscored in Acts 1:8. There has always been—and continues to be—one primary mission for the Christian Church: to make known or "show" Jesus Christ, by word and deed, on land and sea.

In one sense, the history of the Church's mission among people of the sea begins with the history of the Church itself. It was just before Pentecost, the birthday of the Christian Church, that they heard the voice of the risen Christ over the waters of Galilee. The Apostle John (who was there) describes in his last chapter how Jesus welcomed those weary fisherfolk ashore to share a meal of bread and fresh baked fish with him, right there on the beach (21:1-14). In so doing, the Lord offered every generation to become a graphic model for mission among people of the sea.

Jesus not only provided for those sea workers' physical needs. In hindsight, that meal also became a symbol of Jesus' communion meal. Moreover, the way Jesus accepted his remorseful friend Peter on that occasion is also significant. It would dispel the self-doubt of all who might later sense their unworthiness to follow Jesus' call (21:15-19).

Everyday Ministry on the Waterfront

The biggest obstacle the pioneers of maritime mission had to contend with was the negative public image of seafarers of the day. Most people saw them as worthless and hopeless—beyond respectable society. As a result, they believed it themselves. An immediate goal for seafarers' chaplains was therefore to counteract this low self-esteem. They would remind seafarers that they, too, had been created in the image of God, and that Jesus, the very Son of God, had given his life for them no less than for anyone else.

Some of this age-old prejudice persists. Far from family and friends, who can they really trust? Shipowners and maritime unions have important agendas. However, over the years, seafarers have found that none are more concerned with their welfare than seafarers' chaplains. Chaplains try to be a bridge between seafarers and their homes. They also seek to serve their spiritual needs. Many of today's seafarers are sincere believers in other faiths, but strangers to the Christian gospel. These deserve equal respect. They also deserve an opportunity to know the uniqueness of Jesus' saving forgiveness and love.

This underscores the kind of challenge a chaplain has to face. He or she may be the only Bible a seafarer will ever read. A seafarers' chaplain can only "show Christ" in a believable way to those who do not yet know him through a walk of faith that demonstrates Jesus' limitless love. If we can win seafarers as friends, Jesus himself will take care of the conversion part. I have seen this happen again and again during my years on the waterfront.

A Buddhist radio officer from Malaysia was in despair. He had just received news that his mother was seriously ill, and he wanted so badly to see her before she died. The captain would not let him go; and he knew that if he left the ship against orders he would be black-listed for ever. So, I prayed with him in his cabin. Next morning the captain himself met us with the good news—a replacement officer had become available. There were tears of gratitude as we drove to the airport. A mother got to see her eldest son three days before she died. Some years later, I heard someone call my name: "Ibrahim, don't you remember me?" After his mother's death, he had wanted to find out more about the faith of a friend he met in his need. He had then decided to follow Christ himself.

The head nurse at a hospital in Hamburg was exasperated. She told me this Filipino seafarer was critically ill, but steadfastly refused to talk or take either food or medicine. I sat down by his side and began asking him about his family. Still without uttering a word, he reached under his pillow and pulled out a photo. At first he hesitated. Then he said this was his wife and two children. After that, it was as if he just could not stop talking. Before leaving, I offered a short prayer and promised to be back next morning with my mobile phone, so he could be in direct contact with his wife. As soon as I returned, the hospital personnel asked what I had done to him. At last he was willing to talk, eat and cooperate. When I explained, the doctor in charge said the outcome in this case proved how this kind of visit could be a crucial part of the whole healing process. He told me he would leave instructions that, in future, chaplains from the Mission must have access to visit seafarers at this hospital at any time, day or night.

In another hospital, I visited an Egyptian second officer who was gravely ill with a late stage of cancer. I visited him on a daily basis. One day he asked me, "How come you have a Muslim name like me, and yet you are a Christian?" When I explained about my life story, he wanted to know more about the Christian faith. Two weeks later, he told me that he wanted to be a Christian, too, and asked to be baptized before they sent him home to be with his family. A Coptic Christian friend of his assisted me as a witness, there at the hospital. Not long after, this friend wrote to tell me that the officer had kept the faith until the Lord called him home to himself.

The heart of maritime mission is, of course, ship-visiting. Repeatedly, crew members who happen to be Muslim are surprised when they discover that a Christian like me can speak Arabic. But rather than resentment, it raises respect and rapport. On one occasion, as so often happened, some Muslim seafarers asked if I would drive them to a Hamburg mosque, since it was Thursday. Of course I did. Afterwards I took them on a sight-seeing trip, during which I invited them to visit Hamburg's historic St. Michael's Church, a well-known tourist attraction. It seemed they wanted to do me a favor, too, in return for what I had done for them. As we stood by the altar, I explained the story of Abraham and Isaac. They were surprised to hear a story we had in common, and this led to other issues of faith. I read the Lord's Prayer for them in Arabic. They asked for copies of it for themselves and their friends. Since then, we have had to make thousands of copies of the Lord's Prayer for Arabic speaking people.

In "showing Christ" to seafaring friends of other faiths, we seafarers' chaplains have discovered we have no better partners than crew members who are committed to a daily walk of faith, both among their shipmates and ashore. With their shipboard Christian fellowship groups, such seafarers are a constant reminder of the contagious faith and love of members of the Early Church. For us, as seafarers' chaplains, that makes maritime mission so full of *promise*. It also brings to mind what a *privilege* it is to minister among those of whom Jesus once said, "What you did for the least of these, you did for me!"

15

SEAFARING DISCIPLES—THEN AND NOW

Nautical Reflections from a Jewish Christian Perspective

M. Bernard "Buzz" Kahn

M. BERNARD "BUZZ" KAHN was born into a Russian-Jewish immigrant family and raised in San Pedro, California. His Orthodox Jewish grandparents left him with a lasting love for his Judaic roots. After marrying his Danish-born high school friend Betsy, his spiritual search led him to the Christian faith at the age of 28. He soon found himself involved in the youth ministry of the local Lutheran congregation. As a father of five, he later received a call to professional lay ministry. He then continued as Youth and Education Director in the Evangelical Lutheran Church in the Pacific Northwest. As an educator and Associate in Ministry, Buzz Kahn has, for several years, taught the Jewish roots of the Christian faith— in congregational, conference and college settings.

As a student and teacher of Holy Scripture for fifty years, I have come to delight in the magnificent literary style of those selected to record the words of God. Grand story telling! And nowhere more exciting than in Luke's Book of Acts! The writer clearly designs to take the reader through the dramatic actions of God, so as to reveal the Jewish Messiah to the growing movement of Jewish and Gentile believers. Peter, Stephen and Paul still challenge us, as the Acts of the Apostles carry us through the highs and lows of this divine adventure. We can assume that Luke was likely a medical practitioner. However, as we look at chapter 27 and the first 14 verses of chapter 28, his obvious familiarity with seafaring, oceanography and nautical terminology suddenly surprises us.

Having cruised through some of the very waters mentioned in Acts, I can well imagine how those who spend considerable time in the Eastern Mediterranean can sense a special relationship with St. Luke and the others involved. Seeing the islands, the mountain ranges, the coastal cliffs, just as they were when the story unfolded, with all the precariousness of ocean travel in those days, one may easily experience going back in time. In that way, one can participate in the world-shaking events surrounding those first so-called "People of the Way."

My earliest memories as a child in San Pedro, California are of the many ships plying the channel, tied at dockside, or lying at anchor in the inner and outer harbors. With little opportunity to get on board, except for occasional visits to the naval ships in port, still—I was infatuated. I grew up loving the smell of the sea, the sound of the surf, and the melancholy call of the lighthouse foghorn. Alas, seafaring was nevertheless not to be my destiny in life.

Both my parents were Orthodox Jewish. My father's family smuggled him out of Kiev, Russia, so that he would avoid conscription into the Tsar's army. My parents met and married in New York and went west to settle, my father working as a tailor and my mother assisting him. In their shop I helped them and experienced a variety of customers—navy and army men, port pilots, longshoremen and fishermen, also many immigrants from Southeast Europe. Yes, I heard words that spoke of prejudice and hostility between different groups of people, but that was offset by their fascinating variety.

My exposure to "Jewish-ness" came mostly from my grandparents. They were active in an Orthodox Synagogue in Boyle Heights, East Los Angeles. As a teenager, I also became involved in the YMCA and experienced my first feelings of spirituality at one of their camps. Then, in my late teens, my search for meaning in life really began. I read the Old Testament, books about Judaism (out of loyalty to my ancestors), and literature about other religions, including Christianity. I felt that life could only have meaning if there were a God.

Meanwhile, in my last year of high school, I had dated the daughter of Danish immigrants. We married six months after graduation, after which we began raising a family. I agreed to have our children baptized in the Lutheran church. I figured that might be like a vaccination.... Finally, my breakthrough came when, at 28 years old, I experienced the presence of God. It was as I was receiving the Sacrament of Holy Communion for the first time in that Lutheran church. This began a love affair with God and with the Holy Scriptures that has continued to this day. Eventually, after further studies and ministry, I became a youth leader in a Lutheran congregation and began a new career as lay minister.

For 25 years, I had the privilege of serving in the Puget Sound area, near Seattle, Washington. Once again, I was near seafarers and watercraft. While directing camping programs for local congregations, I helped develop water-based activities in the San Juan Islands. By 1971, we had managed to build and launch a 56-foot steel motor-vessel for retreat purposes called the *Christian*. I finally had my opportunity at seamanship—a brief but cherished experience.

It was also here in the Pacific Northwest that I received a personal introduction to modern-day mission among multi-cultural ocean-going seafarers. It then became obvious to me that ministry to and through seafarers was a vital part of the Church's mission. I discovered that no one could have a more strategic site of witness than seafaring disciples aboard today's merchant ships. I also learned that seafarers on these vessels continue to suffer many of the same problems that I observed as a boy among migrant workers ashore.

I found myself asking, why was it that Yeshua, Jesus, chose his first core of followers from the fishing industry? Was that part of his deliberate focus and concern for those on the edges of society? Were Galilean fishers, denigrated by the more conservative Judeans, more motivated to follow the Messiah? Jesus was, after all, a consistent defender of those that upper-class society ignored.

My studies of Acts have led me to regard the figure of *Barnabas* (meaning "son of encouragement") as God's antidote to the arrogance that still afflicts the church today. After sailing from his native Cyprus to the mainland, Barnabas became conspicuous in the early church as the faithful advocate of all who were excluded—always ready to encourage victims of oppression and discrimination.

As a Jewish-Christian myself, I cannot help thinking how wonderful it would be if modern-day mariners were to model the spirit of Barnabas, not least toward the many Jews they encounter on their way around the world. They might not meet so many Jews as *fellow-seafarers* (although the remarkable growth of the Haifa-based ZIM Shipping conglomerate has certainly dented some of the negative stereotypes about Israel and the sea). However, they are bound to encounter Jews *in general,* as dispersed as these have become throughout the world. Given both their own nomadic vocation and inclusive nature, seafarers could be Barnabas-like bridge-builders with Jews everywhere.

That need is indeed acute. As most modern-day Jews still see it, their people have been the victims of 1900 years of terrorism by supposedly "Christian" societies, culminating with the horror of the Holocaust. Not only is there a crying need for repentance and honest apology for centuries of anti-Semitism. The Christian church has not fully recognized its indebtedness to its own Jewish roots. Jesus himself was Jewish, and so were his first followers. Ever since, there have been Jews becoming Christians in every succeeding generation. However, these have all too often had to lose their "Jewish-ness" if they were to gain acceptance within the Christian church.

Fortunately, there is today a growing number of so-called "Messianic" congregations, where Jews who believe in Jesus as the Messiah can retain their Jewish culture and identity. Still, the history of Christianity is fraught with persecution of the kinsfolk of the Jewish Messiah who shed his blood for Jews and non-Jews alike. Much remains for the Christian church to recognize and repent, in order to rebuild bridges with the Jews, bridges it so arrogantly burnt from the first century of its existence. In the meantime, why should not seafarers who model the mindset of Barnabas take the lead in rebuilding those bridges?

I have a vision, maybe a naïve one, that if people of different backgrounds, religious, racial or cultural, come together, whether by choice or necessity, they would be more open to learn from and assist one another to be all that the God of the Universe would have us all be. I imagine that committed Christian seafarers on board ships of today, with their multi-cultural crews, could each become a Barnabas among their shipmates, and in that way help them be a model for the masses in every port and harbor they visit. Picture with me what might happen if every crew were to furnish missionaries of good will to a world in such need of reconciliation—both with God and fellow humans everywhere!

16

THE SCOURGE OF ADDICTION

Recovering and Hope at Sea and in Port

Ruth L. Kverndal

RUTH KVERNDAL was born in Philadelphia, USA, where her Norwegian immigrant grandparents settled. Her school years were in London, where her father, a seafarers' chaplain, was posted at the Norwegian Seamen's Church. Ruth Kverndal served with her husband in a number of port ministries and congregations around the world. Professionally, she has ministered to those with addictions, domestic abuse and family issues. She has a degree in psychology from the University of Washington, Seattle and is a nationally certified addiction counselor and former director of a non-profit treatment center.

Prologue

A sailor brought her to the door of our chaplain home in Melbourne, Australia, late one evening. Her whole body wracked with tremors, the 30-year-old woman bore the marks of a tough life. He pushed her gently into our hallway, this seafarer we were endeavoring to assist with his alcohol problem. "Help her," he said and disappeared into the night. My husband was still down in the port and our small children were asleep. Maria sank on to the couch while she told me she had malaria.

Her helper showed two attributes so common among his fellow seafarers worldwide—an implicit trust in chaplains (and, in this case, their family) and a warm heart for others in need. As for Maria, her alcohol addiction was full blown. Suffering from withdrawal (*delirium tremens*) was a truth she was so reluctant to see. She and I managed to face her reality together, both her physical and her spiritual needs. From this nocturnal visit I was, early in my life, to learn about addiction-related denial and the relentless, subtle, cunning characteristics of a devastating condition. It was also a time to make the acquaintance of Alcoholics Anonymous (AA). Today, AA has two million members in 150 countries. All chaplains and maritime ministry workers would do well to know the AA phone number in their port and to visit an open AA group, for their own information and, not least, for referral. For the Twelve Steps of Alcoholics Anonymous, see the end of this Perspective.

Toward a Definition

The number of addictions is up for debate. However, when we look at the facts cited below, many issues may fall into this category. As a result, different kinds of support groups have proliferated, to the benefit of those who need them.

Through the centuries, alcoholism was treated as a moral issue rather than a disease. People were often told to pull themselves together and just pray more. Even today, there is misunderstanding. True, there were pioneers at the time that forged the way to the disease concept. Toward the end of the 18th century, Dr. *Benjamin Rush* of Philadelphia came to the conclusion that "drunkards" were "addicted" to "spirituous liquor." At about the same time, in England, Dr. *Thomas Trotter* wrote a definition of alcoholism:

> ...I consider drunkenness, strictly speaking, to be a disease; produced by a remote cause, and giving birth to actions and movements in the living body, that disorder the functions of health (Pittman 1988, p. 6).

In the 20th century, there were other significant forerunners with names such as *Jellinek, Twerski, Tiebout, Silkworth* and *Shoemaker*, not to speak of all the thousands of unnamed who followed. The National Council on Alcoholism in the U.S. uses the following definition for alcoholism:

> Alcoholism is a primary, chronic disease with genetic, psychosocial, and environmental factors influencing its development and manifestations. The disease is often progressive and fatal. It is characterized by continuous or periodic impaired control over drinking, preoccupation with the drug alcohol, use of alcohol despite adverse consequences, and distortions in thinking, most notably denial.

This definition will not cover all addictions (not all are genetic as alcohol addiction can be, nor are others necessarily fatal) but it can be a guideline for what to look for.

Addiction as a Disease

Two criteria for an affliction to qualify as a disease are a recognized causative agent and an identifiable group of signs and symptoms.

Agents: Addiction develops with use or behavior involving "agents" such as alcohol, various prescription drugs, caffeine, gambling, sex, eating, the internet, spending and getting into debt. Illegal drugs, such as heroin, hallucinogens, cocaine, marijuana are all addictive, as everyone knows who has experienced this or have worked with those who have. For marijuana (cannabis), there was once a debate about its addictiveness; however, too many people have since found that they have become dependent on this drug, and especially as it increased in potency over the years. In the USA, methamphetamine production and abuse is spreading at an epidemic rate, with global repercussions.

> Fifty years ago, alcohol defined the outer limits of drug use for most Americans. Today the boundaries include a pharmacological candy store of aggressively addicting substances that provide quick fixes. (Roger Curtiss, Past President of the National Association of Drug and Alcohol Addiction Counselors, in 2006).

Signs and Symptoms: Irrational use is a sign of addiction. If she/he is not "working the program," an addicted person will often drink or use *in spite of* physical damage, family problems, financial and general dysfunction. A person's denial, rational defense systems and projection strategy are three barriers that they need help to overcome. ("No, I don't have a problem"..."So, wouldn't you drink/use, too, if you were in my shoes?"... "You're the one that has a problem.")

Other warning signs are: drinking more, or persisting in behavior other than planned; preoccupation with the relevant agent; going to parties where they can drink or use (or drinking/using "enough" before the event); family, legal, financial, social, school, job problems. To recognize a person who needs help is not always easy, especially if they have built up tolerance to the addicting agent and still are on the job. However, such a person might be functioning normally and yet might be in a blackout (alcoholic amnesia). Apart from that, their eyes might not look the same as usual; there can be a change of personality and behavior, irritability, secretiveness and, in the case of some drugs, needle marks, muscle twitching, a strange odor, rage. Protecting one's addiction and the agent of choice becomes paramount to those suffering from such a condition.

In 2003, *The New England Journal of Medicine* reported: "Continued use induces adaptive changes in the central nervous system that lead to tolerance, physical dependence, sensitization, craving and relapse." An important fact, however, is that hope is not lost with relapse. The vital factor is for the person to get and use enough "tools" at that time, for a return to a healthy, recovery state.

The Consequences of Addiction

Addiction is no respecter of persons—either related to gender, social standing or nationality. It is global, a threat to every community, on board ship and in port. A deadly silence has often prevented people and communities from getting the help they deserve. The World Health Organization recognized alcoholism as a disease in the 1950s. Yet, stigma and shame follow addiction. It is a family disease. Everyone is affected. There is even literature for *grand*children of alcoholics; the consequences of addiction continue into adulthood. There are support groups such as "Adult Children of Alcoholics" (ACOA) and "Adult Children Anonymous" (ACA). Addiction is a confusing condition. *Bill Wilson*, a financial broker and the co-founder of A.A. together with *Bob Smith*, a surgeon, in the film about the beginnings of A.A. says to his wife, "I know this sounds insane, Lois, but what I want more than anything else is another drink." (*Lois Wilson* was co-founder of "Alanon" in the early 1950s, leading to support groups for family members.)

Addiction is a spiritual disease. The initial damage impacts the person's spiritual life. Then follow effects on the emotional side, the mental state and the physical system. During the recovery process, however, it is important to care for the physical issues first (heart, liver, esophagus, circulation, malnutrition, etc.) The use of addictive substances can also be factors in different cancers. The recovery process can then incorporate the mental area (a plan for recovery), the emotional (grief, loss, shame, guilt), and the spiritual (making amends, seeking forgiveness, being assured that God loves unconditionally). It is, of course, always important to respect the individual person's situation, also in matters of faith. The sequence of the recovery process has often been misunderstood by church workers. For example, in the case of a splintered limb, a clergyperson would surely call for emergency medical help without delay. A person with an active alcohol problem also needs to be checked medically—as soon as possible—and get help from a chemical dependency professional.

In terms of alcohol, there are three general categories of drinkers: the social drinker, the alcohol abuser, and the alcoholic. Perhaps a third of all adults in the USA do not use alcohol. Most of those who do are social drinkers. Alcohol abusers are those who decide to binge on a weekend, for example, or to drink in excess while in port. While this is dangerous, they might still be in control—in making conscious decisions to drink. Then there are those who become alcoholics. Although there are many who become addicted with their first drink (this was the case with Bill Wilson), the addiction process is often gradual. If the process is not arrested, it will lead to life becoming unmanageable, often with tragic consequences. Addiction is progressive.

The Maritime Context

It is surely a given that an industry such as the maritime deserves employees who are healthy and clear-minded—for security reasons, as well as for their own and their families' sakes. Living in a "total institution" has its special challenges, however. Peer pressure is one. Homesickness, loneliness and stress are others. Additionally, what is a seafarer to do if he/she has information about illegal drug trafficking? "Snitching" is a dirty word, but this is a different scenario. The safety of fellow seafarers and others may hang in the balance and reporting can be lifesaving—and therefore ethical.

The drug trade has made technical/operational "advances" at sea. *Kenneth Luck* describes the transition from the "dumb load" cargo to the driver-accompanied vehicle driven on board, called a Ro-Ro operation. This can become a preferred way of smuggling drugs between countries. All countries need mariners who are faithful to the goals of safety and security. What does a sailor do if she/he knows of illegal drug use or trade? In port, discreetly use the emergency system where you can just lift the phone and ask for the police; the call is free. If you get the customs office, let them handle it. You will have done the right thing (Luck 1992, 87).

It is also a joint responsibility to support seafarers, in handling the brief time they have in port in a healthy way. The use of any free time on board is equally important, including good videos, literature, hobbies, music. And for everyone, seafarers and landlubbers: be a friend. Confront caringly the person you know who has an alcohol or other problem. Are they in denial? Ask a treatment center, or a professional, for "The Twenty Questions" that can indicate whether a person is addicted or not, and that they can use in private. Give further information and say, "When you are ready, these are people who can help." Do not take on the whole situation yourself. Refer, refer, and refer—to support groups and professionals, to anyone on board who is in recovery.

Write about addiction, and the help available, in newsletters on board and on shore. Use bulletin boards and handouts, including phone numbers. The ILO has a helpful manual, *Drug and Alcohol Abuse Prevention Programmes in the Maritime Industry,* originally published in 1996. Another helpful publication, from the U.S. Department of Health and Human Services, is entitled *Join the Voices for Recovery.* Other resources are the Employee Assistance Programs that offer help with problems for employees, and often their family members. See also the World Health Organization's website.

Encourage everyone to take the first step—and then one step at a time.

> **God grant me the serenity to accept the things I cannot change, courage to change the things I can, and wisdom to know the difference.**
> *Reinhold Niebuhr*

THE TWELVE STEPS

1. We admitted we were powerless over alcohol—that our lives had become unmanageable.
2. Came to believe that a Power greater than ourselves could restore us to sanity.
3. Made a decision to turn our will and our lives over to the care of God as we understood Him.
4. Made a searching and fearless moral inventory of ourselves.
5. Admitted to God, to ourselves, and to another human being the exact nature of our wrongs.
6. Were entirely ready to have God remove all these defects of character.
7. Humbly asked Him to remove our shortcomings.
8. Made a list of all persons we had harmed, and became willing to make amends to them all.
9. Made direct amends to such people whenever possible, except when to do so would injure them or others.
10. Continued to take personal inventory and, when we were wrong, promptly admitted it.
11. Sought through prayer and meditation to improve our conscious contact with God as we understood Him, praying only for knowledge of His will for us and the power to carry that out.
12. Having had a spiritual awakening as the result of these steps, we tried to carry this message to alcoholics, and to practice these principles in all our affairs.

The Twelve Steps are reprinted with permission of Alcoholics Anonymous World Services, Inc. (AAWS). Permission to reprint the Twelve Steps does not mean that AAWS has reviewed or approved the contents of this publication, or that AAWS necessarily agrees with the views expressed herein. A.A. is a program of recovery from alcoholism only. Use of the Twelve Steps in connection with programs and activities which are patterned after A.A. but which address other problems, or in any other non-A.A. context, does not imply otherwise. Alcoholics Anonymous, Box 459, Grand Central Station, New York, NY 10163.

17

SHIPVISITING AND FOLLOW-UP MINISTRY

From a Woman's Perspective
Karen Lai

KAREN LAI is Port Chaplain of the Galveston Seaman's Center, Texas. As such, she serves as an AOS Catholic Lay Minister, a calling to which the Archdiocese of Detroit originally commissioned her in 1985, and to which the Archdiocese of Galveston-Houston re-commissioned her in 2005. A graduate of the Houston Port Chaplaincy School in 1990, she has since taught lay ministry on that school's faculty and at maritime ministry training events in several port-cities overseas. During the 1990s, she became the first woman to serve as President of the NCCS, as well as Vice President of NAMMA. She also became co-founder of the support group "Women in Maritime Ministry." Among Chaplain Lai's publications are the maritime ministry-related books An Unconditional Love Story *(1999) and* I am your Song *(2002).*

I have always felt that shipvisiting is the most important part of maritime ministry, with follow-up ministry as the second most important. The first time I ever boarded a ship, the M/V BALSA 6, in April of 1985 in the Port of Detroit, I knew that God had led me to where he needed me to be. It was as a result of that very first shipvisit that I began my correspondence ministry as well. Both ship-visiting and this kind of follow-up ministry are essential in developing positive and strong relationships with seafarers—and with God.

I see St. Paul as an exceptional visionary. As he preached the Word to the people and walked among them, he knew he could not leave them to fend for themselves. He established churches, and then nurtured the people through *correspondence.* He did not abandon them to struggle on alone. He gave them tools to build on the foundation he had given them when they were together.

I have found St. Paul's example and insights extremely inspiring in maritime ministry. However, unlike St. Paul, I believe I have had an advantage in using his methods as a woman. For many years, the only women who boarded vessels were prostitutes. As women came on the scene as port chaplains and shipvisitors, seafarers began to discover the warmth and comfort of a woman in a different way. Although prostitutes are still a prevalent port activity, seafarers who experience the care and concern of a woman port chaplain have found our company a stronger tie to home than sharing a street woman's bed.

Most women have found themselves facing great challenges, simply because they are women. Tradition has dictated that we must not be ambitious, even though our brothers certainly are. We are not supposed to "make waves" on the ocean of life. History and society have engraved this into people's minds. Fortunately, this is beginning to change—including on the waterfront.

On board any ship, I find that I spend 80-90% of my time *listening*. This does not mean that seafarers always have problems. However, they do need someone who cares about them. By placing myself in a listening mode, I give seafarers the opportunity to set the agenda. Male seafarers open up incredibly well when they feel they can trust the chaplain. Once that trust is established, the conversation flows freely. They talk about their families, their wives and maybe serious concerns like personality conflicts on board, deep secrets, and other burdens of life and faith. So many times, when they have finished pouring themselves out, I hear them say, "I have never shared myself like that before."

There are far fewer women seafarers than men. Still, the women seafarers I do come in contact with are happy to see another woman on board ship. Some have spoken about reactions on the part of men when women seafarer workers "invade" their world. I remember one young Thai girl, working on a bulk carrier; she wanted to "hang out" with me all day like a best friend. So we did.

I cannot say I have had any bad experiences when visiting ships, although there have been great challenges. One captain, who had been physically abusing a mess boy, thought I would back down from helping him obtain repatriation. He began throwing things around and screaming at me. When I just stood by the boy, waiting for the next missile, it was this temperamental mariner who backed down. I really do not think he would have thrown such a fit if I had been a man.

Our responsibilities as port chaplains do not stop at the waterfront. To quote a Lutheran colleague (Ray Eckhoff): "In maritime ministry—just like in golf—it is the follow-through that counts." The two main methods of effective follow-up ministry are by shipboard prayer groups and by correspondence. When I try to explain the concept of lay ministry and prayer groups on board, the seafarers' first reaction is that they are not "worthy." They sense they are sinful; they have so often had to miss mass or Sunday services, and feel unfit to lead their peers in prayer. Therefore, when we do identify any potential prayer leaders, we have to encourage them, train them, provide prayer group materials, and network with chaplains in other ports who can continue the contact.

Anytime I am involved in counseling a crewmember, I try to make sure I have a way to correspond with that seafarer, in order to continue the ministry.

Seafarers I correspond with can include lonely cadets, away from home for the first time, captains who may feel torn between the company and the crew, seafarers who have lost a loved one, become ill or injured, experienced wage, safety, or marriage problems, and those who may even be suicidal.

During my 20 years of ministry, I have written many thousands of letters to seafarers. Some have corresponded with me for over ten years. We have been through births, deaths, baptisms, marriages, but mostly their countless days at sea. Correspondence, too, can convey Christ's unconditional love. Seafarers have been around the world and met many people. When you visit them on board, they will always sense when you are genuine and truly care about them. If they then receive a letter from you a few ports down the road, they will realize that their instincts were correct. You came through as a genuine caregiver.

Seafarers often tell me they are not great letter writers. My file cabinet is full of thousands of letters from seafarers that have said just that. However, when they receive a letter from someone who seems to care about their life, they respond anyway. Some have gone on to develop their skills in letter writing. This has helped them to correspond more regularly with their families. I have received several letters from wives thanking me for teaching their husbands about God, and bringing them closer together as a family.

In 1994, I visited the family of a Russian seafarer I had come to know on board his vessel in Galveston. At first, he had no concept of God; but since his ship came back every 10 days, we could continue to plant the seed. I maintained contact by mail with both him and his family. When I entered their home in Kaliningrad, I recognized a portrait of the Risen Christ, given them from my home parish. Victor had attended mass there with my family one Easter Sunday. While in Kaliningrad, Victor's 19 year old daughter, Natasha, took me to the Orthodox Church that her family had begun to attend when her father came home from Galveston. As I left, Victor's mother, once raised in a Soviet military family, blessed me and prayed for safety on my further voyage. Seeing what flowers can grow from such small seeds has been one of my life's greatest joys.

I know the Church's hierarchy wonders how to deal with me. In church language, they cannot call me a regular *chaplain,* because that is only for the ordained—and therefore males. Yet, in my archdiocese, I hold the position of "Port Chaplain" for the Port of Galveston. What I am called or not called has never bothered me. I do the work God has called me to—the best I know how. I do not feel like a pioneer for my sex in this field because unconditional love knows no race, age or gender. Placing limits on women in port ministry means making judgments that are only God's to make. Jesus loves us all—in spite of our imperfections. If he loves us like that, then we must strive to do the same.

Whenever people ask what I do for a living, I answer, "I make sailors smile!" For generations, men have been trying to understand women. I say— stop trying to figure us out and start celebrating our contributions! We complement one another, just as a wife complements a husband and a mother complements a father. Then, if someone asks us what we do as women working in maritime ministry, we can each of us simply say, "I make God smile!"

18

THE CHALLENGE OF FUNDAMENTALISM

Damning or Dumbing?*

Per Lönning

In the space of one generation, "fundamentalism" has become one of the most emotionally charged words in the world— especially since 9/11. Traditionally, seafarers have a reputation for openness and tolerance. Nevertheless, they too, as well as those who serve them, are impacted by individuals and regimes rightly or wrongly seen as "fundamentalist." Dr. Per Lönning is a native of West Norway's major port city, Bergen, where he became Bishop of the Church of Norway, and served as Episcopal Overseer of the Norwegian Seamen's Mission. He holds earned doctorates in both Theology and Philosophy. As a Professor of Systematic Theology, he is known internationally, particularly for his pioneer research with the Lutheran World Federation in the field of ecumenism and inter-religious dialogue. The following is an abridged version of his Norwegian-language study on Fundamentalism (Bergen, 1997).

At Issue

In recent years, the word "fundamentalism" has come into wide, yet varying, usage throughout the world. Since the close of the 20th century, few concepts have become as popular, and yet contested. This does not only apply within Christianity but also Islam and Judaism, in fact any religion. Meanwhile, the word has gained currency far beyond specifically religious reactive movements. It has also established itself in serious societal debate on, for example, political and environmental issues. All this has made the word fundamentalism difficult to dismiss or replace.

Indiscriminate usage poses a double danger: (1) *Confusion* resulting from an unspecific, unreflective use of the word, covering a collection of loosely linked phenomena. (2) A*buse* inflicted by an emotionally charged, unsubstantiated use of the word as a negative stereotype. This constantly expanded usage has contributed to a worldwide phobia concerning the spread of

The term "Dumbing" in the sub-title connotes a simplistic approach (Ed.)

radicalism and reactive movements, and has made the word fundamentalism the core of a contagious fear syndrome.

The overall purpose of this study is to constrain the concept of fundamentalism, based on a study of its origin and current usage. Current fundamentalism research focuses increasingly on the *plural* form of the concept, i.e. "fundamentalisms." Rather than simply categorizing certain movements as "fundamentalisms" or "fundamentalist," it might be more meaningful to speak of "fundamentalist *dispositions"* within different movements, ideologies and religions. Some of these movements appear more readily disposed to develop fundamentalist modes of reaction than others. From a psychological perspective, one might speak of fundamentalism as primarily a question of *attitude.*

History

The word "fundamentalism" originated in the USA in c. 1920, within ultra-Protestant circles committed to the literal "inerrancy" of Scripture, in reaction to the alleged undermining of Scriptural authority by "modernism." The movement also advocated for (1) *"Separatism"*—from churches and institutions considered non-orthodox and (2) *"Pre-millennialism"*—belief in Christ's impending return to institute a literal thousand-year reign on earth, this as a justification for socio-political non-involvement by Christians.

In 1979, a dramatic development in American fundamentalism marked the beginning of an almost explosive proliferation of the fundamentalist phenomenon worldwide. That year, the television evangelist, *Jerry Falwell*, launched "The Moral Majority" to bridge the gap between Fundamentalists and Evangelicals. Seeking to renew American society, the movement represented a radical reversal of former fundamentalist positions on both Separatism and Pre-millennialism. From the late 1980's Falwell's fellow-TV evangelist, *Pat Robertson* took over with a new configuration called "The Christian Coalition" which, like its predecessor, has involved itself heavily in national politics. In terms of traditional "fundamentalistic" positions, the American scene has never been more complex and contradictory than it is today.

In *Catholic usage,* the term "fundamentalism" has become both confined and controversial. During the first half of the 20th century, "traditionalism" or "integrism" remained the preferred designations for the dominant type of anti-modernistic conservatism. However, in the wake of reforms introduced by Vatican II (1962-1965), the concept of fundamentalism began to apply to fellow Catholics who reacted vehemently against those reforms as a betrayal of traditional, "integral" Catholicism. Meanwhile, many Catholics would restrict the designation "fundamentalism," usually preceded by the adjective "biblical," to exponents of extreme Protestantism. This lack of consensus suggests that any similarity of usage among Catholics is really only on an existential level.

In today's Western world, fundamentalism is, at least in public perception, most readily associated with *Islamic militancy*. However, the term "Islamic Fundamentalism" only became widespread around the year 1980. Moreover, this whole concept continues to be highly controversial. Muslim scholars underscore the term's Western origins and see its application to Islam as an example of the continuing "religious imperialism of the Christian West" within the largely Arab world it once sought to colonize.

Certainly, there are conspicuous differences, as well as similarities, between Christian and Muslim manifestations of fundamentalism. On the one hand, there is in Islam the inherent inter-relationship of religion and politics, based on submission to the absolute unity of a sovereign God. On the other hand, there is the uncritical disregard of historic evidence in Muslims' universal acceptance of the literal truth of the Koran and classical Islamic traditions. However, Muslim fundamentalism manifests wide global diversity, all the way from a radical islamization, based on the civic enforcement of Islamic law (*Sharia*), to more modified manifestations. In later years, Islam has demonstrated a greater overall *disposition* toward fundamentalist development than any of the other major world religions.

In contrast to Islamic versions, *Jewish fundamentalism* has been motivated less by resentment over Western colonialism and economic exploitation than by deep-rooted regional enmities in the Middle East. Of the two most striking Jewish versions, the black-dressed, bearded *Haredim* ("The Pious") represents a quietist, introvert, orthodox tradition from the 1700s, adamantly opposed to political activism—in anticipation of the arrival of the Messiah. The politically hyperactive *Gush Emunim* ("The Bloc of Faithful"), on the other hand, emerged in the wake of the 1967 War as an ultra-Zionist movement, fiercely committed to keeping and settling the occupied West Bank as an integral part of the land originally promised to Israel by God himself. This unconditional commitment to the "biblical" territorial rights of the modern state of Israel has also become a fundamentalist feature of several *Protestant* groups worldwide.

Beyond the three Abrahamic religions (Judaism, Christianity and Islam), variants of religious fundamentalism have appeared in virtually every part of the world. Chiefly for reasons of space, only brief mention can be made of such traits within the religions of Asia. In general, the two major religions, Buddhism and Hinduism, both evince an image of toleration rather than confrontation. Nevertheless, in the Asian region, as in the Middle East, any combination of religion and national culture can create a volatile mix and therefore reactive, religious-political movements. Precisely this has happened in Sri Lanka and on the Indian sub-continent. The potential for fundamentalist tension is even more evident in the militant versions of Sikhism and Shintoism.

In recent years, some have expanded the usage of "fundamentalism" to include *secular* movements, whether politically or ideologically motivated (for example, in the case of environmentalism, feminism, etc.). This may well reveal remarkable structural parallels between religious fundamentalism and variants of *cultural fundamentalism*. Further research in this field is clearly called for.

Analysis

Research hitherto defies any attempt at a *universal* definition of fundamentalism. However, as a phenomenon on the international scene in the final quarter of the 20th century, it does display one common characteristic. Specifically, fundamentalism manifests a worldwide radical reaction against features in today's society best summarized as *"modernity."* These include individualism, progressivism, pluralism, and erosion of established values, all of it undergirded by a blind faith in the all-sufficiency of market forces.

Nevertheless, this kind of common ground, in terms of reactivity, allows for wide diversity among fundamentalist movements in other aspects, for example: (a) Fixation on a perceived enemy *within one's own ranks* rather than an external adversary. (b) Wide variation in *outer appearance*, ranging from archaic to modern. (c) Both kinds of *social extremes* as potential sources of recruitment, whether these are poverty-stricken multitudes with little to lose, or a socio-economic elite who see themselves threatened by a loss of privilege.

Although fundamentalist movements show little commonality in what they stand for (in contrast to what they stand against), there are none the less certain typical presuppositions that they tend to share:

(1) Reactivity: The predominant fundamentalist mode of self-expression is one of confrontation with a concrete adversary. The specific nature of that adversary will determine whatever forms of expression the movement adopts.

(2) Absolutism: Predominant fundamentalist thought attributes absolute (*objective*) validity to the movement's own (*subjective*) view of the truth.

(3) Repression: The overriding need to eliminate rival ideologies or movements may require a strategy of coercion that disregards personal integrity.

(4) Restoration: Lending legitimacy to a given fundamentalist movement may require restoring a past golden age, since lost due to "subversive" forces.

(5) Progression: Rather than simply seeking replication of an idealized past, fundamentalist movements seek to pursue progression toward a utopian goal, one which may have been lost from view, but now is seen as within reach.

(6) Apocalypticism: Fundamentalist movements may seek to interpret current events in light of a predictable and indisputably final consummation of history (as with those Christians who see pro-Israeli political involvement as an essential contribution to the Creator's plan of world redemption).

Conclusion

Any movement (including any reactive movement)—if claiming to be ethical—must subject itself to the following test: How far does the movement's actual record correspond not only with its proclaimed intentions but also with the criteria of others? Based on humanistic and religious (especially Christian) criteria, the record of fundamentalist movements falls short in terms of both *segregation* and *intimidation.* Movements that deny valid claims to objective truth by all others readily abuse power in matters of conscience and faith.

Any hope of relating in a meaningful way to fundamentalist movements, groups or individuals—for example in the form of dialogue, however limited— would call for the mutual acceptance of a clear distinction between *commitment* to truth, and *monopoly* of truth. This would require the firm rejection of absolutizing personal, subjective convictions, and demonizing those of others.

19

SHIPPING AND THE HUMAN ELEMENT
Putting the Seafarer First
Efthimios Mitropoulos

EFTHIMIOS E. MITROPOULOS succeeded William O'Neil as Secretary-General of the London-based International Maritime Organization (IMO) in 2004. Born in Piraeus, the port-city of Athens, he served as an officer first in the Greek Merchant Navy, then in its Coast Guard. After advanced maritime studies in Italy and the UK, he worked in different capacities at IMO from 1966. From 2000, he served as Assistant Secretary-General there, until he became Secretary-General in 2004. The following is largely an abbreviated version of his article on "Putting the Seafarer First" in the ITF's Transport International, *20/2005, pp. 25-26.*

IMO's Core Priority

There can be no doubt that shipping plays a pivotal role in underpinning international trade. It has always provided the only cost-effective way to transport large quantities of raw materials, finished goods, fuel and foodstuffs over any great distance. Ships and the seafarers that man them therefore fulfill a vital role in today's global economy. That is why the International Maritime Organization (IMO)—the United Nations specialized agency with responsibility for the safety and security of shipping and the prevention of marine pollution by ships—places consideration of *the human element* at the center of its work.

Issues of concern to seafarers, such as stress, fatigue, workloads, training standards, safety, security and environmental protection, are all of prime importance to the committees and sub-committees of our organization. Experts who serve on committees that develop international standards give special consideration to the "human element," when they review the adequacy of requirements and recommendations for the operation of ships and their equipment.

The Importance of Safety Standards

There exist elements in the shipping industry that operate substandard ships and cut corners on safety, in order to generate quick profits. This "enemy within" needs to be identified and told they have no place in the industry. However, responsible shipowners today clearly recognize the benefits from employing seafarers who display the professional standards and technical competence needed to manage today's ships safely and efficiently. That is why IMO's revised Convention on *Standards of Training, Certification and Watchkeeping for Seafarers (STCW)*, which is designed to make sure that the human resources available to the shipping industry meet the required standards, is one of the most important measures that IMO has considered in recent years.

Another major part of IMO's work, which also closely relates to the human element at sea, has been the introduction of the *International Safety Management (ISM)* Code. This mandatory instrument deals with the responsibility of management to play a full and active part in building a safety culture, on board ship as well as within the company, to the benefit of all concerned. The code puts management squarely in the safety chain. Should something go wrong with the ship at sea, it does not leave the ship's master as solely responsible, but takes the issue as far as the board room.

Addressing Seafarer Shortage

IMO is deeply concerned about the widely reported upcoming shortage of seafarers—an issue requiring action before it reaches unmanageable proportions. Recent decisions in some parts of the world, criminalizing crewmembers who may have inadvertently caused pollution, will do little to encourage youngsters to choose shipping when they are looking at career options.

IMO has now, in cooperation with the International Labour Organisation (ILO), developed guidelines to be published in 2006 for the fair treatment of seafarers in such situations. If the global pool of competent, qualified and efficient seafarers is to increase, seafaring must become a viable career choice for people of the right caliber, with employment conditions at least comparable with those found in other industries.

A troubling complication is the incidence of fraudulent practices related to obtaining statutory certificates for attesting competency. This leads to people in positions of responsibility jeopardizing the lives of others and the entire marine environment. The relevant IMO sub-committee has therefore taken action through a series of circulars that give appropriate guidance.

Strengthening security, protecting rights

At IMO, we have had to join other UN organizations to address the issue of maritime security following the recent terrorist incidents around the world, foreshadowed by the September 11th attacks in the USA. Part of the guiding philosophy has been to ensure that all concerned have the appropriate skills to fulfill the responsibilities entrusted to them. Seafarers have a central role in the maritime security measures that entered into force on 1 July 2004.

In implementing this new security regime, IMO wanted to ensure the correct balance. It needed to tighten security provisions, so that criminals and terrorists cannot gain access to ships and ports by posing as seafarers. At the same time, it wanted to avoid penalizing innocent seafarers themselves—for example, by unfairly denying them shore leave.

Shipping relies on the cooperation and constant vigilance of seafarers, in order to help prevent breaches of maritime security. Without their support, the *International Ship and Port Facility Security (ISPS)* Code will become severely weakened. Fast turnaround times mean that port stays are short and pressures on seafarers keep growing. For the sake of efficiency as well as security, seafarers need adequate opportunity for relaxation and, where possible, shore leave, before they take their ships out to sea again.

Recognizing the Role of the Seafarer

Thanks to the efforts of IMO and others, the standards regulating the design, operation, and manning of ships are now more exacting than ever before. Nevertheless, every year too many seafarers suffer injuries or lose their lives in maritime accidents. More often than not, their injuries and deaths go largely unrecorded and forgotten by all but their families and close friends.

Among those friends, IMO welcomes the observer status filled by the International Christian Maritime Association (ICMA), and values its input in IMO discussions, particularly those related to training and the human element. IMO appreciates the work of church-related maritime mission organizations all over the world in promoting seafarers' welfare and providing support in times of need.

To mark the 50th anniversary of IMO in 1998, we inaugurated a trust fund dedicated to seafarers—generously supported by the ITF. Among other projects, we have used the fund to create a permanent memorial to seafarers at IMO headquarters. This memorial acts as a constant reminder of the important role that seafarers play, and of what the work of our organization is really all about.

Without seafarers, there would be no shipping. Without shipping, there would be no global economy. In pursuing our mission statement of "safe, secure and efficient shipping on clean oceans," we will never forget that achieving these objectives will be impossible without the vital contribution of the seafarer.

20

THE DIACONAL DIMENSION
OF MARITIME MISSION

Being Church in the Seafaring World

Kjell Nordstokke

KJELL NORDSTOKKE has been Director of the Department of Mission and Development of the Geneva-based Lutheran World Federation (LWF) since 2005. Born in the fishing community of Karmöy, Norway, he studied theology in Stavanger and Oslo. He served nine years as missionary and professor in Brazil. In 1991, the University of Oslo awarded him a ThD for his dissertation on Latin American Liberation Theology. From 1990 to 2005, he served at the Diaconal University College in Oslo, eventually as director-general and professor. Besides numerous other publications, Dr. Nordstokke has authored a diaconal-related maritime mission resource book as a consultant to the Norwegian Seafarers' Church (formerly Norwegian Seamen's Mission).

The Biblical Understanding of Diakonia

I have often met maritime clergy confessing to a bad conscience about not being able to perform the "pastoral" role that seminary trained them for. "Why did I have to get a degree in theology to do *this*?" they ask. There are, in fact, those who maintain that modern-day maritime mission has more in common with welfare or social work than authentic missionary outreach.

My understanding is different. Based on experience with the Norwegian Seamen's Mission, I am convinced that maritime mission represents a *diaconal* way of being church. Maritime mission actually implies a profound "Theology of Incarnational Christian Service." To many, maritime mission is easier done than said. In fact, insights gained from the planned action (or "praxis") of maritime mission have significance for the whole church and theology at large..

"Diakonia" is a central concept in the New Testament, meaning *service.* It relates to Jesus' understanding of his mission and the manner in which he carried it out. In the central narrative in Mark 10: 35-38, Jesus rejects the vision of a messianic kingdom based on dominion. His authority, unlike that of the mighty, is rooted in service: "For the Son of man also came not to be served but to serve, and to give his life as a ransom for many" (Matt. 20:28).

Primarily, such service is not only an ethical concept, expressing humility and servility. It is *transformational*. In Luke 22: 27, the emphasis is on the transforming power of service rooted in the authority of the servant. Here Jesus, through his servant role, transforms the last supper with his disciples into a messianic meal: "But I am among you as one who serves." In saying this, Jesus does not want to remind them of his humility but, on the contrary, of his messianic mission, one that manifests itself in his way of preparing a table for his friends. Through his transformational service, he gives sinners access to this table. His death on the cross becomes the ultimate consequence of his diaconal service, and the final fulfillment of his mission as the Lord's Servant.

The story of the washing of the disciples' feet illustrates just this (John 13). Peter's reaction implies the question: "How can *you* do this kind of service?" Jesus' answer is clear. He is the only one able to. It becomes a saving service, one that makes all things new. Diakonia has at its very core a *Christological* message. At the same time, the disciples are called to follow the example of Jesus, of integrating mission and service: "A servant is not greater than his master; nor is he who is sent greater than he who sent him" (v. 16). Sending (mission) and service (diakonia) are interrelated. The ultimate model is that of God: "As the Father has sent me, even so I send you" (John 20:21).

As a theological term, diakonia thus refers not only to Christology but also to *ecclesiology*— to a way of being church. The New Testament Church chose the term "diakonia" (Latin *ministerium;* English *ministry*) in order to designate the leadership of new congregations (Rom. 15:17; 1 Cor. 12:5). Meanwhile, the church also referred to certain activities as "diakonia." In Acts 6, we learn about the "diakonia of the table" as a concern parallel to the "diakonia of the word." Paul calls his campaign to assist the poor in Jerusalem a "diakonia" (2 Cor. 8-9)—the first known example of *international* diakonia.

Diakonia in Historical Perspective

Church history is replete with similar initiatives. In the Middle Ages, monasteries were centers of Christian faith and service, in contrast to an official church that many saw as governed more by lust for power than the will to serve. The modern mission movement that emerged in the 19th century integrated diaconal activities as an important expression of mission. Over the years, it developed medical mission, educational programs and humanitarian projects of different kinds. Missions organized such initiatives in order to serve the needy, change their conditions of life, and to recognize and preserve their human dignity. Roald Kverndal has documented how early organized maritime mission manifested the same holistic approach, seeking to meet seafarers' total human needs, not only their spiritual welfare (Kverndal 1986: 510-26).

However, since the 1960s, there has been a tendency to separate diaconal initiatives from the activities of the church at large. Specialized agencies have emerged, adopting the structures and rationales of secular institutions as the "social action" of the church. Yet if the social activity of Christian mission does not differ from that of secular maritime welfare, why should church-related mission undertake it in the first place? Would it not be better simply to join secular agencies in a common struggle for public social welfare?

This also applies to mission among seafarers. It is vital to overcome the tendency to reduce diaconal activity in maritime mission to "social action," instead of seeing it for what it actually is—*an expression of the church's identity as a serving community in the maritime world.* This is crucial if maritime mission is to lend legitimacy to both its work and its workers.

The Current Context of Human Society

Diaconal ministry has always seen an analysis of social reality as a decisive starting point for identifying tasks and methods. In the 19th century, a major challenge, especially for marginalized groups, was health issues. In the 20th century, human rights and decent living conditions became decisive parameters. As we enter the 21st century, the current context of a postmodern world offers the dual challenges of marginalization and individualism.

Globalization and marginalization represent *one axis* of this postmodern world. Today's world is "market" oriented, delivering prosperity based on the law of the market. Ideologically, this logic is rooted in neo-liberal politics, and its basic presupposition is a perverted application of Matt. 6:33: "Seek first the *Market* and its righteousness, and all these things will be given to you as well!" Consumption and functionality are the major values in this system. Those who fall outside this pattern of thinking become expendable. The growing gap between a prosperous North and a poorer South shows how globalization and marginalization are only two inseparable sides of the same coin.

Individualism and technology represent *another axis* in our postmodern world. The media portray the postmodern individual as young, fit and consumer-oriented. Mercy on the person who looks different or does not correspond to such standards! Within the logic of consumer ideology, technology facilitates the pursuit of happiness, even promising a "virtual reality" if the real world cannot satisfy the individual's longing for extraordinary experiences.

The church must identify its mission in this context. The church's word and deed cannot ignore this reality unless it is to accept secularism. That would lead to a praxis that condones exclusion and allows people to be expendable. In the name of the Jesus of the Bible, who embraced sinners, losers and the poor, and empowered precisely the marginalized to be his disciples, a relevant diaconal praxis must entail the implementation of Jesus' own model of action.

Visitation and Hospitality as Maritime Diaconal Praxis

From my understanding of maritime mission, a main concern has always been to stand alongside seafarers in their everyday life. This has meant a sincere interest in their experiences as maritime workers, a concern for their welfare, a readiness to assist them in all kinds of need, and a willingness to share the faith and hope of the gospel. Christian witness and Christian service have always been integral and inseparable elements of this mission, even if the context has required approaches specific to seafarers and their situation.

Two components seem of fundamental importance in the methodology of maritime mission. The first is *visitation*, a systematic effort to meet seafarers where they work and live. The second is *hospitality*, an equally well-organized effort to receive seafarers as guests in facility space that maritime mission agencies provide for that purpose. Both are basic elements of diaconal praxis everywhere. They are rooted in the biblical message of how God visits and redeems his people through the messianic diakonia of Jesus (Luke 1:68, 7:16).

Whenever maritime mission practitioners visit and invite seafarers, it is important to see these daily routines as a continuation of this messianic visitation and hospitality. Both manifest the true nature of God's kingdom and the diaconal way of being church. *Hospitality* is a key virtue in the New Testament. In Hebrews, it is seen as the mysterious event that makes divine visitation possible (13:2—compare Gen. 18:1-8). *Visitation* fulfills the promise of the Kingdom: That the blind shall see, the lame shall walk, the oppressed shall be free, and the poor shall hear the gospel (Luke 4:18-19; Matt. 11:4-6). As such, visitation also has eschatological significance (Matt. 25:31-46).

Inclusiveness as Maritime Diaconal Witness

In the current context of human society, large portions of the world's population experience marginalization and therefore *exclusion*. Meanwhile, visitation and hospitality form the foundation for a praxis of *inclusion*, one that acknowledges people's dignity and builds relations that empower them.

It is the challenge of maritime mission to bear witness to a way of being church that offers room for the excluded. Lip service cannot suffice. If ethnic or confessional background becomes a deciding factor in the treatment of seafarers, does not this reinforce divisions on board in a way contrary to the gospel? Can religious activities become so exclusive that there is no room for other faiths?

According to the key passage in Galatians 3:28: "There is neither Jew nor Greek, slave nor free, male nor female, for you are all one in Christ Jesus." The church has specific instruments of inclusion: baptism as an open door, holy communion as a table of gracious hospitality, prayer as free access to the Lord's heart, Bible reading as reflection on God's acts among us. While there is always the risk of perverting these elements into instruments of exclusion, the diaconal nature of the church presents them as signs of inclusion, as "vehicles of grace."

Among practitioners of maritime mission, these signs of inclusion combine to make up a distinctive *spirituality* of maritime ministry. This resists injustice while, at the same time, encouraging a lifestyle of simplicity and healthy self-care. Above all, this spirituality transcends the lack of external signs of hope—in the midst of the more mundane daily tasks of maritime mission. It does so, because it looks in the direction of Jesus Christ. In him, hope becomes *transformational*—placing everything within the range of the unconditional and unwavering love of God (Rom. 5:5; Heb. 6:19; 1 Pet. 1:3).

21

MARITIME MISSION AND NATIONALITY

Ethno-Specific Ministry in a Globalized Industry?

Kjell Bertel Nyland

KJELL BERTEL NYLAND has, since 1992, served as General Secretary of the Norwegian Seamen's Mission, renamed the Norwegian Seafarers' Church/Norwegian Church Abroad. Born in Nordfjord, Norway, in 1978 he became Chaplain/Director of the Norwegian Seafarers' Church in New Orleans, USA. Since 1983, he has served in various leadership capacities at his organization's head office in Bergen. He has also pursued graduate studies in market research and authored several studies in maritime mission-related Norwegian-language publications, including (in 2005) Advocate and Servant: A Contribution to the Self-identity and Public Image of the Seafarers' Church.

Historical Background

The founding of the Norwegian Seamen's Mission dates from 1864. This signaled the origin of nationally oriented maritime mission. By 1875, similar national organizations had emerged in Sweden, Denmark and Finland, respectively. All four had close affiliation with the Lutheran denomination of the Nordic national churches. Moreover, all four had historic roots in the pioneer role of Rev. *Johan C. H. Storjohann* of Bergen, Norway. In each case, the target group was fellow-Nordic seafarers in foreign ports, and Storjohann's strategy was strictly contextual, namely to bring them the gospel in the language of the heart—their own mother tongue.

However, the strategy of ministering to seafarers in their native tongue was not something that Storjohann had invented. Long before the year 1864, Scandinavian seafarers were able to benefit from sporadic efforts by both British and American organizations working among international seafarers. Wherever possible, they would also do so in their own languages (Kverndal 1986, 592-8).

Finally, in the winter of 1861, something happened that would prove decisive for the founding of the Norwegian Seamen's Mission. Chaplain *August*

Thiemann of the British and Foreign Sailors' Society had come to Norway to improve his knowledge of Norwegian. This was in order to minister more effectively among Norwegian seafarers on London's River Thames. In Norway, Thiemann happened to meet and make a powerful impression on Johan Storjohann, then a young theological candidate. During post-graduate studies in Scotland in 1863, Storjohann had a chance to verify Thiemann's arguments first-hand in the docklands of Edinburgh.

After this, it was not easy to make Storjohann stop. Back in Bergen in 1864, he established "The Society for Preaching the Gospel to Scandinavian Seamen in Foreign Ports." This was the original name of the Norwegian Seamen's Mission. From the start, it was understood that expatriate fellow nationals would also be included. Once again, the basic strategy was not new. It was the great reformer, Martin Luther, who first turned the Latin Bible and church services into the everyday language of the people. As far back as in Acts chapter 2, we read how, on the day of Pentecost, people from abroad heard the great acts of God preached each in their own tongue. Hearing about the Lord in foreign surroundings, yet in their native language, proved a powerful and effective combination—then as now.

The Challenges of Globalization

During the last quarter of the 20th century, the "ethnic revolution" in the international maritime labor force affected the merchant fleets of the Nordic nations, too. It affected none of them more radically than Norwegian-flag vessels, which made up by far the most in number. Impacted by harsh market pressures in the contemporary climate of globalization, some Norwegian owners started sailing under flags of convenience—simply to survive. In the late 1980s, a Norwegian International Register (NIS) gave them the opportunity to hire foreign lower-cost crews, yet still sail under a Norwegian flag. The result was a dramatic reduction in the number of Norwegian seafarers in international trade. (The other Nordic fleets were also affected, though proportionately less so.)

Confronted by this critical challenge, the Norwegian Seamen's Mission had to face a hard choice: either deliberately broaden its focus by becoming more of an *international seafarers' mission;* or, stay the course by continuing to be an essentially *Norwegian Church Abroad,* only now combining a stronger focus on fellow Norwegians *ashore.* After careful consideration, the Norwegian Seamen's Mission decided to keep the same basic course it had already chosen back in 1864.

Certainly, the overall context of mission had gone through drastic change. Globalization had not only resulted in far *fewer* fellow-Norwegian seafarers in overseas ports. It had also led to far *greater* numbers of fellow Norwegians in other occupational groups residing abroad for shorter or longer periods. When the Norwegian Seamen's Mission chose to keep its historic course, the funda-mental *aim* would therefore be the same—to proclaim the gospel by word and deed among fellow nationals abroad. This meant that the basic *strategy* would also need to be the same—to use a given target-group's own native language in reinforcing a culturally relevant common tradition and identity (cf. 1 Tim. 5:8).

This link between aim and strategy is strong. As a former seafarers' chaplain myself, in the port of New Orleans, I remember the impressive quali- fications required to pilot an ocean-going vessel safely past the banks of the mighty Mississippi River. Similarly, one who is to guide me on the way to heaven needs to know the "shallows" of my heart, the universe of my soul, in short what stirs me in my innermost being. There is an inherent connection between the gospel and culture. It is with good reason that mission schools spend several years educating their students in foreign cultures.

Demographic developments during recent decades, in terms of Norwegians abroad, have resulted in renaming the Norwegian Seamen's Mission the "Norwegian Seafarers' Church/Norwegian Church Abroad." This reflects more accurately the organization's official sphere of responsibility as representing the established Church of Norway abroad. This applies equally to not only the thousands of Norwegian seafarers still sailing in international waters, but also the steadily increasing mobile mass of students, business and professional people, tourists and other Norwegians, temporarily resident abroad.

A similar development has characterized the corresponding organizations of the other Nordic nations. Does this change in name, from "mission" to "church," reflect any theological shift in the original objective of these nationally oriented organizations? Speaking for us as Norwegians, I can confirm that this is certainly not the case. There is absolutely no change in our original commitment—to a holistic verbalization and incarnation of the gospel of Jesus Christ, as expressed in his Great Commission.

From my own experience in the port of Dubai in the United Arab Emirates, I remember how we were woken at 5 in the morning by the cry of prayers from the local minarets. There were no less than six mosques encircling our Norwegian-Swedish seafarers' church within a radius of one square kilometer. We understood they were proclaiming that it was better to pray than to sleep. This caused quite a sense of spiritual stirring among non-Muslims as well. As a result, people eventually filled our church, too, for worship services.

What I saw was a confirmation of a phenomenon defined by the Norwegian sociologist, professor *Otto Krogseth*: When pressures caused by chaos and insecurity impact us most, there emerges a corresponding need for a religious anchorage of identity. Familiar rituals become "fear-suppressing" for the individual, and unifying for the community. In consequence, we find that many fellow nationals from both ship and shore, who may not have been church-goers at home, experience a new relationship to both the church and its message abroad (Kvarme 1995).

National Identity and International Solidarity
"In the industrial mission that our work really is, we should not be guilty of preserving the last vestige of colonialism . . . ." This accusation is quoted from a study document, at the founding consultation of ICMA in Rotterdam in

1969, referring to national seafarers' missions—clearly meaning the Nordic bloc. At ICMA's First World Conference in London in 1972, the Norwegian General Secretary at that time, Rev. *Johannes Aardal*, took up the challenge, delivering a balanced, well-documented paper on the topic. This presented valid reasons for continuing to serve seafarers through "national centres in foreign ports, led by chaplains from their own home countries." The outcome was a compromise resolution. This recognized there was essentially "no conflict" between the promotion of multi-national centers and the "relevance of nationally orientated centres to serve the needs of particular groups."

Obviously, it can pose a difficult dilemma—to remain loyal toward your own church heritage and strategy, while still fulfilling your Christian obligation to those who are not your fellow nationals. In 1986, *Roald Kverndal* (who was then serving as Maritime Ministry Consultant to the Lutheran World Federation) attended as guest speaker at a staff retreat for employees of the Norwegian Seamen's Mission in the USA. Here, he put words to the problem. He gave an example of a Nordic shipvisitor walking past the non-Nordic crew of a typical flag of convenience ship. The shipvisitor felt he had to "concentrate" on his fellow ethnics (the officers). However, for the crew, it became just another version of an old familiar story. The clergyman and his associate were simply too busy with their fellow-ethnic "target group" to be distracted by any Asian seafarer lying by the roadside (Luke 10:30-37).

In response, we introduced a more proactive policy. Then, in 1994, the General Assembly of the Norwegian Seamen's Mission formally revised our constitution by combining our primary national objective with an explicit commitment to minister "also to foreign seamen on board Norwegian ships." However, any talk of regular missionary outreach among non-Nordic seafarers would be quite another matter. That would require a different form of recruitment and education (although this might well be a future possibility— for qualified personnel from cooperating world mission organizations).

Together with our partners in the Nordic Council of Seafarers' Churches, we in the Norwegian Seafarers' Church of today are committed to continue cooperating ecumenically through ICMA, as we have from the very beginning. While the Finns have been able to share their Sailing Chaplaincy Project with ICMA partners in recent years, we Norwegians have been happy to play a similar role with our Oilrig, Crisis Preparedness and Net-Church initiatives.

Is it possible to be ethno-specific without becoming ethno-centric? Based on our own experience, we respond in the affirmative. We continue to believe that we can best serve our joint Savior and Lord by staying loyal to our God-given national identity while, at the same time, remaining committed to international solidarity with the worldwide maritime ministry community.

22

SMALL CHRISTIAN COMMUNITIES
In the Seafaring World and Beyond

James O'Halloran

JAMES O'HALLORAN is an Irish-born Salesian priest who holds degrees in education and theology from London, Oxford, Philadelphia, and Maynooth (Ireland). He has worked with small Christian communities for thirty-five years, as member, coordinator and promoter. He has carried out this mission worldwide—from the halls of universities to parishes and far-flung mission stations. James O'Halloran has become inter-nationally known as one of the most respected writers in the field of small Christian communities.

None of us Goes to Heaven Alone

We are saved through relationships. The Bible says it is not good for us to be alone (cf. Genesis 2:18). A person who cuts her- or himself off from others is a human contradiction because, without one another, we could not even learn to be persons. Without the sunshine of love and the rain of acceptance, neither can we grow as persons. By the power of the Holy Spirit, people are experiencing this through thousands of small Christian communities on every continent.

In modern times, the proposal of the Church as "communion" has come from two sources. After its founding in 1948, the World Council of Churches did much research on the notion of the Church as the "People of God," a model that emphasizes the role of the laity. This research became available to the participants of the Second Vatican Council (1962-65) through a team of fifteen theologians from the World Council of Churches, meeting with fifteen of their Roman Catholic counterparts at the request of *John XXIII*. The Spirit, who is at work at the grassroots, also blew strongly on this theme at Vatican Council II. Paragraph 4 in *Lumen Gentium,* the document on the Church, says, ". . . *the universal Church is seen to be 'a people brought into unity from the unity of the Father, the Son and the Holy Spirit.'"* So, from both of these two sources,

Geneva and Rome, there flowed the understanding of the Church as communion—in the image of the Trinity.

How is this to happen in practice? Certainly, a key way in which it is currently emerging is through the proliferation of small Christian communities, also called "basic ecclesial communities." All over the planet today, people sit down in their neighborhoods, in small groups of about eight, with their Bibles in hand. Here, they converse about their lives, see what is happening to them in light of the word of God, and work out what they are going to do about it. In time, these groups network with one another and thereby form a *communion of communities,* deepening their sense of communion wherever they happen to be.

There are, of course, variations of the neighborhood model. We also find small communities on board ship, in schools, universities and so forth. All are integral parts of the small Christian community phenomenon. Though statistics are available for some areas of the world, this is not universally so. However, a World Consultation on Small Christian Communities held in Bolivia in 1999 noted that they existed in thousands on every continent. It referred to them as "a sleeping giant," because they tended to be low profile. This sleeping giant at the service of the churches and the world could become an immense force for good.

Rooted in the Trinity

How can these small Christian communities implement the communitarian vision of the World Council of Churches and Vatican II? We can find the roots in the community of the Trinity. We are created in the image of the Three in One. In Genesis 1:27 we read how God created human beings "in our own image, after our own likeness . . . male and female." The inclusion here of *male and female* is significant. God did not create us in isolation. Rather, we were created as a community of brothers and sisters without divisions on grounds of race, social condition, or sex (Gal. 3:28).

The Trinity is a community where there is intimate loving and sharing. This is not possible in a parish of thousands, not even in a gathering of one hundred, nor among the entire crew of a ship. Only by reducing groups to about eight, can one achieve intimate sharing and become one. For the Church to be community as the Trinity is community, we need *small* Christian communities. As such, they are visual aids, or sacraments, of the Blessed Trinity.

Each community can truly say of itself that it is Church, because it contains all the ingredients of the universal Church: love, commitment, worship, mission and so forth. In such groups, the universal and the particular inter-penetrate each other in mysterious ways. This is why *Paul VI*, in his *Evangelization of Peoples,* 58, says that the small Christian communities are *cells* of the Church. In this, they are distinct from other groups and movements that may come and go. *They are of the essence.*

The Overall Scenario

Let us look at the bigger picture. God created us a community of brothers and sisters without divisions. We did not remain in this state. Through our weakness and sinfulness, we marred the Lord's plan and sowed division, which is sin. In so doing, we did something that we could not ourselves put right, thereby becoming in need of a Savior. A merciful God sent us that Savior in the figure of Jesus Christ. This "person for others," through his death and resurrection, redeemed us. He reconciled us to ourselves, to God, to our brothers and sisters, and to all creation. In other words, *he restored community.*

The historic Jesus is no longer with us. However, he is present in his Church, which is, of course, the body of Christ (1 Cor. 12:27). Jesus is a sacrament of, or makes present, the loving Trinity on earth (John 14:8-9). Similarly, the Church is a sacrament of Jesus (Matt. 18:20). The Church must now continue the mission of Jesus and reconcile us to ourselves, to our brothers and sisters, and to the environment. It becomes the task of the Church to restore community. Small Christian communities can be a particularly effective means for achieving this since they are, in a special way, visible and palpable sacraments of the Trinity and of Jesus.

God loves us unconditionally. This we know in our heads. Do we know it in our hearts? The journey from the head to the heart is the longest in the world. If, however, we grasp this truth in our hearts, it can change our whole perception of people and the world. It is by befriending fellow humans in the Lord, and giving each other an experience of love, that we can lead one another to God, who is love (1 John 4:8). God is the wonderfully creative Father, the Son as the Word Incarnate is the center and mediator of spirituality, and the exuberant Holy Spirit is deeply embedded as the motivator of consciousness. Spirit consciousness is high in small Christian communities.

People of the Sea

Before I felt called to the priesthood, I had a burning desire to be a sailor. However, because I had such an aversion for water in terms of washing myself, my mother always declared that I would have to be a dry-land sailor. So, early intimations connecting me to the sea were not awfully promising.

For what I know of maritime mission, I am indebted to *Colleen Fleischmann* who first drew my attention to the existence of small Christian communities at sea; to *Ray Eckhoff,* who plied me with valuable material on the subject; finally, to *Roald Kverndal.* Among other favors, Roald provided a splendid historical profile of small communities, in the context of maritime mission, for a book of mine entitled *Small Christian Communities, Vision and Practicalities* (Columba Press: Dublin 2002). The only way I can describe the effect of this profile on myself is to say it felt *exciting.*

I cannot do justice to Roald's profile here. However, I would like to mention one striking thing he said: "Christ could not have been more *explicit* in his choice to head his global mission enterprise. By the shores of the Sea of Galilee it was a small band of *seafarers* he called to be his first followers, and eventually to go with his gospel to the waiting world." May I go on to stress a further point? When these seafarers came to give concrete expression to this gospel, they did so through small Christian communities. These were open to one another and combined together to form a communion of communities (cf. Acts 2:42-47; 4:32-37; 11:14-15; 12:12; 16:3-5). The whole vision and reality that I have tried to describe began with *seafarers!*

The community model of Church that those seafarers launched eventually faded, largely through the influence of the Roman Emperor, *Constantine I* (288?-337 CE). The sea change came with his conversion. The Church ceased to be harassed and Christianity became the favored religion of the Empire. In numbers, the Church greatly increased. However, this was not due to any massive entry of "pagans." It had become fashionable to be "Christian." The Church had lost the momentum of an entity that until then had been lean, persecuted and committed. This blunted the edge of witness. In the mid-fourth century, bishops received recognition as counselors of state, eventually with juridical rights. This gave birth to a Church model that was both hierarchical and strongly institutional, a form that has prevailed until modern times and is only now coming into question.

Though the communitarian vision of Church faded, it was never entirely lost. The memory was kept alive by the charismatic vision of the founders of religious orders such as Basil, Benedict, Francis, and Teresa. It again raised its head with the rise of the Anabaptists and then, significantly, with the coming into being of the Bethel Movement among seafarers in the early 1800s.

To quote Kverndal: "Nurtured by the burgeoning Bible Society Movement that emerged in both Britain and America in the late 1700s, seafarers spontaneously formed a widening network of worshipping and witnessing cell groups at sea. As the Spirit again 'moved upon the waters' (Gen. 1:2), the 'Seafarers' Mission Movement' first took the shape of *Maritime Small Christian Communities,* a typical case of self-empowering, grassroots 'mission from below.'"

So, People of the Sea, you that launched the communitarian Christian project in the first instance, and gave it one of its most invigorating resurgences in the course of history: I now urge you to reclaim your ancient heritage! Foster the grassroots communities that are once again appearing in the seafaring world! That world is changing—with poor, exploited Asians and others of many religions now figuring greatly on the scene. From among them, let Jesus' Nazareth Manifesto ring in our ears:

> *The Spirit of the Lord is upon me, because he has anointed me to bring good news to the poor. He has sent me to bring release to captives and recovery of sight to the blind, to let the oppressed go free, to proclaim the year of the Lord's favor* (Luke 4:18-19).

23

HOPE REGAINED

Seafarers' Mission Facing the Future

Carl Osterwald

CARL OSTERWALD, for more than a decade the General Secretary of the German Seamen's Mission (GSM), grew up in Ostfriesland in Northwest Germany. Indoctrinated from grade school in Hitler's Nazi ideology, by 1945 he was among 1250 teenage naval cadets, hurled into the last bloody battle to defend Berlin before the advancing Russians. Barely 200 of them survived. Realizing later that he had been the victim of a counterfeit, criminal regime, he embarked on an urgent search for truth. He finally found the answer, he recounts, in the New Testament witness of him who said of his own person: "I am the Truth!" After theological studies, he served seafarers in both Bremen and Cape Town before his appointment as General Secretary of the GSM (1973-1984). As such, he was for five years also Chairman of ICMA.

New Directions?

In 1946, *Alexander Mitscherlich* wrote, "Technological developments are causing *a threat to all human existence* (my emphasis)." Technology and economics are increasingly influencing almost every area of life, but without taking into account the human cost. In the maritime world, a quick look at a modern container terminal gives a clear picture of what the problem is. The shipment of goods simply takes center stage.

My question is how can this fixation on material benefits be reconciled with the welfare of seafarers? There is, of course, no going back to a pre-industrial, pre-technological lifestyle. Seafarers' mission should be making the concept of "re-creation" possible by promoting the creation of a new humanity as such. Can we do this by doing what we have always done? Or, will we trust in *the power of hope* to help us visualize new paths?

I am convinced that Christian faith, hope and love constitute the only effective way to counteract the "threat to all human existence" that darkens the horizon and moves inexorably toward us. I would like to show how this can happen in concrete terms and to encourage us to move in new directions.

Modern Shipping—For Humanity an S.O.S.

Shipping has always been international. In that sense, "globalization" is nothing new. Global competition causes shippers to look for the cheapest labor all over the world, but without taking into account each nation's obligation to look after the social needs of its people. The consequences are always detrimental to workers. Shipowners who want to treat their employees fairly and give them a decent wage have trouble maintaining profitability in competition with companies that underpay their seafarers. Therefore, if one wants to bring about change, one must change the system itself.

A seafarer's life has always been a hard one. It has its beauties and attractions, and for people with a good character and a strong backbone it can be mastered. Under today's conditions, however, destructive elements of life on board tend to gain the upper hand. The number of seafarers from the traditional seafaring nations has declined rapidly. Workers from developing countries have replaced them, coming from places in the world where there are few jobs and much poverty. These mariners are willing to work for low wages on substandard ships under contracts that they can barely read.

As a result, seafarers have been reduced from being *homo sapiens* to an expendable, specialized form of *homo oeconomicus*. This degradation of people —to the shrunken version of humanity as a mere commodity—is for us in seafarers' mission unacceptable. Under these conditions, the old emergency signal "SOS" (Save our Souls) takes on a new urgency. No longer is it the forces of nature that primarily threaten the lives of seafarers. Far more threatening and destructive are these new societal pressures. We are in a dire state indeed if we think we cannot change the underlying societal processes.

Seafarers' Mission—a Pathfinder for the Church

Seafarers' mission has a permanent commission based on a biblical view of humanity. People need freedom from all of the forces that enslave them, and to be in a position to live life to the full under the lordship of Jesus Christ. In this Kingdom of God, according to the third article of the Apostles Creed, it is already possible to live in solidarity with others in a new community, bonded by a love that points me in the direction of my neighbor. Love is not only a feeling; it is something I express when I recognize my neighbors, try to understand them, give them respect, care for them, and take responsibility for my actions.

Since organized seafarers' mission began in the early 1800s, the work has undergone radical change. It is clear that we need a new orientation. Seafarers' mission needs to avoid any vestige of condescending care that treats seafarers as though they are unable to help themselves. We need an approach that empowers seafarers to live self-assured lives of hope, spiritual freedom, and solidarity.

Authentic solidarity is an act of conscious human fellowship, even though living conditions on board may stand in the way. This is the hour for seafarers' mission to rise to its calling and become a *pathfinder* for the Church toward the society of the future. For this reason, there should be a lively, institutionalized exchange of information between seafarers' mission and the Church.

Jesus healed and liberated individuals, but that was not all. He also called them to discipleship—to his circle of friends, fellowships that could project love and, in turn, form a worldwide network. In this new community, the deciding factor is not their employability as efficient objects. Here, they become active *subjects*, people who have rediscovered their self-worth and are in control of their own lives.

In the work of seafarers' mission we must demonstrate that the reality of the Kingdom of God—as righteousness, peace and joy (Rom. 14:17)—is available here and now. In that struggle, we are not alone. Seafarers' mission works together with the unions for the human rights of seafarers, in a way that is mutually complementary.

Hope – the Key to Change from Below

Johann Hinrich Wichern, whose *Memorandum* of 1849 led to the founding of the German Inner Mission, and eventually also the German Seamen's Mission, warned that love needed to take its place alongside faith. Significantly, he named here only two constituent elements of Christian existence, ignoring the role of *hope*. We can see now the practical consequences of this. Since hope did not become a foundational force in the church, it "emigrated" into the secular sphere and degenerated into the Marxist expectation of a classless society. In the process, the church lost the working classes—and not only them.

In spite of their nominal Christianity, Europe and North America have histories of conquest, vanity and greed. The Christian life is just the opposite. It is not the glorious victor who is to be worshipped, but rather the One who suffers and agonizes. Behind the Christian façade of Western countries lies a com-pletely different religion, one which *Erich Fromm* calls "industrial religion." Here, things that are "holy" are work, property, profit, power and success. That kind of religion is incompatible with true Christianity, since people become anonymous tools and have to sell themselves to the highest bidder.

In this context, seafarers' mission takes on a clear missionary task, one that has to involve conversion. We need to call people away from this industrial religion and show them another way, a way that leads them to life, to their own life, and to a life with and for others (John 10:10). How can this happen? The powers that oppose us can seem like a huge mountain rising up before us, causing us to overlook the little flower called "hope" that grows at the foot of the mountain. This is dangerous because despair over global abuse of power is bringing about global terrorism.

What collapsed in 1989? It was not the collapse of a socialist vision, but rather the fall of an imperialist domination. This had been just as destructive to the human spirit as any other form of domination. It became evident that the communist ideal of a classless society by means of a dictatorship of the proletariat was totally different from the Kingdom of God on earth. Communism failed, and will inevitably always fail, because people are sinful and slaves to sin. For this reason, we will never be able to bring about the Kingdom of God using only our own strength. However, what we *can* do is to work with passion in hope, love and faith that God will keep his promise to let our work bear fruit (Phil. 4:13; John 15:7-8). We believe in not only the crucifixion but also the resurrection. We need to keep *both* of these momentous events before us. Only then will we avoid exhaustion and despair.

Joseph Weizenbaum, professor of information sciences at MIT in Cambridge, Massachusetts, writes: "In my opinion, all of us today are passengers on the *Titanic*. We are heading for an iceberg, and it is too late to change course." Then he asks if there is any way in which we might be saved. His answer is, "Yes, but we need a miracle." The supposed inability of the individual to change things is a dangerous illusion. It can all too easily become a self-fulfilling prophecy. If one believes that one is powerless, one becomes in fact powerless.

Weizenbaum points to the example of *Rosa Parks*, a middle-aged black woman in Montgomery, Alabama, who was going home from work. Since she was dead tired, she took a bus seat reserved for white people. When she got the order to get up, she would not, and her resistance sparked the Civil Rights Movement. Rosa Parks did not perform a miracle. Yet, that day in 1955, she started a chain of events that would change the world. A miracle comes about when two things merge—action and *kairos* (the right time). God gives the *kairos*. The decisive action, however, has to come from us. Action requires people like Rosa Parks, not a President nor a Prime Minister.

True change always comes from below. I myself have twice been a direct witness to the kind of miracle that change from below can bring about. In November 1989, I was in Rostock when overfilled churches sang "We Shall Overcome," and thousands marched past the "Stasi" secret police building. After that, we heard the news that the Berlin Wall was coming down. In January 1993, I was a Peace Monitor in two townships of Johannesburg, South Africa. The situation was tense in the run-up to the election of *Nelson Mandela* as the nation's first black president. Our multi-racial team was there to intervene in case of a disturbance. A black woman in the enormous crowd came up to me, put her arm around me and said with a smile, "Peace for our land!" I smiled and answered, "Peace for our land!"—and wiped away the tears from my eyes. Is it unrealistic to believe in miracles? It is foolish not to.

The Kingdom of God has not yet come in its fullness anywhere in the world, neither in the former Soviet-dominated countries of Eastern Europe nor in South Africa. This world, in which Auschwitz and Hiroshima were possible, is still a world in which trillions are spent on armaments, while more than ten thousand children starve every day. However, the most revolutionary and relevant book that we possess, the New Testament, reminds us that this is also a world where the cross still stands. Moreover, it is a cross that stands in the light of Easter. That is the ultimate foundation of our hope. It is in this light that we go on board the ships. This is our mission. *We have hope on our side!*

24

WOMEN ON THE WATERFRONT

A Perspective from the Non-Western World

Irette Ramoelinina

IRETTE RAMOELININA is Chaplain-Director of Toamasina Maritime Ministry (Tomami), an affiliate of the Malagasy Lutheran Church, located in Toamasina (Tamatave), primary port city of the island republic of Madagascar. After graduation from the Lutheran Theological Seminary in Fianarantsoa, Madagascar, she received a call in 1991 to head her church body's pioneer ministry in the Port of Toamasina, thereby becoming the first woman seafarers' chaplain in the non-Western world. In 1994, she graduated from the International Training Center of the SCI in New York. From 2005, her church body appointed her Principal Lutheran Port Chaplain in Madagascar.

"No Work for a Woman"?

Maritime mission is not a human invention. It is a mission founded by Jesus Christ himself. It was by the sea that he found those whom he first called to follow him and preach the good news of the gospel to every nation (Matt. 4:18-20, 28:18-20).

I praise the Lord that he also called me, like Peter and his friends, to continue his mission to the nations. Even though my national church is still struggling with issues concerning the status of women in ministry, I am convinced that the Lord, in his love, has called me to this special mission. In connection with the role of women in maritime mission, Mary's Magnificat in the Bible is special. For even though I am a woman, I too can say with all my heart: "My soul magnifies the Lord, for he has regarded the low estate of his handmaiden" (Luke 1:47-49). Mary's mission as the mother of Jesus was, of course, unique. But because he has also entrusted a task to me, however humble, I too will rejoice and praise his name.

I was born into a Christian family in a village called Anosiarivo, about 400 kilometers from Toamasina, Madagascar's main port city, where I now work. This place was at that time like another world to me, because my village is unreachable by road and takes one week to reach by foot. I was the sixth in a family of 12 children. Due to the lack of local school facilities, I had to move from family to family during my early years. I did not have stable family relationships. However, God turned all this to good somehow, because putting my trust in Jesus gave me a sense of security and deepened my faith.

As a young adult, I committed myself to becoming a *Mpiandry* (Shepherd). This is a recognized revival movement within the Malagasy Lutheran Church, now numbering some 10,000 men and women devoted to the care of the suffering and spiritually afflicted. I had heard the call of the Lord in high school. Now it became clear to me that he wanted me to serve as pastor. Based on my exam results, I qualified for a church scholarship, entered a theological college in 1984, and then went on to our main theological seminary. While there, I prepared a thesis comparing the Levitic concept of sacrifice in the Old Testament with the concept of sacrifice in Malagasy traditional religion. I chose this theme because I wanted to explore further the uniqueness and sufficiency of Jesus' sacrifice of himself for the human race (Hebrews 7:27).

I also took a training program in prison chaplaincy led by an American missionary, Rev. *Arthur Shultz*. I would counsel, pray and lead Bible study among some 800 male and female inmates. Little did I know that this would prove to be excellent preparation for chaplaincy in another type of total institution—the world of ships and seafarers.

In August 1990, one year before graduating, I had the privilege of joining a group that attended a pioneer "Maritime Mission Seminar" in the port of Toamasina. We were different "Shepherds", doctors, teachers, port officials, social workers, and students like myself. Dr. *Roald Kverndal*, who had taken this initiative as Maritime Consultant for the Lutheran World Federation, led the seminar. Rev. *Claire Kotosoa*, Evangelism Director of the Toamasina Synod of the Malagasy Lutheran Church, provided local coordination. As a result, our national church decided, for the first time, to launch an indigenous outreach to people of the sea in the port-cities of Madagascar, beginning with Toamasina. I received an invitation to head the local ministry as Port Chaplain and commenced in October 1991, shortly after completing my studies.

Ninety percent of the people who spoke with me, however, tried to discourage me. These people gave good reasons, so it seemed. First, fellow Christians who had not attended the seminar saw no reason for any special mission for seafarers and fishers. Second, visiting ships, and ministering to such people, was certainly no work for a woman, least of all a *young* woman. Anyway, my church body still had problems with the whole issue of women in public ministry—regardless of age. In the beginning, therefore, I felt afraid.

Despite this time of testing, I soon saw I had good reasons for my decision. I may have come from a small rural community, far from any port city. However, as a Malagasy, I knew very well that my country is the world's fourth largest island, surrounded by sea on all sides. I also knew that our very origin as a nation relates us intimately to the sea. Our ancestors were seafarers, often described as the "Vikings of the Indian Ocean." In their simple yet seaworthy outriggers, they navigated thousands of miles from the islands of Indonesia and

Melanesia. In addition, for me as a Christian, that seminar in August 1990 opened up a new horizon of mission. Seafarers are today among those most deprived of the gospel and the love of Christ. Yet, like his first followers by the Sea of Galilee, once given that gospel, seafarers still have unique opportunities to spread it—wherever they go.

Instead of questioning why women should take on public ministry among people of the sea, I found myself asking: *"Why not?"* Some of our most renowned leaders have been women. Several of them were reigning monarchs, like Queen *Ranavalona II*, who converted to Christianity and became one of its warmest promoters. In the Mpiandry Movement, *Nenilava* ("Tall Mother") has been the undisputed leader. More importantly, Jesus is not only our Savior. As our Lord, he offers liberation, both from personal sin and from social sin. This includes the oppression of women. I asked Jesus directly for confirmation of my call. I got the Bible verse given to me at my graduation from seminary, Judges 6:14. Here the Lord says to Gideon at a critical moment in the history of his people: "Go in the strength you have! Am I not sending you?" That settled it.

Seafarers and Port Prostitutes

After accepting my call, I contacted the Chaplain-Director of the Toamasina branch of the Catholic Apostleship of the Sea (AOS). From that moment, I enjoyed excellent relations with Brother *Yves Aubron*, an experienced veteran in this ministry, who has since gone to be with the Lord. Every day he would take me to visit the ships. He patiently helped me to understand the very different life of the seafarer. After a year, I "graduated" and was able to visit freely on my own, often together with one or two volunteers.

The words of Mary's Magnificat make her the model of not only total trust and faith in the Lord (Luke 1:46-50). She also provides a model of prophetic response to the abuse of justice and the arrogance of power (verses 51-53). On the waterfront of Toamasina, I soon discovered how easily seafarers of today become victims of injustice, and then often just abandoned to their fate. While attending the International Training Center of the Seamen's Church Institute of New York/New Jersey in 1994, I learnt, through the Center for Seafarers' Rights there, that there was a lack of coastguard protection in African, and especially Malagasy, waters. This was attracting increased illegal, substandard shipping to the Indian Ocean. Advocating for seafarers' justice is therefore now an integral part of the overall outreach of the Toamasina Maritime Ministry (Tomami).

Shipvisiting remains at the core of this ministry. As I go up the ship's ladder, I try to take Paul's words literally by becoming, for the sake of the gospel, a Filipino for the Filipinos and a Japanese for the Japanese (1 Cor. 9:19-23). I have found that to come on board in this way, as a Christian friend, is a true privilege and a genuine joy. Here is suddenly someone with whom the seafarer can talk and share his or her burdens. There has never been any feeling of rejection because of my gender. On several occasions, I have had the joy of holding Bible study on board with Muslim crewmembers. There have been up to

20 of them at a time. The problem, if any, lies not with seafarers but with cultural prejudice ashore.

In Tomami, we have also developed a broad outreach to seafarers' family members. The families of Madagascar's coastal seafarers and fishers tend to be among the poorest of the poor, with acute social and spiritual needs. We have started counseling services, support groups, job training and Christian education programs, the latter also for the children. In 2005, the Malagasy Lutheran Church decided to make the comprehensive nature of our ministry in Toamasina the official model for an expansion of Lutheran port ministries to five other seaports in Madagascar.

A part of our overall ministry that is especially dear to my heart concerns port prostitution, a form of exploitation of women for which Toamasina has long been notorious. From the very beginning of my ministry, the sheer magnitude of this evil shocked me. At the same time, as a woman myself, I was inspired by Jesus' special compassion for the victims of this traffic. The Lord's solution was for me to become friends with them, which I have done. I uncovered three major problems among them: a lack of love from parents and family, a lack of education and spiritual nurture, and a lack of other employment opportunities. The Prostitutes' Project has worked to meet their needs for alternative income, shelter and re-motivation, as well as combating the AIDS epidemic.

Maritime mission, like all mission, is the Lord's mission, not that of any human agency. In order for it to continue, it is therefore up to him, both whom he chooses to use—men or women (John 15:16), and how he chooses to gift them (1 Cor.12:7-11). I believe he has chosen me, too—to share his good news and saving love with seafarers from around the world and the oppressed women of our port cities. My joy is to see every day how both seafarers and prostitutes accept me and trust me to do just that.

25

THE MERCHANT SHIP
AS A TOTAL INSTITUTION

Some Sociological Reflections

Ricardo Rodriguez-Martos Dauer

RICARDO RODRIGUEZ-MARTOS DAUER, a native of Barcelona, Spain, has combined four careers in his life so far. As seafarer, he sailed until 1975, eventually as master mariner. As theologian, he became a deacon in 1983, and delegate of the AOS in Spain. As lawyer, he co-founded the Center for Seafarers' Rights in Barcelona in 1988. As sociologist, he pioneered the subject "Maritime Sociology" in Spain, earning a doctorate in 1995, with his research on the ship as a total institution.

Characterization

From a sociological point of view, a merchant ship exhibits a number of characteristics that qualify it as a "total institution." According to *Erwing Goffman*, "A total institution can be defined as a place of residence and work where a large number of individuals in the same situation, isolated from society for an appreciable period of time, share in their confinement a daily routine that is formally administered" (Goffman 1972). Total institutions are all encompassing. These "twenty-four hour societies" confine people; they spend their work and leisure time within them, practically without changing their location and always subjected to a controlling authority.

If we turn to another type of total institution, a convent for example, we see that here, too, there is an organized and disciplined lifestyle with a hierarchical structure. The purpose is the development of spiritual life, and often dedication to works of charity. The convent's rules require total commitment of its members. Here, there is a clear difference from, for example, a penal institution, where inmates enter against their will.

In any institution that we can term "total," the individual loses the opportunity to change his or her role (to that of parent, spouse, employee, member of a club or social group, etc.), contrary to how any other citizen lives during the course of a day. This isolated, hierarchical structure and lack of role alternation are elements that seem necessary to fulfill an objective. They do not necessarily imply that the person within such a situation is suffering maltreatment or indignities. The structure of the total institution is, however, readily susceptible to abuse that can lead to a perverse form of communal life.

In light of the criteria cited in Goffman's definition, let us look at what happens on a merchant vessel (Rodriguez-Martos 1997): 1) It is a place for both work and leisure. 2) A varying number of individuals share the same place and situation for a period of time, regardless of rank and background. 3) The crew is physically isolated from society, now often even when in port. 4) Everyone is subject to an authority, whether this be external (the management, the ship-owners themselves) or internal (the captain and the officers).

Exploitation

We can see that structure is unavoidable and necessary, both for a ship to fulfill its objective to travel a specific maritime route, and for its crewmembers to exercise their profession and earn a salary. The problem arises when the person or group exercising authority takes undue advantage of the structure required by life aboard ship for his or her own benefit. This abuse can come from outside—from the shipowners, or from inside—from the captain or officers, abetted frequently by the passivity of governmental authorities.

Governments and administrative authorities violate the terms of international conventions when they fail to take the necessary steps to protect the rights of seafarers. This occurs when weak labor legislation allows companies to exploit a country's shipping register, in order to ignore their social, health and safety obligations toward their crewmembers. The same arises where countries ratify international conventions with strict laws governing their own subjects, but neglect to exert control over ships of other flags that visit their ports.

Shipowners, as business people, have the prime responsibility for crew-members of their ships. Problems arise when shipowners break the link with their own employees, by hiring them through intermediaries that reserve the right to fire a crewmember unilaterally. They may pay salaries below the legal amount and require an excessively long workday, knowing that crewmembers from poor countries will accept such conditions in order to secure a job. Ship-owners may owe months' worth of back pay, or not pay for vacation or insurance. Finally, they may run a ship without sufficient funds or food and, when debts become too high, allow the authorities to seize the ship, leaving their crews to fend for themselves, far from their own country.

In addition to the shipowners, the captain and officers, too, as the responsible authorities on board and colleagues of the rest of the crew, have a decisive influence and responsibility regarding the quality of life on board. The captain, or an officer, may choose to ignore flagrant injustices on board in order to obtain personal favor with the shipowner. However, by doing so, those in command flout their professional and moral obligation to do what is best for the entire crew. When we, as Christians, say that wielding authority is a means of serving others, we are not just saying pretty words. To assume that having authority entails no responsibility is to pervert its fundamental meaning.

Refutation

The IMO subcommittee on norms of training and watch-keeping states—in its November 1990 STCW session—that a ship's captain and officers should be aware of problems that may arise on board vessels with multi-national crews. Such problems may be due to linguistic, social, cultural or religious barriers. The ILO also—in its Convention No. 163 and its Recommendation No. 173—stresses that signatory governments have an obligation to look after the welfare of seafarers, both on board and in port. As a result, illegal manning agencies that charge seafarers as much as several months' pay for getting them a job should not even exist.

Multi-nationalism can create problems of communication and integration among crewmembers. These can bring about isolation, discrimination and personal confrontations that may lead to drug and alcohol dependency. This can again have negative consequences for the entire community on board (Rodriguez-Martos 1997). However, since isolation is a reality intrinsically linked to the seafarer's profession, it is of little use to lament the fact that he must spend months away from home. Rather, one should focus on enabling him to pursue his daily life and work in a way that is fair and respects his human dignity. This includes providing him with the means for constructive leisure time activities that match his cultural needs and customs.

Maritime missions should be *"thirsty for justice"* (Rodriguez-Martos 1992). Then they will receive a blessing themselves while fulfilling their mission of love to their neighbors in the maritime world. They may do this by: 1) Promoting an atmosphere of respect for humanity and justice on shipboard, through direct contact with the people working at sea. 2) Supporting those who suffer injustice with advice, assistance and—if necessary—legal action. 3) Playing a visible role with shipowners and other public and private entities in the maritime industry.

In this way, maritime missions can be truly prophetic. They should not stir up prejudice against those who do not respect the dignity of seafarers. Rather, they should proactively oppose their actions and attempt to persuade them about a better way. Sins of omission tend to be the more common. The gospels call attention to them, both in the parable of the Good Samaritan (Luke 10:25-37), and in the words of the Last Judgment (Matt. 25:31-46). Indifference or passivity is a negative testimony to the great, positive mission to which the gospels call us all. Maritime missions must pursue a policy worthy of their divine vocation!

26

SEAFARERS INTERNATIONAL RESEARCH CENTRE

Purposes, Projects and Priorities

Helen Sampson

 *HELEN SAMPSON has, since 2003, served as Director of the Seafarers International Research Center (SIRC) at the Department of Maritime Studies of the Cardiff-based University of Wales. After graduate studies in Education, Economics and Social Studies, she earned her PhD in Sociology. Before joining the research staff of SIRC in 1999, she served in research, training and education capacities within Sociology and Social Welfare at several other institutions. At SIRC, Dr. Sampson has authored and co-authored a series of publications relating to research projects about multi-national crews, maritime training, women seafarers, seafarers' family life, and broader issues of maritime health and safety.*

Purposes

The Seafarers International Research Centre (SIRC) was set up in 1995, in order to develop research on occupational health and safety issues in the shipping industry. The intention was to produce scientific research that would be of interest to both academic audiences and industry stakeholders. As such, staff at SIRC was aware of the special need to research and write for two quite different audiences—a challenge that they have proved equal to. In doing so, they aimed to inform policy at international, national, and sub-national levels, and to contribute to a raising of standards across the industry in relation to the health and welfare of seafarers.

The Center's purpose has never formally altered, and it remains focused on both the shipping industry and occupational health and safety in their broadest sense. This understanding of occupational health and safety has allowed research at the Center to cover a wide range of topics. These include issues that relate to the regulation of the industry, education and training, fraudulent certification, living and working conditions, gender issues, and seafarers' health.

In the period 2000 to 2003, the Center additionally produced a statistical dataset based upon data gleaned from crew list collection and indicative of the size and composition of the global seafarer labor market. The Director at the time, *Tony Lane*, supplemented this by commissioning a series of regional labor market reports for the SIRC website.

Since 2003, and with the encouragement of its sponsors, the Center has sought to return to a closer focus on occupational health and safety. In 2004, the Lloyd's Register Research Unit developed, within SIRC, a research program related to safety and concerns associated with the interface between ships as technical systems and seafarers as human beings. The Research Unit commenced in April and engaged in two studies in the first year of its operation: a study of the introduction of new technology and training systems; also, a study of perceptions of risk within the industry as these pertain to seafaring.

SIRC was able to welcome a further new development in 2004, with the award of a grant from the Nippon Foundation, allowing students to undertake Mphil/PhD degrees in social science focusing upon seafarers. The first five Nippon Foundation fellows arrived at SIRC in September 2004 and surpassed all expectations in their first year. All things being equal, we expect this program to run for a minimum period of five years. We hope that it will produce scholars capable of establishing an international network of professionals conducting research on seafarers across the world.

Projects

Recent and current formal research projects at SIRC include these topics, commissioned by both governmental and non-governmental organizations:

- Flag State Audit: Analyzing the effectiveness of regulatory regimes
- Port State Control and ILO Conventions
- Fraudulent Practices Associated with Certificates
- Seafarers' Outreach Welfare Schemes: Sailing Chaplains, Worker Priests and Political Commissars
- Transnational Seafarer Communities
- Women Seafarers in World Shipping
- Abandoned Ships and their Crews
- Global Labor Market Database: Ongoing from 2003
- The Transformation of the Chinese Seafarer Labor Market
- Improving the Quality of Maritime Education in Europe & Asia-Pacific
- Fatigue, Health and Injury Among Seafarers
- Seafarers' Sexual Risk Behavior
- Stress Prevention Activities (SPA)

From year to year, SIRC Annual Reports regularly list the many books, journal papers, conference lectures, reports and other publications contributed by SIRC staff, on topics related to seafarers' health, safety and welfare issues.

Candidates connected with the Center are currently undertaking

MPhil/PhD studies on the following topics:
- Risk behavior and collision avoidance
- A study of emotional health and UK cadet recruitment and retention
- A study in collaboration with the Standard P & I Club

Nippon Foundation fellows at the Center are currently planning research projects on the following topics:
- Globalization and the international labor market
- A study of regulatory standards as operated by Second Registers
- The impact of the internet on seafarers and their families
- Safe navigation and collision avoidance
- The implementation of the ISM Code in relation to shore-side occupational health and safety management systems

SIRC is planning future studies with a stronger occupational health and safety link. These include research on food and nutrition, further studies of fraud, regulation, training, and research related specifically to seafarer health.

Priorities

The main priority for SIRC in the coming years is to retain its direction while securing new funding. This will allow it to continue to undertake independent research related to seafarers' health and welfare. The independence of the Center is vital to its success. It originated thanks to the support of two major bodies: Cardiff University and the ITF Seafarers' Trust.

The intention, however, was always to attract funding from a variety of sources, and SIRC has enjoyed some success in this. As well as the recent and substantial support received from the Nippon Foundation and Lloyd's Register, the Center has won grants and contracts from the Economic and Social Research Council (ESRC), International Labour Organisation (ILO), International Maritime Organization (IMO), European Commission, Millennium Challenge Account (MCA), International Shipping Federation (ISF), British Academy and, lately, from Emergency Medical Services Authority (EMSA). The challenge is to secure sufficient funds to remain both independent and significant in scale.

Ultimately, the Center's priority is to produce scientific work of high quality for the benefit of the maritime industry and the welfare of seafarers. To this end, SIRC is committed to publishing as much of its work as possible on-line and in a format that is widely accessible. Additionally, staff members contribute a regular article to the widely distributed seafarers' newspaper, *The Sea,* produced by the Mission to Seafarers. The Center also hosts a symposium every two years at which members of staff report their research findings to a highly diverse audience from across the maritime community. These priorities indicate the importance SIRC attaches to dissemination, also its commitment to both academic rigor and serving the maritime sector and seafarers in particular.

27

LIVING TEMPLES AT SEA
A Call for Physical Health and Wellness

Darrell Schoen

DARRELL. E. SCHOEN grew up far from the ocean, on a farm in Southern Indiana. After completing an M.Div. degree at Concordia Seminary, St. Louis, Missouri, he served a five-year term as missionary in the Philippines, returning to serve as a university campus pastor in California and later Washington State. Meanwhile, he pursued further degree work in Cultural Anthropology at Ateneo de Manila, and Near Eastern Studies at the University of Washington. In recent years, he has served as port chaplain with the Seattle-based Lutheran Maritime Minis-
try of Puget Sound, while also engaging himself in health and wellness issues, both at sea and ashore.

How "Holistic" Are We?

Captain *James Cook* is not only famous for bringing the vast Pacific Ocean within the known world of the late 1700s. He also made history by banishing that bane of deep-sea sailors everywhere—the debilitating disease of scurvy. Despite initial threats of mutiny by his crew, Cook's combination of strict hygiene and a diet rich in citrus fruits and other healthy foods soon paid off. Where others could lose half the ship's company to disease on long voyages, Captain Cook's crews would nearly all survive. This was a time when no one had even heard about "vitamins"—nor yet about "seafarers' mission."

Contrary to widely held stereotypes, the pioneers of such mission were not narrow-minded "sky pilots," only interested in saving souls for heaven. Without any preconceived notion of what has since been termed "holistic" ministry, there is powerful evidence that they, too, did seek to serve the physical as well as spiritual and mental needs of seafarers of their day (Kverndal 1986, 315).

Succeeding decades have seen great improvements in crew conditions since the "coffin-ships" of yesteryear. Nevertheless, recent SIRC studies continue to provide documentation of totally unacceptable levels of ill health, abuse and mortality among modern-day seafarers and fishers. There is today broad consensus on the gospel's call to wholeness and the need for a truly balanced, holistic approach in maritime ministry. However, much still remains to be done. Without adequate attention to seafarers' *physical* health as well, how can maritime ministry claim to be authentically *holistic*? The following explores the shape of a biblical foundation for physical health as an inherent component of a Christian concept of holistic human welfare—in body, mind and spirit.

What Does Scripture Have to Say?

Contemporary theologians have produced a growing list of publications on "Body Theology," highlighting the "incarnational" aspects of creation and redemption as revealed in Scripture. The writer is indebted to the research of *Carl E.* and *LaVonne Braaten.* In their groundbreaking book, *The Living Temple,* the Braatens build on St. Paul's challenge to the early Christians in Corinth: "Do you not know that your body is a temple of the Holy Spirit, who is in you, whom you have received from God? You are not your own, you were bought at a price. Therefore, honor God with your body!" (1 Cor. 6:19-20). In providing a biblical basis for viewing the physical body as a dwelling place of the Spirit, Scripture traces a "Trinitarian" sequence. This may be summarized as follows:

—*Living Temples Created by God:* According to the Genesis account, when God first created human beings as "male and female," they were—like all of his original creation—"very good" (Gen.1:31). Marveling at the sheer miracle of that act, the Psalmist would later exclaim, "I praise you because I am fearfully and wonderfully made!" (Psalm 139:14). Just think, 100 trillion cells interacting in perfect harmony! Yet what really set those first human beings apart was that God made them "in his own image" (Gen. 1:27). In so doing, the Spirit of God that had moved over the face of the waters breathed into those human nostrils "the breath of life"—in all its fullness (Gen. 2:7). See Brand and Yancey 1980.

—*Living Temples Recreated in the Son of God:* After the first humans had reaped the disastrous results of ruptured relations with their Creator, restoring that relationship would make up the central theme of divine revelation. In due time, "the Word became flesh, and made his dwelling among us" (John 1:14). Paraphrasing Martin Luther, Christ in the flesh is the solid certainty of God's love. By his self-embodiment ("incarnation") in his Son, God in his infinite love has opened for all the possibility of a new beginning (2 Cor. 5:17; Phil.2:6-10).

—*Living Temples filled with the Spirit:* What God did for all of creation— through the birth, death and resurrection of Christ—becomes immediately available through the Spirit. It began at Pentecost, when all were "filled with the Holy Spirit" (Acts 1:8; 2:4). Since then, just as the Word became flesh in the *first* incarnation of Christ, his Spirit now becomes embodied in a *second* kind of incarnation—within the body of every believer in him. It is the human body that has now become the vehicle for the reconciling and healing ministry of Christ, through believers acting out the gifts of the Spirit (1 Cor. 12:1-31; Gal. 5:22-26).

What Are the Practical Implications?

If the human body is meant to house the Spirit of God and honor God by serving others, this calls for a corresponding level of holistic care—of body, mind and spirit. History is replete with examples of extremist error, ranging from a "hedonism" that sees physical self-satisfaction as the primary purpose of life to a "spiritualism" that degrades the body to a prison from which the spirit needs to be freed. By contrast, the concept of "Living Temples" calls for a form of "body stewardship" that focuses on the frequently overlooked need for *preventive health care—not just curing disease.*

Christianity was born as a religion of healing (Matthew 10:7-8). Yet what good would it do to give a shot in the arm and then leave a person to repeat the folly that caused the condition in the first place? However wonderfully made, the body cannot function well without the fundamental requirements of healthy living. This does not have to lead to an "idolatry of health" (Denton 2005, 33 ff), one that distorts the balance between ultimate and penultimate concerns (Matt. 16:26). However, leading authorities in the field (like Strand 2004) do agree that healthy living in today's world will normally include three main components:

—*Healthy Diet:* There is now abundant evidence that the overuse of "junk-food" and fatty "fast foods" can lead to both obesity and toxicity. Indiscriminate intake of highly processed ingredients like white flour, sugar and saturated fats, as well as high levels of preservatives and food coloring, can compromise health and displace good alternatives. Gaining attention as a healthy replacement is the "Mediterranean" diet. The people of that part of the world emphasize fish and poultry, fresh fruit and vegetables, accompanied by olive oil, whole-grain bread, pasta, nuts, seeds, beans, garlic, herbs, low-fat cheese and yoghurt.

—*Moderate Exercise:* The old adage "Use it or lose it!" certainly applies to our physical and mental faculties. Studies continue to confirm the health benefits of 30 minutes of appropriate exercise at least three times a week. Those benefits include improving circulation, boosting metabolism, burning up excess calories and body fat, as well as strengthening bones, muscles and the immune system. All of which reduce the risk of heart attacks, stroke, cancer, chronic depression, even Alzheimer's disease. Aerobics, swimming, brisk walking, whatever works to give a safe pulse increase is up to each individual. At all events, nothing can make de-conditioning and disease more inevitable than just doing nothing.

—*Nutritional Supplements: Hippocrates*, the father of medicine in ancient Greece, said, "Let food be thy medicine!" However, given today's depleted food and polluted environment, supplements play a crucial role in making up the resulting deficiencies. With each year of life, the human body's ability to absorb essential nutrients decreases. Natural remedies are available as vitamins (mainly from fruits and vegetables), minerals (from inorganic sources) and herbs (from very select plants). Consulting with medical professionals who are trained in nutritional health is important. While indiscriminate or excessive use may well be detrimental, it is a proven fact that the wise use of nutritional supplements will normally make a real difference to the human body's delicately balanced ecosystem and its ability to repel the many poisons that assail it.

How Does This Relate to Maritime Ministry Today?

Is physical health care really a legitimate concern of Christian-based maritime ministry? After all, a ship has always been basically a floating "total institution," but nowadays personal choices are even further constrained by the severe limitations of time and space imposed by modern-day crew conditions. In principle, however, no concept of maritime mission can be loyal to the diaconal dimension of Christ's Great Commission without an incarnational ministry for the benefit of seafarers' physical welfare. In practice, maritime ministers have themselves promoted seafarers' physical wellbeing wherever possible. They have also engaged with secular agencies in advocating for seafarers' health as an issue of social justice, now in coordination with their own specialized Center for Seafarers' Rights and its associates. Hopefully, the day will come when there will be a corresponding Christian-based *Center for Seafarers' Health.*

In that context, ICMA agencies are already closely involved with the ICSW in its recently launched *Seafarers' Health Information Program (SHIP).* This seeks to maximize whatever opportunities life aboard ship does allow to address specific physical health issues, such as wholesome food, safety concerns, stress, fatigue, fitness programs, weight control, malaria and HIV-AIDS. Physical health at sea not only affects the overall wellbeing of the seafaring community, including, of course, its family members. Healthy and energized crews directly impact the productivity of the shipping industry. Companies can decisively enhance the effectiveness of programs like SHIP through their catering departments and personnel policies, for example in connection with the use of nicotine, alcohol, and other addictive substances. At all these levels, maritime ministry can participate—or at least advocate.

How can the multi-cultural modern-day maritime work-force, with so many active adherents of non-Christian faiths, relate to a typically biblical concept, in this case the human body as a Temple of the Spirit—of Christ? Given the increasing emphasis on "seafarer-centered" maritime ministry, such a connection can, in actual fact, become more realistic than ever. With more and more committed Christians serving as *Ministering Seafarers,* these can each portray—through their daily walk of faith—visible examples of a healthy life-style at sea. They can also promote physical health concerns on board as a witness of practical, unconditional love within the wider shipboard community.

Meanwhile, *professional chaplains* (whether "sailing" or shore-based) can play a decisive supportive role—by both encouragement and (perhaps even more so) by their personal example in healthy living. Besides offering sports and workout opportunities, *seafarers' centers* can (as some already do) integrate items like fruit, wholesome snacks and refreshments into their ministry of hospitality, as well as top-quality supplements in their slop-chest. A segment on physical health care must, of course, become an inherent part of future *training curricula* for both Ministering Seafarers and those who serve them, whether in a professional or volunteer capacity. Together, all can work toward God's intent for everyone—to become *Living Temples at Sea*—and everywhere!

28

OILRIG CHAPLAINCY

Reflections on Offshore Maritime Ministry

Annette Tronsen Spilling

ANNETTE TRONSEN SPILLING was born in Hamburg, Germany, where her father, a pioneer athletics chaplain, was serving as chaplain-director for the Norwegian Seamen's Mission, a calling she, too, would one day follow. After first heading that Mission's shore-based centers in Gothenburg, Sweden, then in San Pedro, California, she became, from 1994, a pioneer herself as the first woman in the world to serve full-time as an oilrig chaplain. Meanwhile, she has also pursued graduate studies in the field of mental health. Currently, she is pastoring a parish of the Church of Norway in Vegårshei, near the south-coast port of Tvedestrand.

How It All Began

In all the years the Norwegian Seamen's Mission has existed, its representatives have always pursued the primary strategy of reaching out to people with some kind of connection to seafaring. My own background, as the daughter of a seafarers' chaplain, has given me a deep love for my church, especially for the "down to earth" way of its maritime mission—meeting people just wherever they happen to be.

The year 1982 saw the appointment of the first chaplain to serve on a permanent basis on Norwegian-owned oilrigs—for all I know perhaps also the first worldwide. Some of us in the Norwegian Seamen's Mission had served on oilrigs during Christmas the previous two years. However, the tragic "Alexander Kjelland" disaster and other accidents showed the North Sea offshore oil industry's leadership how important it could be for their workers to have access to chaplaincy support, not only in general, but especially after experiencing traumatic events.

For some, the idea of having a full-time chaplain on a rig was difficult in the beginning. However, many of the oilrig workers themselves already knew what a seafarers' mission was all about. There, they had personally gained positive experiences and knew they could always count on a warm welcome. By contrast, churches in Norway have not as a rule been equally successful in reaching the many non-churchgoing people.

Rev. *Knut Mölbach*, himself an experienced seafarers' chaplain, became the first Norwegian oilrig chaplain. With the warmth of his personality and his ability to tell good jokes, he opened many doors. The gift of humor has often been a trademark of seafarers' chaplains. For me, however, that did not always come easily. I do not consider myself very funny, and do not appear to have inherited my father's facility for telling good stories. Fortunately, no one has ever seemed to hold that against me.

My Own Oilrig Odyssey

Actually, I started out as a regular seafarers' chaplain. When the Norwegian Seamen's Mission announced another oil rig chaplaincy opening, my husband encouraged me to apply, even though he knew this would mean a more strenuous job for himself, partly alone at home with two small children. We had then already served shore-based seafarers' centers for six years in Gothenburg, Sweden, then two years in San Pedro, California, and I had no regrets. Still, I had really hoped I would get an oilrig position, because this meant I could keep alternating between being a full-time chaplain at work and a 100% mom at home.

I soon discovered that working on oilrigs was like an extended ship-visit. In the beginning, I felt quite a little insecure. Where would I go first? What should I say? Would they appreciate my visiting them? Perhaps seafarers may have a similar sense of insecurity at the thought of entering a church environment. Our challenge is—how can we make people feel at ease and more at home in church? I believe part of the answer is first to meet them on the outside, at work, in their own activities. That way we can come across as fellow human beings, and first become their friends.

To begin with, oilrig workers would confuse us female chaplains with being a nurse or a kitchen worker. Nevertheless, they soon seemed to accept us for what we really were—chaplains by vocation. Sometimes we would even enjoy a special level of goodwill, because they found they did not agree with biases they had heard against women pastors ashore. In addition, if (as in many cases) there were also female workers on board, they and we would tend to feel a special bond of affinity.

It has never seemed to matter that I do not have first-hand knowledge of technical maritime terms about rigs, etc. They accept that. They appreciate talking about family and work relationships. Some people theorize that it is easier for males to be open with a woman. That may often be true, but not necessarily so. Many of my male colleagues have training in family therapy and conflict resolution, and maintain excellent rapport also with their own gender.

Occasionally, oilrig workers have been surprised that I would not feel I should always be at home with my children. It is difficult for them to understand that family life can also be healthy and stable when a father is left with the main responsibility. During a chat in the lunch-room one day, I happened to mention that my husband and I were attending a course on marital communication. One man was startled and exclaimed, "Do *you* really need that?" A good exchange followed, where he admitted that he found family life quite difficult, and we could talk through some of his problems.

In order to be as accessible as possible, I would try to be in a different coffee-shop every work break. When they arranged security meetings, I would participate in order to identify with them and learn all I could about what they were doing. They could also page me if needed, and I would let the radio officer know if I left one platform to go to another, so I could always be on call.

The Gospel and Church Offshore

On the "Ekofisk" rig we would normally have devotion and prayers in the chapel two evenings a week. There was consensus that we would focus on the core content of the gospel that we had in common, not on our denominational differences. Of course, I have also often prayed with individuals—any time, anywhere it might seem right. This would include being outside on a very noisy platform. Here I might not be able to hear the other's prayer, but I would say "Amen" anyway, and could sense the fellowship right there!

Of course, Christmas-time is important for all those from some kind of a Christian background. Seafarers have often said it is just not Christmas if a pastor or his/her representative is not around. Nearly everyone feels they need to attend a Christmas service. Christmas is when they miss their families most, and may well express an increased need to talk with someone other than their workmates. Significantly, around that time someone often becomes ill on board a typical oilrig, usually with heart or gastric problems. In that case, they might need a helicopter for transportation to a hospital ashore.

In many ways, it is an advantage to have women working on board such a male-dominated place of employment. Some industry observers have suggested that more women as chaplains could help "normalize" the gender imbalance in this North Sea work environment. For many, encountering a male church worker might at first seem to pose a threat, at least for oilrig workers who do not normally go to church. These might well feel pre-judged, if they are living with a partner outside of marriage, or have been divorced, or for other reasons do not somehow seem to fit into a "church lifestyle."

A guideline in my work has been to be easily available—but also easily *avoidable*! The church is not there to pressure, but should be easy and comfortable to contact. Oilrig chaplaincy is just such an unbelievably rich ministry—serving the Lord Jesus by living as a Christian among this special type of seafarer, from 7 am to 7 pm. This is a ministry where so often the most effective witness may mean being just a fellow human being—not always a preacher.

29

SEAFARERS AND JUSTICE
The Role of the Church
Douglas B. Stevenson

DOUGLAS B. STEVENSON has been Director of the Center for Seafarers' Rights of the Seamen's Church Institute (SCI) of New York/New Jersey since 1990. Before that, he served twenty years in the US Coast Guard, retiring as Commander after serving in various operational and legal assignments, including command at sea and a diplomatic post at the US Mission to the UN. As a graduate of Miami School of Law, he is also an attorney-at-law, and serves as an advisor in relation to several governmental and non-governmental maritime-related institutions.

When I began my work at the Center for Seafarers' Rights in 1990, there was considerable discussion about whether the Church should be involved in advocacy. Now, the interest seems to have shifted away from *whether* to *how* it should do so. We know, from the Church's own teachings, that the Church does have a role in seeking justice for oppressed seafarers. More significantly, we know this from the Church's actions. I can personally vouch for the Church's commitment here from years of working with port chaplains around the world.

At the Center for Seafarers' Rights, several theological foundations have been our guide. Micah 6:8 says: "And what does the Lord require of you but to do justice, and to love kindness, and to walk humbly with your God?" In our Baptismal Covenant, many of us have promised to "strive for justice and peace among all peoples and respect the dignity of every human being." *John Paul II,* in his 1981 encyclical "Laborem Exercens," provides a pivotal statement of Christians' responsibility for social justice everywhere in this global era.

All this leads me to believe that, for seafarers too, promoting justice is not an optional part of our work, but rather it is mandated. In this context, I like to refer to the familiar parable of the Good Samaritan. This is a particularly appealing biblical passage to me, not just because it involves a lawyer, but because it goes beyond the question of what is the law to how do we apply the law to real life situations.

You will recall that, after telling the parable, Jesus asked the lawyer which of the three—the priest, the Levite or the Samaritan—was truly a neighbor to the stranger. When the lawyer replied, "The one who showed mercy on him," Jesus commanded the lawyer to "Go and do likewise." As maritime ministers, whether we are lawyers, priests, volunteers or professionals, we should not need any reminder of our obligation to be friends to the friendless or to show mercy to strangers in our midst. But we do need to reflect on how we are to do this. How are we to show mercy to strangers or seek justice for oppressed seafarers in real life situations?

Just how do we "go and do likewise" with the dilemma of both ministering to the American or European seafarer whose job has been displaced by a foreign seafarer and, at the same time, ministering to that same foreign seafarer who is the subject of exploitation and discrimination? Or, how do we go and do likewise with the frightened South African seafarer who tells the port chaplain that the aging bulk carrier, on which he has his sole livelihood, has bad drinking water, spoiled food, and a long list of safety violations? Or again, how do we go and do likewise with the Filipino fisherman who tells the port chaplain that he fears for his life, because he has witnessed the officers on his Taiwanese fishing vessel murder one of his countrymen and then cover up the murder?

These, and others like them, are thorny questions. Such cases of blatant oppression challenge both us and our mission in the maritime world. So much is expected of us, yet we often feel alone and ill equipped to respond effectively. This seems like how the disciples must have felt when they were confronted with that huge problem in the wilderness near Bethsaida. Over 5,000 people had followed Jesus there, to hear his words and to feel his healing touch. It was getting late in the day and the crowd was getting hungry. There were no food stores nearby and, even if there had been, the disciples did not have enough money to buy food for such a crowd. They identified the problem. They had a hungry crowd on their hands, and they knew they could not feed them. So they asked Jesus to send the crowd away to fend for themselves.

Instead, Jesus answered, "You give them something to eat." "Lord, we have only five loaves and two fish," the disciples protested. Was their response any different from ours, when we feel overwhelmed by the tasks before us? Jesus blessed the loaves and fish and distributed them among the crowd. After all had eaten and were satisfied, we read there were twelve baskets left over.

That is the Good News. Even though we do not have what it takes to do everything on our own, we know that, with each other and with God's mercy, there is enough—more than enough—to do what we need to do. Identifying seafarers' problems is not so difficult. We do not have to look for problems on ships; the problems will find us. What is difficult, though, is identifying the resources, both within us and around us, to help solve the problems, and to prevent them from recurring.

We in the Church are certainly not the only ones who are working to promote safe and decent conditions for seafarers. Many others have recognized that the maritime industry's health depends upon its ability to operate safe, well-run ships. Let us first look at six of these other institutions.

First, the *shipowners*. These are ultimately responsible for providing decent working and living conditions for seafarers on their ships—and a great many of them still do so. However, since the early 1970s, shipowners are no longer traditional maritime companies that understand the importance of taking good care of their crews. More and more of them are merely investors interested in short-term profits. These hire ship management companies to operate their vessels at the lowest possible cost, leaving their seafarers all too often the losers.

Second, the *International Transport Workers Federation (ITF) and trade unions*: When owners fail in their responsibilities, the ITF and the trade unions become the next maritime institutions in line to seek justice for seafarers. Both have a remarkable record of supporting seafarers' rights and improving living and working standards on ships around the world. However, trade unions do not necessarily protect all seafarers, particularly those from developing countries. Moreover, some countries simply prohibit them.

Third, we should expect the country of the ship's registry, *the flag state,* to guarantee decent standards on their ships. However, in the early 1970s, the maritime industry saw many shipowners changing their ships' registry from their own country to countries that allowed the use of low salaried foreign labor, and where taxes and inspection standards likewise were low. Since then, their number has grown greatly. Many of these countries have no maritime experience, lack the infrastructure or political will to regulate ships flying their flags, and do not adequately protect the seafarers who work on their ships.

The fourth institution that should help protect seafarers is the country of their citizenship, *the labor-supplying country.* For many developing countries, exporting labor is a major source of revenue. These countries know that if their seafarers cost too much or "cause problems," then shipowners will simply hire seafarers from other countries. Their motivation to protect their own revenues often overshadows their interest in protecting the rights of their citizens.

Fifth, when countries seriously seek to establish protections for their seafarers, they look to *two specialized agencies of the United Nations* for help: the International Labour Organisation (ILO) and the International Maritime Organisation (IMO). ILO sets international *labor* standards on ships while IMO sets international *safety* standards on them. However, there are two basic problems frustrating their efforts. First, both IMO and ILO use a system of consensus that produces lowest common denominator standards. Second, once the standards are adopted, there is no international enforcement mechanism.

The sixth industry institution is *the port state.* In order to protect their own interest—especially those related to pollution control and maritime safety—port states are becoming more willing to inspect foreign ships entering their ports. However, their inspection standards are usually just those lowest common denominator standards established by IMO and ILO. Also, port states have resources to inspect only a fraction of the foreign vessels that actually arrive.

Based on these trends, we can expect more and more problems landing in the last safety net for seafarers: *the Church*. The issue is: How will the Church respond to the seafarers' cries for help? In addition to those mentioned above, other pressing problems include discrimination, wage and contract problems, abandonment, denial of medical care, bad food and water, filthy living conditions, fatigue, demoralization and boredom, to name just a few. Now, since 9/11, we need to add the burdens that security regulations impose on seafarers, including new duties, more stress, restrictions on shore leave and restrictions on visitors' access to ships. We need to help the authorities understand that security is enhanced by recognizing merchant mariners as allies in the war on terrorism, rather than treating them as if they were potential terrorists themselves.

The Center for Seafarers' Rights (CSR) is one example of how the Church works to promote justice for seafarers. The CSR is a division of the Seamen's Church Institute of New York and New Jersey. From our offices in the South Street Seaport district of New York City, we conduct three main programs:

In our *legal assistance program*, we provide free legal advice, counseling and referrals to needy merchant seafarers around the world, and to the port chaplains who serve them. We also maintain a library and resource center.

In our *education program,* we try to help seafarers help themselves by informing them of their rights, through booklets that we publish and articles that we write for various periodicals. To help empower also those who minister to seafarers, we have developed a training workshop on seafarers' rights for port chaplains, center directors, volunteers and ship visitors.

In our a*dvocacy program* of "prophetic justice," it is not enough only to seek solutions to individual seafarers' problems. We share our experiences and insights with decision makers in industry and government, in order to change the conditions that cause the problems in the first place. In so doing, we enlist the unique experience of port chaplains. Because seafarers share with chaplains their innermost feelings, no one knows more than they about what life is really like aboard merchant ships. We at the CSR are just one voice. We believe that, by coordinating with the efforts of others, the Church could have a much bigger voice in the maritime industry. To that end, we work closely with not only our justice ministry colleagues in the Mission to Seafarers in London and the Apostleship of the Sea in Barcelona, but also with ICMA and NAMMA.

It is crucial to realize that the Church is not peripheral to the maritime industry, but an essential part of it. In many ports, where nations are beginning to meet their obligation under international law to provide welfare facilities for visiting foreign crewmembers, this is not due to governments but to voluntary church agencies. For our own part, too, it is crucial to understand that we in the Church can make a real difference in the maritime world. We may have only five loaves and two fish. The good news is that by working together in our ports, in our societies, and ecumenically, through God's mercy there will be enough— more than enough—for us to fulfill Christ's command to go and do likewise.

30

MINISTRY AMONG FISHERS
Issues of Justice, Safety and Health
Gérard Tronche

GERARD TRONCHE M.Afr., who was born in Southwestern France, is a Catholic priest belonging to the "Society of Missionaries of Africa." After theological studies in England, his order assigned him to Tanzania in 1960, where he ministered for many years among nomadic fishing communities along Lake Tanganyika. In 1988, the AOS appointed him port chaplain in Dar-es-Salaam. In 1994, the Vatican called him to the AOS International Secretariat in Rome, eventually as General Secretary. After "retiring" to Mauritania in 2004, he has remained active as West Africa's Regional Coordinator for the International Committee on Seafarers' Welfare.

Hard Facts about Fishing and Fishers

Along sea and ocean shores, in coastal waters, great lakes and rivers, human beings have for millennia been fishing to earn a living or simply survive. In our era, modern technology and massive financial investment in ships and fishing-gear have made it possible for fishers to go out onto the high seas, carrying with them a staggering capacity for catching and preserving fish.

Today, the estimated number of fishers in the world is near 50 million. While an estimated half a million of these are industrial or deep-sea fishers—working on sophisticated seagoing vessels—the others are artisinal or coastal fishers, engaged in small-scale fishing in domestic waters. The members of fishers' families probably number over 200 million. Together with the fishers themselves, they make up a population of at least one quarter of a billion people.

Not only fishers as such, but also the whole world population, have a stake in these issues. Fishers risk their lives to satisfy the insatiable appetites of fish-protein eaters in developed countries, with food that their own chronically poor cannot afford. Meanwhile, developing countries earn precious foreign exchange through the labors of fellow-citizens who happen to be fishers, while the latter themselves often have to sell their whole catch simply to survive.

Fishing is among the world's most dangerous professions. Yet few realize that workers on fishing vessels actually rank as the "least protected" among all professions in the maritime world. For the international community at large, it would seem that issues like protecting the marine environment from pollution, saving endangered species of fish and promoting the marketing of fish catches, have become the only matters of public concern. These issues, however valid, have assumed greater importance than the welfare of the people who continue to risk their lives in this hostile environment. That applies also, of course, to the consequences for families who depend on those who are out there.

A Christian Perspective

However sad it may be, fishers are generally taken for granted or just forgotten—like their fellow seafarers on other ships. Travelers on board a cruise ship are visible, but not the crew. Containers piling up in ports are in full view, but not those who have toiled to transport them there from half a world away. Everybody expects to find fish at the market. Yet who wants to hear about those who undergo such incredible hardships in order to bring that same fish ashore?

As a Catholic missionary in Tanzania, I experienced this irony first hand, serving for years on the shores of the 700 km long Lake Tanganyika and later in Dar es Salaam on the coast of the Indian Ocean. How often have I not heard people refer to fishers and their families—whether Christians, Muslims or followers of traditional religions—as "those drunkards, cannabis smokers, foul-mouthed, promiscuous guys whom you simply cannot trust for anything. . . ."

Jesus knew fishers and trusted them. What a contrast! Nowhere do we find more dramatic evidence of how Jesus values fishers than during the first days of his public ministry. It was there, by the Sea of Galilee, that he called his first followers—right in the midst of their daily chores as professional fishers, tending their boats and washing their nets. Jesus saw people who were proud of their work, who would be willing to give him a fair hearing and change their minds if proved wrong. In short, Jesus saw them, loved them—and trusted them.

As the Risen Christ, he never changed that attitude. One of those fishers, the Apostle John, has recorded (in chapter 21 of his narrative) how Jesus, shortly after his resurrection, made a point of meeting them on the same waterfront. Here Jesus renewed the flagging faith of Peter and his colleagues, back on the beach, busy with their original vocation. It was here he now reaffirmed their new calling—this time with no less than a global goal in view. Entrusting them with his message of redemption, he told them to "go into all the world, and proclaim the good news to the whole creation" (Mark 16:15).

The mission of Christian-based seafarers' ministry is to spread that message of hope in the maritime world. This means to witness by both personally working toward that end, and inviting all people of good will to join in. The overall objective is to help facilitate the fulfillment of Jesus' own solemn promise: "I came that they might have life and have it abundantly!" (John 10:10). Christians believe that justice, safety and health are an inherent part of the "abundant life" that Christ came to bring to all his sisters and brothers on land and sea—even to those who may never know him here on earth.

Fishers who accept this Christian perspective can find a unique source of self-respect and face the trials of life without fear. Moreover, those engaged in maritime ministry will find it impossible to address effectively issues of justice, safety and health among fishers unless—just like Jesus—they, too, come to "see, love and trust" those fishers. That means recognizing the dignity of their work, and also their personhood as created in the image of the same God and Father.

Christ loves and trusts fishers— fishers are called to love and trust Christ! Ultimately, it is this truth that represents the Christian perspective, and remains the foremost challenge for all who seek to serve them.

Implications for Maritime Ministry

Compared with this Christian view of ministry among fishers, the harsh realities of today's maritime world are starkly different. At the International Conference of ICMA in South Africa in 1999, Father *Bruno Ciceri* CS, director of the AOS Stella Maris Center in Kaohsiung, Taiwan, offered a paper entitled "Fishermen—the Forgotten Seamen." It became a wake-up call far and wide.

Father Ciceri paints a vivid picture of the vulnerability of today's average fisher. Although many fishworkers are women, most seagoing fishers are very young men, uneducated, usually from developing countries, where widespread unemployment is just a fact of life. Dreaming of job opportunities on deep-sea fishing vessels, they become easy prey for unscrupulous recruiting agents. Hired with fraudulent contracts, they are whisked away thousands of miles to a small floating prison, where they discover how their dream has become a nightmare.

This vicious circle of abuse is also the subject of a report backed by both the Australian Government and the ITF. *The Changing Nature of High Seas Fishing* (2005) describes how Flags of Convenience (FOCs) nowadays provide a "perfect cover" for illegal, unreported and unregulated (IUU) fishing on distant water vessels (DWVs). ITF General Secretary *David Cockroft* joins in condemning this abuse in forceful terms: "In many cases, IUU vessels operate with an unprotected workforce who can be beaten, starved, and worked without pay—all out of sight in one of the world's most dangerous industries...."

It seems obvious that such workers have a legitimate claim on protection of their rights and promotion of their welfare by not only church and society, but most especially by the international maritime ministry community. The crucial question is—how can that community best fulfill its obligation in practice?

First of all, Christian maritime mission has a vital role to play in terms of *advocacy for systemic change* in the fishing industry's impact on its own workforce. Three major UN-related international organizations each seek to address issues of fishers' justice, safety and health: The International Maritime Organisation (IMO), the International Labour Organisation (ILO) and the Food and Agriculture Organisation (FAO). All three have, in recent decades, adopted instruments dealing with such issues. However, most IMO and ILO maritime conventions apply to merchant seafarers only—not fishers. Where instruments do relate to fishers, many states have simply not ratified them. Even where they have, they seldom provide any means of enforcement. Here ICMA, with its observer status in each of these agencies, is seeking to promote needful change.

ICMA and its member agencies also cooperate closely in these matters with the International Transport Workers' Federation (ITF) and its fishers' section. However, a major impediment to ITF effectiveness in this field has been the lack of union representation in the fishing industry. Where this is due to intimidation, it is a matter of common justice, and for maritime mission a call for solidarity. (Still, solidarity cannot, of course, include condoning over-fishing, a practice generated by pressures of soaring demands and disappearing stocks.)

At the same time, fishers' *spiritual* welfare also has to constitute a core component of any truly holistic understanding of their human needs. Here, maritime mission has a role to play that is distinctively its own: How can the worldwide Church bring *an inclusive gospel ministry of pastoral care* to those who are so ready to receive it, but all too often beyond its reach? For deep-sea industrial fishers, this means making sure that those within reach of regular seafarers' centers can also benefit from the shipvisiting and service programs available to merchant seafarers. For small-scale artisinal fishers not far from home for any length of time, it may mean proactively contacting local Christian congregations on their behalf along a regional stretch of coastline. These could respond by offering opportunities for fellowship, counseling and support, all of which can be truly meaningful both for the fishers themselves and their families.

The Least of These—and the Last Word

What is there to say about justice, safety and health for *fishers who are still children?* No one familiar with Jesus' priority for "the least" among society's most marginalized can remain in doubt. In many Asian countries like Myanmar, Indonesia, the Philippines and Thailand, mere children work in *muro-ami* fishing. This is a form of fishing that involves deep-sea diving without the use of protective equipment. The children beat on corral reefs to scare the fish into nets. Each fishing vessel employs up to 300 boys between ages 10 and 15, usually recruited from poor neighborhoods. Divers reset their nets several times a day, so the children are often in the water for up to 12 hours in one stretch.

According to an ILO Report, *World of Work* (1996), this flagrant form of child abuse results in injury and death for countless children every year—from drowning, fatal accidents or decompression sickness. Predatory fish, such as sharks, barracudas and poisonous sea-snakes, also attack them. The full weight of world opinion just has to be brought to bear on this intolerable scandal.

In Matthew 25:31, we learn that when the Son of Man comes in his glory, and all the angels with him, he will sit on his throne and before him will gather all the nations of the world. This is where the Christian perspective on life will one day bring us all, whoever we are. He who sits on that judgment throne is the Risen Christ. This means that he who will have the last word is the very one who once prepared breakfast for his fisher friends, Peter, Andrew and the Zebedee brothers, John and James, tired after a long night's work.

31

TRUTH AND RECONCILIATION
A Paradigm for Conflict Resolution

Desmond Tutu

DESMOND MPILO TUTU was born and raised under the racist regime of the white minority in South Africa. He fought fearlessly from 1975 against the evil of apartheid, first as the Anglican Dean of Johannesburg, eventually as Archbishop of Cape Town. Branded by his own government as "Public Enemy Number One," he was—at the height of the conflict—awarded the 1984 Nobel Peace Prize in Oslo, Norway. A decade later, the world witnessed the miracle of South Africa's transition from despotism to democracy, and Archbishop Tutu was chosen to chair a "Truth and Reconciliation Commis-
sion" to help heal his traumatized nation. Under his leadership, there emerged a biblically based paradigm for justice and healing that also has relevance for the current-day world of seafarers, where exploitation and marginalization remain commonplace. The following Perspective is based, with permission, on selections from Desmond Tutu's book No Future Without Forgiveness *(Doubleday, 1999), his sequel to* The Rainbow People of God: The Making of a Peaceful Revolution *(Doubleday, 1994).*

The Nightmare called Apartheid

When the apartheid government of South Africa came to power in 1948, they engaged from the very word go in an orgy of racist oppression. What we had from then on was essentially a pigmentocracy. This notion claimed that what invested human beings with worth was simply a biological attribute, namely ethnicity, skin color, race. Since it could be enjoyed by only a few, this attribute was by definition exclusive and therefore not a universal phenomenon. It was like what even someone as wise as Aristotle had been guilty of. He claimed that human personality was not a universal possession enjoyed by all, since *slaves* were devoid of this. The absurdity of his position must have given great comfort to slave-owners who thus could ill-treat their chattels with impunity.

The ancients could to some extent be forgiven for holding to such an irrational and immoral position. However, the perpetrators of apartheid in South

Africa could not plead ignorance since they were not benighted pagans. They claimed to be "the last bastion of Western Christian civilization against Soviet Communist expansionism." Many times our people were left perplexed by the remarkable fact that those who treated them so abominably were not heathen, but claimed to be *fellow Christians* who read the same Bible, and went to church. And how they went to church!

But the Bible is quite categorical on this. That which endows every single human being with worth, infinite worth, is not this or that biological attribute, like the color of one's skin or (as I sometimes said of myself) the size of one's nose! No, it is the fact that each one of us has been created in the image of God. This is something intrinsic. It comes, as it were, with the package. It means that each one of us is a God-carrier, God's representative. To treat any such person as if he or she were anything less than that is blasphemous. It is like spitting in the face of God.

This is what filled some of us with such a passionate commitment to fight for justice and freedom. We were inspired not by political motives. No, we were fired by our biblical faith. The Bible turned out to be the most subversive thing around in a situation of such injustice and oppression.

The Evolution of a Miracle

When Nelson Mandela was finally released on February 11, 1990, after twenty-seven years in jail, he was not spewing words of hatred and revenge. He amazed us all by his heroic embodiment of reconciliation and forgiveness. In 1995, now as the President of South Africa, Nelson Mandela appointed me chairperson of the new Truth and Reconciliation Commission (TRC). Later, as we sat listening to the testimony of those who came to the Commission to tell us their stories of unbearable suffering, and as we considered applications for amnesty by those who had committed such horrendous atrocities, I caught myself asking whether God did not sometimes wonder: "What in the name of everything that is good ever got into Me to create that lot?"

First there were those who had wanted to follow the *Nuremberg trial paradigm*—by bringing to trial all perpetrators of gross violations of human rights, and imposing "victor's justice," just like the Allies after World War II. But while the Allies could pack up and go home after Nuremberg, we in South Africa had a military stalemate. We had to go on living with one another. We could very well have had justice. But it would have been "retributive justice," one which would have led to a bloodbath and left South Africa lying in ashes.

Then there were members of the previous government, and those who had carried out their orders, who suggested rather glibly that we "let bygones be bygones." They clamored for blanket or general amnesty, as had already happened in Chile, when General Pinochet and his cohorts gave themselves amnesty as a precondition to handing over from their military junta to a civilian government. But it was felt that general amnesty would simply amount to national amnesia. And to quote George Santayana, "Those who forget the past are doomed to repeat it." The past has a persistent way of returning to haunt us, unless the truth has been fully disclosed and dealt with adequately. The truth may hurt, but silence kills.

The Truth and Reconciliation Commission came about because our negotiators rejected *both* extremes, not only Nuremberg trials but also blanket amnesty. Instead they opted for a "third way," granting *conditional amnesty* in exchange for full disclosure. Ultimately, this third way of "restorative" rather than "retributive" justice was completely consistent with a central feature of our African world view called *ubuntu*—and therefore in accord with traditional African jurisprudence.

When *uhuru* (freedom, independence) came to Kenya and elsewhere in Africa, many had expected an orgy of revenge, leading to the white man's grave. It did not happen, because ubuntu was also there. To have ubuntu is to say that my humanity is inextricably bound up in yours. We belong together in a delicate network of interdependence, a "bundle of life" or greater whole, where what diminishes or dehumanizes you diminishes or dehumanizes me. Revenge, even aggressive competitiveness, corrodes the *community* for which we were all intended. Therefore, to forgive is not just to be altruistic. It is the best form of self-interest.

Many have felt that the TRC process was immoral in that it could be said to encourage impunity, allowing a perpetrator to get off scot-free with only a so-called confession. This is not true. Amnesty is granted only to those who are willing to accept the public humiliation of *pleading guilty,* and in that way take responsibility for what they have done, including carrying out unconscionable orders. Amnesty is *not* given to those who claim to be innocent or those who in effect deny that they have committed a crime. If the process of forgiveness and healing is to become mutually cathartic, and therefore fully successful, the culprit's ultimate acknowledgment of the truth is indispensable.

The same goes for the victim's *willingness to forgive.* In the Commission the victim, we hoped, would be moved to respond to an apology by forgiving the culprit. Many did show extraordinary magnanimity. There were also some that said they would not forgive, though these were the exceptions. To forgive does not mean to forget. It means drawing out that *sting* in the memory which would otherwise threaten to poison our entire system. In the United States, the academic study of forgiveness has now, because of developments such as ours in the TRC, become an academic discipline. Forgiving has even been found to be good for health.

Does the victim depend on the culprit's contrition and confession to be able to forgive? Jesus did not. He did not wait until those who were nailing him to the cross had asked for forgiveness. He was ready, as they drove in the nails, to pray to his Father to forgive them and even provided an excuse for what they were doing. If the victim could forgive only when the culprit confessed, then the victim would be locked into the culprit's whim and therefore remain in victim-hood. That would be palpably unjust.

All of this reminds of some U.S. ex-servicemen standing in front of the Vietnam Memorial in Washington D.C. One asks, "Have you forgiven those who held you prisoner of war?" "I will never forgive them," replies the other. To this his mate responds, "Then it seems they still have you in prison, don't they?" Forgiving means abandoning your right to pay back the perpetrator in his or her own coin. *But it is a loss that liberates!*

Once the wrongdoer has confessed and the victim has forgiven, it does not mean that this is the end of the process. What about *reparation?* Apartheid provided the whites with enormous benefits and privileges, leaving its victims deprived and exploited—not least in tangible, material ways. As we in the TRC said in our report, "Without adequate reparation and rehabilitation there can be no healing and reconciliation, either at an individual or a community level.... The granting of amnesty denies victims the right to institute civil claims against perpetrators. The Government should thus accept responsibility for reparation."

That process has only just begun. What has placed it in such jeopardy is the huge gap between the "haves" and the "have-nots," created and maintained by racism and apartheid. That is why I have exhorted whites to support a fundamental transformation in the lot of the blacks—including zero tolerance for intolerance, by working together for a more inclusive society.

In the spirit of "ubuntu," the central concern is the healing of broken relationships, seeking to rehabilitate both the victim and the perpetrator. *Both* should be given the opportunity to be reintegrated into the community. Confession, forgiveness and reparation, wherever feasible, form part of a *continuum*—in one and the same process of reconciliation. Real reconciliation is neither cheap nor easy. It cost God the death of His only begotten Son.

How Biblical Theology Helped Us

It is interesting that the President appointed an Archbishop as chairperson of the Commission and not, for instance, a judge, since we were a quasi-judicial body. After all, it was more common to have the ethos of "dog eat dog" in the jungle world of politics. The President must have believed that our work would be profoundly spiritual. At all events, as soon as I was appointed I had our Anglican religious communities around the world alerted about our Commission's desperate need for regular intercession. We know that whatever may have been achieved was in large measure due to the love and prayers of all those nuns and monks, as well as so many others, who made up that worldwide "cloud of witnesses."

Certainly, theological insights really did inform much of what we did and how we did it. Frequently we in the Commission were appalled at the depth of depravity to which human beings could sink. But theology reminded us that, however diabolical the act, it did not turn the perpetrator into a demon. We had to condemn the sin while being filled with compassion for the sinner. If perpetrators were to be despaired of as monsters and demons, we were then declaring they were not *moral agents,* to be held responsible for the deeds they had committed. More importantly, it meant that we should, as a Commission, have had to shut up shop. After all, we were operating on the premise that they still had a God-given capacity to change, and at some point confess their dastardly conduct and ask for forgiveness.

In this theology, we can never give up on anyone, because our God is one who has a particularly soft spot for sinners. This God in Christ scandalized the orthodox religious leaders of the day, because he companied not with the elite but with the fringes of society, the prostitutes, the sinners and the ostracized. When Jesus was crucified it was in the company of two thieves. One of them became repentant and Jesus promised that he would be in paradise with him on that day. None of us can ever consign anyone to hell as being ultimately irredeemable, because God is preeminently the God of grace. God does not give up on anyone, for God has loved us from all eternity.

As I listened in the TRC, I realized how each one of us has this capacity for the most awful evil—every one of us. None of us could predict that if we had been subjected to the same conditioning we would not have turned out like these perpetrators. This is not to condone or excuse. We have to say, but not with cheap pietism, "there but for the grace of God go I."

Theology helped us in the TRC to recognize that we inhabit *a moral universe,* that good and evil are real and that they matter. This means that despite all the evidence that seems to be to the contrary, there is no way that evil and injustice can have the last word. For us as Christians, the death and resurrection of Jesus Christ is proof positive that love, light and life are stronger than hate, darkness and death.

In the TRC, we actually saw all this unfolding before our very eyes. Those who had strutted about arrogantly in the days of apartheid, dealing out death and injustice with unrestrained abandon, had never imagined in their wildest dreams that their machinations would ever see the light of day. Now it was gushing forth from the mouths of perpetrators themselves. During the dark days of the struggle, I used to appeal to our white fellow South Africans: "We are being nice to you. Join the winning side!" Finally, we were vindicated. This *was* after all a moral universe. And the victory was for *all* of us, black and white together – the rainbow people of God!

God Does Have a Sense of Humor

God does have a sense of humor. Who in their right mind could ever have imagined *South Africa* to be an example of anything but the most ghastly awfulness—of how *not* to order a nation's race relations? We South Africans were the unlikeliest lot—a hopeless case if ever there was one. And that is precisely why God chose us. God wanted to point to us and say: "Look at South Africa. They had a nightmare called apartheid. It has ended. Your nightmare will end too."

Those of us in the Commission were not some superior breed pontificating about the lot of poor, hapless victims. We were also wounded and traumatized, a house divided against herself and a pariah to the rest of the world. Mercifully for us, the world did not leave us to our own devices, but was fascinated by us, prayed for us, loved us, was exasperated by us, boycotted us, applied sanctions against us, and just went on supporting us until the wonder of April 27, 1994, held the world in awe: the day when we would vote for the first time in a democratic election in the land of our birth.

The world could not quite believe what it was seeing. The world thought that, after a democratically elected government was in place, those who had for so long been trodden underfoot would go on a rampage, unleashing an orgy of revenge and retribution. Instead, there was this remarkable Truth and Reconciliation Commission, with perpetrators asking forgiveness from those they had so grievously wronged and victims expressing their willingness to forgive. True, ours has been the bloodiest century known to human history. Yet there is a movement, not easily discernable, at the heart of things—to *reverse* the awful centrifugal force of alienation, division and hostility. God has set in motion a *centripetal* process, a moving toward the center, toward goodness, peace and justice, to recover that primordial harmony for which the Bible tells us we were once created.

Jesus says, "And when I am lifted up from the earth I shall draw everyone to myself" (John 12:32). From his cross he hangs with out-flung arms, thrown out to clasp all in one cosmic embrace, so that all, everyone, everything, belongs. Here there is no longer Jew nor Greek, male nor female, slave nor free (Galatians 3:28). Instead of separation, all distinctions make for a richer diversity. We are different so that we can know our need of one another. The completely self-sufficient person would be subhuman. From the beginning, it was God's intention to bring all things in heaven and on earth to a unity in Christ, where each one of us participates in this grand movement.

The warring groups in Northern Ireland, the Balkans, the Middle East, Rwanda, the Sudan, Afghanistan, Burma, and elsewhere have seen a beacon of hope, *a possible paradigm* in what we have attempted in South Africa. Our experiment is going to succeed because God wants us to succeed. Not for our glory, but for the sake of God's world. God wants to show that there is life after conflict and repression—that *because of forgiveness there is a future!*

APPENDICES

Appendix 1

THE SEAFARERS' COVENANT

This document represents a maritime adaptation of the Lausanne Covenant *of 1974—one of the 20th century's most significant global mission statements. The* Seafarers' Covenant *emerged at the Second International Congress on World Evangelization ("Lausanne II") in Manila, Philippines, July 10-20, 1989, the first major global mission event where maritime mission was part of the official program. Originating from the Congress Workshops on "Seafarers' Mission," its dual purpose was: (1) To awaken greater awareness within the worldwide Christian Church concerning Christ's continuing mission to and through seafarers. (2) To rally fellow workers ashore and afloat around the biblical basis for such mission. The following slightly abbreviated text appears in its entirety as pages 453-456 in the published Congress Report: J. D. Douglas (ed.),* Proclaim Christ Until He Comes, *Minneapolis, Minnesota, 1990.*

INTRODUCTION

We, as participants in the International Congress on World Evangelization in Manila—on the shores of the South China Sea, are reminded that the very first Christ called to follow him were seafarers—on the shores of the Sea of Galilee. Due to drastic changes in the maritime industry, the majority of today's merchant seafarers are now no longer from a Western-world, nominally Christian context, but instead from an Asian, and largely non-Christian background. Thus, most of today's merchant seafarers make up a vast, floating global mission field of Muslims, Hindus, Buddhists, Shintoists, animists, atheists and others. Convinced as we are that many churches and agencies committed to the Great Commission have not yet become aware of this great global mission opportunity on their own waterfront, we wish to share the following affirmations:

1. A Doubly Deprived People Group

We affirm that, like most people, we have all too often taken the indispensable services of seafarers for granted, unmindful of how doubly deprived they are as a people group. First, they are socially isolated, for long periods totally removed by their very vocation from family and friends, home and country (sociologically speaking, a seagoing "total institution"). Second, they are spiritually isolated, and most of them have been deprived of any authentic offer of the Gospel, much less an accountable relationship within the body of Christ.

2. Our Double Obligation to Respond

We affirm that commitment to the Gospel implies a double duty to respond to the seafarer's social and spiritual isolation. First, in the Great Commandment Christ calls us to love our neighbors as ourselves. That has to include seafaring strangers at the gates of our port-cities. One day he has predicted he will say, "Ï was a stranger," and relate our final fate to whether we welcomed him or not (Es. 20:10; Mt. 22:19, 25:31-46). Second, in the Great Commission Christ calls us to go make disciples of all people. He made no exception for seafarers. On the contrary, he set the example by singling out seafarers as his very first missionaries! He knew that seafarers (as they have always proved wherever they have been given a valid opportunity to accept the Gospel) would become the very best missionaries. And there is reason to believe (as doors close to conventional mission around the world) that they may one day prove to be the very last missionaries (Mt. 4:18-22, 28:18-20; John 20-21; Acts 1:8, 18:3, 27:1-44).

3. Ultimate Nature of Maritime Evangelism

We affirm the ultimate nature of evangelism—in seafarers' mission as in world mission. Through God's general revelation, seafarers in a special sense "see the works of the Lord, his wonderful works in the deep" (Ps. 197:107:23-24; Acts 17:27; Rom. 1:20). However, in the extreme pluralism of the seafaring world, surrounded by a host of other faiths on every side, all more or less pointing out ways to self-salvation, seafarers have an acute need for God's particular revelation—of redemption through Christ alone. To maintain the undiluted uniqueness of salvation through Christ, without making that Gospel universally available—by bold but sensitive, verbalized witness—would be a betrayal of both Christ's supreme sacrifice and the non-Christian seafarer's chance to benefit by it (Mt 16:26; John 14:6; Acts 4:12; Rom 10:13-14; Gal 2:21; 1 Tim 2:4-5). Meanwhile, to be effective, such witness needs to be responsibly followed up (see section 4 below). Furthermore, in order to be credible, it needs to be holistically oriented (see section 5 below).

4. Seafarers' Missionary Fellowships

We affirm that Christ calls not only to decision but also to discipleship. In the seafarer's context of constant mobility, this calls for an intentional form of follow-up, focusing on both shipboard peer ministry and fellowship. Organized seafarers' mission began with spontaneous Scripture-nurtured, Spirit-bonded lay cell groups, similar to those in the Early Church (Acts 2:42). Two reasons make it mandatory to implement the priesthood of all believers and the concept of Christian communion (or "koinonia") within the maritime context of every age. First, given the limited stay of ships in port, shipboard peer ministry, with seafarers witnessing to fellow-seafarers through their daily walk of faith, is the only means by which most of today's non-Christian seafarers can be reached with a genuinely contextualized offer of the Gospel. Second, a worshipping, witnessing shipboard fellowship is essential, if a new-born Christian is to find the strength to be an effective witness—or even survive. Thus, hundreds of so-called "Maritime Base Communities" of (mostly Asian) ministering seafarers have emerged in recent years, and now form a key factor in current-day maritime evangelization. We thank God for these missionary fellowships, as well as for innovative programs designed to promote them. They merit encouragement and support by Great Commission Christians everywhere.

5. Seafarers' Human Rights

We affirm that a faith which does not manifest itself in love and compassion is dead (James 2:14-17). In maritime as in world evangelization, though evangelism is ultimate, social concern is by no means optional, but indispensable to a biblically holistic understanding of the faith. No one can claim to be indwelt by the Spirit of Christ, while remaining indifferent to the sufferings of fellow-humans—in body, mind or spirit (Mt.

7:21, 25:31-46; 2 Cor. 5:14; Gal. 5:6). This applies equally to the prophetic task of confronting the underlying causes of suffering, and seeking to counter them. With the proliferation of so-called "flags of convenience," and mass hiring of two-thirds world maritime labor, cases of blatant abuse of fundamental human rights have become all too frequent. In advocating for seafarers' God-given dignity and humanization of their conditions of life and work, there is a compelling need for specialized resources (as currently provided by the Center for Seafarers' Rights in New York and its associates). However, it must never be forgotten that nothing undermines the human dignity of seafarers (or anyone) more than being deprived of the most basic human right—that of choosing one's own ultimate destiny. Which is what happens when a non-Christian seafarer is not given the means (and therefore freedom) of comparison, through a credible offer of the Gospel alternative.

6. Research and Resources

We affirm the acute need, only increased by recent radical change in the context of seafarers' mission, for ongoing study and research. These activities should be closely connected with current missiological studies on related themes, such as migration ("people on the move"), urban mission, industrial chaplaincy, lay ministry, restricted access ministry, cross-cultural communication, dialogue and witness. Such study and research must also relate to events, issues and studies in all aspects of maritime industry that affect the welfare of seafarers. Since the resources of long-established (Caucasian) and emerging (Asian) seafarers' mission agencies are so sorely inadequate in relation to current challenges, there exists a manifest need for resource sharing by world mission agencies. For example, in terms of personnel, media, training and funding, as well as in the crucial areas of awareness-raising and intercessory prayer.

7. Cooperation without Compromise

We affirm the call of Christ, not to uniformity in specifics, but to unity in the Spirit, in seafarers' mission as in every area of mission. We must not fracture the face of Christ on the waterfront! We see the diversity of agencies and individuals involved in seafarers' mission as a means of achieving together what none could hope to achieve as effectively (if at all) by working in isolation. We therefore pledge ourselves to seek cooperation with both world and seafarers' mission agencies, to the extent that we do not in any way compromise our basic commitment to both seafarers and the Great Commission. In so doing, we will seek to promote inter-agency electronic communication, and gladly share information, plans and resources.

CONCLUSION

In light of the above, we appeal to world mission agencies, churches and committed Christians everywhere to respond to the urgent need and providential opportunity offered by today's maritime migrants, as potential followers of that first great seafaring tentmaker, the Apostle Paul. We endorse the words of the Lausanne Covenant of 1974. But we must remind that the whole Gospel can never be brought to the whole world, so long as the world of seafarers is not reached. At Lausanne II in 1989, we have pledged ourselves to "proclaim Christ until he comes." But only by enlisting the unique witness of the Church Maritime can we expect the glory of the Lord to completely "cover the earth—as the waters cover the sea!" (Hab. 2:14).

Note: In order to avoid ambiguity, the term "ultimate nature" has (as subsequently agreed) replaced the word "primacy" in Section 3.

Appendix 2

NAMMA'S STATEMENT OF MISSION

As unanimously adopted by the Annual Assembly of NAMMA (formerly ICOSA) at the North American Maritime Ministry Conference in New Orleans, September 24, 1990

"In the beginning was the Word, the Word was with God and the Word was God. He was with God in the beginning. Through him all things came to be, not one thing had its being but through him...The Word was made flesh, he lived among us, and we saw his glory, the glory that is his as the only Son of the Father, full of grace and truth" (John 1:1-3, 14).

Through the gift of faith we abide in Jesus Christ. We experience life in new ways. Our discovery is not that of a last word, completed, but of a process. We know his presence. With our lives and our experience, we humbly share our own presence, our being, our values, our convictions, our faith, our beliefs. We have relationships with dimensions that are common and different, distinct and new. Sensitive to one another, we listen attentively in order to understand, to receive, to accept, to respect, to value, and to grow together. We find areas of agreement, areas in question, and even areas of disagreement. Painfully and joyfully, we discover that words can mean different things to different people. In order that Jesus Christ and we may be understood, received, accepted, respected, and valued, we sincerely cherish opportunities to be fully present to one another.

In the name of the Father and of the Son and of the Holy Spirit, we manifest our common belief:

By going to seafarers and their families in person, to acknowledge their dignity, presence and worth, to receive them, to welcome them, to journey with them in life port by port. It is our common belief that God took the initiative in creating, and continues to take the initiative in saving and sustaining his people. We believe that he sent his Son, Jesus Christ, in person to redeem all people and all of creation. We believe that Christ commissioned his followers to be his presence in this world and to proclaim the Good News of the Kingdom of God. Christ entered our story and shared his story, a life of love filled with grace, peace, and justice extending to all peoples.

By standing with seafarers and their families in radical equality, friendship, and unconditional love.

By serving seafarers and their families, and by inviting them in turn to serve others.

By standing up for seafarers and their families as advocates of their human rights and dignity.

We cherish the common foundation we have in the Old and New Testaments, and in the Apostles' and Nicene Creeds. In accordance with Christ's Great Commission to "Go, therefore, make disciples of all nations, baptize them in the name of the Father and of the Son and of the Holy Spirit, and teach them to observe all the commands I gave you" (Mt 28:18-20, JB), we invite all people to follow him. Through witnessing to our faith by word and deed, we seek to evangelize and invite. We proclaim the Word. We do not impose upon others. We long for a unity that respects diversity. We are committed to ecumenical collaboration, and the promotion of community in Christ on land and sea. We affirm a human solidarity that respects plurality of cultures and peoples, and which can be enriched by dialogue with persons of other faiths. We share a passion for life, and compassion not only for seafarers and their families, but also for all people, when life is threatened, diminished, or denied through ignorance, insensitivity, or injustice.

In summary, we journey together with the humble awareness that all of life is a gift from a gracious God, revealed to us in Jesus, the Christ, who invites and values our response through a ministry of presence, witness, service and advocacy to, with, and for seafarers and their families. Conscious of the complexity and incompleteness awaiting the coming of the fullness of the Kingdom of God, we walk together in faith guided by this motto: *Agreement in essentials, freedom in non-essentials, love in everything!*

(Text originally published in *Watermarks* #3-4, December, 1990)

Appendix 3

SHIPVISITING GUIDELINES

1) **GENERAL PREPARATION:** You are going on board as an ambassador for Christ (2 Cor. 5:20). You can therefore confidently look to his Spirit for guidance and wisdom (Acts 1:8).

2) **SPECIAL PREPARATION:** Based on the latest information of ships in port, select materials for ship-visiting, including the following—as far as possible in likely languages: New Testaments, Scripture portions, Bible Study materials, sound Christian literature and videos (not least the *Jesus Video*), the *National Geographic* and other appropriate magazines and newspapers.. Also, remember shipboard worship and follow-up aids as needed.

3) **SHIPVISITING PLAN:** It would be unrealistic to plan on visiting every seafarer—on every ship—every day. However, aim to be among the first on board when a ship arrives. Be flexible, be prepared for the unforeseen—and rely on divine guidance (Eph. 2:10).

4) **ENTERING THE PORT AREA:** Keep yourself updated about port protocol and security regulations. Follow them scrupulously. Park only in designated safe areas. Maintain good working relations with port personnel and always show them due respect.

5) **MAKING CONTACT ON BOARD:** Identify yourself to gangway watch. Ask to see officer of the watch and request permission to visit with captain (if available), officers and crew. Identify yourself to all you meet, welcome them to both the port and your center, and ask how you may be of service. Make port maps and center brochures available. Offer help with mail, low-cost phone cards, cell phones, internet access, etc. If possible, offer transportation to places of worship, shopping facilities, medical services, sightseeing, and/or local host homes. Never solicit, but whenever practicable accept invitations to share a meal—or at least table fellowship.

6) **RELATING PERSONALLY:** Remember you are a guest in the seafarer's home as well as workplace. Never be intrusive, but always courteous and friendly. Learning just a few words in relevant languages can open many doors. Encourage them, through an interpreter if need be, to tell you about their country, family and faith. Be ready to share sensitively about your own. Offer your reading matter judiciously. (No indiscriminate scattering of Scripture or other Christian literature!)

7) **RELATING PASTORALLY:** While visiting on board, make a mental note of any who seem to have something on their mind, and wait for a moment to relate alone. Tactfully identify Christians, if any, in order to give them encouragement and pray with them in private, if they so wish. If any of them are not already involved in a shipboard lay ministry program, explain and motivate. Entrust worship and Bible study materials with any potential leader among them

8) **WORSHIP SERVICES:** Before leaving, if the opportunity presents itself, consider offering a prayer and/or blessing for the ship, the crew and their families. In so doing, it might be natural to form a circle and hold hands. If there is time and interest, offer to lead a brief Bible study or worship service. While so doing, take special care to respect every crewmember's sacramental or other religious loyalties

9) **CONFLICT RESOLUTION:** In case of crew complaints, be sure to hear all sides. There might simply be a need to "vent." However, where there is clear indication of real abuse or injustice, contact the *Center for Seafarers' Rights* in New York (1-212-349-9090) or its associates in London (44-20-7828-0704) or Barcelona (34-3-443-1965). A local representative of the ITF might also be available (44-20-7403-2733). Other referrals: Coast Guard, Port Authorities, police, consul of the vessel's country of registry, and/or—when warranted—the local media.

10) **LEAVING SHIP**: As you leave the ship, pray that your visit may somehow bear fruit (John 12:32). Then, faithfully fulfill whatever any of the crew may have entrusted to you—as both the Lord's and their servant. In so doing, you will honor the heritage of trust built by generations of fellow chaplains around the world.

Note: For a more comprehensive treatment, see also the 50-page manual *ICMA Ship Visiting Handbook,* produced in 2005 and available online.

Appendix 4

A PORT CHAPLAIN'S "SURVIVAL KIT"

Maritime Meditations for Turbulent Times

Bill Down

At NAMMA'S Annual Conference, held in Toronto on June 10-14, 1995, Bishop Bill Down, former Secretary General of the MtS, shared insights from decades of distinguished service in maritime ministry, with a series of four biblical meditations focusing on chaplaincy self-care in turbulent times. Originally offered against the backdrop of a particular time of testing in NAMMA's recent history, the following excerpts also have obvious ongoing relevance.

On October 12, 1973, an Australian coastal freighter, the *Blythe Star,* capsized and sank off the South-West coast of Tasmania. She had a crew of ten. Eventually, seven survivors drifted ashore. Two of these died from the effects of their long ordeal.

I have since wondered: How would I fare—in an open boat adrift at sea? Certainly, I would be scared. I think I would also be aware that it would be vital for all of us in that same boat to act together be sensitive to the needs of each other, accept the leadership of the person in command, suffer without grumbling, and be brave. It would be a time when love for others would be put to the test.

The life of the Christian Church can seem like life at sea in an open boat. Like people in an open boat at sea, we Christians have a common purpose. We have good news to share everywhere—the Gospel of Jesus Christ, of God come to earth in human form, crucified, risen and alive forever. Above all, it is the good news that Jesus Christ died for the sins of every one of us, and was then raised from the dead, victorious over the power of both sin and death. Believing this good news and proclaiming it—by word of mouth, by our actions, and by the quality of our lives—this is the common purpose that has to hold us together!

The Church is set, however, in a world that, like the sea, presents a hostile environment. It must frequently face buffeting. On the global scene, today's Church faces momentous challenges, such as the dark shadows of poverty, hunger and AIDS, rampant drug abuse, ethnic and religious fundamentalist militancy, the proliferation of nuclear and other weapons of mass destruction, continuing erosion of traditional family values, irresponsible environmental policies, and practices threatening the whole human habitat.

It is not as if the Church is not trying to grapple with these problems. Still, its response is often inadequate, even irrelevant, and frequently treated with disdain and ridicule. In fact, the Church of today is very much in an "open boat" situation in a stormy sea. The Bible speaks clearly of this tension between the church and the world, between the people of God and those who want little or nothing to do with either God or the Church.

The Church is human, and its faults are all too apparent. However, it is also "the Body of Christ"—and he is still in control. Like people at sea in an open boat we, as members of that Church, need to pool our resources and pull together if we are to survive and fulfill God's purpose for His Church.

Maritime ministry gives us a golden opportunity to do just that—to witness and contribute to the life of the whole Christian Church, by promoting that unity which is our Lord's express will, "so that the world may believe" (John 17:21). It was a momentous occasion when more than a hundred people, representing all the major Christian denominations and organizations in maritime ministry, came together in Rotterdam in 1969 and brought into being the International Christian Maritime Association (ICMA). In the maritime world, the Christian Church has truly moved forward in terms of collaboration— being in the same boat—than any other part of the Church.

Nevertheless, we still have a long way to go. In maritime ministry, we experience some of the same frustrations as the wider Church. We, too, are still bedeviled by unacceptable denominationalism and sectarian politics. We, too, have experienced problems like personal antagonisms, selfish actions, partisan groupings, opinionated speaking, overwhelming ambitions, and even outright hypocrisy. It is of little comfort to remind ourselves that the Church has always struggled with scandals and unworthy living among its members. Instead, we must ask, what can we do about it?

On a personal level, we each need to examine ourselves carefully to see if we ourselves are guilty of any of this. We need to ask, how honest am I about my own shortcomings? We also need to remember how Jesus dealt with the woman caught in adultery. He did not condemn her. Nor did He condone what she had done. He gave her the chance of a fresh start. He reminded her accusers that they were all "in the same boat."

On a wider level, we need to keep up the momentum, as we pray together and work together to break down the barriers that we know still exist among us. We need to continue to make our voice heard within our own churches and in international secular forums. We need to subjugate our self-interest and personal agendas to the best interest of all.

Last, but most importantly, if the boat is not to be swamped by the buffeting which is bound to keep coming, we need, all of us, to keep our eyes firmly focused on Jesus (Hebrews 12:2). Not only in order to survive, but above all to accomplish His purpose, as He sends us out into the maritime world with a message to share—the message that Jesus Christ is indeed "The Way, the Truth and the Life" (John 14:6).

Appendix 5

Volunteer Chaplain Brings Comfort
To Crews at Port

Lona O'Connor, Palm Beach Post Religion Writer
Monday, February 19, 2007 © 2007 Palm Beach Post
Used by permission

Below deck on the Palm Beach Princess, the cooks are in a pre-cruise frenzy. The chop-chop of their cleavers on cantaloupe punctuates the steady thrum of the engines. The kitchen air is rich with the scent of barbecued meat. In less than an hour, the first daily horde of offshore gamblers and buffet-grazing *bon vivants* will be climbing the gangplank. Though they haven't a moment to spare, the cooks slow their pace just for a moment as John Van Hemert enters the busy galley, passing out big smiles and religious pamphlets from his jacket pockets.

He calls himself "Pastor John," and is, as far as anyone knows, the first harbor chaplain ever in the 89-year history of the Port of Palm Beach. His congregation is composed of the cooks, mechanics and ship's officers - anyone working on the cruise ships and the freighters - in need of the word of God or a sympathetic ear.

Van Hemert, a retired Protestant minister, is a member of Action International Ministries, a nondenominational evangelical missionary group. Van Hemert was born in the Netherlands to a farming family. His father, the organist at the local church, worked with the Resistance and helped hide Jews and others fleeing the Nazis. When they found that someone had stolen food or clothing from them, his mother, the youngest of 17 children, was philosophical. "Must be that somebody needed it more than we did," she told her children. Times were hard and grew worse. By the end of World War II, when he was 8, the family "were eating tulip bulbs and bark off the trees," he recalled.

In 1947, the extended Van Hemert family - 26 in all - moved to Canada, which was seeking immigrants with farming skills. His father grew carrots, lettuce and onions on 150 acres in Ontario's "salad basket." At 17, Van Hemert was a truck driver, transporting vegetables to Toronto. He went back to high school at 21 and later became a minister, preaching in Canada before he retired to Lake Worth. But not for long.

He learned the ropes of chaplaincy in the ports of Bridgeport and New Haven, Conn., where one of his children lives, then Miami and Fort Lauderdale. Then, in 2002, he heard that the Port of Palm Beach had never had a chaplain. He approached port official Jarra Kaczwara about ministering to the crews. "He just showed up and said he wanted to know if there was something he could do," said Kaczwara, who got him security clearance and introduced him around the port. "He really went out and made this happen. It's really proven to be a true blessing for the port."

It's a no-frills ministry. Van Hemert is unpaid, aided by two volunteers and his wife, Jean, and whatever contributions come their way. He goes to schools and other groups to get the word out about his mission. "The first thing we ask for is prayers for these lonely guys and gals. The second thing we ask them for is care packages." After he visited a school in Boynton Beach, the children sent 56 handmade Christmas cards for sailors. "The Van Hemerts are go-for-it type people," said Bill Flansburg, a project manager for Action International Ministries. "Instead of retiring, they took on new challenges. They're a challenge for other people to go out there and be helpful."

Aiding the lonely seafarers

Many sailors come from the Philippines, Europe, Africa and other faraway lands. Their long work days often confine them to the ships, where they eat, sleep and work. They are far from their families, getting home for two or three months a year. "Seafarers are a forgotten group of people," said Van Hemert. "We can hardly imagine how they are starved for some social contact. So I try to bring a little bit of the Sabbath to them."

Among his trophy moments is one cold February day when he brought gifts to a crew of Greeks and Ukrainians who had been at sea for months and not celebrated Christmas. Or the ecumenical moment when he brought three cellphones to a crew of 28 Turkish Muslims so they could call home. The grateful captain invited the Van Hemerts on board for dinner. Undaunted by the religion gap, he based his after-dinner talk on their shared patriarch, the prophet Abraham. "We had such a good time of sharing," Van Hemert said. Or when he managed to find a Chinese newspaper in New Haven to present to a Chinese captain. "He gave everybody a page," said Van Hemert. Later he presented the captain with 10 Bibles in Chinese.

When the weather is cold and the wind cuts, the Van Hemerts buy thrift-shop coats for the sailors working on the windy decks of the container ships. On one particularly cold day, he gave away his own jacket. He takes them shopping onshore when he can. He arranges for cellphone access so they can call home. He has a group of church ladies knitting caps for the sailors. "Sometimes the whole crew is shivering on the deck," Van Hemert said.

Pastor John drives to the port several days a week to conduct brief services, built around the crews' tight work schedule. On a recent Sunday, he arrived at the Princess at 8 a.m., set up a small table on the dance floor of the ship's cocktail lounge, lit two candles and placed a small bowl of communion breads. About 15 crew members joined him to pray, sing hymns and listen to a short sermon. Then he conducted a flying tour of the rest of the Princess, dropping benedictions and smiles on the cooks. They called him "Father" and made the sign of the cross as he passed them. He disembarked just as the passengers started filing in and picking out seats in the dining room or at the slot machines.

He's 'a benefit for all of us'

Later in the week, the Van Hemerts climbed a narrow gangplank up to the Tropical Carib, a container ship. He set up his simple altar in the crew's small dining room, using a small baguette for communion bread. He began a prayer: "Creator of the land and sea - and there's so much sea - we thank you for this precious crew, captain and officers. In the engine room, on the deck, also, Lord, on the bridge, do your utmost, Lord. And their wives and their children and their parents and their families."

The service ends with a beaming crew shaking hands and exchanging the greeting, "Peace be with you." After *What a Friend We Have in Jesus* and *Amazing Grace*, the 16 crew members pick up pamphlets and file out of the little dining room and back to their posts. The ship has to be loaded and ready to leave for St. Croix in a few hours.

Tropical Carib Capt. Johnny Deraper, from the Philippines, lingers a moment so Jean Van Hemert can take a snapshot of him with her husband. Deraper has known Van Hemert since he began his seafarers mission. "He is a benefit for all of us when we are away from our family. He binds us in togetherness on board." Not content just to climb onboard ships, Van Hemert is now working with officials to put up a seafarers' center to provide rest, relaxation and, of course, religion for ships' crews.

Appendix 6

"THE GREATEST OF THESE..."

A Maritime Version of 1 Corinthians 13

Theodore E. Mall

Though I may be able
>	To speak the languages of all seafarers who call at my port,
>	And even understand their cultural distinctiveness,
>	But if I have not love...
>	My speech is like that of FOC owners,
>	Seeking to exploit those who sail their ships.

Though I may be a gifted preacher
>	Rightly dividing the Word of God among all I can reach,
>	Though I may attain knowledge
>	Of seafaring customs and lore throughout the world,
>	Though I may have unflagging faith
>	To deal with shipping agents, maritime unions, and the Coast Guard,
>	But if I have not love...
>	I am nothing.

Though I may give everything I own
>	To the poor and needy seafarers from around the world,
>	And even give my very life for them,
>	But if I have not love...
>	It profits me for naught.

Love is—
>	Feeling their loneliness on the high seas and in port,
>	Truly listening to their concerns for family and friends,
>	Caring enough to intervene in cases of abuse and exploitation,
>	Being their family while away from their own family,
>	Respecting them as God does,
>	Being available in their time of need,
>	And just belonging to them.

Love never ends—
>	Nations will pass away,
>	Theories of contextualized ministries will change,
>	Methods of evangelism and patterns of worship will need to be revised,
>	Maritime industry will be altered, institutions and organizations replaced,
>	Because all these are not ends unto themselves.

Meanwhile, these three abide:
>	Identifying with those whom we serve,
>	Learning all about how we can better serve,
>	Having selfless love for all we serve.

But—the greatest of these is love!

SELECT BIBLIOGRAPHY

The following books, reports and articles are either cited in the text or suggested for further reading. For earlier source materials, see bibliography in Kverndal 1986 (pp. 803-869).

Adeney, Miriam. *Daughter of Islam.* Downers Grove, 2002.
Ad Gentes: Decree on the Mission Activity of the Church. Vatican City, 1965.
Alcoholics Anonymous. 4th Edition. New York, 2006.
Allen, Roland. *The Spontaneous Expansion of the Church.* Grand Rapids, 1962.
Anson, Peter F. *Harbour Head: Maritime Memories.* London, 1944.
———. *The Church and the Sailor: A Survey of the Sea Apostolate Past and Present.* London, 1948.
———. *Christ and the Sailor: A Study of the Maritime Incidents in the New Testament.* London, 1954.
Apostolatus Maris. Quarterly Newsletter of the AOS at the Vatican.
Arterburn, Stephen and Jack Felton. *Faith that Hurts, Faith that Heals.* Nashville, 1992.
Axtell, Silas B. *A Symposium on Andrew Furuseth.* New Bedford, 1948.

Barbosa da Silva, António. "The Phenomenology of Religion as a Philosophical Problem." *Studia Philosophiae Religionis* no. 8 (1982).
Barrett, David et al., eds. *Christian World Encyclopedia.* New York, 2001.
Berentsen, Jan-Martin. "Dialogue: Impossible or Indispensable?" *Areopagus* no. 2 (1993): 10-13.
———. *Det Moderne Areopagus.* Stavanger, 1994.
Bevans, Stephen B. and Roger P. Schroeder. "Missiology after Bosch: Reverencing a Classic by Moving Beyond." *International Bulletin of Missionary Research* (April 2005): 69-72.
Bolster, Jeffrey. *Black Jack: African American Seamen in the Age of Sail.* Cambridge, 1997.
Bosch, David. "Evangelism." *International Bulletin of Missionary Research* (1987).
———. *Transforming Mission: Paradigm Shifts in Theology of Mission.* New York, 1991.
Braaten, Carl E. and LaVonne Braaten. *The Living Temple: A Practical Theology of the Body and the Foods of the Earth.* New York, 1976.
———. *No Other Gospel: Christianity among the World's Religions.* Minneapolis, 1992.
Brand, Paul and Philip Yancey. *Fearfully and Wonderfully Made.* Grand Rapids, 1980.
Bullock, Alan and Oliver Stallybrass, eds. *The Fontana Dictionary of Modern Thought.* London, 1977.

Cabantous, Alain. "Religion et monde maritime" *Annales de Normandie.* St. Malo, 1983.
———. *Le Ciel dans la Mer.* Paris, 1990.
———. *Dix Mille Marins face a l'Océan.* Paris, 1991.

Campolo, Tony. *How to Rescue the Earth Without Worshiping Nature.* Nashville, 1992.
Carey, George L. *In the Market Place.* Harrisburg, 1991.
Carson, Rachel. *Silent Spring.* New York, 1962.
Carter, Jimmy. *Living Faith.* New York, 1996
Chapman, Paul K. *Human Rights for Seafarers.* D.Min.Thesis Project. New York
    Theological Seminary, New York, 1983.
———. *Trouble on Board: The Plight of International Seafarers.* Ithaca, 1992.
Choi, Jonah Won-Jong. *Shalom and the Church Maritime: A Korean Perspective on
    Maritime Missiology.* D.Min. Thesis, NY Theological Seminary, NY, 1996
Coleman, Robert E. *The Master Plan of Evangelism.* Grand Rapids, 1993.
Collins, Francis. *The Language of God.* New York, 2006.
Collison, Christopher J. *Towards a Theology of Seafarers' Rights.* London, 1987.
Corlett, Ewan. *The Ship: The Revolution in Merchant Shipping 1950-1980.* London,
    1981.
Couper, A. D. et al. *Voyages of Abuse: Seafarers Human Rights and International
    Shipping.* London, 1999.

Denton, Jean, ed. *Good is the Flesh: Body, Soul and Christian Faith.* Harrisburg, 2005.
Douglas, J. D., ed. *Proclaim Christ Until He Comes.* Minneapolis, 1990.
Down, Bill. *On Course Together: The Churches' Ministry in the Maritime World Today.*
    Norwich, 1989.
———. *Down to the Sea: A Bishop's Life and Ministry.* Stanhope, 2004.

Eckhoff, Ray. "Maritime Follow-Up Ministry: With Special Reference to Inter-Port and
    Inter-Agency Cooperation." *Maritime Mission Studies,* no. 1 (Spring 1994): 17-21.
Eisler, Riane. *The Power of Partnership.* Novato, 2002.
Engelsviken, Tormod. "Misjonstenkningen i det 20.århundre." *Missiologi idag.*
    Jan-Martin Berentsen et al. Oslo, 1994.
———. "Dialog eller misjon?" *Lys og Liv,* no. 5 (1995).
Escobar, Samuel. "Latin America." *Toward the Twenty-first Century in Christian
    Mission.* James M. Phillips and Robert T. Coots, eds. Grand Rapids, 1993.

Foster, John. "The Sailor's Share in the Spread of the Gospel." *The Expository Time,* vol.
    70 (Jan. 1959): 110-113.
Frayne, Francis S. *What is the Apostleship of the Sea?* Liverpool, 1965.
———. "The Present Situation of the Apostleship of the Sea." *On the Move,* 4/1972.
Freese, Reinhard. *Geschichte der Deutschen Seemannsmission.* Bielefeld, 1991.
Fricke, Peter H., ed. *Seafarer & Community.* London, 1973.
Friend, Stephen. "The Origin of Organised Seafarers' Missions." *IASMM Newsletter*
    (Spring 1992): 11-12.
———. *The Churches' Work Amongst British Fishing Communities During the 19th
    Century.* M.Phil. Thesis, University of Leeds. Leeds, 1994.
———. "Social and Spiritual Work Amongst Fishing Communities." *England's Sea
    Fisheries.* David Starkey et al., eds. London, 2003.
——— ."The 'Devil's Mission Ships': The North Sea Liquor Trade, 1820-1890."
    Maritime Mission Studies, no. 2 (Autumn 1995): 39-48.
Fung, Raymond. *The Isaiah Vision: An Ecumenical Strategy for Congregational
    Evangelism.* Geneva, 1992.
Gannon, Arthur. *Apostolatus Maris 1920-1960.* New Orleans, 1965.

Gardiner, Robert, ed. *The Shipping Revolution: The Modern Merchant Ship.* Annapolis, 1992.

Goffman, Erving. "On the Characteristics of Total Institutions." *Asylums.* NY, 1972

Greenhill, Basil. *The Ship: The Life and Death of the Merchant Sailing Ship.* London, 1980.

Hakluyt, Richard. *Principal Navigations.* Extra Series, vol. 12. Glasgow, 1903.

Healey, James C. *Foc's'l & Glory Hole: A Study of the Merchant Seaman.* NY, 1936.

He Qi. *Look toward the Heavens: The Art of He Qi.* New Haven, 2005.

Held, David and Anthony McGrew. "Globalization." *Oxford Companion to Politics of the World.* Oxford, 2001.

Hertig, Paul. "The Galilee Theme in Matthew." *Missiology,* vol. 25 (April 1997): 155-63.

Hiebert, Paul. "Critical Issues in the Social Sciences." *Missiology* (Jan. 1996): 63-82.

———. *Anthropological Reflections on Missiological Issues.* Grand Rapids, 1994.

Hohman, Elmo P. *Seamen Ashore: A Study of the United Seamen's Service and of Merchant Seamen in Port.* New Haven, 1952.

Hope, Ronald. *Poor Jack: The Perilous History of the Merchant Seaman.* London, 2001.

International Association for the Study of Maritime Mission. *Maritime Mission Studies.*
———. *Occasional Papers.*

International Social Christian Institute. *The Churches and the Welfare of Seamen.* Geneva, 1930.

International Transport Workers' Federation. *Flags of Convenience.* London, n.d.
———. *Solidarity: The First 100 Years of the ITF.* London, 1996.
———. *ITF Women 1996.* London, 1996.
———. *Troubled Waters: Fishing, Pollution and FOCs.* London, 1999.

International Christian Maritime Association. *Plenary Conference Reports.*

Jacob, Michael. *The Flying Angel Story.* London, 1973.

Jenkins, Philip. *The Next Christendom: The Coming of Global Christianity.* NY, 2002

John Paul II. *Laborem Exercens.* Vatican City, 1981.

Jones, Charles J. *From the Forecastle to the Pulpit:* New York, 1884.

Jun, David Chul-Han. *An Historical and Contextual Mission Approach to Seafarers by Korean Churches with Special Reference to Muslim Seafarers.* D.Miss. Dissertation, Fuller School of World Mission, Pasadena, 2001.

Kahveci, Erol, et al. *The Sailing Chaplain & Outreach Welfare Schemes.* Cardiff, 2003.
———. *Port Based Welfare Services for Seafarers.* Cardiff, 2007.

Kalliala, Kaarlo. *Strangership: A Theological Etude on Strangers Aboard and Abroad.* Helsinki, 1997.

Kelley, Harold H. "The Early History of the Church's Work for Seamen in the United States." *Historical Magazine of the Protestant Episcopal Church* (1940): 349-67.

Kennerley, Alston. *British Seamen's Missions and Sailors' Homes—1815 to 1970.* Unpubl. PhD Dissertation, University of Plymouth, Plymouth 1989.
———. "British Seamen's Missions in the Nineteenth Century." *The North Sea.* Stavanger, 1992.
———. "Seafaring Missionary Societies & Maritime Education and Training 1815-1914." *History of Education Seminar Papers.* Dublin, 1997.

Kim, Young-Hwan. *Development of Maritime Mission: Gospel-based Strategies for Ministry to Seafarers.* D.Min. Project, Eastern Baptist Seminary, Philadelphia. 1990

Kitagawa, Daisuke. *Race Relations and Christian Mission.* New York, 1964.

Koenig, John. *New Testament Hospitality: Partnership with Strangers as Promise and Mission.* Philadelphia, 1985.

Kreider, Alan. "Beyond Bosch: The Early Church and the Christendom Shift." *International Bulletin of Missionary Research (*April 2005): 59-68.

Krey, Andrew E. V. and Roald Kverndal. *Maritime Ministry Models.* Geneva, 1994.

Kverndal, Roald. *Sjömannsetikk: Håndbok i Yrkesetikk..* Oslo, 1971.

————. *China, the Sea, and the Gospel: Historical Foundations for Maritime Ministry in Chinese Waters, and the Shape of Today's Challenge.* IASMM Conference Paper, 2007

————. "The Origin and Nature of Nordic Missions to Seamen." *Norwegian Yearbook of Maritime History* (Bergen, 1978): 103-34.

————. *Seamen's Missions: Their Origin and Early Growth.* Pasadena, 1986

————. "The Urgency of Indigenization." *IASMM Newsletter* (Spring 1992): 9.

————. *Lutheran Maritime Ministry Inventory.* Geneva, 1993.

————. "Maritime Christian Fellowship." *Maritime Mission Studies,* no. 1 (Spring 1994): 1-15.

————. "The Origins of IASMM: A Personal Perspective." *Maritime Mission Studies,* no. 2 (Autumn 1995): 1-9.

————. "A New Challenge for the Church in China." *IASMM Newsletter* (Winter 1997-1998): 10-12.

————. "George Charles Smith: Founder of the Seafarers' Mission Movement." *Maritime Mission Studies,* vol. 1 (Spring 1998): 9-23.

————. "Women on the Waterfront: The Status and Roles of Women in Seafarers' Mission." *Maritime Mission Studies,* vol. 2 (Spring 2000): 17-32.

————. "1000 Years Since the Sea Apostolate Arrived in North America." *IASMM Newsletter* (Winter 2000): 8-9.

————. "Globalized Maritime Mission as Charted by Two Twentieth Century Futurists". *Maritime Mission Studies Supplement* (Spring 2004): 29-46.

————. Entries in *Oxford Dictionary of National Biography* (Oxford, 2004): "Grey, Mary," "Marks, Richard," "Rogers, Zebedee," " Smith, George Charles."

Lai, Karen M. *An Unconditional Love Story: Meeting the People of the Sea.* Niles, 1999.

————. *I am Your Song: My Journey of Faith.* Beach Park, 2002.

Lander, John K. "Seamen's Champion, or Unworthy Pastor? The Revd George Charles Smith (1782-1863)." *Journal of the Royal Institute of Cornwall* (2005): 45-58.

Langley, Harold D. *Social Reform in the United States Navy 1798-1862.* Chicago, 1967.

Larom, Peter. "The New Port Security and the Marginalisation of the Seafarer." *Maritime Mission Studies Supplement* (Spring 2004): 47-53.

Lee, Byeong Eun Lee. *A Manual for Equipping Asian Churches in Port Cities of North America to Develop the Reformed Maritime Ministries.* D. Min. Thesis Project, Westminster Theological Seminary, Philadelphia, 2005.

Legood, Giles ed. *Chaplaincy: The Church's Sector Ministries.* London, 1999.

Levinson, Marc. *The Box: How the Shipping Container Made the World Smaller and the World Economy Bigger.* Princeton, 2006.

Livingston, Theodore. "The Gospel Navy." *IASMM Newsletter* (Winter 2002/3): 7-11.

Lookout. Newsletter of Seamen's Church Institute of NY/NJ.

Luck, Kenneth. *Drugs and Ships: Classification, Carriers and Control.* London, 1992.

Lutheran World Federation. *LWF/DMD Workshop on Stewardship of God's Creation.* Geneva, 1996.

Maguire, Hugh. "Fr. Hans Ansgar Reinhold ('Har') 1897-1968." *IASMM Newsletter* (Spring 1994): 6-7.
Mall, Ted. *Developing Ministry to Seafarers.* Beach Park, 2002.
Marks, Richard. *The Retrospect, or, Review of Providential Mercies.* London, 1816.
Matthews, Edward Walter. *The King's Brotherhood.* London, 1911.
Mattison, Robyn D. *Water Words: Sea Readings for People of the Sea.* Beach Park, 2002.
———. *True North: Steering by Scripture at Sea.* Beach Park, 2003.
Masters, David. *The Plimsoll Mark.* London, 1955.
May, Gerald G. *Addiction and Grace.* New York, 1988.
Miller, Robert. *From Shore to Shore: A History of the Church and the Merchant Seafarer.* Nailsworth, 1989.
———. *Charles Plomer Hopkins and the Seamen's Union with Particular Reference to the 1911 Strike.* Unpubl. MA Thesis, Warwick University, Warwick, 1992.
———. *Ship of Peter: The Catholic Sea Apostolate and the Apostleship of the Sea.* Unpubl. MPh. Thesis, University of Plymouth, Plymouth, 1995 (1).
———. "Charles Plomer Hopkins (1861-1922): The Gaps." *Maritime Mission Studies,* no. 2 (Autumn 1995): 57-62 (2).
———. *The Man at the Helm: The Faith and Practice of the Medieval Seafarer.* Unpubl. PhD thesis, University of London, 2000.
Montagu, Ashley. *Man's Most Dangerous Myth.* New York, 1964
Mooney, Paul G. *Maritime Mission: History, Developments, A New Perspective.* Zoetermeer, 2005.
———. "Serving Seafarers Under Sail and Steam: A Missiological Reflection on the Development of Maritime Mission from 1779 to 1945." *IASMM Occasional Papers,* no. 2 (2000).
Moree, Perry. "Serving Two Masters: Preachers and Sick-comforters of the Dutch East India Company." *Maritime Mission Studies,* no. 2 (Autumn 1995) 19-27.
Mostert, Noël. *Supership.* New York, 1974.
Münchmeyer, Reinhard. *Handbuch der deutschen evangelischen Seemannsmission.* Stettin, 1912.
Myklebust, Olav G. "On the Origin of IAMS." *Mission Studies,* 3/1986.
———. "Missiology in Contemporary Theological Education." *Mission Studies,* 6/1989.
Nelson, Bruce. *Workers on the Waterfront.* Urbana, 1990.
Netland, Harold A. *Dissonant Voices.* Grand Rapids, 1991.
———. *Encountering Religious Pluralism.* Downers Grove, 2001.
Nordstokke, Kjell. *Tjeneste i Verdens Hverdag.* Bergen, 1999.

O'Halloran, James. *Small Christian Communities: A Pastoral Companion.* Dublin, 1996.
———. *Small Christian Communities: Vision and Practicalities.* Dublin, 2002.
Osterwald, Carl. *Hope Regained: The Position and Course of Seafarers' Mission at the Dawn of the Third Millennium.* IASMM Occasional Paper, no. 4 (2004).
Otto, Martin. *Seafarers! A Strategic Missionary Vision.* Carlisle, 2002.
———. *Church on the Oceans.* Carlisle, 2007.
Oubre, Sinclair K. *The Apostolatus Maris: Its Structural Development.* Licenciate in Canon Law Thesis, Catholic University of America, Washington DC, 1998.

Padgitt, Clint. "German Seamen's Mission of New York 1907-2001." *IASMM Newsletter* (Spring-Summer 2001): 5-7.
Padilla, René. *Mission Between the Times.* Grand Rapids, 1985.

Pierce, Ronald & Rebecca Groothuis, eds. *Discovering Biblical Equality.* Garden Grove, 2005
Pittman, Bill. *AA The Way It Began.* Seattle, 1988.

Reinhold, Hans Ansgar. *H.A.R.: The Autobiography of Father Reinhold.* New York, 1968.
Rodriguez-Martos Dauer, Ricardo. *The Call of the Gospel to Demand Justice for the Oppressed and How This Must Motivate the Apostleship of the Sea.* Barcelona, 1992.
Rompkey, Ronald. *Grenfell of Labrador: A Biography.* Toronto, 1991.
Royce, James E. *Alcohol Problems and Alcoholism.* New York, 1981.
Ryman, Björn et al. *Nordic Folk Churches: A Contemporary Church History.* Grand Rapids, 2005.

Seafarers International Research Centre. *Symposium 2001.* Cardiff, 2001.
Sherar, Mariam G. *Shipping Out: A Sociological Study.* Cambridge, 1973
Shenk, Wilbert R. "New Wineskin for New Wine." *International Bulletin for Missionary Research,* vol 21 (Oct. 1997): 154-59.
Ships of Shame: Inquiry into Ship Safety. Report from the House of Representatives Standing Committee on Transport, Communication and Infrastructure. Canberra, 1992.
Sider, Ronald J. *Rich Christians in an Age of Hunger.* Downers Grove, 1997.
Skinner, Betty Lee. *Daws: A Man Who Trusted God.* Colorado Springs, 1974.
Stafford, Ward. *New Missionary Field.* New York, 1817.
Smith, Jean R. "The Paducah Project." *IASMM Newsletter* (Winter 1998/1999): 11-13.
———. ed. *ICMA Ship Visiting Handbook.* New York and London, 2005.
Stott, John. *Christian Mission in the Modern World.* Downers Grove, 1975.
Strand, Ray D. *Healthy for Life: Developing Healthy Lifestyles.* Rapid City, 2004.

Thun, R. W. *Werden und Wachsen der Deutschen Evangelischen Seemannsmission.* Bremen/Hamburg-Altona, 1959.
Tippett, Alan R. *The Deep Sea Canoe: The Story of Third World Missionaries in the South Pacific.* Pasadena, 2006.

Waltari, Toivo. *Finska Sjomansmissionen 1875-1925.* Helsingfors, 1925.
Waterlines. Newsletter of NAMMA from 1991.
Watermarks. Newsletter of NAMMA (then ICOSA) 1979-1991.
Weibust, Knut. *Deep Sea Sailors: A Study in Maritime Ethnology.* Stockholm, 1969.
Whittemore, James R. *Seamen's Church Institute: 150 Years and Beyond.* D.Min. Thesis Project, New York Theological Seminary, New York, 1982.
Wilson, Michael J. *World Mission on Your Doorstep: 150 Years of the Seamen's Christian Friend Society 1846-1996.* Alderley Edge, 1996.
Wristers, Jan. *Here is the Sea.* Hong Kong, 1978.

Yzermans, Vincent. *American Catholic Seafarers' Church.* Washington DC, 1995.

Zhao, Minghua, ed. *Women Seafarers.* Geneva, 2003.

INDEX OF PERSONS

SEAMEN'S MISSIONS
Their Origin and Early Growth
A Contribution to the History of the Church Maritime
By Roald Kverndal

This marvelous book gives the definitive history of the beginnings of ministry to seafarers, covering events during the 18th and 19th centuries. The author reveals the social and political conditions that led to the establishment of missions and ministries to the forgotten and mistreated men of the sea.

Over 800 pages of fascinating history with numerous period illustrations. Includes a lengthy *Bibliography*.

Published by William Carey Library, 1986, Hardcover, 902 pages.

$12.97 each plus shipping and handling. Order number WCL440-1

To order:

By phone: Toll free – 1-800-MISSION (1-800-647-7466)
                  Outside the U.S. – 1-423-282-9475
By e-mail: STL@WCLBooks.com
By fax: 1-800-759-2779
By mail: Send The Light/WCL, 129 Mobilization Drive, Waynesboro,
                  Georgia 30830 USA

The subject is almost withering in scope, but the author's meticulous scholarship is persuasive. It will no doubt stand as the definitive study on the subject.
Dr. Gerald E. Morris,
American Maritime Library, Mystic Seaport, Connecticut

A book that is as exciting as it is scholarly, with the best background presentation for a comprehensive study I have ever read. Every institution teaching missiology should offer courses with this book as a text.
Dr. Lucille M. Johnson,
Professor of English, Pacific Lutheran University, Tacoma, Washington

Fills a long felt void in maritime and church history. I commend it whole-heartedly as a unique source of reference, vision and inspiration.
Rev. Prebendary T.P. Kerfoot, OBE,
General Secretary, The Missions to Seamen/ICMA, London